Encyclopedia of Cuba

Encyclopedia of Cuba

People, History, Culture

Volume I

Edited by
Luis Martínez-Fernández,
D. H. Figueredo, Louis A. Pérez, Jr.,
and Luis González

An Oryx Book

Greenwood Press
Westport, Connecticut • London

REF
F
1754
.E53
2003
Vol. 1

Library of Congress Cataloging-in-Publication Data

Encyclopedia of Cuba : people, history, culture / edited by Luis Martínez-Fernández . . . [et al.].
    p. cm.
  Includes bibliographical references and index.
  ISBN 1–57356–334–X (set: alk. paper)—ISBN 1–57356–572–5 (v. 1: alk. paper)—
    ISBN 1–57356–573–3 (v. 2: alk. paper)
    1. Cuba—Encyclopedias.   I. Martínez-Fernández, Luis, 1960–
F1754.E53   2003
972.91′003—dc21   2002070030

British Library Cataloguing in Publication Data is available.

Library of Congress Catalog Card Number: 2002070030
ISBN: 1–57356–334–X (set)
ISBN: 1–57356–572–5 (v. 1)
ISBN: 1–57356–573–5 (v. 2)

First published in 2003

Greenwood Press, 88 Post Road West, Westport, CT 06881
An imprint of Greenwood Publishing Group, Inc.
www.greenwood.com

Printed in the United States of America

The paper used in this book complies with the
Permanent Paper Standard issued by the National
Information Standards Organization (Z39.48–1984).

10 9 8 7 6 5 4 3 2 1

Copyright Acknowledgments

The editors and the publisher gratefully acknowledge permission for use of the following
material:

Every reasonable effort has been made to trace the owners of copyright materials in this book,
but in some instances this has proven impossible. The author and publisher will be glad to
receive information leading to more complete acknowledgments in subsequent printings of this
book and in the meantime extend their apologies for any ommissions.

Contents

List of Entries

Introduction

The study of Cuba and its people attracts attention—and elicits passions—disproportionate to the country's numbers. With its 42,845 square miles (roughly equivalent to the area of Pennsylvania or Guatemala) and its 11.2 million inhabitants (about the population of Ohio or Metropolitan London), Cuba has captured worldwide attention among scholars and the general public—increasingly so since the triumph of the Cuban Revolution in 1959. The Cuban Revolution, in fact, is credited with igniting the ensuing boom in Latin American studies in U.S. universities, think tanks, and government agencies. The unexpected establishment of a pro-Soviet regime in an island state so near to, and with so many affinities with, the United States sparked interest among those who wanted to know "What happened in Cuba?"—either to keep it from happening again or to demonstrate that its alternative path was viable and replicable. Paradoxically, the same circumstances that increased U.S. scholarly interest in Latin America turned the study of Cuba into a challenging and difficult task as the United States imposed a trade embargo on the wayward island and as revolutionary leaders pursued a path of isolation from the West. Increased attention to Cuba, much of it responding to Cold War era political agendas, coupled with difficult access to information and obstacles to sustained research, as well as the absence of dialogue and exchange between island-based and foreign-based Cubanists, hampered the development of Cuban studies over the first few decades of the Cuban Revolution.

Over the last decade many of the old barriers to Cuban studies have begun to crumble, allowing the production of many valuable studies. Yet, some of the grotesque distortions that dominated the first few decades of the revolutionary era linger stubbornly and continue to influence the way many individuals—informed or otherwise—speak, write, and teach about Cuba's past and present. Although the catalogue of distortions is a long one, some of the most prevailing and harmful are highly politicized approaches producing polarized interpretations; a teleological view of Cuba's history that reduces the past to a mere prologue to the Revolution; a before-and-after narrative that fails to recognize continuities before and after 1959; a static view of the Revolution as if 1960s realities are the same as those of the dawn of the twenty-first century; a romanticized and exoticizing portrayal of the island and its people; and the notion that the more than one in ten Cubans who live abroad have somehow turned into something other than Cuban.

The Scope of this Encyclopedia

The editors and authors of this *Encyclopedia* have sought to prevent these distortions by striving to produce a collective work that is balanced and thus avoids a politicized depiction of the Cuban past and present reality. While not shying away from controversial topics—so much about Cuba is controversial—a concerted effort was made to include a variety of entries in which individual contributors could provide information and interpretation on the achievements and shortcomings of various epochs in Cuba's history: colonial, republican, and revolutionary. Biographical entries were selected on the merits and historical relevance of each biographee regardless of where each stood, or stands, vis-à-vis the Revolution or whether they lived, or live, on the island or abroad. Although many more individuals may warrant inclusion in a reference work of this kind, space limitations forced us to select a limited number of people to profile. Although the selection was subjective and certainly not perfect, no one was left out or forced in because of political considerations. Furthermore, much care went into the selection of the *Encyclopedia*'s eighty-one contributors, to ensure not only that each author possessed the necessary knowledge and skills but also that as a whole the contributions presented a balanced and objective picture.

Although the Cuban Revolution and Cuba's recent past has been the overwhelmingly primary object of attention from scholars as well as the general public, the editors of this *Encyclopedia* stress that Cuba has had a long and rich history that merits attention for its own importance and not only as a background to the tumultuous revolutionary period that began in 1959. This work points to the extraordinarily rich and vibrant contributions of generations of Cubans to the arts, literature, the sciences, sports, and many other fields. It also tells of the Cuban peoples' struggles, achievements, and failures, all of which deserve attention (even had the Revolution not taken place) and which will continue to deserve notice long after the Revolution comes to an end.

A related distortion is the before-and-after syndrome that continues to dominate the narrative of Cuban history. Rather than portraying the Cuban Revolution as a profound abyss separating heaven from hell, or conversely hell from heaven, we set out to trace the historical continuities that transcend the different periods of Cuban history. Undoubtedly, Cuba's Revolution was built upon a preexisting culture, and it inherited a tempestuous and complex past. For example, Cuba's contemporary emphasis on medical research and its laudable goal to make health care accessible to the entire population cannot be fully understood without recognizing that even if most physicians left the island shortly after the Revolution—more than half emigrated between 1959 and 1964—Cuba's health revolution grew out of a preexisting ethos of socially conscious medicine and a long tradition of medicine as science dating back to the nineteenth century. Similarly, the recent wave of official corruption and malfeasance is not simply a response to the crisis of the so-called Special Period but rather is heir to an ingrained political culture—again dating back to the colonial era—that has historically viewed political power as the primary source of individual profit and privilege. This *Encyclopedia* also seeks to provide a nuanced and historical view of the revolutionary period which recognizes that much has changed in the forty-odd years since Fidel Castro assumed power. It also seeks to emphasize that one should not generalize for the entire period but should rather be sensitive to change over time when looking at a host of matters ranging from nutrition to foreign relations and from government repression to internal support for the regime. Because the entries on the revolutionary period and contemporary era draw upon the latest available sources and publications, they provide up-to-date information and trace the most recent transformations in Cuban society.

The before-and-after perspective often leads to two related distortions: one that credits all areas of progress in Cuba to the Revolution and another that blames it for all of the island's misfortunes. Comparing pre-1959 Cuba with the island's present reality is both ahistorical and distorting—it assumes that all changes over a four-decade period were the result of actions by the revolutionary regime. It also ignores, for example, that the position of women has changed over the past forty years in Puerto Rico, Venezuela, and other societies that did not go through a revolution. The other side to this distortion, which I call the James Dean distortion, perpetuates a frozen and idealized picture of a late 1950s Cuba that was violently truncated suddenly and unexpectedly. Marlon Brando, we all know, grew old, fat, and bald; but the only James Dean we will ever know is the handsome twenty-four-year-old Hollywood icon who died tragically in 1955. Applied to Cuba, this distortion assumes that the island nation would not have suffered severe economic and social traumas had Castro not taken over in 1959. To conclude that all would have gone well in a Cuba without Revolution is a counterfactual exercise that ignores the past four convulsed and troubled decades of Latin American history.

Comparing Cuba to other neighboring societies, meanwhile, can be equally problematic. Much of what is said and written about the island nation, particularly by those who wish to highlight the achievements of the Revolution, implicitly or explicitly compares Cuba with nations like Guatemala or even Haiti. Such comparisons not only fail to recognize Cuba's particular historical trajectory but also ignore the fact that, dating back to the late eighteenth century, Cubans used European and North American frames of reference for their cultural, political, social, and technological aspirations. Thus, eighteenth-century planters purchased the latest European technology, nineteenth-century annexationists aspired to freedoms similar to those enjoyed in the United States, and present-day scientists and athletes pursue accomplishments comparable to those of their European and U.S. counterparts. When someone highlights Cuba's recent achievements in reducing illiteracy and child mortality, for example, by comparing them to those of, say, El Salvador, that person is engaging in overlapping distortions: first, implying that both societies stood at the same educational and health level fifty years ago—which was not the case; second, assuming that both societies aspire to the same standards—which is not the case either.

Yet another distortion that the editors have sought to avoid is the one that extrapolates the political differences separating Cuba's diaspora from the Cuban regime to the point that Cubans are bifurcated into two distinct peoples, each with its own culture, set of values, and aspirations for the island's future. Cuba has had a long history of massive and recurrent exile and emigration. José Antonio Saco, Félix Varela, José Martí, Tomás Estrada Palma (Cuba's first president), and thousands of other Cubans spent the bulk of their lifetimes abroad. In 1898, as the Cuban War of Independence raged on, one in ten Cubans—roughly the same proportion as today—lived in exile in the United States. These experiences forged a Cuban culture that could remain Cuban and continue to thrive even during prolonged periods of exile. Similarly, the estimated two million Cubans who are scattered throughout the world today continue to contribute to—and arguably preserve—many aspects of Cuban culture. In that vein, anthropologist Fernando Ortiz, one of Cuba's most influential scholars, asserted in 1940 that Cuba was "both a land and a people; and that 'lo cubano' are those things belonging to this country and to its people." Likewise, Guillermo Cabrera Infante later wrote "To be Cuban is to go with Cuba everywhere." Echoing these beliefs, the editors of this work did not separate the contributions of Cubans abroad from those of Cubans on the island. We recognized that what unites Cuban writers, musicians, and even *peloteros* on both sides of the Straits of Florida is more than what sets them apart. That is why, for example, the entry on Cuban American novelist Cristina García—who writes in English—appears in the same chapter as that of writer Cabrera Infante, who sought exile in 1966 and now lives in London, and poet Nicolás Guillén, who died in Havana in 1989, to the end apparently loyal to the Revolution. In short, this *Encyclopedia* subscribes to the notion that there is one Cuban literature, and it includes not only what has been written on the island but also what the Countess of Merlín wrote in mid-nineteenth-century Paris and what Martí later wrote in New York as well as what Oscar Hijuelos writes today in New York and what Zoé Valdés writes in Paris. Given the massive nature and historical importance of the Cuban diaspora, however, we have chosen to include a separate section on the Cuban diaspora that chronicles the activities of Cubans abroad, particularly in the realms of business and politics.

Arrangement of the Encyclopedia

A few words on the *Encyclopedia*'s organization: Rather than structure these volumes along a strict A-to-Z format, the editors decided to arrange the work's more than 700 entries into twelve topical chapters so that readers could easily find clusters of entries touching upon similar topics. Entries within each chapter appear alphabetically. The chapters include a brief opening explanation on Cuba's national symbols, followed by a chapter on geography, the environment, and urbanization. These are followed by three historical chapters, each focusing on a particular period (colonial, republican, and revolutionary) and a sixth chapter covering aspects of the island's contemporary economy and society. Chapters 7, 8, and 9 provide information on literature, the performing arts, and the plastic arts, respectively. Chapter 10 addresses popular culture and religion, and Chapter 11 covers sports. A final chapter is dedicated to the Cuban diaspora. Because of this thematic structure, a reader seeking information on, say, baseball Hall of Famer Atanasio (Tony) Pérez, will find next to his entry those of other Cuban sports legends ranging from Cuba's first Olympic star, fencer Ramón Fonst, to contemporary sluggers Orestes Quindelán and Omar Linares. Pérez's entry also leads to a series of cross-referenced entries such as **Camagüey Province** (where he was born) and related entries such as **Baseball** and **Cubans in the U.S. Major Leagues**. This format also allows someone interested in learning about a given topic, for example, Cuban painting, to encounter information on the leading painters and related subjects within a specific section of the *Encyclopedia*. By reading all the entries in that particular section, the reader will get a good sense of the trajectory and richness of Cuban painting. Most entries include cross references that point to other entries and also include a list of suggested further readings where students and researchers can find expanded information on any particular person or subject matter. All cross references within the entry appear in **bold type**. For those who wish to find information alphabetically in the *Encyclopedia*, there are both a detailed index at the end of the second volume and a list of all the entry headwords in alphabetical order at the front of the volumes. A number of appendixes are also included to provide extra information on some particular topics. The appendixes include historical documents, a chronology of Cuban history and lists of all colonial governors and presidents.

Acknowledgments

This project has been a collective labor of love that has brought together nearly a hundred scholars, photographers, and artists from all over the globe who share a passion for Cuba and its people. Luis González deserves credit for the idea of producing this comprehensive Cuban encyclopedia, the first since the mid-1970s and the first ever in English. He drafted the original proposal for the book and also took the first steps in putting together the team of four editors, which besides him included Louis A. Pérez, Jr., of the University of North Carolina, D. H. Figueredo, of Bloomfield College, and myself, Luis Martínez-Fernández, of Rutgers University. At the early stages of this project, the editors sought the advice of some of the world's foremost experts on Cuban subjects and invited them to join the *Encyclopedia*'s advisory board, which includes Antonio Benítez Rojo, Wilfredo Cancio Isla, Cristóbal Díaz Ayala, Jason Feer, Ada M. Isasi-Díaz, Peter T. Johnson, Juan A. Martínez, Félix Masud-Piloto, Consuelo Naranjo Orovio, Silvia Pedraza, Paula J. Pettavino, Armando H. Portela, and Alan West-Durán. They were instrumental in shaping the work's structure and in tackling the difficult task of establishing the master list of entries. They also wrote a number of the work's entries and recommended many of the other contributors. Consuelo Naranjo Orovio in particular was key to the selection of the Spanish contributors. The team of eighty-one scholars who wrote the work's more than 700 entries includes writers, researchers, and scholars from various parts of the world; we received contributions from Spain, the United Kingdom, Australia, Canada, Cuba, Puerto Rico, and from several states of the United States. The authors ranged from advanced graduate students to middle career scholars to professors emeriti, and they came from various fields: geography, history, literary criticism, journalism, and filmmaking, to name but a few. Unusual for a collaborative project of this magnitude, we had virtually no *embarcadores*—on the contrary, the authors were reliably punctual—and despite the bewildering back-and-forth of hundreds of diskettes and attachments over a three-year period, no cyber-viruses were ever received. Although the editors remain responsible for the selection of the team of contributing scholars and the structural balance of the work, all authors retained the prerogative to write their entries as they saw fit. The editors of the *Encyclopedia* wish to acknowledge their gratitude to the advisers and authors who generously poured their energy and knowledge into this project.

We are also grateful to a number of institutions and individuals who collaborated with and supported the project in a variety of ways. Rutgers University's Research Council provided a grant that helped fund some of the research. The Center for Latin American Studies of the University of Florida awarded a Library Travel Grant to the University of Florida's Smathers Libraries, where Richard Phillips and his staff were enormously helpful. Pat Roos, former Area Dean for Social and Behavioral Sciences at Rutgers University, allotted funds that paid for graduate student assistance. Aracely García Carranza of the Biblioteca Nacional José Martí in Havana, Esperanza Varona of the Cuban Heritage Collection at the Otto G. Richter Library of the University of Miami, and Peter T. Johnson and AnnaLee Pauls of Princeton University's Firestone Library also provided invaluable assistance, as did Lourdes Vázquez and Fernanda Perrone of Rutgers University's Alexander Library. Myra Torres Alamo and the staff of the Digitalization Project of the *El Mundo* Photograph Collection at the University of Puerto Rico, Río Piedras, granted access to their collection. Also generous with his collection was Cristóbal Díaz Ayala of Fundación Musicalia in San Juan, a unique collection of recordings and other materials documenting the trajectory of Cuban and Latin American music. This collection was donated to the Florida International University Library in 2001, which also made these materials available for our use. Frank Argote-Freyre served as assistant editor, writing entries and laboring in various research and administrative tasks.

Numerous cartographers, photographers, and editors allowed us to reproduce their work so that the *Encyclopedia*'s visual component would match the quality of its text. Geographer Armando H. Portela produced many of the maps specially for the *Encyclopedia*. Michael Siegel of Rutgers University Cartography produced the map of nineteenth-century Havana. Jason Feer, former editor of *CubaNews*, graciously allowed us to reproduce several graphs, tables, and maps. My father, Celestino Martínez Lindín, traveled to Havana—his first visit in four decades—to take many of this book's photographs of contemporary Cuba. And my oldest son Luis Alberto Martínez, despite never having worn one, drew the sketch of the traditional Cuban *guayabera* shirt. Dania del Sol of Art & Photo Retouching gave of her technical expertise in photo retouching to improve the quality of many of the illustrations. Alejandro Anreus, Ada Ferrer, and Julio César González Pagés graciously loaned us photographs from their collections. Many other photographers whose work graces the pages of the *Encyclopedia* are properly credited in the captions.

Anne Thompson and the other editors and staff members of the Greenwood Publishing Group took special interest in and devoted particular care to these volumes. We thank them for their support, guidance, and assistance during the various stages leading to their publication.

Numerous other individuals—too many to mention here—contributed to the final result in large and small ways: providing hard-to-find facts, giving leads about illustrations, suggesting potential contributors, or simply encouraging us about the relevance of this work.

We trust that this work will fill an important gap among works of reference on Cuba and that it will serve as the first step in many future studies that shall continue to increase our knowledge and understanding about that alluring and complex island and its brave, tenacious, and creative people. We especially hope that these volumes will find their way to the bookshelves and hearts of Cuban and Cuban American homes so that new generations may get a taste of the *ajiaco* (Cuban stew) with which Fernando Ortiz compared the complex Cuban culture and find ways to connect with the island which Columbus described as "the most beautiful land human eyes have ever seen."

This work, whose publication coincides with the centennial of Cuba's ill-starred independence in 1902, is humbly dedicated to all Cubans, wherever they may live.

Luis Martínez-Fernández
Senior Editor

1

National Symbols

National Anthem

The national anthem "Himno Nacional" of Cuba was written by Pedro (Perucho) Figueredo Cisneros of **Bayamo** in the old Cuban province of Oriente. Figueredo, a landowner, became involved in conspiratorial political clubs and revolutionary plots with **Carlos Manuel de Céspedes** and other Creoles opposed to Spanish rule. He wrote the words and music of the anthem, originally titled "La Bayamesa" after the French Revolutionary "La Marseillaise," on August 14, 1867. The national hymn was first sung during the **Ten Years' War** (1868–1878) on October 20, 1868, after the capture of Bayamo from the Spanish.

A martial piece, the anthem remembers the sacrifice of Cuba's Liberation Army during the Ten Years' War and the rebellion of the oppressed, while calling forth the qualities of heroism, dignity, and duty to the nation. Originally written in three stanzas, only the first is sung when the anthem is played.

After a siege in 1869, the Spanish retook Bayamo but not before the citizens razed their city rather than see it fall into enemy hands. Although the Ten Years' War was ultimately unsuccessful, the anthem remained as an icon of independence among veterans and patriots and was officially designated as the national anthem once the Cuban Republic was established.

"Himno Nacional de Cuba"

Al combate corred bayameses,
que la patria os contempla orgullosa,
no temais una muerte gloriosa
que morir por la patria es vivir.
En cadenas vivir; es vivir
en afrenta y oprobio sumido.
Del clarín, escuchad el sonido
¡A las armas, valientes, corred!

No temais los feroces iberos,
son cobardes cual todo tirano,
no resisten al bravo cubano
para siempre su imperio cayó.
¡Cuba Libre! ¿ Ya España murió,
su poder y su orgullo, do es ido?
Del clarín, escuchad el sonido
¡A las armas, valientes, corred!

Contemplad nuestras huestes
    triunfantes,
contempladlos a ellos caídos,
por cobardes huyeron vencidos:
¡por valientes sabemos triunfar!
¡Cuba Libre! Podemos gritar
del cañón al terrible estampido.
Del clarín, escuchad el sonido
!A las armas, valientes, corred!

Translated, the text of the sung portion of the anthem reads:

> Into combat, run, people of Bayamo,
> for the fatherland looks upon all of you
>   with pride,
> fear not a glorious death,
> for to die for the homeland is to live.
> To live in chains is to live
> plunged in insult and dishonor.
> The bugle calls, hear the sound
> To arms! Run, valiant ones.

Further Readings

Gay-Calbó, Enrique. *Las banderas, el escudo y el himno de Cuba*. Havana: Sociedad Colombista Panamericana, 1956.

Pereda Rodríguez, Justo Luis, Leopoldo Montano Cortina, and Gil Ramos Blanco. *Cuba y sus símbolos*. Havana: Ediciones Abril, 1992.

David C. Carlson

National Bird

The endemic Cuban Trogon, *Priotelus temnurus*, is considered the national bird of Cuba, chosen because its blue head, white chest, and red belly reflect the colors of the Cuban **national flag** and because it has a reputation of not being able to live in captivity. Its Spanish name *tocororo*, or *tocoloro*, is onomatopoeic, deriving from the monotonous phrase of its song.

A member of the bird family that includes the better-known quetzals of Central America, the Cuban Trogon is ten to eleven inches long. Its preferred habitat is forested mountainous regions, where it nests in tree cavities previously dug by woodpeckers, since its beak is not strong enough to make holes in wood. The bird's diet is made up of wild fruits and insects caught in flight. Males help incubate the eggs and feed the nestlings.

Most commonly found in the **Sierra Maestra**, in Cuba's eastern end, it is also fairly widespread throughout the island, present in the **Escambray Mountains** of the center, in the western Sierra de los Órganos, and on la **Isla de la Juventud**. Please see color insert for illustration. *See also* Fauna

Further Reading

Pereda Rodríguez, Justo Luis, Leopoldo Montano Cortina, and Gil Ramos Blanco. *Cuba y sus símbolos*. Havana: Ediciones Abril, 1992.

Roger E. Hernández

National Coat of Arms

Cuba's coat of arms was designed in 1849 by the annexationist patriot and poet **Miguel Teurbe Tolón** and adopted the following year by General **Narciso López**. The original design included annexationist symbolisms such as a circle of thirteen stars on the Phrygian cap and another around the crest of the royal palm, representing the thirteen original states of the United States. A 1906 decree by President **Tomás Estrada Palma** officially established the Cuban Republic's coat of arms based on Teurbe Tolón's design.

The coat of arms' central shield is divided into three fields. The upper field includes a sun rising out of the ocean between two bodies of land and a golden key, allusive to Cuba's historical strategic role as "the Key to the Indies" and its location as the key to the Gulf of Mexico. The bottom left field includes five diagonal stripes in alternating blue and white colors; these are the stripes on the Cuban flag. The bottom right field is composed of a landscape with a valley, a towering royal palm, and two mountains on the background. The shield is supported by a fasces, symbolizing unity, and crowned by a Phrygian cap, symbolizing republicanism. The Phrygian cap is adorned with a solitary silver star, representing Cuban independence. Two branches frame the shield: a laurel branch on the right side, an oak branch (officially described as an *encina* branch) on the left. Please see color insert for illustration. *See also* Annexationism; National Flag; National Tree

Further Readings

Gay-Calbó, Enrique. *Las banderas, el escudo y el himno de Cuba*. Havana: Sociedad Colombista Panamericana, 1956.

Pereda Rodríguez, Justo Luis, Leopoldo Montano Cortina, and Gil Ramos Blanco. *Cuba y sus símbolos*. Havana: Ediciones Abril, 1992.

Luis Martínez-Fernández

National Flag

Cuba's national flag was originally conceived in June 1849 by the Venezuelan-born general **Narciso López** in a meeting of Cuban patriots in New York City. **Miguel Teurbe Tolón**, who participated in that meeting, executed the design, and his wife Emilia sewed the first model. The Cuban flag, sometimes referred to as Narciso López's, drew from a wide array of republican and Masonic symbolisms. Cuban patriots of the mid-nineteenth century, many of whom were Freemasons, aspired to a republican form of government either through independence or annexation to the United States. What eventually became the Cuban flag included the red, white, and blue colors of republicanism, and its red triangle alluded to the revolutionary principles of liberty, equality, and fraternity. The red triangle with the solitary star as well as the numerical symbolisms of the flag's other geometric components also derived from Masonic symbolisms. The Cuban flag was first hoisted on Cuban soil on May 19, 1850, in the town of **Cárdenas**, during its temporary capture by López's invading troops. Thereafter it was used by patriots and revolutionaries and officially adopted by Cuba's Republic-in-Arms in April 1869. On May 20, 1902, the Cuban flag was raised in **El Morro Castle** as the U.S. flag was lowered, marking the transition of power from the U.S. military to the Cuban Republic.

The flag, as officially standardized by presidential decree on April 24, 1906, is shaped rectangularly, with its length being twice as long as its width. It includes five horizontal stripes in alternating deep blue and white colors and a red equilateral triangle on the flag's post side; the side of the triangle on the post side runs vertically and extends from top to bottom. A five-pointed white star is located at the center of the red triangle. Various symbolisms are attributed to the flag's colors and components. The red symbolizes the blood spilled by patriots; the white stands for the purity of the patriots' ideals; and the blue symbolizes their celestial aspirations. The three blue stripes represent the three departments into which the island was divided during the mid-nineteenth century, and the solitary star represents Cuba's sovereignty. Please see color insert for illustration. *See also*: Annexationism; Freemasonry; Ten Years' War

Further Readings

Gay-Calbó, Enrique. *Las banderas, el escudo y el himno de Cuba*. Havana: Sociedad Colombista Panamericana, 1956.

Pereda Rodríguez, Justo Luis, Leopoldo Montano Cortina, and Gil Ramos Blanco. *Cuba y sus símbolos*. Havana: Ediciones Abril, 1992.

Luis Martínez-Fernández

National Flower

La Mariposa (the butterfly), also known as *caña de ámbar* (amber cane), is the popular name given to *Hedychium coronarium Koenig*, the national flower of Cuba. Originally native to India, the fragrant flower of the jasmine family reproduces in great number throughout Cuba by means of rhizomes, which are underground stems that send out roots and spread from the original plant. La Mariposa was designated the national flower of Cuba in 1936. The designation came as a result of a request by botanists in Argentina, working at the Jardín de la Paz (Garden of Peace), to a query about the national flower. Several reasons were given for the selection of la Mariposa: The delicate whiteness of the petals is seen as representative of the purity of Cuban independence ideals and a symbol of peace, while the unity of the petals on the stem symbolizes the unity and strength of the Cuban people. The flower is also seen as a symbol of Cuban femininity, because it is delicate, tall, and graceful. La Mariposa also conjures up images of Cuba's Independence Wars, because in the nineteenth century women would wear them in their hair or draping their shoulders. Sometimes hidden in the flowers were messages to or from the independence fighters. Please see color insert for illustration. *See also* Flora; Ten Years' War; War of Independence

Further Reading

Pereda Rodríguez, Justo Luis, Leopoldo Montano Cortina, and Gil Ramos Blanco. *Cuba y sus símbolos*. Havana: Ediciones Abril, 1992.

Araceli García Carranza

National Tree

The royal palm (*Roystonea regia*) is widely recognized as Cuba's national tree. Believed to be indigenous to Cuba, its majestic splendor and beauty grace the island's landscape and the Cuban coat of arms. Royal palms have long, straight trunks that are crowned by imposing crests of leaves; they usually grow to 40 to 50 feet but can reach heights of 80 to 100 feet.

Besides their beauty, royal palms have multiple uses. The island's rural population and the **mambises** who fought Spain during the last third of the nineteenth century made extensive use of royal palms. Their trunks provide boards for construction; their leaves have been used historically to thatch the roofs of *bohíos* (traditional rural dwellings); their fruit (*palmito*) is used in salads; their seeds (*palmiches*) are used to feed hogs and extract oil; their roots are believed to have medicinal powers; and even their branches, when seedless, are used by rural dwellers as brooms. Please see color insert for illustration. *See also*: Flora; National Coat of Arms

Further Reading

Pereda Rodríguez, Justo Luis, Leopoldo Montano Cortina, and Gil Ramos Blanco. *Cuba y sus símbolos*. Havana: Ediciones Abril, 1992.

Luis Martínez-Fernández

2

Geography, the Environment, and Urbanization

Area and Geographic Location

The territory of the Republic of Cuba spreads over an archipelago composed of the island of Cuba, the **Isla de la Juventud (Isle of Youth)**, and nearly 1,600 other islands and **keys**. The total area for the island of Cuba is 104,945 square kilometers (65,066 square miles), while that of the Cuban archipelago is 110,860 square kilometers (68,733 square miles). Cuba is by far the largest of the islands of the Caribbean; its territorial extension is about the same as that of all the other Caribbean islands combined. The archipelago's second largest island, Isla de la Juventud, measures 2,200 square kilometers (1,364 square miles), making it the sixth largest of all the islands of the Caribbean behind Cuba, Hispaniola, Jamaica, Puerto Rico, and Trinidad.

Cuba is an elongated island located just south of the Tropic of Cancer. The island's length at its longest is 1,250 kilometers (775 miles); its width at its widest is 191 kilometers (118 miles). Its northernmost point is Punta Hicacos, **Matanzas Province** (23° 12′ 20″ N), and its southernmost point is Punta del Inglés, **Granma Province** (19° 49′ 36″ N). The island's westernmost point is Cabo San Antonio, **Pinar del Río Province** (84° 57′ 54″ W), while Punta del Quemado, **Guantánamo Province**, is its easternmost point at 74° 07′ 52″ W.

Cuba's strategic geographic location earned it early on the title of Key to the Indies. Its location has historically made Cuba critical to the defense of the Straits of Florida, the Strait of Yucatán, and the Windward Passage, as well as the Gulf of Mexico and the Isthmus of Central America. During the colonial era, Cuba's location—Havana's in particular—made it the stopping point of the various fleets that linked the New World with Spain. The island's strategic location has continued to shape its historical trajectory as recently as the Cold War era. Please see color insert for map. *See also* Trade and Navigation (1500–1800)

Further Readings

Marrero, Leví. *Geografía de Cuba*. New York: Minerva Books, 1966.

República de Cuba, Comité Estatal de Estadísticas. *Anuario estadístico de Cuba, 1989*. Havana: Comité Estatal de Estadísticas 1991.

República de Cuba, Instituto Cubano de Geodesia y Cartografía. *Atlas de Cuba*. Havana: Instituto Cubano de Geodesia y Cartografía, 1978.

Luis Martínez-Fernández

Baracoa (Municipality)

A port city and municipality located on the northern coast of the present-day eastern province of **Guantánamo**, Baracoa was the first Spanish village established on the island. Discovered by **Columbus** in 1492, it was settled by **Diego Velázquez** in 1512 and remained the only one of Cuba's early settlements that did not move its geographic location. The village served as the new colony's first capital between 1518 and 1522. Following this initial period of importance, Baracoa turned into an isolated backwater settlement, periodically targeted by corsairs and foreign smugglers. The forts built to protect Baracoa are still standing and serve as tourist attractions. During the 1700s and 1800s the region experienced some economic expansion, mostly associated with the production of cocoa and coconuts. The port city, however, remained geographically isolated from the rest of the island until the 1960s when La Farola highway was built. Because of its isolation, Baracoa served as a landing sight for several anti-Spanish expeditions during the nineteenth-century wars of independence. The present-day municipality of Baracoa has a population of 80,601 (estimate 1998), and its economy is based on the production of cocoa, chocolates, and coconut oil; it also boasts considerable deposits of chromium and nickel. Because of its historic importance, Baracoa also attracts a significant number of tourists each year. *See also* Colonial Settlements, Early; Contraband Trade; Corsairs Attacks; Tourism

Further Readings

Alfonso, Carmen R. *Principales ciudades*. Havana: Editorial José Martí, 1997.

Freire Díaz, Joaquín. *Historia de los municipios de Cuba*. Miami: La Moderna Poesía, 1985.

Pichardo Viñales, Hortensia. *La fundación de las primeras villas de la Isla de Cuba*. Havana: Editorial de Ciencias Sociales, 1986.

Luis Martínez-Fernández

Bayamo (Municipality)

Bayamo is a municipality and capital of the province of **Granma**, on the eastern end of Cuba. The city of Bayamo is the second-oldest Spanish settlement on the island; its founding by **Diego Velázquez** dates to 1513. Originally named San Salvador de Bayamo, the city has enormous historical significance that has earned it the title of Cradle of the Cuban Nation and the honor of National Historic City. The region of Bayamo has had a long tradition of rebellion. It was there that Spanish conquerors executed the native warrior **Hatuey**. Settlers later developed independent trade relations with foreign smugglers in violation of exclusivist trade restrictions. **Contraband trade** stimulated the region's cattle and tobacco production during the 1600s and 1700s. The Bayameses' independent spirit was made patent in 1868 when the **Ten Years' War** was ignited at La Demajagua plantation in the outskirts of Bayamo. The Cuban **national anthem**, "La Bayamesa," was first sung in Bayamo; and in 1869 the city's rebel leaders burned down Bayamo rather than allow it to fall back in Spanish hands. Bayamo is the birthplace of several patriots and prominent political figures including **Carlos Manuel de Céspedes, José Antonio Saco, Francisco Vicente Aguilera**, and **Tomás Estrada Palma**. Presently, the municipality of Bayamo is an important **manufacturing** and **transportation** center with a population of 206,336 (est. 1998); the city itself has a population of 143,600 (est. 1999). *See also* Colonial Settlements, Early; Conquest

Further Readings

Freire Díaz, Joaquín. *Historia de los municipios de Cuba*. Miami: La Moderna Poesía, 1985.

Pichardo Viñales, Hortensia. *La fundación de las primeras villas de la Isla de Cuba.* Havana: Editorial de Ciencias Sociales, 1986.

Luis Martínez-Fernández

Beaches

The Cuban coastline is graced by nearly 300 beaches, stretching over 588 kilometers (365 miles). Internationally renowned for their beauty, Cuba's beaches constitute the nation's main tourist attraction. While the majority of Cuba's beaches have not been developed for **tourism**, the recent boom in the tourist industry has led to the rapid development of some beach areas, most notably Varadero, Cayo Coco, Cayo Largo, and the complex known as Playas del Este in the outskirts of Havana.

Varadero is, without doubt, Cuba's most important beach, considered by many the most beautiful beach in the world. Made up of fine, white sand and washed by tranquil, crystalline waters, Varadero extends over 11.5 kilometers (7 miles) along the north coast of the Hicacos Peninsula in the municipality of **Cárdenas**. More than thirty hotels and other accommodations include 12,000 rooms as of 2000.

Their beauty and proximity to Havana make the Playas del Este complex one of the most popular beach destinations; it includes—from west to east—the beaches of Bacuranao, Tarará, El Mégano, Santa María del Mar, Boca Ciega, and Guanabo. Among the other more popular beaches are those of Cayo Coco, Santa Lucía (in **Camagüey Province**), Guardalavaca (in **Holguín Province**), Baconao (in **Santiago de Cuba Province**), Ancón (in **Trinidad**), and Cayo Largo. The **Isla de la Juventud**'s most important beaches are the black-sanded Bibijagua and Punta del Este. *See also* Keys

Further Reading

Núñez Jiménez, Antonio. *Varadero y su entorno maravilloso.* Havana: Ediciones Turísticas de Cuba, 1985.

Luis Martínez-Fernández

Camagüey (Municipality)

With its founding dating back to 1514, Camagüey is one of the island's oldest cities and presently the third largest municipality with a population of 317,427 (est. 1998); the city proper has 306,049 inhabitants (est. 1999). It is the capital of the central province that bears the same name. The city was originally built as a port city on the north coast where Nuevitas stands today and named Santa María del Puerto Príncipe. It was later moved twice until it reached its present inland location in 1528, where it was less vulnerable to **corsairs attacks**. Notwithstanding its safer location, Henry Morgan raided it in 1668. During the first half of the nineteenth century Camagüey temporarily served as the seat of the Royal Audiencia. In 1903 its name was officially changed from Puerto Príncipe to Camagüey, a name derived from the *cacique* who ruled the region at the time of the Spanish **conquest**.

The region's flat terrain allowed the cattle industry to flourish during the colonial era, and large-scale **sugar plantations** sprung up during the twentieth century. The city of Camagüey has served historically as a transportation hub and **manufacturing** center; some of its main industries are linked to food processing. Its urban center is characterized by an intricate system of narrow streets and many plazas; many houses are adorned with large clay containers—thereby the city's nickname as the city of *los tinajones*. Camagüey has a proud heritage of patriotism and fine letters. Among the notable Cubans who were born in Camagüey are the patriots **Ignacio Agramonte** and **Joaquín Agüero y Agüero**, the scientist **Carlos J. Finlay**, and the writers **Gertrudis Gómez de Avellaneda, Enrique José Varona**, and **Nicolás Guillén**. The city has a rich cultural life with its own university and the famed Ballet de Camagüey. *See also* Camagüey Province;

Cattle Ranching; Colonial Institutions; Colonial Settlements, Early; Sugar Industry

Further Readings

Alfonso, Carmen R. *Principales ciudades*. Havana: Ed. José Martí, 1997.

Freire Díaz, Joaquín. *Historia de los municipios de Cuba*. Miami: La Moderna Poesía, 1985.

Pérez de la Lama, Ángela. *El Camagüey legendario*. Camagüey: Imprenta La Moderna, 1944.

Luis Martínez-Fernández

Camagüey Province

Camagüey Province. By Armando H. Portela.

Located toward the central part of the island, Camagüey is the largest Cuban province, with 15,997 square kilometers (6,179 square miles), equivalent to 14.4 percent of the country's surface. Before the changes in the administrative structure of 1976, Camagüey's extension was much larger, comprising most of the current neighboring **Ciego de Ávila Province**, to the west, and part of **Las Tunas**, to the east.

The territory is typically flat, with the exception of a few scattered step hills rising from the plains as relics of prolonged erosion processes. The province's plains developed over a core of Cretaceous turfs and intrusive granites surrounded by more recent Paleocene and Neocene mostly carbonaceous deposits and Quaternary marsh sediments toward the shoreline. A relatively large outcrop of serpentinites with a potent lateritic weathering crust at the San Felipe plateau is the ground for a conspicuous landscape of xerophytic shrubs known as *cuabal* in the Cuban scientific literature.

The province's most prominent elevation is the Sierra de Cubitas, to the north, a belt of overthrusted Mesozoic limestone, with a rough topography of karstic landforms covered by dense semideciduous forests, which rises 330 meters (1,083 feet) above sea level. To the south, the hills of Najasa rise to a top altitude of 312 meters

(1,024 feet). Most of the agricultural lands are brown argillaceous soils of excellent quality with few natural limitations. Lowland coastal areas suffer from poor drainage and local saltwater intrusion.

Camagüey has been shaped by geography and history into a territory of cattle raising, sugarcane plantations, and scarce population. The **sugar industry** spread to Camagüey in the early twentieth century, when the completion of the Central Railroad and the investment of U.S. capital allowed the wild lands to be developed and access to shipping ports was provided. Within a few years, Camagüey lost its reserves of hardwood forests, often used as firewood for the incipient industry. Currently, there are fourteen sugar mills in the province having a nominal capacity in excess of one tenth of the total raw sugar output of the country. The Brasil and Panamá mills (formerly Jaronú and Vertientes) have a daily grinding capacity of 10,200 tons of sugarcane each, among the highest in Cuba. This industry has been badly hit by the economic crisis of the 1990s, when the output of sugar shrank considerably.

Half of the arable lands in Camagüey are devoted to pasture. **Cattle ranching** is extensive, although intensive high-quality dairy cows are bred in the vicinity of the provincial capital and serve as the basis for an important dairy industry. Camagüey hosts roughly 16 percent of the national cattle herd, but the numbers of heads have diminished in recent years. Large areas of grazing lands are currently overgrown and semiabandoned.

Developed by U.S. settlers in the early years of the twentieth century, citrus products are today cultivated in a coastal belt of red ferralitic soils at Sola, to the north, over an area of 10,800 hectares (26,690 acres), two thirds of them consisting of oranges. During its heyday in the 1920s, these citrus orchards exported their output to the United States, rivaling that of the Florida groves. Natural conditions allow rice to be grown in the lowlands of the southwest. Some 16,500 hectares (40,770 acres) produce 10 to 15 percent of the rice grown in Cuba.

The city and port of Nuevitas, to the north, is an important industrial and shipping hub. Some 15 percent of Cuban cement is produced there; there is also a fertilizer plant built in 1975 with Soviet technology, but it largely remains idle as result of the economic collapse of the 1990s. The "10 de Octubre" thermal power plant with 442-megawatt capacity is one of the leading power generators in Cuba. The industrial activity combined with poor environmental practices created in Nuevitas some of the more severe pollution problems on the island.

The fishing port of Santa Cruz del Sur stands among the most important in Cuba. White shrimp, lobster, king fish, and other species are the most valuable captures. Overexploitation and environmental degradation have, however, led to a decline in the volume and quality of captures, in particular of shrimp. Pollution also affects the activity of the northern fishing port at Nuevitas, where a processing plant exists.

For most of its history, Camagüey was a territory of vast unpopulated lands. The improvement of basic communications at the turn of the twentieth century, along with the boom of the sugar industry, attracted immigrants from all over the island and from abroad. Camagüey still is the least densely populated province, with 49 inhabitants per square kilometer (127 per square mile). Its population was estimated at 782,246 in 1999, or roughly 7 percent of the total Cuban population. The capital city, also named **Camagüey**, has a population of 281,000 residents, which makes it the third-largest city, after Havana and **Santiago de Cuba**. Other important cities are Florida (47,000), Nuevitas (42,000), Vertientes (27,000), Guáimaro (19,000), and Santa Cruz del Sur (19,000). The coastal fishing town of Santa Cruz del Sur suffered the worse natural disaster in Cuban records when a hurricane-raised twenty-foot tidal wave took 3,000 lives and wiped out the town of 3,600 inhabitants on November 9, 1932.

The Central Highway and the Central Railroad link Camagüey with the rest of the island, and a network of secondary roads and railroad branches reaches all settlements and economic hubs. The port of Nuevitas is among the most important in Cuba and serves both domestic and international cargo. Its activity has decreased greatly in the last decades, as new sugar shipping ports have been developed. It currently handles over 6 percent of sugar shipments and 3 percent of the international cargo. The **Ignacio Agramonte** International Airport, at the city of Camagüey, is one of the most important in the country. *See also* Fishing Industry; Foreign Investments (Republican Era); Hurricanes; Railroads (Nineteenth Century)

Further Reading

Cruz del Pino, Mary. *Camagüey (Biografía de una provincia).* Havana: Imprenta El Siglo XX, 1955.
Provincia Camagüey. Santiago: Editorial Oriente, 1978.

Armando H. Portela

Cárdenas (Municipality)

Cárdenas is a port city and municipality on the north coast of the province of **Matanzas** in the island's northwest. Cárdenas was founded in 1828 by Juan José Aranguren, and its population and importance increased parallel to the sugar boom of the nineteenth century. Its fine bay became an outlet for the region's sugar production, and many mercantile houses were established in the city. Early on, Cárdenas developed strong commercial and cultural ties with the United States, the main market for its sugar output. Several **manufacturing** industries such as foundries and sugar refineries and **rum** distilleries emerged as linkages of the **sugar industry**. Cárdenas is also known for its fishing tradition and the abundance of crabs. In 1889 Cárdenas earned the distinction of becoming the first Cuban city with electric lighting.

It was in Cárdenas where the Cuban flag was first flown—on May 19, 1850, when **Narciso López's** expeditionaries landed in Cárdenas (see **National Flag**). Because of this honor, Cárdenas is known as la Ciudad Bandera (Flag City); it is also referred to as la Perla del Norte (Pearl of the North), la Ciudad de los Cangrejos (City of Crabs), and la Ciudad de los Coches (City of Carriages). With a population of 95,522 (est. 1998), the municipality of Cárdenas's economy depends on fishing and rum production; many Cardenences find employment in the tourist industry of neighboring Varadero. The city itself has a population of about 68,000. Recently, Cárdenas received international media attention as the hometown of Elián González (see **González Case [Elián]**). *See also* Beaches; Fishing Industry; Sugar Plantations; Tourism

Further Readings
Alfonso, Carmen R. *Principales ciudades*. Havana: Editorial José Martí, 1997.
Freire Díaz, Joaquín. *Historia de los municipios de Cuba*. Miami: La Moderna Poesía, 1985.

Luis Martínez-Fernández

Cauto River Valley

One of the most important geographic features of Cuba due to its physical impression on the land and its importance to the population, the Cauto River Valley is the wide and low valley of the Cauto River, the longest on the island. Located on the eastern end of Cuba, this asymmetrical valley is merely the reflection on the surface of a huge geological structure sunk between faults reaching deep into the mantle of the earth.

On the long and narrow island of Cuba, almost all rivers run toward the south or the north, but the Cauto River, which runs east to west, is an exception. The river's sources are 213 miles away from its mouth, at an altitude of 600 meters (1,970 feet) in the **Sierra Maestra**; some of its tributaries have their sources much higher. Although the Cauto River does not possess the largest water stock in Cuba (that distinction belongs to the Toa River in the northeast), its floods can be devastating, as was the case during Hurricane Flora in 1963 (see **Hurricanes**).

With an area of 8,969 square kilometers (3,464 square miles), equivalent to 8 percent of the country's surface, the Cauto River Basin is one of the island's most important agricultural zones. The land is used for **cattle ranching**, sugarcane cultivation, and rice production. The basin contains 30 percent of Cuba's rice lands. Among the region's thirteen sugar mills is the Urbano Noris (formerly, San Germán, one of Cuba's most important). Unfortunately, the soils are often spoiled by salinization, affecting agricultural output.

Population is not evenly distributed in the valley. Settlements are concentrated toward its edges, keeping distant from the most flood-prone lower parts. Only two roads cross through the valley as well as the southern branch of the Central Railroad. *See also* Agriculture; Communications; Granma Province; Sugar Industry

Further Reading
Portela, Armando H. "The Canto River Valley." *CubaNews* (August 1975): 9.

Armando H. Portela

Ciego de Ávila (Municipality)

Ciego de Ávila is a municipality and capital city of the province of **Ciego de Ávila**, a province that until 1976 was part of the province of **Camagüey**. The region received its name from Jácome de Ávila, an early Spanish settler who received a land concession from the crown. As attested to by extensive archeological finds, the region was an important pre-Columbian population center. The city of Ciego de Ávila was not founded until 1840; in 1877 it was separated from the municipality of Puerto Príncipe (present-day **Camagüey**). Ciego de Ávila was split down the middle, when Spanish troops built the *trocha* of Júcaro-Morón, a fortified line that divided the island in half. Cuban patriots repeatedly penetrated the trocha both during the **Ten Years' War** and the **War of Independence**. Ciego de Ávila is known for its exquisite pineapples and is a major producer of sugarcane and citrus fruits. In 1998 the municipality's population stood at 122,671. *See also* Colonial Settlements, Early; Indigenous Inhabitants; Sugar Industry

Further Readings

Alfonso, Carmen R. *Principales ciudades*. Havana: Editorial José Martí, 1997.

Freire Díaz, Joaquín. *Historia de los municipios de Cuba*. Miami: La Moderna Poesía, 1985.

Luis Martínez-Fernández

Ciego de Ávila Province

The province of Ciego de Ávila was created in November 1976 by combining the western part of **Camagüey Province** with some smaller portions of the eastern part of the old province of Las Villas. It has a total area of 6,910 square kilometers (2,669 square miles), equivalent to 6.2 percent of the country's surface, including 589 square kilometers (227.6 square miles) in the adjacent **keys**.

The territory of Ciego de Ávila is made up almost entirely of flatlands less than 50 meters (164 feet) high, with the exception of scattered step hills to the north, rising to a top altitude of 443 meters (1,453 feet) at the Sierra de Jatibonico and 332 meters (1,089 feet) at the Cunagua Hill. Most of the territory is composed of Miocene limestone and Quaternary marine and alluvial deposits gently sloping toward the sea. Toward the interior, the plains are covered with deep red ferralitic soils, considered among the most productive in Cuba. In the low parts of the coastal plains there are poorly drained gley soils. Brown argillaceous soils are restricted to its foothills and valleys. Consistent with the abundance of karstic limestone in the plains, Ciego de Ávila has an abundant supply of groundwater, but concerns about saltwater intrusions limit the use of aquifers. Over 77,000 hectares (190,271 acres) of lowlands—11 percent of the territory—suffer some degree of saline intrusion in the groundwater and soils. Groundwater is mostly used to irrigate sugarcane, citrus, and other crops. Water for irrigation is brought from **Sancti Spíritus** and Camagücy through canals.

The province's economy depends on **agriculture**, particularly the cultivation of sugarcane. **Tourism** in the keys off the north coast is an increasing source of income. The assimilation of the province's lands occurred mostly after Cuba's independence from Spain, as the sugar boom of the early twentieth century brought capital and immigrants to these plains, at that time still covered with dense hardwood tropical forests that were rapidly cleared to open space for farming. Scattered relics of the original landscapes were spared at the most in marginal locations, mostly the hills, the keys, and in marshlands. Currently there are 9 sugar mills, all of them built in the period between 1906 and 1921. Some of these mills rank among the largest in the country. More than 200,000 hectares

(494,200 acres) are planted with sugar-cane, about 29 percent of the total area. The province accounts for roughly 10 percent of the overall sugar production. The nominal daily grinding capacity of the industry is 70,000 tons, representing 10.6 percent of the country's total. The Ecuador sugar mill (formerly Baraguá) is the province's leading plant and one of the largest in the country. It has a daily grinding capacity of 10,200 tons, 14.6 percent of the province's total capacity and 1.6 percent of all 156 sugar mills existing on the island. This mill includes the only sugar refinery in the province, with a capacity of 95,000 tons annually.

Citrus fruits are grown on 9,900 hectares (24,500 acres) and are an important crop. Farms at Ceballos produce 7 percent of all citrus grown in Cuba and 10 percent of all oranges. Although low by international standards, citrus yields have been customarily among the highest in Cuba, but the quality and yield were severely impacted by the economic crisis of the 1990s. Reportedly some twelve tons/hectare (thirty tons/acre) of fruit were harvested from the fields in the late 1980s, but output had been shrinking since then. A major citrus processing plant exists at Ceballos, in the center of the citrus production zone.

There are few mineral resources in Ciego de Ávila, although the island's largest deposit of gypsum is located at Punta Alegre. Along the length of its border with Sancti Spíritus there are oil fields, some of which have been producing for forty years. The well field at Pina, exploited since 1990, is the main producer in the territory.

The Jardines del Rey (King's Gardens) tourist hub, developed in the 1990s in the keys Coco and Guillermo, off the northern shore, ranks as the third largest in Cuba, only after Havana and Varadero. In 2000 it had over 2,600 rooms, equivalent to 7 percent of all Cuba's hotel capacity, and hosted some 150,000 foreign visitors.

Ciego de Ávila Province. By Armando H. Portela.

Plans foresee a further expansion of capacities and the development of other keys. The development of the keys did not come without problems. A well-known example is the environmental impact on the inland seas and wetlands of the recent construction of an 11-miles-long causeway connecting Key Coco and Key Guillermo to the main island. Interrupting the natural tidal and marine currents flow inside the Bay of Perros, this causeway annihilated the marine life and all but eliminated commercial fishing.

As for most of its history, Ciego de Ávila remains one of the least densely populated regions in Cuba, with 58.5 inhabitants per square kilometer (151 per square mile). Total population was estimated at 403,901 in 1999, with 33.7 percent of those concentrated in two cities, **Ciego de Ávila** (85,000) and Morón (51,000). Other minor settlements have 10,000 dwellers or less and are associated with the sugar mills.

The old two-lanes Central Highway and the Central Railroad link Ciego de Ávila with the rest of the island, and a network of secondary paved roads and railroad branches reaches all its settlements and economic hubs. The province's only port is located at Júcaro, on the province's southern coast. It handles a limited volume of sugar and refined products. Most of the sugar production is shipped through the ports of **Cienfuegos**, Nuevitas, and Guayabal. An international airport, north of the capital city, serves tourism. A second international airport was recently built in an area of dense coastal forests in Key Largo, causing a severe impact on the limited natural reserves of the territory. *See also* Fishing Industry; Foreign Investments (Republican Era); Mining Industry; Sugar Industry

Further Reading

Provincia Ciego de Ávila. Santiago: Editorial Oriente, 1978.

Armando H. Portela

Cienfuegos (Municipality)

Cienfuegos is a municipality and capital city of the southern province that bears the same name. The region was first visited by **Columbus** in 1494. In the 1740s the fort of Jagua was erected to protect the bay of Jagua from foreign attacks; it became Cuba's interim capital during the **British occupation of Havana** in 1762. The founding of Cienfuegos, however, did not take place until 1819, when French settlers

Valle Palace in Cienfuegos. Photograph by Celestino Martínez Lindín.

from Louisiana led by Luis D'Clout were granted permission to immigrate. The city derived its name from that of the island's captain-general at the time of its founding, José Cienfuegos. Cienfuegos soon developed into an important port city, through which passed large quantities of sugar, tobacco, and coffee destined for foreign markets. Known as la Perla del Sur (Pearl of the South), Cienfuegos is considered one of Cuba's most attractive and cultured cities. Among its notable architectural jewels are the Palacio del Valle, Parque **Martí**, Teatro Tomás Terry, and the Paseo del Prado. Cienfuegos is also home to a fine Botanical Garden. Besides being one of the island's main port cities, Cienfuegos is one of Cuba's main industrial centers. Among other industries, Cienfuegos produces cement and thermoelectric energy. Its bay also houses an important naval installation. In 1982 construction began on the controversial Jaraguá nuclear plant in the outskirts of the city; work on the plant has been discontinued since 1992. Currently, the municipality's population stands at 158,384 (est. 1998), the city's at 117,000. *See also* Cienfuegos Province; Coffee Industry; Corsairs Attacks; Manufacturing; Sugar Industry; Tobacco Industry

Further Readings

Alfonso, Carmen R. *Principales ciudades.* Havana: Editorial José Martí, 1997.

Freire Díaz, Joaquín. *Historia de los municipios de Cuba.* Miami: La Moderna Poesía, 1985.

Luis Martínez-Fernández

Cienfuegos Province

Located in the south-central part of the island, the province of Cienfuegos has existed since 1976, when the former province of Las Villas was divided to form three new territories, including the neighboring provinces of **Villa Clara** and **Sancti Spíritus**. Cienfuegos is the second-smallest province in area after the **Ciudad de La Habana Province**, with 4,177 square kilometers (1,613.5 square miles), equivalent to almost 3.8 percent of the national territory. It borders the provinces of **Matanzas** to the west, Villa Clara to the north, and Sancti Spíritus to the east.

The territory is made up of fertile flat and undulating plains and valleys, with crops and grazing lands occupying 75 percent of the area, where most people live, and of sparsely populated mountains, typically covered with dense forests and coffee groves. The **Escambray Mountains**, rising abruptly to the southeast of the province, are an intricate massif of overthrusted Jurassic sequences, including schist, limestone, marble, and amphibolites, deeply cut by narrow flat-bottom valleys. The provinces of Villa Clara and Sancti Spíritus also share this mountain range. Pico San Juan (also known as Pico La Cuca), rising 1,140 meters (3,740 feet), is the tallest peak in the Escambray Mountains and the highest elevation west of the **Sierra Maestra** mountain range in the southeast of the island.

The province's economy is a combination of **agriculture, manufacturing**, and port activities. Cienfuegos's development is closely tied to the bay and port that share its name. The province has 3,156 square kilometers (1,219 square miles) of agricultural lands. Of these, sugarcane accounts for roughly 30 percent and pastureland, 36 percent. Sugarcane plantations and grazing and dairy farms dominate the landscape of plains and hills, while coffee grows in the mountains amid the dense tropical forest. Twelve sugar mills with a daily grinding capacity of 42,800 tons of cane account for 6 to 7 percent of the national sugar output. Compared to Cuban standards, Cienfuegos's sugar mills are typically small.

Major investments in the 1970s and 1980s made Cienfuegos one of the leading industrial hubs on the island, but the hard-ships of the economic crisis at the end of the twentieth century paralyzed or left unfinished most of its facilities. The construction of the Juraguá nuclear power plant, the best-known industrial facility in the area, was halted at the time of the collapse of the Soviet Union and officially abandoned in 2000 even though its first reactor was 75 to 80 percent built and just two years away from completion. The project had aroused deep safety concerns in the United States since the beginning of construction in 1983; the heart of the facility was to have been a Russian-built 440-megawatt reactor similar to the one that exploded in April 1986 at Chernobyl in the Ukraine. Other industrial facilities bear national importance. The **"Carlos Manuel de Céspedes"** thermoelectric plant began operations in 1978 with a generating capacity of 398 megawatts, equivalent to 12 percent of Cuba's total generating capacity. The plant is linked to the backbone of the national power transmission lines through a double extension line of 220 kilovolts and 110 kilovolts running 60 kilometers (37 miles) to **Santa Clara** in the center of the island. Cuba's second-largest cement plant, the "Karl Marx," located northeast of the city of **Cienfuegos**, has a nominal capacity to produce 650,000 tons of cement a year, or over a fifth of the record production in Cuba; hindered by fuel inefficiency, however, the plant drastically slowed production after the onset of the economic crisis in the 1990s. One of the largest industrial facilities in the province, a new oil refinery, remains idle since its completion in 1991. It has a potential refining capacity of 60,000 barrels per day (3 million tons per year), or over one third of the national fuel consumption of the late 1990s. The refinery is connected to the supertankers piers and huge oil storage facilities in **Matanzas** Bay through the also idle Friendship Pipeline, a double 186-kilometer-long (116 miles) pipeline, capable of moving

Cienfuegos Province. By Armando H. Portela.

134,000 barrels per day, upgradeable to 200,000 barrels daily.

Cienfuegos's population was estimated at 392,558 in 1999, equivalent to 3.5 percent of the total Cuban population. The province's capital, also called Cienfuegos, is Cuba's eighth-largest city and concentrates 30 percent of the province's dwellers, with a population of 117,000, a large proportion by Cuban standards. Other important settlements are Cruces (22,000), Cumanayagua (21,000), and Aguada de Pasajeros (15,000).

Founded by French immigrants from Louisiana in 1819 that moved there to grow sugarcane, Cienfuegos originally bore the aboriginal name of Jagua, changed to its current name in 1881 to honor Spanish Captain-General José Cienfuegos, who ruled the island at the time of the city's foundation. Although all settlements and economic hubs are reachable through paved roads and railroads, Cienfuegos lies relatively far from Cuba's primary land routes, the National Expressway and the Central Railroad, connected to them only by sinuous narrow branches. A domestic airport located close to the capital city has limited and nonregular links with the rest of the country. Its broad, sheltered bay hosts one of the busiest and best-outfitted ports on the island, ranking second after Havana's. It is the leading terminal for Cuban sugar shipping, with 30 percent of all exports leaving from it. It also exports citrus, cement, and fuel. A deep-water pier, capable of berthing 50,000-ton ships, was recently built to serve the new oil refinery but remains little used.

Industrial expansion has produced a severe environmental impact. Uncontrolled industrial waste disposal, oil spills, and the untreated runoff from the sugar industry reportedly have ruined some marine ecosystems in the bay. *See also* Coffee Industry; Soviet Union, Cuba's Relations with the; Special Period; Sugar Industry

Further Reading

Provincia Cienfuegos. Santiago: Editorial Oriente, 1978.

Armando H. Portela

Ciudad de La Habana (City of Havana) Province

Following the rearrangement of the administrative layout of the island in 1976, the nation's capital city and its immediate surrounds were detached from the rural areas of the old **Havana Province** to form the new City of Havana Province.

Located in western Cuba around a virtually landlocked harbor, the province faces the Straits of Florida in the north, with 50 kilometers (31 miles) of shoreline—not considering the inner coast of Havana Bay—and is surrounded by Havana Province in all other confines. The City of Havana is the smallest province on the island, with only 724 square kilometers (280 square miles), representing barely 0.6 percent of the country's territory.

Havana originally was founded in 1514 by **Diego Velázquez** on the swampy southwestern coast of the island, near the present town of Batabanó, but mosquitoes and poor access compelled the first residents to move in 1519 to the current location around the port of Carenas, as Havana's Bay was originally named. The city is one of the earliest settlements in the Americas and has served as Cuba's capital since the mid-sixteenth century.

The province consists mainly of the developed lands of the capital and its outskirts, where roughly one fifth of all the

Cuban **population** lives. Nevertheless, one third of its territory is devoted to **agriculture**, mainly to grazing lands but also to sugarcane and vegetables cultivation (see **Cattle Ranching** and **Sugar Industry**).

Havana is built on top of gentle rising marine terraces carved out of Miocene to Quaternary limestone along the shoreline. These terraces are more evident in El Vedado, Miramar, and Marianao neighborhoods to the west and Cojímar, Alamar, and Guanabo beach to the east. A hilly landscape predominates inland, shaped on a core of Cretaceous marls, sandstone, and serpentinites where El Cerro, Luyanó, La Víbora, Lawton, and Guanabacoa neighborhoods sit. To its southern edge, the city is built over a high karstic plain covered with red soils where the districts of El Cotorro, Fontanar, and Santiago de las Vegas stand.

The Almendares River splits the city into two parts, forming a less populated low alluvial plain. The river cuts a relatively deep and narrow canyon in the coastal terraces, reaching the sea in a location known as "la Chorrera" (The Flush).

Havana's top elevation is the Tetas de Managua, at the southern edge of the province, rising to 220 meters (722 feet) above sea level. Scattered hills in the middle section of the city such as Loma del Burro (50 meters), Loma de Chaple (60 meters), Loma del Mazo (70 meters), Loma del Quinto Distrito (80 meters), and Loma de la Cruz, at Guanabacoa (70 meters), all provide a superb view of the city and its surroundings.

A scenic coast with 9 kilometers (5.6 miles) of white-sand **beaches** to the east is a favorite resting place for Havana's residents. Intense erosion since the 1970s has depleted the quality of the beaches, however. The high karstic plain south of the city holds a rich aquifer, utilized since 1893 when the Acueducto de Albear was completed to supply the freshwater needs of the population and its industry: overuse

and pollution have dramatically depleted its quality and reserves. Today this aqueduct still supplies 19 percent of the fresh water Havana uses. Water and sewer services to Havana are a chronic nightmare for authorities. Freshwater shortages, depletion of sources, spillage through the aging system, and improper wastewater disposal are common.

Havana is the heart of the nation. It is not just the decision-making and economic center of the island; it has been a political and cultural reference point in the Americas for centuries. As the principal site of government, most of the official headquarters are concentrated in and around the **Plaza de la Revolución (Revolution's [Civic] Square)**. It is also the center of commerce, **communications, transportation, tourism**, and culture. Furthermore, it boasts the best institutions of learning and the most comprehensive medical services on the island, thus helping to attract a constant stream of immigrants from the countryside.

It accounts for half of the industrial output of the country (see **Manufacturing** and **Energy**). Electric power generation and crude oil refining are leading industries, but Havana also hosts some of the largest and best-known processing plants of the food industry (breweries, dairy, and canning plants). Manufacturing of cigars and cigarettes is a long-established industry in the capital, where most of the legendary cigar brands are made. Havana also has textile, apparel, and shoemaking factories and tanneries. The fast-growing pharmaceutical and biotechnological industry (see **Pharmaceutical Industry** and **Biotechnology**), largely based in Havana, is a leading source of hard **currency** with some $40 million per year in exports during the late 1990s. The capital also has several chemical plants, paper mills, machinery shops, slaughtering houses, two steel mills, print shops, and construction plants, among other industrial facilities.

Havana attracts nearly half the visitors to Cuba in the growing tourism sector. With just under 12,000 rooms in 2000, the city concentrates 29 percent of the hosting capacities nationwide, second only to Varadero Beach. Most tourists visit the historic core of **Habana Vieja (Old Havana)** and Santa María beach, to the east. Once the pride of the nation as a sophisticated, modern, and influential sector, Havana's commercial infrastructure is in dismal condition as its hundreds of elegant convenience stores, illuminated promenades, bohemian cafés, restaurants, night clubs, and even office buildings have suffered decades of official neglect, which has frequently led to the closure of many facilities.

Traditionally, the capital has been the center of enlightenment in the country. Academic and cultural life have flourished in Havana. Its **theaters**, museums, newspapers, journals, editorial houses, academies, and colleges all have had an important and lasting influence on the course of Cuban history. The **University of Havana**, founded in 1728, embodies a symbol for the higher education centers in the country. Havana also hosts the Higher Polytechnic Institute, the Higher Pedagogic Institute, the School of Medicine, the Higher School of Arts, and others. The **Academy of Sciences** and a number of leading research institutions in biotechnology have also been founded in Havana.

Havana has an estimated 2.186 million residents (2000), or 19.5 percent of Cuba's population, which makes the city the largest urban settlement on the island and the Caribbean. Unlike other cities or provinces in Cuba, the size of Havana's population has been shrinking since 1996—after peaking at 2.204 million dwellers—at an annual rate of −0.2 percent. Population loss results from the capital's poor natural growth, the relatively high rate of emigration abroad of its residents, and the severe

Ciudad de La Habana Province. By Armando H. Portela.

restrictions imposed by the government on countryside migrants wishing to settle there. Population density reaches 3,019 settlers per square kilometer as an average, but it is unevenly distributed, peaking at 44,000 residents per square kilometer in the crowded Centro Habana municipality where most of the living quarters are two or three stories high, compared to barely 837 dwellers per square kilometer in the Guanabacoa municipality where ample spaces of vacant or grazing lands prevail.

Havana's **housing** shortage is a problem that has been neglected for decades. More than half of the 568,000 housing units in the city are in urgent need of repair, and one in ten dwellings is officially labeled beyond repair. Other basic urban services such as public transport, telephones, and garbage collection are in a dismal state. As the managerial and economic center of the country, the transport and communication system radiates from Havana to the east and west to reach all economic hubs and settlements on the island. The new eight-lane National Expressway, the old two-lane Central Highway, and the Central Railway are the main links to the rest of the country. Havana is also the center of the national transmission network of radio-electronic and digital communications.

The port of Havana is the most important in Cuba. It has 7,833 meters (25,700 feet) of berthing capacity and supports the most maritime traffic in the country. Its versatile facilities allow handling all kinds of cargo and include the largest

El Morro Castle at the entrance of the Bay of Havana. Photograph by Celestino Martínez Lindín.

cranes, dry docks, and refrigerated warehouses in the country. Careless port activities and improper industrial and urban waste disposal for over a century around Havana Bay have built its reputation as one of the most polluted ports in the world. Frequent spillage from surrounding factories joins hundreds of tons of garbage, waste oil, and sewer waste dumped regularly in the waters. Environmental rules are rarely enforced. Restoration is estimated to cost billions and to last for decades.

The **José Martí** International Airport, located in the southern part of the city, handles the largest air traffic in Cuba. *See also* **Cigars and Cigar Making**; Habana (Havana) Province, La; Habana Vieja (Old Havana) (Municipality), La

Further Readings

Barclay, Juliet, *Havana: Portrait of a City.* London: Cassell Villiers House, 1993.

Carpentier, Alejo. *La ciudad de las columnas.* Barcelona: Editorial Lumen, 1970.

Roig de Leuchsenring, Emilio. *La Habana. Apuntes históricos.* 3 vols. 2nd ed. Havana: Consejo Nacional de Cultura, 1963.

Armando H. Portela

Climate

While located within the tropics, the Cuban archipelago exhibits a climate that is moderated by several factors, including the cooling effect of the trade winds, the influence of surrounding bodies of water, and the impact of cooler air masses flowing from the continent of North America. According to the Koppen classification of world climates, the northern and western parts of the island are tropical monsoon, while the southern part of the island is tropical savannah.

Cuba's yearly mean temperature stands at 25° Celsius (77° F); the mean for the summer is 27° (80.6° F), and the mean for the winter is 21° (69.8° F). The average relative humidity is 81 percent, and the average yearly rainfall is close to 1,400 millimeters (55 inches). Certain parts of the island, such as la **Sierra Maestra**, receive large amounts of rainfall (more than 2,000 millimeters; 78 inches), while places like **Guantánamo** receive only half that amount, and la Punta de Maisí, on the eastern end, receives a little over 500 millimeters (20 inches). The rainy season runs from May to October, and the dry season runs from November to April. Hurricane season begins on June 1 and ends on November 15, with most **hurricanes** striking in October and September.

Further Readings

Davitaya, F.F., and I.I. Trusov. *Los recursos climáticos de Cuba, su utilización en la economía nacional.* Havana: Academia de Ciencias de Cuba, 1965.

Marrero, Leví. *Geografía de Cuba.* New York: Minerva Books, 1966.

República de Cuba, Comité Estatal de Estadísticas. *Anuario estadístico de Cuba, 1989.* Havana: Comité Estatal de Estadísticas, 1991.

República de Cuba, Instituto Cubano de Geodesia y Cartografía. *Atlas climático de Cuba.* Havana: Instituto Cubano de Geodesia y Cartografía, 1987.

Luis Martínez-Fernández

Escambray Mountains

The Escambray is a small group of low mountains located toward the south-central part of the island and surrounded by wavy plains, cattle lands, and some rough hill ranges. The range measures about eighty kilometers (fifty miles) from east to west and forty kilometers (twenty-five miles) from north to south. Before 1959, the range was known by other names such as the mountains of **Trinidad** or **Sancti Spíritus**. Scientific literature, trying to prevent misunderstandings, prefers to use the Indian name *Guamuhaya*, an option rarely used by the population.

The Escambray was the scene of two wars. The first was part of the **struggle against Batista** in the late 1950s. The other erupted a few months into the **Revolution**, as guerrilla forces fought in the region, attempting to bring down the government of **Fidel Castro**. As a result of this last confrontation, the mountains were almost entirely depopulated: Residents were relocated, and after the end of the conflict, new families settled in (see **Segundo Frente del Escambray**).

The region's economy is predominantly agriculturally based, with coffee being its primary product. Other economic activities include **cattle ranching**, sugarcane growing, and tobacco farming. In the recent past, **tourism** has expanded, including hunting and ecotourism. The region's historic cities and **beaches** to the south also attract tourists. *See also* Coffee Industry; Sugar Industry; Tobacco Industry

Further Reading

Ayala Castro, Norberto. *Topes de Collantes, vida silvestre en el Escambray*. Havana: Empresa Industrial de Comunicaciones, 1989.

Armando H. Portela

Fauna

With over 13,000 species of animals, Cuba is a diversified habitat for numerous species of reptiles, amphibians, mollusks, mammals, birds, fish, and insects. Cuba's territory is characterized by extraordinarily high rates of biodiversity and endemism. About 10 percent of the island's fauna, however, is on the verge of extinction. Although animal life in Cuba is similar to that of other Caribbean islands, Cuba's unique geography and separation from other regions have influenced its fauna in very distinct ways. There are no real large fauna on the island; the island, rather, plays habitat for some of the world's smallest animals. The world's smallest bird comes from Cuba: the bee hummingbird, or *zunzuncito* (*Calypte helenae*). It is just slightly larger than a grasshopper and weighs only two grams. The microtytus Cuban froglet (Eleutherodactylus limbatus) and the dwarf bat (*Nyctiellus lepidus*), and the sijucito bird are also among the smallest animal species in the world.

Cuba's most abundant land fauna is reptilian and includes crocodiles, caymans, iguanas, lizards, salamanders, turtles, and snakes. Over 80 percent of the reptiles found in Cuba are endemic. The iguana, a common land reptile on the island, was once a major source of nutrition but is now close to extinction. The most common variety of iguana (*Cyclura nubila*) is about 7.6 to 10 centimeters (three to four inches) in length, has a light green hue, and is fast moving. Snakes on the island are found in over fifteen species, none of which are venomous. The largest snake, the Majá de Santamaría (*Epicrates angulizer*), or thick-bodied snake, range in length from about three feet to nine feet. The island plays host to an abundance of crocodiles, which are found at the mouth of many rivers and in muddy waters. There are two species of crocodiles, the *Crocodylus rhombifer* and the *Crocodylus acutus*, commonly referred to as *caimán*. Lizards, or *lagartijas*, are another abundant reptile and play a large role in controlling the insect population since they prey on small insects.

There are thousands of species of mollusks in Cuba and range from freshwater, saltwater, and land varieties. About 90 per-

Cuban Crocodile (Cocodrilo); *Crocodylus rhombifer.* Nineteenth-century sketch by Samuel Hazard.

cent of the island's mollusks are endemic. Endemic to the island is the tiny and colorful snail *Polymitas picta cubana*, which only breeds on the island's easternmost region. Most marine mollusks are edible. The most common mollusks in and around Cuba include clams, oysters, squids, octopuses, *cobos*, and cuttle fish. The most common crustaceans are shrimp (of various sizes), crabs, and lobsters. These constitute one of Cuba's most sought-after exports (see **Fishing Industry**).

There are over 900 different species of fish in the coastal waters of Cuba; of these, over 500 species are edible. The most common are grouper, or *cherna*, tuna, swordfish, red snapper, and stripped tuna, or *bonito*. The *manjuarí* (*Atractosteus tristoechus*), which can be found on the western part of the island, is not only endemic to the island but also prehistoric. There are over 35 species of sharks. Manta rays, sting rays, and the moray eels are also common.

There are over 300 species of birds in Cuba. As Cuba is situated along a migratory path, most of the bird species on the island are not endemic, however. Among the endemic birds of Cuba are the *tocororo* (*Priotelus temnurus*), from the family of the majestic quetzal, which is the national bird of the island and whose plumage shares the Cuban flag's colors. The parakeet, also known as the *cotorra* or *periquito* (*Amazona leucocephala leucocephala*) was once abundant on the island but is now close to extinction. Other common birds include owls, several varieties of woodpeckers, and black buzzards (*Cathares aura*), pelicans, and flamingoes (Phoenicopterus ruber). The *sinsonte* (mockingbird) (*Mimus polyglottos orpheus*) and *ruiseñor* (nightingale) (*Myadestes elisabeth elisabeth*) are also very common.

The largest land mammal is the *jutía*, a tree rat that grows to about sixty centimeters (twenty-four inches) in length. They are close to extinction, as they are edible. The largest jutía is known as the *conga* (*Capromys pilorides*). Other types of jutía include the *carabalí* (*Capromys prehensilis*) and the *andaraz* (*Capromys melanurus*). Another endemic mammalian is the smaller *almiquí* (*Solendon cubanus*). The *manatí* (*Trichechus manatus*) can be found in some of Cuba's rivers.

There are thousands of insect species in Cuba. Among the most common are ants, roaches, moths, mosquitoes, flies, termites, and weevils. Cuba is habitat to two species of giant harvester ants, *bibi-jaguas* (Atta insularis). *See also* National Bird

Further Readings

Barbour, Thomas. *A Naturalist in Cuba*. Boston: Little, Brown, 1945.

Hernández Ricardo, Luis H. *La fauna cubana*. Havana: Editorial Científico-Técnica, 1997.

Silva Lee, Alfonso. *Natural Cuba*. St. Paul, MN: Pangaea, 1997.

Nilo Jorge Barredo

Flora

Cuba's biodiversity allows for a mosaic of colors and shapes of flora. There are over 7,000 species of plants in Cuba. Over 3,000 of these are endemic. Over half of the endemic flora on the island can be found in the eastern provinces. During the last 350 years, about 900 species of flora have become either endangered or extinct.

There are various theories regarding the origin of Cuba's flora. Most scientists agree that Cuba was attached to North, Central, and South America during the Mesozoic era. The geological proximity of the Mesozoic era allows for the presence of flora such as palm trees and pines, which are common to other areas of the Americas. The island of Hispaniola shares more species of flora with Cuba than any other country in the region. Jamaica and Puerto Rico also share a large degree of flora with Cuba.

Before the arrival of European settlers, more than 90 percent of Cuba was covered with forest. However, clearance for **cattle ranching** and sugarcane reduced this proportion: 75 percent of the land is now savannah or plains, 18 percent mountains, and 4 percent swamps. Besides semideciduous woodland, vegetation types include rainforest, coastal and upland scrub, distinctive limestone vegetation found in the Sierra de los Órganos and similar areas, savannah vegetation found on nutrient-deficient white silica sands, pine forests, xerophytic coastal limestone woodland, mangroves, and other coastal wetlands.

Among the endemic flora in Cuba are the families of *Asteraceae, Rubiaceae, Papilionaceae, Poaceae, Acanthaceae,* and *Myrtaceae.* The majority of the endemic flora on the island can be found in mountainous regions. There are over 400 species of *Poaceae* and *Asteraceae.* The families of *Orchidaceae, Rubiaceae,* and *Euphorbiaceae* are present on the island, with over 300 species each. Among the island's tree varieties are the cedars, ebony, kapok trees, giant figs, mahogany, oaks, pine, and mangroves near the shore. Flower plant varieties include begonias, bromeliads, hibiscus, orchids, oleander, and poinsettias. One of the world's largest flowers, the *Solandra grandiflora,* is endemic to Cuba. There are over 300 species of orchids in Cuba, whose colors and shapes form a unique floral patrimony. The **national flower** is *la mariposa,* or butterfly (*Hedychium coronarium Koenig*), a small white petal flower of the jasmine family. One tiny orchid, the *Pleurothallis shaferi,* which is only one centimeter (less than half an inch), has leaves measuring five millimeters (.20 inch) and flowers of only two millimeters (.08 inch).

Cuba's **national tree** is the royal palm (*Roystonea regia*), which graces the **national coat of arms**. With over thirty species of palm trees, Cuba is said to have a population of over 20 million palms. Within the family of palms, we not only find the royal palm but also a rare and prehistoric cork palm, which can be traced back to the Cretaceous Period. The cork palm is endemic to the island and endangered. *See also* Sugar Industry

Further Readings

Barbour, Thomas. *A Naturalist in Cuba*. Boston: Little, Brown, 1945.

Samkova, Hana, and Veroslav Samek. *Bibliografía botánica cubana*. Havana: Academia de Ciencias de Cuba, 1967.

Silva Lee, Alfonso. *Natural Cuba*. St. Paul, MN: Pangaea, 1997.

Nilo Jorge Barredo

Granma Province

Located on the southeastern part of the island, facing the Caribbean Sea and the inner waters of the Gulf of Guacanayabo, Granma is one of the five provinces founded in 1976 following the division of the old Oriente Province. Its name was given after that of the vessel used in 1956 to carry on to Cuba a belligerent expedition headed by **Fidel Castro** aiming to overthrow the government of **Fulgencio Batista** (see *Granma* **Expedition**). Granma is Cuba's sixth-largest province, with an area of 8,372 square kilometers (3,234 square miles), equivalent to 7.5 percent of the country's total area. It shares borders with the provinces of **Las Tunas** and **Holguín**, to the north, and **Santiago de Cuba**, to the east and south.

The province's territory is a contrasting combination of the broad plains of the lower part of the **Cauto River Valley**, covered with marshes, croplands, and grazing lands, where most people live, and the steep mountains of the western part of the **Sierra Maestra**, the highest and most extensive range in the country, a sparsely populated terrain with coffee groves shaded by tropical forests. Plains make up two thirds of the province. They correspond to a deep structural Tertiary basin filled with argillaceous sequences overlaid by Quaternary alluvial and deltaic sediments gentle sloping to the Gulf of Guacanayabo. The mountains are built on an intricate core of Paleocenic andesites intruded by granitic rocks cut by deep narrow valleys that provide access to the inland. Near Cape Cruz, to the west, the heights gradually disappear, covered by gentle sloping Neocene limestone where some of Cuba's most impressive sinkholes are located. Pico La Bayamesa is the highest point in the province, rising 1,756 meters (5,760 feet) above sea level. Other important summits are Pico **Martí**, with 1,722 meters (5,648 feet); Pico Palma Mocha, rising to 1,388 meters (4,553 feet); and Pico Caracas, topping at 1,234 meters (4,047 feet).

Deep dark clayey soils, very plastic, once considered among the most productive in Cuba, cover the low plains of the Cauto River Valley, but today poor drainage and high salinity are a serious limitation to their quality. Better-drained brown argillaceous soils are restricted to the Sierra Maestra piedmont. The Cauto delta creates a wetland ecosystem with mangrove forests that provides shelter and breeding ground for valuable commercial fishing species caught in nearby waters. Two large freshwater reservoirs were built in the Sierra Maestra to suit the needs of a growing **population** and **agriculture**. They have a combined capacity to hold 255 million cubic meters (67.4 billion gallons). An extensive irrigation system, including hundreds of kilometers of culverts, sends the water mainly to sugarcane and rice lands.

The province has endured considerable environmental damage. Deforestation, river damming, overgrazing in mountains, and improper waste disposal have taken the greatest toll. The original semideciduous tropical forest that once covered plains and mountains have gradually been cleared since colonial times to open space for farming. Even riparian forests spared along riverbanks as protection belts have disappeared in large extensions. Remnants of the forests cover barely 13 percent of the province and can be found in remote areas unsuitable for agriculture or in mountains' highest belts. Salinization of soils is a severe problem largely caused by river damming and irrigation, along with a noticeable decrease of rains and runoff. Roughly 2,773 square kilometers (1,723 square miles), or over one third, of all agricultural lands in the province suffer varying degrees of saline intrusions on soils.

Agriculture is the mainstay of the province's economy. Accounting for approximately 40 percent of the total, Granma is the largest producer of rice in the country, with an average output of 180,000 tons per year in the 1980s, falling sharply three to four times in the 1990s. Eleven sugar mills produce between 6 and 7 percent of the country's sugar. One sugar refinery makes 2 percent of Cuba's refined sugar. Sugarcane fields suffer poor yields, and the industry's wastes rank among the worst offenders to the local environment. Granma is the third largest coffee grower in the country, with 10 to 15 percent of the total output, behind the provinces of **Guantánamo** and Santiago de Cuba. The orchards, located in the Sierra Maestra, have been largely neglected, and yields are generally poor.

The province also houses some factories of national significance. A pipe and sprinkler factory was opened in 1977 in **Bayamo** to satisfy national irrigation needs. The only electric batteries producing factory in the country was opened in Manzanillo in 1979, with a nominal capacity to make 450,000 units per year, enough to cover most of the needs of the island. Untreated industrial wastes of these two plants rank among the most harmful polluters in the province. A marble quarry near Guisa, on the northern slope of Sierra Maestra, produces a highly sought after decorative variety for domestic construction needs and for exports.

The fishing port of Manzanillo stands among the most significant in Cuba. Fisheries are also important in Niquero. White shrimp, lobster, and king fish are the most

Granma Province. By Armando H. Portela.

valuable captures. Also common are oysters, sea turtles, sharks, marlins, and other species. Overexploitation, severe pollution, and the loss of coastal habitats have led to decline in the volume and quality of captures, in particular, of shrimp.

Its population was estimated at 828,324 in 1999, or 7.4 percent of the total Cuban population. Bayamo is the province's capital, with an estimated 113,000 dwellers. It was the second settlement founded in Cuba by **Diego Velázquez** in 1513 with the original name of San Salvador de Bayamo. The second city, Manzanillo, has an estimated 107,000 dwellers. Other important cities are Niquero (19,000), Jiguaní (17,000), Guisa (17,000), Campechuela (17,000), and Media Luna (15,000).

The two-lane Central Highway and the Central Railroad link Granma to the rest of the island. A network of narrow secondary paved roads reaches all major settlements and economic hubs. The mountains are accessible through dirt roads. The sugar bulk-loading terminal at Ceiba Hueca, 25 kilometers (fifteen miles) southwest of Manzanillo, handles 6 percent of all Cuba's sugar exports. The airports at Bayamo and Manzanillo handle modest domestic air traffic. *See also* Coffee Industry; Colonial Settlements, Early; Fishing Industry; Manufacturing; Sugar Industry

Further Reading
Provincia Granma. Santiago: Editorial Oriente, 1977.

Armando H. Portela

Guantánamo Province

Located at the eastern tip of the island, Guantánamo's rugged and poorly accessible topography is the least studied in Cuba. It is a land of high contrasts that holds important natural resources and perhaps the best-preserved wilderness in the country. Guantánamo was detached from the old Oriente Province in 1976, as the ruling **Communist Party** resolved to change the administrative structure of the island. With 6,186 square kilometers (2,388 square miles), equivalent to 5.6 percent of the country's area, Guantánamo is a small province by Cuban standards, not only in terms of its area but also according to the size of its population and the weight of the local economy. It borders with the provinces of **Santiago de Cuba** and **Holguín** to the west.

The thickest and best-preserved forests on the island cover most of the mountains, where the highest average rainfall in Cuba is recorded and ironically also the driest **climate**. The **population** to some extent, with a marked presence of *mestizos* and distinguishable aboriginal features in many individuals, shows a different physiognomy from those born in other regions of Cuba. The local accent and even some staples of the local diet also contrast with the rest of the island. These distinctions make Guantánamo unlike any other place in Cuba. It is so conspicuous that traveling through the province is, to some extent, like being in a different country.

Mountains make up 75 percent of Guantánamo's area. Curiously, there is not a unified name to recognize the mountain range across Guantánamo; rather, they are locally named as the separated ranges of Cuchillas del Toa, Cuchillas de Baracoa, Sierra del Purial, Sierra del Mariana, Sierra del Maquey, and Meseta del Guaso. Together with the Sierra de Nipe and Sierra Cristal in the neighboring Holguín Province, scholars agreed to group them conventionally as the Nipe-Sagua-Baracoa mountain range, a denomination not used by locals. The top elevation in the province is Pico El Gato, at the Sierra del Purial, rising to 1,184 meters (3,884 feet) above sea level. Other important elevations are the Cuchillas del Mate, topping 1,180 meters (3,870 feet); Loma Colorada, with 1,051 meters (3,447 feet); and Pico Galán, with 974 meters (3,195 feet). Blocking the free flow of the Atlantic humid trade winds, the mountains are a formidable barrier to rains and divide two very different landscapes. In the north windward slope of the mountains, average annual rainfall exceeds 3,400 millimeters (134 inches). A dense rainforest, often growing over thick weathering crusts, shelters numerous endemic plants and animals, among them the *almiquí* (*Solenodon cubanus*), an elusive endangered mammal found nowhere else in the world. A colorful terrestrial mollusk of the *Polymita* genus crawls in the forests, but collectors or handcrafters have decimated the populations (see **Fauna**).

South of the watershed, on the lee of winds and rains, a narrow belt along the coast from Guantánamo Bay to the Point of Maisí, receives less than 600 millimeters (24 inches) of rainfall yearly, and xerophytic thorn bushes predominate.

The Guantánamo basin, a tectonic Tertiary depression enclosed by mountains, provides the only relatively wide space for agriculture in the province, although droughts and expanding salinity hamper farming, ruining many croplands.

Another outstanding geographic trait of this part of the island is the series of spectacular marine terraces at Maisí Point. Unique in the world and frequently featured in textbooks of geography, this series of dozens of large steps carved on limestone was created by the combined effects of marine abrasion and tectonic upheaval over millions of years. They rise from the sea level to a top altitude of 660 meters (2,160 feet). Terraces along the southeast-

ern coast are often interrupted by a se-
quence of large amphitheaters resulting
from seismically provoked landslides. This
feature, first described by Cuban scholars
in the early 1990s, represents an exceptional element for the study of Caribbean
seismic history.

Guantánamo's economy is primarily
agricultural, with 40 percent of the province's land devoted to it; but arable lands,
found only in the Guantánamo Basin and
the Caujerí Valley, are scarce and poor.
Salinization of soils is a severe problem
exacerbated by improper agricultural practices. Roughly 276 square kilometers (106
square miles), almost one fifth, of all agricultural lands in the province suffer saline intrusions on soils. Only 6 percent of
the territory is devoted to sugarcane. Its six
sugar mills have a daily grinding capacity
of 11,800 metric tons, or about 1.8 percent
of the country's total. The province accounts for 25 percent of the **coffee** produced in Cuba, ranking second after
Santiago de Cuba. The orchards are located in the mountains where deep soils,
fresh temperatures, and high humidity provide excellent conditions for the bean.
Nevertheless, plantations have been
largely neglected, affecting both yields and
quality. Annual production is less than
5,000 tons. Guantánamo is the first cacao
producer on the island, averaging some
1,700 tons per year, much lower than the
6,800 tons reached in the early years of the
twentieth century, before plantations were
abandoned as a result of sugar expansion.
Helped by the dryness of the climate, a
facility at Caimanera produces 115,000
tons of common salt per year, representing
70 percent of national consumption. A fur-
niture factory in the capital city is oriented
to the tourist industry.

The population was estimated at
512,266 in 1999, or roughly 4.6 percent of
all Cubans. Traditionally, Guantánamo
shows the highest birthrate in the nation
but at the same time the largest emigration

Guantánamo Province. By Armando H. Portela.

rate to other provinces. Poor living conditions and scarce job opportunities feed
the migrant flow. In the late 1990s it was
estimated that 1 percent of the population
leaves the province every year in search of
a better place.

The province's capital, also known as
Guantánamo, had 208,000 dwellers in
1999. The capital city has tripled its population since 1953, when 64,671 inhabitants
lived there. **Baracoa**, the first village
founded in Cuba by **Diego Velázquez** in
1512, is the second-largest city in the province, with 41,000 inhabitants.

The network of roads and railroads is
very limited. Some settlements in the
mountains are inaccessible by modern
means of **transportation**. Sugar production is exported entirely through Bo-
querón, where the facilities for shipping in
bulk can handle about 5,000 tons daily and
storage capacity totals 20,000 tons. The
airport near the city of Guantánamo supports limited domestic traffic. The **Guantánamo U.S. Naval Base** covers an area of
117.6 square kilometers (45.4 square
miles), two thirds of which are highlands,
wetlands, and inland water. A 28-kilometer
(17.4 miles) fence surrounds the military
enclave. *See also* Racial Composition;
Sugar Industry

Further Readings

Magaz, Antonio. *Morfotectonica de Cuba Oriental*.
    Havana: Editorial Academia, 1991.
Provincia Guantánamo. Santiago: Editorial Oriente,
    1977.

Armando H. Portela

Guantánamo U.S. Naval Base

The naval base at Guantánamo Bay, at the southeastern tip of Cuba, was acquired by the United States in 1903, in the aftermath of Spain's defeat in the War of 1898. An ongoing reminder of U.S. power in the Caribbean, its anomalous character emerged more starkly after the Cuban **Revolution**.

An inlet of the Caribbean Sea, Guantánamo Bay measures a capacious 9.5 kilometers by 19 kilometers (six miles by twelve miles) and is one of the world's best sheltered harbors. Thirty-four kilometers (twenty-one miles) to the north, Guantánamo city is linked by rail and road to the base's neighboring ports. The base measures seventy-two square kilometers (forty-five square miles), of which a little over two fifths consists of solid ground—and the rest water and swampland.

U.S. rights to a coaling and naval station at Guantánamo—where Marines under Admiral William T. Sampson had landed in June 1898—were asserted by the 1901 **Platt Amendment**. In 1903, Presidents **Tomás Estrada Palma** and Theodore Roosevelt signed a lease agreement establishing the terms of the base's peculiar status: full U.S. jurisdiction, ultimate Cuban sovereignty, termination only by consent of both parties. This perpetual U.S. control was reaffirmed in a 1934 treaty. In 1952, during a period of Korean War–stimulated expansion, the base's population of 11,000 included some 3,000 Cuban day workers; at their peak, Cuban workers numbered 10,000.

With the 1959 Revolution and subsequent diplomatic break, the persistent anomaly of a U.S. naval enclave on Cuban territory gave rise to recurrent tensions. The Cuban government repeatedly protested the U.S. presence and, from 1960 on, refused to cash Washington's token annual lease check of $4,085. Beginning in

Aerial view of Guantánamo U.S. Naval Base (1960). Courtesy of the Digitalization Project of the *El Mundo* Photographic Collection, University of Puerto Rico, Río Piedras Campus.

1961, the number of Cuban workers was steadily reduced. Probably the worst crisis involving the base came in 1964, amid conflict over Cuban fishing in waters near Florida, when the **Fidel Castro** government cut off water and power to the base. In October 1979, in the wake of the Sandinista victory in Nicaragua, the United States staged a mock amphibious assault on the base area with 2,000 Marines. Despite such conflicts and the base's heavy fortification (barbed wire and land mines, the latter removed beginning in 1998), the base never lost all interaction with the island.

The 1990s saw the internment of large numbers of Cuban and Haitian refugees. Between 1991 and 1996, some 50,000 refugees temporarily settled at the base. Later in the decade, several thousand refugees from Kosovo spent time there. In January 2002 the base began to be used to temporarily house hundreds of al-Qaeda and Taliban prisoners captured during the U.S. intervention in Afghanistan; Cuban officials did not deem the move as threatening to their security and collaborated with the United States. Into the early twenty-first century, all attempts to reexamine the base's status, whether arising in Cuba or the United States, have ended up stillborn.

Only about thirty Cubans continue to work at the base. *See also* Fishing Industry; Guantánamo Province; United States, Cuba's Relations with the; War of Independence

Further Readings

Murphy, Marion Emerson, et al., *The History of Guantánamo Bay, 1494–1964.* Guantánamo Bay, Cuba: U.S. Naval Station Public Affairs Office, 1964.

Ricardo, Roger. *Guantánamo: The Bay of Discord.* Trans. Mary Todd. Melbourne, Australia: Ocean Press, 1994.

Smith, Wayne S. *The Closest of Enemies: A Personal and Diplomatic Account of U.S.-Cuban Relations since 1957.* New York: W.W. Norton, 1987.

Pablo Julián Davis

Habana (Havana) Province, La

The province of Havana has existed since 1976, when the ruling **Communist Party** redrew all the domestic administrative boundaries on the island, separating the rural areas of the old Havana Province and the nation's capital into two new jurisdictions (see **Political and Administrative Divisions**).

Located in western Cuba, Havana Province faces the Straits of Florida in the north and opens to the shallow inner waters of the Gulf of Batabanó in the southern sea shelf. The provinces of **Pinar del Río**, to the west, and **Matanzas**, to the east, flank its territory.

Havana Province is one of the smallest in Cuba, with 5,730 square kilometers (2,212 square miles), nearly 5.2 percent of the country. It is also located on the narrowest part of the island, with an average width between the northern and southern shores of only 50 kilometers (31 miles), reduced to 31 kilometers (19 miles) in the shortest section, between the bay of Mariel, in the north shore, and the Majana Cove, in the south.

The province's terrain is generally undulate to the north and mostly flat south of the watershed, with some striking hill ranges rising abruptly toward the axis. The highest altitude at Sierra de Camarones, near the border with Matanzas, is 358 meters (1,073 feet) high. Other summits include the Loma del Grillo, near Madruga, rising to 317 meters (1,040 feet); the Escaleras de Jaruco, topping 293 meters (961 feet); and the Mesa de Anafe (also called El Esperón), with 275 meters (902 feet).

A core of Cretaceous pyroclastic sequences forming an overthrusted mélange with marls, sandstone, and serpentinites is exposed in ample sectors mostly along the northern part of the province. These complex sequences entrap some deposits of oil and natural gas, mostly used for electric power generation. Roughly 80 percent of the province's territory is formed by karstic Neocene limestone gently sloping toward the sea in the plains or abruptly raised as tectonic pillars in the hilly inlands. These deposits hold important groundwater reserves amounting roughly to 1.5 billion cubic meters (396 billion gallons). Frequently opened to the sea, these aquifers face the constant threat of saltwater intrusion. Some 16,000 hectares (39,500 acres) of agricultural land along the southern shore have been rendered salty. There are another 452 million cubic meters (119 billion gallons) of freshwater dammed in reservoirs.

A network of culverts, pipelines, and pumping stations serves the needs of agriculture, the industry, and population, but its shabby conditions produce chronic water shortages. Furthermore, liquid wastes are poorly treated, polluting the groundwater, the runoff, wetlands, and reservoirs alike. Over the wavy plains and hills of the north and the watershed predominate brown argillaceous carbonated soils, generally poor and eroded, typically sustaining grazing lands. The southern plains are covered with highly productive, deep and well-drained red clayey lateritic soils, intensively cultivated.

Havana Province's economy is a combination of **agriculture** and **manufacturing**. Wrapping the nation's capital with good soils and abundant fresh water, the economy, the infrastructure, and settling patterns of the province are developed under the strong influence of the capital city. Its croplands sustain the large demand of the 2.2 million population of the city of Havana and 0.7 million of its own. But as with the rest of the island's agriculture, low yields and poor management create permanent food shortages.

Sugarcane is the main agricultural product and has been grown there for centuries (see **Sugar Industry**). Over 135,000 hectares (333,600 acres) of sugarcane feed its fifteen sugar mills whose combined production accounts for around 8 percent of the national output. There are also three sugar refineries with a joint capacity of 340,000 tons a year, or 34.6 percent of the total product. The largest of them is the **Camilo Cienfuegos** mill (formerly Hershey sugar mill), in Santa Cruz del Norte.

The province's rich red soils produce more than 40 percent of the potatoes harvested on the island. It also grows large quantities of other tubers, bananas, and vegetables. There are about 8,500 hectares (21,000 acres) devoted to citrus, near Ceiba del Agua, producing just under a tenth of the nation's citrus harvest.

Havana Province grows high-quality wrapping tobacco leaves (*capa*) for cigar manufacturing. This care-demanding crop is concentrated mostly south of San Antonio de los Baños (see **Tobacco Industry** and **Cigars and Cigar Making**).

Pasturelands extend to 40 percent of the territory. Quality livestock is raised in some ranches, but the herd has been decimated by the economic crisis, and dairy production collapsed (see **Cattle Ranching**).

Manufacturing in Havana has been developed under the strong influence of the capital requirements. Some industries have national significance. The economic crisis at the end of the twentieth century largely slowed down or even paralyzed many of the facilities (see **Special Period**). Electric power generation leads the industrial output in the province. The **Máximo Gómez** thermoelectric power plant, at Mariel, with a 600-megawatt generating capacity is one of the largest in the country. The government plans to build a giant 1,200-megawatt thermal power plant at Santa Cruz del Norte connected to the supertankers piers at **Matanzas** were aborted after the collapse of the Soviet bloc, but nonetheless the completed units of this plant remain as one of the most important in the industry. Also at Mariel is the country's top cement plant, capable of manufacturing one fourth of all Cuban cement. The latter, together with the cement plant at the neighboring town of Artemisa, can produce up to 40 percent of the national product.

Santa Cruz also houses the Havana Club liquor distillery, Cuba's largest producer of **rum**. The oil fields located in a narrow belt along the northeastern coast currently produce minor quantities of crude oil and some natural gas for domestic use. The environmental impact of hundreds of wells drilled and abandoned in the belt has been severe. Two major textile mills at Alquízar and Ariguanabo are among the largest in the country. The latter is capable of producing near 60 million square meters (70 million square yards) of textiles yearly, even though it is currently only semioperational. Other industries include plants for the manufacturing of tires, paint, food processing, and electric wire at San José de las Lajas. There are machinery assembling plants at several locations. The cement industry supports a relatively large prefab industry.

Havana's **population** was estimated at 696,610 in 1999, equivalent to 6.3 percent of all Cubans. It is one of the most densely

La Habana Province. By Armando H. Portela.

populated territories after the nation's capital and **Santiago de Cuba**.

There is no provincial capital in Havana; government resides in the City of Havana. With a population evenly distributed in the territory, the most important settlements are Güines (49,000), Artemisa (40,000), San Antonio de los Baños (32,000), San José de las Lajas (32,000), Güira de Melena (25,000), Guanajay (25,000), Bauta (22,000), Bejucal (17,000), Alquízar (15,000), and Mariel (15,000).

The six-lane-wide National Highway, the narrow old Central Highway, and the Central Railroad cross the territory, while a dense secondary network of sinuous paved roads and railroad branches reaches all settlements and economic hubs (see **Transportation**). Four-lane paved roads run along the north coast linking to Matanzas in the east and Mariel in the west.

Although best known as the shipping port of nuclear weapons during the 1962 **missile crisis** and the human stampede of 1980, Mariel's versatile facilities serve as auxiliary to the port of Havana, playing a key role in Cuba's economy (see **Mariel Boatlift**). Over 3 percent of Cuban sugar production is shipped through Mariel. Its terminal for loading sugar in bulk is capable of handling 10,000 tons per day. It handles also bulk cement, fertilizers, fuel, and machinery. The air base at San Antonio, with excellent connection to the capital, could serve civilian needs in the future. *See also* Ciudad de La Habana (City of Havana) Province; Habana Vieja (Old Havana) (Municipality), La

Further Reading

Provincia La Habana. Santiago: Editorial Oriente, 1978.

Armando H. Portela

Habana Vieja (Old Havana) (Municipality), La

La Habana Vieja (Old Havana) is the municipal jurisdiction that encompasses the oldest part of the city of Havana. It includes the territory west of the Bay of Havana up to the Paseo de **Martí** and the Avenida **Máximo Gómez** (formerly known, respectively, as Paseo del Prado and Calzada del Monte). The municipality also includes a band of land encircling the cove of Atarés up to the banks of the Luyanó River. The heart of Old Havana is constituted by the area formerly enclosed by the city's walls; the walls' demolition began in 1863, and today only a few fragments remain standing.

The settlement of Havana was originally established as San Cristóbal de La Habana on the southern coast of the island near where Batabanó stands today. It was founded by Pánfilo de Narváez in 1514. Within a decade the settlement was moved north to its present location on the western shore of the Bay of Havana. Later in the century it supplanted **Santiago de Cuba** as the island's capital. Since then it has been Cuba's largest and most important city, its political, military, and commercial center. During the 1500s, 1600s, and much of the 1700s, the system of fleets gave Havana's port monopolistic privileges and made it an obligatory stop for convoys of vessels bound for Spain. Its geographic importance made Havana one of the Spanish empire's most coveted prizes and a frequent target of foreign aggression; Spain invested heavily in the city's defenses, making it the best-fortified city in the New World. Despite its fortifications and heavy military presence, Havana was captured by British forces in 1762 and occupied for

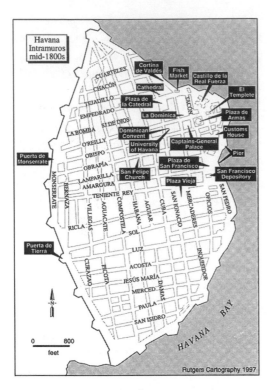

Havana
Intramuros
mid-1800s

Walled Section (Intramuros) of Havana, mid-1800s. By Michael Siegel, Rutgers University Cartography.

Old Havana includes within its confines many architectural jewels and historic sites; it has been declared a Humanity's Heritage site by the United Nations Educational, Scientific, and Cultural Organization (UNESCO). Among its most popular attractions are the **Cathedral of Havana**, the **Palace of the Captains-General**, the Castle of la Real Fuerza, the **Presidential Palace**, the **Capitol Building**, and scores of mansions, churches, plazas, paseos, museums, and monuments. Under the able leadership of **Eusebio Leal Spengler**, the historian of the city of Havana, many colonial buildings have been renovated. Despite the generalized state of decay that Havana exhibits, it continues to deserve the title of Capital of the Antilles. The municipality's population in 1998 was estimated at 97,984; the city's other fourteen municipalities had 2,094,337 inhabitants, for a city total of 2,192,321. *See also* British Occupation of Havana; Ciudad de La Habana (City of Havana) Province; Colonial Settlements, Early; Corsairs Attacks; Fortifications of Havana; Habana (Havana) Province, La; Trade and Navigation (1500–1800)

Further Reading

Carpentier, Alejo. *La ciudad de las columnas*. Havana: Instituto Cubano del Libro, 1998.

Leal Spengler, Eusebio. *Detén el paso caminante . . . : La Habana*. Caribe International Tours, 1987.

Roig de Leuchsenring, Emilio. *La Habana, apuntes históricos*. 3 vols. Havana: Oficina del Historiador de la Ciudad, 1964.

Stout, Nancy, and Jorge Rigau. *Havana/La Habana*. New York: Rizzoli, 1994.

Luis Martínez-Fernández

Holguín (Municipality)

Holguín is a municipality and the capital city of the eastern province of **Holguín**. With 303,389 inhabitants (est. 1998), it is the municipal jurisdiction with the third-largest **population**. The city proper, with

eleven months. Havana expanded as one of the hemisphere's most important port cities during the nineteenth century, a reflection of the sugar boom in the Havana-Matanzas belt. A total of 158,587 people lived in Havana in 1860, by then the majority beyond the city's walls. Havana's importance as the island's main city and capital continued to increase during the republican era. In fact, Havana came close to monopolizing not only political power but many of the republic's resources and institutions such as higher education and hospitals. The **Revolution** of 1959 was, in part, a revolution against Havana's disproportionate dominance. Four decades after the triumph of the Revolution, however, Havana continues to enjoy a privileged position within the country. It has increasingly become a magnet for population from the island's provincial cities and rural areas.

259,300 residents (est. 1999), has the fourth-largest population behind Havana, **Santiago de Cuba**, and **Camagüey**. San Isidro de Holguín was founded in 1523 in a region heavily populated with natives by the Spanish officer Francisco García Holguín; it became a municipality in 1751. The town exhibited the slow growth that characterized most of eastern Cuba during the 1500s to 1800s. Holguín figured prominently during the wars of independence of the late 1800s. Its native son, **Calixto García Íñiguez**, was one of the wars' principal leaders; thirteen other generals were born in Holguín. The city's historic center is graced by many fine buildings and monuments; because of its many parks, Holguín is referred to as la Ciudad de los Parques. On the outskirts of the city, la Loma de la Cruz has historically attracted many religious pilgrims.

The municipality's economy has been characterized by high agricultural output of fruits and vegetables as well as sugar production (see **Agriculture** and **Sugar Industry**). *See also* Indigenous Inhabitants; Ten Years' War; War of Independence

Further Readings

Alfonso, Carmen R. *Principales ciudades*. Havana: Editorial José Martí, 1997.

Freire Díaz, Joaquín. *Historia de los municipios de Cuba*. Miami: La Moderna Poesía, 1985.

Luis Martínez-Fernández

Holguín Province

Holguín is one of the five provinces established in 1976 when the government split up the former province of Oriente. Located on Cuba's northeast coast, facing the Atlantic Ocean, Holguín is the fourth-largest province, with 9,295 square kilometers (3,590 square miles). It consists of fertile plains and valleys, where sugarcane, coffee, plantains, and other vegetable products are grown and most of its population lives, and of mountains and uplands covered with dense forests and pine groves, scarcely populated, representing an important ecological reserve.

The province's topography is a rugged combination of low mountains rising to a top elevation of 900 to 1,200 meters (2,950 to 3,900 feet) above sea level and smooth flat basins gently leaning to the sea. Its highest point is the Pico del Cristal, rising 1,231 meters (4,038 feet) at Sierra del Cristal, southeast of the town of Mayarí. Other outstanding elevations are the Alto del Toldo, 17 kilometers (10.5 miles) south of the city of Moa, and La Mensura, 995 meters high (3,264 feet), in the Sierra de Nipe plateau. To the east, the mountains of Sierra de Nipe, Sierra Cristal, and Sierra de Moa largely consist of massive bodies of serpentinites, peridotites, and other ultrabasics. These bodies have developed lateritic weathering crusts, 15 to 20 feet thick (sometimes 70 to 80 feet), particularly rich in nickel and cobalt (see **Mining Industry**).

Nickel, which is the main natural resource in Holguín, is the basis of one of the most important industries in the country. Nickel ore reserves are estimated at around 800 million tons, representing approximately 37 percent of the world total, more than the combined reserves of Canada and Russia. These vast superficial nickel deposits are relatively easy to mine, but at the same time strip **mining** causes extensive, devastating, and virtually irreversible environmental destruction of the dense forest of the zone, a singular combination of pine groves and rainforests that shelter a large and unique wildlife. Three nickel and cobalt benefiting plants have a combined output of 75,000 tons (a record production of 72,000 tons in 2000), making Cuba one of the largest world producers. Two of these plants were built by U.S.-based companies before 1959: the René Ramos Latour plant (formerly Nicaro Nickel Co.) in 1943, and the Pedro Soto Alba plant (formerly Moa Nickel Co.), which started in 1960. The more recent **Che Guevara** plant was finished in 1986 in Moa with Soviet technology but has been radically refurbished after that. Slated to open in 1995, a fourth plant at Las Camariocas, near Moa, was abandoned in 1991 at the height of the **Special Period** crisis when at 85 percent completion. Untreated liquid and solid wastes, along with emissions to the atmosphere from the nickel benefiting industry, produce one of the most severely polluted zones in Cuba.

Agricultural production is concentrated toward the northern slope of the **Cauto River Valley**, the Nipe Basin, and the valleys and hills of Maniabón. Croplands are predominantly located over brown argillaceous soil, often with poor drainage and saline. Over one third of the soils suffer some degree of saline intrusion. Sugar is by far the largest agricultural product. Large-scale sugarcane growing began toward the end of the nineteenth century. Presently, there are ten sugar mills in the province producing 9 to 10 percent of the country's total output. The Urbano Noris sugar mill (formerly San Germán) is one of the largest in Cuba, with a sugarcane grinding capacity of 12,500 tons per day, 26.8 percent of the province's and almost 2 percent of the total Cuban **sugar industry**.

Coffee is grown in the mountains surrounding Mayarí and Sagua de Tánamo in the east, at altitudes of 300 meters (984 feet) and more above sea level, where fresh temperatures and rains in excess of 1,600 millimeters per year (63 inches) are normal. Holguín accounts for 5 to 10 percent of all coffee grown in Cuba.

An agricultural harvester factory, built with Soviet assistance at the beginning of the 1980s, became one emblematic plant in the country. Its capacity to produce over 600 combines per year (in 1989, it pro-

Holguín Province. By Armando H. Portela.

duced 621 combines) enabled the country to curb the ample use of manpower to carry on the sugar harvest. About 70 percent of the sugarcane is now chopped with harvesters. It is a very versatile installation, capable of producing a variety of complex agricultural equipment and spare parts. A thermal power plant with a 500-megawatt capacity was built in Felton in the 1990s, the newest generating facilities in the country.

With 115 inhabitants per square kilometer, Holguín is one of the most densely populated provinces. Its **population** was estimated at 1,024,943 in 1999, or roughly 9.2 percent of the total Cuban population. Its capital city, also named **Holguín**, has 210,000 residents, which makes it the country's fourth-largest city. Other important provincial cities are Moa (45,000), Banes (35,000), Mayarí (24,000), San Germán (19,000), Sagua de Tánamo (17,000), and Gibara (16,000).

The Central Highway and the Central Railroad link Holguín with the rest of the island, and a dense network of secondary roads and railroads reaches all settlements and economic hubs. Several ports rank among the most important in Cuba and serve both domestic and international cargo. The ports of Moa and Nicaro export all the Cuban nickel. The port of Antilla in Nipe Bay dispatches roughly 3 percent of Cuba's sugar exports. The **Calixto García** International Airport, south of the city of Holguín, is growing in importance. *See also* Agriculture; Coffee Industry; Railroads (Nineteenth Century)

Further Reading

Provincia Holguín. Santiago: Editora Oriente, 1977.

Armando H. Portela

Hurricanes

Cuba, like the rest of the Antilles, lies on a path frequently traveled by tropical storms and hurricanes. Hurricanes are tropical cyclones with sustained winds in excess of 120 kilometers (seventy-five miles) per hour. Over 150 hurricanes have battered the island since 1498, when the ships of **Christopher Columbus** witnessed the first recorded hurricane. The impact of hurricanes on Cuban lives and the Cuban economy has been considerable. Seven of the forty deadliest Atlantic hurricanes recorded in the eighteenth, nineteenth, and twentieth centuries struck the island. Havana was nearly completely destroyed by a hurricane in 1768, when it was reported that over a thousand people lost their lives. A 1791 hurricane is estimated to have killed 3,000 Cubans and wiped out Havana's entire stock of cattle. **Cienfuegos, Pinar del Río**, and other towns were leveled by hurricanes during the 1840s. A hurricane-generated tidal wave that struck the south coast of **Camagüey Province** in 1932 killed more than 3,000 Cubans in the town of Santa Cruz del Sur; in 1963, Hurricane Flora killed 4,200 and destroyed 30,000 homes.

In recent years, several hurricanes have caused much damage on the island: Lili (1996), Georges (1998), Irene (1999), and Michelle in November 2001. Hurricane Michelle, a category four storm, was the worst hurricane to hit Cuba since Flora. It forced the evacuation of 700,000 residents, left a toll of 5 dead, and destroyed livestock, crops, and property to the extent that the Cuban government was forced to accept U.S. shipments of food, the first since the establishment of the embargo in 1960. *See also* Climate; U.S. Trade Embargo and Related Legislation

Further Readings

Díaz, Henry F., and Roger S. Pulwarty, eds. *Hurricanes: Climate and Socioeconomic Impacts.* New York: Springer, 1997.

Pérez, Louis A., Jr. *Winds of Change: Hurricanes and the Transformation of Nineteenth-Century Cuba.* Chapel Hill: University of North Carolina Press, 2001.

Mariola Espinosa

Isla de la Juventud (Isle of Youth)

Believed to be Robert Louis Stevenson's famed Treasure Island, the Isla de la Juventud (Isle of Youth) was known until 1978 as Isla de Pinos (Isle of Pines), when the Cuban government changed its name to commemorate the XI World Festival of Youth and Students. The isle is the second largest of all the islands and islets within Cuban territory, covering 2,200 square kilometers (850 square miles). By its size, it is the sixth-largest island in the Caribbean, larger than any of the Lesser Antilles, with the exception of the island of Trinidad. It is separated from Cuba itself by the shallow waters of the Gulf of Batabanó. The Isla de la Juventud has the status of special municipality since 1976, after the changes in the administrative structure of Cuba were promoted by the ruling **Cuban Communist Party**.

Called Camarcó by its native inhabitants, **Columbus** encountered the island in 1494 and named it Isla Evangelista. The island, however, remained a backwater of the colonial agenda, reaching a **population** of only 300 in 1787 and 2,067 in 1864. After **U.S. intervention** during the **War of Independence**, the Isla de Pinos, as the island was then known, came under U.S. control until 1925, when it was returned to Cuban hands. Until recently, the history of the Isla de la Juventud has been associated with its role as site of prisons. A young **José Martí** was deported to the isle at the start of the **Ten Years' War**, and decades later **Gerardo Machado's** opponents were jailed there. **Fidel Castro** and several of his associates were imprisoned at its Model Prison in the aftermath of the failed attack on the **Moncada Army Barracks** of 1953. After 1959 thousands of Castro's opponents were jailed there in one of the darkest episodes of Cuba's political history. The Model Prison was finally closed in the late 1960s. The island now serves as an educational center where the Cuban government provides education to hundreds of foreign children, predominantly from Africa and Latin America (*see* **Educational System**).

The island is primarily flat, with some step-isolated hills rising from the plains. The highest point rises to 303 meters (903 feet) at Sierra de la Cañada in the central part of the island. Geology determines the existence of two radically different landscapes. A core of eroded Jurassic schist and rising marble towering hills, with citrus orchards and pasturelands, lies to the north, accounting for two thirds of the territory. The south is a low, flat rocky plain, composed of Quaternary carbonaceous deposits covered by dense forests and bushes. Between the agricultural north and the savage south, the Lanier swamp, with thick recent deposits of peat, extends as a natural barrier. Locally, the inaccessible southern plain beyond the Lanier swamp is known as the South.

The island's agricultural soils are mostly sandy, poor in nutrients, and acidic, requiring fertilization and treatment. The low-lying areas have very poor drainage, and the center of the territory has suffered from erosion. A well-developed caolinitic weathering crust covers extensive areas of the higher northern plains, while in the south the soils exist in small pockets, filling the depressions.

Freshwater reservoirs were built in the north after the mid-1960s to suit the needs of a growing population and **agriculture**. As a result, the natural drainage was intensely regulated, and currently the island has a storage capacity exceeding 180 million cubic meters (47.5 billion gallons).

The autochthonous vegetation has receded to open space for agriculture. Originally, it consisted of open pine forests in the north, dense tropical semideciduous forests and bushes in the south, and mangrove in the wetlands. Some residual pine forests have been preserved toward the highest parts inland. In the south, customarily more isolated, the original vegetation is better preserved. This provides habitat for a diverse **fauna**. A marine natural preserve exists on the south shore, east from Point Francés, covering the coral reef ecosystem to the edge of the sea shelf.

The cave of Punta del Este, a national monument located in the southeast corner of the island, was presumably an ancient aborigine dwelling, profusely decorated on the ceiling with pre-Columbian pictographs depicting concentric circles and other geometric figures.

The economy of the Isla de la Juventud depends primarily on agriculture, though there are local developments in fishing and **mining**, and **tourism** is a growing sector. Citrus has been the primary agricultural product since U.S. settlers developed the first farms in the early years of the twentieth century. Totaling some 15,400 hectares (38,000 acres), the groves are grouped in the center of the island, where the land is higher and the drainage better. Roughly half of the grapefruit produced in Cuba is harvested in the Isla de la Juventud. The rest of the agricultural land is mostly devoted to grazing and to growing some vegetables for local consumption. At one time, high-quality dairy cows were raised on the island, including the world record-holder Ubre Blanca, but the herd was considerably depleted as a result of the economic crisis in the 1990s.

From relatively abundant deposits, the island produces a variety of coarse-grain gray marble that has been widely used in

Isle of Youth

Isla de la Juventud. By Armando H. Portela.

Cuban urban construction. Quarries have been operating for over 100 years. Kaolin deposits in the north support a modest china industry. Small quantities of gold and tungsten were mined in the past, but reserves are apparently exhausted.

With a seventeen-mile-long sand beach and over 1,000 hotel rooms, Key Largo del Sur, to the southeast, is a growing tourist destination. Numerous **keys** and **beaches**, such as Key Rosario and Playa Larga, remain undeveloped.

Fisheries and fish-canning industry complete the economy of the island. Lobsters and tunas are the most valuable species captured and processed.

In 1999 the population was estimated at 78,798 inhabitants, mostly concentrated in the principal town of Nueva Gerona, with roughly 52,000 residents. From barely 10,105 inhabitants in the census of 1953, population grew rapidly during the next two decades, largely due to migration from eastern provinces.

The primary link with the rest of the country is by sea, with ferries connecting Nueva Gerona, the island's only port, to Batabanó in **La Habana Province**. A domestic airport links Nueva Gerona to Havana and occasionally to **Pinar del Río** and **Santiago de Cuba**. An international airport at Cayo Largo del Sur serves tourists direct flights from Europe, Canada, and South America. *See also* Fishing Industry; Indigenous Inhabitants

Further Readings

McManus, Jane. *Cuba's Island of Dreams: Voices from the Isle of Pines and Youth*. Gainesville: University Press of Florida, 2000.

Núñez Jiménez, Antonio. *Isla de Pinos: piratas, colonizadores, rebeldes*. Havana: Editorial Arte y Literatura, 1977.

Armando H. Portela

Keys

Among the most remarkable features of Cuban geography are the hundreds of small keys or low islands or reefs that surround the main island. In addition to their beauty, these islands probably contain the least-known and best-preserved ecosystems in the country.

The total area of the 1,300 to 1,600 keys around Cuba, except for the **Isla de la Juventud**, is 3,715 square kilometers, or 1,434 square miles. That is equivalent to 3.3 percent of the country's total land size, or roughly two thirds the size of **La Habana Province**. With a surface area covering 926 square kilometers (357.5 square miles), Key Romano on the northern coast is the biggest of the Cuban keys, but most of the other keys measure only a few acres. In some cases, they are merely a handful of mangrove trees growing on a shelf of land a couple of inches higher than the tides.

The keys are composed mostly of muck, silt, or sand fixed by mangroves. Many are simply ancient coral reefs or sand bars that remained isolated ten to twelve feet above sea level as a result of the upraising of the sea level that followed the onset of climatic global warming 10,000 years ago. Before the warming period began, the keys were actually part of the main island, when it was roughly two thirds bigger than it is today (see **Area and Geographic Location**).

Together with some remote mountains or inaccessible swamps, the keys preserve the least disturbed ecosystem in Cuba and enjoy a high biological diversity, in many cases serving as shelter for **fauna** and **flora** living exclusively in these parts of the world. Many of the most interesting and rare Cuban rodents, reptiles, birds, insects—even bats—live in the keys. Until the end of the 1980s the keys remained essentially underdeveloped, used regularly only as sites for coast guard booths and visited occasionally by fishermen or scavengers in search of charcoal.

In recent times, however, Cuba's keys have attracted growing interest by government officials anxious to expand **tourism** to the virgin and isolated **beaches** that were virtually unknown until very recently. In some cases, the increased interest has resulted in severe ecological damage. In recent years, for example, many beaches have been linked to the mainland by dozens of miles of improvised causeways or roads, known as *pedraplenes*, in an effort to create a minimal infrastructure in order to speed development. Such was the case with the extensive development that occurred during the 1990s in the northern keys Key Coco and Key Guillermo. Presently, they constitute the important tourist hub Los Jardines del Rey, with over 2,600 rooms for tourists.

One of the best developed keys is undoubtedly Key Largo del Sur, a long strip of dunes located east of the Isle of Youth, that boasts more than seventeen miles of coral sand beaches facing the Caribbean Sea and over 1,000 hotel rooms. Key Largo has an airport with a 4,000-meter (13,000-foot) runway capable of receiving passenger jets.

Further Reading

Núñez Jiménez, Antonio. *Pedro en el laberinto de las doce leguas*. Havana: Gente Nueva, 1983.

Armando H. Portela

Matanzas (Municipality)

Matanzas is a municipality and the capital city of the province that bears the same name. Its name, which literally means "massacres," is said to have derived from the slaughter of Spanish settlers at the hands of native Cubans in the early 1500s. Other versions claim that it derives from the massacre of Indians or the slaughter of pigs. Matanzas is located on the shores of the bay of Matanzas, a bay into which flow three rivers: the Yumurí, San Juan, and Canimar. Because so many rivers cut through Matanzas, it is sometimes referred to as the city of bridges. The Yumurí Valley and the Caves of Bellamar are two impressive scenic sites near the city of Matanzas. The city proper was founded in 1693 by thirty immigrant families from the Canary Islands. Matanzas experienced dramatic growth in the nineteenth century when the province became the epicenter of the sugar boom. The number of **sugar plantations** and slaves increased dramatically, and Matanzas became the island's second city after Havana. The city also experienced a cultural boom that earned it the nickname the Athens of Cuba. Several major newspapers, theaters, and cultural centers emerged in nineteenth-century Matanzas. Among the literary figures of Matanzas were **José Jacinto Milanés, Domingo del Monte, Gabriel de la Concepción Valdés (Plácido)**, and **Miguel Teurbe Tolón**.

Matanzas's economy suffered enormously as a result of the **War of Independence** and the **reconcentraciones** of its population by Spanish authorities. During the early decades of the twentieth century, the relative importance of Matanzas waned as sugar production expanded to the island's eastern provinces. Because of its large and deep harbor, however, Matanzas continues to be a major import and export port. Its major industries are distilling, refining, tanning, fishing, and the manufacture of paper, textiles, and fertilizers. Sisal is also produced in the region. Because of its proximity to Varadero, many Matanceros serve in the tourist sector. In 1998 the municipality's **population** was estimated at 135,624; 124,754 lived within the city limits (est. 1999). *See also* Indigenous

Inhabitants; Manufacturing; Matanzas Province; Press and Journalism (Eighteenth and Nineteenth Centuries); Slavery; Sugar Industry; Tourism

Further Readings

Alfonso, Carmen R. *Principales ciudades*. Havana: Editorial José Martí, 1997.

Freire Díaz, Joaquín. *Historia de los municipios de Cuba*. Miami: La Moderna Poesía, 1985.

Ponte Domínguez, Francisco J. *Matanzas (Biografía de una provincia)*. Havana: Imprenta El Siglo XX, 1959.

Luis Martínez-Fernández

Matanzas Province

Matanzas is one of the territories best endowed with natural resources in Cuba. Located in western Cuba, Matanzas faces the Straits of Florida in the north and opens to the Caribbean Sea in the south. The provinces of **La Habana**, to the west, and **Villa Clara** and **Cienfuegos**, to the east, flank its territory.

Barely ninety kilometers (fifty-six miles) east from Havana, Matanzas has excellent agricultural lands, abundant fresh water, an ample and deep bay, good transportation routes, oil deposits, and Cuba's best-known tourist resort, Varadero.

Matanzas is the second-largest province in Cuba, with 11,739 square kilometers (4,532 square miles), and consists mostly of extraordinarily fertile plains, with deep red clayey lateritic soils with good drainage and high productivity, cultivated with sugarcane plantations, citrus groves, rice paddies, orchards, and grazing ranches. A few step hills rise to the north to a top altitude of 381 meters (1,250 feet) at the Pan de Matanzas.

One of Cuba's most important ecological reserves, the Ciénaga de Zapata, the Zapata Swamp, accounts for roughly two thirds of the territory of Matanzas. It represents the largest wetland environment in the Caribbean. It covers 4,520 square kilometers (1,746 square miles) of freshwater swamps, saline marshes, hammocks, and bogs, inhabited by numerous endemic species, among them a few very rare birds found nowhere else in the world and more than a hundred extraordinary plants. Zapata Swamp provides the perfect habitat for the endangered Cuban crocodile (see **Flora** and **Fauna**).

Neocene limestones, gently sloping toward the sea, hide a core of overthrusted Cretaceous sequences of volcanic and intrusive rocks that traps some of the most important crude oil deposits in the island. The **Cárdenas**-Varadero oil field yields over 17,000 barrels per day of a heavy, dense oil containing 6 percent of sulfur, which is used in electric power generation and the cement industries. The Ciénaga de Zapata contains more than 500,000 tons of dry peat, a fuel that, while low in energy yield, could be pressed into service if other fuels are scarce. Dry peat has been used experimentally to fuel some industrial facilities. Full exploitation of the peat deposits would be devastating ecologically, however. There are no major water reservoirs in Matanzas, but the province has 474 billion gallons of usable underground water, which is mostly used to irrigate sugarcane, citrus, and rice crops.

Sugarcane is the first agricultural product and has been grown there since the early nineteenth century, when hundreds of small factories and slave labor proliferated on the rich red soils and flat plains. The province currently operates twenty-one sugar mills, accounting for 10 to 13 percent of the national total sugar output. Two sugar refineries located in Cárdenas and at the España Republicana sugar mill can produce roughly one tenth of the Cuban refined sugar. In Cárdenas, alcohol is distilled and is used in the production of **rum** in the Havana Club factory.

Mostly developed in the early 1970s, in rocky soils north of Jagüey Grande, Matanzas has the largest citrus orchards on the island, accounting for one third of all

Matanzas Province. By Armando H. Portela.

citrus plantations of Cuba, with a production in excess of 300,000 tons per year. Several benefiting plants serve the plantations. Jagüey Grande is the site of a fruit and juice concentrate processing plant. Oranges make up 62 percent of the production, and grapefruit 24 percent.

Tourism is by far the most rewarding sector of the Matanzas economy. Varadero beach, with over twenty kilometers (twelve miles) of white sand **beaches**, is the second tourist destination in Cuba, only after Havana, and attracts more than 40 percent of all foreign visitors to Cuba. New hotel construction in Varadero increased the number of accommodations from 8,000 rooms in 1994 to 12,000 in 2000, when 750,000 visitors were received. In 1999, revenues from tourism in Varadero were 33 percent higher than the earnings from all of Cuba's sugar export and nearly doubled those of all nickel sales abroad. Vast spaces of vacant lands and unexploited beaches are available at Varadero for future developments.

One of the last engineering projects finished with Soviet assistance is the petroleum storage and transporting facilities of the port of Matanzas. This installation is designed for the receiving, storage, and distribution of imported petroleum and, to a lesser extent, the production of the Varadero-Cárdenas oil fields. The petroleum node can receive tankers up to 150,000 tons and warehouse half a million cubic meters of crude (3.665 million barrels), to be shipped later to the port and oil refinery at **Cienfuegos** through a 186-kilometer-long (116 miles) pipeline, ca-

pable of moving 134,000 barrels per day, upgradeable to 200,000 barrels daily. The facilities, however, were finished as the Soviet bloc collapsed and consequently were never used fully. The oil refinery in Cienfuegos, a corner piece of the system, remains hopelessly idle, and supertankers are never moored at the giant peers. Instead, the facility is being partially used to store and distribute domestic crude from Varadero-Cárdenas, coming through a 40-kilometer-long (25 miles) pipeline finished in 2000.

In 1999 the **population** was estimated at 654,994 inhabitants, representing 5.9 percent of all Cubans, down from the ratio at the turn of the twentieth century, when 12.9 percent of Cuba's population lived in the province. Its capital, also called **Matanzas**, has 124,000 residents. Other important cities are Cárdenas (68,000), Colón (40,000), Jovellanos (24,000), and Jagüey Grande (18,000).

The six-lane-wide National Highway, the narrow old Central Highway, and the Central Railroad link Matanzas to the rest of the island, and a dense network of secondary roads and railroad branches reaches all settlements and economic hubs. The Vía Blanca highway links the province with Havana. An electric train, built in 1916 by Central Hershey, still runs between Havana and Matanzas. The port of Matanzas is one of the country's busiest. At its heyday, more than 300 ships called there annually. Sixteen percent of the country's sugar production is exported through the port, second only to Cienfuegos, and the bulk sugar terminal can handle 10,000 tons daily. Six miles east of the city of Matanzas is **Juan Gualberto Gómez** International Airport, currently the second busiest airport in Cuba in number of passengers. It was finished in the 1990s to assimilate the growing tourism traffic, replacing the old Varadero airport. *See also* Agriculture; Soviet Union, Cuba's Relations with the; Sugar Industry

Further Readings

Ponte Domínguez, Francisco J. *Matanzas (Biografía de una provincia)*. Havana: Imprenta El Siglo XX, 1959.

Provincia Matanzas. Santiago: Editorial Oriente, 1978.

Armando H. Portela

Pinar del Río (Municipality)

Pinar del Río is a municipality and the provincial capital of the island's westernmost province: **Pinar del Río**. The western part of Cuba, which had had the lowest concentration of **indigenous inhabitants**, was very sparsely settled during the first few centuries of Spanish colonization. The region was initially called Nueva Filipinas and had its government in Guane; it later moved east to its present location and was named Pinar del Río because a river cut through a pine forest in the place where the village was built. It became a municipality in 1859. Farmers, mostly from the Canary Islands, moved into the region during the 1700s and 1800s and developed farms that produced the world's best tobacco. The province's economy still depends largely on the production of tobacco and rice. The **population** of the municipality was estimated at 185,843 in 1998; according to 1999 estimates, 148,500 lived in the city proper. *See also* Cigars and Cigar Making; Tobacco Industry

Further Readings

Alfonso, Carmen R. *Principales ciudades*. Havana: Editorial José Martí, 1997.

Freire Díaz, Joaquín. *Historia de los municipios de Cuba*. Miami: La Moderna Poesía, 1985.

Luis Martínez-Fernández

Pinar del Río Province

Pinar del Río Province's distinctive landscapes, along with its relative isolation on the western end of the island, and its distinguishing agricultural profile set it apart from the rest of the country. Facing the Gulf of Mexico to the north and the Caribbean Sea to the south, Pinar del Río is the third-largest province in Cuba, with 10,925 square kilometers (4,218 square miles), equivalent to 9.8 percent of the country's land area.

It is shaped by a contrasting and scenic combination of forested low mountains and towering hills with cultivated landlocked valleys and wide flat plains. The Guaniguanico mountain system, formed by two very different ranges (the Sierra del Rosario to the east and the Sierra de los Órganos to the west), outlines a belt along the central part of the territory rising to a height of 692 meters (2,270 feet) above sea level at the Pan de Guajaibón. To the south, an ample alluvial plain is the ground for most agricultural activities and the largest settlements.

Overthrusted Jurassic sequences of massive limestone and schist, Cretaceous sedimentary series, and occasionally imbrications of serpentine form a complex foundation where erosion and karstic processes have carved astonishing unique landscapes. Locals call the large towering hills rising vertically several hundred meters from the bottom of flat valleys at the Sierra de los Órganos *mogotes*. The mogotes are usually bored by a labyrinth of echeloned fluvial caves, some of them many kilometers in length. The Santo Tomás cave, with fifty kilometers (thirty-one miles) of galleries is the largest on the island. The Los Perdidos cave, near Rancho Mundito, exceeds thirty-two kilometers (twenty miles). Majaguas-Cantera cave at the Sierra de los Órganos is twenty-four kilometers (fifteen miles) long.

Pinar del Río's natural drainage has been largely diverted to serve agricultural requirements. The overall water reservoir capacity nears 800 million cubic meters (211 billion gallons). An extensive web of channels and culverts has changed the natural water runoff. Salinized soils and aquifers in the southern coastal flatlands pose a permanent threat to farming and have reportedly ruined the productivity of soils in some places. Excessive regulation of the runoff, faulty irrigation practices, and seawater intrusions are blamed for the problem. Over 54,000 hectares (133,400 acres) of soil, equivalent to one tenth of the agricultural lands, are saline.

Pinar del Río is invariably identified with tobacco cultivation, even though tobacco accounts for only 9 percent of the croplands. Tobacco farming and trade drove the territory's assimilation from the late seventeenth century. The "Vueltabajo" region, an appellation of origin that eventually became the province's surname, produces the best-quality black tobacco in Cuba. Tobacco is cultivated in the west, on high, sandy, loose, and well-drained acid soils (pH < 4.5), commonly eroded and demanding fertilization. Tobacco requires a skilled workforce and is cultivated in relatively small plots cared for by hand, "leaf by leaf," by a family or a few laborers. Consequently, in the tobacco growing areas, rural population is dense. Cured tobacco leaves are sent to the Havana factories, where manufacture of quality cigars and cigarettes takes place. Reportedly the excellence of the province's tobacco has decreased as a result of collectivization and mismanagement.

Pinar del Río accounts for one fifth of the rice produced in Cuba. It is grown in the low, flat alluvial plains south of Los Palacios. Heavy gley-soaked soils with dark mineral concretions forming a hardpan locally known as *mocarrero* fit the grain requirements.

Sugar plays a small part in the province's agricultural economy. The same soggy conditions that make Pinar del Río a good rice-growing region work against it for sugar. Five sugar mills, all located in the eastern portion of the province, produce just fewer than 3 percent of Cuba's total sugar output. Cultivated and spontaneous pastures, often overgrown, make up one third of agricultural lands.

Nearly 40 percent of the province's area is covered with forests, an outstanding ratio compared to the rest of the island. Pine forests—many planted after the 1960s—grow well over the schist and serpentine hills to the west but have disappeared from the loamy plains to open space for agriculture. Semideciduous forests and rainforests cover part of the mountain ranges but have been decimated by precarious farming practices.

Pinar del Río hosts a large number of endangered endemic species of plants and animals mainly in the unique conditions of the Sierra de los Órganos and the quartz sandy plains with acid soils to the west. The best known is the *Microcycas calocoma*, a curious short palm tree, a Jurassic survivor growing in crevasses and humid places in the highlands. Two natural reserves under the patronage of the United Nations, at the eastern part of Sierra del Rosario and the Guanahacabibes Peninsula, have been established to monitor and protect the ecosystems.

Tourism is modest and concentrated in the Viñales Valley, even if the original beauty of the province's landscapes and its tranquil mood could potentially lure more visitors. Better facilities and easier access would increase the number of tourists to other areas.

Some small deposits of lead, zinc, copper, gold, quartz sand, and phosphorite are currently mined. Iron, nickel, and bauxite reserves have been found. A copper mine at Matahambre was closed in 1997 as its ore reserves became exhausted after eighty-four years of activity. Gold is exploited in the Castellanos mine, yielding some 9,600 ounces per year (see **Mining Industry**).

Fisheries and fish-canning industry complete the economy of the province. Lobsters and tunas are the most valuable species captured and processed at La Coloma fishing facilities, one of the most important in Cuba (see **Fishing Industry**).

Pinar del Río Province. By Armando H. Portela.

The Pinar del Río **population** was estimated at 734,864 in 1999, equivalent to 6.6 percent of the total Cuban population. The province's capital, also called **Pinar del Río**, was founded in 1669 as a place to raise cattle and grow tobacco. It is currently Cuba's seventh-largest city, with a population of 148,500. Other settlements are Consolación del Sur (20,000), Los Palacios (16,000), and San Cristóbal (13,000).

The paved road network reaches all settlements and agricultural zones. The main arteries are the four- and six-lane National Highway and the two-lane old Central Highway, both linking the province to Havana. The Central Railroad stretches west to the small village of Guane.

Despite having deep, ample, and well-sheltered bays at Bahía Honda and Cabañas, Pinar del Río lacks important port facilities. Sugar is shipped through the port of Mariel in **La Habana Province**. Shipping of tobacco has traditionally been carried out through Havana. Pinar del Río has no civilian airport with regular services, but a military airport six miles south from the province's capital in the past has supported some charter civilian traffic with Nueva Gerona and Havana. A military air base exists at San Julián, to the west. *See also* Cattle Ranching; Cigars and Cigar Making; Flora; Tobacco Industry

Further Reading

Provincia Pinar del Río. Santiago: Editorial Oriente, 1978.

Armando H. Portela

Political and Administrative Divisions

During the middle of the nineteenth century the Spanish colony of Cuba was divided into two departments and thirty-one districts. Havana was the capital of the Western Department, and **Santiago de Cuba** was the capital of the Eastern Department. The districts were Pinar del Río, Bahía Honda, Guanajay, San Cristóbal, San Antonio de los Baños, Bejucal, Santiago de las Vegas, La Habana, Santa María del Rosario, Guanabacoa, Jaruco, **Matanzas**, Güines, Colón, **Cárdenas**, Sagua la Grande, **Villa Clara, Cienfuegos, Trinidad**, San Juan de los Remedios, **Sancti Spíritus**, Nuevitas, Puerto Príncipe (**Camagüey**), **Las Tunas, Bayamo**, Manzanillo, Jiguaní, **Holguín**, Santiago de Cuba, Guantánamo, and **Baracoa**. In 1878 the island was divided into six provinces: **Pinar del Río, La Habana, Matanzas**, Santa Clara, Puerto Príncipe (**Camagüey**), and **Santiago de Cuba**. This provincial breakdown remained in place until 1976 when **Fidel Castro**'s government increased the number of provinces from six to fourteen and reduced the number of municipalities from 407 to 169. The Isla de Pinos was renamed **Isla de la Juventud**, was segregated from the province of **La Habana**, and was granted a special municipal status. The current provinces and their respective municipal jurisdiction are as follows:

Pinar del Río Province: Sandino, Mantua, Minas de Matahambre, Viñales, La Palma, Bahía Honda, Candelaria, San Cristóbal, Los Palacios, Consolación del Sur, **Pinar del Río**, San Luis, San Juan y Martínez, Guane.

La Habana Province: Mariel, Guanajay, Caimito, Bauta, San Antonio de los Baños, Bejucal, San José de las Lajas, Jaruco, Santa Cruz del Norte, Madruga, Nueva Paz, San Nicolás, Güines, Melena del Sur, Batabanó, Quivicán, Güira de Melena, Alquízar, Artemisa.

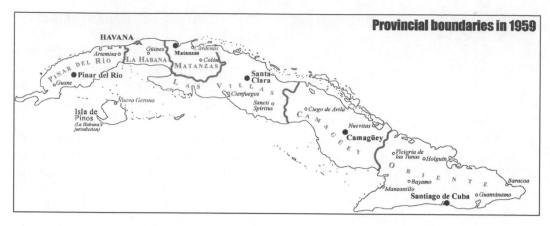

Provincial boundaries in 1959. By Armando H. Portela.

Ciudad de La Habana Province: Playa, Plaza de la Revolución, Centro Habana, **Habana Vieja**, Regla, Habana del Este, Guanabacoa, San Miguel del Padrón, Diez de Octubre, Cerro, Marianao, La Lisa, Boyeros, Arroyo Naranjo, Cotorro.

Matanzas Province: Matanzas, Cárdenas, Varadero, Martí, Colón, Perico, Jovellanos, Pedro Betancourt, Limonar, Unión de Reyes, Ciénaga de Zapata, Jagüey Grande, Calimete, Los Arabos.

Villa Clara Province: Corralillo, Quemado de Güines, Sagua la Grande, Encrucijada, Camajuaní, Caibarién, Remedios, Placetas, **Santa Clara**, Cifuentes, Santo Domingo, Ranchuelo, Manicaragua.

Cienfuegos Province: Aguada de Pasajeros, Rodas, Palmira, Lajas, Cruces, Cumanayagua, Cienfuegos, Abreus.

Sancti Spíritus Province: Yaguajay, Jatibonico, Taguasco, Cabaiguán, Fomento, Trinidad, Sancti Spíritus, La Sierpe.

Ciego de Ávila Province: Chambas, Morón, Bolivia, Primero de Enero, Ciro Redondo, Florencia, Majigua, Ciego de Ávila, Venezuela, Baraguá.

Camagüey Province: Carlos Manuel de Céspedes, Esmeralda, Sierra de Cubitas, Minas, Nuevitas, Guáimaro, Sibanicú, Camagüey, Florida, Vertientes, Jimaguayú, Najasa, Santa Cruz del Sur.

Las Tunas Province: Manatí, Puerto Padre, Jesús Menéndez, Majibacoa, **Las Tunas**, Jobabo, Colombia, Amancio Rodríguez.

Holguín Province: Gibara, Rafael Freyre, Banes, Antilla, Baguanos, Holguín, Calixto García, Cacocum, Urbano Noris, Cueto, Mayarí, Frank País, Sagua de Tánamo, Moa.

Granma Province: Río Cauto, Cauto Cristo, Jiguaní, Bayamo, Yara, Manzanillo, Campechuela, Media Luna, Niquero, Pilón, Bartolomé Masó, Buey Arriba, Guisa.

Santiago de Cuba Province: Contramaestre, Mella, San Luis, Segundo Frente, Songo-La Maya, Santiago de Cuba, Palma Soriano, Tercer Frente, Guamá.

Guantánamo Province: El Salvador, Guantánamo, Yateras, Baracoa, Maisí, Imías, San Antonio del Sur, Manuel Tames, Caimanera, Niceto Pérez.

See also Constitution of 1976.

Further Readings

Freire Díaz, Joaquín. *Historia de los municipios de Cuba*. Miami: La Moderna Poesía, 1985.

Rassi, Reynold. *Cuba: nueva división político-administrativa*. Havana: Editorial Orbe, 1981.

República de Cuba, Instituto Cubano de Geodesia y Cartografía. *Atlas de Cuba*. Havana: Instituto Cubano de Geodesia y Cartografía, 1978.

Luis Martínez-Fernández

Provincial boundaries after 1976. By Armando H. Portela.

Sancti Spíritus (Municipality)

Sancti Spíritus is a municipality and capital city of the central province with the same name. It was founded in 1514 by **Diego Velázquez** and like most of the other early villages was subsequently moved to a safer location; in 1522 it was established in its present site on the margins of the Yayabo River. The object of pirate and **corsair attacks** during the 1500s and 1600s, the region became an important sugar producer in the 1700s and 1800s. Sugar and **cattle ranching** are still its main industries, along with food processing. Its Iglesia Mayor is Cuba's oldest standing place of worship. The municipality had 125,485 inhabitants in 1998; estimates for 1999 place the **population** of the city itself at 104,626. *See also* Colonial Settlements, Early; Sancti Spíritus Province; Sugar Industry; Sugar Plantations

Further Readings

Freire Díaz, Joaquín. *Historia de los municipios de Cuba.* Miami: La Moderna Poesía, 1985.

Pichardo Viñales, Hortensia. *La fundación de las primeras villas de la Isla de Cuba.* Havana: Editorial de Ciencias Sociales, 1986.

Luis Martínez-Fernández

Sancti Spíritus Province

Located in the center of the island, the province of Sancti Spíritus has existed since 1976, when the former province of Las Villas was divided to form the three new territories of **Villa Clara, Cienfuegos**, and Sancti Spíritus. Sancti Spíritus is the seventh province in size, with 6,744 square kilometers (2,604 square miles), including the **keys**. It has boundaries with the provinces of **Ciego de Ávila**, to the cast, and Villa Clara and Cienfuegos, to the west.

The province's territory is made up of fertile plains and valleys, with crops and grazing lands occupying 80 percent of the area, where most people live, and of sparsely populated mountains and hills in the rest of its territory, typically covered with dense forests and coffee groves.

The **Escambray Mountains**, rising abruptly to the southeast of the province, are an intricate massif of overthrusted Jurassic sequences, including schist, limestone, and some amphibolites, deeply cut by narrow valleys. The provinces of Cienfuegos and Villa Clara also share this mountain range. The top altitude in the province, at Pico Potrerillo, rising 931 meters (3,054 feet), is located north of the town of Trinidad. To the north, the Sierra de Jatibonico forms a belt of stepped hills rising over 300 meters (984 feet) near the town of Yaguajay.

Sancti Spíritus has the largest man-made water reservoir in Cuba, the Zaza Dam, built in the low-middle course of the Zaza River (the second largest in Cuba), with a capacity to hold 1.02 billion cubic meters (270 billion gallons). The dam is mostly used, through a system of canals, to irrigate rice and sugar crops and to provide water to neighboring Ciego de Ávila. Other reservoirs complete a total capacity of 1.3 billion cubic meters (345 billion gallons).

Sancti Spíritus's economy is based on **agriculture**. Roughly three quarters of the land is farmland, or more precisely 4,976 square kilometers (1,922 square miles), though 52 percent of this extension remains unused. Almost 30 percent of the territory is labeled as "spontaneous pastures," a euphemism often used to typify vacant, commonly overgrown lands.

Sugarcane plantations, grazing ranches, and tobacco farms are common in the high plains, while large rice paddies cover the lowlands south of the towns of La Sierpe and El Jíbaro. Coffee grows in the Escambray Mountains, but production has declined sharply in the last decades to less than 5 percent of the national output. Nine sugar mills account for 5 to 7 percent of the national sugar output. The Uruguay sugar mill (formerly Jatibonico) is one of the most important on the island. A sugar refinery, located in Fomento, can produce 42,000 metric tons a year (4.2 percent of the national total).

Cement **manufacturing** is the most notable industry in the province after sugar. The Siguaney cement factory, in the center of the province, nominally accounts for 15 percent of the nation's total production capacity. Production, however, sharply declined after 1990.

Some crude oil findings, associated with a deep geological trough known as La Trocha, were made in the 1950s and moved the construction of a domestic crude oil refinery near the city of Cabaiguán. It has a limited refining capacity and has gone largely idle after the gradual exhaustion of the deposits and the energy crisis of the 1990s.

A fishing port at Tunas de Zaza specializes in shrimp, lobster, and shelf fisheries, but the shrinkage of marine populations and the size of specimens, a result of overexploitation and environmental degradation, reportedly affect captures.

The **population** of the province was estimated at 458,874 in 1999, or roughly 4.1 percent of the total Cuban population. With a density of 68 inhabitants per square kilometer (176 inhabitants per square mile), Sancti Spíritus is less densely settled than the nation as a whole.

The province's capital, also named **Sancti Spíritus**, has 104,626 residents (est. 1999), which makes it the smallest provincial capital city along with **Ciego de Ávila**. With 38,000 residents, **Trinidad** is the second city in the province. Trinidad and Sancti Spíritus were founded by **Diego Velázquez** in the sixteenth century and represent two of the earliest settlements in Cuba. Other important cities are Cabaiguán (30,000), Jatibonico (17,000), and Fomento (17,000).

The two-lane old Central Highway and the Central Railroad link Sancti Spíritus with the rest of the island. The four- to six-lane National Highway reaches the town of Taguasco, reducing the driving time to Havana to four hours from six and a half hours through the old Central Highway. A dense network of secondary roads and railroad branches reaches all settlements and economic hubs in the province. The province lacks important port facilities, so its sugar is shipped from the ports of **Cienfuegos** and Caibarién. The port of Casilda, on the south shore, is a secondary facility with limited movement. Air traffic at the local airport in Trinidad is report-

Sancti Spíritus Province. By Armando H. Portela.

edly increasing as the area becomes a growing tourist destination. *See also* Coffee Industry; Colonial Settlements, Early; Fishing Industry; Sugar Industry; Tobacco Industry

Further Reading
Provincia Sancti Spíritus. Santiago: Editorial Oriente, 1978.

Armando H. Portela

Santa Clara (Municipality)

Municipality and capital of the province of **Villa Clara**, Santa Clara is located on the center of the island in the region that Cuba's **indigenous inhabitants** called *Cubanacán*, a native word that means "center." The founding of Santa Clara dates to 1689, when eighteen families from the coastal town of Los Remedios decided to move to a safer inland location. In more recent history Santa Clara became the site of one of the most important battles in the **struggle against Batista**; rebel troops under the command of **Che Guevara** triumphed over the demoralized troops of Batista in the Battle of Santa Clara in December 1958. Santa Clara has recently honored El Che with a monumental statue and mausoleum. Santa Clara has developed into one of Cuba's largest cities with a population of 210,100 (est. 1999). Since the republican era, it is one of Cuba's main **manufacturing** and food processing centers. The municipal limits include 226,900 (est. 1998) residents. Sugar and tobacco are also produced in the vicinity of Santa Clara. *See also* Sugar Industry; Tobacco Industry

Further Readings
Alfonso, Carmen R. *Principales ciudades*, Havana: Editorial José Martí, 1997.
Freire Díaz, Joaquín. *Historia de los municipios de Cuba*, Miami: La Moderna Poesía, 1985.

Luis Martínez-Fernández

Santiago de Cuba (Municipality)

Santiago de Cuba is the municipal jurisdiction with the largest number of inhabitants and the capital city of the province that bears the same name. Founded in 1515 on the banks of the Parada River by **Diego Velázquez**, Santiago was soon moved to its present scenic location, nestled between the Santiago Bay and its surrounding mountains. During much of the first half of the sixteenth century Santiago was the island's colonial capital; its first mayor was none other than Hernán Cortés. As the focus of Spanish colonialism shifted toward Central and South America, Santiago's importance within the empire diminished; the moving of the island's capital to Havana reflected Santiago's waning importance. Like most of eastern Cuba, Santiago endured repeated pirate and **corsairs attacks**, and its economy came to depend on **contraband trade**. The arrival of large numbers of French settlers fleeing St. Domingue (Haiti) in the late 1700s and early 1800s helped spark the region's export economy, particularly coffee production. Because **slavery** was a weaker institution in the region, racial miscegenation was more prevalent in Santiago and neighboring areas than in the west.

Santiago, as the "capital" of Cuba's oriental districts, developed a culture of rebellion against Spain and its colonial capital, Havana. Santiago was the birthplace of scores of officers of the **Wars of Independence**, the **Maceo** brothers among them. During the U.S. intervention of 1898, Santiago and its surrounding areas were the site of major land and naval bat-

Postcard depicting the Church of la Virgen de la Caridad del Cobre near Santiago de Cuba. Luis Martínez-Fernández Collection.

tles. More recently, during the **struggle against Batista**, Santiago became the urban stronghold of the revolutionaries. Interestingly, **Fidel Castro**, who was born in Oriente, momentarily considered transferring Cuba's capital to Santiago in the early months of the **Revolution**. The regime hails Santiago as la Ciudad Héroe (heroic city) and la Cuna de la Revolución (cradle of the Revolution). Santiago, which is also known as la Tierra del **Son**, is famous for its carnivals and for the Sanctuary of the **Virgen de la Caridad del Cobre**, located a few miles outside the city. The Cuban patriot **José Martí** is buried in Santiago's cemetery, and the city is home to many important historic sites, most notably Santiago's Cathedral and its Morro fort. In 1998 the **population** of the municipality was estimated at 472,255; that of the city proper was

441,524 (est. 1999). The region's primary products are sugar, coffee, citrus fruits, and copper. *See also* Coffee Industry; Colonial Settlements, Early; Santiago de Cuba Province; Sugar Industry

Further Readings

Bacardí y Moreau, Emilio. *Crónicas de Santiago de Cuba*. 10 vols. Madrid: Gráficas Breogán, 1972.
Freire Díaz, Joaquín. *Historia de los municipios de Cuba*, Miami: La Moderna Poesía, 1985.

Luis Martínez-Fernández

Santiago de Cuba Province

Santiago de Cuba Province is a centerpiece in Cuba's geography and history. It was established in 1976 when the government redrew all the political boundaries nationwide, dividing the former province of Oriente into several smaller administrative areas. Located on the southeastern end of the island, Santiago encompasses 6,170 square kilometers (2,382 square miles), nearly 5.6 percent of Cuba's territory, but its more meaningful dimension is given by its historic, cultural, demographic, and economic influence on the rest of the island.

Its rough territory embraces most of the southern slope and a large portion of the steep **Sierra Maestra** mountains, the highest mountain system in Cuba; a sparsely populated terrain cut by deep valleys with coffee grows shaded by tropical forests. It also includes the densely populated croplands of the upper **Cauto River Valley**, the Central Valley, and the landlocked tectonic depression of Santiago de Cuba, where most of the population resides. The mountains make up 70 percent of the province. They correspond to an intricate core of Paleocenic andesites and tuffs with granitic intrusions. The top altitude is Pico Turquino, also the tallest peak on the island, rising 1,974 meters (6,474 feet) over sea level, followed by the

Pico Cuba, with 1,872 meters (6,140 feet) and Pico Suecia with 1,734 meters (5,687 feet). Another important summit is the Gran Piedra, rising to 1,214 meters (3,982 feet). The plains correspond with structural Tertiary depressions filled with gently sloping argillaceous sediments partially overlaid by Quaternary alluvial sediments.

Santiago's striking coastline is drawn by a long transforming fault separating the Sierra Maestra from the deep Bartlett Trough, bottoming −7,230 meters (−23,720 feet) south of Pico Turquino. This is the most active seismic zone in Cuba.

The province has endured considerable environmental damage. Deforestation, river damming, overgrazing in mountains, and improper waste disposal have taken the greatest toll.

Three large freshwater reservoirs have been built since the 1960s in the upper Cauto River basin to suit the needs of a growing population, control catastrophic floods, and serve agriculture. They have a combined capacity to hold over 510 million cubic meters (135 billion gallons) of water. An extensive irrigation system sends the water to the croplands in the neighboring **Granma** and **Holguín** provinces. Damming the Cauto River ultimately caused extensive environmental damage to the river and the croplands, including fading runoff, saline intrusions, and aridity of soils downstream, curbing in turn agricultural yields.

The original semideciduous tropical forests that once covered plains and mountains were cleared following colonial times to open space for farming. Today woodlands cover approximately a quarter of the territory, a low ratio considering the extent of mountainous terrain.

The economy of Santiago de Cuba is a combination of **agriculture** and **manufacturing**. Sugarcane cultivation is the primary use for more than 82,500 hectares (204,000 acres) and is the main crop in the

Cauto River basin and Central Valley. Its eight sugar mills have a nominal milling capacity of 27,200 metric tons of sugar daily, representing 4.1 percent of the country's total. In its heyday in the late 1980s they produced in excess of 350,000 tons of sugar each harvest, but since then the sugar tally has dropped at least a third. Refined sugar, **rum**, and torula yeast complete the array of products of the **sugar industry**.

Santiago de Cuba is the first producer of coffee on the island, accounting for 35 percent of the total. Coffee has been grown for 200 years on the fresh, humid, and forested slopes of the Sierra Maestra. Decades of poor care of the orchards along with continuing migration of farmers from the mountains to the cities have depleted the quality and volume of the crops. A third of the province's territory is devoted to pastureland, frequently occupying the deforested slopes of the mountains.

The province represents the second industrial hub in the island after Havana, but the economic crisis at the end of the twentieth century slowed down or even paralyzed many of the facilities. With few exceptions, most industries are concentrated around the city and port of **Santiago de Cuba**. Under normal conditions, a third of the province's industrial production comes from electricity generation and petroleum refining.

The Renté and **Antonio Maceo** thermoelectric plants, with 300 and 500 megawatts of capacity, respectively, rank among the most important of the country, capable of generating together a fourth of all Cuba's electricity. The "Hermanos Díaz" (Renté) petroleum refinery is capable of processing 74,000 barrels of crude oil daily. It remained idle for years after the onset of the economic havoc of the 1990s. A classic example of the Cuban unfeasible mammoth industrial investments of the Soviet era, the **Celia Sánchez** textile factory, designed to produce 95 million

Santiago de Cuba Province. By Armando H. Portela.

square yards of textiles and 2,000 tons of thread per year, was completed in the 1980s but never operated to capacity. Santiago's cement factory can make about 11 percent of the national total. In the 1980s, it produced from 350,000 to 400,000 metric tons, falling to less than half that a decade later. Other industries include a large brewery, six rum distilleries, one of the largest wheat mills in the country, a dairy production plant, and a large prefab plant.

Copper **mining**, a traditional endeavor, was halted in mid-2001 as the mine at El Cobre—the oldest in the Americas—near the city of Santiago de Cuba became exhausted after 471 years of continuous exploitation.

With 167 inhabitants per square kilometer (433.5 per square mile), Santiago de Cuba is the second most densely populated province, only after the **Ciudad de La Habana Province**. In 1999 the population was estimated at 1,032,508 inhabitants, representing 9.2 percent of all Cubans. Two out of five dwellers live in the capital city, also called Santiago de Cuba, which is Cuba's second-largest city only after Havana and one of those experiencing the fastest growth. Founded by **Diego Velázquez** in 1514, Santiago is one of the earliest settlements in the Americas. It served as Cuba's capital in the first half of the sixteenth century. In 1953 the city hosted 163,237 dwellers and in 1999 exceeded 441,000. Other important settlements are Palma Soriano (64,000), San Luis (27,000), Contramaestre (25,000), and Alto Songo-La Maya (17,000).

The province's highway system reaches all its economic centers and settlements. The two-lanes old Central Highway and the Central Railway are the main links with the rest of the country. A very scenic paved road along the Sierra Maestra coastline links Santiago to Pilón in the west. The port of Santiago is the second largest in Cuba. It has thirteen docks with 2,025 meters (6,643 feet) of berthing capacity. Its versatile facilities allow handling different kinds of cargo and over 80,000 tons in stocking capacity. The Antonio Maceo International Airport, located in the southern part of the city of Santiago, was recently expanded, with one of its runways lengthened to 13,400 feet. *See also* Coffee Industry

Further Readings

Bacardí y Moreau, Emilio. *Crónicas de Santiago de Cuba*. 10 vols. Madrid: Gráficas Breogán, 1972.
Santiago de Cuba Provincia. Santiago: Editorial Oriente, 1977.

Armando H. Portela

Sierra Maestra

Located along the southeastern coast of Cuba, facing the Caribbean Sea, the Sierra Maestra is the largest and tallest mountain range in Cuba. It has a total length of 240 kilometers (149 miles) from near Cape Cruz, in the west, to Borrachos Point, close to Guantánamo Bay, in the east end, while the average width is just 30 kilometers (18.6 miles), reaching a maximum 39 kilometers (24 miles) south of the town of Jiguaní. Its total area of 4,769 square kilometers (1,842 square miles) is equivalent to 4.3 percent of the country's territory. Rising 1,974 meters (6,474 feet) above sea level, the Pico Turquino is the top altitude as well as the tallest mountain in Cuba. Other important summits are Pico Bayamesa with 1,730 meters (5,674 feet); Pico **Martí**, 1,722 meters (5,648); Pico Caracas, 1,294 meters (4,244 feet); and the Gran Piedra, 1,214 meters (3,982 feet).

The Sierra Maestra is part of one of the most conspicuous physical features of the Caribbean: the Cayman Rise and the Bartlett Trough, a submarine mountain range and a deep trench, respectively, extending 1,500 kilometers (930 miles) across the bottom of the Caribbean Sea, from the Honduras Gulf in Central America, in the west, to the Windward Passage between Cuba and Haiti, in the east. These large planetary elements resulted from extreme tectonic shifts produced along the border between the Caribbean and Cuban tectonic plates moving in opposite directions. It is also the most seismic territory in Cuba. The Bartlett Trough, south of the Sierra Maestra, sinks to 7,230 meters (23,720 feet).

Centuries of timbering and clearing space for precarious forms of agriculture have swept away most of the original forested landscapes in the mountains. Relatively broad relics of the original ecosystems are found in the highest places at the core of the mountain range represented by mountain rainforests and by cloudy forests around the Pico Turquino. In spite of efforts to revert the devastation of the environment, **cattle ranching** and subsistence **agriculture** have taken an impressive toll over the last decades on its natural environs, posing a permanent threat to rare animals and plants.

Nearly a hundred endemic plants as well as many unique species of birds, mammals, lizards, and other animals find shelter in these mountains. The Pico Turquino alone is home to twenty-three endemic plants. To protect the remains of natural ecosystems as well as the scenery of the guerrilla war fought by **Fidel Castro**'s troops before 1959, the government created in 1980 the Sierra Maestra National Park, comprising most of the mountain territory.

The mountains' economy depends on agriculture, particularly coffee growing, cattle ranching, and vegetables cultivation. **Tourism** on the scenic beaches of the shoreline is becoming an increasing source of income. A traditional grower since the early nineteenth century, the Sierra Maestra produces roughly half of the coffee grown on the island, but mismanagement, along with environmental degradation and high rates of migration from the highlands to the cities, has made coffee production languish to a fraction of its previous splendor.

The dispersed **population** is estimated at 170,000, but some of the most populated cities and towns of eastern Cuba, exceeding a total 750,000 dwellers, lie at its foothills. These are **Santiago de Cuba, Bayamo**, San Luis, Palma Soriano, Contramaestre, Guisa, Jiguaní, Bartolomé Masó (**Estrada Palma**), Buey Arriba, and others.

The Sierra Maestra was a setting where much of the fighting during the wars of independence took place during the nineteenth century; it was also the site for the guerrilla war that launched Fidel Castro's rule over the island in 1959.

A recently finished scenic two-lane road links Santiago de Cuba to Pilón along the south coastline. Meanwhile, the interior is accessible mostly by dirt roads. *See also* Coffee Industry; Fauna; Flora

Further Reading

Fernow, B. E. "The High Sierra Maestra." *Bulletin of the American Geographical Society* 39, no. 5 (1907): 257–268.

Armando H. Portela

Trinidad (Municipality)

Trinidad is a municipality and city in the central province of **Sancti Spíritus**. The village of Trinidad was founded in 1514 by **Diego Velázquez** in an Indian settlement called Manzanillo. It is Cuba's third-oldest city after **Baracoa** and **Bayamo**. During the sixteenth and seventeenth cen-

Tower of San Francisco, Trinidad. Photograph by Luis Martínez-Fernández.

turies, Trinidad was targeted repeatedly by foreign corsairs. The region experienced a dramatic boom in the eighteenth century stemming from the establishment of **sugar plantations**. The opulence of many of Trinidad's palatial homes testifies to the wealth accumulated by the city's planters. Trinidad's historic center, with its quaint cobblestone streets, includes several architectural jewels, among them the Brunet Palace and the Iglesia Mayor. Cubans refer to Trinidad as la Ciudad Museo (Museum City), and in 1988 the United Nations Educational, Scientific, and Cultural Organization (UNESCO) declared it a Humanity's Heritage Site. Because of its historic importance and the beauty of the nearby Ancón beach, Trinidad is a major tourist destination. With 71,776 inhabitants in 1998, the municipality's economy also depends on sugar and **cattle ranching**. Some 38,000 inhabit the city proper.

See also Colonial Settlements, Early; Corsairs Attacks; Indigenous Inhabitants; Sugar Industry; Tourism

Further Readings

Marín Villafuerte, Francisco. *Historia de Trinidad*. Havana: Jesús Montero, 1945.
Alfonso, Carmen R. *Principales ciudades*. Havana: Editorial José Martí, 1997.
Freire Díaz, Joaquín. *Historia de los municipios de Cuba*. Miami: La Moderna Poesía, 1985.

Luis Martínez-Fernández

Tunas (Municipality), Las

Las Tunas is a municipality and the capital city of **Las Tunas Province**. Two Taíno chiefdoms, Maniabón and Cueyba, shared a border in the region known today as Las Tunas. The Spanish conquistador Alonso de Ojeda is said to have ordered the construction of a chapel there in 1510; this was the first Catholic temple erected on Cuban soil. The village of Las Tunas was founded in 1759 within the jurisdiction of **Bayamo**; nine decades later it was granted separate status as a mayoralty. Las Tunas figured prominently during the Cuban **Wars of Independence**. The city was burned to the ground three times between 1869 and 1897. Both sides claimed that the city's new name, Victoria de Las Tunas, alluded to their respective victories. During the twentieth century, Las Tunas evolved into a major producer of sugarcane. More recently, various industries, glass-making and dairy products among them, have been established. Because of its many sculptures, the city of Las Tunas has been nicknamed "Capital de las Esculturas." Also because of its location it is sometimes referred to as Balcón de Oriente (Balcony onto Oriente). In 1998 the municipality's **population** was estimated at 180,103, and 137,331 reside within the city limits (est. 1999). *See also* Colonial Settlements, Early; Indigenous Inhabitants; Sugar Industry

Further Readings

Alfonso, Carmen R. *Principales ciudades*. Havana: Editorial José Martí, 1997.

Freire Díaz, Joaquín. *Historia de los municipios de Cuba*. Miami: La Moderna Poesía, 1985.

Luis Martínez-Fernández

Tunas Province, Las

Located on the eastern part of the island, the province of Las Tunas has existed since 1976, when the former province of Oriente was split into five new territories. Part of the neighboring **Camagüey Province** to the southwest, was also assigned to Las Tunas.

Totaling approximately 6,589 square kilometers (2,544 square miles), its largely flat territory is equivalent to 5.9 percent of the country. Few scattered low hills break the otherwise monotonous topography, rising as relics of prolonged erosion processes. Cerro Verde hill, located toward the watershed, is the highest altitude, 164 meters (538 feet) above sea level.

The plains stretch over a complex foundation of Cretaceous effusive-volcanic rocks and intrusive granites, surrounded by a Paleocene and Neocene cover of mostly carbonaceous deposits and Quaternary marsh sediments toward the shoreline. Inland soils are mostly brown argillaceous of excellent agricultural quality, shifting to dark plastic clayey soils to the lower parts, where bad drainage often hampers farming. Salinity of soils and aquifers limits the land use in low coastal areas. There are some 41,100 hectares (101,560 acres) of saline soils, roughly equivalent to 7.5 percent of the agricultural lands.

The scale assimilation of the province's lands occurred mostly after Cuba's independence, as the sugar boom of the early twentieth century rushed North American capital and immigrants to these plains, at that time still covered with a mixture of tropical forest and shrubby savannas resulting from local clearings for grazing by earlier settlers. Nowadays roughly 12 percent of the territory is covered with forests. Relics of the original landscapes are confined to the rocky shores and mangrove-covered swamps.

Agriculture is the economy's base, with roughly 83 percent of the land devoted to agricultural activities. Large sugarcane plantations and wide spontaneous pasturelands, frequently overgrown, form the typical landscape of the province. One third of the agricultural lands are devoted to sugarcane, the primary crop in the province. Seven sugar mills, some of them among the largest in the country, account for 9 to 10 percent of the national sugar output. The **Antonio Guiteras** mill (formerly Delicias) at Chaparra in the north is the main producer in Cuba, exceeding 100,000 tons of raw sugar per harvest, good for 1.5 to 2.5 percent of the national output. The Guiteras mill, together with the Argelia Libre (formerly Manatí) and Perú (formerly Jobabo) mills have the capacity to grind 57 percent of all sugarcane in the province, or 4.5 percent of the country's total. As a result of the economic crisis of the 1990s, sugar production at Las Tunas declined to two fifths of the traditional level of 725,000 to 750,000 tons of sugar in the late 1980s. Torula yeast for animal feeding and bagasse pressboard are by-products of the sugar industry produced in the province.

Pasturelands extend to 45 percent of the agricultural lands, but **cattle ranching** produces traditionally poor yields. The herd has diminished as a result of the economic havoc of the 1990s.

With the exception of sugar-related activities, the industrial development of Las Tunas is low. The most important installations are the Metallic Structures plant, which produces prefab forms for industrial construction, and a glass bottle factory, which has had only limited success because of its distance from raw materials, which have to be brought from **Pinar del Río** at the opposite end of the country.

Las Tunas Province. By Armando H. Portela.

Its **population** was estimated at 525,227 in 1999, or roughly 4.7 percent of the total Cuban population. The capital city, also named **Las Tunas**, has 137,331 (est. 1999) residents, 26 percent of the province's total. The capital has had one of the fastest rates of growth in the country over the last 40 years, growing from 20,400 residents in 1953. In Las Tunas, explosive growth of urban settlements (partially caused by migration from the countryside) is a prominent feature of its demographics. Some small towns, known in Cuba as *bateyes*, such as Amancio (formerly Francisco), Colombia (formerly Elia), and Jobabo, that in the 1950s had barely 3,000 to 6,000 inhabitants now have 26,000, 20,000, and 18,000 inhabitants, respectively. The second-largest city in the province is Puerto Padre (28,000), a sugar shipping and fishing port in the north.

The two-lane Central Highway and the Central Railroad link Las Tunas with the rest of the island, and a network of secondary roads and railroad branches reaches all settlements and economic hubs. The ports of Guayabal, on the southern coast, and Carúpano, on Puerto Padre Bay in the north, are important bulk loading terminals, each capable of shipping 10,000 metric tons of sugar daily. They serve sugar shipping from the neighboring provinces of Camagüey and **Holguín** and, combined, load over one fifth of the Cuban sugar production. A minor sugar shipping facility exists at Manatí Bay, in the northwest. A domestic airport, at the city of Las Tunas, has only limited traffic. *See also* Foreign Investments (Republican Era); Sugar Industry

Further Reading
Provincia Las Tunas. Santiago: Editorial Oriente, 1977.

Armando H. Portela

Villa Clara Province

Villa Clara is one of the three provinces created in 1976 after the division of the former province of Las Villas. With 8,662 square kilometers (3,344 square miles), or 7.8 percent of Cuba's territory—including 719 square kilometers (278 square miles) of the northern keys—Villa Clara is the fifth-largest province on the island. It bordens with **Matanzas** to the west and the provinces of **Cienfuegos** and **Sancti Spíritus** to the southwest and east, respectively.

Its location in the geographic center of the island, an obliged route for travelers and commerce, is as crucial to its significance as its good soils, varied landscapes, and wide economic profile. The territory is diverse, including densely populated plains and valleys with sugarcane plantations, tobacco farms, and grazing lands. Plains alter with sparsely populated mountains and step rising hills commonly covered with shrubs, dense forests, and coffee groves.

A central plain elevated from 100 to 250 meters (330 to 820 feet) carved out of Cretaceous tuffs and crisscrossed by step rising belts of andesite, serpentinites, and limestone form the core of the territory. The hills top 478 meters (1,568 feet) at Sierra Alta de Agabama, near the city of **Santa Clara**. To the northern coast, a low and narrow deltaic plain, with marshes and mangroves, rarely exceeds 20 meters (65 feet) in altitude. To the south raise abruptly the overthrusted Jurassic metamorphic sequences of the **Escambray Mountains** with a top altitude of 923 meters (3,027 feet) at Pico Tuerto within Villa Clara bounds. Some outcrops of the crystalline Precambrian foundation of the island exist near Rancho Veloz, to the northwest and at the Escambray.

An important reservoir system used primarily for agricultural needs has been developed in the territory. The Alacranes reservoir in the Sagua la Grande River, with a capacity of 352 million cubic meters of water (93 billion gallons), is the country's second largest. Also important are the Minerva reservoir, holding 123 million cubic meters (32.5 billion gallons), and the Hanabanilla dam, a hydroelectric dam built in the late 1950s with 292 million cubic meters (77.1 billion gallons) and a power generation capacity of forty-five megawatts.

Most of the agricultural lands in the elevated plains have brown argillaceous soils of excellent quality with few natural limitations. To the north, however, the deltaic lowlands suffer from poor drainage and local saltwater intrusion. Some 81,200 hectares (200,650 acres) of saline agricultural soils have been surveyed. Brown loamy soils along the edge of the Escambray Mountains provide a superb ground for tobacco cultivation. Poor wastewater management in some densely populated and industrial areas has caused pollution in streams and dams. Reportedly the waters in the Alacranes and Minerva reservoirs are polluted with industrial and agricultural wastes.

The economy of Villa Clara is a combination of **agriculture** and **manufacturing**. Sugarcane is the primary crop, with about 200,000 hectares (494,000 acres). This is concentrated primarily on the northern plains and in a sugarcane belt that runs from Sagua la Grande to Cienfuegos. Villa Clara's twenty-eight sugar mills have a daily combined grinding capacity of 75,000 tons of sugarcane in normal economic times, representing 11.4 percent of Cuba's potential. Three sugar refineries, at the George Washington, **Quintín Banderas**, and Chiquitico Fabregat mills, are able to produce up to 110,000 metric tons year, or 11.2 percent of Cuba's output. A torula yeast factory is located at the Per-

ucho Figueredo mill, and alcohol is produced at the Heriberto Duquesne sugar mill. After topping 1 million tons during the 1980s the province's sugar tally was dramatically cut 60 percent as a result of the economic havoc of the 1990s.

Villa Clara is traditionally the second most important tobacco growing area after **Pinar del Río**. Its strongly scented brands, once in great demand in the United States to blend with local varieties in cigarettes, are devoted primarily to *tripa* for cigars and cigarettes. Tobacco is grown mainly in a narrow, undulating valley along the Escambray foothills, where loose loamy brown soils developed over weathered granites create an ideal environment. It is the "Hoyo de Manicaragua" region, an appellation of origin and a quality brand of cigars (see **Cigars and Cigar Making**).

Over a third of the province's lands are devoted to pasture, but it is generally of poor quality, growing over unattended lands. A dairy industry serving the needs of central Cuba's population reportedly languishes. Coffee is a traditional crop in the fresh, humid, and forested slopes of the Escambray, but decades of poor orchard care have depleted the quality and volume of the crop. Currently less than 5 percent of national production is harvested here.

Some industries in Villa Clara have national significance. One of the few still-working plants built in the early 1960s, as part of the early chaotic effort to diversify the national economy, is the INPUD (National Industry for the Manufacturing of Household Products) plant in Santa Clara. It produces a wide array of domestic appliances, from kitchen hardware to TV sets and refrigerators. A textile mill at Santa Clara, built with Japanese technology, has an output capacity of 60 million square meters (71.8 million yards) of fabrics yearly. South from the town of Manicaragua, a secluded plant produces different kinds of ammunitions, weapons, and explosives for the military. A mechanical plant in Santa Clara serves diverse industrial needs on the island, chiefly the **sugar industry**. A large chemical plant at Sagua la Grande is key for various Cuban industries. It produces a wide array of industrial reactive, acids, alkalis, chlorine compounds, and cleaners. This plant's poorly treated wastes are particularly harmful to the environment. Suited to serve the sugar industry, the "Sakenaf" factory has the capacity to produce 21 million sacks per year, enough to hold up to 3 million tons of sugar. At one time it used locally grown kenaf fibers, but in 1995, it switched to polypropylene. The factory is reportedly producing well below its design capacity.

The fishing ports of Caibarién and Isabela de Sagua rank among the most important in Cuba. Lobster, oysters, and sharks are among the most valuable captures. Oyster harvesting has declined, however, as a result of water pollution and habitat shrinkage.

Villa Clara's **population** was estimated at 834,861 in 1999, equivalent to 7.5 percent of the total Cuban population. Each fourth dweller lives in Santa Clara, the capital city, with 210,100 inhabitants, which is the fifth-largest city on the island. Other important settlements are Sagua la Grande (46,000), Placetas (41,000), Caibarién (35,000), Manicaragua (20,000), Camajuaní (19,000), and Ranchuelo (16,000). The

Villa Clara Province. By Armando H. Portela.

city of Remedios (17,000) was founded in 1515 and is one of the oldest in Cuba.

The six-lane-wide National Highway, the two-lane old Central Highway, and the Central Railroad link Villa Clara to the rest of the island. A dense network of secondary roads and railroad branches reaches all settlements and economic hubs. Driving time to Havana was cut from five to three hours after the completion of the National Highway. Port activity is limited to Caibarién and Isabela de Sagua, both handling little cargo. Sugar is mainly shipped through the port of Cienfuegos. A military/civil airport at Santa Clara, whose importance faded after the completion of the National Highway, has limited domestic service. *See also* Coffee Industry; Fishing Industry; Tobacco Industry

Further Reading

Provincia Villa Clara. Santiago: Editorial Oriente, 1979.

Armando H. Portela

3

History: The Colonial Period (Pre-Columbian Era to 1901)

Abolition and Emancipation

The abolition of **slavery** was the aspiration of **Afro-Cubans** and a small number of white Cubans throughout the nineteenth century. However, for most of the century abolition was viewed as an economic and political threat by Cuba's sugar planters and other elites. The issue of abolition was brought before the Spanish Cortes (parliament) sitting in Cádiz in 1812. In the face of strong opposition from the planters and the captain-general of the island, the measure was defeated. A treaty was signed in 1817 between Spain and Great Britain ending the **slave trade** as of 1820. Under the provisions of that treaty, slaves transported to Cuba after that time would be freed. According to the new laws, slaves acquired illegally were subject to immediate emancipation. Mixed British-Spanish tribunals were established in Havana and Sierra Leone to enforce the treaty, but its provisions went largely ignored. The tribunals were denied access to the plantations where the majority of the violations occurred.

African laborers freed under the provisions of the 1817 treaty were declared *emancipados* and placed under the control of the colonial government until they were granted full liberty. The colonial government frequently put them to work on public works projects, rented them out, and on some occasions, illegally sold them. For a fee, the government rented out the emancipados to the planters for domestic work or fieldwork, and the planters in turn paid the workers a small nominal salary (see **Sugar Plantations**).

Some slaves were allowed to work for themselves for a fee and were allowed to put money aside every month to purchase their freedom. This system of *coartación* allowed some slaves to purchase their freedom gradually after reaching an agreement with their masters about their price.

Abolitionist sentiments gradually found an audience in Cuba. In 1834, prominent writer and thinker **José Antonio Saco** was expelled from the island for espousing abolitionist views. Saco argued for the abolition of slavery because the slave system was no longer economically viable, and the large number of slaves created an undesirable racial and ethnic imbalance on the island (see **Racial Composition**). This imbalance could provoke an armed insurrection by the slaves and other Cubans of color. David Turnbull, the British consul-

Former slaves and other free workers were often paid with tokens that could be redeemed at stores owned by or affiliated with plantations. These are tokens from plantations: La Victoria (Gibara), Santa Lucía (Gibara), San Antonio (Guantánamo), La Cautillera (Guisa), and La Glorieta (Ranchuelo). Luis Martínez-Fernández Collection. Photograph by Celestino Martínez Lindín.

general in Havana from 1840 until his expulsion in 1842, advocated abolition. After slavery was abolished in the United States, a reformist group of planters emerged, arguing for gradual elimination with compensation. The formation of this group was in response to mounting international pressure against slavery and growing abolitionist sentiment in Spain. In 1865, an Abolitionist Society (Sociedad Abolicionista) was established in Madrid, which tried to influence the Spanish government. Among the members was a prominent Cuban, Rafael María de Labra.

The abolitionist movement in Cuba was pushed forward by the **Ten Years' War** (1868–1878), which sought Cuban independence from Spain. On October 27, 1868, Cuban wartime president **Carlos**

Manuel de Céspedes declared that all slaves permitted by their masters to fight against Spain would be freed and their masters compensated. In 1870, the Spanish Cortes approved the Moret Law, paving the way for abolition. The law declared that the children of slaves born after September 17, 1868, slaves over the age of sixty, and the emancipados were declared free. Representatives of the Republic-in-Arms gathered at the Assembly of Guáimaro agreed to honor the Moret Law, which also provided for a complex transition *patronato* system whereby slaves were guaranteed certain rights and privileges and were even allowed to appeal injustices to the courts. On December 25, 1870, Céspedes declared the complete abolition of slavery, but the failure to gain independence limited the significance of that declaration. In 1878, the Pact of Zanjón, ending the Ten Years' War, freed all the slaves that fought in the conflict. The final blow to slavery came on February 13, 1880, when the slave system was officially converted into a patronato of eight years, with the gradual freeing of the slaves over an eight-year period without compensation for the owners. The process was formally concluded ahead of schedule on October 7, 1886, with a final decree ending the patronato and all forced labor in Cuba. *See also* Guáimaro, Constitution of; Spanish Colonialism (Nineteenth Century)

Further Readings

Martínez-Fernández, Luis. *Fighting Slavery in the Caribbean: The Life and Times of a British Family in Nineteenth-Century Havana.* Armonk, NY: M.E. Sharpe, 1998.

Piqueras Arenas, José Antonio. *La revolución democrática (1868–1874). Cuestión social, colonialismo y grupos de presión.* Madrid: Ministerio de Trabajo, 1992.

Roldán de Montaud, Inés. "Origen, evolución y supresión del grupo de negros 'emancipados' en Cuba (1817–1870)." *Revista de Indias* 42 (July–December 1982): 559–641.

Schmidt-Nowara, Christopher. *Empire and Anti-slavery: Spain, Cuba, and Puerto Rico, 1833–1874.* Pittsburgh: University of Pittsburgh Press, 1999.

Scott, Rebecca J. *Slave Emancipation in Cuba: The Transition to Free Labor, 1860–1899.* Princeton, NJ: Princeton University Press, 1985.

José Antonio Piqueras Arenas

Abreu Arencibia, Marta (1845–1909)

Born in **Santa Clara** to a wealthy family, Marta Abreu Arencibia was a prominent patriot and philanthropist. With her sisters, she founded and sustained a wide variety of institutions throughout the province for poor children, including the Santa Rosalía school, the San Pedro Nolasco school, and the San Pedro y Santa Rosalía orphanage. She established the El Amparo clinic for poor children, founded the Colegio Cer-

vantes, built La Caridad theater, funded the construction of an obelisk to honor the priests Juan Martín de Conyedo and Francisco Hurtado de Mendoza, and funded the repair of the road between Villa Clara and Camajuaní.

Among her other philanthropic projects were the construction of four communal washing stations, the establishment of a public lighting works, the purchase of equipment for the Municipal Meteorological Observatory (Observatorio Meteorológico Municipal), and the repair of Santa Clara's parish church. Abreu visited and consoled patients at the San Juan and **San Lázaro** hospital as well as inmates in the jails. She donated a crypt in the municipal cemetery for the poor. As a result of her generosity, the municipality of Villa Clara recognized her as its benefactor. She moved to Paris in 1895 with her husband, Luis Estévez y Romero, and their son, Pedro. She lived in New York in 1898 and 1899, where she provided assistance to many deported patriots. Abreu donated large sums of money during the **War of Independence** under the pseudonym **Ignacio Agramonte**. She moved back to Cuba after the war, where she lived until 1905. Thereafter she returned to Paris with her husband after he resigned as Cuba's vice president. She died in Paris four years later. *See also* Political Exile (Nineteenth Century)

Further Reading

García-Garófalo Mesa, Rafael. *Marta Abreu Arencibia y el Dr. Luis Estévez y Romero.* Havana: Imprenta y Librería La Moderna Poesía, 1925.

María del Carmen Barcia Zequeira

Agramonte y Loynaz, Ignacio (1841–1873)

Ignacio Agramonte y Loynaz was one of the most significant figures in the struggle for Cuban independence. Born in **Camagüey**, he received a law degree from the

Ignacio Agramonte y Loynaz, a patriot leader during the Ten Years' War. Courtesy of the Biblioteca Nacional José Martí, Havana.

University of Havana. He married Amalia Simoni. One of the first to take up arms against the Spanish during the Ten Years' War, he took part in the uprising in Paso de las Clavelinas on November 4, 1868. Agramonte was the author of a key document, along with Antonio Zambrana and Eduardo Machado, at the Assembly of Guáimaro, in which he opposed the leadership and methods of President Carlos Manuel de Céspedes as dictatorial. Along with Zambrana, he drafted the Constitution of Guáimaro, which favored the legislative body over the executive in keeping with liberal and democratic principles. He advocated the civilian role remain dominant over the military in the independence struggle. Agramonte resigned the leadership of the Camagüey Province in April 1870 because of differences with Céspedes. He was reappointed leader of the province the following year by Céspedes when Spanish troops concentrated their efforts there. Agramonte displayed enormous talent in organizing the province

against the Spanish, establishing factories to supply arms, riding gear, uniforms, and shoes for the rebel forces. He established supply warehouses throughout the province and a rapid courier service. Among his more impressive military campaigns were the battle at Cocal del Olimpo and the rescue of General Julio Sanguily, held prisoner by a column of Spanish soldiers. He died in combat on May 11, 1873, at Jimaguayú. The Spanish burned his body and dispersed his ashes into the air. *See also* Spanish Colonialism (Nineteenth Century)

Further Readings

Betancourt Agramonte, Eugenio. *Ignacio Agramonte y la Revolución Cubana*. Havana: Dorrbecker, 1928.

Cruz, Mary. *El Mayor. Biografía en tres movimientos*. Havana: Instituto Cubano del Libro, 1972.

Pastrana, Juan J. *Ignacio Agramonte, documentos*. Havana: Editorial de Ciencias Sociales, 1974.

María del Carmen Barcia Zequeira

Agüero y Agüero, Joaquín (1816–1851)

A member of one of Puerto Príncipe's (Camagüey) most prominent families, Joaquín Agüero y Agüero led that city's revolutionary movement between 1849 and 1851. A lawyer by profession, he was one of the first Cubans to free his slaves and encourage the immigration of white Europeans to farm his lands. Agüero was accused of taking part in the Conspiracy of la Escalera. He was the leader from its inception in 1849 of la Sociedad Libertadora de Puerto Príncipe (The Emancipation Society of Puerto Príncipe). The Puerto Príncipe region was known for its anticolonialism, and Agüero went under the pseudonym "Franklin." His wife, Ana Josefa Agüero Perdomo, shared his revolutionary ideals.

In an effort to support the revolutionary plans of Narciso López, Agüero left Puerto Príncipe for Las Tunas de Bayamo on April 30, 1851. On his way back, he learned that the governor of Puerto Príncipe, José Lemery, had detained twelve revolutionaries. As a result, he hid in the Sierra de Jacinto and at la Piedra de Juan Sánchez in Las Tunas until June 26. On July 4, he was joined by thirty-eight men, including some of his former slaves, and together they signed a declaration of independence at San Francisco de Jucaral, a hacienda in Cascorro. After a battle at the San Carlos farm, he became convinced that the movement had erred, and he left for the coast to flee Cuba. He was apprehended at Punta de Ganado and executed at Puerto Príncipe on August 12, along with other conspirators. *See also* Abolition and Emancipation; Colonization and Population (Nineteenth Century)

Further Readings

Agüero Estrada, Francisco. *Breve reseña sobre los hechos más notables de la vida de Joaquín de Agüero y Agüero, hasta su muerte ocurrida el 12 de agosto de 1851*. New York, 1853.
Morales y Morales, Vidal. *Iniciadores y primeros mártires de la Revolución Cubana*. Vol. 2. Havana: Cultural, S.A., 1931.

María del Carmen Barcia Zequeira

Aguilera e Infante, Francisco Vicente (1821–1877)

A wealthy landowner from **Bayamo**, Francisco Vicente Aguilera was an early advocate of independence and an important leader in the **Ten Years' War**. He was a founding member, along with Francisco Maceo Osorio and Pedro Figueredo, of a Masonic lodge, Estrella Tropical 19, tied into the larger **Freemasonry** movement, Gran Oriente de Cuba y las Antillas, an early catalyst of insurrection.

When **Carlos Manuel de Céspedes**, leader of the revolutionary committee of Manzanillo, decided to move ahead with the insurrection and preside over it, Aguilera, in the interest of unity, opted against challenging his leadership. He also supported Céspedes when Donato Mármol tried to replace him as leader after the loss of Bayamo. He participated in the convention that produced the **Constitution of Guáimaro** and was first elected secretary of war and later vice president of the Republic-in-Arms. He later served as commanding general of the army in the eastern provinces. Aguilera was appointed by the president to reestablish unity among the Cuban exiles in support of the independence movement. The exiles were divided in their allegiances between the partisans of **Miguel Aldama** (*aldamistas*) and Manuel de Quesada (*quesadistas*). Aguilera was never able to reconcile the two factions. When Céspedes foresaw his removal from the presidency, he ordered Aguilera's return so that he could assume the post. However, Aguilera decided to stay in the United States in an effort to secure assistance to continue the revolutionary struggle. He died penniless in New York City. *See also* Political Exile (Nineteenth Century)

Further Readings

Aguilera, Francisco Vicente. *Epistolario*. Havana: Editorial de Ciencias Sociales, 1974.
Aguilera Rojas, Eladio. *Francisco V. Aguilera y la revolución de Cuba de 1868*. Havana: Imprenta La Moderna Poesía, 1909.

María del Carmen Barcia Zequeira

Aldama y Alfonso, Miguel (1821–1888)

Miguel Aldama, one of Cuba's most important sugar planters before 1868, was a member of the **Reformist movement** in the early 1860s and represented the island in the United States during the **Ten Years' War**. The son of Domingo Aldama, a Basque of poor means, he arrived in Cuba in the 1820s and managed to buy sugar mills, slaves, warehouses, and **railroads**. By 1845, Aldama favored annexation to the United States, but later on, during the captaincies-general of Francisco Serrano and Domingo Dulce, he advocated for political reforms, which included the gradual abolition of slavery, an increase in the immigration of white colonists, and political participation in Spain.

In 1869, he went into exile, and all his possessions in Cuba were confiscated after an angry mob of Spanish loyalists sacked his palatial Havana home. In the United States, he managed the office for the Republic-in-Arms and attempted to persuade the U.S. government to recognize the Cuban cause and to force Spain to negotiate the gradual independence of the island. In 1888, Aldama was allowed to return to the island, where he died later that year. *See also* Abolition and Emancipation; Annexationism; Colonization and Population (Nineteenth Century); Palace of Aldama (Palacio de Aldama); Political Exile (Nineteenth Century); Slavery; Sugar Plantations

Further Readings

Barcia Zequeira, María del Carmen. *Élites y grupos de presión: Cuba, 1868–1898*. Havana: Editorial de Ciencias Sociales, 1998.

Martínez-Fernández, Luis. *Torn between Empires: Economy, Society, and Patterns of Political Thought in the Hispanic Caribbean, 1840–1878*. Athens: University of Georgia Press, 1994.

José Antonio Piqueras Arenas

Annexationism

Annexationism refers to the nineteenth-century political movement promoted by Cuban slave owners and their North American counterparts who advocated Cuba's annexation to the United States. During the 1840s many Cubans feared political events in Europe could end **slavery** in Cuba and "Africanize" the island. France had abolished slavery in 1848; some Spanish officials were growing sympathetic toward abolition; and the possibility of war between Great Britain and Spain could result in an invasion of Cuba by the British, who had already abolished slavery in their colonies. Thus, Cuba's annexationists turned to the United States for support. They were aware that in 1845 the republic of Texas had joined the American Union and that three years later Mexico had yielded to the United States, as a result of the Guadalupe-Hidalgo treaty, over 2 million acres of Mexican territory. Furthermore, they knew that white Southerners were eager to incorporate into the Union a proslavery state.

Annexationist activities erupted in several locations in Cuba. In Havana, wealthy plantation owners founded the Club de La Habana with the objective of maintaining slavery. In the cities of **Trinidad, Sancti Spíritus**, and **Cienfuegos**, annexationists rallied around the powerful Iznaga family, who were **sugar industry** moguls, and the military leader **Narciso López**. In the city of Puerto Príncipe (**Camagüey**), **Gaspar Cisneros Betancourt** saw annexation as a means to create a democratic government and encourage free commerce.

Different strategies were employed by the annexationists. One strategy consisted of persuading U.S. politicians to purchase the island: In 1848, President James K. Polk offered $100 million to acquire the island, and in 1854, President Franklin Pierce upped the figure to $130 million. Many Cubans, however, deemed the purchase as a humiliating alternative.

Another approach was to organize an invasion of the island, claim independence from Spain, and then annex Cuba to the United States. With this objective in mind, General **Narciso López** attempted to invade the island in 1850, organizing two military expeditions. Captured by the Spaniards in **Pinar del Río Province** in 1851, the general was later put to death. In 1855, William Walker and Domingo Goicuría organized another military expedition. The plan was to occupy Nicaragua and then launch an invasion of Cuba from that country.

Not all annexationists favored military action. Others realized that annexation might maintain Cuba as a colony rather than a nation. Finally, the advent of the North American Civil War, which distracted Southerners from pursuing the acquisition of the island, ended annexationist activities. Annexationist sentiments resurfaced, however, among some members of the island's economic elites in the early years of the Cuban republic. *See also* Abolition and Emancipation; Escalera, Conspiracy of la; Sugar Plantations; U.S. Expansionism (Nineteenth Century)

Further Readings

Chaffin, Tom. *Fatal Glory: Narciso López and the First Clandestine U.S. War against Cuba.* Charlottesville: University of Virginia Press, 1996.

Martínez-Fernández, Luis. *Torn between Empires: Economy, Society, and Patterns of Political Thought in the Hispanic Caribbean, 1840–1878.* Athens: University of Georgia Press, 1994.

Opatrný, Josef. *U.S. Expansionism and Cuban Annexationism in the 1850s.* Lewiston, NY: E. Mellen Press, 1993.

Portell-Vilá, Herminio. *Narciso López y su época.* 3 vols. Havana: Cultural, 1930.

Luis Miguel García Mora

Aponte y Ulabarra, José Antonio (?–1812)

A free man of color, José Antonio Aponte organized one of the first conspiracies of the nineteenth century. Aponte was a woodcarver and a first corporal in the Militia of Color in Havana. He was discharged because of suspicion that he took part in the 1810 separatist conspiracy led by Luis Francisco Bassave. He was a tireless teacher and possessed his own small library. Aponte had great influence over the **Afro-Cuban** community because he presided over the Shangó Tedum council, a secret Nigerian society. In the religious sphere, he was considered an *Oni Shangó*, who held within himself the power of Oni,

his ancestral African god. The activities of the secret African society took place at his woodcarving shop. Upon the door of the shop he carved an image of Jesus on a pilgrimage (*Jesús Peregrino*), which gave the street its name. The conspirators met at his shop with the pretext of taking part in religious ceremonies, but their objectives were to topple the colonial government and end **slavery**. The conspiracy had followers in **Matanzas**, in Puerto Príncipe (**Camagüey**), and throughout eastern Cuba. In an effort to gain the support of the slaves, they disseminated false rumors that the king of Spain had abolished slavery. The slave owners, supported by the colonial government, refused to accept abolition. Aponte was imprisoned on March 19, 1812, after the seditious movement was discovered, and placed in the Cabaña Fortress. He was hanged on April 9. As part of a scare campaign, Aponte's head was hung in an iron cage on the present-day corner of Belascoaín and Salvador Allende (Carlos III) in Havana. *See also* Abolition and Emancipation; Santería; Slavery; Spanish Colonialism (Nineteenth Century)

Further Readings

Franco, José L. *La conspiración de Aponte.* Havana: Consejo Nacional de Cultura, Publicaciones del Archivo Nacional LVIII, 1963.

Franco, José L. *Las conspiraciones de 1810 y 1812.* Havana: Editorial de Ciencias Sociales, 1977.

María del Carmen Barcia Zequeira

Arango y Parreño, Francisco de (1765–1837)

Planter-lawyer Francisco de Arango y Parreño was the main economic and political ideologue of the landed sugar aristocracy of Cuba during the late eighteenth and early nineteenth centuries. He studied at the San Carlos and San Ambrosio seminary and at the **University of Havana**, where he obtained his bachelor's in civil

Sugar planter and lawyer Francisco de Arango y Parreño. Sketch by Esteban Valderrama.

law. In 1787 he was sent to the Royal Audiencia in Santo Domingo to resolve family matters, and in 1787 he traveled to Spain to continue his studies at the Real Academia de Derecho Patrio y Común de Madrid and at the Real Casa de Estudios de San Isidro, where he became an attorney in 1789. Named representative for the city of Havana in the Spanish Court, he began lobbying for the interests of his constituents, gaining a number of decrees and concessions for the open introduction of African slaves in Cuba.

The revolution in St. Domingue in 1791 and the fall of sugar production there gave Arango y Parreño the opportunity and inspiration to write *Discurso sobre la agricultura de La Habana y medios de fomentarla* (Discourse on Agriculture in Havana and Ways to Promote It) where he expressed his liberal economic ideas on production and commerce, contrary to the restrictions of the mother country. Linked to the **Sociedad Económica de Amigos del País** and main inspirer of the Real Consulado de Agricultura y Comercio (Royal Consulate of Agriculture and Commerce), Arango y Parreño participated in the development of the newspaper *Papel Periódico de La Habana* and in a plan of education for Cuba. The promulgation of his ideas advanced political reform. In 1813, he served as Cuban delegate to the Spanish Cortes. He received several other appointments and duties for the municipality and colony. These included superintendent in charge of tobacco income; honorary judge in the superior court of Mexico; honorary minister in the Council of the Indies; administrator of the army; superintendent of the subdelegation of the royal treasury, and dignitary of the kingdom in 1834. Late in his career, Arango y Parreño recognized the social and political implications of the massive importation of slaves and assumed an anti–slave trade stance, while remaining opposed to the abolition of slavery. He retired to his famous la Ninfa plantation in Güines, where he died in 1837. *See also* Abolition and Emancipation; Press and Journalism (Eighteenth and Nineteenth Centuries); Slave Trade; Sugar Plantations

Further Readings

Arango y Parreño, Francisco de. *Obras de Don Francisco de Arango y Parreño.* 2 vols. Havana: Dirección de Cultura del Ministerio de Educación, 1952.

Argote-Freyre, Frank. "Humboldt and Arango y Parreño: A Dialogue." In *The Island of Cuba by Alexander von Humboldt.* Princeton, NJ: Markus Wiener Publishers, 2001. 273–280.

González-Ripoll Navarro, María Dolores. *Cuba, la isla de los ensayos. Cultura y sociedad (1790–1815).* Madrid: Consejo Superior de Investigaciones Científicas, 1999.

Pierson, William W. "Francisco de Arango y Parreño." *Hispanic American Historical Review* 16, no. 4 (November 1936): 451–478.

María Dolores González-Ripoll Navarro

Asian Contract Laborers

The introduction of Asian contract workers into Cuba in the nineteenth century was the result of a series of economic factors, including the increasing demand for Cuban sugar in the British and U.S. markets, coupled with a shortage of African slave labor. Other factors included the completion of **railroads** across much of the island and the fact that the costs of free labor still exceeded those of slave or contractual labor. The practice of bringing Asian contract workers to Cuba began in 1847 and was a standard activity by the mid-1850s. During the contractual period, the worker lived in conditions closely resembling slavery, in which the contractor played a similar role to that of the slave master. Asian contract workers exhibited appalling rates of mortality, and the suicide rate among them was a hundred times higher than among Cuba's whites. In the case of Asian workers, they were mandated to work a set number of years, usually seven, before they were granted their liberty. These relations were formalized through a series of regulations adopted in 1849 and 1854 and by the royal decree of 1860, known as the *Introducción de asiáticos y reglamento para su gobierno.*

Havana's Barrio Chino (Chinatown). Over 125,000 Asian contract workers arrived in Cuba between 1847 and the 1870s. Photograph by Luis Martínez-Fernández.

Asian workers were primarily from China and specifically from the area adjacent to Macao, the only port authorized to conduct this trade, beginning in 1853. The vast majority were from Canton or Cochin in China. In the first years of the trade, the price per worker was 121 pesos. In the years from 1848 through 1874, roughly 125,000 contract workers were brought to Cuba. The rich profits from the trade discouraged legislative efforts to put a halt to the practice of Asian immigration. Legal immigration was finally accepted in the Treaty of Tien Tsin (1864). As a result of reported abuses, the Chinese empire decided to conduct an investigation of working and living conditions in Cuba. The result was a suspension of immigration from China, although the import of contract workers continued through the Portuguese port of Macao. In 1877, negotiations were renewed between China and Spain, and

immigration was again legalized. The new treaty annulled the provisions of Tien Tsin and required that all new immigrants be "free and arrive voluntarily."

The contract laborers more than exceeded the expectations of the plantation owners by alleviating the labor shortage suffered during the middle decades of the nineteenth century. The poor treatment and difficult working conditions were justified, as in the case of African labor, by scientific notions. In the racial hierarchy of Cuban slave society, Chinese and Asian laborers were considered "superior" to African laborers but "inferior" to whites. Their customs and religious beliefs were deemed "barbaric" by Cuba's elites. The racial, cultural, and political challenges of incorporating the new immigrants into nineteenth-century Cuban society were downplayed by Cuban planters, who were more interested, along with Spanish officials, with the economic gains associated with the practice. *See also* Slave Trade; Slavery; Sugar Plantations

Further Readings

Baltar Rodríguez, José. *Los chinos de Cuba. Apuntes etnográficos*. Havana: Fundación Fernando Ortiz, 1997.
The Cuba Commission Report: A Hidden History of the Chinese in Cuba. Baltimore: Johns Hopkins University Press, 1993.
Jiménez Pastrana, Juan. *Los chinos en la historia de Cuba, 1847–1930*. Havana: Ediciones Políticas, 1983.
Pérez de la Riva, Juan, and Pedro Deschamps Chapeaux. *Contribución a la historia de la gente sin historia*. Havana: Editorial de Ciencias Sociales, 1974.

Consuelo Naranjo Orovio

Autonomism

Autonomism was a political ideology that gained preeminence in Cuba toward the end of the nineteenth century. Though autonomist ideas surfaced at the beginning of the 1800s, it was not until 1878 that a political party representing those ideals, the Partido Liberal Autonomista, was established. The autonomists advocated a large degree of self-rule for Cuba while remaining a colony of Spain.

The autonomist movement had its roots in the reforms proposed by Cubans who did not want separation from Spain. The reformers wanted to reform colonial society, creating a political system that allowed Cubans to run their own government. In 1878, the Autonomist party presented its platform. It revolved around the social, political, and economic issues of the period, advocating abolition of slavery, equal political participation within the Spanish government in all matters pertaining to the island, and free international commerce, especially with the United States. The autonomists also demanded freedom of press and the right to convene and hold political discussions. In addition,

the party advocated emulating the autonomous regime set up in Canada by the British.

The Autonomist party labored for twenty years, from 1878 to 1898, to establish autonomy within the boundaries of the Spanish empire, trying to offer a choice between independence and colonial rule. But the autonomists were successful in establishing such a regime only for a few short months in 1898, at a time when separatist Cubans, who viewed advocating autonomism as treason, were staging the **War of Independence**. *See also* Abolition and Emancipation; Press and Journalism (Eighteenth and Nineteenth Centuries); Reformist Movement

Further Readings

Bizcarrondo, Marta, and Antonio Elozza. *Cuba/España. El dilema autonomista, 1878–1898*. Madrid: Editorial Colibrí, 2001.
García Mora, Luis Miguel. "Del Zanjón al Baire. A propósito de un balance historiográfico sobre el autonomismo cubano." In *Cuba, algunos problemas de su historia*, ed. Josef Opatrný. Prague: Universidad Carolina, 1995. 29–45.
García Mora, Luis Miguel. "La fuerza de la palabra. El autonomismo en Cuba en el último tercio del siglo XIX." *Revista de Indias* 61, no. 222 (August–December 2001): 715–748.
Ogelsby, J.C.M. "The Cuban Autonomist Movement's Perception of Canada, 1865–1898: Its Implication." *The Americas* 48, no. 4 (April 1992): 445–461.
Torre Molina, Mildred de la. *El autonomismo en Cuba, 1878–1898*. Havana: Editorial de Ciencias Sociales, 1997.

Luis Miguel García Mora

Bachiller y Morales, Antonio (1812–1889)

Antonio Bachiller y Morales was a lawyer, historian, and bibliographer who wrote about political economy, anthropology, law, public administration, education, and history in the major journals of the period. Born in Havana, he was a lifetime member of the **Sociedad Económica de Amigos del País**, serving as its secretary, censor, and director. He taught philosophy and law at several institutions, including el Liceo de La Habana and the **University of Havana**. In 1862, he directed Havana's Instituto de Segunda Enseñanza.

Bachiller y Morales was a reformist and an abolitionist. As such, he did not support the insurgents during the **Ten Years' War**: instead, he proposed a plan to bring about the island's autonomy and end the conflict. His initiative angered Spanish authorities, who confiscated his properties and forced him into exile to the United States, where he gave up his Spanish citizenship. At the end of the war, he returned to Cuba. He did not participate in political events but chose to concentrate on intellectual activities, writing for the journal *Revista de Cuba* and participating in the meetings of the Sociedad Antropológica. In 1881, he presented his thesis "Cuba Primitiva" (Pre-Columbian Cuba) at the International Congress of Americanists. He died in Havana in 1889. *See also* Abolition and Emancipation; Autonomism; Political Exile (Nineteenth Century); Press and Journalism (Eighteenth and Nineteenth Centuries); Reformist Movement

Further Readings

Morales y Morales, Vidal. "Antonio Bachiller y Morales." In *3 Biografías*. Havana: Ministerio de Educación y Cultura, 1949. 197–225.

Núñez González, Ana Rosa. *La vida bibliográfica de don Antonio Bachiller y Morales*. Havana: Editorial Librería Martí, 1955.

Peraza Sarausa, Fermín. *Antonio Bachiller y Morales, el padre de la bibliografía cubana*. Havana: Imprenta Molina, 1937.

Luis Miguel García Mora

Banderas Betancourt, Quintín (1834–1906)

Quintín Banderas (or Bandera), a black general of the Cuban Liberation Army, fought in all three armed conflicts of the thirty-year struggle for independence from

General Quintín Banderas Betancourt. Photograph courtesy of the U.S. National Archives, Washington, D.C.

Spain. Born in **Santiago de Cuba**, Banderas was the son of free black parents, like Guillermo Moncada, **Antonio Maceo**, and other leaders who emerged during the **Ten Years' War** (1868–1878). Banderas remained with Maceo during the protest of Baraguá in which Maceo and his troops refused to surrender to the Spanish without guarantees of Cuban independence and the abolition of slavery. Banderas also fought in the brief **Guerra Chiquita** (Little War) (1879–1880) that followed.

During the invasion of the west by Maceo's column in the **War of Independence** (1895–1898), Banderas led a force of infantry to guard the southern flank of the troops under Maceo and **Máximo Gómez**, drawing Spanish soldiers away from the main invading contingent. For much of the remainder of the war, Banderas and his soldiers operated in the **Escambray**

Mountains near **Trinidad**. In August 1897, Banderas was removed from command, ostensibly for not pursuing the enemy with sufficient vigor. However, conflicts within the high command of the Cuban insurgency likely played a role in his dismissal. Banderas was killed during political violence in 1906, amid a revolt against the reelection of President **Tomás Estrada Palma**. *See also* Abolition and Emancipation; Afro-Cubans; Mambises

Further Readings

Ferrer, Ada. *Insurgent Cuba: Race, Nation, and Revolution, 1868–1898*. Chapel Hill: University of North Carolina Press, 1999.

Helg, Aline. *Our Rightful Share: The Afro-Cuban Struggle for Equality, 1886–1912*. Chapel Hill: University of North Carolina Press, 1995.

Savignón, Tomás. *Quintín Banderas: el mambí sacrificado y escarnecido*. Havana: Imprenta P. Hernández, 1948.

David C. Carlson

Banditry

The origins of Cuban banditry as a social phenomenon can be traced to the truce lasting between the **Ten Years' War** (1868–1878) and the **War of Independence** (1895–1898). Social banditry, as theorized by Eric Hobsbawm, typically emerges in rural-agrarian societies in transition and manifests itself in acts of resistance, such as cattle rustling or other forms of "delinquency." Acts of banditry serve important functions for the rural community and include acts against the rich of a redistributive nature. In the case of Cuba, social banditry was linked with the struggle for independence, as many of the so-called social bandits took part in the independence struggle and were members of the Liberation Army (Ejército Libertador), including José Álvarez Arteaga, Matagás, Pedro Delgado, Desiderio Matos, "El Tuerto," José I. Sosa Alfonso, and Gallo Sosa. Many of these social bandits lost their lives during the independence struggle; many of those who survived the conflicts "reformed" their ways after independence.

Cuba's most famous bandit was Manuel García Ponce, known as the "Rey de los Campos de Cuba," (King of the Cuban countryside). García Ponce died in **Matanzas Province** under suspicious circumstances after joining the independence movement. He was the descendant of immigrants from the Canary Islands, as were many of the rural independence fighters, including Andrés Santana Pérez. The tradition of social banditry persisted into the twentieth century with examples such as Ramón Arroyo Suárez, known as "Arroyito" or "Delirio." Many of the postindependence acts of social banditry were manifestations of disillusionment against the injustices of the Republican government. *See also* Mambises

Further Readings

Paz Sánchez, Manuel de, José Fernández Fernández, and Nelson López Novegil. *El bandolerismo en Cuba (1800–1933). Presencia canaria y protesta rural*. Tenerife: Centro de la Cultura Popular Canaria, 1993–1994.

Pérez, Louis A., Jr. *Lords of the Mountain. Social Banditry and Peasant Protest in Cuba. 1878–1918*. Pittsburgh: University of Pittsburgh Press, 1989.

Schwartz, Rosalie. *Lawless Liberators: Political Banditry and Cuban Independence*. Durham, NC: Duke University Press, 1989.

Manuel de Paz Sánchez

Betancourt Agramonte, Ana (1832–1901)

A nineteenth-century advocate for women's rights, Ana Betancourt Agramonte was an active participant in the independence struggle against Spain. During the **Ten Years' War** (1868–1878), Betancourt Agramonte spoke out openly against colonialism, most significantly at the Guáimaro Assembly in April 1869. At that assembly, she advocated for the emancipation of women and compared their status to that of the slaves. This declaration made her one of the founders of the feminist movement in Cuba and placed her at the vanguard of feminism throughout Latin America. Ironically, she had few contacts with feminists prior to her speech and thereafter. She was cofounder, along with her husband Ignacio Mora, of the newspaper *El Mambí*. Betancourt Agramonte suffered great hardships during the independence struggle and was ultimately arrested and exiled. She lived for a time in the United States, before moving to Jamaica and then to El Salvador, where she worked as a teacher. She died in Spain, and her remains were taken to **Camagüey** her native land, in 1968, on the centenary of the Ten Years' War. Betancourt Agramonte's remains are beside those of **Mariana Grajales**, another heroine of the independence wars. *See also* Feminist Movement (Republican Era); Guáimaro, Constitution of; Mambises; Political Exile (Nineteenth Century); Press and Journalism (Eighteenth and Nineteenth Centuries)

Further Readings

Sarabia, Nydia. *Ana Betancourt*. Havana: Editorial de Ciencias Sociales, 1970.

Stoner, K. Lynn, ed. *The Women's Movement in Cuba, 1898–1958*. Stoner Collection on Cuban Feminism. Wilmington, DE: Scholarly Resources, 1991. Microform.

Julio César González Pagés

Betancourt Cisneros, Gaspar (1803–1866)

Gaspar Betancourt Cisneros was a writer and politician born in Puerto Príncipe (present-day **Camagüey**) who used the pseudonym el Lugareño. In 1822, Betancourt Cisneros visited the United States where he contacted pro-independence Cuban exiles. A year later he traveled, along with other exiles, to South America to enlist the help of liberator Simón Bolívar in the fight for Cuban independence.

In 1834, he returned to Cuba where he wrote for the journals *Gaceta de Puerto Príncipe* and *El Fanal*. In his essays, he proposed political reforms and social justice, and in that spirit, he founded a public school and distributed some of his lands to small farmers. In 1839, he became president of the Nuevitas-Puerto Príncipe railroad, the second railroad to run in Cuba.

Influenced by his knowledge of the political chaos in the newly established South American republics and the admiration of the United States, Betancourt Cisneros abandoned his pro-independence stance, favoring Cuba's annexation to the United States during the late 1840s and early 1850s. His political views forced him to leave Cuba, and upon his departure, the Spanish government seized all his properties.

Settling in New York, he wrote for the newspaper *La Verdad*, where he promoted annexation. In 1856, he journeyed to Europe, finally returning to Cuba in 1861. He wrote for the publication *El Siglo*, a reformist periodical that opposed independence. He died in Havana in 1866.

His most influential book was *Ideas sobre la incorporación de Cuba a los Estados Unidos, en contraposición a las que ha publicado D. José Antonio Saco* (New York, 1849). His essays were collected in the volume *Escenas cotidianas* (Havana, 1950). *See also* Annexationism; Political Exile (Nineteenth Century); Press and Journalism (Eighteenth and Nineteenth Centuries); Railroads (Nineteenth Century); Reformist Movement; Saco y López-Cisneros, José Antonio

Further Readings

Córdova, Federico de. *Gaspar Betancourt Cisneros. El Lugareño*. Havana: Editorial Trópico, 1938.

Entralgo, Elías. *Doctrina del progreso + Revolución mecánica—El Lugareño*. Havana: Universidad de la Habana, 1956.

Martínez-Fernández, Luis. *Torn between Empires: Economy, Society, and Patterns of Political Thought in the Hispanic Caribbean, 1840–1878*. Athens: University of Georgia Press, 1994.

Luis Miguel García Mora

Bobadilla y Gomera, Isabel de (1515–1543)

Isabel de Bobadilla y Gomera was the daughter of Pedrarias Dávila, governor of Darién, and Isabel Bobadilla y Peñalosa, influential within the Spanish Court. In 1536 she married Hernando de Soto, one of Cuba's early governors and conquistador of Florida. De Soto had distinguished himself in the conquest of Peru. Two years later they traveled to Cuba, where Isabel de Bobadilla later served as the only female interim governor of the island, as appointed by her husband, from 1539 to 1544 when he left for an expedition of Florida, during which he died in 1542. Hernando de Soto had named Juan de Rojas and Francisco de Guzmán as deputies of Havana and **Santiago de Cuba**, respectively, and authorized his wife to cancel any concessions, giving her control over matters relating to the expedition. She learned of her husband's death in 1543 and lived just a few months thereafter. The statue of *La Giraldilla* atop the fort of la Real Fuerza in Havana bears her likeness. *See also* Colonial Institutions; Conquest; Fortifications of Havana

Further Readings

Albornoz, Miguel. *Hernando de Soto. El Amadís de la Florida*. Madrid: Ediciones de la Revista de Occidente, 1971.
Syme, Ronald. *De Soto, Finder of the Mississippi*. New York: Morrow, 1957.
Wright, Irene A. *The Early History of Cuba, 1492–1586*. New York: Macmillan, 1916.

María Dolores González-Ripoll Navarro

Bourbon Reforms

The Bourbon reforms were attempts to modify the administrative, economic, social, and cultural system in Spain and its territories during the Bourbon dynasty of the eighteenth century, especially under the Enlightenment absolutist monarchs Charles III and Charles IV. In Spain's American colonies, the reforms had the objective of competing against the potential of British commerce, defending the territories from external attacks, and yielding income from their resources, which is why they imposed a number of economic and administrative measures that met with some resistance. While the reforms had different effects on different territories of the Americas, the crown established control throughout the hemisphere with the help of the newly appointed intendants.

The reforms were instituted in Cuba in 1764, just months after Havana was returned to Spain following the **British Occupation of Havana** in 1762. Until then, some measures had been taken so as to solidify Spain's hold over the island's production—for instance, the monopoly over tobacco in 1717 and in 1740 the establishment of the **Real Compañía de Comercio de La Habana** with the purpose of stimulating naval construction and production of tobacco and other exportable products (such as sugar, wood, and leather), along with the introduction of African slaves (see **Slave Trade**). Other initiatives included the creation of an examining board of physicians in Havana (1709), the first publishing operation (1720s), the Seminary of San Basilio el Magno in **Santiago de Cuba** (1722), and the **University of Havana** (1728).

Upon recovering Havana, the Spanish authorities initiated a political-military strategy of defending the territory and training its population with the construction of new forts and the modernization of existing forts, the reactivation of the arsenal and shipyard, and the creation of militia units that included native Cubans. The Count de Ricla (1763–1765) placed limits upon the traditional system of *asientos* (licenses to import slaves) and eliminated trade barriers with the help of *situado* funds from New Spain. His successors, especially the Marquis de la Torre (1771–1777), continued a policy of modernization and repairs (lighting, pavement, sanitation, etc.) and control over the inhabitants (censuses, laws against vagrancy, and so forth) marked by an alliance between the colonial power and the economic elites of the island. This alliance turned Cuba into a great exporter of sugar, thanks to a massive importation of slave labor, giving way to institutions such as las Sociedades Patrióticas de Santiago de Cuba (1787) and Havana (1792), the publication of the newspaper *Papel Periódico de La Habana*, and the establishment of the Real Consulado de Agricultura y Comercio de La Habana. *See also* Fortifications of Havana; Spanish Colonialism (Nineteenth Century); Sugar Plantations; Trade and Navigation (1500–1800)

Further Readings

González-Ripoll Navarro, María Dolores. *Cuba, la isla de los ensayos. Cultura y sociedad (1790–1815)*. Madrid: Consejo Superior de Investigaciones Científicas, 1999.

Johnson, Sherry. *The Social Transformation of 18th-Century Cuba*. Gainesville: University Press of Florida, 2001.

Kuethe, Allan J. *Cuba, 1753–1815: Crown, Military and Society*. Knoxville: University of Tennessee Press, 1986.

Moreno Fraginals, Manuel. *El Ingenio. Complejo económico social cubano del azúcar*. 3 vols., Havana: Editorial de Ciencias Sociales, 1978.

Puig-Samper, Miguel Ángel, Consuelo Naranjo Orovio, and Armando García González, eds. *Ensayo político sobre la Isla de Cuba. Alejandro de Humboldt*. Aranjuez, Spain: Ediciones Doce Calles, 1998.

Puig-Samper, Miguel Ángel, and Mercedes Valero. *Historia del Jardín Botánico de La Habana*. Madrid: Ed. Doce Calles—CSIC, 2000.

María Dolores González-Ripoll Navarro

British Occupation of Havana

In August 1762, during the Seven Years' War (known in the United Sates as the French and Indian War) (1756–1763), Havana came under siege by British troops under the command of Lord Albemarle. Following a forty-two-day siege, Havana fell and was occupied for ten months along with portions of the western part of the island. The region remained under British control until it was returned to Spain in exchange for Florida under the Treaty of Paris (1763). Beyond the military and naval significance of the occupation and the fact that the Spanish realized that they must rely on natives in future military endeavors, the British occupation was also an important and pivotal moment in Cuban history from the standpoint of relations between the island and its metropolis, Spain, especially pertaining to issues of free commerce, the monopolistic nature of colonial dominance, and tensions between Creoles and Spaniards.

Some of the salient military aspects of the British siege and occupation were the defense of the **Morro Castle** by Luis Vicente Velasco, the attacks by guerrillas assembled by the mayor of Guanabacoa, José Antonio Gómez (alias "Pepe Gómez"), and the ineptitude of sitting governor Juan de Prado Portocarrero, who was judged harshly for his defeat upon returning to Spain.

During the British occupation, trade taxes were abolished and a torrent of British and North American colonial products were made available in Havana. Nearly 10,000 slaves were imported during those months. At the same time, Cuban tobacco, sugar, and other products found new vibrant markets in Europe and the British colonies of North America. An estimated 1,000 ships entered Havana's port during the city's occupation. In the aftermath of Havana's capture, Spanish officials implemented a series of reforms known as the **Bourbon reforms**.

Contemporaries involved in the **sugar industry** and some historians consider the period of British occupation as a time of liberty and prosperity that sparked the sugar boom of the late eighteenth and

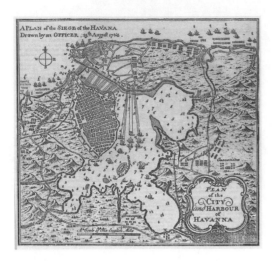

Plan of Havana drawn by a British officer during the city's siege in 1762.

nineteenth centuries. *See also* Fortifications of Havana; Sugar Plantations; Spanish Colonialism (Nineteenth Century)

Further Readings

Kuethe, Allan J. *Cuba, 1753–1815: Crown, Military and Society*. Knoxville: University of Tennessee Press, 1986.

Parcero Torre, Celia María. *La pérdida de La Habana y las reformas borbónicas en Cuba, 1762–1773*. Ávila, Spain: Miján, 1998.

Syrett, David, comp. *The Siege and Capture of Havana, 1762*. London: Naval Records Society, 1970.

María Dolores González-Ripoll Navarro

Cabildos de Nación

Cabildos de nación were organizations of Africans and African-descended people that were important in the creation of **Afro-Cuban** culture and in the construction of African-derived religious practices in urban areas during the nineteenth century. Cabildos dated to the early years of colonization. Cabildos were mainly formed by free Africans from a particular *nación* (ethnic group) to facilitate social interaction, to practice religion, and to continue funerary practices. These mutual aid groups were permitted by the slave-holding class and the colonial government, in part, to perpetuate differences between groups of slaves, thereby reducing the risk of widespread race-based actions. Also, the ruling class saw these organizations as a convenient way to inculcate Catholic practice among the African population. Many cabildos were regularly, though infrequently, visited by a priest who provided the members with some of the sacraments of the Catholic Church.

Some scholars consider cabildos as the pivotal institution in the formation of African-derived systems of religious practice. It was most likely behind the closed doors of these associations that saints and *orishas* (African deities) or *mpungus* became intertwined and African festivals were reconstrued to coincide with saints' days. Some acknowledge this may have been the site of combining saints and orishas but consider it a survival strategy with no real blending of ideas. Others consider this a clear point of syncretism or transculturation in which entirely new forms of Afro-Cuban religion and culture emerged. In either case, the cabildos were important in the maintenance of an identifiably African quality that has informed Cuban identity down to the present. *See also* Abakuá, Sociedad de; Aponte y Ulabarra, José Antonio; Catholicism; Palo Monte; Santería; Slavery

Further Readings

Brandon, George. *Santería from Africa to the New World: The Dead Sell Memories*. Bloomington: Indiana University Press, 1993.

Howard, Philip A. *Changing History: Afro-Cuban Cabildos and Societies of Color in the Nineteenth Century*. Baton Rouge: Louisiana State University Press, 1998.

William Van Norman, Jr.

Cabrales e Isaac, María (1842–1905)

María Cabrales was the wife of Cuban hero **Antonio Maceo** and a participant in the dual struggle for independence and the

María Cabrales e Isaac, protagonist in the struggles against Spain and wife of General Antonio Maceo. Photograph courtesy of the Biblioteca Nacional José Martí, Havana.

abolition of slavery during the last third of the nineteenth century. Cabrales was born in eastern Cuba, on her parents' farm, "San Agustín." Her parents, Ramón Cabrales and Antonia Isaac, enjoyed good economic position as small landowners. In 1866 Cabrales married Antonio Maceo, and they established their own farm, "La Esperanza," which was close to both of their childhood homes. Because of Maceo's participation in the **Ten Years' War** (1868–1878), Cabrales was forced to spend the next twenty years in exile. She lived alternatively in Jamaica, Costa Rica, and the United States, sharing her life during this period with Maceo, as well as with **Máximo Gómez Báez** and his wife Manana Toro. During the late 1880s and early 1890s Cabrales made several trips between the United States and Jamaica in the interests of the Cuban independence movement. She did not return to Cuba until 1899, after Maceo's death. Due to her impoverished condition, she was forced to live in **Santiago de Cuba**'s *Casa de Beneficencia* (charity shelter), and it was not

until 1904, with the assistance of her husband's admirers, that she came to have her own home in Santiago de Cuba. By that time her health was failing, and she died one year later. *See also* Abolition and Emancipation; Political Exile (Nineteenth Century); War of Independence

Further Readings

Graziella Méndez, María. "Cabrales de Maceo." *Mujeres* 8 (December 1968): 65.
Sarabia, Nydia. "María Cabrales." *Bohemia* 66 (July 5, 1974): 86–93.

Marikay McCabe

Céspedes y del Castillo, Carlos Manuel de (1819–1874)

Carlos Manuel de Céspedes was the first leader of Cuban independence and the initiator of the **Ten Years' War** in 1868. He was born in **Bayamo**, where his family owned the sugar mill La Demajagua. He lived and studied law in Spain, returning to Cuba in 1850. A Freemason, he joined revolutionary groups that were organizing an uprising and in August 1868 presided over a meeting of insurgents from Bayamo and **Camagüey**. When Isabella II was dethroned in Spain and several revolutionary leaders were arrested, Céspedes decided to free his slaves, proclaim the island's independence, and begin the war. The date he chose was October 10, 1868. His call to arms is known as the *Grito de Yara*.

Proclaimed chief general, Céspedes organized a liberation army with the help of veterans of the wars in the Dominican Republic. On October 20 he took over the town of Bayamo and successfully persuaded insurgents in other regions, except for those in the province of Camagüey, to recognize him as their leader. Then, in the Guáimaro Assembly of 1869, differences among the revolutionaries were worked out, and Céspedes was elected president of the Republic-in-Arms. His power, how-

Carlos Manuel de Céspedes is regarded as Cuba's founding father. Courtesy of the Biblioteca Nacional José Martí, Havana.

ever, was limited by the creation of the House of Representatives, a legislative body with wide powers. Differences between Céspedes and the House escalated on the subject of political power and military strategy, such as whether or not to invade the province of Occidente.

In 1870, Céspedes abolished slavery in Cuba, despite the opposition of conservative members of the House of Representatives. His commitment to total independence, rejection of any negotiations with Spain, and mistrust of the annexationists alienated him from other rebel leaders. He was accused of being authoritarian and incompetent, and on October 27, 1873, the House of Representatives impeached him. In February 1874, Céspedes was killed combating Spanish troops. He is regarded by Cubans as el Padre de la Patria (Father of the Cuban Nation). *See also* Abolition and Emancipation; Agramonte y Loynaz, Ignacio; Annexationism; Freemasonry; Guáimaro, Constitution of; Mambises; Sugar Plantations

Further Readings

Bueno, Salvador. *Carlos M. de Céspedes*. Havana: Gente Nueva, 1978.

Céspedes, Carlos Manuel de. *Carlos Manuel de Céspedes: El diario perdido*. Ed. Eusebio Leal Spengler. Havana: Editorial de Ciencias Sociales, 1992.

Portell-Vilá, Herminio. *Céspedes, el padre de la patria cubana*. Miami: La Moderna Poesía, 1989.

José Antonio Piqueras Arenas

Cimarrones (Runaway Slaves)

The word *cimarrón* (maroon) is synonymous with "wild"; it was first applied in the Caribbean to wild cattle. It was later applied to Africans and **indigenous inhabitants** who, as a form of resistance to **slavery**, fled to the mountains and countryside. Spanish law considered cimarrones to be fugitive slaves that had fled further than three leagues (nine miles) from their haciendas in groups of up to seven individuals without establishing themselves permanently in a region. If the number of fugitive slaves exceeded seven, and they had established permanent villages, known as *palenques*, they were classified as *apalencados*.

The cimarrones were pursued by parties of men using specially trained hunting dogs (*perros de busca*). On various occasions, Cuban mastiffs were used in Nicaragua, Haiti, and Jamaica to capture runaway slaves. It is believed that the majority of fugitives were African-born slaves, known as *bozales*. Captured slaves were taken to the Cimarrón Depot (*Depósito de cimarrones*) administered by the Royal Consulado. If they went unclaimed by their masters, they were utilized in constructing roads, bridges, and buildings.

The first legislation dealing with cimarrones, *Reglamento de Cimarrones*, was decreed in 1796 and was published in the *Bando de Buen Gobierno* of 1842 with the modifications that were made to the law in 1820 and 1822. New legislation was promulgated in 1845. In 1997 a statue was unveiled in El Cobre to commemorate the unknown runaway slave. *See also* Slave Trade

Further Readings

Montejo, Esteban. *Autobiography of a Runaway Slave, Esteban Montejo*. Ed. Miguel Barnet. New York: Vintage Books, 1973.

Ortiz Fernández, Fernando. *Los Negros esclavos*. Havana: Editorial de Ciencias Sociales, 1975.

Rosa Corzo, Gabino de la. *Los cimarrones de Cuba*. Havana: Editorial de Ciencias Sociales, 1988.

Rosa Corzo, Gabino de la. *Los palenques del Oriente de Cuba. Resistencia y acoso*. Havana: Editorial de Ciencias Sociales, 1991.

María del Carmen Barcia Zequeira

Cisneros Betancourt, Salvador (1828–1914)

Salvador Cisneros Betancourt was a leader of Cuba's wars of independence. Born in Puerto Príncipe (present-day **Camagüey**), Cisneros Betancourt became a Spanish noble who bore the title of marquis de Santa Lucía. In 1851, he joined the annexationist movement, was arrested for his political activities, and was sent to exile in Spain; from there, he escaped to the United States. In 1866, he returned to Cuba and joined a Masonic Lodge, from where he continued to conspire against Spanish rule.

In 1868, along with **Ignacio Agramonte**, he founded the Revolutionary Junta for the planning of the insurrection that was to take place in early 1869. Surprised by **Carlos Manuel de Céspedes**'s call to arms in October 1868, he returned to Camagüey to create Camagüey's Revolutionary Committee, an organ that led the war's vanguard. In 1869, he was elected president of the Cuban House of Representatives, where he monitored the powers used by Céspedes, who was then president of the Republic-in-Arms. After Céspedes's forced resignation from office, Cisneros Betancourt served as the island's president until 1875. Opposed to the Paz del Zanjón treaty, he left Cuba in 1878.

Cisneros Betancourt lived in the United States until 1884 when he returned to the island under orders from Generals **Antonio Maceo** and **Máximo Gómez** to start the **War of Independence**. In 1895, he emerged again as one of the major leaders of the independence movement and served as president of Cuba for the next two years. Once the island freed itself from Spain, Cisneros Betancourt was one of the writers of the Cuban **Constitution of 1901** and was a strong opponent of the **Platt Amendment**. Elected senator, he used his office to promote social and political rights for people of color and members of the working class. He was also a vocal advocate of the separation of church and state. *See also* Annexationism; Freemasonry; Guáimaro, Constitution of; Political Exile (Nineteenth Century)

Further Readings

Bernal, Fernando. *Salvador Cisneros Betancourt: Marqués de Santa Lucía y presidente de la República de Cuba*. Madrid: Editorial Verbum, 1993.

Carbonell y Rivero, Néstor. *En torno a una gran vida*. Havana: Academia de la Historia de Cuba, 1948.

Luis Miguel García Mora

Colonial Institutions

Seven early settlements were established in the early 1500s as part of the voyages of exploration and **conquest** commanded by **Diego Velázquez**. Havana, the principal seaport, became the staging ground for further conquest of mainland Central and South America. The city later became the primary transshipment point for silver and other goods going from the Americas back to Spain. As a result the economic, political, and social life of the city evolved around the regularly scheduled visits of the Spanish *flota* (trade convoy).

The first government institution on the island was the *cabildo* (municipal government), which was responsible for governing the early towns. The cabildo consisted of a mayor (*alcalde*), city council members (*regidores*), secretaries, a prosecuting attorney, and other functionaries. The cabildos were responsible for administering the "Ordenanzas de Cáceres," or land distributions authorized by the Spanish crown in 1574.

For the purposes of governing the island, Spain divided it into two administrative departments; the western part (Occidental) centered around Havana, and the eastern part (Oriental) centered around **Santiago de Cuba**. Each department was administered separately, although military jurisdiction remained in Havana. The concentration of military command in Havana had certain disadvantages and was discontinued in 1698.

The church organized along similar geographical lines, and new parishes were established as population centers emerged. As donations and church revenue increased, the church established a number of schools throughout the island, including San Ambrosio and San Francisco de Salles in Havana, San Basilio el Magno in Santiago, and Santa Inés in Puerto Príncipe (**Camagüey**). In addition, the Franciscan and Dominican orders established a presence in Havana in 1574 and 1578, respectively.

In the eighteenth century, as occurred throughout Latin America, the Bourbon dynasty attempted to gain greater economic and political control of its colonies. One of the crown decrees in 1717 established a royal monopoly on tobacco, which led to a series of insurrections among Cuban tobacco growers (the **Vegueros' Revolts**). The Bourbons placed a greater emphasis on public works and other technological improvements. In 1720, the first printing press was established in Cuba. Eight years later, the **University of Havana** was created, and in 1754 a post office was established. The **Real Com-**

pañía de Comercio de La Habana** began operations in 1749. In the 1790s, the crown appointed Luis de las Casas governor of Cuba, and he took a lead role in fostering the economic and cultural development of the island. At his urging, a number of important economic and social organizations were founded, including the **Sociedad Económica de Amigos del País** and the Real Consulado de Agricultura y Comercio. Also in the 1790s, a newspaper, *Papel Periódico de La Habana*, was established, the first library was opened, and the first *Casa de Beneficencia* (House of Charity) began its charitable work. After the Treaty of Basel (1795), the Spanish ceded part of the island of Santo Domingo to the French. As a result the Real Audiencia (a regional court of appeals) was transferred from Santo Domingo to Puerto Príncipe in 1800. *See also* Bourbon Reforms; Colonial Settlements, Early; Spanish Colonialism (Nineteenth Century); Tobacco Industry; Trade and Navigation (1500–1800)

Further Readings

González-Ripoll Navarro, María Dolores. *Cuba, la isla de los ensayos. Cultura y sociedad (1790–1815)*. Madrid: Consejo Superior de Investigaciones Científicas, 1999.

Instituto de Historia. *Historia de Cuba. La Colonia, evolución socioeconómica y formación nacional de los orígenes hasta 1867*. Havana: Editora Política, 1994.

Johnson, Sherry. *The Social Transformation of 18th-Century Cuba*. Gainesville: University Press of Florida, 2001.

Marrero, Leví. *Cuba, economía y sociedad*. 15 vols. Madrid: Ed. Playor, 1972–1992.

Wright, Irene A. *The Early History of Cuba, 1492–1586*. New York: Macmillan Company, 1916.

María Dolores González-Ripoll Navarro

Colonial Settlements, Early

Seven original settlements were founded in Cuba by Spanish settlers during the first years of **conquest** and colonization organized and initiated from Hispaniola. Au-

Map of Cuba by G. Mercator (1607) showing early settlements and detail of Havana.

Further Readings

Pichardo Viñales, Hortensia. *La fundación de las primeras villas de la isla de Cuba*. Havana: Editorial de Ciencias Sociales, 1986.

Sauer, Carl O. *The Early Spanish Main*. Berkeley: University of California Press, 1966.

Wright, Irene A. *The Early History of Cuba, 1492–1586*. New York: Macmillan, 1916.

Sherry Johnson

thority to do so was granted to **Diego Velázquez** who, as the de facto governor of the western portion of Hispaniola, simply crossed the Windward Passage to the neighboring island in 1511. He established the first settlement at **Baracoa** on the remote northeastern coast in 1511, and **Bayamo**, inland on the Caribbean coast, was founded by Velázquez's associate Pánfilo de Narváez in 1513. After the conquest other settlements quickly followed as settlers migrated westward from Hispaniola. Their most pressing concern was finding gold, and when placer gold was discovered in the rivers that emptied into the bay of Jagua, European settlements were created nearby at **Trinidad** (1514) and at **Sancti Spíritus** (1514). Puerto Príncipe (present-day **Camagüey**) originally was founded in 1514 on the north coast on Nuevitas Bay but later was relocated inland. It was the primary settlement near large native populations, and the Indian laborers awarded to Spanish *encomenderos* were rented out to the mining centers. The original location of San Cristóbal de La Habana (1514) was on the southern coast near present-day Batabanó, but it was relocated to Carenas Bay on the northern coast in 1519. The seventh settlement, **Santiago de Cuba**, was established as the administrative capital in 1515. Velázquez built his residence in Santiago de Cuba, and it also became the religious center of the island. *See also* Colonial Institutions; Labor Institutions, Early; Indigenous Inhabitants

Colonization and Population (Nineteenth Century)

Government strategies to attract immigrants to Cuba throughout the nineteenth century were based on achieving a variety of goals, including populating sparsely settled areas and efforts to "whiten" the population. Influenced by liberal reformist ideas, the elites sought to restructure the labor force, systems of production, and the future development of Cuba. At the time, there was a great fear that Cuba would be "Africanized" because of the growing **Afro-Cuban** population. Slave revolts were a cause of concern and thus the emphasis on modifying the makeup of the population. The elites tried to create a *Cuba pequeña* (Little Cuba) that would offset the large **sugar plantations** of the Cuban countryside dominated by a labor force of slaves. Cuba pequeña would be dominated by small white farmers dedicated to growing crops for domestic consumption. By the 1830s, it was believed that sugar production could be achieved by using a combination of slaves and salaried workers.

Policies aimed at attracting white immigrants to Cuba were proposed to the Comisión de Población Blanca (Commission on White Colonization) in 1812, which was later renamed the Real Junta de Población Blanca (Royal Board on White Colonization). In 1842 this Junta was replaced by the Junta de Fomento, Agricul-

Cuba's Population, Nineteenth Century

Year	Total	Whites (%)	Free of Color (%)	Slaves (%)	of Color (%)
1827	704,487	44.2	15.1	40.7	55.8
1841	1,007,624	41.5	15.2	43.3	58.5
1861	1,396,530	56.8	16.7	26.5	43.2
1877	1,434,747	67.1	18.9	13.9	32.9
1887	1,631,687	68.0	—	—	32.0
1899	1,572,977	67.0	—	—	33.0

Sources: Official Censuses.

tura y Comercio (Board of Development, Agriculture and Commerce), which was advised by the Comisión Permanente de Población Blanca (Permanent Commission on White Colonization). As the century wore on, there was less emphasis on populating sparsely settled areas, a major concern in earlier centuries because of English and French raids along the coasts. The emphasis shifted to concerns about attracting more whites to diminish the chances of a major slave revolt. A massive influx of slaves, in the aftermath of the Haitian Revolution, drastically changed the demographic composition of the island. As a result of the rise in the **Afro-Cuban** population, the Cuban elite supported an end to the **slave trade** and an increase in the price of slaves. The need for additional labor stimulated efforts to attract contract laborers from the Yucatán and China, and although they were considered free laborers, they were subjected to conditions bordering on slavery. White immigrants were treated considerably better.

The necessity of reducing the cost of production required the continual entry of migrant laborers. In the early 1870s, Cuban planters and a variety of societies dedicated to colonization and immigration led efforts to secure cheap and temporary labor. In the aftermath of the **Ten Years' War**, which concluded in 1878, efforts to attract permanent colonists to the Cuban

countryside intensified. The goal was to "whiten" the country by attracting Spanish immigrants to settle in small military or agricultural colonies. The plan served two purposes: First, it would change the demographic composition of the island. Second, the new colonists would be loyal to Spain in the event Cubans sought independence. *See also* Asian Contract Laborers; Slavery

Further Readings

Naranjo Orovio, Consuelo, and Armando García González. *Racismo e inmigración en Cuba, siglo XIX.* Madrid-Aranjuez: Ed. Doce Calles—FIM, 1996.

Paz, Manuel de, and Manuel Hernández. *La esclavitud blanca. Contribución a la historia del inmigrante canario en América. Siglo XIX.* Santa Cruz de Tenerife: Taller de Historia, Centro de la Cultura Canaria, 1992.

Consuelo Naranjo Orovio

Columbus, Christopher (1451–1506)

Christopher Columbus led the first European exploration to come into contact with Cuban territory (See **Appendix 2**). Sailing for the kingdom of Castile, the Genoan mariner reached Cuba during his first voyage in 1492, disembarking at a spot near present-day Gibara, **Holguín Province**, on October 28. He named the island "Juana" in honor of Queen Isabella's daughter and wrote in his diary that the island was "the most beautiful land human eyes have ever seen."

Columbus believed that Cuba was part of the Asian continent, though he was surprised by the lack of wealth, cultural sophistication, and resources in the villages he found and among the natives he met. During his second voyage in 1494, Columbus determined the depth of Puerto Escondido (Guantánamo Bay), visited the Bay of Santiago, and sailed along the south of the island, spotting numerous **keys**, which he described as "little gardens," with the objective of determining whether or not Cuba was part of a continent. Before returning east, Columbus, still adhering to his notion that Cuba was an Asian peninsula, forced several of his crew members to sign an affidavit certifying that Cuba was not an island. Eventually, Columbus reached the Isla de Pinos, later renamed the **Isla de la Juventud**. He gave it the name Isla Evangelista. Still he did not dismiss the notion that Cuba was a peninsula sticking out of mainland Asia.

Due to the capitalist nature of Columbus's enterprise, the absence of precious minerals on the island, the dearth of villages, and the swampy nature of the southern coast of Cuba, Columbus became more interested in the exploration of the island of Hispaniola, as a possible departure site for further journeys and expeditions. Columbus encountered numerous challenges as the administrator of Hispaniola. Disappointed, he returned to Spain in November 1504. He died on May 20, 1506. Columbus's remains were taken to Cuba in 1795 after being removed from Santo Domingo. They were later removed from Havana's Cathedral after Spain lost control over Cuba in 1898.

Further Reading

Columbus, Christopher. *The Log of Christopher Columbus.* Camden, ME: International Marine, 1987.

Crosby, Alfred W. *The Columbian Exchange: Biological and Cultural Consequences of 1492.* Westport, CT: Greenwood Press, 1972.

Manzano Manzano, Juan. *Colón y su secreto. El predescubrimiento.* Madrid: Ed. Cultura Hispánica, 1982.

Morison, Samuel Eliot. *Admiral of the Ocean Sea: A Life of Christopher Columbus.* Boston: Little, Brown, 1942.

Núñez Jiménez, Antonio. *El almirante en la tierra más hermosa: los viajes de Colón a Cuba.* Cádiz, Spain: Diputación Provincial de Cádiz, 1985.

María Dolores González-Ripoll Navarro

Conquest

Beginning in 1511, **Diego Velázquez** organized and led the conquest of Cuba from the territory he governed on the western portion of Hispaniola. The Europeans drew upon their previous knowledge of Cuba, especially the circumnavigation voyage of Sebastián de Ocampo (1508), and slave raidings on nearby islands. Even before they sailed, the leaders had identified the bays at Jagua (**Cienfuegos**) and Carenas (Havana) as potential sites for settlement. Velázquez also drew upon his experience with the **indigenous inhabitants** in the western part of Hispaniola. The cacique **Hatuey**, a veteran of Spanish "pacification" methods, fled westward from Hispaniola to Cuba, bringing his knowledge of the Europeans to the neighboring island. Reputedly, one of Velázquez's justifications for his incursion into Cuba was the capture of the indigenous leader as well as the search for gold deposits.

After the Spanish monarch Ferdinand granted approval for Velázquez's expedition, 300 men set out from Hispaniola. The group included Pánfilo de Narváez, who recently had subjugated Jamaica. In addition, the man who would become the most famous chronicler of Spanish activities in the Caribbean, **Bartolomé de las Casas**, came to Cuba on the first European incursion in the hope of gaining an *encomienda* (grant of indigenous labor), which he did receive near the gold mines close to the bay of Jagua.

Velázquez landed on the eastern tip of Cuba near Punta Maisí, and he established his center of operations at **Baracoa** in 1511. Narváez landed on the south side of the **Sierra Maestra**, and the two armies moved throughout the eastern end of the island in a pincer effect. Velázquez remained in the southeast, but Narváez moved northwestward into what later became **Camagüey Province**. At Caonao, the Cuban chiefs greeted Narváez and his men with a banquet. After the meal, the Spaniards rose and massacred the natives, eliminating the aristocracy of indigenous society and, therefore, indigenous resistance in one strike. Narváez proceeded westward overland to Sagua la Grande and from there by canoe to Carenas Bay, the site of present-day Havana, marking the farthest western progress of the initial venture. The Cuban natives fled before the advancing Spaniards, and in four months, native resistance was crushed. Las Casas was so horrified by the wholesale slaughter of the innocent Cuban natives that he renounced his encomienda and spent the remainder of his long life championing their cause. The massacre at Caonao and the subsequent trail of blood became the impetus for his campaign that earned him the title "Protector of the Indians." *See also* Appendix 3; Colonial Institutions; Colonial Settlements, Early; Labor Institutions, Early

Further Readings

Andrews, Kenneth R. *The Spanish Caribbean: Trade and Plunder, 1530–1630*. (New Haven: Yale University Press, 1978).

Sauer, Carl O. *The Early Spanish Main*. Berkeley: University of California Press, 1966.

Wright, Irene A. *The Early History of Cuba, 1492–1586*. New York: Macmillan, 1916.

Sherry Johnson

Contraband Trade

Operating under restrictive mercantilist doctrine and through an inefficient system that granted licenses to foreign-owned merchant houses in Seville, Spain was unable to supply what was wanted in her colonial settlements, much less at prices that the inhabitants could pay. The answer to high demand and insufficient supply was the contraband trade conducted by other European nations operating with local complicity. Contraband flourished in areas that were bypassed by the *flotas* (trading convoys) and by the Spanish navy. In the early sixteenth century, the French were the vanguard of the contraband traders. When France and Spain signed an armistice in 1567, dominance in the contraband trade passed to the Protestant nations England and Holland. Both established entrepôts on neighboring Caribbean islands with the intent of introducing illicit products into Cuba. When Spanish Jamaica fell to England in 1655, the situation became even more propitious for widespread smuggling to the southern coast. The illicit trade consisted of the importation of finished goods such as china, textiles, and iron pots and pans that were traded for Cuban tobacco and hides. By the late seventeenth century, calculations estimate that more than half of the island's profits from trade were siphoned off illegally.

Another way that contraband was introduced was under the guise of the *asiento*. The asiento was the privilege of importing slaves into Cuba, granted to England from 1714 to 1739 as a consequence of the Treaty of Utrecht (1713). British ships, with permission to enter Cuban ports with slaves, more frequently introduced far greater quantities of finished goods with the full knowledge and cooperation of local officials. The creation of the **Real Compañía de Comercio de La Habana** (1740) was intended to eliminate contraband, but it, too, was unable to meet the residents' demands, either for products or for slaves. The first movement toward free trade began in 1765, which led to an increasing liberalization of commercial relations in the Atlantic world. Trade linkages between Cuba and the United States were established during the North American Revolution, and after the war, in the 1780s, North Americans perpetuated the illegal trade by smuggling goods concealed in legally introduced barrels of flour. *See also* Bourbon Reforms; Slave Trade; Tobacco Industry; Trade and Navigation (1500–1800)

Further Readings

Lane, Kris E. *Pillaging the Empire: Piracy in the Americas, 1500–1750.* Armonk, NY: M.E. Sharpe, 1998.

Wright, Irene A. "'Rescates': With Special Reference to Cuba, 1599–1610." *Hispanic American Historical Review* 3 (August 1920): 333–361.

Sherry Johnson

Corsairs Attacks

Early Mediterranean maritime plunderers were called *corsairs*, and later this name was used interchangeably with *pirates* in the Western Hemisphere. Since the early years of Spanish colonization, Cuba was a recurring target for piracy, largely because of its strategic location in the path of riches bound for Europe. The Gulf Stream's rapid currents carried ships through the Florida and Bahamas channels. Yearly the Spanish trade convoy (the combined Mexican *Flota* and Panama *Galeones*) met in Havana for the last stretch of the *Carrera de Indias* toward Spain. Thus, independent pirates, called buccaneers, and pirates officially licensed by foreign nations, called privateers, raided in and off Cuba, usually with little profits but always with lots of violence.

In 1554, François le Clerc (Jambe de Bois) looted **Santiago de Cuba**, then the

principal Spanish settlement on the island. The following year, Jacques de Sores captured Havana: When he failed to secure a ransom, he burned the city. A stunned Spanish government charged Pedro Menéndez de Avilés with fortifying Cuban and other Caribbean ports. In the 1580s, the Italian engineer Juan Bautista Antoneli erected Havana's **Morro Castle** and other fortifications in response to pirates' attacks. These defensive works were completed by the end of the eighteenth century. Despite these measures, attacks continued along Cuban coasts. In 1628, the Dutchman Piet Heyn seized an entire Spanish treasure fleet off Cuba and forced it into the Matanzas River. The age of the buccaneers ended in the late seventeenth century when Dutch, English, and French authorities, now with a legitimized presence in the Caribbean, found lawful trade more profitable than plunder. *See also* Contraband Trade; Fortifications of Havana

Further Readings

Konstam, Angus. *Buccaneers*. Mechanisburg, PA: Stackpole Books, 2000.

Mota, Francisco. M. *Piratas y corsarios en las costas de Cuba*. Havana: Editorial Gente Nueva, 1997.

Núñez Jiménez, Antonio. *Piratas en el Archipiélago Cubano*. Havana: Publicaciones Gente Nueva, 1986.

Pyle, Howard. *The Book of Pirates*. Mineola, NY: Dover Publications, 2000.

Dennis R. Hidalgo

Del Monte, Domingo (1804–1851)

Domingo del Monte was one of Cuba's principal literary and intellectual figures of the first half of the nineteenth century. This writer, literary critic, and promoter of Cuban culture was born in Maracaibo, Venezuela, but moved to Cuba when he was six years old. He studied at the Seminario de San Carlos, where he befriended **Félix**

Varela, and later attended the **University of Havana**, becoming a longtime friend of the poet **José María Heredia**. Graduating from law school in 1827, he traveled to the United States and Europe. Upon his return to Cuba in 1829, he was elected president of the **Sociedad Económica de Amigos del País**. He wrote for such influential journals as *Revista Bimestre Cubana* and founded the weeklies *La Moda* and *El Punto Literario*, where he introduced to Cuba literary works produced in Europe. He sponsored symposiums where he promoted the talents of emerging Cuban writers. He mentored **Juan Francisco Manzano**, a black poet who was a slave, securing him his freedom; later on, he helped Manzano write his autobiography, an abolitionist tract.

His constant promotion of Cuban culture, his antislavery stance, and his work with Manzano and other writers who favored abolition made him suspect before the Spanish authorities, and in 1843, he fled Cuba. A year later, while living in Paris, he was accused of participating in the **Conspiracy of la Escalera**, but even though he knew the conspirators, he was able to prove his innocence. He was allowed to relocate to Madrid from where he opposed annexation and promoted colonial reforms to improve relations between Cuba and Spain.

His correspondence with hundreds of literary figures, which took up seven volumes and was published under the title of *Centón epistolario de Domingo del Monte* (Havana, 1926–1957), offered an in-depth portrait of nineteenth-century culture. *See also* Abolition and Emancipation; Abolitionist Literature; Annexationism; Press and Journalism (Eighteenth and Nineteenth Centuries); Reformist Movement

Further Readings

Bueno, Salvador. *Domingo del Monte*. Havana: Unión de Escritores y Artistas de Cuba, 1986.
Entralgo, Elías José. *Domingo del Monte y su época*. Havana: Hermes, 1924.
Martínez Carmenate, Urbano. *Domingo del Monte y su tiempo*. Maracaibo, Venezuela: Dirección de Cultura de la Universidad del Zulia, 1996.

Luis Miguel García Mora

Dolz y Arango, María Luisa (1854–1928)

María Luisa Dolz y Arango was a distinguished teacher and feminist leader. She received a comprehensive education in a wide range of subjects including English, French, German, and music. She graduated as a primary school teacher in 1876 and as a middle school teacher the following year. In 1884 she completed high school, and in 1890 she went to college to study natural sciences and completed a doctorate in that field in 1898. In 1879 she founded a school for girls, Isabel la Católica, which years later was named for her. At her school she applied the pedagogical principles of Johan Heinrich Pestalozzi. She was a pioneer in girls' education, introducing sports, physical education, and more advanced courses into the school's curriculum. Dolz believed the central goal of women's education was to prepare capable mothers to shape the men and women of the future. Her school won awards at the Pan American Exhibition in Buffalo in 1901, in Charleston in 1902, Saint Louis in 1904, and later on at Chicago. Dolz's interest in the plight of destitute children intensified in the 1880s, an interest that was magnified as the result of the cruel consequences of the **reconcentraciones** of the Spanish government during the **War for Independence** (1895–1898). She focused on the establishment of reformatories for Cuban children. To educate herself on the issue, Dolz visited La Roquette school in Paris and the Institución de Reforma Am Urbam in Berlin. She was a member of the Club Femenino de Cuba and participated in the First Women's Congress (Primer Congreso Feminista) in 1923. She was a member of the Pan American Women's Commission. *See also* Feminist Movement (Republican Era)

Further Reading
De la Cruz, Dania, et al. *María Luisa Dolz: documentos para el estudio de su labor pedagógica y social*. Havana: Editorial Academia, 1990.

María del Carmen Barcia Zequeira

Escalera, Conspiracy of La

In 1843 several slave uprisings erupted in **Cárdenas** and **Matanzas**. Toward the end of that year, rumors spread that a vast abolitionist conspiracy was under way. Already terrified, white landowners found themselves at a point in history where pressure from British abolitionists had intensified and the black slave population had surpassed the number of white inhabitants. The ruling authorities initiated a period of bloody repression against the slaves as well as free blacks and mulattoes. Some whites associated with the British Consul, David Turnbull, and others who had condemned the continuation of the **slave trade**, such as **José de la Luz y Caballero** and **Domingo del Monte**, were prosecuted. It is estimated that under the Executive Military Commission more than 300 blacks and mulattoes died under their torturous tactics for obtaining information. There were 78 death sentences and executions, half of which were slaves, half free. More than 1,200 were jailed; another 435 were banished. The conspiracy's name was derived from the *escaleras* (ladders) used to tie down those being lashed during the repression.

To this day, it is not known whether there was in fact a conspiracy. Some historians figure that it was fabricated by Captain-General Leopoldo O'Donnell and the slaveholders so as to rid themselves of all abolitionist movements. Others believe that is was a way of curbing the annexationist movement. It is also said that the island's sugar barons wanted to halt the freeing of slaves. For this reason, prominent blacks such as the poet **Gabriel de la Concepción Valdés (Plácido)** and other members of the black middle classes were executed, and many free blacks were deported to other countries. *See also* Abolition and Emancipation; Annexationism; Slavery; Spanish Colonialism (Nineteenth Century); Sugar Plantations

Further Readings
Llanes Miqueli, Rita. *Víctimas del año del cuero*. Havana: Editorial de Ciencias Sociales, 1988.
Morales y Morales, Vidal. *Iniciadores y primeros mártires de la revolución cubana*. Havana: Editorial Nacional de Cuba, 1963.
Paquette, Robert L. *Sugar Is Made with Blood: The Conspiracy of La Escalera and the Conflict between Empires over Slavery in Cuba*. Middletown, CT: Wesleyan University Press, 1988.

Inés Roldán de Montaud

Escobar Laredo, María (1866–1919)

María Escobar Laredo was an active participant in the **War of Independence** from its inception in 1895. She was a member of several revolutionary organizations operating in Caibarién, including the clubs "Patria," "El Diablo," and "Vencedor." Escobar Laredo directed the Vencedor club, which was dedicated to procuring medicine, clothing, shoes, money, and weapons for the pro-independence forces. To avoid detection, she used the pseudonyms "Esmeralda," "Vencedor," and "la Coronela." She worked closely with Brigadier José González Planas, General Francisco Carrillo, and Commander-in-Chief **Máximo Gómez**. She maintained an ongoing correspondence with Gómez regarding her covert activities and missions. After the war, she abandoned her political activities, because of disillusionment with the outcome of the revolutionary struggles. Even though out of the public eye, she was frequently honored for her efforts during the independence struggle. A few days after her death, an important street in Caibarién was named after her. *See also* Mambises

Further Readings
La mujer cubana en los 100 años de lucha, 1868–1968. Havana: Instituto Cubano del Libro, 1968.
Las mujeres en la Revolución Cubana. Havana, 1960.

Julio César González Pagés

Finlay de Barres, Carlos J. (1833–1915)

One of the most prominent scientists in Cuban history, Carlos J. Finlay did vital research in the 1880s that determined that a specific type of mosquito was responsible for the spread of yellow fever, a leading cause of death on the island. The son of a Scottish father, a medical doctor, and a French mother, he received his early education in France, England, and Germany and returned to Cuba in 1851. Two years later, he was accepted to the Jefferson Medical College in Philadelphia, where he received a medical degree in 1855. Nine years later, Finlay presented a research paper on yellow fever to the Royal Academy of Medical, Physical and Natural Sciences in Havana (see **Academy of Sciences**). The Academy would later admit him as a member in 1872. Finlay's groundbreaking research on yellow fever was again presented to the Academy in 1881 in his work *El mosquito hipotéticamente considerado como agente de transmisión de la fiebre amarilla* (The Mosquito Hypothetically Considered as Agent in the Spread of Yellow Fever). In the work, he identified the disease-causing agent as the Culex mosquito (later known as *Aedes aegypti*). Although his investigations uncovered a new avenue of research into various diseases, his findings were largely ignored by the international scientific community. The acceptance of his work did not come until

after the U.S. takeover of Cuba in 1898. The following year, a medical commission was appointed, directed by Walter Reed, to find the cause of yellow fever. Using the work of Finlay and Jesse Lazear, a member of the commission, Reed confirmed the earlier findings in 1901.

In addition to his research on yellow fever, Finlay wrote extensively on a broad range of medical issues, including tuberculosis, tetanus, leprosy, beriberi, goiter, and ophthalmology. After independence, he was appointed public health minister by the Cuban government in 1902. Later the government would establish the Finlay Institute for Investigations in Tropical Medicine. *See also* Science and Scientists (Eighteenth and Nineteenth Centuries)

Further Reading
López Sánchez, José. *Finlay. El hombre y la verdad científica*. Havana: Editorial Científico-Técnica, 1987.

Miguel Ángel Puig-Samper Mulero

García Íñiguez, Calixto (1839–1898)

An important insurgent leader in the Cuban **War of Independence**, Major General Calixto García Íñiguez commanded the Liberation Army in eastern Cuba from 1896 to 1898. When the earlier uprising against Spanish colonialism began on October 10, 1868, García served as a colonel. He was promoted to major general in 1872. Captured by Spanish irregular troops in 1874, García survived a self-inflicted gunshot to the head. After spending four years in Spanish prisons, García received an amnesty and moved with his family to New York, where he headed the Cuban Revolutionary Committee.

Back in Cuba, García was recaptured in 1880 during **la Guerra Chiquita** (Little War), while attempting to join the main insurgent forces. He remained in Spain for fifteen years but traveled to the United

States when the War of Independence broke out in 1895.

In 1896, García arrived in Cuba, where he led several important battles, noted for the insurgents' effective use of artillery. Late in the war, troops under his command captured the towns Guáimaro, **Las Tunas**, and Guisa. During the 1898 North American intervention in the Spanish-Cuban-American War, García cooperated with the U.S. Army during the **Santiago de Cuba** campaign. When it became clear that the United States would sideline Cubans in surrender negotiations and deny them control of the island, García resigned from his command in protest, sending a strong letter to U.S. General William R. Shafter (see Appendix 9). García died in late 1898 during a diplomatic mission to Washington, D.C. *See also* Mambises; Political Exile (Nineteenth Century); Ten Years' War; U.S. Interventions

Further Readings

Foner, Philip S. *The Spanish-Cuban-American War and the Birth of U.S. Imperialism.* 2 vols. New York: Monthly Review Press, 1972.

Pérez, Louis A., Jr. *Cuba between Empires, 1878–1902.* Pittsburgh: University of Pittsburgh Press, 1983.

Pérez, Louis A., Jr. *The War of 1898: The United States and Cuba in History and Historiography.* Chapel Hill: University of North Carolina Press, 1998.

David C. Carlson

Gómez Báez, Máximo (1836–1905)

A general in both of Cuba's independence wars, Máximo Gómez was born in the Dominican Republic on November 18, 1836. He joined the Dominican Army in 1856 and rose to the rank of captain in the cavalry. During Spain's annexation of the Dominican Republic (1863–1865), he served in the Dominican Reserves of the Spanish army. After the Spanish evacuation from the Dominican Republic and his discharge

from the army in 1865, Gómez came to Cuba. He rented lands on the sugar plantation Guanarrubianí in the Jiguaní region, while at the same time joining Casa Ramírez y Oro, owned by fellow Dominican Miguel Lavastida, as a lumber salesman. While working at the company, he met Eduardo Bertot, who encouraged him to join the Cuban independence movement.

Gómez joined the Liberation Army on October 16, 1868, under the command of José Joaquín Palma, who granted him the rank of sergeant. He would later serve under Donato Mármol, who promoted him to general. Gómez directed the first machete charge on November 4, 1868, at a place known as Tienda del Pino (also known as Ventas de Casanova). Upon the death of Donato Mármol on July 26, 1870, he took command of the Cuba Division (encompassing **Santiago de Cuba**, Guantánamo, **Baracoa**, and El Cobre) and created six battalions. In the period between June 1871 and May 1872, he invaded the wealthy coffee region of Guantánamo and liberated hundreds of slaves in the process. In June 1872 he was relieved of his command by President **Carlos Manuel de Céspedes** because of differences between the two. Despite their differences, Gómez opposed efforts to oust Céspedes as president, arguing it would undermine the war effort. After the death of **Ignacio Agramonte** he was named military commander of **Camagüey Province**. It was here that he fought some of the most significant battles of the war in 1873 and 1874.

Gómez expressed a strong belief that the only way to win the **Ten Years' War** (1868–1878) was to expand the struggle to the western part of the island, but that desire was thwarted by the regionalism of other revolutionary leaders. On six occasions, he crossed the border between Camagüey and Las Villas, bypassing Spanish fortifications. In 1877, a disastrous year for the rebels, he occupied the post of secretary of war for the Republic-in-Arms.

On March 6, 1878, after consultations with General **Antonio Maceo** where he argued that further military campaigns by the rebels would be futile, he left Cuba and went to Jamaica, where he was met by his wife Manana Toro and children. He lived there in great poverty until General Julio Sanguily and Coronel Manuel Codina helped him buy a ranch and a tobacco plantation. At the suggestion of José Joaquín Palma, former president of Honduras, Gómez was given a military commission in that country. During that time he again began to conspire against the Spanish government in Cuba and developed, along with Maceo, the plan of San Pedro de Sula, known as the *Plan Gómez Maceo*.

José Martí sought his collaboration in preparing the final **War of Independence**, and Gómez was appointed commanding general. On March 25, 1895, he signed, along with Martí, the Manifesto of Montecristi in the Dominican Republic. The manifesto set forth the goals of the independence struggle. The document reached Cuba on April 11 by way of Cajobabo Beach. After the death of Martí, Gómez continued the rebel march to Camagüey, where he initiated his "circular campaign." At the ranch of Lázaro López, he awaited the eastern rebel forces, led by Antonio Maceo, so that they could mount a major invasion, which he saw as critical to the success of the war effort. The invading column of men, selected by Maceo in Baraguá, began the march on October 22, 1895. On December 15, the rebels fought and won a pitched battle against the Spanish, the Battle of Mal Tiempo. The victory permitted rebel forces to enter **Matanzas Province**, where two more decisive battles were fought, the Battle of Coliseo and the Battle of Calimete. Those victories allowed Cuban rebel forces to advance into the Province of Havana, the advance forces reaching Bauta (Hoyo Colorado) on the outskirts of the capital. Gómez's forces remained in **La Habana Province** with the goal of bogging down Spanish troops, so that Maceo could enter the westernmost province of Pinar del Río. Maceo reached the town of Mantua in **Pinar del Río Province** on January 22, 1896. At that point, Gómez decided to deploy troops to the eastern part of the island in an effort to take pressure off the western front. In the middle of 1896, he won the Battle of Saratoga in Camagüey, after which Spanish forces in that province were confined to the cities. Despite his victories, Gómez became dissatisfied with actions by the Governing Council, such as the promotion of several commanders without consultation, the diversion of reinforcements intended for Maceo, and various acts of indiscipline. For a time, he considered resigning his post. Despite the deaths of Maceo and his son Panchito Gómez Toro, the Governing Council convinced him to remain as chief of the rebel army.

Shortly thereafter, he unveiled a new strategy, known as La Reforma Campaign, to weaken and demoralize Spanish forces. By day, his troops would snipe at Spanish columns, forcing them to chase rebel columns until they were exhausted. At night, the **mambises** would lead Spanish troops into areas heavily infested with mosquitoes and then retreat. The Spanish soldiers, unaccustomed to conditions in the tropics, were given little time to rest and recover.

After U.S. intervention in the War of Independence and Spain's surrender, a Constituent Assembly was organized to draft a new constitution for the country. A quarrel ensued between Gómez and some representatives over his advocacy of a loan to pay the veterans of the Independence War. The dispute led to his removal as commanding general. After his removal, Gómez remained a figure of enormous popularity, a beloved symbol for the Cuban people. He was offered the chance to run in the presidential race of 1901, but he declined. He retired and lived with his wife, who had accompanied him through-

General Máximo Gómez Báez, Dominican-born leader of Cuba's wars of independence. Photograph courtesy of the Biblioteca Nacional José Martí, Havana.

out the war, surrounded by his children, Clemencia, Máximo, Bernardo, Urbano, Andrés, and Margarita. He died at his home in Havana on Galeano Street in 1905. *See also* Abolition and Emancipation; Coffee Industry; Constitution of 1901; Sugar Plantations; U.S. Interventions

Further Readings

Beningno Souza, Benigno. *Máximo Gómez, el Generalísimo*. Havana: Editorial de Ciencias Sociales, 1972.

Ferrer, Ada. *Insurgent Cuba: Race, Nation, and Revolution, 1868–1898*. Chapel Hill: University of North Carolina Press, 1999.

Gómez, Máximo. *Obras escogidas de Máximo Gómez*. Havana: Editorial Letras Cubanas, 1979.

María del Carmen Barcia Zequeira

Grajales, Mariana (1808/1815–1893)

Mariana Grajales is considered the epitome of Cuban self-abnegation, heroism, and love of a country. The mother of **Antonio Maceo** and thirteen other children, eleven of Grajales's children fought in the wars of independence, nine of them dying during the struggle. It is said that when her husband was killed on the battlefield, Grajales told her children not to cry, that she disliked tears.

Grajales was born in **Santiago de Cuba**, the daughter of Dominican parents. As a child, she heard stories about oppression and the cruelty of **slavery** in St. Domingue and the Dominican Republic. At the age of twenty-three she married for the first time. In 1840, her husband passed away—though some accounts suggest that he deserted her and that they were divorced. Years later, Grajales, a hardworking and prosperous woman, attracted the attention of the Venezuelan Marcos Maceo. Upon their marriage, Grajales and Maceo moved to his farm in the countryside. Familiar with the wars of independence in South America, Maceo had great interest in politics and the cause of Cuban freedom. As their family grew, Grajales and Maceo instilled in their children abolitionist and patriotic values.

After the first battle of the **Ten Years' War** in October 1868, Maceo and Grajales offered their house to the Cuban soldiers. When the soldiers moved on to the jungle and the mountains, the couple joined them. Maceo and his sons Antonio and José proved fierce soldiers, gaining recognition in the battlefield. Meanwhile, Grajales and her daughters prepared meals for the soldiers and nursed the wounded. As the war progressed, Grajales encouraged her other children to join the Cuban forces. Once she told one of her youngest sons, "Hurry up and grow up quickly. Cuba needs you."

At the end of the war in 1878, Grajales, now a widow, moved to Jamaica. Upon meeting her, the poet **José Martí** wrote an eloquent essay celebrating Grajales's commitment to independence, the abolition of slavery, and equality. Grajales died in Jamaica in 1893.

Today, Cubans on the island and elsewhere honor her memory by naming civic organizations, schools, and hospitals after her. For many, Mariana Grajales is regarded as the mother of Cuba. *See also* Abolition and Emancipation; Mambises; War of Independence

Further Readings

Cupull, Adys. *Mariana, raíz del alma cubana*. Havana: Editorial Política, 1998.

Danger, Matilde, and Delfina Rodríguez, comps. *Mariana Grajales*. Santiago: Editorial Oriente, 1977.

Foner, Philip S. *Antonio Maceo: The "Bronze Titan" of Cuba's Struggle for Independence*. New York: Monthly Labor Review, 1977.

D.H. Figueredo

Guáimaro, Constitution of

Cuba's first constitution was promulgated in Guáimaro in 1869 early in the **Ten Years' War** (1868–1878) (see Appendix 7). The Constitution of Guáimaro was intended to be temporary until the end of the conflict. It was drafted by a constitutional assembly consisting of delegates from Oriente, Las Villas, and **Camagüey**, the provinces up in arms. It was adopted on April 10, 1869. The constitution recognized three separate branches of government, the executive, the legislative, and the judicial. Maximum authority was placed in civilian hands, and military decisions were to be approved by civilian leaders, an issue that led to numerous disputes during the war. Under the provisions of the constitution the House of Representatives (Cámara de Representantes) designated the president of the Republic-in-Arms and the commander in chief of the military forces, but the commander was to answer to the president. The legislative body held the greatest power and could overrule the president under certain circumstances. It also had the power to review charges against the president and the military lead-

Proclamation of the Constitution of Guáimaro in 1869. Courtesy of the Biblioteca Nacional José Martí, Havana.

ers and replace them, if necessary. The governing body was ultimately responsible for declaring and concluding the war as well as recruiting and maintaining the troops. Cabinet officials were named by the House of Representatives after their names were submitted by the president. The House was divided along federal lines with an equal number of representatives from the four provinces of the island. The Constitution of Guáimaro guaranteed a wide range of liberties including freedom of religion, press, assembly, teaching, and dissent. It declared all the citizens of Cuba soldiers of the Liberation Army and affirmed that all were free, foreshadowing the ultimate demise of slavery. *See also* Agramonte y Loynaz, Ignacio; Céspedes, Carlos Manuel de

Futher Readings

Guerra, Ramiro. *Guerra de los Diez Años, 1868–1878*. Havana: Editorial de Ciencias Sociales, 1972.

Llerena, María Cristina, ed. *Sobre la Guerra de los 10 Años*. Havana: Instituto Cubano del Libro, 1973.

José Antonio Piqueras Arenas

Guerra Chiquita, la

Guerra Chiquita (Little War) is the name given to the group of separatist military actions following shortly after the peace of

Zanjón, which had ended the **Ten Years' War**. Since the early part of 1879, some (such as **Antonio Maceo**) who had mounted protests in Baraguá, in exile and on the island, prepared a new armed movement. The organizers on the eastern part of the island included Flor Crombet, Pedro Martínez Freyre, and Mayía Rodríguez. In Havana, key figures included a young **José Martí**. The Spanish authorities learned of the revolutionary plot and began detaining suspects. Some leaders precipitated the military mobilization, without waiting for the commander **Calixto García** and Antonio Maceo, head of the army in the east. On August 24 there were uprisings in Gibara and **Holguín**, just two days after Guillermo Moncada, José Maceo, and **Quintín Banderas** clashed with the Civil Guard. In September there were confrontations in **Baracoa, Las Tunas**, and Baire, but the deportation of Martí frustrated the movement in Havana. Calixto García, with his small expedition, did not arrive until June 1880, at which point some insurgent bands had succumbed. Isolated and lacking support, García was captured shortly thereafter. Others were held until October.

Contributing to the failure of the movement was the Spanish government's propaganda as well as the press. These spread the idea that this was a race war whose objective was to establish a black republic in the east. This shook white landowners in the western part of the island. Further, the lack of coordination and scarcity of resources and arms put an end to the movement.

Further Readings

Ferrer, Ada. *Insurgent Cuba: Race, Nation, and Revolution, 1868–1898*. Chapel Hill: University of North Carolina Press, 1999.

Pérez Guzmán, Francisco, and Rodolfo Sarracino. *La Guerra Chiquita, una experiencia necesaria*. Havana: Editorial Letras Cubanas, 1982.

Inés Roldán de Montaud

Hatuey (?–1512)

Hatuey was a legendary Taíno cacique who led the resistance to the Spanish colonization of Cuba. An indigenous chief in Guahába (Hispaniola), Hatuey fled the island for Cuba with the arrival of Spanish colonists under **Diego Velázquez**. With Velázquez's eventual arrival in Cuba, Hatuey organized some of the island's indigenous groups to fight against Spanish colonization. According to **Bartolomé de las Casas**, once captured and sentenced to death, Hatuey was asked by a Spanish priest to convert to Christianity so that he might go to heaven. He refused, reportedly saying, "If Christians go to heaven I don't want to go to heaven, father, because Christians kill and enslave Indians." Over the years, Cubans came to view Hatuey's resistance to Spanish authority as a symbol of both Cuban independence and Spanish brutality. Hatuey has become a symbol of Cuban nationality; a brand of Cuban beer and malt uses his name and his likeness on its label. *See also* Conquest; Indigenous Inhabitants

Further Readings

Harrington, M.R. *Cuba before Columbus*. 2 vols. New York: Museum of the American Indian, 1921.

Rodríguez Expósito, César. *Hatuey: el primer libertador de Cuba*. Havana: Editorial Cubanacán, 1944.

John A. Gutiérrez

Humboldt, Alexander von (1769–1859)

German scientist and author Alexander von Humboldt is considered Cuba's second discoverer. In the company of the French scientist Aimé Bonpland, Humboldt visited Cuba in 1800–1801 as part of a scientific expedition that spanned vast territories in the Americas. Humboldt visited Cuba again in 1804, conducting geological and mineralogical studies commissioned by the **Sociedad Económica de Amigos del País**. During his Cuban expeditions Humboldt made numerous scientific observations and collected documentation and specimens that he later used to write his *Political Essay on the Island of Cuba*, part of his voluminous work on the equinoctial regions of the New World. The *Political Essay* covered a multitude of topics ranging from the island's **climate, flora**, and **fauna** to its **population, agriculture**, and **foreign trade**. He underscored the fact that Cuba remained relatively depopulated and its economic and commercial potential had not been reached. Humboldt's abolitionist views—he once called **slavery** "the greatest of all evils which have afflicted mankind"—clashed with the views of **Francisco de Arango y Parreño** and other Cuban aristocrats who had collaborated with Humboldt during his visits to the island. The *Political Essay* remains one of the most important books ever published on Cuba; it has been translated into many languages and reedited numerous times. *See also* Abolition and Emancipation; Science and Scientists (Eighteenth and Nineteenth Centuries)

Further Readings

Holl, Frank, ed. *Alejandro de Humboldt en Cuba*. Augsburg, Germany: Wissner, 1997.

Humboldt, Alexander von. *The Island of Cuba: A Political Essay by Alexander von Humboldt*. Princeton, NJ: Markus Wiener, 2001.

Puig-Samper, Miguel Ángel, Consuelo Naranjo Orovio, and Armando García González, eds. *Ensayo político sobre la isla de Cuba. Alejandro de Humboldt*. Aranjuez, Spain: Ediciones Doce Calles, 1998.

Luis Martínez-Fernández

Indigenous Inhabitants

The indigenous population of Cuba resulted from numerous migrations over thousands of years. By 1492, the population hovered at around 112,000, a number that was reduced by disease and other ravages of the **conquest** to 893 by 1544, according to Father Diego Sarmiento y Castilla. The first wave of migration occurred around 8000 B.C., but those early cultural groups were virtually extinct by the time of the **conquest**. They came from North America and consisted of hunters and gatherers that traveled the extensive territory made up by the Bahamas archipelago. The second wave of immigrants arrived around 2000 B.C. and originated from a broad area between Venezuela and Honduras. They settled in what today is called **Isla de la Juventud**, the Guanahacabibes Peninsula, and the Ciénaga de Zapata (Zapata Swamps). They reached the eastern part of Cuba, where they later coexisted with the Arawaks. The third wave occurred in three stages beginning around 500 B.C. In the first stage, Amerindians migrated from Florida and the Mississippi basin. The second and third stages consisted of Arawak communities from the island of Hispaniola. They settled in eastern Cuba. The last phase of this immigration occurred shortly before the arrival of **Columbus**, and they settled in the Maisí Peninsula, the island's easternmost point.

The first studies of the indigenous population were based on information provided by the early chroniclers, typically Spanish settlers and missionaries such as **Bartolomé de las Casas** and Ramón Pané. These early studies identified three groups: the Guanahatabeyes, the Siboneys, and the Taínos (also known as Arawaks). The Guanahatabeyes were the least technologically developed. They lived primarily in caves and fashioned their tools from conch shells and other rustic materials. The Siboneys lived along the coasts and were renowned for their fishing techniques and their use of carved stones as tools. The Taínos were accomplished farmers and skilled in making pottery. Later studies attempted to classify the Amerindian groups based on their level of technological development, utilizing categories such as Paleolithic, Mesolithic, and Neolithic. Some scholars concentrated on distinguishing between the economic activities of the various groups, such as collector-gatherers and producers. Still others classified them based on their specific activities, as hunters, fishermen, collectors, proto-agriculturalists, and agriculturalists.

When the conquistadors arrived, there were still Amerindian cultural groups descending from the second migration wave. This group carved stones, used conch shells, and dedicated itself to hunting, gathering, and fishing. They practiced ritual ceremonies to bury their dead, and some of these groups produced very elaborate pottery. Archaeological evidence of these cultural groups can be found throughout Cuba.

The most widespread Amerindian group at the time of the conquest was the Arawaks, which can be divided into two separate classifications: Taíno and Sub-taíno. They were agriculturalists and pottery makers. These different groups were culturally and linguistically homogeneous. In general, the Arawaks were short of stature with Asian features. For aesthetic purposes, they flattened the forehead of newborns by tying a piece of wood to the front of the head and securing it to the back of the skull.

Their homes were either circular or rectangular, the first termed *caneyes*, and the second, *bohíos*. They lived with their extended families. Inside their homes they strung *hamacas* (hammocks) made of cotton and other vegetable fibers. Alongside their homes, they built adjoining structures, known as *barbacoas*, where they stored food and supplies.

The Taínos plowed fields to plant yucca from which they drew their primary staple, cassava. They also planted beans, peppers, sweet potatoes, corn, cotton, tobacco, and fruit trees, including guava and calabash (*güira*). With the fruit, they were able to create receptacles and buoys used for their fishing reels. They used fish hooks made out of conch and fish spines as well as employing "glue fish" (*guaycán*). In order to maintain a steady supply of fish, they dammed rivers and lagoons and bred them. In addition, they captured seashells, crabs, iguanas, and turtles. The Taínos succeeded in domesticating various species of birds and a type of mute dog that was utilized to hunt tree rats (*jutías*).

The first written accounts of Amerindian life note a division of labor based on sex and age. In the area of **agriculture**, the men were responsible for clearing trees and bushes and planting, while the women were charged with harvesting crops. The women wove hammocks and *naguas*, skirts that covered only the front of the body, in addition to arm and leg bands. It was also the responsibility of the women to make cassava by shredding and scraping the yucca. The cassava was then placed in a closed sleeve, known as a *sibucán*, and squeezed to extract the poisonous acid it contains. It was then placed on clay dishes (*burenes*) and cooked. They were unfamiliar with the potter's wheel, so they made their pottery by measuring it with chords and baking it over an open flame.

By polishing and carving stones, conch shells, and the bones and teeth of animals, they were able to make a wide variety of implements including axes and crushers, as well as a wide range of decorative objects, some of which held religious and magical significance. With wood they manufactured *coas*, sticks in which the tip was hardened by fire and then used in agriculture. From wood they also crafted a type of club weapon (*macana*) and canoes, which they used to fish, transport goods, and fight wars. They manufactured ceremonial trays and chairs (*dujos*) that were decorated with zoomorphic figures and engraved with conch shells and gold (*guanín*).

Taíno communities or clans were linked by webs of alliance and were pre-

Indigenous behique (shaman) treating patient; hammock in the background. From Girolamo Benzoni, *La historia del Mondo Nuovo* (1565).

sided over by chiefs, known as *caciques*, whose authority was based on blood lines, experience, and prestige. Religious and magical ceremonies were presided over by *behiques*, also known as *hechiceros*, who also served as *curanderos* (healers). The *naborias* constituted the servant class. The soldiers and fighters were known as *baquías*.

Funeral and burial practices varied widely. Some cadavers were buried with ceremonial offerings, while others were left in grottoes or caverns. Their religious beliefs included the following concepts: Humanity was born from the earth; the soul transmigrates into another body after death; an afterlife exists. They worshiped idols, known as *cemies*. Their religious leaders practiced exorcism. They also practiced the ritual of *cohoba*, whereby they inhaled hallucinogenic powders, derived from potent tobacco, or tobacco smoke itself, before making important decisions. During their religious ceremonies Taínos decorated their bodies with vegetable dyes, particularly *annatto*. The game of *batos* had religious overtones. In the game two opposing teams attempted to move a ball from one end of a field to the other without using their hands and with-

out letting it fall. One of the more important ceremonies was the *areíto*, in which participants danced for hours, singing and chanting about their family lineages and accomplishments.

The arrival of the Spanish conquistadors swiftly brought an end to many of the customs and practices of the Amerindians. The land and its inhabitants were divided through *encomiendas* and *repartimientos* among the Spanish settlers. The practice of the encomiendas was legalized in 1503. The Amerindians were put to work washing gold and in subsistence agriculture. The population declined dramatically as a result of excessive work, poor nutrition, the dispersion of their communities, and the introduction of deadly diseases for which they had no natural defenses, including smallpox, measles, and a variety of bronchiopulmonary ailments. The overwhelming cultural, psychological, and social impact of the conquest led to many instances of individual and collective suicide.

Some Amerindian groups tried to actively resist the conquistadors, as was the case with **Hatuey**, the cacique Guamá, and the bands of Amerindians (*indios cayos*) who chose to build defenses on the small **keys** that dot the Cuban archipelago. Others chose to flee to the mountains where they built small villages (*palenques*). In 1542, as a result of new laws mandated by the crown, the encomiendas were abolished, and Amerindian labor was replaced by African slaves. *See also* Cimarrones (Runaway Slaves); Fauna; Flora; Labor Institutions, Early; Slave Trade; Slavery; Tobacco Industry

Further Readings

Dacal, Ramón, and Manuel Rivero de la Calle. *Arqueología aborigen de Cuba*. Havana: Editorial Gente Nueva, 1986.

Pané, Ramón. *An Account of the Antiquities of the Indians*. Durham, NC: Duke University Press, 1999.

Rouse, Irving. *The Taínos: Rise and Decline of the People Who Greeted Columbus*. New Haven, CT: Yale University Press, 1992.

Tabío, Ernesto, and Estrella Rey. *Prehistoria de Cuba*. Havana: Editorial de Ciencias Sociales, 1979.

María del Carmen Barcia Zequeira

Junta de Información de Ultramar

In November 1865, the Spanish government, influenced by General Francisco Serrano, convocated a Junta de Información de Ultramar (Overseas Information Board) in Madrid with the purpose of studying the issue of reforming the colonial system, given the growing **reformist movement** in Cuba and Puerto Rico. The board consisted of delegates designated by the largest contributors and by the government. Albeit mistrustful of the government, the reformists opted to accept this initiative and elected fourteen delegates, among them the Count of Pozos Dulces, Nicolás de Azcárate, **José Antonio Saco**, and **José Morales Lemus**, head of the Cuban delegation.

The meetings began in November 1866, posing difficulties that nearly broke off the conference. On the matter of **slavery**, the more progressive Puerto Rican delegates wanted immediate abolition. The Cuban reformists preferred gradual abolition with indemnification, the end of the **slave trade**, and the promotion of white immigration. The Spanish representatives, meanwhile, opposed abolition and favored Asian immigration. With regard to political reform, the reformists wanted for the Antilles the separation of civilian and military authority, all the rights outlined by the Constitution for Spaniards, and the establishment of an autonomous regime with representation in the Spanish Cortes, which delegate Saco was opposed to. The insular delegates insisted on the end of customs tariffs and the introduction of a direct taxation system based upon economic activities. However, the government

of Isabel II paid no attention to the recommendations of the Junta de Información. The failure of the Junta meeting to bring about change, together with the growing financial crisis, gave way to the uprising at Yara that began the **Ten Years' War**. *See also* Abolition and Emancipation; Asian Contract Laborers; Autonomism; Colonization and Population (Nineteenth Century); Spanish Colonialism (Nineteenth Century)

Further Readings

Corwin, Arthur F. *Spain and the Abolition of Slavery in Cuba, 1817–1886*. Austin: University of Texas Press, 1967.
Martínez-Fernández, Luis. *Torn between Empires: Economy, Society, and Patterns of Political Thought in the Hispanic Caribbean, 1840–1878*. Athens: University of Georgia Press, 1994.
"Un emigrado cubano." *Información sobre reformas en Cuba y Puerto Rico*. 2nd ed. New York: Hallet and Green, 1877.

Inés Roldán de Montaud

Labor Institutions, Early

Although the Europeans' early primary goal in Cuba was to find gold, more frequently their source of wealth derived from the privilege of exploiting indigenous labor. The precedent that the conquered people owed tribute to the conquerors was established on Hispaniola during the administration of the **Columbus** family (1494), and it was they who took the decision to distribute (*repartir*) the conquered people among the victorious Spaniards. Uneasy with the assumption of such privilege and even more concerned over increasing mortality among the Caribbean natives, Queen Isabella mandated that the receipt of indigenous labor would come with the responsibility to care for (*encomendar*) and Christianize the natives, a practice that evolved into the *encomienda*. Specifically, the receipt of an encomienda granted the recipient (*enco-mendero*) the privilege of using native labor for his/her economic pursuits.

The practice established in Hispaniola was transferred to Cuba, and the earliest labor demands were in **mining**, especially near **Sancti Spíritus** and **Trinidad** where placer gold was discovered in the nearby rivers in 1514. The holders of encomiendas in other areas, especially Puerto Príncipe (**Camagüey**), rented their encomienda natives to the mining enterprises. Labor proved to be a problem since Cuba was more sparsely populated than Hispaniola, and disease, overwork, and exploitation caused the native populations to decline rapidly. Although Indian slavery was forbidden in 1512, in 1514 the governor of Cuba, **Diego Velázquez**, authorized slave raids on nearby areas under the rationalization that the inhabitants had rejected Christianity or had rebelled against his authority and could be enslaved under a "just war."

One of the foremost champions of humane treatment of the indigenous people was **Bartolomé de las Casas**, who advocated the substitution of African labor for the rapidly dwindling Caribbean natives. Although African slaves had been introduced into Hispaniola as early as 1502 and were brought to Cuba in 1515, royal permission that allowed Africans to be brought to the Americas as a substitute for indigenous labor was granted in 1517. With the discovery of advanced and complex civilizations on the mainland, Cuba diminished in economic importance. Various schemes to increase the European population, such as mandating the immigration of entire families rather than single men, an initiative to encourage artisan immigration, and the prohibition on leaving the island, all failed to promote population increase and to address the chronic labor problem. *See also* Colonial Settlements, Early; Conquest; Indigenous Inhabitants; Slave Trade; Slavery

Further Readings

Sauer, Carl O. *The Early Spanish Main*. Berkeley: University of California Press, 1966.
Wright, Irene A. *The Early History of Cuba, 1492–1586*. New York: Macmillan, 1916.

Sherry Johnson

Las Casas, Bartolomé de (1474–1566)

Bartolomé de las Casas was an *encomendero*, priest, missionary, historian, and theologian who played a leading role in the defense of the native inhabitants of Cuba and other Spanish colonies. He was born in 1474 in Seville and died on July 17, 1566, in Madrid. He arrived in Cuba in 1512, accepting an invitation from the new governor, **Diego Velázquez**, and was given an *encomienda*, a royal grant of Indian labor. Though he was a compassionate encomendero, he utilized Indian labor in a fashion he later condemned. This was neither the first time he had participated in the Spanish **conquest** of the Americas nor the first time he had Indians working for him. Following the example of his father who earlier accompanied **Christopher Columbus**, las Casas himself joined the colonizing efforts of Gonzalo Fernández de Oviedo in 1502. On the island of Hispaniola he helped suppress an Indian rebellion and was rewarded with an encomienda.

In 1510, las Casas became the first priest ordained in the New World, and with these credentials he set out to participate in the conquest of Cuba (see **Catholicism**). His life, however, changed forever as a result of his experiences as an encomendero on the island. After meditating over the Indians' condition, he joined voices with other Dominican priests like Antonio de Montesinos in protesting the cruelty against the indigenous population. It happened while studying Ecclesiastes 34 that las Casas found himself convicted for the Indians' mistreatment. Convinced that this injustice must cease, he renounced his encomienda in Cuba and began preaching passionately against Indian oppression. Las Casas then left Cuba for Spain to argue for the natives and was named "Protector of the Indians." His writings and forceful advocacy for this exploited population helped create the "New Laws" and forced a dialogue over the legitimacy of the Spanish Empire. *See also* Appendix 3; Colonial Settlements, Early; Indigenous Inhabitants; Labor Institutions, Early; Slave Trade; Slavery

Further Readings

Las Casas, Bartolomé de. *The Devastation of the Indies: A Brief Account.* Baltimore: Johns Hopkins University Press, 1994.

Keen, Benjamin, and Juan Friede, eds. *Bartolomé de las Casas in History.* De Kalb: Northern Illinois University Press, 1971.

Traoulay, David M. *Columbus and las Casas: The Conquest and Christianization of America, 1492–1566.* Lanham, MD: University Press of America, 1994.

Dennis R. Hidalgo

López de Uriolaz, Narciso (1797–1851)

Narciso López was a former general in the Spanish army who planned several expeditions to Cuba in the mid-nineteenth century with the goal of liberating the island from the Spanish crown and annexing it to the United States.

Born in Venezuela, López fought with the royal army against liberator Simón Bolívar, opposed conservative Spanish Carlist forces, was promoted to general, and participated in revolutionary plots in Spain. He traveled to Cuba where he married the sister of the count of Pozos Dulces, an annexationist conspirator. Befriending slaveholders, López felt that the island could only achieve freedom from Spain and maintain **slavery** by being annexed to the United States.

In 1848, he plotted a rebellion against the Spanish government, was discovered,

and had to flee Cuba. The following year, he organized in New Orleans a military expedition to the island that did not materialize. In the meantime, he sought help from John Quitman, the governor of Mississippi, and Southern planters to fund another filibustering enterprise. In May 1850, he landed in **Cárdenas** with 600 soldiers but did not find local support and had to return to the United States. In 1851, he returned to the island with 400 soldiers, many of whom were veterans of the Mexican War of 1848. Defeated by the Spanish, he was captured, sentenced as a traitor, and garroted to death.

López was a precursor of the Cuban struggle for independence, though he was criticized by many as an annexationist. The flag that he hoisted during his 1850 expedition became the official Cuban banner in 1869. *See also* Annexationism; National Flag; Political Exile (Nineteenth Century); U.S. Expansionism (Nineteenth Century)

Further Readings

Chaffin, Tom. *Fatal Glory: Narciso López and the First Clandestine U.S. War against Cuba.* Charlottesville: University Press of Virginia, 1996.

Portell-Vilá, Herminio. *Narciso López y su época.* Havana: Cultural, 1930.

José Antonio Piqueras Arenas

Maceo Grajales, Antonio (1845–1896)

Antonio Maceo was one of the principal figures in the struggle for Cuban independence. A man of color who joined the Cuban rebel army as a private in 1868 during the **Ten Years' War** (1868–1878), he ascended through the ranks to hold the second-highest position in the Cuban Liberation Army during the **War of Independence** (1895–1898). Well-known and respected for his bravery and military talents, he also took important political positions, advocating not only Cuban independence from Spain but also the abolition of **slavery** and the advancement of racial equality.

Maceo was born in **Santiago de Cuba** on June 14, 1845. His father, Marcos Maceo, served in the Spanish army in Venezuela and migrated to Cuba in 1825, marrying **Mariana Grajales**, of Dominican ancestry, in 1843. The family owned a house in the city of Santiago and several farms on its outskirts. The most important, La Delicia located in Majaguabo, San Luis, consisted of 9 *caballerías* (120 hectares) and produced coffee, tobacco, plantains, minor fruits, and livestock. As a boy, Antonio attended a school for free children of color in Santiago. At home, his father was said to read the children stories and biographies of Simón Bolívar, Toussaint Louverture, and other heroes. In the period before the outbreak of the Ten Years' War, Maceo was working as a mule driver, traveling often between the family farm and the city of Santiago, where he was also involved in Masonic lodges.

The Ten Years' War began on October 10, 1868, when **Carlos Manuel de Céspedes** issued a declaration calling for Cuban independence, freed his slaves, and recruited them to the war against Spanish rule. Other slave owners from the region joined the Cuban forces. Maceo joined the armed movement later that month. He quickly started gaining promotions: to sergeant almost immediately after enlisting, to commander, and then to lieutenant colonel early in 1869. In 1871, he was one of the officers under General **Máximo Gómez** leading the "invasion" of the Guantánamo area, where slaveholders tended to support Spain and reject the Cuban insurgency. The Cuban rebels set about destroying farms and estates and liberating and recruiting slaves, and staged important defeats of Spanish troops. Gómez advocated a similar and larger-scale insurgent invasion of western Cuba, which had remained

relatively free of insurgent activity and where most of the island's **sugar plantations** were concentrated. He further proposed that Maceo be designated leader of that invasion. The plan exacerbated divisions among nationalist forces, stemming from the unwillingness to alienate western planters and the refusal to order a multiracial army into territory where slavery was still powerful and entrenched. Opponents further rejected the leadership of Maceo and spoke of the dangers of "Africanization" (black domination). In response to such allegations, Maceo wrote his famous letter to **Tomás Estrada Palma**, then president of the rebel republic, in which he proclaimed himself to be a man of color and a patriot and in which he condemned the racist maneuvers and rumors of fellow nationalists.

On February 11, 1878, rebel forces in **Camagüey** accepted the Treaty of Zanjón, ending the war. The pact granted freedom to slaves who fought on either side of the conflict, but it did not abolish slavery. Nor did the pact end Spanish rule in Cuba. Maceo condemned the treaty, arguing that peace could not be achieved until slavery was abolished and independence won. In March, he met Spanish general Arsenio Martínez Campos and rejected the treaty in person. Days later, he met with other insurgent officers and troops to continue the war, a meeting generally known as the Protest of Baraguá. Gradually, the remaining rebel leaders laid down their arms, and Maceo left for Jamaica in May.

The Cuban Revolutionary Committee in New York, led by Cuban general **Calixto García**, organized a new independence rebellion in 1879. This second insurrection, known as **la Guerra Chiquita**, broke out in eastern Cuba in August 1879. Maceo's brother José became one of its principal military leaders on the island. Antonio himself expected to be dispatched to Cuba to lead the army, but García refused to send him, arguing that rumors of race war and racial fears made it unwise to dispatch a man of color. Throughout the insurgency, Spanish authorities labeled the movement a race war and stressed the black character of the rebellion. The war ended, again without independence or abolition, in August 1880.

In the period between the end of the Guerra Chiquita and the start of the final War of Independence, Maceo spent most of his time in exile, in and out of revolutionary activity and subject to multiple attempts on his life. He traveled through the Caribbean and Central America, spending brief periods also in the United States and Cuba. In the early 1880s, he settled in Honduras, working first as a judge and then as a commander of ports. In 1886–1888, he lived in Panama, where he negotiated a contract for the building of wooden houses in the Panama Canal Zone. In 1892–1893, he spent time in Costa Rica, where he contracted with the Costa Rican government to establish a farm colony on the Pacific coast. Throughout the entire period, he was in communication with other nationalist figures, among them Máximo Gómez, Flor Crombet, Enrique Trujillo, and **José Martí**, who founded the **Partido Revolucionario Cubano** (Cuban Revolutionary Party) in New York in 1892.

On February 25, 1895, the War of Independence began. Initial efforts at rebellion in the west were largely put down by Spanish forces, but insurrection took root in the east. Maceo arrived on the island in late March and enjoyed immediate military successes. Under Gómez's instructions, he began preparing for an insurgent invasion of western Cuba. Though some within the nationalist ranks had the same doubts about a Maceo-led invasion that had surfaced in the mid-1870s, this time the invasion went forward, led by Gómez and Maceo and assisted by black general **Quintín Banderas**, who commanded a

General Antonio Maceo, hero of Cuba's wars of independence. Photograph courtesy of the Biblioteca Nacional José Martí, Havana.

third column to help divert attention from the other two groups. They set out in November 1895 and by January had reached the outskirts of Havana. Along the way, Maceo's forces recruited many workers and former slaves from the western sugar regions. Maceo spent the last months of his life fighting in **Pinar del Río**, the island's westernmost province. In January 1896, attempting to march eastward, he was ambushed in Havana province and killed, together with Panchito Gómez Toro, son of Máximo Gómez. The death of Maceo, who had become a figure of national proportions, sent shock waves throughout the rebel movement. The troops became dispirited, and the level of recruitment and activity fell dramatically.

Though clearly one of the most significant military and political figures of Cuban nationalism, Maceo was also an important symbolic figure. A man of color and of humble origins, he is often represented as the personification of national integration as well as of the popular and antiracist promise of Cuban nationalism. Outside of Cuba, he is a well-known figure among people of African descent, especially in the United States, where some African Americans have named sons Maceo in his honor. *See also* Abolition and Emancipation; Afro-Cubans; Freemasonry; Mambises; Political Exile (Nineteenth Century)

Further Readings

Aparicio, Raúl. *Hombradía de Antonio Maceo*. Havana: Editorial de Ciencias Sociales, 1996.

Ferrer, Ada. *Insurgent Cuba: Race, Nation, and Revolution, 1868–1898*. Chapel Hill: University of North Carolina Press, 1999.

Foner, Philip S. *Antonio Maceo: The "Bronze Titan" of Cuba's Struggle for Independence*. New York: Monthly Review Press, 1977.

Franco, José Luciano. *Antonio Maceo: apuntes para una historia de su vida*. 3 vols. Havana: Editorial de Ciencias Sociales, 1989.

Weiss Fagen, Patricia. "Antonio Maceo: Heroes, History, and Historiography." *Latin American Research Review* 11 (1976): 69–93.

Ada Ferrer

Madan y Madan, Cristóbal F. (1807–1859)

Cristóbal F. Madan y Madan, **Matanzas**'s biggest sugar planter and active participant in the **slave trade**, was an annexationist leader during the 1840s and 1850s. Related to the **Aldama** family and the Alfonso y Poey family, who were major supporters of **slavery**, Madan advocated annexation to the United States to curb British pressures to end the slave trade and Spain's own ambivalence on the matter. He founded the annexationist Club de La Habana, which had branches in New Orleans and New York, and had the support of major merchants and proponents of **U.S. expansionism**, such as tycoon John L. O'Sullivan, the creator of the concept of Manifest Destiny. O'Sullivan, who was also Madan's brother-in-law, actively promoted the purchase of Cuba by the United States. But after the failure of **Narciso Ló**pez's expedition of 1851 and given the strength of the Spanish army, Madan distanced himself from **annexationism**.

In 1855, he wrote *Llamamiento de la Isla de Cuba a la nación Española* (A Call to Spain from the Cuban Nation). This pamphlet highlighted labor problems on the island and demanded that the Spanish government assist Cuba with a workforce in the countryside. *See also* Colonization and Population (Nineteenth Century); Sugar Plantations

Further Reading

Martínez-Fernández, Luis. *Torn between Empires: Economy, Society, and Patterns of Political Thought in the Hispanic Caribbean, 1840–1878*. Athens: University of Georgia Press, 1994.

José Antonio Piqueras Arenas

Maine, USS

The USS *Maine*, a battleship of the U.S. Navy, was sent to Havana's harbor in January 1898 with the stated purpose of protecting the lives and property of U.S. citizens in Cuba during the Cuban **War of Independence** that had begun in 1895. On February 15, 1898, the *Maine* exploded, killing 265 of the 354 sailors and officers onboard.

Although later investigations found the evidence inconclusive, many observers in the United States resolved almost immediately that Spain was responsible for the destruction and loss of life, a sentiment spread by the sensationalist newspapers of the time. When the United States declared war on Spain in April 1898, "Remember the *Maine*" became a rallying cry of the U.S. troops fighting to evict Spain from Cuba. Many contemporary accounts describe the explosion of the *Maine* as the decisive cause of the U.S. entry into the conflict, but scholars disagree on its actual significance. *See also* U.S. Expansionism (Nineteenth Century)

Remains of the USS *Maine* in the Bay of Havana (1898). Photograph by Fernando López Ortiz.

Further Readings

Pérez, Louis A., Jr. "Meaning of the *Maine*." In *The War of 1898: The United States and Cuba in History and Historiography*. Chapel Hill: University of North Carolina Press, 1998. 57–80.
Placer Cervera, Gustavo. *La explosión del* Maine: *el pretexto*. Havana: Editorial Política, 1998.

Mariola Espinosa

Mambises

Mambises is the term frequently used to describe the combatants in the Cuban Liberation Army during the nineteenth-century wars for independence. *Mambí* is used as a noun and an adjective, *mambises* being the plural form of the word. Originally a pejorative and racist label for the rebels used by the Spanish, the Cuban insurgents adopted the expression to proudly refer to themselves. While stories of the word's presumed African origins abound, the elderly former slave Esteban Montejo told Miguel Barnet in *Autobiography of a Runaway Slave* (Pantheon, 1968) that the word denoted the offspring of a vulture and a monkey. The origins of the name *mambí* are also thought to lie in the Dominican Republic. A black Dominican officer, Juan Ethninius Mamby, led irregular troops against the Spanish in 1864. The Spanish later applied the word *mambises* to the Cuban insurrectionists in the **Ten Year's War** (1868–1878) and the **War of Independence** (1895–1898). During the unequal contest between the well-supplied Spanish army and the mambises of the Cuban Liberation Army—perennially short of firearms, ammunition, and equipment—the insurgents primarily fought the Spanish using guerrilla hit-and-run tactics. Today, the Cuban independence fighters are still popularly referred to as mambises. A popular Miami anti-Castro radio station is called Radio Mambí. *See also* Cimarrones (Runaway Slaves)

Further Readings

Ferrer, Ada. *Insurgent Cuba: Race, Nation, and Revolution, 1868–1898*. Chapel Hill: University of North Carolina Press, 1999.
Foner, Philip S. *The Spanish-Cuban-American War and the Birth of U.S. Imperialism*. New York: Monthly Review Press, 1972.

Pérez, Louis A., Jr, *Cuba between Empires, 1878–1902*. Pittsburgh: University of Pittsburgh Press, 1983.

David C. Carlson

Martí, José (as Political Leader) (1853–1895)

Politician, thinker, and writer, José Martí was the principal leader of the nationalist and revolutionary movement in Cuba and among Cuban exiles that led to the **War of Independence**. Falling dead during the conflict in 1895, Martí became the most salient symbol of patriotism in Cuba after independence.

Mariano Martí, José's father, was a Spaniard who arrived in Cuba as an artillery sergeant. Leaving the army, he worked as a night guard and at other jobs that paid poorly. Although he went back to Spain for two years, he returned to Cuba with his family in 1858, never to leave the island again. Upon his father's return, young Martí attended school, even though the family had limited financial resources. Poet and educator **Rafael María Mendive** mentored Martí, supporting his education. Through his mentor, Martí developed a love for literature as well as patriotic inclinations and a strong Cuban identity.

The uprising of 1868 inspired Martí's pro-independence sentiments, and he wrote patriotic poems and pamphlets. Accused in 1869 of penning a letter in support of the war against Spain, he was arrested and sentenced in 1870 to six years of imprisonment. He served six months of forced labor, working at a quarry, and was then sent to Isla de Pinos (today **Isla de la Juventud**) and eventually deported to Spain in 1871.

In Madrid, Martí studied law, graduating from the University of Zaragoza, where he also studied literature and philosophy. During his stay in Spain, he frequented discussion groups sponsored by Cuban exiles, was influenced by the democratic ideas of Calixto Bernal, and espoused the philosophy of Karl Christian Krause, which became the foundation of his own philosophy of harmonious ideals. He also joined the Freemasons and published the monograph, *El presidio político en Cuba* (Political Imprisonment in Cuba).

In 1875, Martí traveled to Mexico where he worked as a journalist and began to achieve recognition as a poet. In 1877, he visited Cuba incognito before moving on to Guatemala, where he worked as a professor. He married Carmen Zayas Bazán, the daughter of a wealthy Cuban exile, but soon the couple separated. After the Treaty of Zanjón, which ended the **Ten Years' War** in 1878, he returned to Cuba, working in the law firm of Nicolás de Azcárate, whom Martí had met while in exile. A year later, he was again banished from Cuba by the Spanish authorities for participating in antigovernment activities. He relocated to New York in 1880, where he lived for fifteen years.

In the United States, Martí collaborated with the Cuban Revolutionary Committee and was displeased with the political tensions and disagreements among the Cubans in exile. He earned his living as a journalist, writing for several newspapers about Latin American customs and traditions. He also wrote poems, essays, and children's stories for numerous newspapers in Latin America. Appointed as consul to the United States by the nations of Uruguay, Argentina, and Paraguay, he was inspired to write his observations on the culture and politics of Latin America, attempting to develop a consciousness for Latin America that was distinct from North American and European influences. Eventually, these writings were gathered together under the volume *Nuestra América* and were published in 1891.

In 1884, Martí met Cuban revolutionary leaders **Máximo Gómez** and **Antonio Maceo** in New York City and detected authoritarian tendencies in Gómez and dis-

José Martí (1894). Leader of the War of Independence and major literary figure. Photograph by Fernando López Ortiz.

agreements between the two leaders. From 1887, he became identified with the struggles of the Latin American exiles in the United States, founding La Liga, a cultural and educational society for Latin Americans. His fame as an orator resulted in an invitation to the Cuban exile enclave of Tampa in 1891. During this period, the common people and workers of New York and Tampa embraced him as a teacher and an apostle of the Cuban cause. In that spirit, his fame grew, eventually molding him into Cuba's supreme symbol of love and patriotism.

In 1892, Martí founded the **Partido Revolucionario Cubano**, which he represented as a delegate, and edited the journal *Patria*, which served as a vehicle to broadcast his political views. The next few years, Martí labored to attract to the Cuban cause the support of Latin America émigrés. He also agreed that Gómez should serve as the chief of the Cuban army, while he would be the civilian leader in charge of preparing the insurrection.

In 1895, he authorized the uprising against Spain. He reunited with Gómez in the Dominican Republic, and on March 25, he signed the Manifesto de Montecristi, where he proclaimed the need for an armed rebellion against Spain and promoted the creation of a democratic Cuban republic where the rights of all men would be respected and protected. On April 11, he arrived in Cuba, and days later he was appointed to the rank of major general in spite of his lack of military experience. Despite this recognition, Martí could not come to terms with the military and political views of Gómez and Maceo, and he was asked to return to New York but refused to do so in order to have the opportunity to participate in combat. On May 19, during a skirmish, Martí was killed near Dos Ríos, Oriente Province.

His extensive bibliography, his political speeches and articles published in patriotic journals, and his diary reveal a humanitarian philosophy influenced by Ralph Waldo Emerson and Henry George as well as Karl Christian Krause. His views, often expressed in a poetic language, were nationalistic and democratic, advocating political and social reforms where he promoted the rights of all to live in freedom and equality. *See also* Appendix 8; Freemasonry; Martí, José (as Writer); Political Exile (Nineteenth Century); Press and Journalism (Eighteenth and Nineteenth Centuries)

Further Readings

Agramonte Pichardo, Roberto D. *Martí y su concepción de la sociedad*. Río Piedras: Editorial de la Universidad de Puerto Rico, 1984.

Estrade, Paul. *José Martí. Los fundamentos de la democracia en Latinoamérica*. Aranjuez, Spain: Ediciónes Doce Calles, 2000.

Ette, Ottmar. *José Martí. Apóstol, poeta revolucionario: Una historia de su recepción*. México City: UNAM, 1995.

Kirk, John M. *José Martí, Mentor of the Cuban Nation*. Tampa: University Press of Florida, 1983.

Mañach, Jorge. *El Apóstol*. Madrid: Espasa Calpe, 1975.

Martí, José. *Obras completas*. 28 vols. Havana: Editorial Nacional, 1963–1980.

Pérez, Louis A., Jr., ed. *Jose Martí in the United States: The Florida Experience*. Tempe: Arizona State University Press, 1995.

José Antonio Piqueras Arenas

Masó y Márquez, Bartolomé (1830–1907)

Bartolomé Masó was a prominent patriot who took part in the three Cuban wars of independence. Born in **Bayamo**, his mother was a local woman and his father was from Catalonia, Spain. He attended school at the Santo Domingo Convent in his hometown and later worked as a businessman in Manzanillo. A lover of literature, he published verses in several magazines. Masó began his political life in 1851 when he edited a proclamation against the execution of **Narciso López**. Under the pseudonym Báguano, he helped establish the Masonic lodge Buena Fe del Gran Oriente de Cuba y las Antillas. He joined **Carlos Manuel de Céspedes** in the Revolutionary Junta of Manzanillo and with him rose up in arms against the Spanish at La Demajagua sugar mill on October 10, 1868, which triggered the **Ten Years' War**. He was recognized as second in command but willingly handed over the post to Luis Marcano, a man with military training. He served as chief of the rebel army and finance minister until 1869. In 1872 he served as secretary of war for the rebel government and later secretary of the House of Representatives. In 1877 he was named chief of the Yara Regiment. He later fought against the Spanish in the **Guerra Chiquita** and was deported to Spain as a prisoner. On February 24, 1895, Masó led an uprising against the Spanish in Bayate. He was elected vice president of the Republic-in-Arms at the Assembly of Jimaguayú and later selected as president at the Assembly of La Yaya. He resigned as president on November 7, 1898, at the Assembly of Santa Cruz del Sur. After the successful independence struggle, he returned to his ranch, La Jagüita, in Manzanillo. He ran against **Tomás Estrada Palma** in the presidential election of 1901 but pulled out charging irregularities and retired from public life. *See also* Freemasonry; Political Exile (Nineteenth Century)

Further Reading

Pérez Landa, Rufino. *Bartolomé Masó y Márquez. Estudio biográfico documentado*. Havana: Imprenta el Siglo XX, 1947.

María del Carmen Barcia Zequeira

Montoro, Rafael (1852–1933)

Rafael Montoro was one of the leading figures of Cuban **autonomism** during the last decade of the nineteenth century. Born in Havana, Montoro studied at El Salvador, an exclusive school for the elite. A sickly child, he traveled extensively throughout the United States, Great Britain, and France. While in New York, he perfected his knowledge of the English language. Upon returning to Cuba, he enrolled at the school of San Francisco de Asís, where he befriended future leaders and members of the Autonomist Party. Due to continuing health problems, he left Cuba again and settled in Madrid in 1867. While the **Ten Years' War** was taking place in Cuba, he unsuccessfully attempted to foster support for the Cuban cause.

Upon his father's death, Montoro returned to Cuba in 1878 to take charge of the family fortune. He joined the Partido Liberal Autonomista, becoming its principal ideologue, member of its executive board, and its representative before the Spanish Cortes from 1886 to 1896. He opposed the **War of Independence**, favoring autonomy within colonial rule. For this, the Spanish government awarded him a nobility title.

With the end of Spanish rule over Cuba, Montoro was pushed out of public office. Eventually, though, he was able to serve the new Cuban government as ambassador to London and Berlin, was a founding member of the Academia Nacional de Artes y Letras, and was appointed secretary to Cuban president **Mario García Menocal** in 1912.

Further Readings

García Mora, Luis Miguel. "Un cubano en la corte de la Restauración: la labor intelectual de Rafael Montoro, 1875–1878." *Revista de Indias*, nos. 195–196 (1992): 443–477.

Martínez Bello, Antonio. *Montoro: Temperamento y clase social.* Havana: Imprenta El Siglo XX, 1952.

Menocal y Cueto, Raimundo. *Rafael Montoro, una interpretación histórica.* Havana: Aquiles, 1952.

Montoro, Rafael. *Rafael Montoro: discursos y escritos.* Ed. Rafael Tarragó. Miami: Editorial Cubana, 2000.

Luis Miguel García Mora

Morales Lemus, José (1808–1870)

A well-known Cuban political figure, reformist José Morales Lemus was born in Gibara. His parents were from the Canary Islands and were of scarce financial resources. Morales Lemus studied at the San Francisco seminary in Havana and later obtained his law degree in 1835. In the mid-1800s he enjoyed much prestige practicing as an attorney in Havana. An unexpected inheritance allowed him to acquire or gain participation in a number of mercantile and financial corporations, especially those involved with the **railroads**. Morales Lemus participated in several political movements of his time. An annexationist since the 1850s, Morales Lemus supported the expeditions of **Narciso López** and the annexationist conspiracies of 1854–1855. Along with other Cubans of high social standing, Morales Lemus later propelled the **reformist movement**. He

was president of the reformist newspaper *El Siglo*. He played a pivotal role as head of the reformist delegation in the **Junta de Información de Ultramar** sanctioned in Madrid by the Spanish government in 1866. Following el Grito de Yara, after initial vacillations, he actively promoted the revolutionary movement in the western part of the island. Toward the end of January 1869, he left Havana, and his property was seized. In the United States he formed part of the Revolutionary Delegation. Designated as minister of the Republic of Cuba in April 1869, he met with U.S. President Ulysses S. Grant and Secretary of State Hamilton Fish, pressing for the recognition of Cuba's status as a belligerent force. Until his death in New York in 1870, he worked tirelessly for the cause of independence. *See also* Annexationism; Political Exile (Nineteenth Century); Press and Journalism (Eighteenth and Nineteenth Centuries); Ten Years' War

Further Reading

Piñeyro, Enrique. *Morales Lemus y la Revolución de Cuba.* New York, 1871.

Inés Roldán de Montaud

Organized Labor (Nineteenth Century)

Organized labor in Cuba emerged and expanded during the second half of the nineteenth century, particularly in Havana and other western cities, where tobacco manufacturing had gained preeminence. At that juncture, colonial government authorities momentarily eased restrictions on labor organizing as a reward for the working class' loyalty to Spain during the annexationist conspiracies of 1847–1855 (see **annexationism**). The first artisans' organization, Sociedad Artística y Literaria Nuestra Señora del Pilar, was founded in 1848 in the Havana suburb of El Horcón. It limited membership, however, to "white, educated persons." Blacks and mulattos, meanwhile, continued to associate within the **cabildos de nación**. As a result of the financial crisis of 1857, colonial administrators acquiesced to the formation of racially segregated mutual benefit associations whose membership was limited to small geographic jurisdictions.

As in many other countries at the time, the workers' dominant ideology was labor reformism, with the goal of improving working conditions without resorting to radical tactics. The first significant strikes took place in 1865 among cigar makers of Havana; soon thereafter the Cuban **reformist movement** created a newspaper directed toward artisans, *La Aurora* (1865–1867), whose writers included Asturian cigar maker Saturnino Martínez, Havana machinist José de Jesús Márquez, and Cuban typographer Juan María Reyes. Because of lingering restrictions on labor organizing, labor reformism focused on popular education through means such as the spoken reading of newspapers and books in cigar shop floors.

The return of harsh colonial repression in mid-1866 supported by Cuba's pro-Spanish elite truncated the first phase of labor organization on the island and fueled the mounting dissatisfactions that led to the **Ten Years' War**. Many workers sympathized with the separatist movement and joined or supported their ranks; by contrast, Spanish-born workers gravitated to the loyalist **Voluntarios**. The increasingly violent actions of the Voluntarios forced many Cuban workers to seek exile in Key West, New Orleans, Philadelphia, New York, and other destinations, where they established separatist labor, educational, and recreational institutions (see **Political Exile** [Nineteenth century]).

Meanwhile, in Cuba, a labor movement led almost exclusively by Spaniards began to reemerge, especially during the period of the First Spanish Republic (1873). The arrival of the conciliatory General Arsenio Martínez Campos to Cuba in November 1876 and the end of the Ten Years' War in 1878 allowed for a new wave of labor organizations. Black and mulatto Cuban workers established their own mutual benefit organizations as did Asian laborers (see **Asian Contract Laborers**). Organizations attempting to break origin (Spanish or Creole) and probably race barriers also emerged, such as the Sociedad Recreo de Obreros (Havana, 1876–1879). Despite legal limitations, this organization produced a reformist labor weekly *La Razón* (1876–1884). Following the path opened by the "Recreo," various labor organizations in western Cuba coalesced through institutions in Havana such as the Centro de Artesanos (1880–1885), the anarcho-collectivist Círculo de Trabajadores (1885–1892), and the anarchist Sociedad General de Trabajadores (1892–1896).

After the end of the Ten Years' War, thousands of exiled workers returned to Cuba, inflating the ranks of trade unions such as the Gremio de Obreros del Ramo de Tabaquerías (GORT). In this period, class identity and conflict began to become more important than the traditional divisions of origin and race. From then on, both the labor movement inside Cuba and that of the émigré communities gradually strengthened their ties and distanced themselves from elite-led political movements, either the pro-Spanish insular lobby or the exile separatist movement, respectively. Gradually, the reformist tactics of the labor struggle proved inadequate to improve labor conditions and to affect colonial society. Rank-and-file workers replaced the still dominant moderate labor leaders, most of them Spaniards, by steering committees in which both white Creoles and Spaniards accepted radical tactics of the labor struggle and anarcho-collectivist ideas. For instance, the moderate-led GORT failed to achieve significant gains during the strike of 1886 in western Cuba and disintegrated shortly thereafter. Then its increasingly conservative Spanish-born leader, Saturnino Martínez, was rejected in favor of anarchist labor leaders such as Enrique Roig San Martín and Enrique Messonier, both representing Havana tobacco.

The end of slavery in November 1886 favored the advance of important colonial reforms that increased civil liberties. This allowed the labor movement to expand and reach the bulk of urban workers throughout the island. Shortly after, Roig San Martín began to edit *El Productor* (Havana, 1887–1892), a periodical that reached a broad readership and audience, the latter through the spoken readings in tobacco factories and workers' hangouts. During the late 1880s, the anarchist-led labor movement won long pitched strikes and lockouts involving thousands of workers throughout western Cuba and forced both the colonial administration and employers to grant them significant concessions. By this time race barriers in the labor movement were disappearing, and black workers were starting to reach mid-rank leadership positions in some major unions.

Economic crisis and above all Spain's shift toward a purely reactionary colonial position between 1890 and 1892 weakened the labor movement and compelled a growing number of workers to join the most progressive wing of the separatist movement, led by leaders such as **Juan Gualberto Gómez** and **José Martí** who sought to mobilize a cross-class and cross-race separatist alliance against Spanish rule. Although the United States' occupation of Cuba in 1898 frustrated many of the social aspirations of the Cuban labor movement, the end of Spanish colonialism allowed greater freedoms of association and the press that permitted the expansion of the labor movement into Cuba's rural areas. Thousands of sugarcane and rural workers joined the new unions, and labor developed into a mass movement with formidable political force. *See also* Cigars and Cigar Making; Press and Journalism (Eighteenth and Nineteenth Centuries); Tobacco Industry

Further Readings

Casanovas, Joan. *Bread, or Bullets!: Urban Labor and Spanish Colonialism in Cuba, 1850–1898.* Pittsburgh: University of Pittsburgh Press, 1998.

Stubbs, Jean. *Tobacco in the Periphery: A Case Study in Cuban Labour History, 1860–1958.* Cambridge, United Kingdom: Cambridge University Press, 1985.

Joan Casanovas

Partido Revolucionario Cubano (Cuban Revolutionary Party)

Founded in April 1892 by **José Martí** while he was in exile in New York, the Cuban Revolutionary Party (Partido Revolucionario Cubano, or PRC) was created to fight for the independence of Cuba from Spain and the establishment of a democratic republic in Cuba. It sought to unite the separatist movements both on the island and in exile in common revolutionary action, define the bases on which the independence struggle would be waged, and prepare Cuba for war. The party included a Puerto Rico section, as it also aspired for the smaller island's independence.

In April 1895, the Cuban Revolutionary Party issued the call for revolution from its headquarters in New York City and thereby began the **War of Independence**. Its leaders, José Martí, **Antonio Maceo**, and **Máximo Gómez**, then returned to the island to lead the insurgent troops against the Spanish. After the death of Martí on May 19, 1895, **Tomás Estrada Palma** ascended to the leadership of the party and refocused its efforts on organization and fund-raising. After the entry of the United States into the conflict and the defeat of the Spanish in 1898, the party was disbanded. *See also* Political Exile (Nineteenth Century)

Further Readings

Armas, Ramón de. *La revolución pospuesta: contenido y alcance de la revolución martiana por la independencia*. Havana: Editorial de Ciencias Sociales, Instituto Cubano del Libro, 1975.

Pérez, Louis A., Jr. *Cuba between Empires, 1878–1902*. Pittsburgh: University of Pittsburgh Press, 1983.

Mariola Espinosa

Political Exile (Nineteenth Century)

Political exile illustrates some of the most important issues in nineteenth-century Cuba, including the character of **Spanish colonialism**. Support of the abolitionist cause and independence from Spain were the two primary reasons Cubans were forced into exile. Many of the most renowned intellectual activists and political leaders of the century spent the majority of their adult lives in places other than Cuba. Dissidents from the early part of the century such as **Félix Varela** and **José Antonio Saco** found themselves in Spain publishing pamphlets that advocated for the abolition of slavery in Cuba, as well as demanding a more liberal political relationship between Cuba and Spain. As strict censorship of mail and all printed material was maintained on the island by the Captain-General's Office, it was easier for Cuban radicals to publish their political tracts in Spain than in Cuba. Varela later lived for years in New York helping to establish the city as a center for the organization of the Cuban independence movement. **Cirilio Villaverde** and **Domingo del Monte**, both writers and activists, were exiled to the United States in the 1840s due to problems with the censors and their relationships with British abolitionists.

The strategy of exiling people whose words and actions were a threat to the colonial government had the unintended effect of creating communities of dissatisfied Cubans, mostly in the United States, who could then work together more freely for the cause of Cuban independence. While the **Ten Years' War** (1868–1878) raged on, an estimated 4,500 Cubans lived in New York City, 5,000 in Key West, and 5,500 in other parts of the United States. Following the war, as many exiles returned to Cuba, military leaders like **Antonio Maceo, Máximo Gómez**, and **Calixto García** left the island. Upon his arrival in New York, García founded the Cuban Revolutionary Committee. In addition to New York, North American cities such as Philadelphia, Key West, Tampa, and New Orleans were important centers for Cuban political organization. Revolutionaries also organized in other Caribbean and Central American locations, such as Jamaica, the Dominican Republic, Mexico, and Costa Rica.

José Martí, the most celebrated of Cuban patriots, is emblematic of the virtues and contradictions of nineteenth-century political exile. Deported to Spain at an early age for political reasons, he, like his forebears, went on to publish in the Peninsula political pamphlets that would have put one in jail if published or circulated in Cuba. In 1874, Martí received degrees in philosophy and law from the University of Zaragoza. He then traveled for several years in Europe and Latin America, ultimately deciding to make New York his base in 1881. Politically, he remained active and, with lessened censorship in the 1880s, was able to publish regularly not only in the exile press but also in newspapers and magazines in Cuba. In 1892 he founded the **Partido Revolucionario Cubano** (Cuban Revolutionary Party), and in its platform he advocated for immediate independence for Cuba and Puerto Rico and for recognition of Cuba's role in international political trends, particularly encroaching U.S. imperialism in Latin America. Political exile reached its nineteenth-century peak during the **War of Independence** (1875–1878), when an estimated 100,000 Cubans went into temporary exile, close to one out of every ten Cubans. *See also* Abolition and Emancipation; Press and Journalism (Eighteenth and Nineteenth Centuries)

Further Readings

Álvarez Estévez, Rolando. *La emigración cubana en Estados Unidos, 1868–1878*. Havana: Editorial de Ciencias Sociales, 1986.

Casanovas, Joan. *Bread, or Bullets!: Urban Labor and Spanish Colonialism in Cuba, 1850–1898*. Pittsburgh: University of Pittsburgh Press, 1998.

Poyo, Gerald. *"With All and for the Good of All": The Emergence of Popular Nationalism in the Cuban Communities in the United States, 1848–1898*. Durham, NC: Duke University Press, 1989.

Marikay McCabe

Press and Journalism (Eighteenth and Nineteenth Centuries)

The periodic press in Cuba was established after the British evacuation of Havana in 1763. The first newspaper, the *Gaceta de La Habana*, began circulating the following year. It concentrated on reporting commercial, political, and government news, but it lasted only two years, and no copies of it have been preserved. A second newspaper, *El Pensador*, was established in 1764, but again no copies of that publication are extant. In 1782 and 1783 another newspaper, also known as the *Gaceta de La Habana*, was edited by Diego de la Barrera. In 1790, Governor Luis de las Casas encouraged the creation of a newspaper, *Papel Periódico de La Habana*, and placed it under the control of the **Sociedad Económica de Amigos del País**, a prominent Creole organization dedicated to promoting the economic interests of Cuban planters. Over time the number of publications gradually increased. In 1805, *El Amigo de los Cubanos* was founded in Santiago, and in 1812 the *Espejo de Puerto Príncipe* was founded in Puerto Príncipe (**Camagüey**). A decree in 1812 guaranteeing freedom of the press encouraged the proliferation of newspapers. Among those founded shortly after the decree were *El Regañón de La Habana, El Criticón de La Habana, El Patriota Americano, El Argos, La Lira de Apolo*, and *El Mosquito*. Other important newspapers of the nineteenth century included *El Observador Habanero, El Americano Libre*, and *El Revisor Político y Literario*.

Within Cuba there were several prominent political newspapers during the nineteenth century, most notably *Diario de la Marina* and *La Prensa*, which were powerful voices for peninsular interests. In opposition to them was *El Siglo*, a reformist newspaper advocating changes in government. The newspaper was a powerful voice for autonomist political causes during the political openness of the 1860s (see **Reformist Movement** and **Autonomism**). A torrent of newspapers, most of them short-lived, saw the light during 1869–1873, when Spanish revolutionaries extended press freedoms to Cuba and Puerto Rico. Spanish loyalists responded from the pages of their conservative organ: *La Voz de Cuba*.

Throughout the nineteenth century, Cuban exiles published scores of newspapers while in exile in New York, Key West, Tampa, New Orleans, and other U.S. locations (see **Political Exile [Nineteenth Century]**). These included *La Verdad, La Revolución, El Republicano*, and dozens of others. Two of the most influential Cuban exile newspapers published in the United States were *El Habanero* (1824–1826), edited by **Félix Varela**, and *Patria* (1892), edited by Cuban independence leader **José Martí**. *See also* British Occupation of Havana

Further Readings

Álvarez Cuartero, Izaskun. *Memorias de la Ilustración: las Sociedades Económicas de Amigos del País en Cuba (1783–1832)*. Madrid: Real Sociedad Bascongada de los Amigos del País, Delegación en Corte, Madrid: 2000.

Cepero Bonilla, Raúl. *"El Siglo* (1862–1868). Un periódico en lucha contra la censura." In *Es-*

tudios históricos. Havana: Editorial de Ciencias Sociales, 1989: 173–208.

Jensen, Larry R. Children of Colonial Despotism: Press, Politics, and Culture in Cuba, 1790–1840. Tampa: University of South Florida Press, 1988.

Vitier, Cintio, Fina García Marruz, and Roberto Friol, eds. La literatura en el Papel Periódico de La Habana, 1790–1805. Havana: Ed. Letras Cubanas, 1990.

María Dolores González-Ripoll Navarro

Railroads (Nineteenth Century)

On November 19, 1837, Cuba's first railroad began operations. It was the first in all of Latin America and within the Spanish empire. The pressing needs of the **sugar industry** made Cuba the seventh country in the world to have a railroad system. Plans for the construction of the first railroad began soon after the Junta de Fomento (Board of Development) was formed in 1832 under the presidency of Claudio Pinillos. Actual work on the railroad began in 1835. Two years later work was completed on the Havana-Bejucal length of the railway, and a year later, the entire Havana-Güines railroad began operations.

In the light of the success and economic advantages of the first railway, others were soon built, mostly linking the port cities of the northwest with their respective hinterlands. In 1870, as the very first railroads began working in other Latin American countries, Cuba already had an impressive network extending over 1,238 kilometers (768 miles). At about that time, Cuba's railways were reorganized and consolidated to reduce problems arising from out-of-control competition. This process continued during the 1880s and beyond, when British capital, especially the Schroeder Company, began acquiring railroads and integrating them into the United Railways of Habana & Regla Warehouses.

The company managed to monopolize the western network by 1921. Before that date, it coexisted with another large British company, Cuban Central Railways, which in 1899 consolidated the railroads of the central region. Up to that time, most of the railway infrastructure had been built and managed by private Cuban and Spanish capital linked to **sugar plantations** and **tobacco industry** activities.

From the beginning, the expansion of Cuba's railroads was intimately tied to sugar production. That is why the least populated and least developed eastern provinces were slow in establishing that mode of transportation. Only 20 percent of the island's railroads in 1899 were located in those provinces. Efforts to connect the east with the west with a single cross-island line also failed. At the end of the nineteenth century, large sugar centrales began to build their own railroads to transport their own cane and sugar without having to depend on the public rail system. The practice continued during the early decades of the twentieth century to the point that in 1930 there were 12,000 kilometers (7,440 miles) of private lines, compared to 5,214 kilometers (3,233 miles) of public ones.

Further Readings

Santamaría García, Antonio. "Los ferrocarriles de servicio público cubanos (1837–1959). La doble naturaleza de la dependencia azucarera." Revista de Indias 55, no. 204 (1995): 485–515.

Zanetti Lecuona, Oscar, and Alejandro García Álvarez. Sugar and Railroads: A Cuban History, 1837–1959. Chapel Hill: University of North Carolina Press, 1998.

Antonio Santamaría García

Real Compañía de Comercio de La Habana

Based upon the successful examples of the Dutch and the English, in the early eighteenth century, the Spanish monarch decided to modify the established but unworkable mercantilist policy and entrust the commerce of select colonies to private monopoly companies. This was an intermediary step between the rigid mercantilism and the Enlightenment-inspired policy of free trade. In Cuba, this decision led to the establishment of the Real Compañía de Comercio de La Habana in 1740. The company's investors were wealthy subscribers from Cuba and from Spain, including the monarch and members of the court. The function of the Real Compañía was to control all commerce of the island and of Florida by extracting the products of the island and providing goods desired by the residents. Implicit was the presumption that the monopoly company would eliminate **contraband trade**. One of its primary functions was to ship tobacco, at the time Cuba's most important product, that was purchased by the royal factory, but the Real Compañía also shipped other products such as sugar and hides. Another of its responsibilities was to construct ships for the royal navy, and the shipyard in Havana became the pride of the island.

The Real Compañía enjoyed only limited success, and it was very unpopular with the island's residents. It made huge profits for the investors by buying cheap and selling dear. It did increase the amount of revenue that was sent to Spain, but by virtue of being the only legal method of obtaining goods, particularly food, the inhabitants resorted to smuggling on a grand scale. Between 1741 and 1748, periodic charges of corruption led to an investigation in 1752, and in 1760 its responsibility to ship tobacco was rescinded. After the fall and the restoration of Havana (see **British Occupation of Havana**), royal decisions beginning in 1765 undermined the Compañía's privileges and led to a series of declarations that fostered free trade. *See also* Bourbon Reforms; Colonial Institutions; Sugar Plantations; Tobacco Industry

Further Readings

Johnson, Sherry. *The Social Transformation of 18th-Century Cuba*. Gainesville: University Press of Florida, 2001.
McNeill, John Robert. *Atlantic Empires of France and Spain: Louisbourg and Havana, 1700–1763*. Chapel Hill: University of North Carolina Press, 1985.

Sherry Johnson

Reconcentraciones (Reconcentrations)

The *reconcentraciones* were concentration camps created by the Spanish for Cuba's rural population during the **War of Independence** (1895–1898). Under the direction of General Valeriano Weyler, in 1896 Spanish troops began relocating civilians living in the countryside to designated cities that were fortified against the insurgents. To deprive the insurgents of supplies and support, Spanish troops burned dwellings, crops, and anything else that could not be taken to the cities. The countryside was evacuated, and the Spanish considered those found outside the cities to be insurgents.

Conditions in the camps were poor: overcrowded, unsanitary, and disease-ridden. It is estimated that over 500,000 Cubans were removed from their homes under the reconcentration policy, and as many as half of them died in the camps. Rather than undermining the insurgency, the brutality of the reconcentraciones led many Cubans who previously had remained neutral to join the independence struggle. In addition, the reconcentration disrupted traditional patterns of rural life and left the Cuban countryside physically and economically devastated. *See also* Mambises

Further Readings

Foner, Philip S. *The Spanish-Cuban-American War and the Birth of American Imperialism, 1895–1902*. 2 vols. New York: Monthly Review Press, 1972.

Reconcentrados in Remedios (present-day Villa Clara Province) during the War of Independence. Luis Martínez-Fernández Collection.

Izquierdo Canosa, Raúl, *El último hombre y la última peseta*. Havana: Ediciones Verde Olivo, 1997.

Offner, John L. *An Unwanted War: The Diplomacy of the United States & Spain over Cuba, 1895–1898*. Chapel Hill: University of North Carolina Press, 1992.

Pérez Guzmán, Francisco. *Herida profunda*. Havana: Ediciones Unión, 1998.

Mariola Espinosa

Reformist Movement

The Cuban reformist political movement emerged in the 1830s in opposition to **annexationism**. **José Antonio Saco** was one of the principal promoters of this movement when it first emerged. The reformist movement was reenergized during the second half of the 1860s, under the protection of progressive Captains-General Francisco Serrano and Domingo Dulce. This time the movement included several former annexationists such as **Miguel Aldama**, the count of Pozos Dulces, and **José Morales Lemus**, along with longtime reformists Rafael María de Labra and Nicolás de Azcárate, among others. The main goal of the movement was to establish and solidify the cultural and social foundations of Cuban identity. The movement advocated a series of economic and administrative reforms in an effort to create a more harmonious and mutually beneficial relation between Spain and Cuba. Among the tenets of reformism were freedom of the press, creation of an insular legislature, reduction of taxes, and improvements in the system of justice. The primary goal was to establish Cuba as a province of Spain, rather than a colony. As a result of this movement, a new Cuban consciousness (*Cubanidad*) began to crystallize among the Creoles. A central theme of the movement was the creation of a white peasantry and labor force in rural areas, which would gradually reduce the need for slave labor (see **Slavery**). The white farmers would dedicate themselves, at least in part, to the cultivation of small crops such as oranges and rice. These independent farmers would hopefully expand the island's internal market. Reformists advocated wide-ranging agricultural reforms, particularly in the area of sugar production. The reformers wanted to separate the agricultural process of sugarcane production from the industrial aspects. These proposals were presented in 1865 to the **Junta de Información de Ultramar**, a consultative body established by the crown. They were also published in newspapers such as *El Siglo. See also* Autonomism; Colonization and Population (Nineteenth Century); Press and Journalism (Eighteenth and Nineteenth Centuries); Spanish Colonialism (Nineteenth Century); Sugar Plantations

Further Readings

Corwin, Arthur F. *Spain and the Abolition of Slavery in Cuba, 1817–1886*. Austin: University of Texas Press, 1967.

Frías y Jacott, Francisco. *La cuestión de Cuba*. Paris: E. Dentu, 1859.

Martínez-Fernández, Luis. *Torn between Empires: Economy, Society, and Patterns of Political Thought in the Hispanic Caribbean, 1840–1878*. Athens: University of Georgia Press, 1994.

Opatrný, Josef. "Algunos aspectos del estudio de la formación de la nación cubana." In *Cuba, la perla de las Antillas*, ed. Consuelo Naranjo and Tomás Mallo. Madrid: Ediciones Doce Calles—CSIC, 1994. 261–278.

Consuelo Naranjo Orovio

Saco y López-Cisneros, José Antonio (1797–1879)

José Antonio Saco was a distinguished writer and political leader. A graduate of philosophy from the **University of Havana**, Saco was the successor to Professor **Félix Varela** at the Seminary of San Carlos. Spending long periods in exile, he lived in different countries, including Spain, the United States, Great Britain, and France, where he continued his writings and political activities. His polemical style led to a series of confrontations with government officials and other intellectuals.

Saco first went into exile in 1834; the following year he was nominated as Cuba's representative to the Spanish Cortes. Although he early on favored annexation to the United States, he later became the most vocal opponent of **annexationism**, believing that union with the United States would destroy Cuban culture. In the 1830s, he was a leading proponent of the **reformist movement**. A native of **Bayamo**, on the island's east, Saco was among the first to propose an expanded vision of Cuban identity, at the time perceived as the purview of the residents of Havana. His concept of *Cubanidad*, however, was limited to white Cubans. As Saco saw it, the African population should be returned to Africa because it would be impossible and undesirable to assimilate them into Cuban society. The presence of **Afro-Cubans**, Saco believed, would retard the cultural and social progress of the island. In 1865, he served as commissioner on the **Junta de Información de Ultramar** in Madrid and was a proponent of a series of government and social reforms regarding the administration of Cuba.

José Antonio Saco was a distinguished historian and politician. Photograph courtesy of the Biblioteca Nacional José Martí, Havana.

Saco also had a distinguished career as an author and historian. He directed *El Mensajero Semanal*, which he founded in the United States along with Varela in 1823. Saco also directed the *Revista Bimestre Cubana*. He published a great number of essays and articles on a broad range of topics, including vagrancy, **slavery**, the arts, and culture. *See also* Political Exile (Nineteenth Century); Press and Journalism (Eighteenth and Nineteenth Centuries)

Further Readings

Opatrný, Josef. "José Antonio Saco's Path toward the Idea of Cubanidad." *Cuban Studies* 24 (1994): 39–56.

Saco, José Antonio. *Colección póstuma de papeles científicos, históricos, políticos y de otros ramos sobre la Isla de Cuba, ya publicados, ya inéditos*. Havana: Editor Miguel de Villa, 1881.

Saco, José Antonio. *Historia de la esclavitud de la raza negra africana en el Nuevo Mundo y en especial en los países américo-hispanos*. 2 vols. Havana: Editora Cultural, 1938.

Consuelo Naranjo Orovio

Science and Scientists (Eighteenth and Nineteenth Centuries)

The first scientific work published in Cuba, *Descripción de diferentes piezas de historia natural, las más del ramo marítimo*, dates to 1787. The book was written by Portuguese resident Antonio Parra, who went on to establish the island's first natural history collection. Interest in the pursuit of scientific endeavors was spurred by the publication in 1790 of the newspaper *Papel Periódico de La Habana* and the establishment three years later of the Patriotic Society of Havana (Sociedad Patriótica). Two members of that society, **Francisco de Arango y Parreño** and Nicolás Calvo de la Puerta, solicited the Spanish government to establish professorships in botany and chemistry. At the same time, Tomás Romay established a foundation for medical science in Cuba.

In 1795 the royal botanical expedition to New Spain visited Cuba, directed by Martín de Sessé, and trained the first Cuban botanist, José Estévez. In 1797, the Royal Commission of Guantánamo arrived in Cuba, led by the count of Mopox and Jaruco, to study economic, scientific, and military issues on the island. **Alexander von Humboldt**, a prominent German scientist, visited Cuba in 1800–1801 and 1804, and as a result of his research he authored *Political Essay on the Island of Cuba* in 1826.

There were several significant scientific milestones in the first three decades of the nineteenth century, including the publication of the works of **Félix Varela**, who introduced modern physics at the San Carlos Seminary. The first botanical garden was founded in Havana in 1817 under the direction of José Antonio de la Ossa. Several years later, the Anatomical Museum was established in the Military Hospital. Another breakthrough was the establishment in 1827 of the journal *Anales de Ciencias, Agricultura, Comercio y Artes* by Ramón de la Sagra. Ten years later, the first **railroads** began operation, while at the same time José Luis Casaseca began offering classes in chemistry, a development that led to the founding of the Instituto de Investigaciones Químicas (Institute for Chemical Research) in 1848. Álvaro Reynoso later succeeded Casaseca and authored the pioneering work on sugar cultivation, *Ensayo sobre el cultivo de la caña de azúcar* (1862).

In addition to advances in medicine and chemistry, there were numerous other important scientific developments, including Esteban Pichardo's maps and the founding of the Physical-Meteorological Observatory in Havana by Andrés Poey (1856) and the establishment of the Observatory of Colegio Belén (1857), where Benito Viñes played a leading role. In this period, Felipe Poey, director of the Natural History Museum, was one of the island's most prominent scientists, publishing in 1851 his *Memorias sobre la historia natural de la Isla de Cuba*. Poey followed this up with *Ictiología cubana*, on Cuba's fish species, which received an award in Amsterdam in 1883. Other prominent Cuban scientists were Pedro A. Auber and Emilio Auber in natural history, Francisco Sauvalle in botany, Juan Cristóbal Gundlach and Carlos de la Torre in zoology, Manuel Fernández de Castro in paleontology, and Luis Montané in anthropology. In terms of scientific institutions, the most significant breakthrough was the founding of the Royal Academy of Medical, Physical and Natural Sciences of Havana in 1861. This academy attracted some of the brightest Cuban scientists and doctors, who published their research findings in the journal *Anales*, which was directed by Antonio Mestre.

In the closing years of the century there were several significant technological accomplishments: the establishment of telephone service (1881), the more effective supply of drinking water to Havana in an aqueduct project led by Francisco de Albear, and the establishment of electric service (1889). Perhaps the best-known scientific achievement in the island's history was the biological research conducted by **Carlos J. Finlay** at the **Academy of Sciences** in the 1880s, which determined that a certain type of mosquito was responsible for the spread of yellow fever. *See also* Press and Journalism (Eighteenth and Nineteenth Centuries); University of Havana

Further Readings

González, Rosa M. *Felipe Poey. Estudio biográfico.* Havana: Editorial Academia, 1999.

Pruna, Pedro M. *Momentos y figuras de la ciencia en Cuba.* Havana: Academia de Ciencias de Cuba, 1988.

Pruna, Pedro M. "National Science in a Colonial Context. The Royal Academy of Sciences of Havana, 1861–1898." *Isis* 85 (1994): 412–426.

Puig-Samper, Miguel Ángel, and Mercedes Valero González. *El Jardín Botánico de la Habana.* Aranjuez, Spain: Ediciones Doce Calles—, 2000.

Valero González, Mercedes. *Instituciones científicas cubanas del siglo XIX.* Havana: Editorial Academia, 1994.

Miguel Ángel Puig-Samper Mulero

Simoni, Amalia (1841–1918)

A Cuban patriot and the wife of war hero **Ignacio Agramonte**, Amalia Simoni was born in Puerto Príncipe (also known as **Camagüey**). She married on August 2, 1868, and within three months, Agramonte left her with her family as he went to lead Cuban rebels in the beginning of the **Ten Years' War** (1868–1878). In 1873, Agramonte died in battle, leaving Simoni a young widow. Living on her family's estate in the countryside throughout the war she gained recognition as a *mambisa* (feminine for *mambí*; see **Mambises**). Simoni gained additional fame as she was from a wealthy family and was seen to have compromised her comfortable eco-

nomic position in the interests of ending Spanish colonialism and the institution of slavery. *See also* Abolition and Emancipation

Further Readings

Méndez, María Graziella. "Amalia Simoni de Agramonte." *Mujeres* 8 (October 1968): 65–66.

Portell-Vilá, Herminio. "Las mambisas: Amalia Simoni." *Bohemia* 35 (June 13, 1943): 4–5, 57–58.

Marikay McCabe

Slave Trade

The slave trade was the principal source of labor for Cuba during much of the colonial era as well as a means employed by many to accumulate capital. The Cuban slave trade can be divided into two distinct periods: The first covers the period from the early 1500s through 1820, when it was legal; the second period covers from 1821 through 1873, when the trade was carried out clandestinely.

The importation of slaves began in the 1510s and was handled primarily by a number of foreign companies under special licenses (*asientos*) with the colonial government. This arrangement persisted until 1789 when the crown allowed direct trade with the African coast. The economic importance of the slave trade increased throughout the seventeenth and eighteenth centuries with the expansion of sugar cultivation, the development of large **sugar plantations**, and the Treaty of Utrecht (1713), which granted the English dominance over the trade. Spanish government officials and Spanish and Creole merchants and planters took control of the Cuban slave trade after 1789, a process spurred by the Haitian Revolution, which made Cuba the main Caribbean destination for slaves. In 1817, the Spanish and British governments negotiated a treaty to suppress the slave trade as of 1820. However, the Spanish government's enforcement of the treaty was spotty, a record that led to recurrent conflict with Great Britain, which sought to enforce the accord. Great Britain forced Spain to sign yet another treaty for the suppression of the slave trade in 1835, this time with more teeth in it and severer penalties for those caught trafficking slaves. Although Spanish authorities abolished the trade in 1845, slaves continued to be illegally introduced for three decades, as intercolonial trade flourished with slaves imported from Puerto Rico. Other illegal shipments continued to arrive from Africa.

In the period between 1518 and 1820, an estimated 385,000 African slaves were brought into Cuba. Ironically the trade boomed after it was made illegal, and an estimated 468,000 slaves were brought to Cuba from 1821 through 1873. Increased risk amounted to increased profits for those involved in the slave trade from merchants, planters, and sailors up to the captain-general of Cuba, who was frequently bribed to look the other way when slave ships disembarked. From 1850 forward, **Asian contract laborers** were used to supplement the slave trade, although they worked under similarly atrocious conditions. The slave trade financed the acquisition and construction of new sugar plantations and spurred the development of a merchant class. The profits accrued by the Spanish financed the construction of **railroads** and industry. The most prominent members of the planter society, including **Francisco de Arango y Parreño, Miguel Aldama**, José Luis Alfonso, **Cristóbal F. Madan**, Tomás Terry, and Julián Zulueta, took part in the clandestine trade. Many prominent Spanish merchants participated in the trade, and it is believed that even Queen Regent María Cristina directly profited from it. *See also* Abolition and Emancipation; Labor Institutions, Early; Slavery

Further Readings
Bergad, Laird W., Fe Iglesias, and María del Carmen Barcia. *The Cuban Slave Market, 1790–1880.* Cambridge, United Kingdom: Cambridge University Press, 1995.
Eltis, David. *Economic Growth and the Ending of the Transatlantic Slave Trade.* New York: Oxford University Press, 1987.
Eltis, David. "The Nineteenth-Century Transatlantic Slave Trade: An Annual Time Series of Imports into the Americas Broken Down by Region." *Hispanic American Historical Review* 67, no. 1 (February 1987): 109–138.
Martínez-Fernández, Luis. *Fighting Slavery in the Caribbean: The Life and Times of a British Family in Nineteenth-Century Havana.* Armonk, NY: M.E. Sharpe, 1998.
Murray, David R. *Odious Commerce: Britain, Spain, and the Abolition of the Cuban Slave Trade.* Cambridge, United Kingdom: Cambridge University Press, 1980.

José Antonio Piqueras Arenas

Slavery

As an institution, slavery in Cuba dates back to the early sixteenth century, but it became the dominant system of labor from the eighteenth century until the last quarter of the nineteenth century. The expansion of slavery coincided with the expansion of the plantation system. The institution had a profound impact on the creation of wealth on the island, the development of society, the formation of a national identity, and Cuba's colonial relationship with Spain.

African slaves began to arrive in Cuba in the 1510s. The importation of slaves was the result of a labor shortage created by the decline of the Amerindian population. The Spanish wanted a workforce to perform heavy labor as well as domestic tasks. Cuba's economic expansion and the advantages of a low-cost labor force led to an increase in the **slave trade**. The slave population increased steadily from the end of the eighteenth century onward. Slaves numbered approximately 50,000 prior to 1790, but their number surpassed 239,000 by 1817. The total slave population climbed to a high of 436,000 by 1841. The

Estimated Annual Imports of Slaves into Cuba, 1811–1867

Year	Number	Year	Number
1811	8,500	1840	13,700
1812	8,100	1841	11,600
1813	6,400	1842	4,100
1814	5,800	1843	7,100
1815	12,100	1844	10,000
1816	23,600	1845	2,600
1817	34,500	1846	1,000
1818	26,500	1847	1,700
1819	20,200	1848	2,000
1820	22,900	1849	7,400
1821	4,500	1850	3,300
1822	4,000	1851	5,000
1823	1,900	1852	7,000
1824	7,700	1853	12,500
1825	13,800	1854	11,400
1826	4,000	1855	6,400
1827	5,000	1856	7,300
1828	12,900	1857	10,400
1829	14,900	1858	15,000
1830	14,400	1859	25,000
1831	16,100	1860	21,000
1832	13,600	1861	13,800
1833	13,800	1862	10,100
1834	16,700	1863	3,800
1835	25,700	1864	2,400
1836	20,200	1865	800
1837	20,900	1866	700
1838	21,000	1867	1,000
1839	19,900	Total	
		1811–67	637,700

Source: Davis Eltis, "The Nineteenth-Century Transatlantic Slave Trade: An Annual Time Series of Imports into the Americas Broken Down by Region," *Hispanic American Historical Review* 67:1 (February 1987): 109–38.

number of slaves declined thereafter, but until 1869 the figure never dropped below 350,000. As late as 1877 there were still 200,000 slaves, a number that steadily decreased with the establishment of the transitional labor institution known as *patronato* in 1880. The patronato was a system in which slaves were gradually freed over an eight-year period, without compensation to their owners. During that period the slaves served an apprenticeship to prepare them to become wage laborers. By the time the patronato was eliminated in 1886, there were only 25,000 *patrocinados* left.

At its height, slavery in Cuba was concentrated in large measure on the western part of the island. In the central and eastern parts of the island, many of the small sugar mills operated with a combination of forced and free labor. Slavery in those areas was largely patriarchal in nature.

Initially, slaves worked a variety of jobs in both rural and urban settings as well as domestic and field jobs. However, in the period around 1840 the labor demands were most acute on the island's **sugar plantations** and coffee plantations, so the slave labor force became primarily rural. Some slaves also worked on cattle ranches or in tobacco cultivation. Over time, sugar production became the primary economic force on the island, and the labor-intensive **sugar industry** required large numbers of slaves. Rising demand and higher prices in international markets fueled sugar's growing dominance. Slaves took part in all aspects of the sugar production process from the fields to the mill. In urban areas, slaves worked as artisans, merchants, servants, and stevedores.

The slave system created a series of unequal relationships throughout society. Slave traders concentrated on exporting young African males to Cuba, because they were thought to be stronger and more likely to survive the harrowing journey. Cuban planters also preferred male slaves because they could be put to work immediately and were likely to live long enough to bring a return on their investment. This preference for males created an imbalance in the sexes in the slave population. In rural Cuba there were three male slaves for each female. The imbalance began to correct itself during the illegal slave trade after 1820. Forty years later, males made up 60 percent of the slave population. Reproduction rates were low among the slaves and the abortion rate high. The suicide rate among slaves was several times higher than among the free population. The slave system made it difficult for slaves to establish a family life, because slave children were frequently sold. The regimentation of slaves in barracks also discouraged family formation. Sexual abuse of female slaves by masters and *mayorales* (overseers) was commonplace.

Nutrition for the slaves consisted primarily of two meals a day that might include rice, corn flour, jerked beef (tasajo), salted fish, root crops, and plantains. During the nineteenth century some slaves were permitted to farm small provisions grounds, known as *conucos*, to supplement their diets. Slaves typically received two sets of clothes a year, but this generally did not include shoes. In the evenings, slaves slept in a rectangular-shaped building, known as a slave *barracón* (barracks), which had only one door and poor ventilation.

Newly arrived slaves, known as *bozales*, came from many different parts of Africa and consisted of numerous ethnic groups, including Congos, Lucumíes, and Carabalíes. Imported slaves underwent a continuous and prolonged process of deculturation. Some aspects of African culture survived and were adapted to the new environment, such as their community organizations (see **Cabildos de Nación**), syncretic religious beliefs, music, storytelling traditions, and dance (see **Afro-Cubans**).

Slaves resisted their plight in a wide variety of ways from flight (*cimarronería*; see **Cimarrones**) to more subtle and covert resistance strategies relating to their levels of production and discipline. Corporal punishment was commonplace at the sugar mill and included the use of stocks and shackles, which replaced lashings. The use of stocks and shackles was finally prohibited by government decree in 1883. The Spanish system allowed a slave to buy his liberty from his owner by means of a regular payment, a process known as *coartación*. This was more common in urban areas where slaves were frequently rented

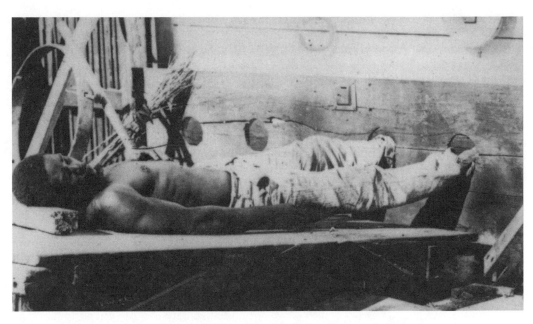

Slave posing in stocks. From the Collection of Keith de Lellis, New York.

out to perform wage-earning jobs. The prospects of a rural slave buying his freedom were much more remote.

The expansion of the slave trade in Cuba throughout the nineteenth century molded the perceptions of the Creole elites regarding independence. Fear of a Haiti-style revolt in Cuba led them to seek closer ties with Spain at the same time that other colonies were in the process of gaining their independence. Later many Creoles favored annexation to the United States as a means of preserving the slave system. This same desire led many to spurn independence efforts launched in 1868. The influence of the slave owners played an important role in shaping Spanish colonial policy.

The impact of slavery on Cuban history continues to be widely debated. Some scholars argue slavery was a specific system of production that fostered the development of a planter class, with some feudal overtones, wedded to the forced labor system. Others view slavery as part of the worldwide spread of capitalism dating back to the sixteenth century and argue the

planters were part of the bourgeoisie. There is also a lively debate over the causes of abolition. One central argument is that the development of new technologies in the sugar industry rendered slavery unnecessary and unprofitable. Furthermore, the slave system entered a period of crisis around 1860, and the supply of slaves was reduced for a large number of reasons. While some attribute the decline of slavery to technological-economic factors, still others emphasize resistance on the part of the slaves and free people of color for its demise. Most scholars agree that the unique role of slavery in Cuba created a situation in which the interests of the Cuban planter class coincided with the political and economic interests of Spain and as a result delayed the emergence of an independence movement. *See also* Abolition and Emancipation; Annexationism; Appendix 6; Escalera, Conspiracy of La; Indigenous Inhabitants; Population and Demographic Indicators; Santería

Further Readings

Deschamps Chapeaux, Pedro. *El negro en la economía habanera del siglo XIX*. Havana: Unión de Escritores y Artistas Cubanos, 1971.

García, Gloria. *La esclavitud desde la esclavitud.* Mexico City: Centro de Investigación Científica "Ing. Jorge L. Tamayo," 1996.

Knight, Franklin W. *Slave Society in Cuba during the Nineteenth Century.* Madison: University of Wisconsin Press, 1970.

Moreno Fraginals, Manuel. *The Sugarmill: The Socioeconomic Complex of Sugar in Cuba, 1760–1860.* Trans. Cedric Belfrage. New York: Monthly Review Press, 1976.

Paquette, Robert L. *Sugar Is Made with Blood: The Conspiracy of La Escalera and the Conflict between Empires over Slavery in Cuba.* Middletown, CT: Wesleyan University Press, 1988.

Scott, Rebecca J. *Slave Emancipation in Cuba: The Transition to Free Labor, 1860–1899.* Princeton, NJ: Princeton University Press, 1985.

José Antonio Piqueras Arenas

Sociedad Económica de Amigos del País

The Sociedad Económica de Amigos del País (Economic Society of Friends of the Country) was one of the earliest and most influential Creole institutions of the colonial period. It was formally established in Havana by Royal Decree in 1792. Five years earlier, a similar society was founded in **Santiago de Cuba**, but it was short-lived. The Sociedad Económica de Amigos del País lasted for more than 100 years, until 1959. It was modeled on the economic societies of Spain and Latin America and played active roles in the economic, social, and cultural life of the island. Throughout its long history, the society was known by a variety of names including the Real Sociedad Económica de La Habana, Real Sociedad Patriótica de La Habana, and Real Junta de Fomento. It was only in 1899 that it came to be known as the Sociedad Económica de Amigos del País. The Havana-based organization established chapters throughout the island. There were separate sections within the society dedicated to education, commerce, industry, economic studies, social studies, history, literature, and the fine arts. In ad-

dition to publishing a newspaper, *Papel Periódico de La Habana*, the society established the country's first public library. It founded the Botanical Gardens and the Academy of Fine Arts. The society was a major sponsor of professorships in political economy, chemistry, and mathematics. It was an important patron of Havana's Casa de Beneficencia, an important charitable organization. In 1831 it began publishing the magazine *Revista Bimestre Cubana*. Several of Cuba's most distinguished citizens were affiliated with the Sociedad at one point or another; among them we find the likes of **Francisco de Arango y Parreño, Félix Varela, Domingo del Monte**, and **José Antonio Saco**. After the colonial era, the society lost its official function and became a private organization dedicated to promoting cultural activities. *See also* Colonial Institutions; Press and Journalism (Eighteenth and Nineteenth Centuries); Science and Scientists (Eighteenth and Nineteenth Centuries)

Further Readings
Álvarez Cuartero, Izaskun. *Memorias de la ilustración: las Sociedades Económicas de Amigos del País en Cuba (1783–1832).* Madrid: Real Sociedad Bascongada de Amigos del País Delegación en Cortes, 2000.

Shafer, Robert J. *The Economic Societies in the Spanish World (1763–1821).* Syracuse, NY: Syracuse University Press, 1958.

María Dolores González-Ripoll Navarro

Spanish Colonialism (Nineteenth Century)

Spanish colonialism over Cuba extended for almost four centuries, from 1511, when **Baracoa** was established as the first Spanish settlement on the island, until January 1, 1899, when Spanish authorities yielded control of the island to the U.S. government. After the final collapse of Spain's continental empire in the Americas in 1824, Cuba became a valued colonial possession, and Spanish colonialism became more intense and far-reaching. In 1825, in order to retain Cuba, the absolutist monarch Ferdinand VII granted to Captain-General Dionisio Vives absolute powers to rule over the island, powers that were ratified and expanded when Miguel Tacón became the island's captain-general a decade later (see **Appendix 5**). The Spanish constitution of 1836 was not made extensive to Cuba; on the contrary, colonial representation was terminated in 1837, and repression of the colonial subjects intensified under Tacón (1834–1838).

During the first half of the nineteenth century, the island's colonial political-administrative structure consisted of three major components: the captain-general and the governor (political and military authority in one individual) (see **Appendixes 4** and **5**), the Audiencia (judiciary authority), and the Intendencia (fiscal authority). Of the three, the captain-general prevailed with the recourse to absolute powers that remained in place during the balance of the century with some adjustments such as the granting of colonial representation to Cuba in 1878, in response to an assimilationist move on the part of Spain.

Beginning in the latter decades of the eighteenth century and up to the 1830s, Cuba's elites, mostly the sugar barons, managed to influence Spain's policy makers to open the island's trade to markets outside the Spanish empire. By mid-century, the U.S. market surpassed Spain's and other European markets as the main recipient of Cuba's exports. While sugar dominated within these trade links, tobacco, coffee, and other products were also traded. Also toward the end of the century foreign investments began to flow into the island, especially into the **railroads** and the **sugar industry**. The expansion of sugar was paralleled by the expansion of **slavery**, as large numbers of slaves were introduced to the island even as the **slave trade** was officially declared illegal in 1820. Slavery

declined, however, beginning in the second half of the 1860s. Because of pressures from planters, merchants, and other interested parties, slavery did not end until 1886.

During the middle decades of the nineteenth century, the fear of a race war, like the one that shook St. Domingue in 1789–1804, weakened the abolitionist inclinations of the island's white Creoles and actually turned many of them into annexationists seeking to turn Cuba into a state of the United States to stop the emancipation of Cuba's slaves. Earlier in the century the liberal-autonomist alternative proposed by **Francisco de Arango y Parreño** and other Creoles had failed during the 1830s. With the growth of the Spanish-born population during the second half of the century, Cuba became increasingly polarized ethnically (Creoles versus Spaniards) and racially. Spain took advantage of the increasingly tense colonial situation to increase the extent of fiscal and commercial exploitation through protectionist taxation, particularly after 1882. The concurrent militarization of the colony allowed the colony's rulers to repress any sort of liberal or progressive movement.

Naturally, many Cubans desired to achieve a greater degree of freedom and liberties. While most sought the reformist route, more radical voices favored independence. Following the collapse of the earlier annexationist movement, in 1857 Captain-General Francisco Serrano relaxed colonial rule, and for the next ten years Cubans enjoyed a larger measure of freedom. Cultural associations, mutual aid and social organizations, newspapers, and journals flourished under the protection of the newfound freedoms; many of these allowed the participation of artisans and free Cubans of color. This period also fostered the emergence of a vigorous **reformist movement** that was active in pursuit of the rights of Cuba's whites but shy with regard to the long-overdue abolition of slavery.

The reformist impetus of the late 1850s and early 1860s collapsed in 1866, when reformist delegates to Madrid's **Junta de Información de Ultramar**, led by **José Morales Lemus**, returned empty-handed and frustrated. Soon thereafter, separatism reemerged, manifesting itself as the **Ten Years' War**. In the war's aftermath, Spain granted Cuba some long-expected reforms, but dissatisfaction with colonial rule lingered.

Under the limited constitutional provisions afforded by the peace terms that ended the Ten Years' War, political parties were formed on the island. Also, despite obstacles posed by colonial authorities, a vigorous and well-organized labor movement emerged with links to U.S. exile enclaves such as Key West, Tampa, and New York, where Cuban workers also organized. Nevertheless, Cuba's Creoles failed to form a common front vis-à-vis the colonial regime. Planters, tobacco workers, and merchants defended their own sectoral interests, thus allowing Spain to continue to divide and conquer. In the light of a shifting balance of power that favored continued colonial rule and in response to the economic crisis of the 1890s, a large segment of the Cuban population saw no alternative but to go to war again to wrest independence from Spain (1895–1898) (see **War of Independence**).

During the last two decades of Spanish colonial rule over Cuba, the island's Creole and Peninsular elites, with few exceptions, remained opposed to each other. On the one hand, Creoles gravitated to the Liberal Autonomist Party; they were mostly sugar planters, agriculturalists, and members of the liberal professions. As Spanish oppression intensified, they tended to flow away from **autonomism** into the ranks of open separatism. On the other hand, the party of the Spanish elites was the Spanish or Constitutional Union Party. It represented the clergy, the army, and the colonial bureaucracy in addition to wealthy merchants, shippers, tobacco manufacturers, and the growing ranks of Peninsular planters. A few wealthy Cubans joined them later on. Spanish colonialism officially ended at the end of 1898, when Spanish authorities yielded control over the island to the U.S. military. *See also* Abolition and Emancipation; Annexationism; Colonial Institutions; Colonization and Population (Nineteenth Century); Organized Labor (Nineteenth Century); Political Exile (Nineteenth Century); Press and Journalism (Eighteenth and Nineteenth Centuries)

Further Readings

Barcia Zequeira, María del Carmen. *Élites y grupos de presión: Cuba, 1868–1898*. Havana: Editorial de Ciencias Sociales, 1998.

Casanovas, Joan. *Bread, or Bullets!: Urban Labor and Spanish Colonialism in Cuba, 1850–1898*. Pittsburgh: University of Pittsburgh Press, 1998.

Martínez-Fernández, Luis. *Torn between Empires: Economy, Society, and Patterns of Political Thought in the Hispanic Caribbean, 1840–1878*. Athens: University of Georgia Press, 1994.

Roldán de Montaud, Inés. *La Restauración en Cuba. El fracaso de un proyecto reformista*. Madrid: CSIC, 2000.

Elena Hernández Sandoica

Sugar Plantations

Sugar plantations, known as *ingenios*, worked by slave labor, constituted Cuba's primary socioeconomic system and the dynamo of the island's economy during most of the nineteenth century. Several factors coincided in the late eighteenth and early nineteenth centuries that set Cuba on the path to becoming the world's premier sugar exporter. The **British occupation of Havana** (1762) opened trade routes and spurred the **slave trade**; the independence of the former thirteen colonies of North America ended British colonial exports to the newly established United States; the

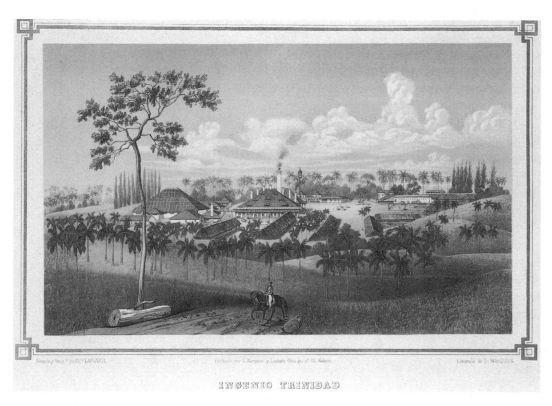

Ingenio Trinidad, circa 1846. Lithograph by Eduardo Laplante, gift of Marshall Stewart, courtesy of the Museum of Arts and Sciences, Daytona Beach, Florida.

revolution in St. Domingue (Haiti) destroyed the exporting capacity of what had been the world's biggest sugar exporter and exiled to Cuba a large number of planters along with their capital; and the collapse of Spain's New World empire redirected capital, migrants, and imperial attention to the still faithful island of Cuba. Spain, furthermore, contributed to the sugar boom by liberalizing the slave trade in exchange for a new tax system; by promoting immigration; by facilitating the importation of foreign capital, machinery, and technicians; and by opening up the island's land market.

The sugar plantations that emerged in the light of such favorable circumstances were characterized by the integration of the agrarian and industrial facets of production, the incorporation of modern technology, and modern organizational and commercial techniques, all of this occur-

ring while remaining dependent on slave labor. In the early part of the nineteenth century the primitive sugar mills were transformed into mechanized ingenios, progressively incorporating steam power and other technological advances. As a result, production skyrocketed from 25,000 tons in 1800 to 113,000 in 1836, an amount equivalent to 19 percent of the world's sugar output. During the 1830s and 1840s Cuba's planters faced the challenges of the expanding European beet sugar producers by further mechanizing their production with vacuum pans, **railroads**, and other new technologies. During the 1860s centrifuges were incorporated into the filtering phase, and thus the entire sugar production process became mechanized. These advances allowed production to reach 770,000 tons in 1868 (29 percent of the world's output). In spite of growing international pressures against the continuation of the slave trade and **slavery** itself, the island's plantations continued to depend on slave labor.

During the **Ten Years' War**, plantations were further modernized. Cuba's insurgents focused their attacks on the eastern half of the island where they destroyed many plantations, actually the most primitive ingenios, and liberated slaves. These actions forced Spain to begin moving toward the abolition of slavery, finally ending the institution in 1886. In the light of the new labor situation and falling sugar prices during the 1880s, sugar producers began a process of centralization. The new sugar *centrales* were completely mechanized and employed free labor; they milled their own cane as well as cane produced by *colonos* (sugar growers), whom they controlled through the ownership of the land and railroads. In order to make the most effective use of their expensive technology, the centrales acquired vast tracks of land and built railroads to transport the cane and sugar.

A new generation of sugar barons, mostly Spanish-born former slave traders, merchants, and financiers, played a major role in the transition from the old ingenios to the new centrales. The Spaniard Julián Zulueta was the first to build a central with its own railroad (1873). *See also* Abolition and Emancipation; Colonization and Population (Nineteenth Century); Science and Scientists (Eighteenth and Nineteenth Centuries)

Further Readings

Bergad, Laird W. *Cuban Rural Society in the Nineteenth Century: The Social and Economic History of Monoculture in Matanzas*. Princeton, NJ: Princeton University Press, 1990.

Deer, Noel. *The History of Sugar*. 2 vols. London: Chapman & Hall, 1950.

Elly, Roland T. *Cuando reinaba su majestad el azúcar. Estudio histórico y sociológico de una tragedia latinoamericana*. Buenos Aires: Editorial Sudamericana, 1963.

Iglesias García, Fe. *Del ingenio al central*. Havana: Editorial de Ciencias Sociales, 1999.

Moreno Fraginals, Manuel. *El Ingenio: Complejo económico social cubano del azúcar*. 3 vols. Havana: Editorial de Ciencias Sociales, 1968.

Antonio Santamaría García

Tejera Calzado, Diego Vicente (1848–1903)

A writer, journalist, and politician, Diego Vicente Tejera dedicated his life to literature, poetry, and Cuba's independence. An admirer of **José Martí**, he traveled throughout Latin America and Europe. He studied medicine abroad in Caracas and Barcelona, but he never practiced. Tejera returned to Cuba in 1879 and founded *El Almendares* and *Revista Habanera*. At the same time, he worked on a variety of general and literary publications. On the eve of the **War of Independence** (1895–1898), Tejera conducted a public relations campaign promoting the revolutionary cause in New York and Key West, Florida. He gave a series of lectures and speeches on social policy, which were later edited. During the first U.S. intervention (1898–1902), he moved back to Cuba where he published the newspaper *La Victoria* and directed another, *Patria*. A utopian socialist, Tejera founded the Cuban Socialist Party (Partido Socialista Cubano) in 1899, which lasted only four months. He conceived of society as consisting of five social groups or classes, ranging from the miserably poor to the opulent. The three stages between miserably poor and opulent were poor, comfortable, and rich. Tejera believed it was possible to rise in social category by means of culture and education. He did not believe it was necessary to eliminate private property and socialize the means of production in order to build an equitable society. In 1900, he founded the Popular Party (Partido Popular), which was also short-lived. Among his poetry collections are *Un ramo de violetas* (Paris, 1877); *Poesías completas* (Havana, 1879); and *Poesías* (Paris, 1893). *See also* Organized Labor (Nineteenth Century); Political Exile (Nineteenth Century); Press and Journalism (Eighteenth and Nineteenth Centuries)

Further Readings
Rivero Muñiz, José. *El primer Partido Socialista Cubano*. Las Villas: Universidad Central, 1962.

Tejera, Diego Vicente. *Textos escogidos*. Ed. Carlos del Toro. Havana: Editorial de Ciencias Sociales, 1981.

Manuel de Paz Sánchez

Ten Years' War

The Ten Years' War is the name given to the bloody armed conflict between Cuba and Spain fought on Cuban soil between 1868 and 1878.

Prior to 1868, Cuba had remained on the fringe of the independence movement that swept over Latin America at the beginning of the nineteenth century. There had been many reasons for Cubans to shy away from confrontation with Spain: A large Spanish army was stationed on the island; rules for commerce with Spain were not as stringent as in the rest of Latin America; Cubans were momentarily allowed participation in the political process by inclusion in the Spanish Cortes; and Cuba's elites desired to maintain and support the **slave trade**. The slave trade was deemed a necessity for Cuban plantation owners who sought to turn the island into the world's principal exporter of sugar. Any insurrection against Spain would threaten the slave trade as well as the **sugar industry**. An insurrection of that sort had taken place in Haiti, when Toussaint Louverture rebelled against the French at the turn of the century, abolishing slavery and propelling into exile to Cuba the former colony's white aristocracy. The example of Haiti haunted Cuba's propertied classes during the entire nineteenth century, turning many of its prominent members into political conservatives.

Relations between Cuba and Spain, however, changed in the 1820s as the Spanish government started to exert harsher authority on the island without input from Cubans, culminating in 1837 with the expulsions of Cubans from the Spanish Cortes. Such actions fueled antagonism between Cubans and Spaniards. Still, the Cuban aristocracy attempted to rectify conditions without endangering the slave trade. **Annexationism** and political reformism of colonial rule were explored. But by 1860, it was evident that **slavery** could not be maintained much longer: Slaves were becoming very costly, and the Confederate states of North America, which had favored annexing Cuba to the United States, lost the Civil War in 1865. Cubans, then, tried to persuade Spain to end slavery by compensating owners for each freed slave. Such an idea, along with democratic reforms, were presented in 1866 at a conference known as the **Junta de Información de Ultramar**. But the Spaniards did not accept the reforms.

In the meantime, Masonic lodges, which served as meeting places for those who favored independence, were proliferating throughout the island. These pro-independence Cubans saw in Spain's failure to regain Mexico and to successfully annex the Dominican Republic in the 1860s evidence that victory was possible in a conflict against Spain. Thus in 1868, Cuban leaders planned an insurrection to take place at the end of the sugarcane harvest in 1869. However, leaders in the province of Oriente precipitated the insurrection.

On October 10, 1868, a plantation owner named **Carlos Manuel de Céspedes** gathered together his friends, followers, and slaves. Freeing his slaves, Céspedes demanded independence for Cuba as well as the gradual abolition of slavery. This initial act of insurrection was known as "el Grito de Yara," the start of the Ten Years' War. Eventually assembling 12,000 men under his command, Céspedes began the long struggle against Spain.

Céspedes proved an effective military leader, taking over the towns of **Holguín** and **Bayamo**, in Oriente. His troops marched under a Cuban flag similar to that of Chile and to the tune of what eventually became Cuba's **national anthem**. Pedro (Perucho) Figueredo had composed the anthem for Céspedes. Soon, the insurrection spread to the center of the island. A year later, a constitution was written at Guáimaro (see **Guáimaro, Constitution of**). Céspedes was elected president of the Cuban republic, a House of Representatives was established, and a military general was appointed. The House abolished slavery, did not rule out annexation, and designated the flag first flown by **Narciso López** in 1850 as the **national flag**.

The war, which was initially led by wealthy, white landowners, attracted the attention of poor whites, blacks, and mullattoes, both former slaves and free people of color, as fighting spread throughout the countryside in the island's central and eastern districts. **Antonio Maceo**, an Afro-Cuban, emerged as an important leader. So did **Máximo Gómez**, who was originally from the Dominican Republic. By 1873, the insurgents, known as the Ejército Libertador, or **mambises**, had full control of the province of Oriente. General Gómez advocated an invasion of the western part of the island and the burning of the sugarcane fields. While Céspedes agreed with Gómez, other generals, as well as the **Camagüey**-dominated House of Representatives, opposed this plan. A schism evolved, and in 1873, Céspedes was forced to resign as president. A year later, he died on the battlefield.

In 1875, Gómez was finally authorized to implement his aggressive battle plan, and in a little over a month, the general torched eighty-three sugarcane fields and mills. However, the members of the more conservative sector within the pro-independence movement were leery of Gómez's tactics as well as of the increasing presence of **Afro-Cubans** among the troops.

While divisions continued among the insurgents, a new Spanish governor, Joaquín Jovellar, arrived on the island in 1876. Prior to his arrival, the previous governor had been content to curb the insurrection within central Cuba. Now, Jovellar was determined to end the conflict at once. The governor appointed a new military leader, Arsenio Martínez Campos, and increased the armed forces to 70,000 troops. In October 1877, the Spanish captured the new president of the Cuban republic, **Tomás Estrada Palma**. In December, his successor began negotiations for an armistice. As part of the truce, the Cubans wanted freedom for the slaves who fought in the Ejército Libertador, a general pardon for the Cuban leaders who were willing to leave the island, and representative parity for Cuba and Puerto Rico before the Spanish Cortes. The agreement was signed in 1878 and was known as la Paz del Zanjón.

Not all who fought in the war accepted the truce. General Maceo met with Martínez Campos and demanded the immediate abolition of slavery and independence for Cuba. His demands were known as the Protest of Baraguá, after the town in Oriente where the meeting took place. This action catapulted Maceo into the leadership of the independence movement. Thus, the war that had started under the leadership of a wealthy white man was now in the hands of an Afro-Cuban.

Cuba did not win the Ten Years' War. But the conflict allowed the island to negotiate with Spain as an equal, consolidated a Cuban national conscience, and placed men such as Gómez and Maceo in the forefront of the independence movement. *See also* Abolition and Emancipation; Freemasonry; Reformist Movement

Further Readings

Barcia, María del Carmen, Gloria García, and Eduardo Torres-Cuevas, eds. *Las luchas por la independencia nacional y las transformaciones*

Cuban 1869 bill issued by the Republic-in-Arms. Such currency circulated in regions controlled by Cuban insurgents. Luis Martínez-Fernández Collection.

estructurales, 1868–1898. Havana: Editora Política—Instituto de Historia, 1996.

Ferrer, Ada. *Insurgent Cuba: Race, Nation, and Revolution, 1868–1898*. Chapel Hill: University of North Carolina Press, 1999.

Guerra, Ramiro. *Guerra de los Diez Años*. Havana: Pueblo y Educación, 1986.

Llerena, María Cristina, ed. *Sobre la Guerra de los 10 Años*. Havana: Instituto Cubano del Libro, 1973.

Plasencia Moro, Aleida. *Bibliografía de la Guerra de los Diez Años*. Havana: Instituto del Libro, 1968.

Luis Miguel García Mora

Trade and Navigation (1500–1800)

During the first centuries of **Spanish colonialism**, trade and navigation between Spain and the New World was based upon mercantilism, a rigid economic system designed to benefit the mother country and exclude other nations. Trade between Spain and Spanish America was regulated by the Casa de Contratación located in Seville. Spain's rivals, France, England, and Holland, all wanted a share of the New World's silver and other riches, and they struck at Spain's wealth in the form of privateer attacks against Spanish shipping. Spain retaliated by limiting the number of sailings and by ordering that ships sail in convoys with a naval escort, the famed *flo-*

View of Havana. By Alain Manesson Mallet (Paris, 1683), from *Description de l'Univers*, Luis Martínez-Fernández Collection.

tas. Originally, only two mainland cities were approved as ports of entry and exit, Portobelo in Panama and Veracruz in Mexico. Ships laden with silver, gold, precious gemstones, or products from individual colonies (for example, hides from Cuba or cacao from Mexico) left the mainland ports for Havana, where they would rendezvous with other ships before sailing in convoy to Spain. The flota system contributed to the development of Havana as the most important port city in the Caribbean.

The rigid flota system was designed to exclude outsiders, but it failed to supply the colonies with desired goods and led to resentment and local complicity in the **contraband trade**. It also failed to protect imperial shipping, exemplified in the daring and successful raid carried out by Dutch admiral Piet Heyn, sailing for the Dutch West India Company, who attacked and captured the entire flota off **Matanzas** in 1628. *See also* Colonial Institutions; Corsairs Attacks

Further Readings
De la Fuente, Alejandro, et al. "Havana and the Fleet System: Trade and Growth in the Periphery of the Spanish Empire, 1550–1610." *Colonial Latin American Review* 5, no. 1 (June 1996): 95–115.
Hoffman, Paul E. *The Spanish Crown and the Defense of the Caribbean, 1535–1568: Precedent, Patrimonialism, and Royal Parsimony*. Baton Rouge: Louisiana State University Press, 1980.
Lane, Kris E. *Pillaging the Empire: Piracy in the Americas, 1500–1750*. Armonk, NY: M.E. Sharpe, 1998.

Sherry Johnson

U.S. Expansionism (Nineteenth Century)

Since independence in 1776, territorial expansionism was a constant in U.S. history, and Cuba figured prominently as a target of those expansionist aspirations. The United States purchased Louisiana in 1803 and Florida in 1819. It annexed Texas in 1845 and Oregon a year later. At the end of the Mexican War in 1848, it incorporated into the Union what later became the western states of New Mexico, Arizona, Nevada, and California.

Thomas Jefferson, in negotiations prior to the acquisition of Florida, did not dismiss war with Spain to take over Cuba, which he deemed part of the continental United States, because a navy was not required for its protection due to the island's geographic proximity. What stopped him was the knowledge that other European nations would side with Spain in case of a conflict, especially Great Britain, which preferred Cuba as a small colonial nation rather than a state within the Union. Thus, by 1823 Secretary of State John Quincy Adams was claiming that the United States would protect the status quo in the Caribbean while quietly anticipating annexation of the island. That same year, the Monroe Doctrine proclaimed that the United States would not allow any European intervention in the Americas. However, three years later, Spain's fears of losing the island were assuaged when Secretary of State Henry Clay indicated that as long as Spain did not try to regain old colonial territories, no nation in the Americas would be allowed to intervene in Cuban affairs.

By the mid-1800s, American policy toward Cuba changed as Southern expansionists demonstrated a desire to add new proslavery states. During the presidencies of James K. Polk (1846–1849), Franklin Pierce (1853–1857), and James Buchanan (1857–1861), the United States repeatedly pressured Spain into selling the island, and to that end, the belligerent Ostend Manifesto was written in 1854. This was a document that threatened war against Spain if it did not sell Cuba to the United States.

After the U.S. Civil War, the United States again became interested in expansionism. The purchase of Alaska in 1867 expanded the United States beyond its continental domains, but the need for a foothold in the Caribbean became increasingly pressing. The **Ten Years' War** offered the United States yet another opportunity for annexation, especially when considering the many insurgents who favored making the island part of the Union. President Ulysses S. Grant's plan was first to recognize the Cuban insurgents and then, upon achieving independence from Spain, to incorporate the island into the Union. However, Secretary of State Hamilton Fish opposed the scheme, expressing concerns that annexation would strain relations between the United States and Great Britain. Then the idea of selling the island surfaced in Spain but was dropped after the assassination of its main proponent, president Juan Prim. As a result, Cuba remained a Spanish colony. By the end of the nineteenth century, Great Britain was notably less interested in Cuban affairs, concentrating on expanding its own empire in Africa and Asia. This reduction in interest afforded the United States the freedom to pursue annexation. Furthermore, the outbreak of the **War of Independence** in 1895 threatened U.S. business interests on the island. In 1896, the United States proposed that Spain maintain nominal control of Cuba while the island practiced autonomy under North American guidance. Then, in 1898, the United States declared war on Spain and intervened in Cuba, occupying the island despite the fact that the Teller Amendment of April 1898 assured the transfer of political power to the Cubans. In 1901, the **Platt Amendment** to the Cuban Constitution afforded the United States the right to control Cuban affairs, thus completing the expansionist cycle that began with the administration of Thomas Jefferson. *See also* Annexationism; Appendix 10; Autonomism; Spanish Colonialism (Nineteenth Century)

Further Readings

Foner, Philip S. *A History of Cuba and Its Relations with the United States*. 2 vols. New York: International Publishers, 1962–1963.

Guerra, Ramiro. *La expansión territorial de los Estados Unidos a expensas de España y de los países hispanoamericanos*. 3rd ed. Havana: Editorial de Ciencias Sociales, 1973.

Martínez-Fernández, Luis. *Torn between Empires: Economy, Society, and Patterns of Political Thought in the Hispanic Caribbean, 1840–1878*. Athens: University of Georgia Press, 1994.

May, Robert E. *The Southern Dream of a Caribbean Empire, 1854–1961*. Baton Rouge: Louisiana State University Press, 1973.

Portell-Vilá, Herminio. *Historia de Cuba en sus relaciones con los Estados Unidos y España*. Havana: Editorial Jesús Montero, 1938–1941.

Luis Miguel García Mora

Varela y Morales, Félix (1788–1853)

Félix Varela was a cleric, teacher, thinker, and promoter of liberal philosophy. He was the son of a Spanish officer stationed in St. Augustine, Florida, where he lived the first fourteen years of his life. Relocating to Cuba against his father's wishes—who wanted him to join the army—Varela matriculated at the San Carlos y San Ambrosio Seminary, where he studied Latin and philosophy. In 1811, after earning a bachelor's degree in theology at the **University of Havana**, Varela was ordained into the priesthood. He taught philosophy at the seminary where he had studied, mentoring and befriending students who later on had great influence in Cuban education, politics, and culture; among these students were **José Antonio Saco, Domingo del Monte**, and **José de la Luz y Caballero**.

As a teacher, Varela taught in Spanish, rather than Latin, and applied experimentation in the study of science. In 1817, he joined the Real Sociedad Económica, which later on awarded him with the title of Socio de Mérito (member of honor). He published speeches and articles in several periodicals: *Diario de Gobierno, El Observador Habanero*, and *Memorias de la Real Sociedad Económica de La Habana*.

In 1822, Varela began his political work with the publication of his essay "Observaciones sobre la constitución política de la monarquía española" and his election to the Spanish Cortes. An abolitionist, Varela offered, along with other representatives from the Americas, a proposal for the independence of the Latin American nations. Sentenced to death by the Spanish crown for sedition, Varela sought refuge in Gibraltar and then managed to escape to New York. In the United States, where he lived the rest of his life, he worked as a journalist and promoted the Cuban cause for independence, primarily through his newspaper *El Habanero*, which was regularly smuggled into Cuba.

With his former student José Antonio Saco, Varela edited in 1830 the weekly *El Mensajero Semanal*, a publication that defended the Catholic faith against Protestant attacks made in the American peri-

Félix Varela y Morales, cleric, philosopher, and patriot. Nineteenth-century sketch by Esteban Valderrama.

odicals *The Protestant Abridger* and *Annotator*. He also collaborated with the journals *El Revisor Político y Literario*, the *Revista Bimestre Cubana*, and *La Moda*. During this period, Varela founded several schools for children and was active in numerous social and church-related activities.

In 1832, he rejected an amnesty offer from the Spanish government, adhering to his pro-independence beliefs. In 1837, he was named vicar of New York. Four years later, he earned a doctorate in theology and began editing with Charles C. Pise the monthly publication *The Catholic Expositor and Literary Magazine*. During the 1840s he wrote dozens of articles on religious themes. One of his best works was *Cartas a Elpidio*, a criticism of superstition and fanaticism. He also wrote articles on pedagogy and the teaching of young children, translated into Spanish texts on parliamentary procedures, and published the first edition of a book of poetry by **Manuel de Zequeira**. In poor health, he left New York City for St. Augustine, where he died in 1853.

Varela's ideas produced much discussion during his lifetime. After his death, his pro-independence sentiments influenced the poet-patriot **José Martí**. In the twentieth century, Cuban intellectuals studied Varela's writings and celebrated him as "the one who first taught us how to think." In the 1990s, there was a move within the Catholic Church to canonize Varela, and in the United States the Postal Service issued a stamp honoring his memory and contributions. In 2002 a Cuban dissident group called Proyecto Varela collected 11,000 signatures petitioning democratic reforms. *See also* Abolition and Emancipation; Political Exile (Nineteenth Century); Press and Journalism (Eighteenth and Nineteenth Centuries); Science and Scientists (Eighteenth and Nineteenth Centuries)

Further Readings

Céspedes García-Menocal, Carlos Manuel de. *Pasión por Cuba y por la iglesia: aproximación biográfica al P. Félix Varela*. Madrid: Biblioteca de Autores Cristianos, 1998.

Torres-Cuevas, Eduardo. *Félix Varela: los orígenes de la ciencia y con-ciencia cubanas*. Havana: Editorial de Ciencias Sociales, 1995.

Varela, Félix. *Obras*. Havana: Editorial Cultura Popular, 1997.

María Dolores González-Ripoll Navarro

Vegueros' Revolts

The Vegueros' Revolts were a series of armed conflicts that arose as a result of a decision by the Spanish crown in 1717 to create a government monopoly on the sale of tobacco, a measure that was considered economically unjust by the tobacco growers (*vegueros*), plantation owners, and mill owners. An uprising by the tobacco growers in 1717 forced Governor Vicente Raja and the officials sent to enforce the monopoly to return to Spain. Raja's replacement, Gregorio Guazo Calderón, reestablished the monopoly, but he was plagued by further problems when Spanish military forces revolted because they went unpaid. Divisions among the rebels led some to make a pact with the Factoría, the commercial establishment created by the crown to sell tobacco. The conflict continued sporadically for several years and reached another climax in 1723 when the government executed twelve insurgent tobacco growers. Violence by the authorities led many tobacco growers to relocate to new agricultural zones away from the grip of the colonial government, particularly into **Pinar del Río**. In 1740 the crown established the **Real Compañía de Comercio de La Habana**, which took over the tobacco monopoly as well as responsibility for the export of Cuban sugar, wood, and leather. The revolt of the tobacco growers merits a prominent place in Cuban history because it was one of the first instances when Cuban interests were in sharp conflict with the interests of the crown. The conflict is viewed by some as a precursor to the economic disputes that would eventually sharply divide the Creoles and the crown and contribute to the desire for independence. *See also* Bourbon Reforms; Cigars and Cigar Making; Colonial Institutions; Tobacco Industry

Further Readings

Johnson, Sherry. *The Social Transformation of 18th-Century Cuba* Gainesville: University Press of Florida, 2001.

Rivero Muñiz, José. *Tabaco, su historia en Cuba.* Havana: Instituto de Historia, Academia de Ciencias de la República de Cuba, 1965.

María Dolores González-Ripoll Navarro

Velázquez, Diego (1465–1524)

Diego Velázquez was Cuba's conqueror and first Spanish governor. After fighting in Spain's campaign against the kingdom of Naples, Velázquez participated in **Columbus**'s second voyage to the New World. As governor in the island of Hispaniola, he founded several villages to the north of the island and became a powerful landowner. With intentions of incorporating Cuba to Diego Columbus's viceregal domains, he prepared an expedition to Cuba, taking with him several conquistadors whose exploits and fame would outshine his own: Hernán Cortés, Bernal Díaz del Castillo, Pedro de Alvarado, Francisco Hernández de Córdova, Cristóbal de Olid, Juan de Grijalba, and Diego de Ordaz.

The expedition left for Cuba in 1510 and disembarked on the port of Palmas, near Guantánamo Bay. After capturing and sentencing to death the Indian chief **Hatuey**, considered Cuba's first hero, Velázquez and his men established Cuba's first Spanish settlement, the town of Nuestra Señora de la Asunción de **Baracoa** (1511). From there, he founded a few other villages throughout the island, including San Cristóbal de La Habana and **Santiago de Cuba**.

Velázquez was in charge of distributing Indians to the Spanish colonizers and also offered landholdings to members of his expedition. In 1519, Hernán Cortés, whom Velázquez had appointed as mayor of Santiago de Cuba, was chosen to lead an expedition to Mexico. Though Velázquez sent Pánfilo de Narváez to curtail Cortés's plans of conquering Mexico and to bring him back to Cuba, Narváez failed in his mission. Cortés conquered Mexico and renamed it New Spain, and his fame and influence grew, while Velázquez's reputation and importance diminished. Velázquez died in Santiago de Cuba in 1524 as he prepared to return to Spain. *See also* Colonial Settlements, Early; Conquest; Labor Institutions, Early

Further Readings

Artiles Rodríguez, Jenaro. *La Habana de Velázquez.* Havana: Municipio de La Habana, 1946.

Instituto de Havana Historia, Historia de Cuba. *La Colonia, evolución socioeconómica y formación nacional de los orígenes hasta 1867.* Havana: Editora Política, 1994

Wright, Irene A. *The Early History of Cuba, 1492–1586*. New York: Macmillan, 1916.

María Dolores González-Ripoll Navarro

Voluntarios (Volunteer Corps), Cuerpo de

The Cuerpo de Voluntarios was an armed citizenry militia that figured prominently during the **Ten Years' War** and the **War of Independence**. These corps were overwhelmingly composed of Spaniards who opposed Cuba's independence and the application of social and political reforms. Prior to the planned invasion of Cuba by **Narciso López** in 1850, there was already in the city of **Cárdenas** a group of so-called noble neighbors who preceded the formal establishment of the Voluntarios. With the outbreak of war in 1868, Captain-General Francisco Lersundi reorganized the existing corps and created new ones. The number of volunteers grew rapidly, with battalions being established in nearly every town on the island. They were particularly important in the large mercantile cities. In June 1869, there were 30,000 volunteers, of which 4,000 resided in Havana. Volunteer colonels in Havana included José Eugenio Moré, Julián de Zulueta, Manuel Martínez Rico, Feliciano Ibáñez, Nicolás Martínez Valdivieso, all of the wealthy landowners, and peninsular businessmen who supported them, as did the Church and the Bank of Spain. These armed citizens were the military might of the Peninsular counterrevolution against the reforms that threatened the so-called national integrity. Fueled by the press, they adopted a violent stance against those they considered upstarts. They planted the seeds of terror in the streets of Havana, with which they were entrusted when the regular forces were sent on campaigns, giving place to events such as the attack on the Teatro Villanueva or the assault on the **Palace of Aldama** (also see **Miguel Aldama**). They deposed General Domingo Dulce and imposed harsh decisions such as the execution of the medical students in 1871 for their alleged profanation of a loyalist's tomb. Beginning in 1874, with the change of regime in Spain and the abandonment of the proposed reforms, the government channeled the volunteers' rabid pro-Spanish sentiment. The voluntarios also played a critical role during the War of Independence.

Further Readings

Barcia Zequeira, María del Carmen. *Élites y grupos de presión: Cuba, 1868–1898*. Havana: Editorial de Ciencias Sociales, 1998.

Ribó, José J. *Historia de los voluntarios cubanos*. 2 vols. Madrid: Imprenta de N. González, 1872–1874.

Roldán de Montaud, Inés. *La Restauracion en Cuba: el fracaso de un proceso reformista*. Madrid: CSIC, 2001.

Inés Roldán de Montaud

War of Independence

The Cuban War of Independence was a three-year-long conflict (1895–1898) between Cuban insurgents and Spanish authorities culminating in the intervention of the United States (1898) and the eventual establishment of a Cuban republic (1902). In the United States, the conflict is often referred to as the War of 1898 or the Hispanic-American War; Cuban scholars have insisted on the more accurate term Guerra Hispano-Cubana-Americana (Spanish-Cuban-American War).

Beginning in 1868, Cuban *patriots* fought to free the island of Spanish colonial rule. The **Ten Years' War**, which lasted from 1868 to 1878, devastated much of the island's economic infrastructure but failed to resolve the question of Cuba's independence. In 1895, as Cuban frustrations with Spanish rule again mounted, Cuban guerrillas launched an offensive beginning with the Grito de Baire.

The early stages of the war were characterized by debilitating setbacks for the revolutionary movement. Shortly after the February 24, 1895, Grito de Baire that ignited the war, Spanish authorities arrested rebel leaders in Cuba's major cities. Without the support of these areas, the revolt was restricted to the eastern provinces. In May 1895, the movement suffered a major loss when **José Martí**, a poet and journalist who had coordinated the disparate strains of Cuban separatism into the **Partido Revolucionario Cubano (Cuban Revolutionary Party)**, was killed in action near the town of Dos Ríos.

The Spanish response to the revolt in Cuba was characterized, at first, by attempts at conciliation. General Antonio Martínez Campos, who had led the Spanish army during the Ten Years' War and earned a reputation among Cuban Creoles as a moderate, was dispatched to Havana in 1895 to end the uprising either by force or negotiation. Efforts at a compromise failed. When Cuban rebels rejected his offer of amnesty, Martínez Campos was forced to amass his troops on the eastern end of the island and to enforce a naval blockade. Nearly 120,000 Spanish troops were stationed in Cuba by the end of 1895.

Nevertheless, the Spanish army's numerical superiority counted for little in the face of Cuban guerrilla attacks and the inhospitable and insalubrious terrain of the island. By January 1896, Cuban rebels had reached the environs surrounding Havana. Spanish authorities, sensing they were losing the island, accepted Martínez Campos's resignation and replaced him with General Valeriano Weyler y Nicolau. Unlike his predecessor, Weyler embraced the concept of "total war" in order to defeat the Cubans. He targeted Cuba's rural communities, from which Spanish authorities knew Cuban insurgents drew material support, with a policy of forced removal. These **reconcentraciones**, as they came to be known, herded Cubans into provincial cities where local infrastructures, already burdened by the disruptions of the war,

could not meet the most basic needs. Nearly 500,000 people were displaced by the reconcentrations; about half of these died. It has been estimated that another 100,000 Cubans were forced into temporary exile during the war. As news of Weyler's policy spread around the world, and especially in the United States, Weyler became known as "the Butcher" and came to symbolize the worst of Spanish rule on the island.

By early 1897, Weyler's military strategy—pacifying the western end of the island before moving on the mass of Cuban insurgents in Oriente province—was proving successful. In December 1896 Spanish troops ambushed and killed **Antonio Maceo** and Francisco (Panchito) Gómez, son of **Máximo Gómez**, dealing a severe blow to the insurgent army's leadership and morale. Despite the death of Maceo and the ever-increasing number of Spanish soldiers arriving on the island, Weyler was unable to defeat the insurgency. Disease, mainly in the form of yellow fever, decimated unacclimated Spanish troops, and the rugged terrain of eastern Cuba made movement difficult—all this against the backdrop of mounting debt and frustration in Spain.

For its part, the insurgent army confronted its share of problems. The United States declared its neutrality vis-à-vis the conflict in June 1895. It enforced a ban, albeit imperfectly, on U.S. military or financial support to the Cubans. Denied this support, Cuban forces were plagued with chronic shortages of supplies and weapons. Cuban insurgents, known as **mambises**, often resorted to suicidal machete charges against better-equipped Spanish regular troops. Internally, the Cuban army contended with racial and class conflicts. **Afro-Cubans** who regarded the war as a mission to create Martí's republic of racial equality were confronted by white Cubans who were unprepared and often unwilling to regard black and mulatto soldiers as equals.

Cuban insurgents during the War of Independence (1895). Gift of Ramiro Fernández, courtesy of the Museum of Arts and Sciences, Daytona Beach, Florida.

In February 1898 the equilibrium of the Spanish-Cuban conflict was altered with the explosion of the **USS *Maine***. The New York–based ship was anchored in Havana when it was destroyed and sunk. More than 260 crew members lost their lives in the blast. Newspapers in the United States, and especially in New York City, blared accusations of sabotage at the Spanish government. Despite President William McKinley's attempts to defuse the crisis, the U.S. public, already outraged by the actions of Weyler, demanded retribution. By early April, the U.S. Congress approved a resolution not only recognizing Cuba's independence but also calling for the immediate withdrawal of Spanish forces. Spain responded to the United States by breaking off diplomatic relations. By April 25, the United States and Spain were formally at war.

The war between Spain and the United States was short in duration. Within a month of the declaration of war by Congress, the American navy under Admiral George Dewey had routed the Spanish navy in the Pacific. By mid-May 1898, the United States took hold of Guam, and the theater of operations turned to the Caribbean. The first U.S. ground forces arrived in Cuba in late June 1898, and after vic-

tories at Las Guásimas, at El Caney, and most famously at San Juan Hill, the war was all but over. Overcome by the superiority of the U.S. military, the debilitating biological milieu of the island, and internal pressures to surrender, Spanish troops in **Santiago de Cuba** capitulated on July 17, 1898. In December of that year, the United States and Spain signed a peace treaty in Paris. Spanish control of Cuba ended on January 1, 1899. For the United States, the cost of the war with Spain was high. American troops were more likely to succumb to yellow fever than to die in combat. In addition, the need for a rapid deployment of soldiers exposed grave weaknesses in U.S. military preparedness.

Although the intervention of armed forces from the United States helped to secure the end of Spanish rule in Cuba, relations between leaders of Cuba's fledgling army and their U.S. counterparts were often strained. U.S. military leaders in Santiago, for example, excluded Cuban general **Calixto García** from the formal procedures surrounding the Spanish surrender of the city (see **Appendix 9**). Moreover, some U.S. leaders regularly complained that Cuban insurgents were not only ill-suited to combat but ill-prepared for self-government. U.S. troops left Cuba in 1902 and handed a mediated control of the island's government to president **Tomás Estrada Palma**. Thereafter, the **Platt Amendment** to the Cuban Constitution ensured, among other things, that the United States would continue to have a direct influence on Cuba's affairs (see **Appendix 10**). *See also* Political Exile (Nineteenth Century); Spanish Colonialism (Nineteenth Century); U.S. Expansionism (Nineteenth Century)

Further Readings

Ferrer, Ada. *Insurgent Cuba: Race, Nation, and Revolution, 1868–1898*. Chapel Hill: University of North Carolina Press, 1999.

Foner, Philip S. *The Spanish-Cuban-American War and the Birth of American Imperialism, 1895–*

1902. New York: Monthly Review Press, 1972.

Offner, John L. *An Unwanted War: The Diplomacy of the United States & Spain over Cuba, 1895–1898*. Chapel Hill: University of North Carolina Press, 1992.

Pérez, Louis A., Jr. *The War of 1898: The United States and Cuba in History and Historiography*. Chapel Hill: University of North Carolina Press, 1998.

John A. Gutiérrez

4

History: The Republican Period (1902–1958)

ABC Revolutionary Society

The ABC Revolutionary Society was the single largest mass movement against the government of **Gerardo Machado** during the 1930s. The ABC was founded in 1931, and the organization quickly developed a mass following, especially among young professionals. Its leaders were prominent Cuban intellectuals like **Jorge Mañach**, Joaquín Martínez-Sáenz, and Carlos Saladrigas, and its ideology was a mélange of nationalism, corporatism, and liberal democratic principles. The ABC, at least in its rhetoric, was firmly opposed to foreign control of the Cuban economy, and its program promised a nationalist path to capitalist development. The organization's name derived from its secretive structure: The leading cell of the movement was "A," the second level cell "B," and so on. Each cell had around ten members. Despite this internal structure, the ABC was more of a mass movement than it was a political party, and it was never ideologically unified. The ABC's leadership was elitist, believing that Cuba was not ready for liberal democracy and that state intervention, directed by an intellectual elite, was required to prepare Cubans to assume their civic re-

sponsibilities. The popularity of the ABC had much less to do with the group's program than with its tactics. The ABC carried out bombings and assassinations in order to maintain an environment of insurrectionary violence, which its leaders believed would bring down Machado. When the ABC accepted U.S. Ambassador Sumner Welles's mediation efforts in July 1933, they abandoned the ranks of the anti-Machado opposition. Thereafter the ABC declined rapidly. In the 1940s and 1950s it played only a minor role in Cuban politics. *See also* Foreign Investments (Republican Era); Revolution of 1933

Further Readings

ABC. *El ABC en la mediación*. Havana: Mazo, Caso y Cía, 1934.

ABC. *Doctrina del ABC*. Havana: Publicaciones del Partido ABC, 1942.

Aguilar, Luis E. *Cuba 1933: Prologue to Revolution*. New York: W.W. Norton, 1972.

Cuba y el ABC. Miami: Editora Rex Press, 1977.

Pérez, Louis A., Jr. *Cuba under the Platt Amendment*. Pittsburgh: University of Pittsburgh Press, 1986.

Tabares del Real, José. *La revolución del 30: Sus dos últimos años*. Havana: Editorial de Ciencias Sociales, 1973.

Robert W. Whitney

Agramonte y Pichardo, Roberto (1904–1995)

Roberto Agramonte y Pichardo was a university professor, writer, and politician. He was born in **Santa Clara** on May 3, 1904. He studied at Havana's Instituto de Segunda Enseñanza and later at the **University of Havana**, where he earned two doctorates in 1925. In 1926 he was appointed professor of sociology and history at the University of Havana. Agramonte later served as ambassador to Mexico under President **Ramón Grau San Martín**, later joining the **Ortodoxos (Partido del Pueblo Cubano)** for which he ran unsuccessfully for the vice presidency in 1948. Following **Eduardo Chibás**'s death in 1951, Agramonte became the Ortodoxos's top leader and presidential candidate for the 1952 elections, which were canceled by **Fulgencio Batista**, whose own candidacy lagged behind those of Agramonte and **Carlos Hevia**. Following Batista's fall in 1959, Agramonte returned to Cuba and joined **Fidel Castro**'s original cabinet as foreign minister. A few months later, Castro replaced him, and Agramonte sought exile in Puerto Rico, where he joined the faculty of the University of Puerto Rico and remained active in the anti-Castro movement. His sociological and historical publications include sociology and psychology textbooks and biographical studies on **José Martí**, **Enrique José Varona**, and **José de la Luz y Caballero**. *See also* Coup of 1952 (March 10); Puerto Rico, Cubans in

Further Reading
Portell-Vilá, Herminio. *Nueva historia de la República de Cuba*. Miami: La Moderna Poesía, 1986.

Luis Martínez-Fernández

Auténticos (Partido Revolucionario Cubano)

The Partido Revolucionario Cubano (Auténticos) was organized in 1934 following the demise of the "one hundred days" of the **Ramón Grau San Martín** provisional government in 1933. A party founded by **José Martí** in 1892 had first carried the name **Partido Revolucionario Cubano**. The Auténticos, as the members of the new party were commonly referred to, came to power, when Grau was elected in 1944, upon defeating **Fulgencio Batista**'s prime minister Carlos Saladrigas. They swept five out of six provinces. In part because of the heady reform sentiment of 1933, the Auténticos' government of Grau raised enormous popular expectations, as they held power from 1944 to 1948 under Grau, and from 1948 to 1952 under **Carlos Prío Socarrás**. However, after decades of political exile and disillusionment, the Auténticos were ready to use public office to enrich themselves, rather than to implement reform, just as all other Cuban governments had done. Because of their uncertainty about the length of their time in office, Auténticos transformed government service into an opportunity to acquire as much personal wealth as possible. The ranks of the civil service grew fat with those who wanted their turn at the public till. *Gangsterismo* described the system of party thuggery. Auténtico rule became synonymous with corruption, graft, violence, and terror. By 1950, 11 percent of the working population was on the government payroll, earning 80 percent of the national budget. Another 8 percent of the budget went toward pensions. The minister of education was accused of stealing $20 million, while the figure attributed to Grau himself was $174 million. When Batista overthrew them in 1952, the Auténticos left behind a thoroughly discredited government and a demoralized Cuban population. As a result of their overwhelming graft and corruption, few Cubans were sorry to see the Auténticos, who had symbolized such hope for reform, go the way of other Cuban politicians.

In 1947, a group split off from the Auténticos and formed the **Ortodoxos (Par-**

tido del Pueblo Cubano). This party, led by the charismatic **Eduardo Chibás**, grew quickly and drew many who became instrumental in the 1959 **Revolution**, most notably **Fidel Castro**.

The Auténticos, along with the Ortodoxos, supplied a large number of the new provisional revolutionary government leaders in 1959. Although they had contributed to Batista's fall, it was not clear at first if they stood to gain from the 1959 Revolution. Eventually, they did not unless they became Fidelistas. *See also* Coup of 1952 (March 10); Revolution of 1933

Further Readings

Ameringer, Charles D. *The Cuban Democratic Experience: The Auténtico Years, 1944–1952*. Gainesville: University Press of Florida, 2000.

Portell-Vilá, Herminio. *Nueva historia de la República de Cuba*. Miami: La Moderna Poesía, 1986.

Riera, Mario. *Cuba política, 1899–1955* Havana: Imprenta Modelo, S.A., 1955.

Vignier, E., and G. Alonso. *La corrupción política y administrativa en Cuba, 1944–1952*. Havana: Editorial de Ciencias Sociales, 1973.

Paula J. Pettavino

Bacardí Moreau, Emilio (1844–1922)

Emilio Bacardí Moreau was a prolific and talented writer as well as a politician and successful entrepreneur. Born in **Santiago de Cuba**, he displayed a natural talent for writing from a very early age. After completing his primary education, he moved to Barcelona. During his career he authored numerous books including *Vía Crucis* (1914), *Magdalena, Doña Giomar* (1916), *El abismo*, and the monumental *Crónicas de Santiago de Cuba* (1908–1909). His works also include the travel chronicle *Hacia tierras viejas* and a wide variety of articles of a historical and philosophical nature.

A dedicated advocate of Cuban independence, Bacardí was twice deported to Africa, where he was imprisoned in Spanish jails. After independence, he was elected mayor of Santiago in 1901 and senator in 1905. Bacardí was regarded as an honest and capable public servant. A gifted businessman, his liquor company, which carried the family name, expanded under his leadership. At his funeral, Dr. Antonio Bravo Correoso commented on the diversity of his talents: "Bacardí was of sincere spirit, generous and philanthropic. A novelist, benefactor, dramatist, chronicler, politician and businessman." *See also* Bacardí Family; Rum

Further Readings

Bacardí y Moreau, Emilio. *Crónicas de Santiago de Cuba*. 10 vols. Madrid: Gráficas Breogán, 1972.

Foster, Peter. *Family Spirits: The Bacardí Saga*. Toronto: Mcfarlane Walter & Ross, 1990.

Julio Domínguez García

Baliño, Carlos (1848–1926)

Carlos Baliño was one of the founding figures of Cuban socialism and communism. An early supporter of Cuban independence, he spent thirty-three years in exile in the United States (1869–1902). Making his living as a tobacco worker in Tampa and Key West, Baliño made contact with socialist thinkers and activists linked with the work of Daniel de León (founder of the Socialist Labor Party) and the Knights of Labor as well as with the independence group around **José Martí**, who founded the **Partido Revolucionario Cubano** in 1892. On his return to Cuba in 1902, Baliño began an active career of socialist proselytism beginning with the establishment of a Socialist Propaganda Club in 1903, then the writing of a pamphlet titled *Verdades socialistas* (Socialist Truths), and culminating in the creation of the Socialist Party of Cuba in 1906. Between 1908 and 1917 he withdrew from political activities.

Under the influence of the 1917 Russian Revolution he wrote pro-Soviet tracts, and in 1923, together with a small number of early Cuban Marxists, he contributed to the creation of the Communist Group of Havana, whose newspaper *Lucha de Clases* he founded the following year. The Havana group, together with a number of similar communist groupings in other regions of Cuba, constituted the nucleus of the first Cuban communist party (**Partido Comunista**), established in 1925, in which Baliño was a founding member. Although Baliño's thought was permeated with utopian socialist and Lasallean concepts, contemporary Cuban historiography considers him as the founding figure of Cuban Marxism. *See also* Communist Party, Cuban (Partido Comunista Cubana [PCC]); Political Exile (Nineteenth Century); Tobacco Industry; War of Independence

Further Readings

Gómez García, Carmen. *Carlos Baliño: primer pensador marxista cubano.* Havana: Editorial de Ciencies Sociales, 1985.
Tellería Toca, Evelio. *Carlos B. Baliño López en el periodismo revolucionario cubano.* Havana: Editorial Pablo de la Torriente, 1989.

Barry Carr

Barquín López, Ramón María (1914–)

Colonel Ramón Barquín was the leader of a group of progressive army officers who unsuccessfully attempted to overthrow **Fulgencio Batista** in 1956; after the fall of Batista, Barquín commanded the old armed forces for a few hours before **Fidel Castro** took power on January 1, 1959.

Unlike many officers in the Cuban army, Barquín was a professional soldier, having graduated from service academies in Cuba and Mexico, and he studied warfare in the United States. After Batista's 1952 coup d'état, Barquín—then military attaché in Washington, D.C.—began to conspire against the dictatorship with

Colonel Ramón Barquín López endured three years of imprisonment for his involvement in an anti-Batista democratic conspiracy. Photograph courtesy of Ramón Barquín López.

other democratically oriented young officers. But in April 1956 "the Conspiracy of the Pure" (the group became known as "los Puros") was discovered, and Barquín was imprisoned.

In mid-December 1958, with Batista's army near collapse as Castro's troops advanced, members of the high command schemed to oust Batista and appoint Barquín military head of a junta to negotiate with the rebel leader. They failed to carry out the plan.

Barquín was freed from prison on January 1, 1959, as Batista fled Cuba, and was placed in command of the shattered forces of the outgoing regime. He arrested several of its chiefs, then ceded control to the Rebel Army.

The new government sent him to Europe as ambassador-at-large. Disillusioned with the **Revolution**, he resigned in 1960 and went into exile in Puerto Rico, where he wrote *El día que Fidel Castro se apoderó de Cuba* (1978) and *Las luchas guerrilleras en Cuba* (1975). He also founded various educational and civic institutions, among them the American Military Academy. Almost ninety years old, Barquín remains active in educational and athletic endeavors. Each year, he runs in the New York Marathon and other races. *See also* Batista, Struggle Against; Carrillo, Justo; Coup of 1952 (March 10); Puerto Rico, Cubans in

Further Reading

Barquín López, Ramón M. *El día que Fidel Castro se apoderó de Cuba*. San Juan: Editorial Rambar, 1978.

Roger E. Hernández

Batista, Struggle Against

Shortly after ascending to power as a result of the military **coup of 1952, Fulgencio Batista** faced widespread opposition that culminated in a revolutionary struggle that toppled his regime on January 1, 1959. The anti-Batista insurrection was a complex multistranded process that combined legal and clandestine actions by students, workers, members of the bourgeoisie, dissident figures within the military, and sections of the peasantry. Well-established parties such as the **Ortodoxos** and **Auténticos** participated alongside new formations such as the Directorio Estudiantil and the **Twenty-sixth (26th) of July Movement**. The struggle involved the construction of an elaborate urban underground, the building of an extensive international network providing protection and funds for the insurrectionists, and the creation of several guerrilla organizations based in eastern Cuba. Although the guerrillas of the **Sierra Maestra** wing of the 26th of July Movement and their chroniclers have dominated the story of the struggle, they

were only one of many anti-Batista organizations, which ranged from conservative religious groups to the Cuban Communists of the **Partido Socialista Popular** (PSP) whose actions became important in the second half of 1958.

Initially, responses to Batista's 1952 coup were weak. Traditional parties like the Auténticos and Ortodoxos were disorganized and demobilized by the arrests and exile of many of their leaders, and while they spawned several clandestine organizations, they provided no platform of immediate action or program to orient their members, preferring instead to call on their rank and file to prepare for participation in the 1954 elections.

The first dramatic act of resistance came in the summer of 1953 when a young Ortodoxo, **Fidel Castro**, launched an assault on the **Moncada Army Barracks** in **Santiago de Cuba**, the country's second largest military base. The assault on Moncada was of enormous significance. It brought Fidel Castro to national prominence, radicalized sections of urban youth, and convinced many that the struggle against Batista had both a military and political dimension. Castro survived the almost suicidal assault, and his defense speech, later published as *History Will Absolve Me* (1953), became a key document in the anti-Batista underground (see **Appendix 11**).

Supporters of an armed strategy grew in numbers in 1953 and 1954. The 1954 elections were widely regarded as a sham, and most parties refused to participate, the result being that Batista, unopposed, won a new term. In 1955 during a series of meetings between representatives of the traditional political parties and Batista, known as the Diálogo Cívico (Civic Dialogue), political moderates tried to negotiate a political settlement that included the holding of new elections. The failure of the Civic Dialogue opened up a new stage in the struggle, one in which the initiative passed to groups and individuals advocating armed resistance.

The path of armed struggle attracted many supporters. In 1955 two important insurrectionary movements were formed: The Directorio Revolucionario (DR) and the 26th of July Movement. The two movements differed as to goals and strategy. The Directorio emerged from the ranks of the university student movement. Unlike other opposition movements it did not concern itself with elaborating a detailed program of government. Its focus, developed by the charismatic **José Antonio Echeverría**, leader of Cuba's main student organization **Federation of University Students** (FEU), was on the immediate overthrow of the Batista regime to be achieved by assassinating the dictator. In January 1957 plans were launched for an assault on the **Presidential Palace**. The assault, which took place on March 13, was a disaster. Batista had been aware of preparations for the attack, and the balance sheet of the March 13 action was the death of more than fifty DR members including Echevarría, who was shot after an assault on the CMQ radio station. Following the attack on the Presidential Palace, the DR continued its urban work while at the same time it launched a guerrilla front in Las Villas province that became known as the **Segundo Frente del Escambray**.

Armed struggle in the countryside was also to be a major strategy of the second insurrectionary movement formed in 1955—the 26th of July Movement. Initially, however, the movement had envisaged its role as the architect of a series of armed uprisings to be followed by a revolutionary general strike. Fidel Castro, released after a general amnesty in May 1955, had moved first to the United States and then to Mexico, where he commenced plans for an expedition to Cuba. The original concept was to have the *Granma* **expedition** land on Cuban soil to coincide with armed uprisings in Santiago de Cuba

and other towns in Oriente province. Unfortunately for the *Granma* expeditionaries the uprisings had already been suppressed by the time they landed on December 2. A small group of about twelve surviving expeditionaries, among them Castro and **Che Guevara**, managed to secure refuge in the Sierra Maestra. The tiny group of sierra guerrillas survived largely due to the aid, men, and munitions provided them by the urban or *llano* (lowlands) wing of the 26th of July Movement led by **Frank País**. Guerrilla victories at La Plata (January 1957) and El Uvero (in May) inspired the urban underground and secured a small but steady flow of peasant recruits, in particular squatters, or *precaristas*, to the largely urban-sourced guerrilla forces. The failure of the DR's attack on the Presidential Palace in March 1957 and the death of Echeverría altered the balance of power among the insurrectionists in favor of Castro and his fighters. The death of Frank País in July 1957 further strengthened the rural wing of the 26th of July Movement and made Fidel Castro the most nationally recognized figure in the anti-Batista movement. Tension steadily rose between the urban or llano wing and the sierra guerrillas as well as between the 26th of July Movement and the surviving cadres of the DR who had established their own guerrilla front with about 800 fighters in the **Escambray Mountains**. But the military weight of the 26th of July Movement guerrillas was given a major boost with the establishment of the **Segundo Frente Oriental "Frank País"** in 1958, which added several thousand peasant recruits to the guerrilla movement. By late 1958 the guerrillas of the 26th of July Movement had over 7,000 recruits.

In spite of the failure of the April 9 general strike, reduced U.S. support for the regime and dissent within the armed forces enabled the guerrillas to defeat Batista's final summer offensive in summer 1958. As the demoralized Batista forces retreated,

Anti-Batista political cartoon with racist overtones from *Patria* (April-June, 1954). Robert J. Alexander Papers, courtesy of Special Collections and University Archives, Rutgers University Libraries.

Batista y Zaldívar, Fulgencio (1901–1973)

One of the most controversial figures in twentieth-century Cuban history, Fulgencio Batista played a key role in both Cuban revolutions. In the **Revolution of 1933**, he was the leader of the Sergeants' Revolt, which allied itself with the Directorio Estudiantil Universitario (University Student Directory) to topple a U.S.-backed government. In the **Revolution** of 1959, he was the disgraced dictator fleeing in the middle of the night.

Batista was born into abject poverty in Banes, a municipality in what was then northern Oriente Province (now **Holguín Province**). His racial and ethnic origins are the subject of debate. His friends referred to him as *el indio*, while his enemies called him *el negro* (the black man). In addition to Amerindian and Afro-Cuban origins, others speculated that Batista was of Chinese, Mexican, or Greek background. Financial necessity forced Batista to leave school at an early age and work in the sugarcane fields near the giant Boston sugar mill, owned by the United Fruit Company, which economically dominated the region. He went on to work as a railroad brakeman, for a little over a year, before joining the Cuban Army in 1921. His early military career was modestly successful. During his first twelve years he advanced from private to sergeant major, specializing in stenography and typing.

The chaos created by the struggle against the dictatorship of **Gerardo Machado** gave Batista his opportunity to emerge as a revolutionary leader. After Machado fled Cuba in August 1933, the army command structure was in disarray, and the military was held in low regard by the public. Furthermore, the replacement of Machado by Carlos Manuel de Céspedes y Quesada, in a deal orchestrated by

virtually the whole of eastern Cuba fell to the armed opposition and the urban Civic Resistance. Strengthened by the last-minute incorporation of PSP elements, the guerrilla forces raced westward across the island, entering Havana on January 1, 1959. *See also* Coup of 1952 (March 10); Partido Comunista (Partido Socialista Popular [Republican Era]); Students' Movement (Republican Era)

Further Readings

Bonachea, Ramón L., and Marta San Martín. *The Cuban Insurrection 1952–1959*. New Brunswick, NJ: Transaction Books, 1974.

Giménez, Armando. *Sierra Maestra. La Revolución de Fidel Castro*. Buenos Aires: Editorial Lautaro, 1959.

San Martín, Rafael. *El grito de la Sierra Maestra*. Buenos Aires: Ediciones Gure, 1960.

Sweig, Julia E. *Inside the Cuban Revolution: Fidel Castro and the Urban Underground*. Cambridge, MA: Harvard University Press.

Barry Carr

U.S. Ambassador Sumner Welles, left nationalist aspirations unfulfilled. In this climate, Sergeant Batista and a group of enlisted men organized an uprising against the officer corps, which was put into action on September 4, 1933. Batista quickly emerged as the military leader and formed an alliance with several civilian revolutionary groups, principally the Directorio, to topple the government. After solidifying his control of the military, he was promoted to the rank of colonel and army chief of staff.

The alliance between the students and enlisted men was a study in uneasy contrasts from its inception. Batista's followers were primarily men of action from the poorest segments of society, many of them **Afro-Cubans**. The students were idealists and ideologues. They were men and women with years of academic and political training, who spent hours in meetings vigorously debating every nuance of political and public policy. For the most part, the students were from the middle and upper classes of Cuban society and primarily of European background. The marriage of students and soldiers was a troubled one and destined to be short-lived. After four months, Batista's relationship with the Directorio and Provisional President **Ramón Grau San Martín** soured, and he removed the president from power.

The removal of Grau in January 1934 inaugurated the "Period of the Puppet Presidents" (1934–1939) in which Batista dominated Cuban political life behind a constitutional facade. However, much of the far-reaching labor legislation enacted by the revolutionary government was preserved by Batista. In addition, the United States agreed to abrogate the hated **Platt Amendment**, which gave it the right to directly intervene in Cuban political affairs. In the late 1930s, Batista reached agreement with his former allies and the other major political parties on a transition process to democracy, beginning with elections for a Constitutional Assembly in 1939. A new constitution was drafted the following year.

In 1939, Batista resigned as army chief of staff to run in the 1940 presidential elections. Batista, with the help of an unusual alliance forged with the Communist (**Partido Socialista Popular**) and Conservative Parties, defeated Grau and served as chief executive from 1940 to 1944. During World War II, Cuba strongly backed the United States and entered the war just days after the attack on Pearl Harbor. The Constitution prohibited Batista from seeking a second term, but he supported Carlos Saladrigas in the 1944 elections against his old rival Grau. Saladrigas was defeated, and despite speculation that Batista would refuse to hand over power, he took part in a peaceful transfer. After leaving office, he toured Latin America and was hailed as a great democratic leader. Thereafter, he went into self-imposed exile in Daytona Beach, Florida, where he lived for several years.

If his career had ended there, he might be remembered as the man who established/restored democracy to Cuba. But it did not. Batista was elected to the Cuban Senate in 1948 and shortly thereafter began to prepare for the presidential election of 1952. Polls indicated that Batista was unlikely to win the race, and he began to plot a military coup to take power, which he did on March 10, 1952, toppling the government of President **Carlos Prío Socarrás**. Shortly after the coup, Batista partially reestablished the **Constitution of 1940** and pledged to remain in power for only a short time. He was never able to establish a sense of legitimacy and, despite assurances to the contrary, he would remain in power for more than six years. His second stint in power would degenerate into an orgy of corruption and political violence. There were allegations that Batista

Colonel Fulgencio Batista y Zaldívar in 1934. AP/ Wide World Photos.

and his political associates made millions from mob-run casino operations, graft, and the national lottery. Bombing attacks and sabotage by the opposition led inevitably to reprisal by the government in the form of repression of political rallies and the torture and murder of political enemies. There is some doubt about whether Batista authorized the murder of political opponents, but what is certain is that those carrying them out went unpunished.

The Batista government captured **Fidel** and **Raúl Castro** after the failed attack on the **Moncada Army Barracks** on July 26, 1953. But as a result of internal and external pressure, Batista signed an amnesty bill two years later, setting them free. In the late 1950s, the Batista government was buffeted by an urban guerrilla campaign and a military uprising led by Fidel Castro in the **Sierra Maestra**. He was nearly killed during an attack on the **Presidential Palace** in 1957. After the defeat of the Cuban Army in the summer of 1958, high-ranking military leaders began to plot against Batista. A master political strategist, Batista knew it was time to leave. He surprised many friends and foes by departing in the middle of the night on January 1, 1959.

At the age of fifty-eight, Batista fled into ignominious exile, first to the Domin-

ican Republic, then Portugal, and finally Franco's Spain, where he died in 1973. He never set foot in Cuba or the United States again. Batista would spend the last years of his life writing book after book, none of which would garner much attention, in a vain effort to rebuild his image as the "revolutionary leader" of the 1930s. *See also* Batista, Struggle against; Coup of 1952 (March 10); Racial Composition; U.S. Interventions

Further Readings

Acosta Rubio, Raúl. *Ensayo biográfico Batista: reportaje histórico*. Havana: Imp. ÚCAR, García y Cía, 1943.

Adam y Silva, Ricardo. *La gran mentira: 4 de Septiembre de 1933*. Havana: Editorial Lex, 1947.

Argote-Freyre, Frank. "Fulgencio Batista: The Making of a Dictator." Ph.D. Dissertation, Rutgers University, 2003.

Batista, Fulgencio. *Respuesta*. Mexico City: Imp. Manuel León Sánchez, 1960.

Carrillo, Justo. *Cuba 1933: estudiantes, yanquis y soldados*. Miami: Instituto de Estudios Interamericanos, 1985.

Chester, Edmund A. *A Sergeant Named Batista*. New York: Henry Holt, 1954.

Vega Cobiellas, Ulpiano. *La personalidad y la obra del General Fulgencio Batista Zaldívar*. Havana: Cultural, S.A., 1943.

Whitney, Robert. "The Architect of the Cuban State: Fulgencio Batista and Populism in Cuba, 1937–1940." *Journal of Latin American Studies* 32 (May 2000): 435–459.

Whitney, Robert. *State and Revolution in Cuba: Mass Mobilization and Political Change, 1920–1940*. Chapel Hill: University of North Carolina Press, 2001.

Frank Argote-Freyre

Carbó Morera, Sergio (1892–1971)

Sergio Carbó was one of Cuba's most influential journalists and pamphleteers of the twentieth century. As a young journalist, Carbó wrote for the newspapers *La Discusión* and *El Día*. In the early 1920s he edited the newspaper *La Libertad*. Under the *Machadato* (regime of **Gerardo Machado**) Carbó directed the satirical weekly *La Semana*. It was in *La Semana* that Carbó created the popular satirical character "El Bobo." Carbó was a member of General **Mario García Menocal**'s Conservative Party. It was as a *Menocalista* that Carbó participated in the armed uprising against Machado at Gibara in 1931. In early September 1933 Carbó joined the short-lived Pentarchy under **Ramón Grau San Martín**, but thereafter he did not hold any official government position. Nonetheless, Carbó had a strong influence on the first Grau government. It was Carbó who promoted **Fulgencio Batista** to the rank of colonel, and at times he acted as an intermediary between *Batistiano* and the *Guiterista* (pro **Antonio Guiteras**) factions in the government. One reason Carbó could play this role was because he was generally respected (if not always admired) as an astute observer of Cuban political culture, especially during the chaotic events of 1933. Carbó regarded himself as both a realist and a revolutionary. He believed that Cuba should become more democratic after 1933, but he also thought that authoritarian rule was a necessary prerequisite for democracy. Thus Carbó supported Batista over Grau between 1934 and 1940. After 1940 Carbó concentrated on journalism, and he edited the newspaper *Prensa Libre*. He opposed **Fidel Castro** and died in Miami in 1971. *See also* Newspapers (Republican Era); Revolution of 1933

Further Readings

Aguilar, Luis E. *Cuba 1933: Prologue to Revolution*. New York: W.W. Norton, 1973.

De la Osa, Enrique. *En Cuba, primer tiempo, 1943–1946*. Havana: Editorial de Ciencias Sociales, 1990.

Robert W. Whitney

Caribbean Immigration

After the end of Spanish colonial rule in Cuba in 1898 the island experienced a significant demographic change. Caribbean migrant workers played a role in this change, as neighboring islands became an important source of labor. Over 351,500 islanders migrated to Cuba between 1898 and 1938. Estimates for those forty years are of 190,398 Haitians, 116,220 Jamaicans, 23,391 immigrants from the eastern Caribbean, and 33,461 from Puerto Rico, the Dominican Republic, and Central America. Most of these migrants worked in the **sugar industry**, but others worked in the railways as well as coffee and fruit plantations. Female migrants mainly worked as domestics or as seamstresses and dressmakers.

The trends and patterns of Caribbean migration to Cuba differed geographically and numerically. **Santiago de Cuba** was the main port of arrival for most Jamaicans and Haitians, while other groups such as eastern Caribbean islanders arrived directly through northeastern ports in Puerto Padre (present-day **Las Tunas Province**) and Nipe (present-day **Holguín Province**). In particular, Puerto Padre—controlled by the Cuban-American Sugar Company—was the main entrance for Windward and Leeward islanders, the preferred labor force for the administration of that company. Haitians were brought directly to the ports of Nipe and Sagua de Tánamo at different stages. Small groups classified as Central Americans, possibly descendants of Caribbean migrants to the banana plantations and the Panama Canal, arrived through the southern ports of Manzanillo and Júcaro, along with many Jamaicans. Figures on passenger movements suggest that the number of Caribbean workers in Cuba might have been more than what can be inferred from immigration figures.

Caribbean migrants were present in Cuba since the nineteenth century. The 1899 census recorded 1,712 persons born in the "West Indies," most of whom were field laborers, tailors, and carpenters. Some of these individuals were socially active in the Salvation Army. An increase in Caribbean migration took place between 1908 and 1911 when 13,685 non-specified Antilleans entered the country. During those years, they constituted the second largest migrant group in Cuba after Spaniards. But it was during the late 1910s when Caribbean migration increased significantly. Between 1916 and 1920, Cuba received 149,432 Caribbean islanders, amounting to more than a third of the total arriving in the first four decades of the century (351,530). But after the economic crisis of 1921, immigration decreased in the same dramatic way it had increased in the previous years.

During the 1920s, the migration trends of Caribbean workers varied from group to group. Although Jamaican migration experienced a limited increase in 1923 and 1924, immigration from that country started a process of gradual decline during the late 1920s. Haitian migration, however, skyrocketed again in 1924 and experienced dramatic increases in the late 1920s. Between 1920 and 1930, the number of Haitians entering Cuba (150,420) more than doubled that of Jamaicans (65,800), thus reflecting a marked difference in the migration trends of these two groups. In the 1930s, Cuban nationalism, economic depression, the **Revolution of 1933**, and the Nationalization of Labor Law led to the virtual end of Caribbean migration to Cuba. At that time, the government started the repatriation and deportation of migrants. Most British Caribbean islanders, who were already departing from Cuba, left the country in those years, but many who were already settled with family decided to stay. British Windward and Leeward islanders suffered the repatriation process more than the Jamaicans, who had the support of a Jamaican Secretary of Immigration. Haitians, more numerous than the other migrant groups by the early 1930s, experienced more troubles with repatriation, especially in the second half of that decade, when thousands were forcefully expelled from Cuba.

Caribbean islanders, particularly black workers from Haiti, Jamaica, and the eastern Caribbean, experienced social, ethnic, and racial discrimination by sugar entrepreneurs and the wider Cuban society of the time. The Cuban government and the intellectual elites accused them of trying to create a black republic, of bringing diseases to Cuba, and of damaging the nation. The migrants confronted discrimination through different social and cultural practices. Some of them joined the labor movement, particularly in the 1930s. Others created a sense of community and identity through the creation of their own societies, clubs, organizations, and churches. Many of these communities and societies remained active even beyond the 1930s and in some cases still exist today. In towns and cities like Baraguá, Banes, Chaparra, Delicias, and Guantánamo, one can notice the cultural presence and impact of the Haitian and British Caribbean migrants. Their transculturation in the Cuban society is a reality, yet their sense as a distinct community also remains alive. *See also* Afro-Cubans, Immigration (Twentieth Century), Sugar Industry

Further Readings

Carr, Barry. "Identity, Class, and Nation: Black Immigrant Workers, Cuban Communism, and the Sugar Insurgency, 1925–1933." *Hispanic American Historical Review* 78, no. 1 (February 1998): 83–116.

De la Fuente, Alejandro. "Two Dangers, One Solution: Immigration, Race, and Labor in Cuba, 1900–1930." *International Labor and Working-Class History* 51 (Spring 1997): 30–49.

McLeod, Marc C. "Undesirable Aliens: Race, Ethnicity and Nationalism in the Comparison of Haitian and British West Indian Immigrant Workers in Cuba, 1912–1939." *Journal of Social History* 31, no. 3 (1998): 599–623.

Pérez de la Riva, Juan. "Cuba y la migración antillana, 1900–1931." In *La república neocolonial: Anuario de Estudios Cubanos*. Havana: Editorial de Ciencias Sociales, 1979. 2: 3–75.

Jorge L. Giovannetti

Carrillo Hernández, Justo (1912–1998)

Justo Carrillo was a student leader, economist, and politician. During the early 1930s, Carrillo was a student leader of the Directorio Estudiantil Universitario. In 1951 President **Carlos Prío Socarrás** appointed him president of the newly formed Banco Nacional de Fomento Agrícola e Industrial. Carrillo joined the anti-**Batista** struggle, forming the Acción Libertadora organization in 1953. He later led the Montecristi Movement and plotted a coup to liberate Colonel **Ramón Barquín** from his prison cell in Isla de Pinos (now **Isla de la Juventud**). Considered a serious candidate for the presidency in the post-Batista government, **Fidel Castro** reinstated him to his former post at the head of the Banco Nacional de Fomento Agrícola e Industrial in 1959. He broke, however, with Castro and formed the opposition group Movimiento de Rescate Revolucionario. Soon after, Carrillo went into exile in Miami. *See also* Batista, Struggle against

Further Readings

Aguilar, Luis E. *Cuba 1933: Prologue to Revolution*. New York: W.W. Norton, 1973.
Carrillo, Justo. *Cuba 1933: estudiantes, yanquis y soldados*. Miami: Instituto de Estudios Interamericanos, 1985.

Luis Martínez-Fernández

Chibás, Eduardo (1907–1951)

A fiery political orator, Eduardo Chibás stunned Cuba by shooting himself in the stomach at the conclusion of his weekly radio program on August 5, 1951. The shooting, known as his *aldabonazo*, or warning, was intended to alert the Cuban people to the corruption that was destroying their democratic institutions. He died eleven days later.

Born into the wealthy and politically prominent Agramonte family in **Santiago de Cuba**, he would distinguish himself as a student activist in the struggle against **Gerardo Machado**. A lifelong dissident, he had the distinction of serving jail terms under three Cuban presidents, Machado, **Fulgencio Batista**, and **Carlos Prío Socarrás**. Chibás helped establish the **Auténticos (Partido Revolucionario Cubano)**, which swept into power in 1944, defeating a candidate backed by Batista. He became disillusioned with the administration of **Ramón Grau San Martín** (1944–1948), which was plagued by one corruption scandal after another, and decided to organize the **Ortodoxos (Partido del Pueblo Cubano)**. Grau's decision to support Prío in the 1948 presidential election contributed to his decision to break with the Auténticos.

In the late 1940s, he railed against political corruption on his weekly radio program, which was among the most popular in Cuba. The Ortodoxos attracted some of the most talented and revolutionary-minded youth in the country, including **Fidel Castro**, who considered Chibás his political mentor. During his weekly show he would fire off accusations of corruption against the Prío administration (1948–1952) but seldom provide any proof. On one occasion, he accused Education Minister Aureliano Sánchez Arango of stealing money appropriated for school breakfasts to construct a private housing development in Guatemala. Arango denied the charges and dared Chibás to provide the proofs. It was on the night that he was scheduled to unveil the evidence against Arango that Chibás shot himself.

Chibás remained a powerful political symbol in Cuba for years after his death. During the attack on the **Moncada Army Barracks** on July 26, 1953, followers of Castro planned to take over a local radio station and play Chibás's final address to the nation as a clarion call to revolt. The attack failed, and the radio station was not

CUBA CORREOS 65
2001

VERGUENZA
CONTRA DINERO

50 ANIVERSARIO DE LA MUERTE DE
EDUARDO R. CHIBAS

Stamp commemorating the fiftieth anniversary of
Eduardo Chibás's death by suicide, 2001. Luis
Martínez-Fernández Collection.

captured. After the success of the Cuban
Revolution, Fidel Castro gave a graveside
eulogy to Chibás's memory. In the eulogy,
Castro declared that without Chibás the
"Cuban Revolution would not have been
possible."

Further Readings

Argote-Freyre, Frank. "The Political Afterlife of Eduardo Chibás: Evolution of a Symbol, 1951–1991." *Cuban Studies* 32 (2002): 74–97.

Conte Agüero, Luis. *Eduardo Chibás, el adalid de Cuba*. Miami: La Moderna Poesía, 1987.

Frank Argote-Freyre

Colonos

The term *colonos* refers to sugarcane
growers who do not produce sugar but
rather sell cane to other parties, usually
large *centrales*, which take the process beyond the cane harvesting stage. The term
colonos originates from their role as colonizers of new lands. The colono system
of production contrasted with the older
slave-based system and gained preeminence toward the end of the nineteenth
century, when the first sugar centrales
emerged. The new centrales produced
sugar from cane cultivated within their
lands and also purchased from colonos.

The colonos were a diverse group.
Some were former slaves, others were former planters who failed to convert their
sugar plantations into modern centrales,
and many were immigrants, mostly Spaniards. Socially, they ranged from small
landholders to proprietors of large tracts of
land. Colonos of various productive capacities established contractual obligations
with the centrales and were categorized as
either independent colonos (they owned
their land) or *arrendatarios* (they rented
land from the centrales). Typically, sugar
centrales sought to control the colonos
through a variety of mechanisms such as
the ownership over land or **railroads** used
to transport the cane in order to impose
price levels and the timing of the cane's
delivery. While the extent of control over
the colonos varied over time, it was generally more effective among colonos established after 1900 on the eastern half of
the island.

Traditionally, but particularly after the
crisis of 1920–1921, when most centrales
came under U.S. financial control, Cuba's
intelligentsia and nationalist politicians
recognized the predominantly white Creole colono as a symbol of *Cubanidad* (Cubanness) in contraposition to oppressive
foreign interests. This association helped
colonos secure certain protections from
state laws, specifically under the Law of
Sugar Coordination (1937), which assigned colonos a quota of cane production,
established favorable prices, and forced
centrales to grind the colonos' cane. In
1934 the colonos organized as the Na-

tional Association of Colonos to lobby and further their interests. *See also* Foreign Investments (Republican Era); Slavery; Sugar Industry

Further Readings

Guerra y Sánchez, Ramiro. *Azúcar y población en las Antillas*. Havana: Cultural, S.A., 1927.

Martínez-Alier, Juan, and Verena Martínez-Alier. *Cuba, economía y sociedad*. Paris: Editorial Ruedo Ibérico, 1972.

Santamaría García, Antonio, and Luis Miguel García Mora. "Colonos. Agricultores cañeros ¿clase media rural en Cuba ?, 1880–1898." *Revista de Indias* 43, no. 212 (1998): 131–161.

Antonio Santamaría García

Constitution of 1901

The first constitution of the independent Republic of Cuba dates to 1901. The island's independence was compromised to a large degree by the insertion of the **Platt Amendment** into the constitution, which gave the United States the authority to militarily intervene if its interests were imperiled. The Constitution of 1901 remained in place through 1928, although it was briefly reestablished in 1933–1934. A Constitutional Convention to draft the document was called by the United States, then occupying the island, on July 25, 1900. The convention began meeting on November 5, 1900, and drafted a constitution on February 21, 1901; however, revisions to the draft and debate of its contents would go on for another four months. It established a democratic republic and provided for a wide range of individual liberties including freedom of expression, association, press, petition, and religion, among others. The Constitution of 1901 was modeled on the U.S. Constitution. The document established three separate branches of power: the executive, legislative, and judicial. The president was elected by indirect popular vote for a period of four years and was permitted to seek only one additional four-year term. It

established a bicameral legislature, with a House of Representatives, elected every four years by direct popular vote, and a Senate, made up of four senators from each of the six provinces. Senators, who served eight-year terms, were selected by elected provincial legislators and party leaders. The Senate came to exert an important influence, particularly over foreign affairs. The provinces were administered by a directly elected governor and a Provincial Council. The municipal governing system was ill defined by the constitution, however. The constitution provided for equal rights under the law for all citizens. All men over the age of twenty-one were granted the right to vote. It did not provide for the establishment of a military. The Platt Amendment restricted Cuba's national sovereignty. *See also* U.S. Expansionism (Nineteenth Century); U.S. Interventions

Further Readings

Guerra, Ramiro, et al. "La Convención Constituyente." In *Historia de la Nación Cubana*. Havana: Editorial de Historia de la Nación Cubana, 1952. 7: 73–116.

Ibarra, Jorge. *Cuba: partidos políticos y clases sociales (1898–1923)*. Havana: Editorial de Ciencias Sociales, 1992.

López Rivero, Sergio, and Francisco Ibarra. "En torno a 1898. Una exploración en el curso de la aprobación de la Enmienda Platt en la convención constituyente cubana durante el año 1901." *Millars* 18 (1995): 35–66.

Pérez, Louis A., Jr. *Cuba between Empires, 1878–1902*. Pittsburgh: University of Pittsburgh Press, 1983.

José Antonio Piqueras Arenas

Constitution of 1940

The Constitution of 1940 became the fundamental law of the Cuban Republic on July 5, 1940. It replaced the **Constitution of 1901**, the republic's first. Following the social conflicts of the 1920s and 1930s that had culminated with the **Revolution of 1933**, the abrogation of the **Platt Amend-**

ment, and the signing of the new Reciprocity Treaty (1934), a national consensus formed in recognition of the need for a new constitution to consolidate the many social and political accomplishments of the social mobilizations of the previous two decades. Those aspirations led to the passing of the 1939 law for the election of a constitutional assembly.

The elections were originally scheduled to take place in August 1939 but were delayed until November 15 due to pressures from certain U.S. interests seeking to have in place a Residency and Navigation Treaty that would provide guarantees to U.S. citizens residing on the island. **Fulgencio Batista** proposed postponing the treaty negotiations until after the ratification of the new constitution, and the constitutional delegates finally assembled on February 9, 1940. The delegates represented eleven political parties that coalesced into two main blocks: the Socialist Democratic Coalition of Batista, Cuba's strongman and chief of the armed forces since the Sergeants' Revolt of 1934, and the block led by the **Auténticos (Partido Revolucionario Cubano)** of **Ramón Grau San Martín**. While at first Grau's block enjoyed a majority, the balance shifted later on to the other block.

The constitution was finally promulgated on June 5 after several months of intense debates. Although marked by a liberal-bourgeois imprint, the constitution included very progressive measures of democratic governance and social justice, reflecting the influence of progressive voices within the assembly. The document recognized equality among all citizens without distinctions of race and sex; the right of women to vote and hold elective office; and the right to private property along with the state's right to expropriate properties in the interest of society. The constitution also established (1) the need for government intervention in the economy and its ultimate ownership over sub-soil riches and (2) the protection of small farmers and laborers with measures such as the eight-hour workday, the right to unionization, and compensated periods of rest. The constitution also called for the creation of a Tribunal de Cuentas (Accounts Tribunal) and a National Bank to implement the nation's financial and monetary policies; it prohibited the holding of vast extensions of land and set limits on foreign ownership of land. It also established equality within the family, although not applicable to illegitimate children, and supported a democratic, egalitarian, and progressive school system.

The progressive character of the Constitution of 1940 was limited, however, by the fact that many of its articles were to be further defined by future legislation, something that did not fully occur. It remained in vigor until Batista's **coup of 1952**.

Further Readings

Ameringer, Charles D. *The Cuban Democratic Experience: The Auténtico Years, 1944–1952*. Gainesville: University Press of Florida, 2000.

Carbonell Cortina, Néstor. *El espíritu de la constitución cubana de 1940*. Madrid: Playor, 1974.

Marqués Dolz, María Antonia. *Estado y economía en la antesala de la Revolución, 1940–1952*. Havana: Editorial de Ciencias Sociales, 1994.

Riera, Mario. *Cuba política, 1899–1955*. Havana: Imprenta Modelo, S.A., 1955.

Antonio Santamaría García

Coup of 1952 (March 10)

The **Fulgencio Batista**–led coup of March 10, 1952, toppled the constitutionally elected government of **Carlos Prío Socarrás** and was the final nail in the coffin of Cuban democracy. Virtually no one fought to save Prío's corrupt regime, not even Prío, who sought exile in Mexico rather than challenge the conspiracy led by former Cuban President Batista. Although the coup leaders promised a quick return to constitutional government, Batista remained in power for more than six years.

In that time, the failure of the government and the opposition to negotiate a political settlement led to armed struggle against the regime and the triumph of the Cuban **Revolution**.

The road to the coup was paved by eight years of unceasing scandal, graft, and *gangsterismo* (political thuggery) (1944–1952) by the **Auténticos (Partido Revolucionario Cubano)** governments of Prío and his predecessor **Ramón Grau San Martín**. Presidential elections were scheduled for June 1952, and there were three principal candidates, **Carlos Hevia** for the Auténticos, **Roberto Agramonte** for the **Ortodoxos (Partido del Pueblo Cubano)**, and Batista for the Partido de Acción Unitaria (PAU). Election surveys conducted by the news weekly magazines *Bohemia* and *Carteles* indicate that Agramonte was in the lead. In the *Carteles* survey of February 1952, Agramonte was the choice of 30 percent, Batista 23 percent, and Hevia 16 percent, with another 31 percent committed to minor candidates or undecided. In the months leading up to the coup there were clear indications that questions of political power would not be settled at the ballot box. Prío allegedly contemplated his own coup to ensure that the Ortodoxos, who promised to put him on trial, would not gain power. In turn, Batista was approached by several military and civilian factions urging him to lead a takeover. The conspirators were primarily former Batistiano army officers, gradually replaced by the Auténticos after Batista left power in 1944, although several young officers were involved as well. The coup itself was carefully planned and precisely implemented in the early morning hours of March 10. Within several hours, Batista and his fellow conspirators were in control of military installations, police stations, media outlets, and utilities throughout the island. The new government was never able to establish its legitimacy, although it tried to gain acceptance by holding sham elections in 1954 and 1958. *See also* Batista, Struggle Against; Newspapers (Republican Era)

Further Readings

Chester, Edmund. *A Sergeant Named Batista*. New York: Henry Holt, 1954.

Portell-Vilá, Herminio. *Nueva historia de la República de Cuba (1898–1979)*. Miami: La Moderna Poesía, 1986.

"Survey nacional de *Carteles*." *Carteles*, February 10, 1952, 28–34.

Frank Argote-Freyre

Domínguez Navarro, Ofelia (1894–1976)

A journalist, lawyer, and teacher, Ofelia Domínguez Navarro devoted her life to the ideals of feminism. She was a founder of influential women's organizations such as the Alianza Nacional Feminista (National Feminist Alliance) and the Unión Radical de Mujeres (Women's Radical Union). She was a delegate to numerous women's conferences in the 1920s and 1930s. In 1922, she passed the test for notary, becoming the first woman in Cuba to hold such position. A passionate opponent of the government of **Gerardo Machado** (1925–1933), Domínguez Navarro was jailed and exiled for her beliefs. While in exile, she lived in Mexico, where she gained fame as an attorney for her defense of Jacques Monnard, the killer of Leon Trotsky. She was an avowed pacifist and opposed Cuba's entry into World War II. In 1946, she was named vice president of the Federación Internacional de Abogados (International Federation of Lawyers). The following year, she was named secretary general of the Asociación Cubana de las Naciones Unidas (Cuban Association of the United Nations). In 1962, she retired from her work with the United Nations due to health problems. *See also* Feminist Movement (Republican Era); Women's Suffrage Movement.

Further Readings

Domínguez Navarro, Ofelia. *50 años de una vida.* Havana: Instituto Cubano del Libro, 1971.

Núñez Machín, Ana. *Mujeres en el periodismo cubano.* Santiago de Cuba: Editorial Oriente, 1989.

Julio César González Pagés

Echeverría, José Antonio (1932–1957)

José Antonio Echeverría was a beloved student leader and martyr of the **struggle against Batista**'s dictatorship, better known for his participation in a daring but futile attack on **Fulgencio Batista**'s **Presidential Palace** in March 1975.

Echeverría was the president of the **Federation of University Students (FEU)** at the **University of Havana** and founder of the Directorio Revolucionario, an urban guerrilla group. Echeverría was **Fidel Castro**'s friendly rival. Concerned over the publicity that Castro had received after his interview with *New York Times* correspondent Herbert Matthews in early 1957, Echeverría and members of the Directorio Revolucionario decided to escalate their revolutionary activities. They developed a plan to assassinate Batista by storming the Presidential Palace.

On the afternoon of March 13, the members of the Directorio broke in two groups. One group raided the palace, fighting off the guards and soldiers protecting the dictator. The second group, led by Echeverría, took over the CMQ radio station. The objective was to broadcast to Cubans a call to arms against the regime. Announcing, prematurely, that rebel forces had taken over the Presidential Palace and murdered Batista, Echeverría then blew up the station's central power unit.

Leaving the radio station, Echeverría was unaware that the attempt had been a failure, with many of his co-conspirators dead or on the run. Echeverría himself tried to reach the University of Havana, where he would seek sanctuary, but the police chased him and shot him near the steps to the university.

Echeverría's death, and Batista's harsh repression against Echeverría's colleagues after the attack, became a rallying cry for those who opposed the dictatorship. It also created a leadership vacuum that helped Fidel Castro solidify his position in the **Revolution**.

Today a university in Havana bears his name: Colegio Universitario José Antonio Echeverría (commonly referred to as la CUJAE).

Further Reading

Harnecker, Marta. *José Antonio Echeverría: el movimiento estudiantil en la Revolución Cubana.* Buenos Aires: Dialéctica, 1988.

D.H. Figueredo

Estrada Palma, Tomás (1835–1908)

Tomás Estrada Palma, the first president of the Cuban Republic, was born in 1835 to well-to-do parents in **Bayamo**, in the old province of Oriente. He studied law in Seville and, in 1868, joined the **Ten Years' Wars** against Spain. He held different posts in the insurgents' government and in 1875 was named president of the Republic-in-Arms. Two years later he was arrested by the Spanish and deported to Spain. During this period, he embraced **annexationism**.

Returning to the Americas, he married the daughter of the president of Honduras and later moved to the United States, settling in Central Valley, New York, where he was principal of a high school serving mostly Hispanic students. He remained retired from political life until 1887 when revolutionary **José Martí** invited him to preside over political activities and events held in the United States to commemorate the tenth anniversary the Ten Years' War. When the **Partido Revolucionario Cubano** was founded in 1892, Martí ap-

Tomás Estrada Palma, Cuba's first president (1902–1906). Courtesy of the Cuban Heritage Collection of the Otto G. Richter Library of the University of Miami.

pointed Estrada Palma as an adviser and later, in 1895, placed him in charge of the organization.

During the **War of Independence**, he served in the United States as representative of the Republic-in-Arms and distributed over 2 million Cuban pesos to members of Congress whom he lobbied to support the Teller Amendment. This amendment demanded Spain's departure from Cuba and promised that the U.S. government would not intervene in Cuban affairs and would let Cubans control their own political future. In 1898, Estrada Palma dissolved the Partido Revolucionario Cubano.

After Cuba won independence, Estrada Palma was elected president of the republic in 1902. His government was characterized by austere budgetary measures, promotion of education, repayment of debts incurred during the war, and the approval of two agreements with the United States: The Permanent Relations Accord—which established the **Guantánamo U.S. Naval Base**—and the U.S.-Cuba **Reciprocity Treaty** of 1902. Relying on the conservatives, he allowed fraud in the 1904 elections and opted for reelection in the general elections of 1906, against the wishes of the Liberals. Once reelected, he tried to suppress a Liberal uprising using the Rural Guard. Rejecting an offer by veteran generals to mediate his dispute with the Liberals, Estrada Palma requested U.S. military intervention and resigned from his post. The intervention lasted from 1906 to 1909. He retired to his farm in Oriente and died in **Santiago de Cuba** on November 4, 1908. *See also* U.S. Interventions

Further Readings

Camacho, Pánfilo D. *Estrada Palma, el gobernante honrado*. Havana: Editorial Trópico, 1938.

Márquez Sterling, Carlos. *Don Tomás, biografía de una época*. Havana: Editorial Lex, 1953.

Pérez, Louis A., Jr. *Cuba under the Platt Amendment, 1902–1934*. Pittsburgh: University of Pittsburgh Press, 1986.

Pérez-Stable, Marifeli. "Estrada Palma's Civic March: From Oriente to Havana, April 20–May 11, 1902." *Cuban Studies* 30 (1999): 113–121.

José Antonio Piqueras Arenas

Feminist Movement (Republican Era)

The struggle for women's rights in Cuba can be viewed as a series of evolving struggles that advanced through different stages. The first stage, predating Cuban independence, runs roughly from 1880 through 1912 and centers around the concepts of social feminism. In this stage, the focus was on improving conditions for women within their traditional spheres but maintaining traditional roles. The second stage commenced in 1912 and saw the development of feminist suffragettes whose primary goal was to obtain the vote for women. The third stage began in 1918 with the development of liberal feminism, which saw the right to vote as part of a broader struggle to remedy racial, class, and educational inequalities. Liberal feminists sought to extend the right to vote to illiterates. The feminist movement lost a great deal of its impetus after 1934, when women secured the right to vote and run for office. The **Constitution of 1940** guaranteed the rights of women to vote. With the achievement of this goal, the feminist agenda was principally defined by the political Left. *See also* Women's Rights; Women's Suffrage Movement

Further Reading
Stoner, K. Lynn. *From the House to the Streets. The Cuban Woman's Movement for Legal Reform, 1898–1940*. Durham, NC: Duke University Press, 1991.

Julio César González Pagés

Ferrara y Marino, Orestes (1876–1972)

Orestes Ferrara was a politician, diplomat, and essayist. At an early age, he moved to the United States from his native Naples, where he came into contact with Cuban revolutionaries (see **War of Independence**). He enrolled in the first expedition of the steamer *Dauntless*, which landed in Punta Brava in **Camagüey Province** in 1897. He ended with the rank of colonel in the Liberation Army (Ejército Libertador). Thereafter, he became a professor at the **University of Havana** and a lawyer for major corporations. He was a member of the Liberal Party from the time of **José Miguel Gómez** through the presidency of **Gerardo Machado**. He served in a variety of positions, including governor, member of the House of Representatives for Las Villas Province, president of the House of Representatives, ambassador to Washington, and secretary of state. In 1928, Ferrara praised U.S. policy toward Cuba and Latin America during the VI Inter-American Conference celebrated that year in Havana. He fled Cuba after the fall of Machado in 1933 and did not return until 1940, when he was elected as delegate to the Constitutional Assembly. In 1941, he was named ambassador to Madrid. He was active in journalism, particularly at the *Heraldo de Cuba*, which he controlled. Ferrara was also a member of the Academy of History.

He was the author of numerous books, including *Las ideas políticas de José Antonio Saco* (1909), *La Guerra Europea, causas y pretextos* (1916), *Las ideas jurídico-sociales en las constituciones cubanas* (1945), *Maquiavelo: la vida, las obras, la fama* (1943), *El Cardenal Contarini, un gran embajador veneciano* (1956), and *El Papa Borgia* (1943). *See also* Constitution of 1940; Newspapers (Republican Era)

Further Readings
Ferrara, Orestes. *Mis relaciones con Máximo Gómez*. Miami: Ediciones Universal, 1987.
Riera, Mario. *Cuba política, 1899–1955*. Havana: Imprenta Modelo, S.A., 1955.

Manuel de Paz Sánchez

Foreign Investments (Republican Era)

The first major foreign investments in Cuba began in the 1870s, as British capital flowed into the construction of **railroads**. Smaller U.S. investments began to arrive at about the same time into sugar-related activities. In 1901 U.S. investments on the island totaled an estimated $8 million.

Following the signing of the **U.S.-Cuba Reciprocity Treaty** of 1902, U.S. investments in Cuba skyrocketed, surpassing $200 million on the eve of World War I. At the time, however, U.S. investments in Cuba were still second to those of Great Britain. British and U.S. capital dominated the rail industry, most visibly the United Railways of Habana & Regla Warehouses and the William Van Horne companies.

The possibilities for the expansion of the **sugar industry** during World War I and the boom-bust cycle of 1920–1921 left the bulk of Cuba's sugar industry in the hands of U.S. banks and financial institutions. These circumstances allowed a massive wave of U.S. investments that reached $1.1 billion by 1921. Foreign capital from other countries remained minimal. Eighty percent of U.S. investments in Cuba flowed into the sugar industry, particularly into the development of new *centrales* in the eastern half of the island (see **Colonos**). The balance went into the **tobacco industry**, banking, utilities, and other industries.

U.S. investments continued to increase during the balance of the 1920s. They are estimated to have reached at least $1.75 billion in 1928. The level dropped considerably during the depression years, reaching $1 billion in 1940. Monetary devaluation during the depression, the overcapitalization of the sugar industry during the 1920s, and the gradual withdrawal of U.S. capital from the sugar industry explain the decrease in U.S. investments, which reached $568 million in 1946. Investment levels recuperated during the 1950s, reaching $1 billion in 1958; at the time, only 27 percent of those investments were in **agriculture**.

Besides direct investments, Cuba received massive foreign loans. Between 1904 and 1909 the island borrowed $51 million from Speyer & Co.; between 1914 and 1927 it received $109 million in loans from Morgan & Co.; and it received $200 million from the Chase National Bank between 1926 and 1931 to face the capital needs during the sugar crisis. When the world's financial markets contracted during the 1930s, the flow of loans came to a halt. New loans amounting to $155 million, however, came to Cuba during the second half of the 1950s to help confront the new difficulties of the sugar industry. *See also* Railroads (Nineteenth Century); U.S. Interventions

Further Readings

Ayala, César J. *American Sugar Kingdom: The Plantation Economy of the Spanish Caribbean, 1898–1934*. Chapel Hill: University of North Carolina Press, 1999.

Jenks, Leland H. *Our Cuban Colony*. New York: Vanguard Press, 1928.

Pino Santos, Oscar. *Cuba, historia y economía*. Havana: Editorial de Ciencias Sociales, 1984.

Wallich, Henry C. *Problemas monetarios de una economía de exportación. La experiencia cubana, 1914–1947*. Havana: Banco Nacional de Cuba, 1953.

Antonio Santamaría García

García Menocal, Mario (1866–1941)

Mario García Menocal, who went by his second last name (Menocal), was president of Cuba from 1912 to 1920. Born in **Matanzas**, Menocal's family fled Cuba during the **Ten Years' War** and settled in Mexico. In the late 1870s, Menocal went to study in the United States, eventually earning a degree in engineering from Cornell University. Soon after, he joined his uncle, Aniceto Menocal, in Nicaragua, where the latter was working on a transoceanic canal project. By 1891, Menocal returned to Cuba and was soon involved in the island's **War of Independence**. An able soldier and strategist, Menocal attained the rank of major general and after the intervention of the United States was appointed chief of police in Havana. Eventually, Menocal returned to private industry, turning the Chaparra estate into one of the island's most productive sugar concerns. In 1908, Menocal ran for president but lost to **José Miguel Gómez**. In 1912, he ran for president again and won. Menocal's administration attacked corruption, promoted education, strengthened relations with the United States, and promoted financial reforms. In 1917, Menocal was reelected president through a widely contested election. Opponents of his reelection rebelled in a failed uprising known as "la Cham-

General Mario García Menocal, who later became Cuba's president, 1912–1921. Courtesy of the Biblioteca Nacional José Martí, Havana.

belona." During World War I, Menocal's government supplied the Allies with sugar and benefited from a short-lived era of prosperity known as "la Danza de los Millones." The sugar market crashed, and Cuba entered a financial depression. In 1921, with **Alfredo Zayas** as the new president, Menocal returned to the private sector. In the 1930s, he opposed the dictatorship of **Gerardo Machado** and ran unsuccessfully for president in 1936. *See also* Presidents; U.S. Interventions

Further Readings

Cortina, José Manuel. *Carácteres de Cuba*. Havana: Molina y Compañía, 1945.

Pérez, Louis A., Jr. *Cuba under the Platt Amendment, 1902–1934*. Pittsburgh: University of Pittsburgh Press, 1986.

John A. Gutiérrez

Gómez, José Miguel (1858–1921)

José Miguel Gómez served as Cuba's second president from 1908 to 1912. Born in **Sancti Spíritus**, Gómez fought in the **Ten Years' War**, the **Guerra Chiquita**, and the **War of Independence**, during which he earned the rank of major general. In 1905, when **Tomás Estrada Palma** ran for reelection to the Cuban presidency, Gómez, a Liberal Party leader, opposed him militarily and later as a candidate. Fearing a civil war, Gómez withdrew from the election. In 1908, under the supervision of the United States, Gómez was elected president. His administration mounted public works campaigns and increased the size of the Cuban government bureaucracy. Throughout his tenure Gómez was hounded by charges of corruption; his opponents called him "el Tiburón" (the Shark). In 1912, Gómez faced an uprising led by the Partido Independiente de Color and defeated it with military force. In 1916, he was a leader of the Chambelona revolt against the reelection pretensions of **Mario García Menocal**. And four years later, Gómez ran for reelection against his former ally **Alfredo Zayas** and lost. His son, Miguel Mariano Gómez, served briefly as president in 1936. *See also* Presidents; "Race War" of 1912; U.S. Interventions.

Further Readings

Helg, Aline. *Our Rightful Share: The Afro-Cuban Struggle for Equality, 1886–1912*. Chapel Hill: University of North Carolina Press, 1995.

Pérez, Louis A., Jr. *Intervention, Revolution, and Politics in Cuba, 1913–1921*. Pittsburgh: University of Pittsburgh Press, 1978.

Riera, Mario. *Cuba política, 1899–1955*. Havana: Imprenta Modelo, S.A., 1955.

John A. Gutiérrez

Gómez, Juan Gualberto (1854–1933)

The son of slaves, Juan Gualberto Gómez would become the most prominent voice in Cuban politics for **Afro-Cubans** and

Juan Gualberto Gómez was a distinguished politician and journalist (1880). From *Juan Gualberto Gómez: su labor patriótica y sociológica* (Havana, 1934).

mestizos. Born in **Matanzas Province**, he attended night school and later while in exile went to the Engineering Preparatory School in Paris. While at the school, he developed an interest in journalism and would remain a dominant voice in the field for much of his life. He returned to Cuba in 1878 and was introduced to **José Martí** by abolitionist attorney Nicolás de Azcárate. Shortly thereafter they began to conspire together against the Spanish colonial government. In 1879, Gómez took part in the **Guerra Chiquita** (Little War). As a result, he was imprisoned and deported to Spain. In 1882, he was granted conditional liberty and allowed to travel to Madrid, where he began a long friendship and political association with Rafael María de Labra, a liberal politician and member of the Cuban Liberal Autonomist Party, who

presided over the Sociedad Abolicionista Española (Spanish Abolitionist Society). He returned to Cuba in 1890 and directed, until its dissolution in 1894, the Directorio Central de las Sociedades de la Raza de Color (Central Directory of the Societies of the Colored Races). Since 1879 he had served as editor of *La Fraternidad* newspaper; he would later edit *La Igualdad* and *Patria*. Inside Cuba he was a delegate for the **Partido Revolucionario Cubano (Cuban Revolutionary Party)** and worked to organize the war effort against the Spanish. In 1895 he led a revolt in Ibarra, in Matanzas Province, and was again arrested and deported to Spain. He was elected in 1900 to the Constituent Assembly and would later oppose the inclusion of the **Platt Amendment** in the **Constitution of 1901**. He went on to oppose the presidential reelection plans of **Tomás Estrada Palma**. He was a member of the Liberal Party and served as a member of the House of Representatives and senator. He later fought against the **Gerardo Machado** dictatorship. *See also* Abolition and Emancipation; Autonomism; Political Exile (Nineteenth Century); Press and Journalism (Eighteenth and Nineteenth Centuries)

Further Readings

Costa, Octavio R. *Juan Gualberto Gómez*. Havana: Siglo XX, 1950.

Gómez, Juan G. *Por Cuba libre*. Havana: Editorial de Ciencias Sociales, 1974.

Horrego Estuch, Leopoldo. *Juan Gualberto Gómez, un gran inconforme*. Havana: Editorial Mecenas, 1954.

María del Carmen Barcia Zequeira

Gómez y Arias, Miguel Mariano (1890–1950)

Miguel Mariano Gómez was president at a time when Colonel **Fulgencio Batista** was the strongman of Cuban politics; he served only briefly (1936), losing a power struggle against the Batista-controlled Congress.

The son of President **José Miguel Gómez**, Miguel Mariano entered national politics as a congressman in the 1920s. He inherited his father's popular touch but had the reputation of being more honest. While in the United States during the **Gerardo Machado** dictatorship, Gómez represented the Liberal Party in an exile junta that united factions opposing the regime. After Machado's fall in 1933, he brokered negotiations between the U.S. embassy, **Ramón Grau San Martín**'s young reformers, and the group of noncommissioned officers that included an ascendant Sergeant Batista.

After serving as mayor of Havana, Gómez in January 1936 became the first elected president of the post-Machado era. It was the first election in which women voted and the first in which voters chose a president directly rather than through an electoral college. One month after taking office on May 20, Gómez angered Batista—who had risen to chief of the military—by firing 3,000 government employees, mostly army reservists. The final clash came that December, when Congress approved a tax of nine cents on each bag of sugar to fund a Batista-sponsored project under which soldiers were to go teach in rural schools. Fearing that the plan would militarize Cuban youth and subvert civil control over education, Gómez vetoed the bill. But the Senate impeached him, removing him from office. He never again played a prominent role in Cuban politics. *See also* Presidents; Revolution of 1933; Women's Suffrage Movement

Further Readings

Riera, Mario. *Cuba política, 1899–1955*. Havana: Imprenta Modelo, S.A., 1955.

Del Río, Pastor. *Miguel Mariano Gómez: dos cuestiones incidentales en la Cámara y un discurso en Palacio*. Havana: Empresa Editora de Publicaciones, 1951.

Roger E. Hernández

Granma Expedition

The yacht *Granma* was acquired by **Fidel Castro** and the **26th of July Movement** with the help of funds supplied by, among others, deposed Cuban president **Carlos Prío Socarrás** to land fighters and initiate a guerrilla war against the regime of **Fulgencio Batista**. The *Granma* expedition, which landed eighty-two fighters in Oriente Province, trained in Mexico and took its name from the boat that transported them to Cuba. The revolutionaries, under the command of Fidel Castro, departed from Tuxpan, México, on November 25, 1956, and landed on December 2. The expedition was scheduled to land on November 30 but was delayed by poor weather and mechanical problems with the yacht. As a result, the landing did not coincide with an armed uprising in **Santiago de Cuba**, led by **Frank País**. After a slow and dangerous journey, the revolutionaries landed in Belic on the Playa de las Coloradas, near the town of Niquero on the southern coast of Oriente. They landed in daylight in a swampy region not far from an area where members of the 26th of July Movement were waiting to assist them. Attacked and decimated by Batista's forces, about a dozen reached safety with the assistance of local farmers; the survivors included Fidel and **Raúl Castro, Camilo Cienfuegos**, **Juan Almeida**, José Ponce, Efigenio Ameijeiras, Ciro Redondo, Julio Díaz, Calixto García, Luis Crespo, and Univesro Sánchez. They made their way to the **Sierra Maestra** from where they launched the guerrilla war. The first guerrilla victory occurred on January 14, 1957, with the destruction of a military installation at La Plata. The *Granma* yacht is currently displayed at Havana's Museo de la

The *Granma* yacht transported Fidel Castro and eighty-one other revolutionaries from Mexico to Cuba in 1956. Drawing in a 1959 Cuban children's album depicts an idealized version of the events. Fidel Castro Photograph Collection, Manuscripts Division, Department of Rare Books and Special Collections, Princeton University Library.

Revolución, located in the former **Presidential Palace**. *See also* Batista, Struggle against

Further Readings

Ferrera, Alberto. *El* Granma: *La aventura del siglo*. Havana: Editorial Capitán San Luis, 1990.

Franqui, Carlos. *Vida, aventuras y desastres de un hombre llamado Castro*. Barcelona: Editorial Planeta, 1988.

Manuel de Paz Sánchez

Grau San Martín, Ramón (1887–1969)

A paradoxical historical figure, Ramón Grau San Martín was one of the most inspiring Cuban political leaders of the twentieth century and one of its most disappointing. He and **Fulgencio Batista** were, arguably, the two most influential leaders in the period between 1933 and 1959. Grau San Martín was born in **Pinar del Río Province**, the son of a local woman and an immigrant from Catalonia who made a sizable fortune as a merchant and a tobacco grower (see **Tobacco Industry**). Grau studied medicine at the **University of Havana** and graduated with a medical degree in 1908. In addition to a successful medical practice, he was a popular professor at the university. In 1927, he sided with student leaders in their struggle against the dictatorship of **Gerardo Machado** and was imprisoned and forced into exile. Grau returned to Cuba after the fall of Machado and was selected as one of the "pentarchs" when the students and soldiers joined forces to oust the U.S.-backed government of President Carlos Manuel de Céspedes y Quesada on September 4,

1933. The pentarchy quickly disintegrated, and the student leaders selected him as provisional president on September 10, 1933. The Grau administration, which lasted until January 15, 1934, was one of the most significant in Cuban history and is known in the historical literature for overseeing the **Revolution of 1933**. A wide range of social reforms were initiated in the period, including the eight-hour workday, minimum wage legislation, and **women's suffrage**, but the regime was deemed anticapitalist and was never recognized by the United States. In a move seen as hostile to Washington, Grau unilaterally abrogated the **Platt Amendment**, a codicil to the Cuban **Constitution of 1901** that allowed the United States to invade Cuba when its interests were endangered. In an effort to oust Grau, the United States courted Colonel Batista, chief of the army, who ultimately removed Grau from power.

After his ouster, Grau organized the Cuban Revolutionary Party (**Auténticos [Partido Revolucionario Cubano]**). Through the party, Grau would remain a formidable opponent to Batista, who ran the government through a series of puppet presidents throughout the 1930s. In 1944, Grau was elected to the presidency, and the Auténticos were swept into power, a victory that raised great hopes throughout the nation. Unfortunately, the Grau government was one of the most corrupt in Cuban history, a tradition that was continued by his Auténtico successor, **Carlos Prío Socarrás**. The Grau government, among other charges, was accused of stealing $50 million from union pension funds. It was said that Grau himself declined bribes, but eager businessmen were referred to his sister-in-law, Paulina Alsina de Grau.

After he left office in 1948, Grau became an elder statesman of Cuban politics. In 1954, after a coup placed Batista in power, he decided to run against his old nemesis and was widely criticized for tak-

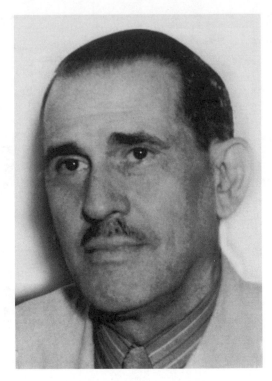

Ramón Grau San Martín, Cuban president (1944–1948). Courtesy of the Digitalization Project of the *El Mundo* Photographic Collection, University of Puerto Rico, Río Piedras Campus.

ing part in the questionable elections. However, days before the elections (October 1954) were to take place, he withdrew from the race, casting another cloud over the entire process. After the triumph of the **Revolution** in 1959, Grau remained in Cuba, even though several of his family members were imprisoned. He died in Havana in 1969, an event that was largely ignored by the revolutionary government. *See also* Presidents; Coup of 1952 (March 10)

Further Readings

Ameringer, Charles D. *The Cuban Democratic Experience: The Auténtico Years, 1944–1952.* Gainesville: University Press of Florida, 2000.

Hernández-Bauzá, Miguel. *Biografía de una emoción popular: el Dr. Grau.* Miami: Ediciones Universal, 1986.

Lancís y Sánchez, Antonio. *Grau, estadista y político.* Miami: Ediciones Universal, 1985.

Frank Argote-Freyre

Grupo Minorista

Under the name Grupo Minorista, a small group of leftist intellectuals promoted a series of programs, beginning in 1923, aimed at fostering *"virtud doméstica"* (domestic virtue). This group sought cultural, political, social, and moral regeneration of Cuban society. In 1927, the group issued its "Manifiesto del Grupo Minorista," a declaration of principles that was woven through the group's literary works, which were preoccupied with the decadence and moral degeneration of society. The group spoke out against Cuba's economic dependence on the United States, imperialism, the fragility of the Cuban state, and the political corruption of the government of President **Alfredo Zayas** (1921–1925).

The views expressed by the group received widespread attention because many of its members were journalists, writers, poets, and student leaders. Members of the Grupo Minorista included **Emilio Roig de Leuchsenring, Rubén Martínez Villena, Juan Marinello**, Félix Lizaso, José Antonio Fernández de Castro, **Alejo Carpentier**, Francisco Ichaso, and **Jorge Mañach**. The largest body of their work was published in *Revista Avance* and *Carteles*, with a smaller sampling appearing in *Atuei*, which was founded in 1927. Among the most significant contributions of this group was in the area of poetry as captured in "La poesía moderna en Cuba (1882 a 1925)." Although the group was short-lived, it served to bring together intellectuals from throughout Latin America preoccupied with similar social concerns. Political persecution and changing interests led to the disbanding of the group in 1927. *See also* Foreign Investments (Republican Era); Literary Journals; Machado Morales, Gerardo; Newspapers (Republican Era); U.S. Interventions

Further Readings

Cairo, Ana. *El Grupo Minorista y su tiempo*. Havana: Editorial Arte y Literatura, 1976.

"Manifiesto del Grupo Minorista." *Carteles*, May 22, 1927, 16, 25.

"La protesta del grupo Minorista." *Carteles*, May 16, 1926, 16.

Roig de Leuchsenring, Emilio. *El Grupo Minorista de intelectuales y artistas habaneros*. Havana: Oficina del Historiador de la Ciudad, 1961.

Consuelo Naranjo Orovio

Guiteras Holmes, Antonio "Tony" (1906–1935)

Antonio Guiteras Holmes was the single most important radical nationalist leader during the revolutionary period between 1931 and 1935. Guiteras was a student at the **University of Havana** between 1924 and 1927. He joined the Directorio Estudiantil Universitario (DEU) (University Student Directorate) in 1927, and like many DEU members, collaborated with the anti-Machado Unión Nacionalista (UN). After the defeat of the UN rebellion at Río Verde in 1931, Guiteras broke with the UN because he believed the organization was not serious about overthrowing **Gerardo Machado**. Thereafter Guiteras and his followers organized armed struggle against Machado, especially in eastern Cuba where Guiteras had strong support among students and young professionals. Largely because of Guiteras's influence in eastern Cuba, he became minister of the interior, war, and navy in the short-lived government of **Ramón Grau San Martín** (September 1933 to January 1934). Some of the radical measures of Grau's first government are attributed to Guiteras, especially the attempted land reform, the worker- and peasant-based militias, and the attempts to build trade union support for the Grau government. As a result of these and other policies, Guiteras became the object of intense hostility from anti-government groups as well as from members of the followers of Sergeant **Fulgencio Batista**. After the overthrow of Grau, Guiteras organized the political-military organization **Joven Cuba**. Guiteras fought not only to overthrow Batista; he also wanted to install a more radical government than Grau's. Guiteras was killed on May 8, 1935, in a clash with Batista's forces. *See also* Revolution of 1933; Students' Movement (Republican Era)

Further Readings

Briones Montoto, Newton. *Aquella decisión callada*. Havana: Editorial de Ciencias Sociales, 1998.

Cabrera, Olga. *Guiteras: la época, el hombre*. Havana: Editorial de Arte y Literatura, 1974.

Cabrera, Olga. *Guiteras: su pensamiento revolucionario*. Havana: Editorial de Ciencias Sociales, 1974.

Masferrer Landa, Rafael. *El pensamiento político del Dr. Guiteras*. Manzanillo, Cuba: Editorial El Arte, 1944.

Tabares del Real, José. *Guiteras*. Havana: Editorial de Ciencias Sociales, 1973.

Robert W. Whitney

Hawley-Smoot Tariff Act

The Hawley-Smoot Tariff Act was passed by the U.S. Congress on June 18, 1930, and remained in effect until June 8, 1934. Seeking to protect domestic sugar producers in the wake of the crisis of 1929, the U.S. government raised the tariff on raw, imported sugar from 2.206 cents to 2.5 cents per pound. Cuban sugar, which enjoyed a 20 percent tariff discount since the **Reciprocity Treaty** of 1902, saw its duties increase from 1.765 cents to 2 cents.

The new, higher tariffs aggravated the economic crisis in Cuba. Between 1929 and 1933 the average price of unrefined sugar fell from 1.8 to 1.13 cents per pound, and the export volume dropped precipitously from 4,821,800 tons to 2,244,000 tons. With adjustments for the new tariffs, Cuban sugar was valued at below production costs. These dramatic changes produced a fall in Cuba's gross national product, averaging 11 percent per year between 1929 and 1933.

Cuba's sugar producers were partially to blame for the increments in U.S. sugar tariffs during the years following World War I. While aware of the growing saturation of the U.S. market, they continued to increase output, thus injuring the least profitable producers: U.S. beet sugar producers. It was precisely the beet sugar producers who led the successful lobbying efforts to raise duties on foreign sugar. Eventually recognizing the damaging results of overproduction, Cuba's producers reduced output and were now in a better position to demand lower tariffs and the revision of the Reciprocity Treaty. They succeeded on both counts in 1934.

The Hawley-Smoot Tariff Act destabilized the political and economic bases upon which the Cuban Republic had been built: sugar monoproduction for export to the United States, the country that forced a protectorate over the island with the sanction of the **Platt Amendment**. Thus, the new tariff contributed to the social and political chaos that culminated with the **Revolution of 1933**. *See also* Batista y Zaldívar, Fulgencio; Jones-Costigan Act; Sugar Industry

Further Readings

Dye, Alan D. *Cuban Sugar in the Age of Mass Production*. Stanford, CA: Stanford University Press, 1998.

Le Riverend, Julio. *Historia económica de Cuba*. Havana: Editorial Pueblo y Educación, 1985.

Santamaría García, Antonio. *La industria azucarera y la economía cubana en los años veinte y treinta. La crisis del sector exportador, comercial y azucarero y su incidencia en la sociedad y economía insular*. Madrid: Ediciones de la Universidad Complutense de Madrid, 1995.

Zanetti Lecuona, Oscar. *Los cautivos de la reciprocidad. La burguesía cubana y la dependencia comercial, 1899–1959*. Havana: Empresa de Producción de la Educación Superior, 1989.

Antonio Santamaría García

Hevia y de los Reyes Gavilán, Carlos (1900–1964)

Carlos Hevia was president for two days during the political turmoil of 1934 and figured prominently in key moments of Cuban history over three decades.

The son of a colonel in the **War of Independence**, Hevia was an engineer and graduate of the U.S. Naval Academy. He gained prominence in 1931 as a leader of the failed Gibara expedition, launched by exiles out of New York City against dictator **Gerardo Machado**. After Machado's overthrow in 1933, Hevia became minister of agriculture under President **Ramón Grau San Martín**. Both helped found the **Auténticos (Partido Revolucionario Cubano)**.

In 1934 Grau was ousted under pressure from the United States and army chief **Fulgencio Batista**. Hevia had succeed Grau—a compromise between Batista and nationalistic factions—taking office on January 16. But unrest instigated by radical students gave Batista an excuse to withdraw his halfhearted support. Hevia resigned on January 18.

Hevia later served as minister of state under President **Carlos Prío Socarrás**. With a reputation for honesty his party badly needed after a decade of corrupt leadership, Hevia became the Auténticos presidential candidate for 1952. But Batista's March 10, 1952, coup d'état canceled the election.

Hevia fled to the United States, remaining active in the Auténtico Batista opposition. He returned after the revolutionaries' triumph in 1959 but soon went back to exile. Hevia was a member of the Consejo Revolucionario Cubano, the Miami-based civilian group that was to govern Cuba on an interim basis, had the **Bay of Pigs Invasion** succeeded. He died in Lantana, Florida, in 1964. *See also* Batista, Struggle Against; Coup of 1952 (March 10); Presidents; Revolution of 1933

Further Readings

Portell-Vilá, Herminio. *Nueva historia de la República de Cuba*. Miami: La Moderna Poesía, 1986.

Riera, Mario. *Cuba política, 1899–1955*. Havana: Imprenta Modelo, S.A., 1955.

Roger E. Hernández

Immigration (Twentieth Century)

Cuban immigration policy throughout the first half of the twentieth century was geared toward providing cheap labor and settling underpopulated areas of the island. The policy also aimed to control the immigration of those deemed "undesirables," particularly unskilled laborers brought to Cuba temporarily to work in the sugarcane fields. Race was a central factor in determining desirability, and Jamaican, Haitian, and Chinese immigration was discouraged because these groups were seen as undermining national unity. They were also stereotyped as lacking morals, such as the case of Chinese immigrants who were labeled opium addicts, alcoholics, and homosexuals. The political debate frequently centered on issues of health and hygiene, and many policies reflected the influence of eugenics on government officials.

An economic boom in Cuba in the first quarter of the twentieth century, as a result of rising world sugar prices, encouraged new waves of immigration (see **Sugar Industry**). The greatest inflow of new immigrants occurred in the years between 1912 and 1921. The numbers grew exponentially during World War I, when Cuba became the primary source of sugar for the Western powers. This initiated an economic boom in Cuba often referred to as the "Danza de los Millones" (Dance of the Millions). The Immigration Law of 1917 served as the legal foundation for this growing immigration. The immigrants were drawn primarily from Spain, which accounted for 74 percent of the total in the years between 1912 and 1916. However, as the need for cane cutters increased in the period between 1917 and 1921, the percentage of Jamaican and Haitian immigrants grew. At the same time, the Spanish migration decreased to about 27 percent.

The banking and economic crisis of 1921 had a profound impact on immigration policy. As often occurs during periods of economic crisis, new legislation was drafted to restrict immigration and protect national workers from foreign labor. But 1921 was just the prelude to a tightening of immigration practices throughout the Americas, leading up to the economic collapse of 1929. In Cuba, immigration policy was severely tightened in the period leading up to 1933. The number of Spanish immigrants declined precipitously and never again reached prior levels. Legislation passed in 1933 requiring that all businesses employ at least 50 percent native workers further reduced immigration (see **Revolution of 1933**).

Spaniards were the largest immigrant group throughout the twentieth century. The large immigration flow from Spain began in the 1880s and was uninterrupted by Cuba's independence. Cuba was the primary destination for most Spanish immigrants up until 1904. After that, Argentina became the primary destination for Spanish immigrants, but Cuba remained the second-most popular destination until the early 1930s. In the period from 1880 through 1930, Cuba received 34 percent of all Spanish immigrants. The Spaniards would become a powerful economic force in Cuba, monopolizing certain sectors of commerce. Most of the Spanish immigrants were from the northern provinces of Galicia and Asturias. In the nineteenth century, most of the Spanish migration had come from the Canary Islands, but their percentage declined in the twentieth century. Spanish immigrants also came from Aragón, Valencia, Catalonia, Andalucía, and the Basque regions. Like other immigrant groups, the Spaniards created a variety of recreational, educational, and health organizations. Immigrants from each of the Spanish provinces established separate organizations to encourage contact among fellow countrymen and women. These organizations played an important social and cultural role and it was not unusual for prominent members of the commercial and industrial elite to sit on their governing boards.

After the Spanish, the second largest immigrant group came from Haiti. In the period between 1912 and 1930 Spaniards accounted for 41 percent of Cuban immigration, while Haitians made up 10 percent. Haitians were preferred by the **sugar industry** because they were easily isolated and exploited as a result of language and cultural differences.

As of 1931, Spaniards accounted for 59 percent of the foreign population living in Cuba. Haitians made up nearly 18 percent of the foreign population, followed by Jamaicans (6.5 percent), Chinese (5.8 percent) and North Americans (1.6 percent). The percentage of Mexicans, English, Polish, French, Africans, and Germans was below 1 percent. The Civil War in Spain (1936–1939) forced many to seek refuge in Cuba and thousands of Caribbean immigrants continued to arrive as seasonal labor until 1959. *See also* Asian Contract Laborers; Caribbean Immigration; Colonization and Population (Nineteenth Century); Population and Demographic Indicators; Racial Compositon

Further Readings

Álvarez Estévez, Rolando. *Azúcar e inmigración: 1900–1940*. Havana: Editorial de Ciencias Sociales, 1988.

Inmigración y movimiento de pasajeros. Havana: Secretaría de Hacienda, 1913.

Knight, Franklin W. "Jamaican Migrants and the Cuban Sugar Industry, 1900–1934." In *Between Slavery and Free Labor: The Spanish Speaking Caribbean in the Nineteenth Century*. Baltimore, MD: Johns Hopkins University Press, 1985: 94–114.

Maluquer de Motes, Jordi. *Nación e inmigración: los españoles en Cuba (ss. XIX y XX)*. Colombres: Ediciones Júcar, 1992.

Naranjo Orovio, Consuelo. "Trabajo libre e inmigración española en Cuba: 1880–1930." *Revista de Indias* 195–196 (1992): 749–794.

Consuelo Naranjo Orovio

Jones-Costigan Act

The Jones-Costigan Act, also known as the James Costigan Act, was approved by the U.S. Congress on June 8, 1934. It reduced the sugar duty rates of the **Hawley-Smoot Tariff Act** from 2.5 to 1.857 cents per pound of raw sugar. Since Cuba's sugar enjoyed a 20 percent discount in its duties since the **Reciprocity Treaty** of 1902, its corresponding reduction was from 2 cents to 1.5 cents. The Jones-Costigan Act also assigned specific sugar quotas to domestic and foreign sugar producers. Cuba was included in that system in 1934 with a sugar quota equivalent to 28.6 percent of U.S. demand. That quota could, and often did, increase if other producers failed to meet theirs. These provisions allowed Cuba to increase its sugar exports to the United States from 1,377,200 tons in 1933 to 2,454,500 tons in 1937. An additional 1,000,000 tons or so were sold to other markets at prices less favorable than those enjoyed in the U.S. market.

In 1934 a new Reciprocity Treaty between Cuba and the United States halted the Jones-Costigan Act. In 1937, it was extended by the United States following the signing in London of the International Sugar Agreement, which also assigned Cuba a quota within the free world market. These provisions, while not reestablishing predepression levels of production, allowed Cuba to continue its path as a single-crop economy. The favorable trade conditions also allowed the island's economy and society to regain stability. Production quotas were distributed in Cuba among the various sugar producers so that they could all share in the benefit of the higher prices offered by the U.S. market. With a few ad-

justments, particularly during World War II, this system continued to operate until 1959. *See also* Sugar Indusry

Further Readings
Santamaría García, Antonio. *La industria azucarera y la economía cubana en los años veinte y treinta. La crisis del sector exportador, comercial y azucarero y su incidencia en la sociedad y economía insular*. Madrid: Ediciones de la Universidad Complutense de Madrid, 1995.
Silva, Arnaldo. *Cuba y el mercado internacional azucarero*. Havana: Editorial de Ciencias Sociales, 1971.
Zanetti Lecuona, Oscar. *Los cautivos de la reciprocidad. La burguesía cubana y la dependencia comercial, 1899–1959*. Havana: Empresa de Producción de la Educación Superior, 1989.

Antonio Santamanía García

Joven Cuba

Joven Cuba was the most important radical nationalist political-military organization before the founding of the **Twenty-sixth of July Movement** in the early 1950s. Joven Cuba was founded in May 1934 by **Antonio Guiteras** and his followers. The organization tried to keep the militant **struggle against Batista** and the Cuban left wing alive after the downfall of **Ramón Grau San Martín** in January 1934. The program of Joven Cuba was broadly antiimperialist and nationalist. The program advocated decentralized democracy, the reorganization of the army and police, land reform, and **women's rights**. Guiteras wanted Joven Cuba to be both ideologically united and organizationally disciplined. According to Guiteras, it was precisely the lack of political unity and tight organization that had undermined Grau's government. Joven Cuba was created to both militarily defeat **Fulgencio Batista** and provide a foundation for a more radical government than the one Guiteras had served in under Grau. Nothing came of his plans. Joven Cuba was too involved with small-scale attacks on Batista's army and police. From its very foundation Joven Cuba was on the defensive. When Guiteras was killed in May 1935 Joven Cuba lost the only leader capable of keeping the group together. Many of the remaining leaders of Joven Cuba were not as politically motivated as was Guiteras, and personalistic factionalism and violent vendettas undermined the group's effectiveness. For two more years, Joven Cuba carried out armed actions against the government. By 1937 most surviving members had joined the **Auténticos (Partido Revolucionario Cubano)**, while others formed smaller "action groups." *See also* Revolution of 1933

Further Readings

Briones Montoto, Newton. *Aquella decisión callada*. Havana: Editorial de Ciencias Sociales, 1998.

Cabrera, Olga. *Guiteras: la época, el hombre*. Havana: Editorial de Arte y Literatura, 1974.

Cabrera, Olga. *Guiteras: su pensamiento revolucionario*. Havana: Editorial de Ciencias Sociales, 1974.

Tabares del Real, José. *Guiteras*. Havana: Editorial de Ciencias Sociales, 1973.

Robert W. Whitney

Labor Movement (Republican Era)

As in most of Latin America, the Cuban organized labor movement had its beginnings in the last decades of the nineteenth century (see **Organized Labor [Nineteenth Century]**). However, it was considerably hampered by the persistence of **slavery**, which was not finally abolished until 1886. The tobacco workers were particularly prominent among the pioneers of Cuban organized labor. Many of those active in the early Cuban labor movement were Spanish immigrants, who had experience with unions in their native country.

During the first two decades of the twentieth century, factions with three ideological tendencies were notable in the Cuban labor movement: anarcho-syndicalists, Marxist Socialists, and the so-called reformists, the first of these being predominant. Also, during that period regional central labor groups were established in various Cuban cities, the most notable of these being the Federación Obrera de La Habana (FOH), in the capital, which was founded in 1920.

In 1925, the first national labor confederation, the Confederación Nacional Obrera de Cuba (CNOC), was established. It was dominated at its inception by the anarchists, but by the end of the decade it had been captured by the communists, whose party (**Partido Comunista**) had also been established in 1925. Outside of the CNOC were the Federación Obrera de La Habana and several specialized national union groups, particularly those of **railroads** and maritime workers. In the early 1930s, the communists launched a major effort to organize the workers in the country's largest industry, sugar. A national union, affiliated with the CNOC, was established.

During the dictatorial administration of President **Gerardo Machado** (1924–1933) the labor movement suffered extensive persecution from the government. As a consequence, labor support was virtually unanimous for the revolutionary general strike of early August 1933. However, the leader of the CNOC worked out a deal with Machado, with him agreeing to legalize the CNOC and the Partido Comunista, in return for which the CNOC leaders promised to try to end the strike, an effort that failed. Machado was soon thereafter forced to flee into exile.

Organized labor was split insofar as the "social nationalist" government of President **Ramón Grau San Martín** (September 1933–January 1934) was concerned. The FOH and most other union groups not controlled by the communists were more or less favorably disposed to the Grau regime. The CNOC, on the contrary, was violently

Cuba's national flower: Butterfly Jasmine (La Mariposa); *Hedychium coronarium Koenig*. Mixed media on paper by Heriberto Rodríguez. Luis Martínez-Fernández Collection.

Cuba's national bird: Cuban Trogon (Tocororo); *Priotelus temnurus*. Mixed media on paper by Adolfo Manuel del Toro Hernández. Luis Martínez-Fernández Collection.

Cuba's national tree: Royal Palm (Palma Real); *Roystonea regia*. Mixed media on paper by Heriberto Rodríguez. Luis Martínez-Fernández Collection.

Coat of arms of the Republic of Cuba.

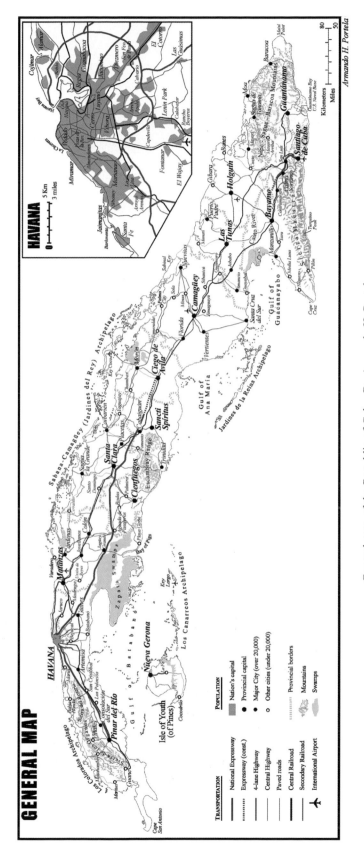

General map of the Republic of Cuba. By Armando H. Portela.

Flag of the Republic of Cuba.

A group of musicians rehearse a *salsa* number in El Cerro, Havana; a portrait of a smiling Fidel Castro looms behind. Photograph by Luis Martínez-Fernández.

Fort of Cojímar, outside of Havana. Photograph by Celestino Martínez Lindín.

Capitol Building, Havana. Photograph by Celestino Martínez Lindín.

Joven campesino (*Peasant Child*) (left) by Armando Menocal (1936) oil on board. Gift of the Cuban Foundation. Courtesy of the Museum of Arts and Sciences, Daytona Beach, Florida.

Figura gris (*Figure in Grey*) (below) (1957) oil on canvas by René Portocarrero. Gift of the Cuban Foundation; Courtesy of the Museum of Arts and Sciences, Daytona Beach, Florida.

Con la fuerza del ejemplo by Lázaro Saavedra, serigraph, 2000. Courtesy of Edge Art, Inc.

Monument to Cuban patriot José Martí by Juan José Sicre in the Plaza of the Revolution, Havana. Photograph by Luis Martínez-Fernández.

Presidential Palace, Havana; today it is the Museum of the Revolution. Photograph by Celestino Martínez Lindín.

Vintage Partagas cigar box label (*litografía*) and cigar rings (*vitolas*). Luis Martínez-Fernández Collection.

Guajiro family in Cienfuegos Province. Photograph by Celestino Martínez Lindín.

opposed to it, in conformity with the Communist International's "line" of that period, which denounced all the leftist parties and regimes that were not Stalinist as being "social fascist."

With the overthrow of Grau by Colonel **Fulgencio Batista**, the government became increasingly hostile toward organized labor. This situation culminated in a revolutionary general strike in March 1935, which failed. Thereafter, organized labor of all ideological orientations was severely persecuted. This persecution continued until late 1937, when negotiations began between the communists and General Batista, which led to communist support for his presidential aspirations and Batista's agreeing to legalize the Communist Party and agree to the reestablishment of a viable labor movement under their control. After this agreement, the labor movement recovered rapidly. The process culminated in the establishment in January 1939 of a new central labor group, the Confederación de Trabajadores de Cuba (CTC), led by the communists' tobacco workers' leader **Lázaro Peña**, who had been the last secretary general of the CNOC.

This recovery of the labor movement began a period in which collective bargaining became "customary." Workers in most key sectors of the national economy were unionized, and their unions periodically negotiated agreements with the employers. Also, the Ministry of Labor intervened extensively in this process. The ability of their union leaders to win gains for them increasingly seemed to matter more to the union members than did those leaders' ideology.

The CTC remained under predominantly communist leadership until 1947. In that year, President Grau having been elected in 1944, the trade union leaders of his **Auténticos** moved to take CTC control away from the communists. This led to a split in the Confederación, and in the

next five years the Auténtico-dominated faction became overwhelmingly dominant.

The second dictatorship of Batista (1952–1958) was a trying period for the labor movement. CTC leaders called a general strike to try to prevent Batista's seizure of power, but when it failed, they reached an agreement to cancel the strike call, and he promised to leave the labor movement alone. However, the Batista regime remained widely unpopular with the workers as with the rest of the populace. In the face of this, CTC Secretary General **Eusebio Mujal**, supposedly fearful that Batista would crack down on and destroy the labor movement, took an increasingly strong position in support of the dictator. For its part, the government gave more and more support to Mujal and his colleagues, allowing him to establish a virtual dictatorship within the CTC.

With the overthrow of Batista on January 1, 1959, members of **Fidel Castro**'s **26th of July Movement** seized control of the CTC and most of the country's unions. Elections within the unions proved that the communists were a small minority, although some 26th of July union leaders sympathized with them. A showdown between the majority of the 26th of July union leadership and the communists and their sympathizers came at the CTC's Tenth Congress in November 1959. There, Fidel Castro, his brother **Raúl**, and the minister of labor all demanded that the communists be given equality with the 26th of July in the CTC leadership. Although this was not accepted, a CTC leadership more or less imposed by the government leaders was elected.

In the months that followed, that new CTC leadership carried out a widespread purge, removing the elected leaders of a majority of the country's national unions and replacing them with pro-communists. This process culminated in 1961 with the election of Lázaro Peña as CTC secretary general, at the Confederation's eleventh Congress. As a result of these purges, the Cuban labor movement was converted into an institution patterned on that established in the Soviet Union by Stalin, concerned primarily with increasing production and productivity and with mobilizing support for the Castro government, rather than with the interests and needs of the workers. *See also* Revolution of 1933; Sugar Industry

Further Readings

Cabrera, Olga. *El movimiento obrero cubano en 1920*. Havana: Instituto Cubano del Libro, 1969.

Sims, Harold D. "Cuban Labor and the Communist Party, 1937–1958: An Interpretation." *Cuban Studies* 15, no. 1 (Winter 1985): 43–58.

Clavijo Aguilera, Fausto. *Los sindicatos en Cuba*. Havana: Editorial Lex, 1954.

Robert J. Alexander

Laredo Brú, Federico (1875–1946)

Best known as one of the "puppet presidents" during the period (1934–1939) when Colonel **Fulgencio Batista** ran Cuba behind a constitutional facade, Federico Laredo Brú was sworn in as president in December 1936, after the impeachment of **Miguel Mariano Gómez**, who opposed Batista's rural education program. He served as president until October 1940, when Batista, who had won in clean elections, replaced him.

Born in Los Remedios in what was then the province of Las Villas, Laredo Brú fought in the **War of Independence** (1895–1898) and rose to the rank of colonel. An accomplished lawyer, after independence he served as secretary to the Audiencia in Las Villas and later as an assistant prosecutor for the Supreme Court. He was appointed interior minister by President **José Miguel Gómez**, father of the man he later succeeded as chief executive. He retired from politics in 1913 to practice law in **Cienfuegos**. In the 1920s, he was active in the opposition to the corrupt government of President **Alfredo Zayas**. In that capacity, he helped organize the **Veterans' and Patriots' Movement**. He led an armed uprising against the Zayas government in 1923, a revolt that was quickly put down. Laredo Brú resurfaced in the 1933 cabinet of Carlos Manuel de Céspedes y Quesada, a government that lasted less than a month. Elected as vice president in January 1936, in a rigged election, he took office in May.

During his tenure as president, Laredo Brú did Batista's bidding. Major policy initiatives, such as the Triennial Plan of 1937, were developed and initiated by Batista. The literature of the period credited the colonel with many of the social initiatives and not the sitting president. Furthermore, the president's cabinet consisted mainly of Batista's friends and associates. When Batista resigned from the army in December 1939 to run for the presidency, Laredo Brú worked to promote his candidacy. Just weeks before leaving office, he signed legislation (Casanova Bill) accepting U.S. loans to pay off Cuba's **foreign debt**. *See also* Presidents

Further Readings

Portell-Vilá, Herminio. *Nueva historia de la República de Cuba*. Miami: La Moderna Poesía, 1986.

Thomas, Hugh. *Cuba: The Pursuit of Freedom*. New York: Harper & Row, 1971.

Frank Argote-Freyre

Lobo, Julio (1898–1983)

Julio Lobo, a sugar trader, wholesaler, and mill owner, was one of Cuba's wealthiest individuals in the 1940s and 1950s. Born in Venezuela, Lobo began working at his family's Galbán Lobo sugar-trading firm after graduating from Louisiana State University in 1919. By the 1930s he controlled a large portion of the Cuban sugar trade, and he began acquiring mills aggressively in the 1940s. One decade later, Lobo owned eleven mills and refineries (with partial interests in two more), including the Hershey estates, central Tinguaro in **Matanzas**, and central Niquero in Oriente, where rebel troops frequently camped. He also had extensive interests in hotels, banking, shipping, and communications. An outspoken lobbyist for the **sugar industry**, Lobo frequently saw his efforts to mechanize sugar production and end restrictions on production frustrated by politicians and labor leaders. Lobo publicly and financially supported the overthrow of dictator **Fulgencio Batista** but came into conflict with **Fidel Castro**'s government when it expropriated his properties and assets (see **Agrarian Reform Acts**). Lobo refused **Che Guevara**'s offer to manage the sugar industry under the new government and left Cuba in October 1960. After managing Galbán Lobo from New York and the Bahamas for several years, he lived the rest of his life in Madrid. *See also* Batista, Struggle Against; Rionda y Polledo, Manuel

Further Readings

Lincoln, Freeman. "Julio Lobo, Colossus of Sugar." *Fortune* 57 (September 1958): 150–152, 189–192.

Robinson, Linda. "The Final Homecoming of Cuba's Sugar Queen." *U.S. News and World Report*, March 22, 1999, 42.

Thomas, Hugh. *Cuba: The Pursuit of Freedom*. New York: Harper & Row, 1971.

David A. Sartorius

Machado y Morales, Gerardo (1871–1939)

Gerardo Machado was elected president of Cuba on the Liberal Party ticket in 1924. He was a veteran of the **War of Independence**, during which he had attained the rank of brigadier general. He later served as mayor of **Santa Clara**, inspector general of the army, and secretary of *gobernación*.

When he ran for president in 1924, Machado adopted what he called the "Platform of Regeneration," in which he called for an end to political corruption, as well as new roads, new schools, and new social services. His campaign invoked nationalism, supported no presidential reelection, called for the abrogation of the **Platt Amendment**, and urged the diversification of the economy. For the first time in decades, reform seemed possible, and Machado won widespread support. Furthermore, Machado entered office a wealthy man, thus raising the hope that he would not use his office for personal gain. He owned a sugar mill, a construction company, and various other enterprises, including a soap factory and a beer brewery.

Yet it was unclear how ill gotten his fortune actually had been. He had worked as a butcher in Camajuaní in the old province of Las Villas. In fact, his left hand, shorn of one finger, attested to that early trade. Before his experience in the War of Independence, he and his father allegedly had been cattle robbers. When he became mayor of Santa Clara in 1899, the Audiencia was mysteriously burned, which held all records of his alleged criminal activity. During the War of Independence, he spent most of his time in Santa Clara, where he handled the disbursements of the army. As a cabinet member in the government of **José Miguel Gómez** in 1911, Machado brutally put down an anarchist strike among the sewer workers.

During the first two years of his administration, Machado made good on his promises of reform. The Customs-Tariff Law of 1927 provided a state subsidy for the expansion of national industry and **agriculture**. Tariffs and duties on raw materials were reduced to promote local **manufacturing**. By 1929, the government had issued permits for fifty new industries, and agricultural and livestock production became more diversified. Higher tariffs on foreign products that Cuba produced were raised to protect and promote national industries. In addition, he created the Central Highway system, the nationalist answer to the foreign-owned **railroads** system, which facilitated the transportation and distribution of locally grown fruit and vegetables.

Then the depression hit Cuba early. In the mid-1920s, the price of sugar began to fall. The annual sugar crop was reduced by 10 percent, and the length of the *zafra* (sugarcane harvest) was shortened from 136 to 87 days, which meant even less work for thousands of Cubans already underemployed. The planting of the new harvest was also postponed by a month. In 1928, Machado decided that he needed to seek reelection to steady the declining economy. He forced a constitutional change that would allow him to extend his term in office. It was unlikely that he would win, so through intimidation and bribery, he secured his nomination through *cooperativismo*, an arrangement whereby the Liberal, Conservative, and Popular Parties agreed to Machado as the *candidato único*, for a new six-year term.

Just after he was inaugurated in 1929, the worldwide depression hit the already weak Cuban economy. In 1930, the United States passed the **Hawley-Smoot Tariff Act**, which raised the tariff on Cuban sugar. Sugar production dropped by 60 percent, the same rate of decline as the price of sugar worldwide. Total Cuban exports declined by 80 percent. The length of time of the zafra was reduced again to sixty-two days, which gave tens of thousands of workers two months' work for the entire year. Approximately 1 million people, out of a population of 3.9 million, found themselves unemployed. By 1933, 60 percent of the population lived on less than $300 in annual real income, while another 30 percent earned between $300 and $600. Salaries of public servants had fallen six months behind in payment.

Political opposition spread. Union membership grew, and labor unions continued to organize. The incidence of strikes, mass demonstrations, and hunger marches skyrocketed. The illegitimate Machado government responded with brutal repression, including firing into the crowds and arresting all who were suspect. By October 1930, Machado had suspended constitutional guarantees in **La Habana Province**, which immediately prompted nationwide demonstrations and clashes with police. **The University of Havana** was closed, and classes were suspended.

The result resembled civil war. Canefields and harvested cane were torched. Armed bands roamed throughout the island, ambushing railroads, disrupting communications and transportation. By November 1930, constitutional guarantees were suspended throughout the island as a state of siege was declared. In January 1931, Machado invoked a never-used colonial law of public order to suspend the publication of fifteen newspapers and to arrest their editors. As the government began to eliminate both real and imagined opposition, arrests, torture, and assassination became commonplace. Having been *el carnicero* in his early professional life, Machado reverted to type and rearmed the moniker because of his brutal methods of repression in this period of time, which came to be called *el Machadato*.

New political forces rose to oppose the dictator. The swelling ranks of the opposition included students, intellectuals, professors, women's groups, and schoolteachers. Open warfare broke out; all members of Machado's government became targets, and all suspected opponents of the regime were either jailed or executed on the spot.

The Cuban conflict became a social crisis, which began to concern the United States. In 1933, the new administration of Franklin D. Roosevelt appointed Sumner Welles as ambassador to Cuba, who arrived in Havana as a "friendly mediator" but one who began encouraging Machado

Gerardo Machado y Morales was elected president in 1924 and later assumed dictatorial powers. Courtesy of the Cuban Heritage Collection of the Otto G. Richter Library of the University of Miami.

Benjamin, Jules R. "The 'Machadato' and Cuban Nationalism, 1928–1932." *Hispanic American Historical Review* 55 (February 1975): 66–91.

Jorge, Guillermo J. *Administración del presidente general Gerardo Machado y Morales*. Miami: Ramón Guiteras Intercultural Center, 1985.

Whitney, Robert. *State and Revolution in Cuba: Mass Mobilization and Political Change, 1920–1940*. Chapel Hill: University of North Carolina Press, 2001.

Paula J. Pettavino

Magoon, Charles E. (1861–1920)

Charles E. Magoon acted as provisional governor of Cuba from 1906 to 1909. Minnesota born and Nebraska raised, Magoon was a prominent member of the Lincoln, Nebraska, legal community. In 1899 he was appointed by the William McKinley administration to serve as a law officer in the newly established Bureau of Insular Affairs. There, in 1902, he published "Report on the Law of Civil Government in Territory Subject to Military Occupation by the Military Forces of the United States." Magoon's expertise in the area of civil administration attracted the attention of his superiors. He was appointed to serve on the Isthmian Canal Commission in 1904 and, by the following year, was promoted to serve as both U.S. minister to Panama and governor of the Canal Zone, positions he held until September 1906. In that same year, he was appointed by the Theodore Roosevelt administration to serve as the provisional governor of Cuba after **Tomás Estrada Palma** abdicated the Cuban presidency. As provisional governor, Magoon created a professional Cuban armed forces, nationalized sanitation and public health programs, began the movement toward a civil service system, mounted a massive public works effort, and conducted the census of 1907. Cuban historians have criticized Magoon for expanding the use of *botellas* (no-show jobs)

to resign. When he refused, the opposition mobilized, strikes began anew, and the army moved against the president out of fear of **U.S. intervention**. On August 12, 1933, Machado boarded a plane for the Bahamas, along with five revolvers, seven bags of gold, and five friends in pajamas. His family arrived later in the day by ship from Havana. In 1939, **Fulgencio Batista** declared that Machado could return to Cuba, but by that time he was already dying in the United States. *See also* Newspapers (Republican Era); Presidents; Revolution of 1933; Students' Movement (Republican Era)

Further Readings

Beals, Carleton. *The Crime of Cuba*. Philadelphia: J.B. Lippincott, 1933.

in the political system. Several large government contracts, including the extension of the Havana Electric Railway, were awarded by Magoon to close friends and associates. After the election of **José Miguel Gómez**, Magoon returned to Washington, D.C., where he practiced law. *See also* Platt Amendment; U.S. Interventions

Further Readings

Lockmiller, David A. *Magoon in Cuba: A History of the Second Intervention, 1906–1909*. Chapel Hill: University of North Carolina Press, 1938.

Mellander, Gustavo A., and Nelly Mellander. *Charles Edward Magoon: The Panama Years*. Puerto Rico: Editorial Plaza Mayor, 1999.

Millett, Allan Reed. *The Politics of Intervention: The Military Occupation of Cuba, 1906–1909*. Columbus: Ohio State University Press, 1968.

John A. Gutiérrez

Marinello, Juan (1898–1977)

Juan Marinello was Cuba's most distinguished communist intellectual and for many years the president of the **Partido Comunista**. He received a law degree at the **University of Havana** in 1920 and a doctorate there nine years later. Subsequently, when the political situation permitted, he served on that university's faculty and, when in exile, taught at the National University of Mexico. His scholarly activities included editing several different political and **literary journals** and extensive research on the career of **José Martí**.

Marinello became involved in the struggle against the dictatorship of **Gerardo Machado** in the 1920s and early 1930s, as a result of which he was forced into exile between 1930 and 1933.

The emergence of Marinello as a major communist leader began with his organization and leadership of the Unión Revolucionaria, which in 1937 was legalized by **Fulgencio Batista**, and Marinello served as the spokesman for the illegal Communist Party. With the formation of the alliance between Batista and the Communist Party, Unión Revolucionaria merged with the Communist Party in 1939 to form the Unión Revolucionaria Comunista (URC), of which Marinello was president. When, in 1944, the URC changed its name to Partido Socialista Popular (PSP), Marinello continued to be its titular head.

Reflecting the Batista-Communist alliance, Marinello held legislative and administrative offices during the early 1940s. He was elected to the 1940 constitutional convention and subsequently to the House of Representatives. Then in 1944 President Batista appointed Marinello as one of the two communist members of the cabinet, as minister without portfolio.

Marinello continued to be the official head of the PSP during the eight years of rule of the **Auténticos (Partido Revolucionario Cubano)** (1944–1952) and the second dictatorship of Batista (1952–1958). Although the Partido Socialista Popular was officially illegal during the second Batista regime, Marinello remained in the country and was able to carry out his tasks as party president.

With the advent of the **Fidel Castro** regime, the PSP was soon merged into the single party of the revolutionary regime, thus ending Marinello's long tenure as party chieftain. He held some secondary posts in the Castro regime, including that of Cuban ambassador to the United Nations Educational, Scientific, and Cultural Organization (UNESCO). *See also* Constitution of 1940; Labor Movement (Republican Era)

Further Readings

Marinello, Juan. *Un hombre de todos los tiempos, Juan Marinello*. Havana: Editorial de Ciencias Sociales, 1998.

Suárez Díaz, Ana, comp. *Cuba, cultura/Juan Marinello*. Havana: Editorial Letras Cubanas, 1989.

Robert J. Alexander

Márquez Sterling, Manuel (1872–1934)

Manuel Márquez Sterling was a renowned journalist and diplomat who fought vigorously for the abolition of the **Platt Amendment**, which prohibited Cuba from entering treaties or contracting debts without U.S. approval. It also allowed the United States to intervene in Cuba to preserve Cuban independence and its government (see Appendix 10). He lived long enough to achieve his goal and was present in Washington, D.C., as Cuban ambassador to the United States when the hated amendment was abrogated. He died shortly thereafter in 1934 while still in the U.S. capital.

Márquez Sterling was attracted to journalism at a young age. He entered the field after graduating high school from the Instituto of Puerto Príncipe (**Camagüey**) in 1889. That year he joined the editorial staff of *El Camagüeyano*. He was residing in Mexico in 1894 when he met **José Martí** and joined the Cuban independence movement. Gonzalo de Quesada entrusted Márquez Sterling with the organization of Martí's personal papers after his death in 1895. As a journalist, he spearheaded a publicity campaign in support of Cuban independence in Paris and Mexico, establishing the newspaper *La Lucha* in the latter. In 1907 he was designated Cuban consul to Argentina, an appointment that initiated his diplomatic career. He would serve in various Latin American countries in addition to the United States. In Havana, he founded the *Heraldo de Cuba* and *La Nación* newspapers. He was awarded the degree of Doctor Honoris Causa by the National University of Mexico in 1921. In 1924 he was named director of the Foreign Ministry's Pan American Office. In addition to his diplomatic achievements, he was a professor at the Foreign Service Institute of the **University of Havana** and a member of the Academy of History and the National Academy of Arts and Letters.

He served as secretary of state in the first government of President **Ramón Grau San Martín**.

Besides his journalistic writings, Márquez Sterling authored various works on chess. His work *Proceso histórico de la Enmienda Platt* was completed posthumously by his nephew, historian Carlos Márquez Sterling. *See also* Newspapers (Republican Era); Press and Journalism (Eighteenth and Nineteenth Centuries)

Further Reading
Cortina, José Manuel. *El periodista, el diplomático y la nacionalidad*. Havana: Imprenta El Siglo XX, 1930.

Manuel de Paz Sánchez

Martínez Villena, Rubén (1899–1934)

Rubén Martínez Villena was a leading writer, poet, journalist, and political activist who participated in several of the radical nationalist movements that critiqued the so called Plattist Republic during the 1920s (see **Platt Amendment**). Moving sharply to the Left in the second half of the 1920s, he became the most important intellectual and political influence in the first eight years of the Cuban Communist Party.

Born into a middle-class family in Havana, Martínez Villena studied law at the **University of Havana**, graduating in 1917. For a period he worked for *El Heraldo* newspaper and then as secretary of the eminent Cuban ethnographer **Fernando Ortiz**. His first major entrance onto the political-cultural stage was as one of the founding members of the **Grupo Minorista**, established in 1923, and as a signatory to the Group's Protest of the Thirteen, which condemned the corruption of political and intellectual life under the **Alfredo Zayas** presidency. His involvement in the **Veterans' and Patriots' Movement** in 1923 and 1924 led to exile in the United

States from where he returned to Cuba in August 1924. Determined to link the struggles of radical intellectuals to the masses, he joined together with the student leader **Julio Antonio Mella** in the establishment of the **José Martí** Popular University, a crucial turning point in his career. In 1927, after working with the Cuban branch of the Anti-Imperialist League of the Americas, he joined the Communist Party where, in the absence of Mella (in exile in Mexico), he became the party's most influential intellectual leader and chief legal adviser to leftist trade unions affiliated with the Confederación Nacional Obrera de Cuba (CNOC). He was one of the chief organizers of the March 20, 1930 general strike, the largest labor protest registered thus far in Cuban history.

His public profile, poor health, and threats made by the **Gerardo Machado** dictatorship forced Martínez Villena to abandon Cuba in April 1930 for the United States and then the Soviet Union. Working for the Comintern, he followed the rising tide of popular mobilizations against Machado and in particular the struggles of unionized sugar workers with growing excitement. Ignoring medical advice to stay in the Soviet Union, he returned clandestinely to Cuba via the United States in mid-May 1933 several months before the overthrow of the Machado regime. In what was to become one of the most controversial episodes in the history of Cuban communism at the height of the general strike that preceded Machado's fall, he recommended the acceptance of the dictator's offer to recognize the Communist Party in exchange for the party urging a return to work. He died of tuberculosis at age thirty-five. *See also* Labor Movement (Republican Era); Newspapers (Republican Era); Partido Comunista (Partido Socialista Popular [Republican Era])

Further Readings

Martínez Villena, Rubén. *Órbita de Rubén Martínez Villena*. Havana: Ediciones Unión, 1964.
Núñez Machín, Ana. *Rubén Martínez Villena*. Havana: Unión Nacional de Escritores y Artistas Cubanos, 1971.

Barry Carr

Mella, Julio Antonio (1903–1929)

Student leader, public speaker, social reformer, and nationalist critic of U.S. exploitation of Cuba, Julio Antonio Mella served as the secretary general of the **Federation of University Students** and was the first head of Cuba's Communist Party in 1925. Julio Antonio Mella was born into a wealthy family in Havana. He completed his high school and then entered law school and studied philosophy and letters at the **University of Havana** in 1921. Mella rose to prominence in the reformist student movement and initiated the **José Martí** Popular University to provide courses for workers and people of modest means. A fierce critic of government corruption and a fervent nationalist opposed to U.S. economic dominance and political interference within Cuba, Mella gravitated to socialist politics, participating in the founding of the Anti-Imperialist League of the Americas and the Communist Party of Cuba in 1925. Arrested during the **Gerardo Machado** dictatorship, Mella was compelled to go into exile in Mexico, where he published numerous articles and pamphlets. In 1927, he traveled to the Soviet Union. Upon his return to Mexico, Mella continued to organize against Machado and to write and speak on Latin American issues, Cuba, and social questions. Mella was assassinated early in 1929 in Mexico City, likely at the behest of Machado. Today, his remains are interred in a monument outside the entrance to the University of Havana. *See also* Foreign In-

Julio Antonio Mella was a prominent student leader during the 1920s. Photograph courtesy of the Biblioteca Nacional José Martí, Havana.

vestments (Republican Era); Partido Comunista (Partido Socialista Popular [Republican Era])

Further Readings

Contrera, Nelio. *Julio Antonio Mella: el joven precursor*. Havana: Editora Política, 1987.

Dumpierre, Erasmo. *Julio Antonio Mella: biografía*. Havana: Secretaría de Trabajo Ideológico, 1975.

Mella, Julio Antonio. *Escritos revolucionarios*. Mexico City: Siglo Veintiuno Editores, S.A., 1978.

David C. Carlson

Mendieta Montefur, Carlos (1873–1960)

Carlos Mendieta is best known as one of Cuba's "puppet presidents" under Colonel **Fulgencio Batista** from 1934 through 1935, but prior to that Mendieta had a long and distinguished military and political career. A supporter of Cuban independence, he personally armed and equipped a contingent of 125 men to fight against the Spanish and rose to the rank of colonel. After the **War of Independence**, he graduated from the **University of Havana** with a degree in medicine. He served several terms in the Cuban House of Representatives, before becoming vice president of the Liberal Party in 1916. He was the favorite to win the Liberal nomination for the presidency in 1924, but he was outmaneuvered by **Gerardo Machado**, who was elected and served from 1925 to 1933. As the Machado government evolved into a brutal dictatorship, Mendieta emerged as one of its most visible opponents. He was imprisoned in 1931 for plotting an uprising in Gibara, which was quickly put down by Machado. Mendieta was opposed to the revolutionary government that took power on September 4, 1933, led by the Directorio Estudiantil Universitario and the army's enlisted men. As support for the presidency of **Ramón Grau San Martín** began to crumble, he was courted by Batista, the leader of the enlisted men, and the United States as a possible replacement. Mendieta became provisional president in January 1934, despite his concerns about the growing power of the military. His administration was marked by widespread labor unrest and political opposition. Mendieta and Batista brutally suppressed the strikes of March 1935 in order to maintain their hold on power. During his administration the United States agreed to abrogate the hated **Platt Amendment**, and a new reciprocal trade agreement between the two nations was negotiated (see **Jones-Costigan Act**). The University of Havana was granted autonomy by Mendieta and soon became the center of political opposition, both violent and nonviolent. There was a good deal of corruption during his administration, although he was personally regarded as a model of honesty. Mendieta resigned the provisional presidency in December 1935, because of his inability to get the support of the political opposition on a date for new elections. From the time of his resignation till the time of his death, some twenty-five years later, he seldom re-emerged into the public limelight. *See also* Presidents; Revolution of 1933

Further Readings

Portell-Vilá, Herminio. *Nueva historia de la República de Cuba*. Miami: La Moderna Poesía, 1986.

Riera, Mario. *Cuba política, 1899–1955*. Havana: Imprenta Modelo, S.A., 1955.

Thomas, Hugh. *Cuba: The Pursuit of Freedom*. New York: Harper & Row, 1971.

Julio Domínguez García

Moncada Army Barracks, Attack on the

The attack on the Moncada Army Barracks, located in **Santiago de Cuba**, occurred on July 26, 1953. The installation served as headquarters of Regiment 1 of the Cuban Rural Guard. The barracks, originally a Spanish base, were renamed after **War of Independence** hero Guillermo Moncada. They were rebuilt in 1937 after a fire had ravaged the facility.

The attack on Moncada was undertaken by about 50 men under the orders of **Fidel Castro** in order to seize control of the barracks and call for the overthrow of **Fulgencio Batista**. Another 50 men took a wrong turn, were lost inside the city, and were unable to take part in the attack. Several months before the attack, Castro organized a small revolutionary movement consisting of members of the left wing of the **Ortodoxos (Partido del Pueblo Cubano)** in an effort to bring down the government of Fulgencio Batista. Abel Santamaría, a lieutenant of Castro's, led the attack on the Saturnino Lora Hospital, accompanied by 20 fighters, including two women, **Haydée Santamaría** (his sister) and Melba Hernández. **Raúl Castro**, with seven men, led the attack on the Justice Palace. Both buildings were of strategic importance because of their location. At the same time, about 20 men, led by Raúl Martínez, attacked the **Carlos Manuel de Céspedes** barracks in **Bayamo**. The rebels, who were transported from Havana in seventeen automobiles, were informed of the attack by Fidel Castro only hours before it was to begin. Several of them decided against taking part in the attack. The number of participants, including the attackers at Bayamo, did not exceed 157. The date of the attack was determined by the fact that Santiago was celebrating its annual **carnival** at the time, and the movement of large numbers of people would generate less suspicion. The attack failed as a result of a lack of military equipment, tactical errors, including the lack of familiarity with the city, and the strong resistance offered by the soldiers.

Only six attackers died during the conflict (Flores Betancourt, Gildo Fleitas, Renato Guitart, José de Jesús Madera, Pedro Marrero, and Carmelo Noa), while another fifty-five died in the aftermath as a result of torture. Another fifty were tried, while seven were tried in absentia. Of the seven, two received diplomatic asylum and were allowed to go into exile. Fidel Castro, who organized his own defense, publicized and distributed his defense speech before the tribunal, which became known as *La historia me absolverá* (History Will Absolve Me) (see **Appendix 11**). Castro and several of his associates were handed long prison sentences. They received amnesty, however, after serving twenty-two months in jail. Upon their release, the Castro brothers went to Mexico, where they resumed anti-Batista activities culminating with the *Granma* **expedition** of 1956. Although the attack on Moncada failed, it inspired the growing movement against Batista whose name (**Twenty-sixth of July Movement**) commemorated the date of the attack. *See also* Batista, Struggle against; Twenty-sixth of July (Holiday)

Bullet riddled facade of the Moncada Army Barracks in Santiago de Cuba. Photograph by Ernesto Sagás.

Further Readings

Castro, Fidel. *History Will Absolve Me*. Several editions, first published in 1953 in Havana by Impresor Económico en General.

Mencía, Mario. *El grito del Moncada*. Havana: Editora Política, 1986.

Rojas, Marta. *El juicio del Moncada*. Havana: Editorial de Ciencias Sociales, 1983.

Manuel de Paz Sánchez

Morúa Delgado, Martín (1857–1910)

Martín Morua Delgado was a prominent patriot and intellectual. His mother was a freed slave and his father a Basque baker. He was trained as a cooper and organized others in the trade into several unions throughout the **Matanzas Province**. He was self-educated, and early on in life he became interested in the press as an exponent of ideas. In 1879, he founded the newspaper *El Pueblo* in **Matanzas**. He was imprisoned in 1880 for conspiring against the government and emigrated to the United States. While in the United States, he was trained as a typesetter and learned to speak English, French, Portuguese, and Italian. In exile, he worked as a reader in a tobacco factory, organized labor unions, and continued his interest in journalism, establishing *La República* newspaper in New York and *Revista Popular* in Key West. He returned to Cuba in the 1890s and joined the Liberal Autonomist Party and published *La Nueva Era*, frequently writing articles along with **Juan Gualberto Gómez**. In 1896, he again left Cuba for a period of two years. During the **War of Independence** he reached the rank of captain, while at the same time editing *Cuba Libre*. During the first U.S. occupation of Cuba (1898–1902) he published *El Republicano*. He served as a member of the Constitutional Assembly, which drafted Cuba's first constitution. In later years, he was elected to the Senate, became Senate president, and was appointed secretary of agriculture, commerce and labor. He was firmly opposed to the establishment of the Partido Independiente de Color (Independent Party of Color), believing that parties or associations consisting of members of only one racial group or class were divisive for the nation. His publications include two novels, *Sofía* and *La familia Unzuazu*. He also authored a political essay on **Afro-Cubans** titled *Ensayo político o Cuba y la raza de color*. *See also* Autonomism; Constitution of 1901; Organized Labor (Nineteenth Century); Political Exile (Nineteenth Century); Press and Journalism (Eighteenth and Nineteenth Centuries); "Race War" of 1912; Tobacco Industry; U.S. Interventions

Further Readings

De la Fuente, Alejandro. *A Nation for All: Race, Inequality, and Politics in Twentieth-Century Cuba*. Chapel Hill: University of North Carolina Press, 2001.

Horrego Estuch, Leopoldo. *Martín Morúa Delgado, vida y mensaje*. Havana: Editorial Sánchez, S.A., 1957.

Morúa Delgado, Martín. *Obras completas*. Havana: Edición de la Comisión del Centenario de Don Martín Morúa Delgado, 1957.

María del Carmen Barcia Zequeira

Mujal, Eusebio (1915–1985)

Eusebio Mujal was a politician and key trade union leader. As a youth he was a member of Cuba's Communist Party. When a Trotskyist split in that party occurred in 1929–1930, Mujal was one of its leaders and became second in command to Sandalio Junco, the head of the Federación Obrera de La Habana (FOH), which was largely controlled by the Trotskyists. The FOH generally supported the September 1933–January 1934 reformist regime of President **Ramón Grau San Martín**. After Grau's overthrow, Junco and Mujal joined **Joven Cuba**, a political organization formed by Grau's ex-Minister of the Interior **Antonio Guiteras**. However, after the murder of Guiteras during the failed revolutionary general strike against the **Fulgencio Batista** dictatorship in 1935, Junco, Mujal, and other Joven Cuba leaders joined the new **Auténticos (Partido Revolucionario Cubano)** of ex-President Grau. Junco soon became head of that party's Comisión Obrera Nacional (CON), and Mujal became his second in command. When Junco was murdered by the communists in 1942, Mujal became head of the CON.

Mujal undoubtedly was influential in the successful move of the Auténticos (and their "Independent" allies) in 1947 to take control of the Confederación de Trabajadores de Cubanos (CTC) away from the communists. In the split in the Confederación that resulted from this effort, the Auténtico-controlled faction of the CTC came to include the great majority of the organized workers. In April 1949, Mujal was elected secretary general of the CTC at its Sixth Congress. Meanwhile, he had been elected a senator by the Auténtico Party and was undoubtedly one of the most influential of the country's politicians.

The coup d'état of Fulgencio Batista in March 1952 that overthrew the Auténtico government presented Mujal and other CTC leaders with a quandary. After their effort to organize a general strike against the coup was unsuccessful, they finally reached an agreement with Batista to call off the strike in return for a promise by him not to interfere with the labor movement. However, as opposition to the Batista dictatorship, particularly opposition from within the labor movement, grew, Mujal became increasingly committed to the Batista regime. To curb labor opposition, Mujal pushed through a high degree of centralization of the Confederación and removed from office many trade union leaders who were in opposition to the regime.

With the final overthrow of Batista by the forces of **Fidel Castro**, Mujal succeeded in escaping abroad. He lived the rest of his life in exile in the United States. *See also* Coup of 1952 (March 10); Labor Movement (Republican Era); Partido Comunista (Partido Socialista Popular [Republican Era])

Further Reading
Pérez Stable, Marifeli. *The Cuban Revolution: Origins, Course, and Legacy*. 2nd ed. New York: Oxford University Press, 1999.

Robert J. Alexander

Newspapers (Republican Era)

The enormous proliferation and variety of newspapers and magazines, some of general interest and others literary, is the hallmark of the history of Cuban journalism during the republican period. In addition to their abundance, the publications are notable for the high quality of their content, print quality, photographs, and illustrations. A notable example is the newsmagazine *Bohemia*, which from its inception in 1910 was a pioneer in journalism with its unique brand of social critique, satire, literary criticism, and political and lifestyle reporting. In January 1959, *Bohemia*, in a historic issue, offered "one million" reasons for the triumph of the **Revolution**.

The dean of Cuban newspapers in this period was the *Diario de la Marina*, founded in 1844, which lasted until 1960, when it was closed as a result of its opposition to the Revolution. There were many other important newspapers including *The Havana Post* (established 1900), *El Mundo* (founded 1901), *La Prensa* (started 1909), *El Día* (1911), and *Heraldo de Cuba* (1913), which was run by **Manuel Márquez Sterling**, who in 1915 transferred it to **Orestes Ferrara**. A second wave of newspapers was established beginning in the 1920s, including *El País* (1923), *Información* (1931), *El Crisol* (1934), *Pueblo* (1937), and *Prensa Libre* (1941). Some of the newspapers, such as *El Mundo*, published literary supplements in which writers and intellectuals of the era exchanged views and collaborated with essays. By 1939, there were as many as fourteen daily newspapers being sold on the streets of Havana. While many of the larger newspapers were centered in the capital, a vibrant newspaper tradition existed in the provinces as well with such important publications as *El Camagüeyano, Diario de Cuba* (**Santiago**), and *Adelante* and *El Republicano* (**Matanzas**). In addition to newspapers, there were a number of newsmagazines in circulation, including the aforementioned *Bohemia, Gráfico* (1913), *Social* (1916), and *Carteles* (see **Literary Journals**).

The newspaper *Revolución*, written and edited clandestinely during the second **Fulgencio Batista** dictatorship (1952–1958), began to appear on a regular basis after the triumph of the Revolution. It was the official voice of the **26th of July Movement** under the direction of **Carlos Franqui**. It contained a weekly literary supplement, *Lunes de Revolución*. The Communist Party newspaper *Hoy*, previously known as *Noticias de Hoy*, re-emerged as an important voice in the aftermath of the Revolution. A little more than a year after the triumph of the Revolution, the independent press disappeared, and many of the giants of Cuban journalism, such as José Ignacio Rivero and **Sergio Carbó**, fled into exile. In 1965, *Revolución* and *Hoy* were merged into what became known as *Granma*, which is still published today. *See also Ciclón*; Newspapers and Magazines; Partido Comunista (Partido Socialista Popular [Republican Era]); Press and Journalism (Eighteenth and Nineteenth Centuries)

Further Reading

Ricardo, José G. *La imprenta en Cuba*. Havana: Letras Cubanas, 1989.

Manuel de Paz Sánchez

Organized Crime

Organized crime expanded its presence in Cuba during the 1950s, when some of the interests of the **Fulgencio Batista** government (1952–1958) coincided with those of crime organizations, at a time when expanding North American **tourism** created new market possibilities. At about the same time, the Estes Kefauver congressional crime hearings had a deleterious effect on crime interests operating in the United States, thereby forcing underworld elements to relocate gambling interests to Cuba. The Batista government obligingly modified existing gambling regulations to permit any nightclub or hotel in Havana worth $1 million or more and more than $500,000 outside the capital to operate gambling casinos.

By the late 1950s, the principal hotels and casinos had passed under the control of the various crime syndicates. Tens of millions of dollars were invested in luxury hotels, nightclubs, and gambling casinos. Some of the most glamorous hotels and casinos of Havana, including the Parisién Casino of the Hotel Nacional, the **Tropicana** casino, the Sans Souci, the Capri, the Riviera Hotel, the Montmartre, the Seville-Biltmore, the Internacional, the Comodoro, and the Havana Hilton, were operated by underworld interests.

The underworld presence became a familiar sight in Havana, ranging from the high-profile mobster to the small-time hood and hustler. During the 1950s, gambling receipts surpassed $500,000 monthly. Crime interests expanded into **prostitution** and illegal drugs, and by the late 1950s Cuba was poised to become the base of international drug trafficking.

Profits on so lavish a scale inevitably implicated Cuban officials high and low. Millions of dollars were distributed to politicians and law enforcement agents in the form of "gifts," outright bribes, and direct payoffs, designed principally to permit crime interests to operate without interference from local officials. With the overthrow of the Batista government, organized crime interests were expelled from the island.

Further Readings

Coe, Andrew. "Mobsters in Paradise." In id. *Cuba.* Hong Kong: Odyssey Guides, 1997. Pp. 134–139.

Schwartz, Rosalie. *Pleasure Island: Tourism and Temptation in Cuba.* Lincoln: University of Nebraska Press, 1997.

Louis A. Pérez, Jr.

Ortodoxos (Partido del Pueblo Cubano)

When the **Auténticos (Partido Revolucionario Cubano)** were in office during the administrations of **Ramón Grau San Martín** and **Carlos Prío Socarrás** (1944–1952), the party proved itself to be even

Political pamphlet of the Partido del Pueblo Cubano (Ortodoxos) founded by Eduardo Chibás. Courtesy of Special Collections and University Archives, Rutgers University Libraries.

more corrupt than previous Cuban governments had been. On May 15, 1947, **Eduardo Chibás**, a former student leader from the **Revolution of 1933**, and others split off to form a new political organization called the Partido del Pueblo Cubano (Ortodoxos). Within several months, the new party ranked fifth in number of members among political parties in Cuba.

The program of the Ortodoxos called for economic independence, agricultural diversification, nationalization of public services, elimination of political gangsterism, state control over production and exports, and the end of racial and class discrimination, among other things. The only conditions for party membership included acceptance of these party positions and of the leadership of Eduardo Chibás. Party membership was very heterogeneous; it included communists, intellectuals, large landowners, and even more conservative members of the Catholic Church (see **Partido Comunista** and **Catholicism**).

The symbol of the Ortodoxos was a broom, indicative of its goal to sweep away the corruption that was seen as the main evil of successive Cuban governments. **Fidel Castro** and many others who were to become instrumental during the **Revolution** of 1959 were Ortodoxos. They lost their spark when Chibás, a rising political star, committed suicide on the air during his radio program in 1951 after failing to produce evidence to sustain the corruption charges he had made against the minister of education. *See also* Agramonte y Pichardo, Roberto

Further Readings

Ameringer, Charles D. *The Cuban Democratic Experience: The Auténtico Years, 1944–1952.* Gainesville: University Press of Florida, 2000.

Conte Agüero, Luis. *Eduardo Chibás, el adalid de Cuba.* Miami: La Moderna Poesía, 1987.

Portell-Vilá, Herminio. *Nueva historia de la República de Cuba.* Miami: La Moderna Poesía, 1986.

Riera, Mario. *Cuba política, 1899–1955.* Havana: Editora Modelo, S.A., 1955.

Paula J. Pettavino

País, Frank (1934–1957)

Best known for his leadership role in the **Santiago de Cuba** branch of the **26th of July Movement**, Frank País (known to his comrades by the pseudonyms "David" and "Cristián") was a key figure in the urban underground opposition to the **Fulgencio Batista** dictatorship. Heavily influenced by his Baptist background (his father was a Baptist minister and a Spanish immigrant of modest means), País's activism went back to his teenage years in 1952, one year before **Fidel Castro**'s attack on the **Moncada Army Barracks**. Trained as a teacher at the National Teachers School in Santiago, he founded and led the Santiago wing of Acción Nacional Revolucionaria, an organization that toward the end of 1955 agreed to join forces with the 26th of July Movement as part of the preparation for Castro's plans to launch an expedition to southeastern Cuba. He quickly came to be the dominant figure in the clandestine apparatus of the 26th of July Movement. The *Granma* **expedition** that left Mexico at the end of November 1956 was planned to coincide with an armed insurrection in Santiago de Cuba on November 30. País, however, was one of several urban activists who had reservations about the viability of the project, and he spoke frankly to Castro about these doubts during a visit to Mexico where plans for the expedition were being made. In fact, the *Granma* and its crew arrived two days late. Although the Santiago insurrectionists were briefly successful in occupying key positions in the city, most of the leaders of the uprising were arrested or, in the case of País's closest collaborators, Pepito Tey, Otto Parellada, and Tony Alomá, killed.

As one of the key figures in the *llano*, or urban wing, of the 26th of July Movement, it was País's responsibility (along with **Vilma Espín, Celia Sánchez** and **Haydée Santamaría**) to supply the **Sierra Maestra**–based guerrillas with medicines, money, food, and above all a stream of recruits in spite of their doubts about the overemphasis on guerrilla struggle that proponents of the sierra wing of the movement had developed. País employed his exceptional organizational skills to construct an elaborate underground movement in major Oriente cities such as Guantánamo, **Holguín**, Manzanillo, and **Bayamo**, and he was a frequent visitor to Las Villas and **La Habana** provinces to extend the reach of the revolutionary movement. However, País never lived to see the overthrow of the dictatorship or even the launching of a second guerrilla front that had become a constant preoccupation during his last few months. On July 30, 1957, aged twenty-two, he was killed by the police in his house in Santiago. A spontaneous general strike was declared by Santiago workers, but the lack of preparation for the action made the planned extension of the strike to the rest of Cuba impossible. In commemoration of País's heroism, Castro named the second front (see **Segundo Frente Oriental "Frank País"**), finally launched by his brother Raúl in March 1958 in the Sierra Cristal, after the murdered Santiago leader. *See also* Batista, Struggle Against; Castro, Raúl

Further Reading

Malo de Molina, Gustavo F. *Frank País: apuntes sobre un luchador clandestino*. Havana: Gente Nueva, 1979.

Barry Carr

Partido Comunista (Partido Socialista Popular [Republican Era])

The Russian Bolshevik Revolution had a strong impact on Cuba, particularly on its fledgling labor movement, and among the country's student organizations. Cuban sympathizers of both the socialists and the anarchists who had dominated organized labor were attracted to the Bolshevik regime and to the Communist International (Comintern), to which it gave rise.

In 1925, Cuba's Communist Party (**Partido Comunista**) was founded, its early leaders including the student activists **Julio Antonio Mella**, the trade union leader **Carlos Baliño**, and the poet **Rubén Martínez Villena**. It immediately began to seek to penetrate the newly established central labor group, the Confederación Nacional Obrera de Cuba (CNOC). By 1929 the communists had displaced the anarchists in the leadership of the CNOC, César Villar soon becoming its secretary general.

The communists participated in the struggle against the dictatorship of President **Gerardo Machado**. They also under-took for virtually the first time the unionization of the sugar workers, the country's largest group of wage earners. By 1933, the CNOC was the country's strongest labor group, although it faced various rivals in Havana and some other cities.

In early August 1933, a left-wing nationalist regime headed by Professor **Ramón Grau San Martín** seized power; the communists strongly opposed this government. In doing so, they followed the Comintern's "Third Period" line then in effect, according to which all non-Stalinist left-wing groups were deemed "social fascist" and to be fought at all costs. Grau San Martín was overthrown in January 1934 by **Fulgencio Batista**, the former sergeant who had originally brought him to power. Batista soon established a dictatorship, which the communists opposed for several years. However, in mid-1938, the Communist Party reached an agreement with Batista, whereby he agreed to legalize their party and to allow them to lead the establishment of a new central labor organization, in return for which the communists would back Batista's presidential aspirations.

The Partido Unión Revolucionaria, a front for the Communist Party, had already been legalized in 1937. Two years later, it merged with the underground Communist Party to form the Partido Unión Revolucionaria Comunista, which was likewise legalized. The communists officially formed part of the electoral bloc formed under the Batista leadership. As part of this coalition, they elected members of the 1940 constitutional convention and then members of the Senate and Chamber of Deputies (see Constitution of 1940). In 1944, two of the party's leaders, **Juan Marinello** and **Carlos Rafael Rodríguez**, became members of Batista's cabinet. That year, the communists, by then known as the Partido Socialista Popular (PSP), supported Batista's candidate for president, who was defeated by ex-President Grau

San Martín. Three years later, Grau's **Auténticos** were able, with the government's help, to take control of the Confederación de Trabajadores de Cuba away from the communists. By the time of Batista's overthrow of the Auténtico regime in March 1952, the communists' influence in organized labor and general politics had been drastically reduced. Although upon his return to power Batista formally outlawed the Communist Party, it was able to function without major difficulties—for instance, most of its periodicals continued to appear legally.

The party long denounced **Fidel Castro**'s attempt to overthrow Batista by guerrilla warfare. Only in the summer of 1958, a few months before Castro's victory, did **Carlos Rafael Rodríguez** join Castro's forces, seeking an alliance with him for the party. With the Castro forces' victory on January 1, 1959, the PSP offered its "critical" support. However, its efforts to regain control of the labor movement were largely defeated by the trade unionists of Castro's **26th of July Movement**, until Castro himself, in November 1959, finally forced the "cooperation" of his followers with the PSP. This led to massive purges of the newly elected trade union leadership and ultimately brought the return of **Lázaro Peña**, who had headed the communist-led Confederación de Trabajadores de Cuba (CTC) from 1939 onward, to be once again the CTC secretary general.

The PSP finally disappeared with the formation of the single party of the Castro regime, which in 1965 became the country's second Communist Party. *See also* Communist Party, Cuban (Partido Comunista Cubano [PCC]; Labor Movement (Republican Era); Organized Labor (Nineteenth Century); Students' Movement (Republican Era)

Further Readings

Montes, Jorge, and Antonio Alonso Ávila. *Historia del Partido Comunista de Cuba*. Miami: Ediciones Universal, 1970.

Sims, Harold D. "Cuban Labor and the Communist Party, 1937–1958: An Interpretation." *Cuban Studies* 15, no. 1 (Winter 1985): 43–58.

Robert J. Alexander

Peña, Lázaro (1911–1974)

Lázaro Peña was for many years the most outstanding Communist Party trade union leader. He first emerged as a leader of the tobacco workers, and his first success was in getting control of that group for the Communist Party. In recognition of that, he became the secretary general of the Confederación Nacional Obrera de Cuba.

When General **Fulgencio Batista** reached an agreement with the Communist Party in 1939 to permit the revival of the **labor movement** under communist leadership, a new central labor group, the Confederación de Trabajadores de Cuba (CTC), was established in January 1939, with Peña as its secretary general. He continued to hold that post in the united CTC for about a decade. During this period, Peña gained a reputation for being a very competent administrator and politician. Even his strong political opponents conceded that he had the capacity of defusing confrontations and finding a way out of critical situations, at least so long as power within the CTC remained in the hands of the communists and they had the support of the Batista government. However, in 1947 these conditions no longer prevailed. Almost three years earlier, ex-President **Ramón Grau San Martín** had been elected to succeed Batista. In 1946, Grau's **Auténticos** had also won control of the legislature. In the face of those developments, the Auténticos decided to move to gain control of the Confederación de Trabajadores de Cuba. This effort resulted in a split in the CTC, leaving the communist-controlled faction with only a small part of the labor movement in its ranks. Peña remained secretary general of the communist version of the CTC.

By the overthrow of the second Batista dictatorship on January 1, 1959, the only

CTC in existence was that which had originally been under Auténtico control. In the beginning, **Fidel Castro**'s **26th of July Movement** was overwhelmingly in control of the CTC and most of its constituent unions. However, by the end of 1959 Castro and other top figures in the government demanded that CTC control be turned over to the communists and their fellow travelers, a demand that resulted in a massive purge of the newly elected union leadership.

This purge process culminated in 1961, when Peña was once again made secretary general of the CTC. However, in 1966 after having some disagreements with the government, he was removed from that post, only to be restored to it two years later. Peña died in 1974 while serving as secretary general of the CTC. *See also* Tobacco Industry

Further Reading

Peña, Lázaro. *Lázaro Peña, capitán de la clase obrera Cubana*. Havana: Editorial de Ciencias Sociales, 1984.

Robert J. Alexander

Platt Amendment

The Platt Amendment defined Cuba's relations with the United States and the international community until it was repealed by treaty in 1934 (see **Appendix 10**). Sponsored by Senator Orville Platt, it was enacted by the U.S. Congress in February 1901 and included in the Cuban **Constitution of 1901**. The Cuban government was prohibited from entering treaties or contracting debts without U.S. approval, and the United States was authorized "to intervene for the preservation of Cuban independence [and] the maintenance of a government adequate for the protection of life, property, and individual liberty." The Platt Amendment also authorized the U.S. naval base at Guantánamo Bay. This provision was retained when the amendment's other provisions were repealed, and the naval base remained even after the Cuban **Revolution** of 1959.

The adoption of the Platt Amendment without modification by the Cuban constitutional assembly was a condition imposed by the U.S. government for the removal of the forces that had occupied the island since 1898. Although outright annexation of the island was barred by the Teller Amendment of 1898, the imposition of the Platt Amendment allowed the United States to grant formal independence while retaining control over Cuba. Cubans and North Americans alike justified the repeated interventions of the United States in Cuba in later years by reference to the Platt Amendment's provisions. *See also* Guantánamo U.S. Naval Base; U.S. Interventions; Reciprocity Treaty (1902), U.S.–Cuba

Further Readings

Hitchman, James H. "The Platt Amendment Revisited: A Bibliographical Survey." *The Americas* 23 (April 1967): 343–69.

Pérez, Louis A. Jr. *Cuba under the Platt Amendment, 1902–1934*. Pittsburgh: University of Pittsburgh Press, 1986.

Roig de Leuchsenring, Emilo. *Historia de la Enmienda Platt*. 2nd ed. 2 vols. Havana: Oficina del Historiador de la Ciudad, 1961

Mariola Espinosa

Presidents

Between the inauguration of the Cuban Republic in 1902 and the **Revolution** of 1959, Cuba had seventeen different presidents; some held that position for a few days or even just a few hours; two of them, **Ramón Grau San Martín** and **Fulgencio Batista**, presided over Cuba on two different occasions (see **Appendix 15**).

Between 1902 and the **Revolution of 1933**, Cuba elected five different presidents. Cuba's first president was **Tomás Estrada Palma**, who ran uncontested in 1901. An acceptable candidate for U.S. interests, he was elected without having set foot on the island since going into exile in 1877. Estrada Palma sought reelection in 1906 and won through widespread electoral fraud. The opposition Liberal Party under **José Miguel Gómez** opposed the ruling Conservatives militarily, and Estrada Palma resigned the presidency on September 28, 1906, requesting the intervention of U.S. troops. Under the U.S. occupation, elections were held in 1908, and Liberal *caudillo* José Miguel Gómez ascended to the presidency on January 28, 1909, under circumstances that provided further guarantees to U.S. interests. In 1912 **Mario García Menocal** of the Conservative Party won against **Alfredo Zayas** of the divided Liberal Party. This was the first peaceful government transition since the advent of the republic. When Menocal retained the presidency through fraud in the 1916 elections, the Liberals revolted again, this time in larger numbers in what came to be known as the revolt of la Chambelona. At that juncture, U.S. troops intervened for a third time, remaining on the island until the end of Menocal's second term in 1921. In 1921 Alfredo Zayas was elected president under the new Partido Popular ticket. Recognized as the most corrupt government to date, Zayas's administration ended on May 20, 1925, as **Gerardo Machado** of the Liberal Party assumed the presidency. Machado maneuvered to extend his term in power, altering the constitution so that he could be reelected in 1928 for a new six-year term.

Machado's presidency turned despotic and came to an end with his resignation on August 12, 1933, against the backdrop of the Revolution of 1933; he fled Cuba, never to return. The next three years were chaotic, with eight different "administrations" between August 12, 1933, and May 20, 1936. General Alberto Herrera filled the presidency for a few hours, following Machado's resignation. Then Carlos Manuel de Céspedes y Quesada presided for three weeks and was succeeded on September 4 by the so-called Pentarquía, a ruling junta composed of Porfirio Franca, Ramón Grau San Martín, Guillermo Portela, José Miguel Irisarri, and **Sergio Carbó**. The Pentarquía was also short-lived, and one of its members, Grau, ascended to the presidency between September 10, 1933, and January 15, 1934. **Carlos Hevia** succeeded Grau for little over two days, and **Manuel Márquez Sterling** assumed the interim presidency for just a few hours. Two Batista puppet presidents followed: **Carlos Mendieta Montefur**, who presided between January 18, 1934, and December 11, 1935, and the Spanish-born José Agripino Barnet, who presided until May 20, 1936. **Miguel Mariano Gómez**, son of former president José Miguel Gómez, assumed the presidency on May 20, 1936; his independence from Batista, who insisted on ruling behind the throne, escalated into a constitutional confrontation that culminated in his impeachment and destitution. **Federico Laredo Brú**, another Batista puppet, became president on December 24, 1936.

In what by most accounts was a fair election, Batista was elected president in 1940 under the auspices of the progressive **Constitution of 1940**. The new constitution prohibited the reelection of presidents, by then widely feared as the first step toward dictatorship. Abiding by the democratic rules he himself helped craft, Batista moved out of the **Presidential Palace** after his own candidate, Carlos Saladrigas of the Socialist-Democratic Coalition, was defeated by the opposition **Auténticos (Partido Revolucionario Cubano)**'s candidate Grau. Peaceful transition occurred again in 1948, when Grau's political heir, **Carlos Prío Socarrás** was elected president, defeating Ricardo Núñez Portuondo of the Liberal and Democratic Parties and **Eduardo Chibás** of the **Ortodoxos (Partido del Pueblo Cubano)**. This was the third straight regularly held, fairly clean and peaceful election. Cuba's democratic, albeit corrupt and violent, political experience was cut short on March 10, 1952, when a military coup brought Batista back to power. While Batista held on to power, yet another puppet president did his bidding: Andrés Domingo y Morales del Castillo was president from April 6, 1954, to February 24, 1955. Batista's dictatorship came to an end on January 1, 1959, with the triumph of **Fidel Castro**'s revolutionary forces. **Manuel Urrutia Lleó** presided briefly over the revolutionary government until Castro, who wielded actual power, forced him out of office. **Osvaldo Dorticós Torrado** succeeded Urrutia on July 16, 1959, and held what was then a mostly ceremonial role while Castro served as prime minister. No presidential elections have been held since the advent of the Revolution and dictator Fidel Castro assumed the title of president in 1976. His heir-designate is his younger brother **Raúl Castro**.

Further Readings

Portell-Vilá, Herminio. *Nueva historia de la República de Cuba*. Miami: La Moderna Poesía, 1986.

Riera, Mario. *Cuba política, 1899–1955*. Havana: Editora Modelo, S.A., 1955.

Luis Martínez-Fernández

Prío Socarrás, Carlos (1903–1977)

Carlos Prío Socarrás was Cuba's last democratically elected president; he served between October 1948 and March 10, 1952, when his term was cut short by **Fulgencio Batista**'s military coup. Born in Bahía Honda (then part of **Pinar del Río Province**) on July 14, 1903, Prío began his political career as a student leader in the opposition against **Gerardo Machado**'s dictatorship. While studying law at the **University of Havana**, he founded the Directorio Estudiantil Universitario, which

became instrumental in the struggle against Machado. In 1933 Prío presided over the Junta Revolucionaria Cubana, and the following year he figured among the founders of the **Auténticos (Partido Revolucionario Cubano)**. In 1939 he represented his party at the Constitutional Convention and in 1940 was elected to the Cuban Senate; he was reelected four years later, when his political mentor **Ramón Grau San Martín** gained the presidency. Prío's appointment as prime minister in October 1945 signaled Grau's intentions to have him succeed him as the Auténticos' next presidential candidate. During 1947–1948 Prío served as labor minister, a position from which he orchestrated the removal of **Lázaro Peña** and other communists from leadership positions in the Confederación de Trabajadores de Cuba (CTC). **Eusebio Mujal** and other Auténtico labor leaders eventually gained control of the powerful CTC.

Prío's administration, known as the "cordial presidency," was characterized by adherence to the democratic principles of the **Constitution of 1940**, but it was tarnished by growing corruption and the continuation of political gangsterism; it was estimated that Prío illegally appropriated $90 million. While passing legislation to combat gangsterism, his administration continued to support and fund those practices. Some progressive social legislation was enacted during Prío's presidential term, including the expansion of retirement programs for workers and some land reform efforts. Prío established the Banco Nacional de Cuba in 1950 and the Banco Nacional de Fomento Agrícola e Industrial de Cuba in 1951.

Following his ouster from the presidency, Prío sought exile in Mexico and later moved to Miami, where he led efforts against the Batista regime; taking advantage of a political amnesty, Prío returned to Cuba in mid-1955 and organized several anti-Batista rallies. He was once again

Carlos Prío Socarrás, Cuba's last democratically-elected president (1948-1952). Courtesy of the Digitalization Project of the *El Mundo* Photographic Collection, University of Puerto Rico, Río Piedras Campus.

forced to flee in May 1956. From exile, Prío coordinated and financed several anti-Batista movements and operations including the failed attack on the Goicuría Barracks in **Matanzas** (April 1956) and the insurrectionary activities of Carlos Gutiérrez Menoyo, Eufemio Fernández, and Aureliano Sánchez Arango. While helping finance **Fidel Castro**'s guerrilla movement, he financed the *Corinthia* expedition (May 1957), designed to rival Castro's forces in the island's Oriental districts. The U.S. government opposed these activities and brought charges against Prío; he was incarcerated in the United States in 1953 and again in 1957. The former recipient of the Legion of Merit Medal at the hands of President Harry S Truman was paraded in handcuffs by U.S. marshals in the streets of Miami and later found guilty by a federal judge. Upon the triumph of Castro's guerrillas, Prío returned to Cuba and pub-

licly supported the new government. Soon thereafter, Prío distanced himself from the Castro regime, seeking exile in 1961. He settled in Miami, where he committed suicide in April 1977. *See also* Batista, Struggle Against; Communist Party, Cuban (Partido Comunista Cubano [PCC]); Coup of 1952 (March 10); *Granma* Expedition Carrillo Hernández, Justo; Labor Movement (Republican Era); Presidents; Students' Movement (Republican Era)

Further Readings
Ameringer, Charles D. *The Cuban Democratic Experience: The Auténtico Years, 1944–1952.* Gainesville: University Press of Florida, 2000.
Riera Hernández, Mario. *Un presidente cordial: Carlos Prío Socarrás, 1927–1964.* n.p. n.d.

Luis Martínez-Fernández

"Race War" of 1912

The three-day armed protest organized by the Partido Independiente de Color (PIC), and the scattered violence that surrounded it in May and June of 1912, fundamentally altered the terms on which **Afro-Cubans** participated in public life. Accusations of a "race war" by newspapers and politicians fueled a backlash that led to the killing of thousands of Afro-Cubans, including PIC leaders Evaristo Estenoz and Pedro Ivonnet, and forced the abandonment of the party as a means to political inclusion. Formed in 1907, the PIC had been declared illegal in 1910 with an amendment to the electoral law by **Martín Morúa Delgado**, an Afro-Cuban Liberal senator. Facing exclusion from running in upcoming elections, the PIC organized an armed protest for May 20, 1912, in order to pressure the administration of President **José Miguel Gómez** to repeal the Morúa amendment. Several hundred *independientes* and sympathizers gathered in southern Oriente and threatened the destruction of foreign property. Two fugitive bands operated in **Santa Clara**, but uprisings by the party outside of Oriente were largely muted. The actions of the PIC, however, ignited broader social unrest as black and mulatto peasants attacked foreign property, especially sugar estates, and cut off lines of communication.

Simultaneously, inflammatory reports of black rebellion circulated throughout the island in the popular press, and white volunteers mobilized militias. In late May, the United States sent marines to garrison railroads and North American property. The Cuban Army took control when a forty-five-day suspension of constitutional guarantees began on June 5. Additional troops converged on Oriente to forcibly relocate the rural population to towns, to restrict civil liberties, and to prevent the entry of Jamaican and Haitian workers of African descent. Soldiers, policemen, and militias patrolled the cities and countryside, arresting, assaulting, and killing Afro-Cubans indiscriminately. The repression ebbed by late June, but white fears of black violence did not. Few Cubans raised their voices to condemn the killings, and the public display of the bodies of Estenoz and Ivonnet in **Santiago de Cuba** evinced a powerful message of retribution. With the memory of the brutal violence and the extinction of the PIC, Afro-Cubans after 1912 had to develop alternative strategies to exercise their political voice. *See also* Immigration (Twentieth Century); Newspapers (Republican Era); Racial Composition; U.S. Interventions

Further Readings

De la Fuente, Alejandro. *A Nation for All: Race, Inequality, and Politics in Twentieth-Century Cuba.* Chapel Hill: University of North Carolina Press, 2001.

Fermoselle, Rafael. *Política y color en Cuba: la guerrita de 1912.* Montevideo: Editorial Géminis, 1974.

Helg, Aline. *Our Rightful Share: The Afro-Cuban Struggle for Equality, 1886–1912.* Chapel Hill: University of North Carolina Press, 1995.

Pérez, Louis A., Jr. "Politics, Peasants, and People of Color: The 1912 'Race War' in Cuba Reconsidered." *Hispanic American Historical Review* 66, no. 3 (1986): 509–539.

David A. Sartorius

Reciprocity Treaty (1902), U.S.-Cuba

A major trade agreement between Cuba and the United States, the Reciprocity Treaty of 1902 granted preferential treatment to exports from both nations in each other's markets. Cuba's sugar exports received a 20 percent discount at U.S. customs, while U.S. exports received discounts of between 20 and 40 percent (26 percent on average) when entering Cuba. This treaty helped consolidate a commercial structure based on the exchange of insular sugar and tobacco for U.S. manufactures and capital goods. In combination with the **Platt Amendment**, the Reciprocity Treaty became a major juridical prop to the establishment of a U.S. protectorate over Cuba in the aftermath of the **U.S. intervention** in the Cuban **War of Independence**.

The Reciprocity Treaty helped establish a sugar monoculture for virtually a single market and helped propel an accelerated growth in sugar production from 888,000 tons in 1902 to 2.5 million tons in 1913. Eighty percent of that output headed to the United States. In the other direction, the proportion of U.S.-made imports in Cuba nearly doubled, from 40 percent in 1900 to 70 to 75 percent during the 1920s.

The raising of U.S. duties on Cuban sugar during the 1920s altered the previous spirit of reciprocity. Cuba, however, was able to renegotiate a favorable sugar preference in 1934. As a result of the **Jones-Costigan Act** of 1934, Cuba was granted a large portion of the U.S. sugar quota. While other Cuban agroexports also benefited, tobacco secured only 18 percent of U.S. demand. With slight alterations, the

Meeting of two of the protagonists of the Revolution of 1933, Batista and Grau San Martín. AP/Wide World Photos.

agreements of 1934 remained in place until 1959. *See also* Hawley-Smoot Tariff Act; Sugar Industry; Tobacco Industry

Further Readings

Alienes, Julián. *Características fundamentales de la economía cubana*. Havana: Banco Nacional de Cuba, 1950.

Ayala, César J. *American Sugar Kingdom: The Plantation Economy of the Spanish Caribbean, 1898–1934*. Chapel Hill: University of North Carolina Press, 1999.

Zanetti Lecuona, Oscar. *Los cautivos de la reciprocidad. La burguesía cubana y la dependencia comercial, 1899–1959*. Havana: Empresa de Producción de la Educación Superior, 1989.

Antonio Santamaría García

Revolution of 1933

An important watershed in Cuban history, the Revolution of 1933 redefined relations between the United States and Cuba, workers and business, and men and women and the state. The failure of the revolutionary government, at least partially as a result of U.S. interference, served as a powerful symbol for revolutionaries a generation later.

What started as a revolt by the sergeants and enlisted men of the army, led by Sergeant **Fulgencio Batista**, against the officers turned into a broad social movement as a result of an alliance between the enlisted men and the Directorio Estudiantil Universitario (University Student Directory). The enlisted men and students agreed to form a new government on September 4, 1933, and ousted President Carlos Manuel de Céspedes y Quesada, an ally of the United States, the following day. Céspedes was replaced by a five-man executive commission, known as the Pentarchy, which functioned for only a few days. The confusion created by the shared presidency led the student leaders to abandon it and appoint **Ramón Grau San Martín**, a popular professor of medicine at the **University of Havana**, as president. Grau was sworn in on September 10 and appointed his cabinet several days later, including

Antonio Guiteras as minister of the interior. Grau, Guiteras, and Batista would form three sides of a political triangle vying for control of the government and the revolutions. Batista, a man without a defined political agenda, was willing to negotiate with the political opposition, including the United States, to ensure his own survival. In contrast, Guiteras, a devoted nationalist and socialist, would do everything in his power to undermine U.S. influence on the island. Grau attempted to steer a middle course, trying to placate the cry for radical reform from Guiteras and the Left, while at the same time negotiating with the political opposition. In the end, while trying to satisfy everyone a little bit, Grau antagonized everyone a great deal.

Amidst the violence, political treachery, shifting alliances, and U.S. interference, the revolutionary government enacted by decree a breathtaking series of laws that profoundly changed Cuban society. During the revolutionary government's four-month hold on power (September 1933–January 1934), workers were granted an eight-hour workday and a minimum wage. Women were granted the right to vote and allowed to run for public office. The government reduced electric rates and took over the U.S.-owned Cuban Electric Company to settle a strike on behalf of the workers. The government targeted foreign companies by requiring that at least 50 percent of their workforce be Cuban. In terms of rural issues, the government forced sugar mills to grind more sugarcane produced by small independent farmers (**colonos**). It forbade companies, a common practice in sugar growing areas, from paying their employees with vouchers or tokens that could only be used at company stores. On the foreign policy front, the revolutionary government failed to recognize the **Platt Amendment**, which gave the United States the right to intervene in Cuban affairs, and declined to pay back loans made by the Chase National Bank.

As a result of these wide-ranging measures, the revolutionary government was unable to secure support from the middle and upper classes in Cuban society. The United States, represented by Ambassador Sumner Welles and later Jefferson Caffery, was hostile to the Grau government from its inception. It undermined the revolutionary government by failing to recognize it, which encouraged political unrest and violent uprisings. The government succeeded in putting down several dangerous challenges, first at the Hotel Nacional (October 2) by the deposed officer corps and then a military uprising supported by the **ABC Revolutionary Society** (November 8–9).

But with no end to the violence in sight, Batista negotiated an agreement with the political opposition and agreed to support **Carlos Mendieta**, a veteran of the **War of Independence**, for the presidency. Grau, abandoned by the students, left power on January 15 and sailed a few days later to Mexico. Guiteras, unable to block Batista, went into hiding and was killed in a shootout with the army the following year. Grau was replaced briefly by Agriculture and Commerce Minister **Carlos Hevia**, a compromise candidate, who resigned on January 18, unable to secure the support of the political opposition. Mendieta then assumed the presidency, ushering in what has come to be known as the era of the "Puppet Presidents" (1934–1939), because behind a constitutional facade, Batista effectively ruled the island.

In the aftermath of the Revolution of 1933, the United States agreed to abrogate the hated **Platt Amendment**. The Cuban governments that followed the revolution did not rescind the far-reaching labor and social legislation, and most of those measures were codified and expanded by the **Constitution of 1940**.

Still there is the sense that the Revolution of 1933 was a missed opportunity.

The problems of land reform, U.S. economic domination, and the need to establish an equal relationship between Cuba and the United States were never completely addressed. Just as important as the failure of the revolutionary government was the failure over the next twenty-five years to live up to the promise of the revolution. The democratic principles and nationalist agenda of the revolution were ultimately derailed by the corruption, violence, and decadence of the generation of political leaders that led it. Their failure laid the groundwork for the **Revolution** of 1959. *See also* Students' Movement (Republican Era); U.S. Interventions

Further Readings

Adam y Silva, Ricardo. *La gran mentira: 4 de Septiembre de 1933*. Havana: Editorial Lex, 1947.

Aguilar, Luis E. *Cuba 1933: Prologue to Revolution*. Ithaca, NY.: Cornell University Press, 1972.

Carrillo, Justo. *Cuba 1933: estudiantes, yanquis y soldados*. Miami: Instituto de Estudios Interamericanos, 1985.

Soto, Lionel. *La Revolución del 33*. 3 vols. Havana: Editorial Pueblo y Educación, 1985.

Tabares del Real, José A. *La Revolución del 30: sus dos últimos años*. Havana: Editorial de Ciencias Sociales, 1973.

Whitney, Robert. *State and Revolution in Cuba: Mass Mobilization and Political Change, 1920–1940*. Chapel Hill: University of North Carolina Press, 2001.

Frank Argote-Freyre

Rionda y Polledo, Manuel (1854–1943)

Sugar tycoon Manuel Rionda was born in Norena, Asturias, Spain, and migrated to New York in 1870, where he worked for the Czarnikow-MacDougall Company. In 1891, he founded with his brother Francisco, who was living in Cuba, a company to repair and restore the sugar mill Tuinicú. This sugar mill was one of the first Spanish business enterprises to receive funding from U.S. sources.

Work ceased during the **War of Independence**, but at the end of the conflict, and with financial help from sugar barons Henry O. Havemeyer and Walter E. Ogilvie, Rionda reactivated the mill. In 1899, his brother died, and Rionda took over the company and erected the sugar mill Francisco in **Camagüey Province**, in memory of his brother. In 1907 he founded the Cuban Trading Company. Later on, he created the Regla Coal Company to supply coal to his sugar mills.

In 1912, after the death of Caesar Czarnikow and the retirement of his partner MacDougall, the company was reorganized with a new name—Czarnikow-Rionda Co.—with Rionda y Polledo serving as its president. In association with the American companies Sullivan & Cromwell, and J. & W. Seligman, Rionda y Polledo then founded the Manatí sugar mill. Three years later, taking advantage of the need for sugar production during World War I, the three companies, along with Morgan & Company and Chase National Bank, created the Cuba Cane Sugar Company. This consortium controlled seventeen sugar mills throughout Cuba and processed 14 percent of the sugar produced on the island.

Rionda presided over the Cuba Cane Sugar Company until 1921 when the company was reorganized due to a drop in the price of sugar. Rionda, however, continued to manage the Cuban Trading Company successfully, and when he died in 1943, the company owned eight sugar mills and was the second largest producer of sugar in the Caribbean. Rionda's heirs maintained ownership and management of the company until the advent of the **Cuban Revolution** (see **Agrarian Reform Acts**). *See also* Foreign Investments (Republican Era); Lobo, Julio; Sugar Industry

Further Readings

Ayala, César J. *American Sugar Kingdom: The Plantation Economy of the Spanish Caribbean, 1898–1934*. Chapel Hill: University of North Carolina Press, 1999.

Dye, Alan D. *Cuban Sugar in the Age of Mass Production*. Stanford, CA: Stanford University Press, 1998.

Santamaría García, Antonio. *Sin azúcar no hay país. La industria azucarera y la economía cubana*. Seville: Universidad de Sevilla-Consejo Superior de Investigaciones Científicas, 2001.

Antonio Santamaría García

Sabas Alomá, Mariblanca (1901–1983)

Mariblanca Sabas Alomá, journalist and feminist leader. Photograph from *Memoria del Segundo Congreso Nacional de Mujeres* (Havana, 1925).

A journalist with a direct and precise style, Mariblanca Sabas Alomá was an important advocate for **women's rights** in Cuba. She was a delegate to the Congresos Nacionales de Mujeres (National Women's Congresses) celebrated in Havana in 1923 and 1925. Her books and articles were widely read during the 1920s by members of the feminist movement, of which she was a prominent leader. She gained great fame in Cuba, and, significantly, her face was featured on match boxes. Sabas Alomá was widely criticized by revolutionary groups for taking a public information post in the government of President **Gerardo Machado**, a dictator who would later be forced from power. In the 1920s, she was a member of the **Grupo Minorista**, which advocated for the moral, social, and political regeneration of Cuban society. She was also a member of El Club Femenino de Cuba. She was a journalist for more than forty years working at *Bohemia* (1927–1930), *Carteles* (1928–1933), *Avance* (1940–1946), and *El Mundo* (1961–1968). She ended her career as a reporter for *Romances*. *See also* Feminist Movement (Republican Era); Newspapers (Republican Era); Women's Suffrage Movement

Further Readings

Núñez Machín, Ana. *Mujeres en el periodismo cubano*. Santiago de Cuba: Editorial Oriente, 1989.

Stoner, Lynn K. *From the House to the Streets: The Cuban Women's Movement for Legal Reform, 1898–1940*. Durham, NC: Duke University Press, 1991.

Julio César González Pagés

Sanguily Garritte, Manuel (1848–1925)

A passionate advocate and polemicist for Cuban independence, Manuel Sanguily, like many Cuban leaders of his generation, was fervently dedicated to the establishment of a Cuban nation and believed fervently that journalism could be used as a powerful weapon to attain that goal. A native of Havana, Sanguily fought with great courage, like his brother General Julio Sanguily, during the **Ten Years' War**. He rose to the rank of colonel during that conflict. In exile, he worked with **José Martí** in the United States in preparing for the final **War of Independence** (1895–1898).

His initial studies were at the Colegio de El Salvador, but his legal studies were interrupted by the Ten Years' War. He completed his education in Madrid after the signing of the Pact of Zanjón, ending the war. He worked at a number of newspapers and magazines, including *El Heraldo de Cuba*, *El Triunfo*, *La Habana Literaria*, and *El País*. He returned to Cuba in 1898 after being designated to serve as a delegate to the Assembly at Santa Cruz del Sur. In 1900, he was a delegate to the Constitutional Convention, which drafted Cuba's first constitution the following year. In 1902, he was elected senator from **Matanzas Province** and became a strong advocate of national interests. He coined the slogan: "No vendan, que la tierra es la Patria" (Do not sell, for our land is our homeland). He represented Cuba at the Second International Conference at The Hague in 1907. He served in a wide variety of government positions, including Senate president and secretary of state under President **José Miguel Gómez**. In the military, he served as inspector general of the armed forces, brigadier general, and director general of the Military Schools. A scholar and historian, he was an honorary dean of the Faculty of Arts and Sciences at the **University of Havana**. He also served as a member of the Permanent Arbitration Tribunal at The Hague. Several collections of his speeches have been published. *See also* Constitution of 1901; Newspapers (Republican Era); Press and Journalism (Eighteenth and Nineteenth Centuries)

Further Readings

Cepeda, Rafael. *Manuel Sanguily frente a la dominación yanqui*. Havana: Letras Cubanas, 1986.

Chacón y Calvo, José. *Manuel Sanguily y Garritte. Discursos y conferencias*. Havana: Ministerio de Educación, 1949.

Manuel de Paz Sánchez

Segundo Frente Oriental "Frank País"

The strategy of **Fidel Castro** and the revolutionary **26th of July Movement** against **Fulgencio Batista**'s military regime was based on both rural and urban forces. Under the leadership of **Frank País, Santiago de Cuba**'s revolutionaries in late 1956 prepared diversionary actions to facilitate the landing of the expeditionary forces in Oriente Province (see *Granma* **Expedition**). Urban activists remained indispensable by

recruiting and training troops, procuring materials, raising money, and organizing growing numbers of supporters inside and outside Cuba. By February 1958, Castro, as commander in chief of the Rebel Army, decided that conditions were ripe and the fighters sufficiently mature to open another front in the **struggle against Batista**. Captains **Juan Almeida** and **Raúl Castro** were promoted to commanders and led a new column in the northeastern part of Oriente Province. The Segundo Frente Oriental "Frank País" was named to honor the highly respected popular leader who had been martyred in 1957 in Santiago de Cuba.

As in the **Sierra Maestra**, the Second Front developed a government in the territories they controlled on the eastern part of the island with systems of education, public health, medicine, justice, communications, pubic works, police and public order, inspections, political propagation, finances, intelligence, a bureau of agriculture and technology, and an air force. They facilitated a Peasants' Congress in September 1958 and a Workers' Congress the following month. In November the revolutionaries launched the final offensive, and the Second Front captured more than fourteen major military quarters, including Santiago's **Moncada Barracks**.

Further Readings

Giménez, Armando. *Sierra Maestra. La Revolución de Fidel Castro*. Buenos Aires: Editorial Lautaro 1959.

Núñez Jiménez, Antonio. *El Segundo Frente Oriental "Frank País."* Lima: Peru [Industrial] 1974.

San Martín, Rafael. *El grito de la Sierra Maestra*. Buenos Aires: Ediciones Gure 1960.

Eloise Linger

Serra y Montalvo, Rafael (1858–1909)

Rafael Serra was a prominent Afro-Cuban patriot whose major political activities took place while in exile. Born in **Matan-**

zas, where from the age of thirteen he worked as a cigar maker, he was self-educated. Serra was concerned about the cultural and educational development of the Afro-Cuban community, and in 1879 he founded the free school La Armonía. He left Cuba for political reasons in 1880 and lived in Jamaica, Key West, and New York, where he collaborated with **José Martí** on the creation of the **Partido Revolucionario Cubano (Cuban Revolutionary Party)**. While in exile, he wrote for various newspapers, principal among those *Patria*. Serra was a member of the Bartolomé Masó Club in Veracruz, Mexico, part of the directorate of the San Carlos Club in Key West, and distinguished associate of Club Los Independientes (The Independents Club) of New York. While living in New York, he founded La Liga, a school dedicated to the intellectual development of Cuban and Puerto Rican men of color. Serra helped found Club Labra in **Santiago de Cuba**, which functioned as a branch of La Liga. He authored numerous works including *Ecos del Alma*, in Jamaica (1885), *Discursos sobre política y educación*, in New York (1890), and his *Ensayos políticos*, in three series (1892, 1896, and 1899). During the early Republican Period he was a member of the Moderate Party and served as a member of the House of Representatives. In 1904, he began editing the newspaper *El Nuevo Criollo*, committed to the advancement of Afro-Cubans and mestizos. His final work, *La República posible*, was published in 1909. He married Gertrudis Heredia y del Monte, with whom he had four children, only one of whom, Consuelo, survived him. He died in Havana in 1909. *See also* Afro-Cubans; Newspapers (Republican Era); Political Exile (Nineteenth Century); Press and Journalism (Eighteenth and Nineteenth Centuries); Cigars and Cigar Making

Further Readings

De la Fuente, Alejandro. *A Nation for All: Race, Inequality, and Politics in Twentieth-Century Cuba*. Chapel Hill: University of North Carolina Press, 2001.
González Veranes, Pedro N. *Rafael Serra, patriota y revolucionario, fraternal amigo de Martí*. Havana: Oficina del Historiador de la Ciudad de la Habana, 1959.

María del Carmen Barcia Zequeira

St. Louis Affair

The *St. Louis* affair of 1939 focused international attention on the policies of Nazi Germany, Cuba, and the United States toward Jewish refugees. As part of an anti-Semitic strategy to whip up international opposition to destitute Jewish emigrants in the Americas, a special voyage of the Hamburg-Amerika line brought nearly a thousand Jewish refugees to Cuba in May 1939. Unbeknownst to the refugees, the Cuban government had revoked their landing permits days before the *St. Louis* left Hamburg. The voyage of the *St. Louis* was closely followed in the Cuban media and provoked much anti-Semitic comment and public demonstrations. When the ship reached Havana on May 27 the Cuban authorities, acting under orders from President **Federico Laredo Brú**, prevented the Jewish refugees from disembarking. Intensive efforts by the U.S.-based Jewish welfare agency, the Joint Distribution Committee, involving lobbying and offers of money as well as intervention by Cuba's substantial Jewish colony, failed to alter the government's position. Finally the captain of the *St. Louis* turned the ship around for the return journey to Europe. Although the ship anchored briefly off Miami Beach in the hope of landing its passengers on U.S. territory, the U.S. government refused to intercede. However, pressured by public opinion and some lukewarm diplomatic efforts by the United States and Britain, the refugees were admitted to Belgium, Holland, France, and Great Britain.

With the coming of World War II and Nazi occupation of Western European nations, less than a quarter of the 907 *St. Louis* passengers survived the war. Although the *St. Louis* incident was just one of many examples of Allied nations' refusal to open their doors to anti-Nazi refugees, the *St. Louis* affair has received considerable publicity, especially after the release of *Voyage of the Damned*, a Hollywood film based on the affair. However, in spite of the notoriety of the case, Cuba's overall record in receiving Jewish refugees (6,000 arrived between 1933 and 1942) was, according to historian Robert M. Levine, "among the best in the world." *See also* Immigration (Twentieth Century); Judaism

Further Reading
Levine, Robert M. *Tropical Diaspora. The Jewish Experience in Cuba*. Gainesville: University Press of Florida, 1993.

Barry Carr

Students' Movement (Republican Era)

Students and their political movements have played a critical role throughout Cuban history. At no time was their influence greater than during the Republican era (1902–1958), but student activism, at the university and high school level, can be traced back to the eighteenth century.

One of the first recorded acts of student protest was a November 1781 dispute over a decree by the Spanish Crown that students must pass examinations or go into the military. In the 1820s, students, including seminary student **Félix Varela**, were part of the Constitutionalist movement, and in subsequent decades they would participate in the anticolonial movements that swept the island. Many lost their lives during the independence struggles of the last three decades of the nineteenth century, including the execution on November 27, 1871, of eight University of Havana medi-

cal students accused of vandalizing the tomb of a well-known Spanish loyalist. Although Spain's General Arsenio Martínez Campos had agreed in the 1878 Treaty of Zanjón (ending the **Ten Years' War**) that the **University of Havana** could grant doctoral degrees, in 1892 Spain denied the right of the university to offer doctoral studies. This led to the first full-scale student strike in Cuba.

The early years of the twentieth century were consumed by efforts to increase funding and expand the educational mission of the University of Havana. Student activism gradually began to focus on the overwhelmingly political and economic influence of the United States on Cuban affairs. In 1921, when the university considered granting an honorary degree to U.S. Special Envoy Enoch Crowder, students organized violent protests against the United States. Two years later, students at the University of Havana, under the leadership of **Julio Antonio Mella**, formed a national organization, the Federación Estudiantil Universitaria (**Federation of University Students**; FEU), also known as the Confederación Nacional de Estudiantes de Cuba. They held the First National Student Congress on October 14–26, 1923, and organized the Popular University of **José Martí** to provide free education for organized workers.

The dictatorship of **Gerardo Machado** (1925–1933) forced Mella to leave Cuba in January 1926, thus removing a radical voice within the leadership of the FEU. In response, students created in 1927 the Directorio Estudiantil Universitario (University Student Directorate; DEU) to oppose the government of Machado. The exiled Mella was named honorary president. The Directorio became a revolutionary magnet, but repression forced many of its members underground or into exile. The September 1930 assassination of student leader Rafael Trejo radicalized the movement, and many of the students took up arms against the Machado government as active participants in an urban guerrilla war. While the university students took up arms, high school students organized protests and demonstrations against Machado. Education on all levels was disrupted for extended periods of time, as the Machado government found it necessary to suspend classes on a regular basis. Machado fled Cuba in August 1933 and was replaced by the U.S.-supported government of President Carlos Manuel de Céspedes y Quesada, a change that did nothing to abate the revolutionary fervor of the students. Although the student movement split into reformist and revolutionary wings, all subgroups participated actively in the **Revolution of 1933**. On September 4, 1933, the DEU, in alliance with **Fulgencio Batista** and the enlisted men of the army, toppled the Céspedes regime and installed university professor **Ramón Grau San Martín** as president. The student/soldier government enacted a series of wide-ranging political and economic reforms, but the alliance was undermined by the vastly different agendas of the two groups and by U.S. pressure, which led Batista to oust Grau and the students from power in January 1934. The students would not forget their removal from power by Batista and, in subsequent years, would become among his fiercest opponents, organizing strikes, protests, and armed revolts against Batista and the military.

The student movement, under its national organization FEU, was politically active during the 1940s. Student politics took another violent turn during the period. Many students organized into action groups, each one representing a different national political party or organization. Armed conflicts between different action groups, resulting in deaths and other casualties, were not unusual. After an armed conflict, the students had the advantage of fleeing to the grounds of the University of Havana, which was granted autonomy by the **Constitution of 1940**, and from which the army and national police were banned. Students helped mobilize the opposition to the **coup of 1952** by Batista that toppled the democratically elected government of **Carlos Prío Socarrás**. Under the leadership of **José Antonio Echeverría**, the FEU led an open opposition movement to the Batista government and sought to keep the university open in the 1950s. In 1955, Echeverría organized the primarily student-based Directorio Revolucionario (Revolutionary Directorate), a group dedicated to armed struggle against the Batista dictatorship. In March 1957, the Revolutionary Directorate launched a daring attack on the **Presidential Place** in Havana in an effort to assassinate Batista. The attack failed, and Echeverría was killed.

The various groups of the student movement, and specifically the FEU, were consolidated and incorporated into a mass organization by the revolutionary government of 1959. The FEU, especially at the University of Havana, continues to be a training ground for political leaders of Cuba since the **Revolution**. *See also* Batista; Struggle against; Educational System

Further Readings

Aguirre, Sergio. *Eco de caminos*. Havana: Editorial de Ciencias Sociales, 1974.

García Oliveras, Julio A. *José Antonio Echeverría: la lucha estudiantil contra Batista*. Havana: Editora Política, 1979.

Guzmán de Armas, Luis. "Desarrollo del proceso revolucionario de los años 30." In *Historia de la Revolución Cubana,* ed. Nicolás Garófolo Fernández, et al. Havana: Editorial Pueblo y Educación, 1994.

Pérez Rojas, Niurka. *El movimiento estudiantil universitario de 1934 a 1940*. Havana: Editorial de Ciencias Sociales, 1975.

Suchlicki, Jaime. *University Students and Revolution in Cuba, 1920–1968*. Coral Gables, FL, University of Miami Press, 1969.

Eloise Linger

Torriente, Cosme de la (1872–1956)

Cosme de la Torriente fought against Spain during the **War of Independence** and went on to become one of the leading Cuban political and diplomatic figures of the first half of the twentieth century. Born near Jovellanos in **Matanzas Province**, he joined the struggle against Spain under **Máximo Gómez** and **Calixto García**. He rose to the rank of colonel and served as a member of the liberation army's chiefs of staff. He was a delegate to the assemblies of Jimaguayú and La Yaya. He was a student at the **University of Havana** where he earned a degree in philosophy and letters in 1892 and a law degree in 1898. During the U.S. occupation, Torriente was designated magistrate of the **Santa Clara** Court of Appeals. Later he would hold the same post in Matanzas Province.

In 1903, he was appointed secretary to Cuba's delegation to Spain, where in 1906 he was named minister plenipotentiary. Torriente returned to Cuba and went on to found the Conservative Party, along with General **Mario García Menocal** and **Enrique José Varona**. The Conservative Party ruled Cuba between 1913 and 1921. In this period, he was elected senator and was appointed secretary of state. He was later named ambassador to the United States and president of the IV Assembly of the League of Nations in 1923. Torriente was also a member of the Permanent Tribunal at The Hague and president of the International Commission of Intellectual Cooperation. During the **Gerardo Machado** presidency (1925–1933), he founded the Partido Unión Nacionalista (Union Nationalist Party) to oppose the reelection designs of Machado. In the final years of his life, Torriente criticized the **Coup of 1952** led by **Fulgencio Batista**. Also an accomplished writer, Torriente's publications included *Libertad y democracia* (1941) and *Actividades de la Liga de las Naciones*. (1923) *See also* U.S. Interventions

Further Readings
Lancís y Sánchez, Antonio. *D. Cosme*. Havana: 1958.
Santovenia, Emeterio. *Cosme de la Torriente: estadista*. Havana: Úcar, García, & Cía., 1944.

Manuel de Paz Sánchez

Twenty-Sixth of July Movement

The revolutionary 26th of July Movement led by **Fidel Castro** received its name from the date of the attack on the **Moncada Army Barracks** in **Santiago de Cuba** on July 26, 1953. Captured after the failed attack, Castro and several of his followers were imprisoned in the Boniato jail, and after being convicted were transferred to the Model Prison on Isla de Pinos (today **Isla de la Juventud**). While serving time, the members of the movement met together and reinforced their revolutionary convictions and continued to conspire against the government.

Fidel Castro and his comrades were granted amnesty in 1955 and released from jail. Shortly thereafter Castro left Cuba for Mexico. While in Mexico, he aired his sharp differences with the mainstream leadership of the **Ortodoxos**, the party to which he had belonged, and began organizing the 26th of July Movement. Among the early participants in the movement were **Raúl Castro**, Faustino Pérez, **Ernesto "Che" Guevara, Camilo Cienfuegos**, and others, including several who had participated in the attack at Moncada. The members of the movement received military training in Mexico under Alberto Bayo, a retired Spanish colonel. At the same time organizers in Cuba were preparing for an armed struggle against the government. Among the most successful

Flag of the 26th of July Movement. Luis Martínez-Fernández Collection.

organizers were **Frank País** in Oriente Province. Other members were drawn from a host of revolutionary groups including the Movimiento Nacionalista Revolucionario (National Revolutionary Movement), Acción Libertadora (Liberating Action), and Acción Revolucionaria Nacional (National Revolutionary Action).

The 26th of July Movement advocated armed struggle as the only means of toppling the illegitimate Batista government, given the inefficiency and corruption of the existing political parties. The movement viewed itself as the heir of Cuba's revolutionary tradition dating back to the wars of independence (see **Ten Years' War** and **War of Independence**). In March 1956, Castro declared that the movement was not a tendency within the Ortodoxos but rather an independent revolutionary apparatus of *Chibasismo* (named for former Ortodoxo leader and Castro mentor **Eduardo Chibás**), which emerged from the masses to battle the dictatorship. In September 1956, a revolutionary pact was reached in Mexico between the 26th of July Movement and the Directorio Estudiantil Revolucionario (Revolutionary Student Directory) led by **José Antonio Echeverría**. The pact symbolized the unity of a new generation in the revolutionary struggle as it pursued democratic and nationalist goals. The 26th of July Movement succeeded in toppling Batista on January 1 1959. In 1961 the movement merged with other parties and revolutionary organizations under the umbrella of Organizaciones Revolucionarias Integradas as part of the process establishing the regime's only political party. *See also* Batista, Struggle against; Students' Movement (Republican Era); Twenty-sixth of July (Holiday)

Further Readings

Franqui, Carlos. *Diario de la Revolución Cubana.* Barcelona: Ediciones R. Torres, 1976.
Mencía, Mario. *La prisión fecunda.* Havana: Editora Política, 1980.

Manuel de Paz Sánchez

U.S. Interventions

The United States occupied Cuba in 1898, and after Cuba's independence in 1902, it repeatedly intervened militarily on the island. In April 1898, President William McKinley requested and received authorization from the U.S. Congress "to take measures to secure a full and final termination of hostilities between the Government of Spain and the people of Cuba, and to secure in the island the establishment of a stable government, capable of maintaining order and observing its international obligations." Following the U.S. entry into the Cuban **War of Independence** in 1898 and the defeat of the Spanish, a U.S. military government headed by Governor General John R. Brooke was installed on the island on January 1, 1899. Governor General Leonard Wood succeeded Brooke in 1900 and over the next two years initiated sweeping programs of public works, sanitation, and education to reconstruct Cuba's social and economic infrastructure. The occupation ended in 1902 with the reluctant adoption of the **Platt Amendment** by the Cuban constitutional assembly and the installation of **Tomás Estrada Palma** as the first Cuban president.

When Estrada Palma was reelected in 1906, the opposition Liberal Party re-

Political cartoon depicting U.S. paternalism toward Cuba. *Baltimore News* (1906).

belled. Pointing to the U.S. guarantee of a stable Cuban government in the Platt Amendment, Estrada Palma called for aid to put down the rebellion, and the U.S. military returned to the island. President Howard Taft appointed **Charles E. Magoon**, a judge from Minnesota, to preside over the provisional government that ruled Cuba for the next three years. Political disorder prompted additional U.S. armed interventions in 1912 and 1917.

Disputes over the presidential elections of 1920 brought U.S. troops back to Cuba in January 1921. General Enoch H. Crowder, as special representative of President Warren Harding, quickly resolved the electoral dispute in favor of Partido Popular candidate **Alfredo Zayas**. The U.S. forces, however, remained in Cuba. Crowder acted as the effective head of state and directed a complete restructuring of the Cuban government at the national, provincial, and municipal levels. In 1923, with the completion of this restructuring, U.S. forces left the island. This marked the last U.S. military intervention in Cuba. With the repeal by treaty of the Platt

Amendment in 1934, the United States no longer had a constitutionally sanctioned right to intervene. *See also* Constitution of 1901

Further Readings

Hernández, José M. *Cuba and the United States: Intervention and Militarism, 1868–1933*. Austin: University of Texas Press, 1993.

Lockmiller, David A. *Magoon in Cuba: A History of the Second Intervention, 1906–1909*. Chapel Hill: University of North Carolina Press, 1938.

Millett, Allan Reed. *The Politics of Intervention: The Military Occupation of Cuba, 1906–1909*. Columbus: Ohio State University of Pittsburgh, 1968.

Pérez, Louis A., Jr. *Intervention, Revolution, and Politics in Cuba, 1913–1921*. Pittsburgh: University of Pittsburgh Press, 1978.

Mariola Espinosa

Varona, Enrique José (1849–1933)

Enrique José Varona was one of the greatest Cuban intellectuals of the nineteenth and twentieth centuries. Born in **Camagüey Province**, Varona began his literary production with *Arpas amigas* (1879) and continued in publications such as *Almanaque Cómico Político y Literario de Juan Palomo, La Lucha*, and *Revista de Cuba*. An influential essayist, Varona authored *Conferencias filosóficas* (1880–1888). His body of work was diverse, including contemporary philosophical, psychological, pedagogical, and scientific issues. He participated in the academic sessions of the Lyceum of Guanabacoa in 1869 and became a member of that learned society in 1878. He also conducted research with the Anthropological Society of Cuba in 1877, joining that society the following year and eventually becoming its president. In 1884, Varona was a deputy to the Spanish Cortes for the Partido Liberal Autonomista (Liberal Autonomist Party). He abandoned the party the following year, however, to join the independence movement.

In a series of essays in *Cuba Contemporánea, Archipiélago, Revista Bimestre Cubana, Avance, El Triunfo, El Heraldo de Cuba*, and *El Fígaro*, Varona sought to explain the factors that led Cuba to war against Spain. His most influential pro-independence work was the essay *Contra España* (1896). In 1885, he founded *Revista Cubana*, which he directed until it closed in 1896. He also founded *Patria*, which lasted from 1895 to 1898. He was awarded a doctorate in philosophy and letters from the **University of Havana** in 1893.

Varona's intellectual pursuits reflect the transition period from the nineteenth to the twentieth century with an emphasis on consolidating Cuban independence and sovereignty and contributing to the advancement of Cuban society. He was a major proponent of educational reforms in 1900. After the second U.S. intervention in 1906, Varona strongly advocated the development of a national industrial base and control of Cuban industries by Cubans. In 1912, he was elected vice president and served under President **Mario García Menocal**. After completing his term he returned to teaching at the University. In the last year of his life, 1933, he was a vocal opponent of the **Gerardo Machado** dictatorship. *See also* Autonomism; Press and Journalism (Eighteenth and Nineteenth Centuries); U.S. Interventions

Further Readings

Agramonte, Roberto. *Enrique José Varona. Su vida, su obra y su influencia*. Havana: Cultural, S.A., 1937.

Varona, Enrique José. *Conferencias filosóficas*. Havana: M. de Villa, 1880–1888.

Varona, Enrique José. *De la Colonia a la República*. Havana: Sociedad Editorial Cuba Contemporánea, 1919.

Vitier, Medardo. Prologue. *Enrique José Varona. Páginas cubanas*. Cuadernos de Cultura, Segunda Serie, 3. Havana: Publicaciones de la Secretaría de Educación, 1936.

Consuelo Naranjo Orovio

Veterans' and Patriots' Movement

Political morality in the Cuban republic had sunk to a new low during the early 1920s. Members of the **Alfredo Zayas** administration, including the president himself and members of his family, had sanctioned or were themselves implicated in graft and malfeasance on an unprecedented scale. Nepotism, bribery, illegal transfers of public lands to private control, and tax fraud were only some of the most common illicit activities with which the Zayas administration became associated.

Against this backdrop, rumors in 1923 that the Zayas government planned to reduce the pensions of the former soldiers and officers of the old Liberation Army served to spark a protest by the prestigious Veterans' Association (see **War of Independence**). The protest generalized into a broad indictment of public life in Cuba and quickly obtained support from a broad cross section of civic and professional organizations. Under the slogan "For the Regeneration of Cuba," the Veterans' and Patriots' Movement, as it became known, called for sweeping political, social, and economic reforms in all facets of political practices and public administration. Within months, the government banned the public meetings of the Veterans and Patriots, forcing the organization to plot the overthrow of the Zayas administration. Drawing support from both civilian organizations and active army officers, the movement posed an imminent threat to Zayas. All through early 1924, the Zayas government moved swiftly to arrest the leadership and retire suspected army collaborators and obtained a public endorsement from the U.S. government. In April 1924, the Veterans and Patriots issued a call to insurrection. Deprived of its principal leaders and army support, the movement collapsed within days, however. The most lasting legacy of the Veterans' and Patriots' Movement was having brought into public forums the issue of reforms in public life, thereby transforming the nature of political debate in the republic.

Further Readings

Cairo Ballester, Ana. *El Movimiento de Veteranos y Patriotas*. Havana: Editorial Arte y Literatura, 1976.

Pérez, Louis A., Jr. *Cuba under the Platt Amendment, 1902–1934*. Pittsburgh: University of Pittsburgh Press, 1986.

Louis A. Pérez, Jr.

Women's Suffrage Movement

The women's suffrage movement in Cuba emerged in the first decade of the twentieth century. Feminist organizations created to promote women's suffrage tackled a variety of other important issues, including **divorce** and parental rights. Those struggles were crowned with success with the passage in 1917 of the Ley de la Patria Potestad (Law on Parental Rights) and the following year with the passage of the Divorce Law. Cuba was the first nation in Latin America to enact comprehensive legislation on parental rights and divorce. In the aftermath of World War I, many nations granted women the right to vote, a development that motivated Cuba's suffrage movement. One of the most prominent organizations in the suffragist movement was the Club Femenino de Cuba (Women's Club of Cuba), which promoted the concept of an umbrella organization of women's groups. That umbrella organization, the Federación Nacional de Asociaciones Femeninas de Cuba (National Federation of Cuban Women's Associations), organized two women's congresses in Havana, the first in 1923 and the second in 1925. The congresses were a fertile forum for debate and the promotion of new ideas and strategies on the national stage. Women's suffrage was finally achieved in

1934 and later codified in the **Constitution of 1940**. *See also* Feminist Movement (Republican Era); Women's Rights

Further Reading

Stoner, K. Lynn. *From the House to the Streets. The Cuban Women's Movement for Legal Reform, 1898–1940*. Durham, NC: Duke University Press, 1991.

Julio César González Pagés

Zayas y Alfonso, Alfredo (1861–1934)

Alfredo Zayas was president of Cuba from 1921 to 1925. He was an accomplished writer and orator as well. The Zayas administration was marked by outlandish corruption schemes, but there were some notable accomplishments, such as securing Cuban sovereignty over the Isla de Pinos (now **Isla de la Juventud**) from the United States.

Zayas strongly supported Cuban independence from Spain during the **War of Independence**. He was a member of the Liberal Autonomist Party and wrote numerous articles criticizing Spanish rule. As a result, he was arrested in 1896 and forced into exile the following year. After independence, he entered politics and held a variety of offices, including mayor of Havana. In 1905, he became senator and was chosen president of that body. He served as vice president of Cuba under President **José Miguel Gómez** (1909–1913). He founded a third party, the Partido Popular (Popular Party), as an alternative to the two major Cuban parties of the early twentieth century, the Liberal Party and the Conservative Party.

During his administration, Zayas was pressured by U.S. Special Envoy Enoch Crowder to establish the "Honest Cabinet," a group of Cuban leaders whose goal was to reduce corruption and trim the bloated bureaucracy. While the government was corrupt, the effort by Crowder was another example of Cuba's limited sovereignty in the years after independence. Zayas would later disband this cabinet, much to the dismay of the United States. The corruption of the Zayas government became legendary. His opponents estimated that at one time he had as many as fourteen relatives on the payroll, most of them in government enterprises. As a backlash to the corruption, a movement led by the Cuban Council of Civic Renovation was established to push for social reforms. After his term of office, he retired from political life.

A prolific writer, Zayas's works include *El presbítero don José Agustín Caballero y su vida y sus obras* (1891) and *Cuba autonómica; lexicografía antillana* (1914). *See also* Autonomism; Political Exile (Nineteenth Century); Presidents

Further Readings

Beals, Carleton. *The Crime of Cuba*. Philadelphia: J.B. Lippincott, 1934.

Pérez, Louis A., Jr. *Cuba under the Platt Amendment, 1902–1934*. Pittsburgh: Pittsburgh University Press, 1991.

Portell-Vilá, Herminio. *Nueva historia de la República de Cuba*. Miami: La Moderna Poesía, 1986.

Frank Argote-Freyre

5

History and Government: The Revolutionary Period (1959–   )

Agrarian Reform Acts

Pre-1959 efforts to implement agrarian reform, including the progressive provisions of the **Constitution of 1940**, failed to curb *latifundia* (large estates), extensive foreign ownership of Cuban soil, and landlessness among most of the island's peasants and agricultural workers. On the eve of the **Revolution**, U.S.- and Cuban-owned sugar companies controlled 2,483,000 hectares (6,135,741 acres) of land, and **cattle ranching** interests controlled huge extensions of the national territory, while hundreds of thousands of agrarian laborers worked land that did not belong to them.

The sweeping revolutionary agrarian reform was enacted in two phases, one responding to the agrarian reform law of May 17, 1959, and the other as the implementation of the agrarian reform law of October 3, 1963 (see **Appendix 12**). Originally presided over by **Fidel Castro**, the massive and far-reaching Instituto Nacional de la Reforma Agraria (INRA) oversaw the reform process and ran a multitude of programs in the Cuban countryside, including **housing**, education, health care, and the building of infrastructure. During the first two years of its existence,

the INRA came to control three fourths of Cuba's industrial structure until those activities came under the purview of the newly created Ministerio de Industrias. The 1959 agrarian reform law limited landownership to a maximum of 30 *caballerías* (403 hectares, or 996 acres); in cases of exceptionally productive farms, the maximum extension was raised to 100 caballerías (1,343 hectares, or 3,319 acres). The law also established that foreign nationals and corporations could not own land in Cuba. While the law provided for compensation to owners whose land was confiscated by the INRA, the promised bonds were never issued and compensation was never paid. Large agricultural estates, while taken from their previous owners, were neither broken down nor distributed; instead, these were briefly turned into cooperatives and later into state farms. Actual land distributions benefited only a small proportion of the agrarian workforce. Two years into the reform, some 33,000 former squatters, tenants, and sharecroppers, half of them from Oriente Province, had become landowners. By the end of 1961, the government owned 41 percent of the land.

The second agrarian reform law (1963) was intended to further weaken Cuba's

Area Controlled by the Largest Sugar Companies (1959) (30,000 + hectacres)

Name	Area in hectacres	U.S. or Cuban Ownership
Cuban Atlantic Sugar Co.	284,404	US
Julio Lobo	164,543	Cuban
Sucesores de Falla Gutiérrez	144,265	Cuban
Cuban American Sugar Co.	143,862	US
American Sugar Refining Co.	136,750	US
United Fruit Co.	109,480	US
West Indies Sugar Co.	109,146	US
Vertientes-Camagüey Sugar Co.	106,595	US
Gómez Mena	84,707	Cuban
Manatí Sugar Co.	78,252	US
Francisco Sugar Co.*	71,703	US
The Cuba Co.	68,388	US
Central Cuba	65,946	Cuban
Punta Alegre Sugar Co.	46,594	US
Fernando de la Riva	38,556	Cuban
Jesús Azqueta	36,127	Cuban
Manuel Aspuru	34,610	Cuban
García Díaz	30,168	Cuban

*Controlled by Cuban Trading Co.
Adapted from Antonio Gayoso Quintana, "The Cuban Agrarian Reform" (M.A. Thesis, University of Florida), 1965, p. 58.

midsize farmers. This time, the maximum ownership of land was limited to 5 caballerías (67 hectares, or 166 acres). Unlike during the first agrarian reform, this time the government paid compensations of 10 to 15 pesos per caballería per month for ten years. In no case was the compensation to exceed 250 pesos per month. When the second round of reform was completed the government controlled 70 percent of the land and 66 percent of **agriculture**. See also Educational System; Foreign Investments (Republican Era); Health-Care System; Sugar Industry

Further Readings
Dumont, René. *Cuba: Socialist Development*. New York: Grove Press, 1970.
Gayoso Quintana, Antonio. "The Cuban Agrarian Reform." Master's thesis, University of Florida, 1965.
Núñez Jiménez, Antonio. *La Ley de Reforma Agraria en su aplicación*. Havana: Capitolio Nacional, 1959.
O'Connor, James. "Agrarian Reform in Cuba, 1959–1963." *Science and Society* 32, no. 2 (Spring 1968): 167–217.

Luis Martínez-Fernández

Alarcón de Quesada, Ricardo (1937–)

Ricardo Alarcón de Quesada is a Cuban diplomat and politician who in the 1990s became one of the closest advisers of **Fidel Castro** and the main negotiator with U.S. officials.

Alarcón studied law at the **University of Havana** in the 1950s, when he was also involved with the **26th of July Movement**.

Ricardo Alarcón, President of the National Assembly (2000). AP/Wide World Photos. Photograph by José Goitía.

After the triumph of the **Revolution**, he was active in the **Federation of University Students** (FEU). In 1962, Alarcón was appointed to work for the Ministry of **Foreign Relations** as head of the Latin American Directorate. Four years later, he was appointed ambassador to the United Nations in New York, until 1978, when he returned to Cuba as deputy minister of foreign relations.

In the 1980s, Alarcón was part of the negotiation team that discussed, signed, and reestablished the **Migration Accords** with the United States (1984, 1987) and participated in the Tripartite Negotiations between Angola, Cuba, and South Africa (1988). In 1989 Cuba was elected a member of the Security Council of the United Nations, and Alarcón was again appointed ambassador to the United Nations (1990–1991). In 1992, he became minister of foreign relations and member of the **Cuban Communist Party**'s politburo. In 1993, he was elected president of the **National Assembly of People's Power** and reelected

in 1998. In the Fifth Congress of the Communist Party (1997) he was reelected a member of the politburo. He led the negotiations with the United States on migratory issues (1994–1995) and was one of the main advisers of the Cuban government during the **Elián González case** (1999–2000). *See also* Angola, Cuba's Involvement in; United States, Cuba's relations with the

Further Readings

Mead, Walter Russell. "Castro's Successor?" *The New Yorker*, January 26, 1998, 42–49.

Romero, Ana. "Voces del milenio: Ricardo Alarcón." *El Mundo*, November 21, 1999.

Zenén Santana Delgado

Almeida Bosque, Juan (1927–)

A veteran of the attack on the **Moncada Army barracks** (1953) and the *Granma* **expedition** (1956), Juan Almeida Bosque is one of the **Revolution**'s highest ranking officials and its most visible Afro-Cuban leader (see **Afro-Cubans**).

Almeida Bosque came in contact with **Fidel Castro** at the **University of Havana** and joined the band of revolutionaries that launched the attack on the Moncada barracks. Apprehended in the failed operation's aftermath, he spent time in prison at the Isle of Pines (now **Isla de la Juventud**), and upon his release he rejoined Fidel Castro in Mexico, where they prepared for the *Granma* expedition. Almeida Bosque was one of the dozen survivors of the landing in Oriente that became the revolutionary core that launched the guerrilla war against the **Fulgencio Batista** regime. Almeida Bosque was soon promoted to commander of the Santiago de Cuba column.

After the triumph of the Revolution, Almeida Bosque served in various leadership capacities within the **Revolutionary Armed Forces**, the **Cuban Communist**

Party, and the **National Assembly of People's Power**, often as the token Afro-Cuban within an overwhelmingly white power elite. Since its inception in 1976, he has been a delegate to the National Assembly. He has also been a long time member of the Political Bureau of the Central Committee of the Cuban Communist Party and one of the vice presidents of the Council of State. Since 1993 Almeida has presided over the Association of Combatants of the Revolution. Aside from his political career, Almeida Bosque is also an author and composer of romantic popular songs such as "Es soledad," "Un beso de recuerdo," and "Decide tú."

Further Reading

Almeida Bosque, Juan. *La Sierra*. Havana: Prensa Latina-World Data Research Center, 1997.

Luis Martínez-Fernández

Angola, Cuba's Involvement in

Cuba's military involvement in Angola is its largest military engagement ever in a foreign conflict. The motivation for Cuba's intervention in Angola (1975) is a contested topic in the analysis of Cuban policy toward Africa and its relations with the Soviet Union. The aid from Cuba allowed the MPLA (People's Movement for the Liberation of Angola) to defeat the other guerrilla groups (National Front for the Liberation of Angola [FNLA] and the União Nacional para a Independência Total de Angola [UNITA]) and the South African and Zairian troops that supported them in the struggle for power in independent Angola. Nearly 400,000 Cubans participated in military and civil projects in Angola between 1975 and 1991.

Cuban interest in Africa intensified in the 1960s. As early as 1966, Cuban advisers began to train MPLA fighters, following a meeting between **Che Guevara** and MPLA leaders in Congo Brazzaville in 1965. Cuba continued to support the MPLA without interruption, while the Soviet Union stopped it twice. Independence for Angola was fixed for November 1975, after the end of Portuguese authoritarian rule in 1974. Hopes for shared power after the Alvor Accord in January 1975 were dashed when the FNLA reignited the armed struggle in March with the covert support of the United States, China, and Zaire. MPLA's leader Agostinho Neto requested Cuban help in May. In August, Cuba sent a delegation to assess the situation. By mid-October, around 500 military advisers and cargoes of weapons had arrived in Angola to staff and supply four training centers for the future Angolan army (FAPLA). The advisers and FAPLA units were soon involved in combats against FNLA, Zairian troops, UNITA, and South African forces. On November 4, the Cuban government decided to send combat troops to Angola (Carlotta Operation), at the request of the MPLA. In the spring of 1976 Cuban-FAPLA forces expelled the Zairian and South African armies, but a coup organized in 1977 by a pro-Soviet faction against Neto, and guerrilla and South African incursions kept Angola in a war situation.

In 1987, when South Africa invaded Angola once more, Cuba and Angola launched a massive counteroffensive in Namibia as a way to put pressure on South Africa for a definitive political solution to the conflict. The military actions were successful, and the tripartite diplomatic negotiations ended in 1988 with an agreement. By 1991, all Cuban troops had left Angola, thus disengaging from the conflict at the same time that South Africa granted independence to Namibia and stopped military actions against Angola. *See also* Ethiopia, Cuba's Involvement in; Revolutionary Armed Forces (Fuerzas Armadas Revolucionarias [FAR]); Soviet Union, Cuba's Relations with the

Further Readings

Domínguez, Jorge I. *To Make a World Safe for Revolution: Cuba's Foreign Policy*. Cambridge, MA: Harvard University Press, 1989.

Gleijeses, Piero. *Conflicting Missions: Havana, Washington, and Africa, 1959–1976*. Chapel Hill: University of North Carolina Press, 2002.

LeoGrande, William M. *Cuba's Policy in Africa, 1959–1980*. Berkeley: University of California Press, 1980.

Mesa Lago, Carmelo, and June Belkin, eds. *Cuba in Africa*. Pittsburgh: University of Pittsburgh Press, 1982.

Zenén Santana Delgado

Arcos Bergnes, Gustavo (1926–   )

Gustavo Arcos is one of Cuba's leading **human rights** activists and dissidents. He has been the leader of the Comité Cubano por Derechos Humanos, the Cuban Committee for Human Rights, since 1988. This organization informs the international community about human rights violations in Cuba and shares information with Cubans about the rights guarantees of the Universal Declaration of Human Rights. Born in Caibarién, Las Villas Province, Arcos was an original member of the **26th of July Movement**, was a student at the **University of Havana** when **Fulgencio Batista** staged the 1952 coup, and accompanied **Fidel Castro** during the **Moncada Army Barracks** attack in 1953. He was wounded during the attack and imprisoned. After being released from prison in 1955, he left Cuba, ultimately joining Castro in Mexico. Instead of returning to Cuba with the *Granma* **expedition**, he raised support for the movement in the United States and Latin America. After Castro assumed power in 1959, Arcos was named ambassador to Belgium. By the mid-1960s, he had become disillusioned with the authoritarian nature of the Castro regime, and after expressing some of his discontent in private conversations, Arcos was imprisoned in 1966 for three years,

accused of counterrevolutionary activity. Upon his release, he applied for permission to leave the island, but his request was denied. In 1981, he and his brother Sebastián, who worked with him in the human rights efforts, were imprisoned for attempting to leave the island illegally. In 1983, while imprisoned, he helped form the human rights group he now heads. In 1988 he was released from prison. Arcos's unfailing commitment to the cause of human rights in Cuba has earned him international respect. He continues to serve as executive secretary of the Cuban Committe for Human Rights. *See also* Crime; Dissidence and Defections (1959–   )

Further Readings

Cabrera Infante, Guillermo. *Mea Cuba*. Madrid: Alfaguara, 1999.

"Gustavo Arcos." *Dissenting Voices* (International Republican Institute) 1, no. 1 (May 19, 1995).

Treaster, Joseph B. "In or Out of Jail, Castro's Old Ally Is a Defiant Foe." *New York Times*, August 11, 1988, sec. A, 4.

Catherine Moses

Bay of Pigs (Playa Girón) Invasion

In the early dawn hours of April 17, 1961, the frogmen and advance forces of the anti-Castro Brigade 2506 invaded Cuba. The number of the brigade was taken from the serial code of a fallen member, who died during training exercises. The brigade consisted of Cuban exiles trained and financed by the United States in Guatemala and other locations. A few days before the invasion, the brigade departed from Nicaragua under the command of Manuel Artime, a former officer of the Rebel Army and ex-inspector of the Instituto Nacional de la Reforma Agraria (INRA; see **Agrarian Reform Acts**) and José Pérez San Román. Artime served as political director of the unit, while San Román was its military leader. The leaders of the brigade's six battalions were Alejandro del Valle, Hugo

Sueiro, Valentín Bacallao, Roberto Pérez San Román, Ricardo Montero, and Francisco Montiel.

The site chosen for the landing is part of a coastal marsh in central Cuba measuring 170 kilometers (105 miles) in length and 50 kilometers (31 miles) in width in the Zapata Peninsula, which extends to the outskirts of the city of **Cienfuegos**, on the southern part of the island. Swampland dominates the coasts of this peninsula, surrounded by jungle, populated by crocodiles and other animal species native to the region. The Bay of Pigs Invasion, known in Cuba as the Girón Beach Invasion, draws its name from the wild pigs that roamed the region since colonial times. The muddy portions, covered by jungle and forests, open up along the coastline to beautiful coralline **beaches** with little vegetation. At the point where the brigade landed, the coastline is separated from mainland Cuba by 12 kilometers (7.5 miles) of swamp to the north and six kilometers (3.7 miles) to the east.

The strategic rationale for landing at this location was that the beachhead could be easily defended by advanced positions in the north and northeast. It was also near an airfield at Playa Girón, built by the revolutionary government. The members of the Consejo Revolucionario de Cuba (Cuban Revolutionary Council), including former Prime Minister **José Miró Cardona**, were to be flown to this site. Once established, the Revolutionary Council would declare a government-in-arms and request recognition and direct aid from the United States. However, the swamps created a formidable barrier and effectively sealed off the landing site from mainland Cuba. The land routes leading out from the embarkation point, built on muddy ground, turned out to be ideal for defense on the part of revolutionary troops and unsuitable for attack by the landing forces. The narrow passages through the swamps hindered the attack of the invading bri-

gade. As a result, revolutionary forces concentrated on capturing at least one of the advanced positions so that their soldiers could gain access to the coastline. Besides the failure to achieve its original military objectives, several other factors contributed to the defeat of the landing party, including the rapid and effective counterattack response of revolutionary forces. Perhaps the most decisive factor was the role of the Cuban Air Force. Two days earlier, Cuban airfields had been bombed in an effort to destroy the rebel air force, but several aircraft survived the raids. Cuban planes sank several landing crafts containing supplies and ammunition. The landing party did not have the element of surprise in its favor. There was also no air support provided by the United States, despite the fact that the U.S. aircraft carrier *Essex* was just offshore. The lack of air support was a severe blow to the landing party's efforts to establish a beachhead.

Another key element in the brigade's strategy was the expectation that the invasion would be met with widespread public support. The Central Intelligence Agency (CIA) assured President John F. Kennedy that the invasion would receive public support. However, after Cuban airfields were bombed on April 15, **Fidel Castro** ordered the detention of thousands of potential supporters throughout the island. The last remnants of the invading force were captured by the Rebel Army in the late afternoon of April 19. After the victory, Castro issued Communiqué Number 4, which read as follows: "The Revolution has emerged victorious, although we have paid a high price in valiant lives and revolutionary fighters, who confronted the invaders and attacked them incessantly without even a minute of truce, destroying in 72 hours the army organized over a period of months by the imperialist government of the United States."

Of the approximately 1,300 members of the attacking brigade, 1,180 were taken

Prime Minister Fidel Castro with soldiers during the Bay of Pigs Invasion. CP Photo/Granma/Raúl Corrales

prisoner or killed in the battle. Among the prisoners were three Catholic priests with Spanish citizenship, who like the other prisoners were returned to the United States in December 1962. There is no consensus on the number of dead on the revolutionary side. Officially "multiple" deaths have been acknowledged among the civilian population and more than 300 dead in the armed forces, but some sources estimate the losses at more than a thousand.

The Bay of Pigs Invasion is widely recognized as one of the greatest fiascos in U.S. foreign policy. The invasion's exact date was known by Cuba's forces, which prepared for the attack and rounded up potential opposition. The site of the landing proved to be highly inadequate: isolated marshlands. U.S. intelligence crassly overestimated the extent of internal support for the invasion. And the United States withheld vital air support it had promised to deliver because Kennedy was concerned about a confrontation with the Soviet Union. The result of the botched invasion was the opposite of what its organizers sought to achieve; rather than bring Castro down, it strengthened his position in the eyes of the Cuban populace and the international community.

The Brigade's banner was not captured by revolutionary forces but rather found its way to an embassy. The Brigade's standard was later presented to President Kennedy at a special celebration at Miami's Orange Bowl welcoming back the participants of the attack. In order to secure the return of Brigade members, the Kennedy administration agreed to pay $62 million in indemnization levied on the attackers by a revolutionary court. In the alternative, the prisoners were sentenced to thirty years of forced labor. After receiving the Brigade 2506's flag, Kennedy, who had withheld the promised air support for the brigade, stated: "I can assure you that this flag will be returned to you in a free Havana. The most fervent desire of our nation, and the nations of this hemisphere, is that Cuba one day be free again. When that day comes, this Brigade deserves to march at the head of the liberating column." *See also* Revolution; Revolutionary Armed Forces (Fuerzas Armadas Revolucionarias [FAR]); United States, Cuba's Relations with the

Further Readings

Johnson, Haynes. *The Bay of Pigs: The Leaders' Story of Brigade 2506*. New York: W.W. Norton, 1964.

Kornbluh, Peter, ed. *Bay of Pigs Declassified: The Secret CIA Report on the Invasion of Cuba*. New York: New Press, 1998.

Pino Machado, Quintón. *La Batalla de Girón. Razones de una victoria*. Havana: Editorial de Ciencias Sociales, 1983.

Triay, Víctor Andrés. *Bay of Pigs: An Oral History of Brigade 2506*. Gainesville: University Press of Florida, 2001.

White, Mark J., ed. *The Kennedys and Cuba. The Declassified Documentary History*. Chicago: Ivan R. See, 1999.

Wyden, Peter. *Bay of Pigs: The Untold Story*. New York: Simon and Schuster, 1979.

Manuel de Paz Sánchez

Castro Ruz, Fidel (1926–)

Fidel Castro Ruz, the leader of the Cuban **Revolution**, premier of Cuba since 1959, first secretary of the **Cuban Communist**

Fidel Castro Ruz. Fidel Castro Photograph Collection, Manuscripts Division, Department of Rare Books and Special Collections, Princeton University Library. Photograph by Raúl Corrales. (CP Photo/Granma/ Raúl Corrales).

Party after 1975, president from 1976, is the most important political figure in the latter portion of the nation's twentieth-century history.

Castro was born on August 13, 1926, near the city of Birán in the eastern province then called Oriente (today **Holguín Province**). He was one of seven children of Ángel Castro, a wealthy Spanish-born landowner, and his second wife, Lina Ruz González. Enjoying a privileged childhood, Fidel entered the exclusive Colegio Belén in Havana in 1941. Castro excelled at both sports and academics, earning the respect, if not the appreciation, of his Jesuit superiors, who resented his quick temper and rebellious attitude. Graduating with distinction in 1945, Castro entered the law school at the **University of Ha-**

vana. He quickly became involved in the internecine squabbles between rival student political factions at the university, which often turned violent. Castro read deeply into Marxist literature during these years and probably had contact with Cuba's communists, the Partido Socialista Popular (PSP) (see **Partido Comunista**), but he apparently found the party too unorganized, and the anticommunist prejudices of the Cuban populace too strong, to enroll in its ranks. A fiery speech in 1946 during a demonstration against the unconstitutional plan of president **Ramón Grau San Martín** (1944–1948) to try for reelection brought Fidel his first national media exposure and also aligned him with the new anti-Grau party, the **Ortodoxos (Partido del Pueblo Cubano)** founded by

Senator **Eduardo Chibás**. Taking his degree in 1950, the young lawyer married Mirta Díaz-Balart. The couple produced one son, Fidelito, but divorced in 1954.

Preparing to run for the House of Representatives on the Ortodoxo ticket in 1952, Castro had his plans cut short by the military **coup of 1952**, instigated by General **Fulgencio Batista**. Publicly, Castro railed against Batista and filed a legal brief charging him with violating the **Constitution of 1940**, while secretly he laid the basis for an armed conspiracy to oust the dictator. Dubbing themselves the "Centennial Generation," in honor of the hundredth anniversary of the birth of **José Martí**, Fidel, his brother **Raúl Castro**, and friends from university days joined forces to seize control of the **Moncada Army Barracks** in the city of **Santiago de Cuba** in Oriente on July 26, 1953, and call for the overthrow of Batista. The attack was a disaster. The guards at the barracks were forewarned when Castro's own automobile broke down, and the general strike planned to coincide with the assault failed to materialize. The army captured Castro and most of his followers after they had fled into the nearby hills, and only the intervention of civic leaders from Santiago spared them immediate execution.

During his trial for sedition in September, Castro outlined a political program that called for a return to the 1940 Constitution, land reform (see **Agrarian Reform Acts**), and greater rights for tenants and rural laborers. Sentenced to twenty year's imprisonment on Isla de Pinos (later renamed **Isla de la Juventud**), Fidel, Raúl, and other political prisoners were released after two years under an amnesty granted by Batista. They resettled in Mexico and reorganized the **26th of July Movement** with additional members, among them Argentine physician **Ernesto "Che" Guevara**. Together with Guevara, Castro had come to the conclusion that only an invasion of Cuba, undertaken by men trained in guerrilla warfare, could succeed in toppling Batista. In December of 1956 he sailed for the island on the boat *Granma*, landing in Oriente Province (see **Granma Expedition**). The initial contact with Batista's troops decimated rebel ranks but won them support among the local peasantry. More important, news of the landing galvanized the growing urban resistance against Batista. The communists mobilized the trade unions on Castro's behalf, while student groups rallied to the 26th of July Movement.

The insurrection produced relatively few genuine battles but won Castro domination over the anti-Batista opposition. The U.S.-equipped Cuban Army proved an abject failure at counterinsurgency warfare. The inability of the government to put down the revolt, and the suppression of civil liberties, caused the middle class to abandon the dictatorship. After the fall of Santiago de Cuba to the rebels in December 1958 Batista fled the country, and the last of his troops surrendered on January 1, 1959. Castro entered Havana on January 8 and became provisional premier of Cuba in February. He soon dismissed his own handpicked president, **Manuel Urrutia**, and named a cabinet composed of followers from the 26th of July Movement and the old communist party. Castro proceeded to carry out radical measures not enunciated during the insurrection. Hundreds of Batista's henchmen and others deemed counterrevolutionary were executed. The amount of land that could be privately owned was severely curtailed, and most urban real estate was proclaimed property of the state. These decrees cost Castro the support of the middle class, many of whom sought exile in the United States. When the Cuban government seized U.S. petroleum refineries that had refused to process Soviet crude oil, President Dwight D. Eisenhower broke off diplomatic relations with Cuba in January 1961 (just before he left office) and instigated a plot by the Central Intelligence Agency to invade the island using exiles from the revolution. The invasion, staged at the **Bay of Pigs** in April under the Kennedy administration, proved a fiasco and actually strengthened Castro's grip on power. He declared the revolution officially socialist, and Cuba turned to the Soviet Union and Eastern Europe for military support. Soviet nuclear missiles were placed in Cuba in 1962, but their removal under a U.S. naval blockade was a political defeat for Castro, who lost prestige at home and in Latin America.

Castro soon turned his energies elsewhere. In 1965 he proclaimed himself chairman of the Central Committee of a new **Cuban Communist Party** (PCC), molded along Soviet lines. The Cuban Trade Union Confederation (CTC), the **Federation of Cuban Women** (FMC), and other newly formed mass organizations owed their loyalty to the party. Attempts to export revolution throughout the rest of Latin America and Africa met with most disappointing results, including the death of Guevara in combat in Bolivia in 1967. The effort to industrialize Cuba had failed by the end of the 1960s, and Castro instead pledged an extremely high goal of a **ten million ton harvest** of sugar in 1970 (which resulted in 8.5 million tons harvested).

The years 1975–1991 witnessed the waxing and waning of Castro's authority. Army troops were sent to Angola and Ethiopia to support Marxist regimes, elevating Cuba's stature in the Third World. Soviet oil supplies and subsidies for sugar allowed Cubans to enjoy a higher standard of living. But corruption and privileges crept into the regime, while the rise to power of Mikhail Gorbachev signaled a twist in Cuban-Soviet relations, as the Russian leader moved to end the Cold War with the United States. The fall of communism in Eastern Europe in 1989 and the disintegration of the Soviet Union in 1991 proved problematic for Cuba, which lost its most important trade partners. Castro searched for other sources of investment from Western Europe and Canada, and in 1998 he invited Pope John Paul II (see **Pope John Paul II's Visit to Cuba**) to the island in order to restore some of his own credibility.

Bearing the banners of both **José Martí** and Karl Marx, Castro turned the insurrection against Batista into the first and only successful socialist revolution in the Western Hemisphere. A patriot to some, tyrant to others, once he achieved power, Fidel Castro altered every aspect of Cuban life, from the arts to religion, from labor to the family. He assumed a critical role in international affairs during the Cold War, becoming a key player in the foreign policy of the United States, the former Soviet Union, and the underdeveloped nations. But at the dawn of the twenty-first century his primary tasks were to save socialism and retain power in Cuba while surrounded by enemies in a world largely hostile to his brand of communism. *See also*: Angola, Cuba's Involvement in; Ethiopia, Cuba's Involvement in; Soviet Union, Cuba's Relations with the; Special Period; Sugar Industry; Appendix II

Further Readings

Castro, Fidel. *Speeches*. New York: Pathfinder Press, 1981.

Franqui, Carlos. *Family Portrait with Fidel: A Memoir*. New York: Random House, 1984.

Geyer, Georgie Anne. *Guerrilla Prince: The Untold Story of Fidel Castro*. Boston: Little, Brown, 1991.

Lockwood, Lee. *Castro's Cuba, Cuba's Fidel*. Boulder, CO: Westview Press, 1990.

Mathews, Herbert L. *Fidel Castro*. New York: Simon and Schuster, 1969.

Quirk, Robert E. *Fidel Castro*. New York: W.W. Norton, 1993.

Szulc, Tad. *Fidel: A Critical Portrait*. New York: Morrow, 1986.

Julio César Pino

Castro Ruz, Raúl (1931–   )

Raúl Castro is the leader of the Cuban **Revolution**, along with his older brother **Fidel Castro**, second secretary of the Central Committee of the **Cuban Communist Party**, first vice president of the Councils of State and Ministers, general of the Army, and minister of the **Revolutionary Armed Forces** since 1959. He has also been designated by Fidel Castro to be his successor.

Raúl Castro was born on his father's estate near Birán in Oriente Province on January 3, 1931, the youngest son of Ángel Castro and Lina Ruz González. Five years younger than his brother Fidel, both boys attended the La Salle primary school. Raúl actively participated in his brother's plan to overthrow dictator **Fulgencio Batista** by seizing the **Moncada Army Barracks** in **Santiago de Cuba** on July 26, 1953. His own mission was to take control of the Palace of Justice, but the troops under his command were quickly repelled by the guards. Condemned for sedition by Batista's courts, Raúl and Fidel shared the same jail cell on Isla de Pinos (later renamed **Isla de la Juventud**).

Granted amnesty after serving twenty-two months, Raúl traveled with Fidel to Mexico but both soon sailed for Cuba to launch a guerrilla war against Batista (see *Granma* **Expedition**). During the insurrection (1956–1959) Raúl Castro was put in charge of the important **Segundo Frente Oriental "Frank País"** that operated widely throughout the northeastern part of Cuba. After the victory over Batista on January 1, 1959, Fidel named Raúl minister of the Revolutionary Armed Forces. During the first years of the Revolution, Raúl ordered the execution of hundreds of Batista's soldiers found guilty of war crimes, reorganized the guerrillas of the **26th of July Movement** into a modern army equipped with weaponry purchased from Western Europe and the Soviet Union, and helped supervise the first attempts to join Castro's followers into a single monolithic party. Raúl also married his longtime companion **Vilma Espín**.

After the birth of the Cuban Communist Party (PCC) in 1965, Raúl became Fidel's second in command, and unofficial successor, in both party and government. His duties and powers broadened considerably. Cuba integrated its armed forces with those of the Soviet bloc, holding joint exercises and permitting the stationing of Soviet military personnel on the island (see **Soviet Union, Cuba's Relations with the**). In 1975 he oversaw the dispatch of tens of thousands of Cuban troops to support Marxist regimes in Angola and Ethiopia. In his capacity as second secretary of the party he purged factions deemed disloyal to Fidel, and in 1989 he arranged the trial of General Arnaldo Ochoa for treason and drug running (see Ochoa Sánchez (Case), Arnaldo).

With the collapse of the Soviet Union in 1991, Cuba's economy was dragged into a severe and prolonged crisis (see **Special Period**), and the military, with Raúl Castro's encouragement, became directly involved in reviving both **manufacturing** and **agriculture**. Soldiers participated in food production drives while officers managed important factories and even tourist resorts built with **foreign investments**. At the same time, Raúl Castro toured the country reminding the party faithful that Cuba would never succumb to capitalist restoration and that the PCC had to remain ideologically pure, lest the United States undermine the revolution through peaceful methods such as **tourism** or the growing use of dollars on the island.

Raúl Castro seems destined to lead Cuba after his brother's death. Whether he will choose to side with the pragmatists who want to introduce more market measures into the economy or the ideologues

Raúl Castro Ruz, Fidel's younger brother and heir apparent with his brother, after bidding farewell to Russian President Vladimir Putin in 2000. AP/ Wide World Photos. Photography by José Goitía.

desiring to preserve socialism at all costs is still unclear. *See also* Angola, Cuba's Involvement in; Batista, Struggle Against; Ethiopia, Cuba's Involvement in

Further Readings

Domínguez, Jorge I. "Political Succession in Cuba." *Third World Quarterly* 10, no. 1 (January 1988): 229–236.

Núñez Jiménez, Antonio. *El Segundo Frente Oriental "Frank País."* Lima, Peru: Industrial, 1974.

Julio César Pino

Cienfuegos Gorriarán, Camilo (1932–1959)

In life, Camilo Cienfuegos was one of the most popular revolutionary heroes and in death one of the **Revolution**'s most venerated martyrs. The circumstances surrounding his death are still clouded in mystery, and some suspect he was killed by members of the **Fidel Castro** government concerned about his popularity.

Of working-class origins, Cienfuegos was born in Havana. His involvement in the revolutionary struggle against **Fulgencio Batista** began in 1955 when he was wounded during a protest march. A tailor by trade, Cienfuegos joined Fidel Castro in Mexico in August 1956 to plot the overthrow of the Batista government. He was a member of the *Granma* **expedition** that landed in Oriente Province on December 2, 1956. Most of the eighty-two expedition members were either killed or captured, but Cienfuegos, and about eleven others, survived and eventually rejoined Castro. This small nucleus would gradually draw recruits from across Cuba and lead a daring guerrilla campaign in the countryside. Cienfuegos distinguished himself during several battles throughout 1957 and 1958. After the collapse of the army offensive in the summer of 1958, Cienfuegos and **Ernesto "Che" Guevara** were ordered to march on western Cuba with the goal of militarily cutting the island in two. As they traveled west, Cienfuegos and Guevara won a series of victories and occupied numerous towns in the center of the island. When Batista fled in the early morning hours of January 1, 1959, they marched on Havana and took control of the city. In the early days of the Revolution, Cienfuegos became a popular hero, arguably the second most popular figure after Fidel Castro. He was named commander in chief of the Rebel Army.

There is some dispute over Cienfuegos's ideological leanings. Many argue that he was virulently anticommunist, a stance that may have cost him his life. Others claim that he was apolitical and would likely have supported Castro regardless of his ideology. In October 1959, Cienfuegos's flight from **Camagüey** to Havana was lost over the sea. The wreckage of the airplane and his body were never recovered. This happened just days after Cien-

Camilo Cienfuegos Gorrirán, charismatic revolutionary leader who died in a mysterious air crash in 1959. Fidel Castro Photograph Collection, Manuscripts Division, Department of Rare Books and Special Collections, Princeton University Library.

Mural celebrating the Committees for the Defense of the Revolution. Photograph by Celestino Martínez Lindín.

fuegos reluctantly arrested Commander **Huber Matos** for decrying the infiltration of the army by communists. Some suspect that **Raúl Castro** had him killed because he was going to object publicly to Matos's arrest. *See also* Batista, Struggle Against

Further Readings

Franqui, Carlos. *Camilo Cienfuegos*. Barcelona: Seix Barral, 2001.
Gálvez, William. *Camilo, señor de la vanguardia*. Havana: Editorial de Ciencias Sociales, 1988.
Thomas, Hugh. *Cuba: The Pursuit of Freedom*. New York: Harper & Row, 1971.

Paula J. Pettavino

Committees for the Defense of the Revolution (Comités de Defensa de la Revolución [CDRs])

Committees for the Defense of the Revolution (CDRs) are neighborhood-level organizations that were designed to allow political participation of the masses and to protect the state from internal subversion. CDRs were established in the wake of a speech made by **Fidel Castro** in September 1960. The organizations, which were created to protect the **Revolution** from internal opponents and from the perceived menace of the United States, function under the supervision of the **Ministry of the Interior**. Committees for the Defense of the Revolution serve a variety of purposes. They provide a conduit for complaints, promote health-care and education programs, encourage voting (see **Elections**), and bring local problems to the attention of government authorities. However, they also monitor the activities of people who live in the neighborhood. Cubans are often under surveillance, and the watchful eye of the CDRs is a key factor in attaining that object. CDRs are particularly alert for people who display actions that could be considered counterrevolutionary or subversive, including homosexuals, dissidents, and people having unauthorized contact with foreigners. *See also* Dissent and Defections (1959–); Educational System; Gays and Lesbians; Health-Care System

Further Readings

Colomer, Josep M. "Watching Neighbors: The Cuban Model for Social Control." *Cuban Studies* 31 (2000): 118–138.

LeoGrande, William. "Mass Political Participation in Socialist Cuba." In *The Cuba Reader: The Making of a Revolutionary Society*, ed. Philip Brenner, William LeoGrande, Donna Rich, and Daniel Siegel. New York: Grove Press, 1989. 186–199.

Salas, Luis P. *Social Control and Deviance in Cuba*. New York: Praeger, 1979.

Sieqelbaum, Portia. "CDRs: Security and Service." *Cuba Review* 7, no. 3 (October 1977): 19–25.

Suchlicki, Jaime. *Cuba, Castro, and Revolution*. Coral Gables, FL: University of Miami Press, 1972.

Catherine Moses

Communist Party, Cuban (Partido Comunista Cubano [PCC])

The Cuban Communist Party is the only legal political party in Cuba, entrusted by the **Constitution of 1976** to be the "guiding force of society and the state" and to "organize and lead efforts" to build socialism. The most powerful and influential political institution in the country, its high-ranking party members control most key government and military posts, so that in fact there is little distinction between the party and the government.

At the top of the party structure is the Political Bureau headed by First Secretary **Fidel Castro** and Second Secretary **Raúl Castro**. The governing body of the party is the Central Committee, which directs party affairs in between party congresses. The Secretariat serves as the administrative arm of the Party. In addition to the national structure, there are party committees in each of the island's fourteen provinces and 169 municipalities. Party organizations operate at military facilities, schools, neighborhoods, and workplaces. Ironically, the communists and the party, known prior to 1961 as the Popular Socialist Party (**Partido Comunista**, PSP), played only a small role in the struggle against **Fulgencio Batista** in the 1950s. It was not until mid-1958 that elements of

the party openly supported Fidel Castro. In the first year of the **Revolution**, the PSP often urged Castro to take a more conciliatory approach to the United States. As relations with Washington soured, Castro merged the PSP with his own **26th of July Movement** and the Directorio Revolucionario in 1961 to form the Organizaciones Revolucionarias Integradas [ORI] (Integrated Revolutionary Organizations). Over time, Castro would clash with several of the old-line communists and purge them from power, including Anibal Escalante and Joaquín Ordoqui. ORI was later organized into the Partido Unido de la Revolución Socialista [PURS] (United Party of the Socialist Revolution), which in 1965 became the Partido Comunista Cubano [PCC] (Cuban Communist Party). Party membership remained stagnant throughout the 1960s as a result of Castro's personalistic leadership and his desire to operate outside the party structure.

In the 1970s, the reshaped Communist Party emerged as a key factor in the Revolution's efforts to consolidate and centralize power. Castro expanded the size of the party's Political Bureau and began to delegate authority to a small cadre of trusted and loyal followers. Its authority over the government and society was heralded by Castro at the First Party Congress in 1975, when he declared that the party was the "soul of the Cuban Revolution."

The party's right to rule stems from the perceived moral authority of its members and their qualifications as exemplary revolutionaries. As a result, membership in the party has traditionally been limited to an elite group, although it has risen steadily over time. In 1965, party membership numbered 50,000, or roughly 2 out of every 1,000 Cubans. By 1975, membership had increased to 203,000, or 21 of every 1,000. The numbers jumped even more dramatically in the 1990s as a result of the collapse of the Soviet Union and the additional hardships suffered by the popu-

Stamp commemorating the celebration of the Second Congress of the Cuban Communist Party in 1980. Luis Martínez-Fernández Collection.

lation, since party affiliation provided some tangible benefits to members. By 1997, party membership had risen to 780,000. The party has held five party congresses since its reorganization in 1965, all of which served as rubber stamps for policies introduced by the government. The most recent party congress held in Havana in 1997 reaffirmed government efforts to diversify the economy and combat economic aggression by the United States. *See also* Bastista, Struggle Against; Government Structure; Soviet Union, Cuba's Relations with the; United States, Cuba's Relations with the

Further Readings

Domínguez, Jorge I. *Cuba: Order and Revolution.* Cambridge, MA: Belknap Press of Harvard University Press, 1978.
González, Edward. *Cuba under Castro: The Limits of Charisma.* Boston: Houghton Mifflin, 1974.
Suárez, Andrés. *Cuba: Castroism and Communism, 1959–1966.* Cambridge: MIT Press, 1967.

Frank Argote-Freyre

Communist Youth Union (Unión de Jóvenes Comunistas [UJC])

The Communist Youth Union is one of Cuba's so-called mass organizations, those that were created in the early 1960s to support the regime and to terminate all the pre-**Revolution** civic and professional groups. The **Constitution of 1976** charges it with the job of teaching the tenets of communism to a new generation, as well as inspiring revolutionary fervor. Members must be under the age of thirty and are drawn from all sectors of society, including students, workers, and farmers. As of 1997, there were 530,000 members.

In an effort to get out its message, the UJC publishes a weekly newspaper, the *Juventud Rebelde*, and supports a wide range of community activities including government construction projects. The UJC works through a variety of student organizations, such as the Organización de Pioneros **José Martí** (José Martí Pioneers Organization) for primary school students, the Federación de Estudiantes de la Enseñanza Media (Federation of Middle School Students), and the Federación Estudiantil Universitaria [FEU] (**Federation of University Students**).

Prior to 1959, there were a number of youth organizations involved in the **struggle against Batista**, all of which were merged into the Asociación de Jóvenes Rebeldes (Association of Rebel Youth) in 1961. The following year, as the Revolution veered to the Left, the Association was replaced by the UJC. In the early years, membership plunged by more than 75 percent, from 100,000 to about 18,000, as noncommunists were expelled and strict membership guidelines established.

Havana billboard celebrating the fortieth anniversary of the founding of the Unión de Jóvenes Comunistas (UJC). Photograph by Luis Martínez-Fernández.

In the early 1970s, charges of elitism were made against the UJC, and efforts were made to expand its membership. In the past, the UJC was accused of ignoring the qualifications of agricultural workers and blue-collar workers in favor of recruiting students and white-collar workers. By the mid-1970s, the UJC was placed firmly under the control of the **Cuban Communist Party**. Membership in the UJC strengthens the candidacy of those wishing to join the party. *See also* Newspapers and Magazines; Students' Movement (Republican Era); University of Havana

Further Readings

Domínguez, Jorge I. *Cuba: Order and Revolution.* Cambridge, MA: Belknap Press of Harvard University Press, 1978.

LeoGrande, William. "Mass Political Participation in Socialist Cuba." In *The Cuba Reader: The Making of a Revolutionary Society*, ed. Philip Brenner, William LeoGrande, Donna Rich, and Daniel Siegel. New York: Grove Press, 1989. 186–199.

Frank Argote-Freyre

Constitution of 1976

The Constitution of 1976 codified and institutionalized the **government structure** put in place by **Fidel Castro** and the **Revolution** of 1959. It mandates the preservation of a socialist state and anoints the **Cuban Communist Party** as the "guiding force of the society." The Constitution grants the rights of artistic, religious, and political expression as long as "their content is not contrary to the revolution." Article 61 of the Constitution clearly states that no rights can be exercised "against the existence or goals of the socialist state." According to the Constitution, ultimate power rests with the **National Assembly of People's Power**, which meets twice a year. However, when not in session, much of the Assembly's authority is delegated to a State Council, headed by President Fidel Castro. The Constitution also grants the president sweeping powers over internal and external affairs. On the local level, the document establishes provincial and municipal assemblies. Discrimination based on race, color, sex, or national origin is prohibited by the Constitution.

The Constitution was substantially amended in 1992 to reflect the new-world reality created by the collapse of the Soviet Union and the Communist bloc. References to Cuba as part of a "socialist community" of nations were stricken from the Constitution and replaced by greater emphasis on "solidarity" with the nations of Latin America and the Caribbean. Also stricken was Cuba's commitment to the "internationalist" mission of assisting countries fighting wars of national liberation. In recognition of Cuba's precarious economic and political situation, the 1992 amendments permit the president, without the prior consent of the National Assembly, to declare a state of emergency and "mobilize the population." The amended Constitution takes a softer stance to organized religion by striking language that made it illegal to use one's faith to "oppose the Revolution, the education system or compliance with the responsibilities to work, defense of the nation with arms and reverence for its symbols." One of the new amendments, Article 8, specifically guarantees "religious liberty" and the separation of church and state. *See also* Guerrillas, Cuba's Support for; Religion under Castro; Soviet Union, Cuba's Relations with the

Further Readings

Álvarez Tabío, Fernando. *Comentarios a la constitución socialista*. Havana: Editorial de Ciencias Sociales, 1981.

De la Cuesta, Leonel Antonio. "The Cuban Socialist Constitution: Its Originality and Role in Institutionalization." *Cuban Studies* 6, no. 2 (July 1976): 15–30.

Domínguez, Jorge I. *Cuba: Order and Revolution*. Cambridge, MA: Belknap Press of Harvard University Press, 1978.

Frank Argote-Freyre

Dissent and Defections (1959–)

Dissent, or openly disagreeing with **Fidel Castro**'s regime, is punishable in Cuba because it is considered counterrevolutionary behavior. There are no open channels for such dissent. The news media only present ideas that are consistent with the dominant political ideology. Artists and writers who express ideas counter to those espoused by the government and the **Cuban Communist Party** are harshly criticized. At the neighborhood level, the **Committees for the Defense of the Revolution** discourage dissent by monitoring individuals' behavior and comments about the regime.

In the first few years of the **Revolution**, the punishments for dissent were lengthy prison terms or, in some cases of counterrevolutionary activity, execution. Now, those who actively dissent are likely to face job loss, harassment, imprisonment, and involuntary exile. To avoid punishment, citizens have learned not to criticize government policies or the Revolution. Few Cubans who do not fully support the government risk expressing their political beliefs for fear of losing their jobs and facing harassment. Those who choose to voice their opposition have two choices:

stay and face the consequences or leave the island.

Those who dissent and stay may join one of a small number of loosely organized **human rights** and independent professional organizations. These groups face great challenges, because they are illegal and the government seeks to undermine and discredit them. Some groups have only a few members, while others have membership numbering in the hundreds. The professional groups work to present a different view from that of the government about what is happening in politics, law, medicine, or economics. The human rights groups seek to inform the outside world of the human rights situation within Cuba and to inform Cubans of their fundamental rights (see **Independent Journalists**). In May 2002, during a visit to Cuba of former U.S. President Jimmy Carter, groups of dissidents called the Varela Project presented the Cuban government with a petition with 11,000 signatures demanding political reforms.

The other option for those who disagree with the regime's political and economic system is to leave the island. Many Cubans who have the opportunity to travel abroad seek political asylum or otherwise adjust their immigration status. Others, denied permission by the Cuban government to leave the island, try to leave by raft or fast boat (see **Balseros**). On a few occasions, defectors have hijacked boats and airplanes in their efforts to leave Cuba.

One dramatic instance of defection was the case of Orestes Lorenzo, who in 1991 escaped Cuba by flying a Cuban Airforce Soviet-made MIG 23. He promised to return for his family and did so seventeen months later. He flew a Cessna plane under radar, landed on the Vía Blanca highway, and picked up his wife and two children. Perhaps the most tragic attempt was that of the *13 de Marzo* tugboat. On July 14, 1995, the boat left Havana harbor loaded with people seeking to flee Cuba.

Seven miles off shore, Cuban vessels sank the *13 de Marzo*, killing forty-one people, including women and children. *See also* Appendix 14; Arcos Bergnes, Gustavo; Communications; Crime; Human Rights; Newspapers and Magazines

Further Readings

Del Águila, Juan M. "The Politics of Dissidence: A Challenge to the Monolith." In *Conflict and Change in Cuba*, ed. Enrique A. Baloyra and James A. Morris. Albuquerque: University of New Mexico Press, 1993. 164–188.

Lorenzo, Orestes. *Wings of the Morning*. New York: St. Martin's Press, 1994.

Moses, Catherine. *Real Life in Castro's Cuba*. Wilmington, DE: Scholarly Resources, 2000.

Salas, Luis P. *Social Control and Deviance in Cuba*. New York: Praeger, 1979.

Vargas Llosa, Álvaro. *El exilio indomable: historia de la disidencia cubana en el destierro*. Madrid: Espasa, 1998.

Catherine Moses

Dorticós Torrado, Osvaldo (1919–1983)

A lawyer and politician, Osvaldo Dorticós served as figurehead president of Cuba between 1959 and 1976. Born to a wealthy **Cienfuegos** family, Dorticós studied law at the **University of Havana** and in his youth joined the Communist Party (see **Partido Comunista**), serving as personal secretary to its president, **Juan Marinello**. In his hometown of Cienfuegos, Dorticós legally represented corporate interests and acted as commodore of the exclusive Cienfuegos Yacht Club. He also served as vice president of the National Bar Association. During **Fulgencio Batista**'s dictatorship, he played a minor role in the **26th of July Movement** but was briefly arrested for his political activities.

Following the triumph of the **Revolution**, Dorticós joined the revolutionary cabinet as head of a new ministry in charge of studying revolutionary legislation. Following **Manuel Urrutia**'s resignation in July 1959, Castro designated him president of the republic. Throughout his presidency, Dorticós remained loyal to Castro, who as prime minister remained Cuba's dictator and undisputed authority. With the government restructuring mandated by the **Constitution of 1976**, Castro assumed the presidency and Dorticós was designated vice president of the Council of Ministers and member of the Council of State. He committed suicide in 1983. *See also* Government Structure; Presidents

Further Reading

Domínguez, Jorge I. *Cuba: Order and Revolution*. Cambridge, MA: Belknap Press of Harvard University Press, 1978.

Luis Martínez-Fernández

Elections (1959–   )

In Cuba, elections take place regularly, though they follow a different logic from those in Western democracies. General elections to elect the members of the **National Assembly of People's Power**, and the delegates of the provincial and municipal assemblies, take place every five years; midterm elections to renew the mandate of the delegates take place every two and a half years; and special elections to cover vacancies take place as they are required by circumstances. In 1993 direct elections were held for the first time to select the members of the National Assembly. Elections are not held, however, for the office of president or vice president. Citizens over the age of sixteen are eligible to vote (including the military), except the mentally ill, criminals (see **Crime**), and those who have requested permission to emigrate. All voters are also eligible to run for office, except for the National Assembly, which requires a minimum age of eighteen. Only the **Cuban Communist Party** is legally recognized, though independent candidates technically may run. Candidates for municipal office are nominated at neighborhood meetings by show of hands. Except for the distribution of the candidates' biographies and photographs, all other forms of political campaigning are prohibited. Winners are determined by a simple majority. The ballot is secret, and voting is not mandatory. Voting, however, is considered a fundamental patriotic duty; repeatedly failing to vote can label an individual as politically untrustworthy. Participation rates are thus very high—usually in the 90 percent–plus range. Opposition to the regime is voiced by voters who turn in blank or damaged ballots; this practice has increased over the past few years. Castro has generally ignored the international community's call for free elections in Cuba. *See also* Government Structure

Further Readings

LeoGrande, William. "Mass Political Participation in Socialist Cuba." In *The Cuba Reader: The Making of a Revolutionary Society*, ed. Philip Brenner, William LeoGrande, Donna Rich, and Daniel Siegel. New York: Grove Press, 1989. 186–199.

Rudolph, James D., ed. *Cuba: A Country Study*. Washington, DC: U.S. Government Printing Office, 1985.

Ernesto Sagás

Espín Guillois, Vilma (1930–)

Vilma Espín has been the president of the **Federation of Cuban Women (Federación de Mujeres Cubanas [FMC])** since its inception in 1960. A fierce opponent of the **Fulgencio Batista** dictatorship, she joined the revolutionary movement in 1953 under the leadership of **Frank País**. In 1957, she was named provincial coordinator for the **26th of July Movement** in Oriente Province. With the triumph of the **Revolution**, Espín emerged as the most influential leader in the Cuban women's movement. She married **Raúl Castro** in 1959. In 1975, she was elected to the Central Committee of the **Cuban Communist Party**, and in 1982 she became a member

Vilma Espín, long-time chief of the Federation of Cuban Women and wife of Raúl Castro. AP/Wide World Photos. Photograph by José Goitía.

of the Politburo. She has served on three occasions (1975, 1980, and 1995) as the vice president for Latin America and the Caribbean for the United Nations World Conferences on Women. She has served as the first lady of Cuba at a wide range of events, because of her marriage in 1959 to Raúl Castro, a union that ended in separation in the 1980s. **Fidel Castro** designated Espín to serve in that capacity at the Encuentros Iberoamericanos de Primeras Damas (Summits of Latin American First Ladies) held throughout the 1990s. *See also* Women's Rights

Further Readings

De La Cruz, Dania. *Movimiento femenino cubano. Bibliografía*. Havana: Editora Política, 1980.

Stone, Elizabeth, ed. *Women and the Cuban Revolution*. New York: Pathfinder Press, 1981.

Stoner, Lynn K., ed. *The Women's Movement in Cuba, 1898–1958*. Stoner Collection on Cuban Feminism. Wilmington, DE: Scholarly Resources, Microform. 1991.

Julio César González Pagés

Ethiopia, Cuba's Involvement in

The Cuban military (see **Revolutionary Armed Forces**) participated in the conflict between Somalia and Ethiopia (1977–1978), at the request of the Ethiopian government, in close cooperation with the Soviet Union. Earlier Cuban intervention in Angola (1975–1976) served as a model for the new involvement. Cuba's motivations and aims for intervening in Ethiopia remain subject to debate by foreign policy scholars.

In 1975 **Fidel Castro** welcomed the revolutionary developments in Ethiopia, and diplomatic relations were established with the new regime. The triumph of Megistu Mariam's faction in Ethiopia's government in February 1977 was well received by Cuba's government. Castro visited both Ethiopia and Somalia in March, during a diplomatic tour to Africa and the Middle East. Somalia had established diplomatic relations with Cuba in 1972, and Cuba had a military mission there. Castro arranged a meeting with the leaders of the two states in Aden (South Yemen) to seek a solution to their territorial disputes. Although the meeting did not solve the conflict, Somalia pledged not to invade Ethiopia. They broke the pledge in July 1977 when the Somali army entered the Ogaden desert. At first, Cuba sent only military advisers to Ethiopia. By the end of November, after Somalia severed relations with them, Cuba sent around 15,000 troops, led by Cuban General Arnaldo Ochoa, in close coordination with the Soviet Union. The Somali army was expelled from Ethiopian territory by spring 1978. Cuba maintained reduced numbers of troops in Ethiopia until 1989 and participated in several civil projects. *See also* Angola, Cuba's Involvement in; Soviet Union, Cuba's Relations with the; Ochoa Sánchez (Case), Arnaldo

Further Readings

Domínguez, Jorge I. *To Make a World Safe for Revolution: Cuba's Foreign Policy.* Cambridge, MA: Harvard University Press, 1989.
Gleijeses, Piero. *Conflicting Missions: Havana, Washington, and Africa, 1959–1976.* Chapel Hill: University of North Carolina Press, 2002.
Mesa Lago, Carmelo, and June Belkin, eds. *Cuba in Africa.* Pittsburgh: University of Pittsburgh Press, 1982.

Zenén Santana Delgado

Federation of Cuban Women (Federación de Mujeres Cubanas [FMC])

The primary women's organization in Cuba, the Federation of Cuban Women (FMC) was formed on August 23, 1960, by the merger of forty existing women's associations. In 1961, the FMC consisted of 17,000 members, a number that climbed to nearly 240,000 by 1962. Members are called *federadas*, rather than *feminists*, the latter term associated with capitalist society. Throughout the years, membership, which is virtually mandatory, has climbed steadily, reaching 3.2 million by the 1990s, or roughly 81 percent of the female population over the age of fourteen. In, 1999 the number of members had reached 3.6 million. The organization has been recognized by the United Nations for efforts to improve conditions for women and children in rural areas, promoting better education for women and equitable treatment in the workplace. Prior to the FMC, there were two other organizations that attempted to mobilize women on a national scale. The first was the Federación Nacional de Asociaciones Femeninas de Cuba (National Federation of Cuban Women's Associations) in 1921 and the second, the Federación Democrática de Mujeres Cubanas (Democratic Federation of Cuban Women) in 1947. *See also* Educational System; Feminist Movement (Republican Era); Women's Rights

Logo of the Federation of Cuban Women, mass organization created in 1960.

Further Readings

Molyneux, Maxime. "State, Gender and Institutional Change. The Federación de Mujeres Cubanas." In *Hidden Histories of Gender and the State in Latin America*, ed. Elizabeth Dore and Maxime Molyneux, Durham, NC: Duke University Press, 2000. 291–321.

Smith, Lois M., and Alfred Padula. *Sex and Revolution: Women in Socialist Cuba*. New York: Oxford University Press, 1996.

Julio César González Pagés

Federation of University Students (Federación Estudiantil Universitaria [FEU])

One of Cuba's mass organizations, the Federation of University Students (Federación Estudiantil Universitaria [FEU]) was charged by the **Constitution of 1976** with representing the interests of university students to the Cuban government and working to organize and support revolutionary initiatives. The FEU receives guidance in how to perform its revolutionary mission from the Unión de Jóvenes Comunistas (UJC) **(Communist Youth Union)**. Leaders of the FEU are almost always members of the UJC. FEU branches exist at all of the island's universities, and membership numbers nearly 100,000.

Historically, the FEU, founded in 1922, was a hotbed of political dissent and debate, frequently in violent opposition to a variety of Cuban governments. Members of FEU were among the most vocal and active opponents of the **Fulgencio Batista** government of the 1950s. After the triumph of the **Revolution**, the Cuban government sought to control the volatile student movement and secure its support for the Revolution. In the fall of 1959, **Fidel Castro** interceded in FEU elections to secure the selection of a candidate favorable to the revolutionary cause. This was a prelude to the eventual takeover of the **University of Havana** by administrators and scholars sympathetic to the government. In 1962, UJC branches were established at university campuses, and the functions of the Federation and the UJC were gradually merged. In 1967, the FEU was dissolved and reestablished in its current form in 1971.

Periodically members gather for congresses to set FEU policies and priorities. Recent organizational goals include the placement of all university graduates in appropriate jobs and the expansion of scientific studies at the university level. In between congresses, FEU activities are administered by a national secretariat. *See also* Students' Movement (Republican Era)

Further Reading

Suchlicki, Jaime. *University Students and Revolution in Cuba, 1920–1968*. Coral Gables, FL: University of Miami Press, 1969.

Frank Argote-Freyre

Foreign Relations

Cuba's foreign relations have constituted one of the pillars of the revolutionary regime since the triumph of the **Revolution** in 1959. They have, however, exposed tensions between the goal of changing the way human societies are organized and relate to each other and the necessity to adapt to an international system, where Cuba has had to play according to the rules established by the world powers.

The ideology behind Cuba's foreign policy merges Marxism-Leninism and nationalism. One of its most enduring tenets is the strong hostility to the United States, a state seen as a threat to the Cuban nation and its independence and as the leader of the capitalist system that the Cuban **Revolution** had rejected. Cuba's foreign policy strategies have proven flexible, depending on the domestic situation and the opportunities and constraints in the international system. However, its main goal has remained constant: to design and implement objectives that secure the revolutionary state, particularly against U.S. actions, through traditional state-to-state alliances, international organizations, and world public opinion. Other objectives include avoiding isolation in the international system, promoting economic relations, and supporting revolutionary movements and civil society groups that share Cuba's values. The principal foreign policy instruments have been bilateral and multilateral diplomatic relations, civil and military assistance, material and political support for revolutionary groups, propaganda, and sports.

The decision-making process of foreign policy involves several high officials and agencies. **Fidel Castro** holds a special position as main decision maker, advised by a group of close associates. Among the most influential Cuban officials in foreign policy have been **Raúl Castro, Ernesto "Che" Guevara, Osvaldo Dorticós, Raúl Roa, Carlos Rafael Rodríguez**, Manuel Piñeiro, Osmani Cienfuegos, and **Ricardo Alarcón**. The Politburo of the **Cuban Communist Party** (PCC) has occupied a central institutional position since the mid-

1970s. Other important agencies are the Ministry of External Relations (MINREX), the America and the International Relations Departments of the Central Committee of the PCC, the General Directorate of Intelligence (DGI) of the **Ministry of the Interior** (MININT), the Directorate of Military Intelligence (DIM), and the External Relations Department (DRE) of the **Revolutionary Armed Forces** (MINFAR); also the Ministry of External Trade (MINCEX), the Ministry of External Investment and Collaboration (MINVEC), and the Cuban Institute of Friendship with the Peoples (ICAP). A secondary role is played by the International Relations Departments of the **Communist Youth Union** (UJC), the so-called mass organizations and trade unions.

Cuba's foreign policy can be divided into two distinctive stages: 1959–1990, marked by the alliance with the Soviet Union; and 1991–present, when for the first time in history Cuba has not been under the hegemony of any external power but remains partially isolated in the international system. In the first decade of the Revolution, Cuba had to deal with increased U.S. hostility. In the early 1960s, the U.S. government carried out several covert and overt operations, including economic sanctions, the **Bay of Pigs Invasion** (1961), and Operation Mongoose (1962) with the objective to defeat, or at least isolate and contain, the Cuban Revolution. Cuba's leaders sought to forge an alliance with the Soviet Union in order to solve the security and economic problems that confronted them. The Soviet Union, albeit cautious at first, decided to support the new revolutionary state. The outcome of the **Missile Crisis** (1962) constrained U.S. hostile policies. However, the relations with the Soviets in this period were affected by Cuba's support for the strategy of armed struggle in Latin America. In the 1960s Cuba took the first steps toward the formulation of a global policy. It supported revolutionary movements in Latin

America and Africa, participated in the **Nonaligned Movement**'s summits and began to work with Third World states in the United Nations. Cuba maintained diplomatic and expanded trade relations with developed capitalist states, avoiding isolation and seeking to break the **U.S. trade embargo**.

In the second decade of the Revolution, Cuba became a significant actor in the international arena, unlike most small states. Cuba became a member of the Soviet-sponsored Council for Mutual Economic Aid (CMEA) in 1972, economic integration that allowed the island to receive considerable development aid. In the early 1970s, Cuba focused on state-to-state relations in Latin America and the Caribbean, establishing diplomatic relations with several states. In 1975, the **Organization of American States (OAS)** ended the collective sanctions against Cuba. The Nicaragua and Grenada revolutions (1979) represented a fulfillment of the Cuban leaders' dreams. Castro participated in the IV Summit of the Nonaligned Movement (NAM) in Algiers (1973) and went on diplomatic tours through Africa, the Middle East, and the Socialist bloc (1972, 1977). Cuba continued to support National Liberation Movements (MLN) and progressive states in Africa and the Middle East and increased tenfold civil and military assistance. Military troops were sent to aid states that were interested in pursuing a "socialist orientation" path. Cuba was elected to hold the VI Summit of the NAM, acquiring a position of leadership and the role of broker between the Third World and the Socialist bloc. The relations with the United States, despite certain thawing and the establishment of Interest Sections (1977), did not improve satisfactorily as conditions requested by each side were beyond what they were prepared to negotiate.

The third decade began with some troubles. Cuba's credentials in the NAM were affected by its pro-Soviet Union position toward the Afghanistan and Kampuchea cases. In Latin America, Cuba's relations were affected by its position on asylum rights and the ways Cuba dealt with the Embassies Crisis (1980). In the Caribbean, conservative forces began to occupy dominant positions. Furthermore, the new U.S. administration of Ronald Reagan (1981–1989) enacted very aggressive policies against any revolutionary states or movements, threatening to go to the source of instability in the Caribbean Basin, meaning Cuba. Although the Soviet Union increased the military supply, they communicated to the Cuban leaders that the Soviet Union would not come to its aid in case of U.S. attack. Confronted with these problems, Cuba adopted less active policies and focused on issues where there was broad consensus, such as supporting Argentina during the Malvinas/Falklands Islands conflict with Great Britain (1982) and the organization of conferences to analyze the external debts of the developing countries (1985). However, in the second half of the 1980s Cuba's international image improved with the diplomatic solution to the conflict in southern Africa (1988). In 1989, Cuba was elected to the Security Council of the United Nations.

The fourth decade of the Revolution began with deep changes in the international system brought by the fall of the Socialist bloc (1989) and the disintegration of the Soviet Union (1991). Those events had a marked negative effect on Cuba's economy and security. Furthermore, the viability of the revolutionary state was brought into question. The United States considerably increased pressure for a change in Cuba, a position that is shared by other states, such as Spain and the United Kingdom though they do not approve the U.S. strategy. However, **Pope John Paul II's visit to Cuba** (1998) and the hosting of the IX Ibero-American summit (1999) were important successes of

Cuba's foreign policy. The Summit of the 77 Group held in Havana (2000) and the support of the African, Caribbean, and Pacific states to include Cuba in the Lomé Convention demonstrate the important role Cuba continues to play in the Third World. *See also* Angola, Cuba's Involvement in; Ethiopia, Cuba's Involvement in; Government Structure; Grenada, Cuba's Involvement in; Guerrillas, Cuba's Support for; Nicaragua, Cuba's Relations with; Revolutionary Armed Forces (Fuerzas Armadas Revolucionarias [FAR]); Soviet Union, Cuba's Relations with the; United States, Cuba's Relations with the

Further Readings

Domínguez, Jorge I. *To Make a World Safe for Revolution: Cuba's Foreign Policy*. Cambridge, MA: Harvard University Press, 1989.

Erisman, H. Michael. *Cuba's Foreign Relations in a Post-Soviet World*. Gainesville: University Press of Florida, 2000.

Falk, Pamela S. *Cuban Foreign Policy: Caribbean Tempest*. Lexington, MA: Lexington Books, 1986.

Fernández, Damián J. *Cuba's Foreign Policy in the Middle East*. Boulder, Co: Westview Press, 1988.

Ritter, Archibald R.M., and John M. Kirk, eds., *Cuba in the International System: Normalization and Integration*. London: Macmillan, 1995.

Zenén Santana Delgado

Franqui, Carlos (1921–   )

A prominent member of the **26th of July Movement**, Carlos Franqui was involved with the armed struggle of the **Revolution**, as well as with the creation and dissemination of its information. As director of Radio Rebelde in the **Sierra Maestra** and the founder and editor in chief of *Revolución* (the underground newspaper and later official paper until 1965), Franqui became the archivist of the Revolution, given his broad access to information and contact with the principal participants.

Born in Clavellinas (old Province of Las Villas) and reared in a peasant family on a sugarcane plantation, Franqui engaged in efforts to overthrow General Rafael L. Trujillo of the Dominican Republic in 1947. He proofread for the communist newspaper *Hoy* in Oriente Province. After breaking with the Partido Socialista Popular (see **Partido Comunista**), he became a collaborator with **Fidel Castro**, working the underground movement in urban areas. Jailed by **Fulgencio Batista**'s police, upon release in 1955 he served on the Committee in Exile while in Mexico and the United States.

With the closure of *Revolución* and the growing influence of the USSR, Franqui turned to representing Cuba in various European cultural and informational ventures. His commitment to democracy led to exile in Italy in 1968. Among his principal works are *Diary of the Cuban Revolution* (1976), which is a selective editing of texts, correspondence, and reports by the major figures of the Revolution. A vocal opponent of the Castro government, Franqui remains active publishing articles and books, most recently a biography of **Camilo Cienfuegos** (2001). *See also* Communications; Dissent and Defections (1959–   ); Newspapers and Magazines

Further Readings

Franqui, Carlos. *Family Portrait with Fidel: A Memoir*. New York: Random House, 1984.

Franqui, Carlos. *The Twelve*. New York: Lyle Stuart, 1968.

Peter T. Johnson

González (Case), Elián

The Elián González case will certainly be remembered as one of the most intense and prickly confrontations between Cuba and the United States since the triumph of the **Revolution**. Beyond the struggle over parental rights and custody over the child Elián González, the case developed into a protracted battle among Cuba, its exile community, and the U.S. government, generating domestic and international debates on its legal, political, and social ramifications.

The Elián saga began with the sinking of the rustic boat (see **Balseros**) in which the child, his mother, several of his family members, and others illegally fled Cuba from the coast of **Cárdenas** on November 22, 1999. The boat with fourteen people on board capsized near Florida's coast, and only three of its passengers survived, Elián, aged five, among them. He was rescued on Thanksgiving Day three miles off the coast north of Miami by clinging to a tire's inner tube. His mother Elizabeth Brotons and his stepfather Lázaro Munero had drowned. After providing Elián with medical assistance, the U.S. Immigration and Naturalization Service (INS) gave temporary custody of the boy to his grandfather's brother Lázaro González, who had abandoned Cuba in 1983 and now resided in a modest home in the **Little Havana** section of Miami.

After establishing communication with his Miami relatives, Elián's father, Juan Miguel González, petitioned the Cuban Ministry of Foreign Relations to seek the child's return to Cuba. **Fidel Castro** spoke with González on December 2, 1999, and then apparently conceived the idea of turning the request for Elián's return into a major international political campaign. Meanwhile, the boy's Miami relatives challenged the father's desires, claiming that his deceased mother had risked and lost her life so that Elián could grow up in a free country. Almost immediately, Cuban exile organizations, Cuban American congresspersons, and wide sectors of the Cuban community in the United States mobilized to block Elián's return to Cuba, thus turning his case into a bone of contention among Miami, Washington, and Havana.

Elián turned six on December 6, 1999, while remaining with his Miami relatives. Four days later a legal battle ensued, even-

tually reaching high levels of the U.S. court system. A group of lawyers representing Lázaro González filed a petition for political asylum on behalf of Elián, while a Miami circuit judge granted temporary custody over the child to Lázaro González. Meanwhile, on the other side of the Florida Straits, huge rallies were organized to demand Elián's return to the island. Early in 2000 the INS recognized the child's father as the only person who could legally speak on behalf of Elián and demanded the return of the child. U.S. Attorney general Janet Reno supported that decision.

Defying the government's orders, a group of Cuban exiles camped outside the González residence in Little Havana, and Lázaro González and his daughter made many public appearances to plead their cause to gain permanent custody of the boy and keep him from returning to Cuba. Among the many issues surrounding the debate were children's rights, political indoctrination, the **educational system** on the island, parental rights, the state of civil rights in Cuba, the rule of law, and the possibility of Elián and his father remaining indefinitely in the United States. A proposal was discussed in the U.S. Congress to grant Elián U.S. citizenship. In January 2000 the child's two grandmothers flew to the United States with the object of taking Elián back to Cuba but were unable to accomplish that. Meanwhile, on March 21, federal judge Michael Moore rejected the request to grant asylum to the boy, stating that he recognized the father's paternal rights. Juan Miguel González arrived to fetch his son on April 6, 2000, as appeals continued to be heard in court.

With decisions still pending in court, in the early morning hours of April 22, 2000, a heavily armed federal operative broke into the house were Elián lived and forcibly removed him. A few hours later Elián joined his father in Washington. The armed assault provoked mass protests on

Famous photograph of the forceful removal of Elián González from his relatives' Miami home (April 22, 2000). AP/Wide World Photos. Photograph by Alan Díaz.

the streets of Miami, resulting in several arrests for public disturbance. Spontaneous protests also occurred in Union City, New Jersey. Following rejections by the Atlanta Appeals Court and the Supreme Court to consider asylum petitions for Elián, the boy and his father returned to Cuba on June 28, 2000.

Elián's saga did not end with his return to Cuba. On both sides of the Florida Straits the boy's image still carries emotional overtones and continues to be used politically. The operation to remove Elián from his relative's home yielded two lawsuits in federal court for alleged violations of civil rights and excessive use of force. Elián's Miami relatives have since turned part of their house into a small museum; massive signs have been erected in Miami comparing Elián with victims of Stalinism and Nazism; a commemorative coin was issued with Elián's likeness; and more than one film has been made chronicling the boy's saga.

In Cuba, meanwhile, Castro often presides over events in which Elián and his family are present and pays visits to the school in Cárdenas that the boy attends. In the city's old fire station, a museum, Museo de la Batalla de Ideas, was opened early in 2001, chronicling the mobilizations and propaganda campaign that accompanied the petition for the boy's return. *See also* Cuban Politics in the United States; United States, Cuban Population in the

Further Reading

Bardach, Ann Louise. *Cuba Confidential: Love and Hate in Two Havanas*. New York: Random House, 2001.

Wilfredo Cancio Isla

Government Structure

Cuba is a socialist republic, as officially stated in its **Constitution of 1976**, the country's supreme law. The 1976 Consti-

Cuba's Power Structure

Communist Party of Cuba (CPC)
Union of Young Communists (UJOTACE)

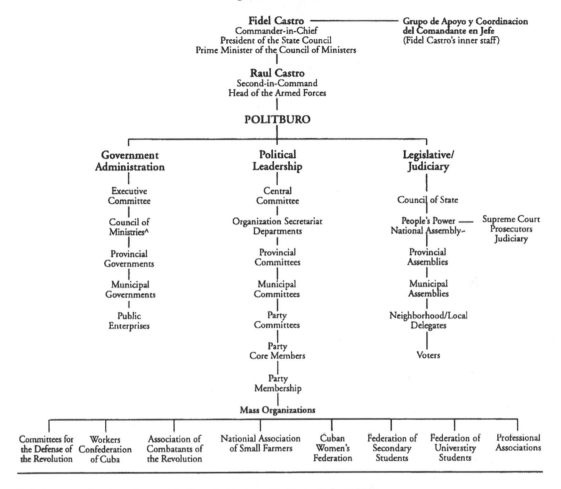

Cuba's power structure. From CubaNews's *Business Guide to Cuba* (2000).

tution replaced the Fundamental Law of the Revolution—enacted in February 1959—which had endured numerous modifications over the years. It is based on the former Soviet Union's 1936 Constitution and proclaims that "all power belongs to the working people." Cuba has a unicameral, semiparliamentary political system, in which the highest state organ is the **National Assembly of People's Power**. The Constitution also established a Council of State, a Council of Ministers, a People's Supreme Court, and assemblies of

people's power for local government at the provincial and municipal levels.

The National Assembly of People's Power is constitutionally vested with the power to declare war, to approve the budget, and to make economic plans, monetary policies, and foreign and domestic policies. It also elects the members of the Council of State, Council of Ministers, the president and vice president, and the judges of the People's Supreme Court. About half of the delegates to the National Assembly are elected by municipal assemblies, while the rest are usually nominated by the **Cuban Communist Party** and appointed by the assemblies. In spite of its constitutional preeminence, the National Assembly has little real power. It only meets for two days twice a year, usually to approve legislation and policies initiated by the Council of State and the Council of Ministers. It rarely initiates legislation or objects to important bills. Government officials and party cadres also tend to dominate the debates in this "ratifying" body.

The Council of State is composed of thirty-one elected members, presided over by the head of state and head of government, **Fidel Castro**. It assumes most of the powers of the National Assembly when the latter is not in session, ruling through decree laws that only the National Assembly can repeal. It is, essentially, the most important decision-making component of Cuba's government structure. Most of its members are also members of the Political Bureau of the Central Committee of the Cuban Communist Party and of the National Assembly.

Finally, the Council of Ministers oversees the various ministries, state committees and institutes, and the provincial and municipal assemblies that administer the state. However, the real power lies in its Executive Committee: fourteen top members who oversee the activities of groups of ministries and state committees. **Fidel Castro**, for example, has under his jurisdiction the **Ministry of the Interior** and the Ministry of the **Revolutionary Armed Forces**. *See also* Elections (1959–   )

Further Readings

Constitution of the Republic of Cuba. Havana: Ministry of Justice, 1977.

Domínguez, Jorge I. *Cuba: Order and Revolution.* Cambridge, MA: Belknap Press of Harvard University Press, 1978.

Rudolph, James D., ed. *Cuba: A Country Study.* Washington, DC: U.S. Government Printing Office, 1985.

Ernesto Sagás

Grenada, Cuba's Involvement in

There was extensive cooperation between Cuba and Grenada's People's Revolutionary Government (PRG) from 1979 to 1983 and a special relationship between **Fidel Castro** and PRG leader Maurice Bishop. The U.S. invasion of Grenada in October 1983, following the coup that resulted in the toppling and death of Bishop, was a great setback for Cuba's external relations in the 1980s.

The **Cuban Communist Party** had enjoyed good relations with the New Jewel Movement (NJM) in the 1970s but was not involved in the coup that brought it to power in 1979. Cuba soon endorsed the PRG, and diplomatic relations followed. Cooperation ranged from sending military advisers and small weapons to several civil projects, including medical personnel, scholarships, various technical assistance, and donations of fishing boats. The biggest project in which Cuba was involved with funding and several hundred workers was the construction of the Point Salines' airport. Moreover, Cuba was the main promoter of Grenada's revolution in Moscow, which earned the PRG some further Soviet military and economic aid.

After the coup against Bishop in 1983 by a faction in the NJM, Castro sent a critical letter to the Central Committee of the NJM. Despite Cuban criticism of the internal events that gave the pretext for the U.S. invasion, the Cuban workers and officers fought against the invasion, surrendering only after severe casualties.

After 1990, Cuba reestablished diplomatic relations with Grenada and has since collaborated on several civil projects. Grenada's Prime Minister Keith Mitchell visited Cuba in April 1997 and Fidel Castro visited Grenada the following year. *See also* Foreign Relations; Guerrillas, Cuba's Support for

Further Readings

Domínguez, Jorge I. *To Make a World Safe for Revolution: Cuba's Foreign Policy.* Cambridge, MA: Harvard University Press, 1989.

Matos, Huber. *La crisis en Grenada y sus implicaciones para Cuba.* Miami: Florida International University, 1983

Meeks, Brian. *Caribbean Revolutions and Revolutionary Theory: An Assessment of Cuba, Nicaragua and Grenada.* London: Macmillan Caribbean, 1993.

Zenén Santana Delgado

Guerrillas, Cuba's Support for

One of the strategies in Cuba's **foreign relations** has been to aid National Liberation Movements (NLMs) or leftist guerrillas, mainly in Latin America and Africa. This type of "internationalism" was driven by strategic and ideological reasons, as well as by the personal inclinations of **Fidel Castro** and other Cuban leaders.

The first expeditions of this sort were launched against the Dominican Republic and Panama in 1959 and partly contributed to the later imposition of sanctions against Cuba by the **Organization of American States**. Cuba responded by increasing aid for guerrilla movements almost everywhere in Latin America (except Mexico), often in opposition to the communist parties in those countries and the Soviet Union. In 1966 Cuba created the Organization of Solidarity with Asia, Africa and Latin-America (OSPAAAL) and in 1967 the Organization of Solidarity with Latin America (OLAS) to support armed struggle as the revolutionary way to transform underdeveloped societies in the Third World. However, the 1967 death of **Che Guevara** in the Bolivian jungle, while trying to implement his *foco* strategy, made Cuba accept that support should be given only when there were conditions for victory. In the late 1970s and early 1980s, Cuba began to aid the guerrilla movements in Central America, the Nicaraguan revolution being the most significant success.

In Africa, Cuba supported various NLMs such as the FLN (National Liberation Front, Algeria), the MPLA (People's Movement for the Liberation of Angola, Angola), PAIGC (Partido Africano para a Independência da Guiné e Cabo Verde, Guinea-Bissau), SWAPO (South West Africa People's Organization, [Namibia]), and ANC (African National Congress, South Africa).

In the 1990s Cuba stopped giving material aid to guerrilla movements. This shift responded to both the expansion of democratic regimes in the Americas and the economic crisis affecting Cuba (see **Special Period**). *See also* Nicaragua, Cuba's Relations with; Soviet Union, Cuba's Relations with the

Further Readings

Castañeda, Jorge G. *La utopía desarmada: intrigas, dilemas y promesa de la izquierda en América Latina.* Mexico City: Planeta, 1993.

Domínguez, Jorge I. *To Make a World Safe for Revolution: Cuba's Foreign Policy.* Cambridge, MA: Harvard University Press, 1989.

Guevara, Ernesto Che. *Guerrilla Warfare.* Lincoln: University of Nebraska Press, 1985.

Zenén Santana Delgado

Guevara de la Serna, Ernesto "Che" (1928–1967)

The name of Ernesto "Che" Guevara is almost synonymous with the Cuban **Revolution**, so much so that few people realize that he was not Cuban by birth. His visage is displayed everywhere throughout the island, indeed, throughout the world: on posters, t-shirts, flags, coins, murals; sometimes his photo is the only decoration on the walls of meagerly supplied Cuban stores (see **Bodegas**; **Nutrition and Food Rationing**). A photograph of Guevara taken by **Alberto Korda** is universally known: the black beret, the curly hair, the scruffy beard, and the determined, unwavering expression.

Ernesto Guevara was born in Rosario, Argentina, on June 14, 1928, to Ernesto

Guevara Lynch and Celia de la Serna, a decidedly upper-middle-class family. Yet his actions in the service of the Cuban Revolution prompted **Fidel Castro** to declare him a *native* Cuban citizen in February 1959, an act that also allowed him to hold office in Cuba. While Che's revolutionary ideas and beliefs only came to fruition in revolutionary Cuba, they had been born back in Argentina and during Guevara's journeys throughout Latin America. Ultimately, despite his efforts to export revolution outside of Cuba, he failed and paid with his life in Bolivia in October 1967.

Young Guevara was plagued with severe asthma throughout his life, which in part prompted him to pursue a medical career. He received a medical degree from the University of Buenos Aires in 1953. His revolutionary education, however, began in earnest when he traveled around Central and South America by motorcycle in the early 1950s. But his class consciousness had been formed much earlier, during his unusual early schooling. When Ernesto was nine years old, the Guevara family moved to Alta Gracia, Argentina, where students of all social classes studied together. His friends tended to come from families far poorer than his own, and they all seemed to gather at the Guevara home, often staying for meals. Discrimination was not taught at home. Although Ernesto was an active child, his asthma attacks often kept him bed-ridden, which led to his love of reading and his thirst for ideas.

His series of trips throughout Latin America, chronicled in *Motorcycle Diaries: A Journey around South America* (1996), began in 1950. By 1953, he had spent time in Argentina, Chile, Peru, Colombia, and Venezuela. The year 1954 found him working in Guatemala as the inspector for the Jacobo Arbenz Guzmán reformist government's agrarian reform agency (see **Agrarian Reform Acts**). When a Central Intelligence Agency (CIA)-organized and -financed coup overthrew the Guatemalan government later that year, Guevara took refuge in the Argentine embassy before fleeing to Mexico. His Guatemala experience taught the twenty-six-year-old Guevara that revolutions needed firepower rather than electoral legitimacy.

During his travels, Guevara's early forays into the medical field exhibited his philosophy of treatment: Regardless of their ability to pay for services, everyone is entitled to the same quality of medical care (see **Health-Care System**). Further, the exposure to myriad people and their suffering greatly increased Guevara's political awareness. Over and over again, he concluded that the most significant cause of the continent's problems was capitalism, in general, and U.S. imperialism, in particular. In his travels through Peru, for example, he saw firsthand the practical results of centuries of colonial rule on indigenous people. Che was greatly influenced by the works of Dr. Hugo Pesce, a communist who was director of Peru's leper treatment program. When Guevara published *Guerra de guerrillas* (*Guerrilla Warfare*) in 1960, he sent Pesce a copy, thanking him for changing his "attitude toward life and society."

Mexico in 1954 served as a refuge for a range of progressives and revolutionaries, including Che Guevara, Rómulo Betancourt of Venezuela, Juan Bosch of the Dominican Republic, and the Castro brothers. The Castros' experience at Moncada (see **Moncada Army Barracks, Attack on**) inspired the erstwhile doctor to sign on as physician for the **26th of July Movement**. Mexico was also where he met and married his first wife, Hilda Gadea, a Peruvian revolutionary, with whom he had a daughter, Hilda. By all indications, it was a loveless marriage, at least on Guevara's part.

In December 1956, Guevara was among the eighty-two guerrillas (and the only non-Cuban) who sailed to Cuba on the *Granma*, as well as one of the twelve who survived the landing and the rout by the Cuban Army. Che became a trusted political and military adviser to **Fidel Castro**, as well as commander of the second guerrilla column. He is most famous for his victory over the Cuban Army in the **Escambray Mountains** in the old Las Villas Province, when his sorely outnumbered guerrillas destroyed an armored train carrying reinforcements for **Fulgencio Batista**'s army near **Santa Clara**.

After Batista fled Cuba on January 1, 1959, Guevara's rebel force was the first into Havana. The year 1959 also brought significant changes to Guevara's personal life. Although Hilda Gadea (and Hildita) came to live in Cuba, Che divorced her. In June, he married Aleida March, a fellow revolutionary from the Santa Clara campaign. Together, they had four children: Ernesto, Camilo, Aleida, and Celia, the youngest of whom would have no memories of him.

Che Guevara's strategic and tactical talents once again brought him to the fore during the next few years. In April 1961, he commanded the westernmost military zone of **Pinar del Río Province**, inspiring the troops with the now-famous "Patria o muerte. ¡Venceremos!" (Homeland or death. We will triumph!) However, as the Revolution began to settle, Guevara held various offices in the Cuban government. Throughout 1959, he served as the military commander of the La Cabaña fortress in Havana and as a high-level official in the National Institute of Agrarian Reform. From 1959 to 1961, Che was president of the National Bank of Cuba, a position for which the Marxist physician was not well suited. In the years from 1961 through 1965, Guevara served the Cuban revolutionary government as minister of industries, where he was responsible for ending the dependence on the production of sugar (see **Sugar Industry**) and trade with the

United States. With the imposition of the **U.S. trade embargo**, he negotiated trading pacts with the Soviet Union and Eastern European countries. Bureaucratic administration proved not to be his forte. Revolutionary ideals and practical policy making apparently did not mix well.

It was not long before Guevara's peculiar blend of revolutionary fervor and wanderlust sent him on the road again. Weary of the pace of policy making, which produced few tangible, expected results, a sorely disillusioned Guevara headed off to the Congo in 1965. But Africa was not what Guevara had expected—the degree of internal tribal conflict and the lack of commitment to the cause, which made his brand of revolution impossible, disheartened him. Illness also took its toll on the Cuban revolutionaries in Africa. His spirits and resolve were dampened even further when he received news of the death of his beloved mother Celia, who ended her last letter to him by describing herself as "an old woman who hopes to see the whole world converted to socialism."

Guevara's final attempt at revolution came in Bolivia. He had considered Peru and Venezuela, but conditions seemed more favorable in this land-locked country with a large indigenous population. Bolivia also bordered his homeland of Argentina, where Che had hoped to ultimately prevail. Unfortunately, the Bolivian Communist Party did not agree with Guevara's assessment of revolutionary conditions in Bolivia. Much has been written about the betrayal that caused the ambush of Che and his revolutionary *foco* in October 1967. Some blame the peasants who were not very revolutionary and certainly unwilling to follow an outsider. Others blame the Bolivian Communist Party for not submitting to Guevara's leadership. Then there are the rumors that Castro himself had betrayed Che, telling the Bolivians that he was merely passing through Bolivia to enter Argentina. Whatever the

Sculpture of "Che" Guevara on the building of the Ministry of the Interior in the Plaza de la Revolución, Havana. Photograph by Luis Martínez-Fernández.

truth, it is clear that Che's final days came in October 1967, when Bolivian and CIA forces killed him. His hands were severed and sent to Castro as positive identification that the great revolutionary had failed.

Che Guevara's body was not recovered until October 1997, thirty years after his death. Then, based on interviews with those who claimed to have buried him, Che's corpse was found buried along an airstrip near Vallegrande, Bolivia. His remains were given a hero's welcome in Cuba and entombed in a special mausoleum in Santa Clara, the site of his famous victory. *See also* Guerrillas, Cuba's Support for; Soviet Union, Cuba's Relations with the

Further Readings

Anderson, Jon Lee. *Che Guevara: A Revolutionary Life*. New York: Grove Press, 1997.

Castañeda, Jorge G. *Compañero: The Life and Death of Che Guevara*. New York: Alfred A. Knopf, 1997.

Guevara, Ernesto Che. *The Motorcycle Diaries: A Journey around South America*. Trans. Ann Wright. London: Verso, 1995.

Guevara, Ernesto Che. *Obras*. 2 vols. Havana: Casa de las Américas, 1970.

Guillermoprieto, Alma. *Looking for History: Dispatches from Latin America*. New York: Pantheon Books, 2001.

Luther, Eric, with Ted Henken. *The Life and Work of Che Guevara*. Indianapolis, IN: Alpha Press, 2001.

Rodríguez, Félix. *Shadow Warrior*. London: W.H. Allen, 1990.

Paula J. Pettavino

Gutiérrez Menoyo, Eloy (1934–   )

Eloy Gutiérrez Menoyo is a pro-dialogue and moderate exile leader who leads the **Cambio Cubano** organization in Miami as a peaceful opposition alternative to **Fidel Castro**'s regime, seeking dialogue with the Cuban government and an eventual democratic change on the island. Menoyo (he is usually known by his maternal last name) was born in Madrid, the son and brother of anti-Franco fighters. One brother died in combat in Majadahonda; another, Carlos, was decorated twice for fighting in France against the Nazis and later, on March 13, 1957, died in the attack on **Fulgencio Batista**'s **Presidential Palace** in Havana. Eight months later, Menoyo founded the guerrilla **Segundo Frente del Escambray** to fight the Batista dictatorship. In January 1959, Menoyo arrived in Havana as one of the commanders of the **Revolution**, but very soon he broke away from Castro and went into exile, where he founded the original version of **Alpha 66**, a commando-type anti-Castro organization. On December 28, 1964, Menoyo returned to Cuba with an armed group of men, but after thirty days of combat, they were defeated and captured. Menoyo spent twenty-two years in Cuban prisons, where he suffered physical and psychological tortures, losing one eye's vision and one ear's hearing. Menoyo was freed in 1986 through a petition of the Spanish government after many years of international campaigns for his release. Once exiled in Madrid, he turned to a peaceful change for Cuba. He moved to Miami in 1987 and in 1992 he founded Cambio Cubano, which has relatively little support in Miami and inside Cuba because of its pro-dialogue stance. *See also* Dissent and Defections (1959–   ); Political Prisoners; Spain, Cuba's Relations with

Further Readings

Gutiérrez Menoyo, Eloy. *El Radarista*. Madrid: Playor, 1985.

Orihuela, Roberto. *Nunca fui un traidor: retrato de un farsante*. Havana: Editorial Capitán San Luis, 1991.

Vargas Llosa, Álvaro. *El exilio indomable: historia de la disidencia cubana en el destierro*. Madrid: Espasa, 1998.

Moisés Asís

Hart Dávalos, Armando E. (1930–   )

A member of the **26th of July Movement** and long-serving member of the **Cuban Communist Party**'s governing bodies, Hart was for many years minister of education and of culture (see **Educational System**). Recognized as a moderate ideologue when handling demands and pressures for more open debate within culture, Hart sought expression that served the **Revolution**, yet allowed partial artistic license.

The son of a Supreme Court judge, Hart was educated and trained to be a lawyer. In 1955 he became involved in Civic Resistance and, as the national coordinator of the 26th of July Movement's efforts to overthrow **Fulgencio Batista**, was jailed in 1958. In 1961 Hart was named minister of education, a post he held until 1967 when he became the first minister of culture. As minister of culture Hart directed the creation of state support and control for culture, including the Cuban Institute of Art and Motion Picture Industry (ICAIC) (see **Cinema**), **Casa de las Américas** (directed by his wife **Haydée Santamaría**), virtually all publishing, and specialized dance and music programming. Maintaining **Fidel Castro**'s policy for intellectuals on expression and publishing only in support of the Revolution, Hart oversaw various purges, banishments, and acts of censorship. In 1997 Abel Prieto replaced him as minister of culture.

Hart's political participation in the Cuban Communist Party includes that of organizational secretary, appointment to the Central Committee in 1965, and membership in the Political Bureau (1975–1991). He served in the **National Assembly of the People's Power** and the Council of State. In 1997 the party created a position for him devoted to publishing and promotion of **José Martí**'s life and work. *See also* Batista, Struggle Against; Padilla Affair; Unión de Escritores y Artistas de Cuba (UNEAC; Union of Cuban Writers and Artists)

Further Readings

Hart Dávalos, Armando. *Cambiar las reglas del juego. Entrevista de Luis Báez*. Havana: Editorial Letras Cubanas, 1983.
Hart Dávalos, Armando. *Cultura en revolución*. Mexico City: Editorial Nuestro Tiempo, 1990.

Peter T. Johnson

Lage Dávila, Carlos (1951–)

A prominent and influential figure in the Cuban government, Carlos Lage spearheaded the economic reforms adopted in the early 1990s after the collapse of the Soviet bloc. Trained as a medical doctor, he also holds a degree in the social sciences from the **University of Havana**. Lage serves as vice president of the State Council and as executive secretary of the Council of Ministers since 1992.

His political activity dates back to the 1960s, when he was a leader of the Unión de Jóvenes Comunistas [UJC] **(Communist Youth Union)** and other student organizations. As a pediatrician, Lage was a member of a medical mission sent to Ethiopia in the 1970s (see **Ethiopia, Cuba's Involvement in**). He was elected president of the **Federation of University Students** (FEU). At the age of twenty-five, he became a member of the **Cuban Communist Party** (PCC) and was elected as a deputy to the **National Assembly of People's Power**. From 1981 through 1987 he served as first secretary of the Communist Youth Union. In 1987, he was selected as a member to a special advisory body to Fidel Castro, known as the Equipo de Coordinación y Apoyo del Comandante en Jefe, a carefully selected group of individuals considered among the future leaders of Cuba. With the onset of the economic crisis brought about by the collapse of the Soviet bloc, Lage was chosen to preside over the National Commission for the **Special Period** in 1990. The commission was crucial in harnessing economic resources and maintaining social control on the island. In 1990, he was promoted to the Politburo of the Communist Party. Lage remains one of the most visible leaders of the **Revolution** and is considered by some to be a possible successor to **Fidel Castro** and **Raúl Castro**.

Further Readings

Lage, Carlos. *Comenzamos el proceso de recuperación económica*. Havana: Editora Política, 1996.
Lage, Carlos. *El desafío económico de Cuba*. Havana: Ediciones Entorno, 1992.

Wilfredo Cancio Isla

Leal Spengler, Eusebio (1942–   )

Eusebio Leal holds the important position of historian of the City of Havana, a post from which he has led efforts to preserve the historic district of Havana, which was declared a world historic site by UNESCO (the United Nations Educational, Scientific, and Cultural Organization) in 1982. Leal has a Ph.D. in history from the **University of Havana** with a specialty in archaeology. A protégé of historian **Emilio Roig de Leuschenring**, in 1967 Leal replaced him as director of the Museum of the City of Havana. From that time forward, he led efforts to restore important buildings and fortifications of the colonial era. A close associate of **Fidel Castro**, Leal is a member of the National Commission on Monuments. He also serves as a delegate to the **National Assembly of People's Power**. He joined the **Cuban Communist Party** in 1972 and was elected to the party's Central Committee in 1991. Leal is a member of the Cuban Academy of Language and a corresponding member of the Spanish Royal Academy. He is the recipient of numerous national and international awards including Knight of the National Order of the Legion of Honor of the French Republic (Caballero de la Orden Nacional de la Legion de Honor de la República Francesa) and Knight of the American Order of Isabel the Catholic of Spain (Caballero de la Orden Americana Isabel la Católica).

His writings include *Regresar en el tiempo* (1986), *Detén el paso, caminante* (1987), and *La Habana, ciudad antigua* (1988). Leal led the effort to retrieve and publish the lost diary of Cuban independence leader **Carlos Manuel de Céspedes** (1819–1874). He wrote the prologue to the diary in 1994. As the historian of the city, Leal supervises a project to use tourist revenues to save buildings of historical value (see **Tourism**). The funds are also used to repair homes and improve living conditions for residents of **La Habana Vieja** (Old Havana). *See also* Fortifications of Havana

Further Reading

Leal Spengler, Eusebio. *Detén el paso, caminante.* Caribe International Tours, 1987.

Wilfredo Cancio Isla

Literacy Campaign

The 1961 Literacy Campaign was the largest and politically most significant example of mass mobilization in the first decade of the Cuban **Revolution**. As far back as 1953, during the trial that followed the failed attack on the **Moncada Army Barracks**, **Fidel Castro** had made a pointed reference to the high rate of illiteracy among Cuban peasants (see Appendix 11). According to the census of 1953, the illiteracy rate for the entire population was 23.6 percent, though much higher among the poor and rural dwellers. Cuba's rate of illiteracy, though high when compared to those of industrial societies, was among the lowest in Latin America; Mexico's, for example, was 43.2 percent in 1950.

In 1957 in the Manifesto of the **Sierra Maestra** the anti-**Batista** guerrillas committed themselves to a campaign against illiteracy as part of the program of a victorious provisional government seeking to incorporate Cuba's marginalized poor into a more just society. When the Literacy Campaign was finally launched in 1961 it was, therefore, both an educational exercise and an opportunity to promote revolutionary commitment among teachers and students. The campaign must therefore be seen as part of a more general revolutionary offensive during 1961, a year in which Cuba successfully defeated the U.S.-sponsored **Bay of Pigs Invasion**, relations with the United States were broken, and the Marxist-Leninist character of the Revolution was announced.

Preparations for the campaign began in late 1960 when a newly formed National Literacy Commission produced two key manuals to be used in the campaign—*Alfabeticemos* and *Venceremos*. In order to count and identify illiterates a census was initiated in November 1960. By August 1960 when the census had been completed 985,000 illiterates had been identified. The literacy workers were originally drawn from the ranks of student volunteers, members of the Rebel Army, and other organizations. In mid-April the government closed all secondary and preuniversity schools in order to release students over the age of thirteen years for training as literacy workers in what were called the Conrado Benítez Brigades, named after an eighteen-year-old literacy worker killed by counterrevolutionaries while undertaking literacy work in the mountains of Las Villas (see **Segundo Frente del Escambray**). By the end of August, 1961, 105,000 students had received training as literacy workers in a specially constructed orientation center at the beach resort of Varadero.

In addition to the Conrado Benítez Brigades, other groups were mobilized to teach in the campaign—volunteer schoolteachers released from work by the closure of schools and 30,000 worker members of the Confederation of Cuban Workers (CTC)—while members of the newly formed **Committees for the Defense of the Revolution (CDRs)** and of the **Federation of Cuban Women (FMC)** scoured the countryside and poorer urban areas to identify illiterates.

The 1961 Literacy Campaign was both a spectacular example of state-directed mass mobilization and political socialization and an impressive moment in educational history. In 1962 Cuba reported a national literacy rate of over 96 percent, by far the highest figure in Latin America. But the goal of the Literacy Campaign was also to radically change social and political attitudes and relationships among both *brigadistas* and students, each group learning from the other. *See also* Educational System

Further Readings

Fagen, Richard. *The Transformation of Political Culture in Cuba*. Stanford, CA: Stanford University Press, 1969.

Kozol, Jonathan. "A New Look at the Literacy Campaign in Cuba." *Harvard Educational Review* 48, no. 3 (August 1978): 341–377.

McDonald, Theodore. *Making a New People: Education in Revolutionary Cuba*. Vancouver: New Star Books, 1985.

Barry Carr

Matos, Huber (1918–   )

Huber Matos was a member of the **Ortodoxos** (the heterogeneous political party formed in 1947) and the owner of a small rice farm in the old Oriente Province. A member of the Manzanillo Masonic lodge, he was active in the struggle in the **Sierra Maestra** and successfully brought the first large group of reinforcements from **Santiago de Cuba** to the Sierra in March 1957. After 1959, he became the military governor of **Camagüey**, the most seigniorial province in Cuba.

While not a veteran of the attack on the **Moncada Army Barracks** nor of the *Granma* expedition, Matos was still seen as a hero of the **Revolution**. He resigned his position with the revolutionary government because he perceived that communists were infiltrating the Revolution. He thought that **Fidel Castro** was unaware of the communist conspiracy directed by **Raúl Castro**, his brother.

Castro came to Camagüey on October 20, 1959, to meet Matos after **Camilo Cienfuegos** had arrested him on Castro's orders. Castro did not allow him to speak at his own trial, and he was sentenced to twenty years in jail for "anti-revolutionary conduct." Cienfuegos took over his command. In protest, the entire **26th of July Movement** executive committee in Ca-

Huber Matos was an early leader of the Revolution. He served twenty years in prison for criticizing the Revolution's veering toward communism. Courtesy of the Digitalization Project of the *El Mundo* Photographic Collection, University of Puerto Rico, Río Piedras Campus.

magüey resigned. They were subsequently tried for "uncertain, anti-patriotic and anti-revolutionary conduct."

In 1968, Castro refused a proposal by Bolivian President René Barrientos to exchange Matos for French revolutionary Jules Régis Debray who had been arrested when seeking to interview **Ernesto Che Guevara**. Matos served every minute of his twenty-year sentence, and upon his release in 1979, he moved to the United States and settled in Miami. He founded the anti-Castro exile group called Cuba Independiente y Democrática (Cuba Independent and Democratic). He was a prominent protester during the Cuban-Baltimore Orioles baseball series in 1999 (see **Baseball**). In September 2001, he won the

Spanish literary award el Premio Comillas for his autobiography titled *Cómo llegó la noche. See also* Dissidence and Defections (1959–); Freemasonry; Human Rights; Political Prisoners

Further Reading

Matos, Huber. *Cómo llegó la noche.* Barcelona: Tusquets Editores, 2002.

Paula J. Pettavino

Ministry of the Interior

The Ministerio del Interior (Ministry of the Interior [MININT]) was officially established by the revolutionary government on June 6, 1961, but its origins date back to the **struggle against Batista** and the guerrilla movement in the **Sierra Maestra**. The need for an intelligence-gathering network was underlined by the discovery of a plot in 1958 to kill **Fidel Castro**. At the suggestion of fellow revolutionary **Juan Almeida Bosque**, a special force was established to protect Castro. The new intelligence organization, known as the Organización de Observación Campesina (Rural Intelligence Organization), was also responsible for keeping the Rebel Army informed of government troop movements. At the same time, a secret organization was established within the Rebel Army and the **26th of July Movement** to detect efforts by enemy agents to infiltrate the **Revolution**, to identify revolutionaries vulnerable to recruitment by the government, and to infiltrate the ranks of the police and government army. This group was originally directed by Commander Ramiro Valdés and was the forerunner of MININT.

After the triumph of the Revolution, Valdés was named to head the Rebel Army's Departamento de Información del Ejército Rebelde [DIER] (Department of Information). The new department, established in January 1959, was charged with capturing those deemed as war criminals by the Revolution and with infiltrating and neutralizing organizations seeking to undermine the government. The intelligence-gathering network underwent another metamorphosis in the middle of 1959, when Castro decided to separate the DIER from the Rebel Army and establish it as the Departamento de Seguridad del Estado [DSE] (Department of State Security). The new department immediately began to establish a nationwide intelligence network, which would ultimately penetrate all major organizations on the island. Among the earliest secret structures within the DSE were Section Q and Section K. Section Q was charged with monitoring enemy agents working with groups believed to be hostile to the Revolution, while Section K specialized in personal and telephonic surveillance. The DSE was later incorporated into the Ministry of the Interior, and the intelligence-gathering functions of that agency were further expanded.

The ministry structure currently consists of a minister, a vice minister, seven independent departments, seven provincial delegations, and two special sections. The Ministry of the Interior, which includes 5,000 officials, officers, and soldiers, monitors a wide range of security activities, including border safety, prison supervision, immigration, special forces, and the issuance of personal identification cards (*carnets de identidad*).

The MININT is under the direct supervision of Chief of State Fidel Castro. Its principal office is located in a large building overlooking the **Plaza de la Revolución (Revolution's [Civic] Square)**. The most serious crisis within the organization occurred in 1989 when several high-level officials, including then Interior Minister José Abrantes, were implicated in corruption and narco-trafficking. Abrantes was removed from his post in 1989 and replaced by General Abelardo Colomé Ibarra. Colomé Ibarra is a member of the Council of State and the Politburo of the **Cuban Communist Party**. *See also* Dissent and Defections (1959–) Committees for the Defense of the Revolution (Comités de Defensa de la Revolución [CDRs])

Further Reading

Rodríguez Menier, Juan A. *Cuba por dentro: el MININT*. Miami: Ediciones Universal, 1994.

Wilfredo Cancio Isla

Miró Cardona, José (1902–1974)

José Miró Cardona was a distinguished jurist, university professor, and political leader. As president of the Cuban Bar Association, Miró Cardona was active in the opposition against **Fulgencio Batista** as one of the leaders of the Civic Dialogue. In 1958 he sought exile in the Uruguayan embassy and soon thereafter left the island. Upon the collapse of the Batista regime, he returned to Cuba, becoming the revolutionary government's first prime minister. Within a few weeks he resigned the appointment over differences with **Fidel Castro**, who replaced him as prime minister. After serving briefly as ambassador to Spain, Miró Cardona broke completely with Castro's government and assumed the presidency of the exile organization Concilio Revolucionario Cubano that helped plan the **Bay of Pigs Invasion**. In the event that the invasion had been successful, Miró Cardona would have been appointed provisional president of Cuba. Miró Cardona later resettled in Puerto Rico, where he taught law at the University of Puerto Rico. *See also* Batista, Struggle Against; Puerto Rico, Cubans in

Further Reading

Thomas, Hugh. *The Cuban Revolution*. New York: Harper & Row, 1977.

Luis Martínez-Fernández

Missile Crisis

The triumph of **Fidel Castro** and the Cuban **Revolution** and growing tensions between Washington and Havana and between revolutionary and counterrevolutionary forces served as the backdrop for the Cuban Missile Crisis of October 1962, a diplomatic confrontation that came close to sparking a nuclear war between the United States and the Soviet Union. The immediate catalysts of the crisis were Castro's declaration that the Revolution was Marxist-Leninist on April 16, 1961, and the decision by the Soviet Union to send dozens of short-range and medium-range nuclear missiles to Cuba. Along with the missiles, the Soviets deployed equipment and advisers to maintain the missiles. The discovery of the missiles by the United States led to one of the most serious crises in recent history. It led to a show of force and a strategic duel between the world's two superpowers.

There has been considerable debate about the emergence of John F. Kennedy as the hero of the West, who succeeded in defeating the threat posed by the Soviet Union by means of a naval blockade of Cuba, begun on October 24, 1962, which prevented further Soviet supplies from entering the island. Shortly thereafter the missile platforms were dismantled, and the Soviet bombs returned to Russia. In return the United States tacitly agreed not to invade Cuba. President Kennedy was criticized for agreeing to remove U.S. missiles from Turkey and Italy. Some polemicists argued that Kennedy should have used the occasion to pressure the Soviet Union to permit the elimination of the Cuban revolutionary government.

Politics aside, at the end of the crisis, several objective realities emerged. Soviet Premier Nikita Khrushchev was forced to concede. Cuba's revolutionary ambitions in Latin America were curtailed and the United States was able to continue its dominant relationship vis-à-vis the region. In addition, as a result of the outcome, in the coming decades the Soviet Union would sink the greater part of its resources in an effort to compete militarily with the United States. Finally, Cuban exiles were forced to accept the long-term survival of the Castro government.

During the crisis, Castro maintained that the missiles and military bases were solely defensive in nature. However, on October 27, 1962, a U.S. U2 spy plane was shot down by the Cubans over Oriente Province, and the next day the Cuban representative to the United Nations issued a set of demands. A letter from the Cuban government declared that use of the bases could not be guaranteed unless the United States agreed to abandon the **Guantánamo U.S. Naval Base**, lift the economic embargo (see **U.S. Trade Embargo and Related Legislation**) against Cuba, and forbid subversive activities by Cuban exiles on U.S. territory. *See also* Bay of Pigs (Playa Girón) Invasion; Soviet Union, Cuba's Relations with the; United States, Cuba's Relations with the

Further Readings

Chang, Laurence, and Peter Kornbluh, eds. *The Cuban Missile Crisis. 1962: A National Security Archive. Documents Reader*. New York: New Press, 1998.

Fursenko, Aleksandr, and Timothy Naftali. *One Hell of a Gamble: Khrushchev, Castro, and Kennedy, 1958–1964*. New York: W.W. Norton, 1997.

Kennedy, Robert F. *Thirteen Days: A Memoir of the Cuban Missile Crisis*. New York: W.W. Norton, 1971.

Manuel de Paz Sánchez

National Assembly of People's Power (Asamblea Nacional del Poder Popular)

The National Assembly of People's Power (Asamblea Nacional del Poder Popular) is the supreme legislative body, according to

Cuba's **Constitution of 1976**. It is legally vested with the power to declare war, to approve the budget, and to make economic plans, monetary policies, and domestic and foreign policies. It also elects the members of the Council of State, Council of Ministers, the president and vice president, and the judges of the People's Supreme Court. It decides on the constitutionality of laws and may organize national referenda to amend the Constitution. Delegates to the National Assembly are elected or appointed by municipal assemblies for a five-year term, at the rate of one delegate for every 20,000 citizens or fraction greater than 10,000. Delegates must be at least eighteen years old. About half of the delegates to the National Assembly are elected by municipal assemblies, while the rest are usually nominated by the **Cuban Communist Party** and appointed by the assemblies.

In spite of its constitutional preeminence, the National Assembly has little real power. It only meets for two days twice a year, usually to approve legislation and policies initiated by the Council of State and the Council of Ministers. It rarely initiates legislation or objects to important bills coming from these two bodies. Debates in the National Assembly are usually dominated by top-level bureaucrats and party cadres, thus giving it more of a "ratifying" function than an autonomous legislative one. *See also* Elections (1959–); Foreign Relations; Government Structure

Further Readings

Asamblea Nacional del Poder Popular de Cuba. Havana: Editorial Orbe, 1981.

Constitution of the Republic of Cuba. Havana: Ministry of Justice, 1977.

Domínguez, Jorge I. *Cuba: Order and Revolution*. Cambridge, MA: Belknap Press, 1978.

Rudolph, James D., ed. *Cuba: A Country Study*. Washington, DC: U.S. Government Printing Office, 1985.

Ernesto Sagás

Nicaragua, Cuba's Relations with

Nicaragua was the closest ally of Cuba in Latin America between 1979 and 1990. The triumph of the Nicaraguan Revolution (1979) was a vindication of the Cuban strategy of aiding revolutionary armed struggle (see **Guerrillas, Cuba's Support for**). Cuba provided material support to the Sandinista National Liberation Front (FSLN) from its foundation in 1961 until the end of the 1960s, then reinitiated it in the late 1970s. This included weapons, guerrilla experts, intelligence, and communications. Following advice from Cuba, the different factions of the FSLN united in 1978 and formed a broad coalition with moderate forces the following year. Cuba helped the FSLN establish contact with other revolutionary groups and states, increasing the standing of the movement in Latin America and the world. The FSLN received massive aid from Cuba after the triumph of the Revolution. Cuban advisers played a significant role in the development of the Sandinista army and the Ministry of the Interior. Civil projects involved Cuban teachers, medical personnel, construction workers, scholarships, and donations such as a sugar factory and supplies of oil. Cuba also persuaded the Soviet Union to aid Nicaragua.

Cuba advocated moderate policies to the Sandinista government. By 1982, Cuba supported the negotiation of a settlement to the Central American conflict as a way to consolidate the Sandinista regime. However, in 1990 Cuba advised against the decision of the FSLN to organize elections, and their subsequent defeat represented a great blow to Cuba in Latin America. Since the end of Sandinista rule in 1990, Nicaragua and Cuba have become distant. *See also* Foreign Relations

Further Readings

Castañeda, Jorge G. *La utopía desarmada: intrigas, dilemas y promesa de la izquierda en América Latina*. Mexico City: Planeta, 1993.

Domínguez, Jorge I. *To Make a World Safe for Rev-olution: Cuba's Foreign Policy.* Cambridge, MA: Harvard University Press, 1989.

Zenén Santana Delgado

Nonaligned Movement (NAM), Cuba in the

Some of the most significant achievements of Cuban foreign policy have related to Cuba's influence in the Third World, such as its leadership of the Nonaligned Movement (NAM) (1979–1982), the gaining of a seat in the Security Council of the United Nations (1990–1991), and hosting the first summit of heads of states of the Group of 77 (2000). The NAM sought to increase the political influence of Third World nations through a policy of nonalignment with the two superpowers of the Cold War era.

Cuba's dual identity as a socialist state and a Third World country provoked tensions in its **foreign relations** until 1990. Although Cuba gave the highest priority to its relations with the Soviet Union and the Socialist bloc, the Third World has occupied a significant place on the Cuban agenda, a position strengthened since the collapse of the Soviet Union in 1991. Cuba has managed its relations with Third World countries at both bilateral and multilateral diplomatic levels. The multilateral relations have taken place in international organizations such as the United Nations, the NAM, and the Group of 77.

Cuba was the only Latin American country present at the first NAM summit in Belgrade (1961). Since then, Cuba has participated regularly in these events, succeeding in including issues of national interest in the Final Declarations. In the 1960s, the main issues of interest to Cuba were decolonization and development. **Fidel Castro** headed the delegation to the IVth summit in Algiers (1973), where he tried to discredit the thesis of the two imperialist powers, insisting on the value of forging an alliance between the Soviet Un-

ion and the NAM. Castro also supported the creation of a New International Economic Order. Mostly due to Cuban aid to the new government of Angola (1975–1976), Cuba was selected to host the VIth summit of the NAM (1979). In order to have a successful summit, Cuba lowered its political agenda, focusing more on the economic issues, where there was greater consensus in the movement. However, Cuba's position as chair of the NAM was affected by Cuba's clearly pro-Soviet approach to the Kampuchea and Afghanistan issues. During the 1980s, Cuba concentrated mainly on development issues, namely the foreign debt of Third World states. In 1989, Cuba was elected to occupy a seat in the Security Council of the United Nations, with the support of the NAM. Since the 1990s Cuba has strongly argued the necessity of keeping the NAM alive as a forum to analyze the conflicts between wealthy and poor nations and to design cooperation strategies within the Third World. *See also* Angola, Cuba's Involvement in; Guerrillas, Cuba's Support for; Organization of American States (OAS), Cuba and the; Soviet Union, Cuba's Relations with the

Further Readings
Domínguez, Jorge I., ed. *Cuba: Internal and International Affairs.* Beverly Hills, CA: Sage Publications, 1982.
Domínguez, Jorge I. *To Make a World Safe for Revolution: Cuba's Foreign Policy.* Cambridge, MA: Harvard University Press, 1989.
Fernández, Damián J. *Cuba's Foreign Policy in the Middle East.* Boulder, CO: Westview Press, 1988.
Smith, Wayne S. *Castro's Cuba: Soviet Partner or Nonaligned?* Washington, DC: Woodrow Wilson Center for Scholars, 1984.

Zenén Santana Delgado

Núñez, Pastora (1926–   )

During the 1950s Pastora Núñez was one of the most active and influential members of the **Ortodoxos (Partido del Pueblo**

Cubano), serving as a member of its National Council. Along with other prominent Cuban women, including Carmen Castro Porta and Aida Pelayo Pelayo, she also organized the Frente Cívico de Mujeres Martianas, which vigorously opposed the **Fulgencio Batista** dictatorship. Núñez joined the **26th of July Movement** and was assigned to collect war taxes from supporters to combat the Batista regime. In May 1957, she nominated **Fidel Castro** for leadership of the Ortodoxos, a move that failed. After the **Revolution**, she was appointed president of the Instituto Nacional de Ahorro y Vivienda (INAV; National Institute for Financing and Housing). Beginning in 1959, she oversaw the construction of many new neighborhoods for workers, and her name became associated with a specific architectural style of affordable housing. In two years, INAV constructed more than 8,500 new homes. The homes were known as "los edificios de Pastorita" (Pastorita's buildings). Retired, she resides in Havana. *See also* Batista, Struggle Against; Housing; Women's Suffrage Movement

Further Readings

Castro Porta, Carmen. *La lección del Maestro*. Havana: Editorial de Ciencias Sociales, 1990.

Mujeres en Revolución. Havana: Dirección Política de las FAR, 1974.

Rodríguez Calderón, Mirtha. "Pupila frente a pupila." *Bohemia*, February 10, 1989, 34.

Julio César González Pagés

Ochoa Sánchez (Case), Arnaldo

General Arnaldo Ochoa (1940–1989) was a popular hero of the **Revolution** who began his career as a guerrilla in the **struggle against Batista**. The commander of Cuba's armed forces in Angola and Ethiopia, he went on to become one of the most popular and decorated officers in the Cuban military. He later commanded troops in Venezuela, Yemen, and Nicaragua.

In January 1989, in **Fidel Castro**'s **New Year's Day** address, Ochoa was designated an "exceptional warrior of the homeland." His closeness to Castro was evidenced by his use of the familiar *tú* form with him, one of the few people who addressed Castro thusly. Ochoa was arrested on June 14, 1989, and charged with drug-trafficking and corruption, as well as smuggling ivory, diamonds, and hardwoods into Cuba. He was accused of maintaining close contacts with the Medellín cartel, of facilitating drug shipments to the United States, and of engaging in money laundering. **Raúl Castro** also accused him of "unbridled populism," saying that there was no place in the military for those "tempted to accept Gorbachev's vision of glasnost."

Ochoa had disagreed with Castro's strategy in Angola and had criticized him openly. His trial and execution were designed to keep the army loyal. Both Castros denounced him openly and at length at his trial. On July 13, 1989, he was executed along with three other defendants: Antonio de la Guardia Font, Jorge Martínez Valdés, and Amado Bruno Padrón. Ochoa walked on his own to the execution post and asked that he be allowed to give the order for his own execution, in the tradition of Cuban heroes executed by Spanish firing squads. It was denied. He rejected the kerchief to cover his eyes. Ever the good soldier, he turned to his executioners and said, "I just wanted to let you know that I am no traitor."

Rumors swept the island that he and the de la Guardia brothers had been plotting to overthrow Castro. The Ochoa affair contributed to a change in the bond of trust between Castro and the Cuban people. There was evidence that Ochoa had been involved in some illegal commercial activities and it is unlikely that Castro was not aware of them. Pro-Ochoa graffiti began to appear—the number 8 was written, followed by the letter A—for *ocho-A*. Some dissidents have claimed that Ochoa had been drugged and tortured, since he cooperated with his own conviction. During his trial, he admitted that he had done "atrocious things" but clarified that the Castro brothers had known nothing of his activities. *See also* Crime; Revolutionary Armed Forces (Fuerzas Armadas Revolucionarias [FAR]); Dissent and Defections (1959–   ); Human Rights; Political Prisoners

Further Reading

Ferrer Castro, Armando. *Conexión en Cuba: un testimonio del caso Ochoa-La Guardia*. Mexico City: Editorial Planeta Mexicana, 1990.

Oppenheimer, Andrés. *Castro's Final Hour*. New York: Simon and Schuster, 1993.

Paula J. Pettavino

Organization of American States (OAS), Cuba and the

Cuba had an ambivalent position at the beginning of the **Revolution** toward the Organization of American States (OAS). Early on, the OAS approved sanctions against Cuba, which increased its isolation in the international system and the legitimacy of the U.S. policies toward the island state. Cuba reacted by increasing support for revolutionary movements in Latin America.

Cuba was first discussed in the meeting of Inter American foreign ministers (August 1959) in relation to threats to peace in the Caribbean. In August 1960, the member states approved the "Declaration of San José," which did not mention Cuba by name but condemned extracontinental intervention in the affairs of the Americas and totalitarian systems as alien to the region. In January 1962, the OAS suspended Cuba from the organization because the island had implemented a Marxist-Leninist regime. Cuba responded to these events with the "First" and "Second Declaration of Havana" in which **Fidel Castro** stated that the duty of the revolutionaries was to bring about revolution. In July 1964, based on evidence that Cuba had intervened in the internal affairs of Venezuela, the OAS approved a resolution imposing sanctions against Cuba, including the breaking of diplomatic relations and the suspension of trade and transport **communications**. Only Mexico did not comply with the resolution. In July 1975 the OAS ended the collective sanctions against Cuba. In spite of overtures by some member states in the 1990s, Cuba continues to be suspended from the organization. *See also* Foreign Relations; Guerrillas, Cuba's Support for; Nicaragua, Cuba's Relations with; United States, Cuba's Relations with the

Further Reading

Domínguez, Jorge I. *To Make a World Safe for Revolution: Cuba's Foreign Policy*. Cambridge, MA: Harvard University Press, 1989.

Zenén Santana Delgado

Pérez, Humberto (1937–   )

Humberto Pérez rose through the ranks of Cuba's **government structure**, eventually becoming the country's vice prime minister. Born in December 1937 into a poor peasant family near **Santa Clara**, Pérez lived in a dirt-floor home but nevertheless learned to read by the age of four. His father, a member of the **Partido Comunista (Partido Socialista Popular)**, provided *Hoy*, the communist newspaper, for reading material. The boy attended mostly Presbyterian schools and graduated from La Progresiva de **Cárdenas**, a renowned Presbyterian high school (see **Protestantism**). By working a full day from 4 A.M., then attending night classes, Pérez pursued a business degree at the University of Santa Clara. In 1957, he dropped his studies, joined the **26th of July Movement**, and worked under the political direction of Miguel Reyes, a provincial leader of the Tobacco Workers' Union.

As a young man after the triumph of the **Revolution**, he first worked for national labor leader Jesús Soto and with communist leader Vicente Pérez, then returned to Santa Clara in late 1959 as a delegate for the Ministry of Labor. A member of the provincial leadership of the 26th of July Movement, he later became a governor of Las Villas. After attending the newly formed National Revolutionary School, he specialized in political economy and would hold many teaching and administrative posts while rising through the ranks to become in 1979 the vice prime minister, working directly under Prime Minister **Fidel Castro**. He was relieved of his duties in the mid-1980s, when the "Rectification of Errors" process began, challenging the Soviet models of glasnost and perestroika and its defenders at high levels of the Cuban state (see **Rectification of Errors Campaign**). *See also* Labor Movement (Republican Era)

Further Reading

Pérez-Stable, Marifeli. *The Cuban Revolution: Origins, Course, and Legacy*. 2nd. ed. New York: Oxford University Press, 1999.

Eloise Linger

Rectification of Errors Campaign

The rectification of errors campaign, launched by **Fidel Castro** in 1986, was an attempt by the Cuban revolutionary leadership to reestablish its control over the economy and revitalize a failing economy by employing traditional concepts of nationalism, revolutionary consciousness, and volunteer work. In short, it was a political means to an economic end. By the mid-1980s the Cuban socialist model was showing signs of exhaustion. Production levels were low, a hard-currency **foreign debt** besieged the government, and the Castro regime felt that people had slackened off and lost their revolutionary zeal.

Led by the **Cuban Communist Party**— and not by economic planners—the rectification campaign eliminated the popular **farmers' markets** (where agricultural goods were sold by private citizens), attacked corruption and inefficiency, and politically mobilized the people for the achievement of economic goals. For example, microbrigades, which had been sporadically used in the past to build **housing** units, were now commonly employed. Work in the microbrigades was ostensibly voluntary, and appeals were made to the revolutionary consciousness and sense of duty of Cubans to actively participate in them. Still, the rectification campaign did not produce the intended results, partly because of its political underpinnings and partly because by 1990 Cuba had entered into its worst economic crisis since the Revolution, as the communist system collapsed in the Soviet Union and Eastern Europe (see **Special Period**). The dollarization of the economy, the expansion of **self-employment**, and other economic and social reforms have moved the regime in the opposite direction of the goals of the rectification efforts of the late 1980s. *Also see* Currency

Further Reading

Pérez-Stable, Marifeli. *The Cuban Revolution: Origins, Course, and Legacy*. 2nd ed. New York: Oxford University Press, 1999.

Ernesto Sagás

Revolution, Cuban

The triumph of the armed insurrection led by **Fidel Castro** in January 1959 signaled more than the overthrow of the government of **Fulgencio Batista**. It brought to political power a new generation at a time of deepening social and economic tensions, under circumstances of popular mobilization and high expectations. Under the charismatic leadership of Fidel Castro, reforms began immediately and gained momentum rapidly. In the first nine months of 1959, an estimated 1,500 decrees, laws, and edicts were enacted. The provisional government lowered postal rates and reduced pharmaceutical prices. The Cuban Telephone Company was intervened and its rates reduced. The Cuban Electricity Company fees were lowered by 30 percent. The Urban Reform Law decreed rent reductions ranging between 50 and 30 percent (see **Housing**). Tax codes were rewritten. More than 200 taxes were reduced, particularly those falling directly upon middle- and working-class households. Virtually all labor contracts were renegotiated and wages raised; minimum wages were increased in **agriculture, manufacturing**, and commerce. Health and education reforms were promulgated at dizzying speeds. Antidiscrimination measures were enacted. By far the most ambitious and controversial measure was enacted in the Agrarian Reform Law of May 1959 (see **Agrarian Reform Acts**). By the terms of the new law, all real estate holdings were reduced to a maximum of 1,000 acres, with the exception of lands engaged in the production of sugar, rice, and livestock, where the maximum size was fixed at 3,333 acres.

Early reform measures were dramatic and historic and provided immediate relief to vast numbers of Cubans. Egalitarian policies, if justified by historic conditions of inequality and injustice, also served as sources of social integration and national mobilization. The net effect of the early strategies of the Revolution was to fuse social justice and popular mobilization and thereby provide an explicit ideological content to the meaning of *revolution*. The reform measures won for the new government widespread popular support, and within the short space of several years, hundreds of thousands of Cubans acquired an immediate and lasting stake in the success of the Revolution.

But reforms also made the new government powerful enemies. Reforms may have provided immediate relief to vast numbers of people, but at the expense of property owners, many of whom were North American. The Revolution's commitment to egalitarian reform required more than changing the internal structures that had sanctioned privilege. It also placed Cubans and North Americans on a collision course (see **United States, Cuba's Relations with the**). So profoundly institutional, so intrinsically structural, were the sources of U.S. hegemony that Cuban determination to advance national interests over foreign ones could not fail to produce an international crisis. The reduction of telephone and electricity rates affected the vital interests of U.S. utilities. The Agrarian Reform Law, in particular, vitally affected North American property interests. Confrontation with the United States could not but have accelerated radicalization of the Revolution and centralization in government. It aroused powerful nationalist sentiments, revived historic grievances, and in the process promoted a national unanimity of purpose previously unimaginable and perhaps unattainable by any other means.

The conflict with the United States necessitated Cuban realignment, both within the internal calculus of power relationships and in the context of international relations. The ensuing realignments further deepened the confrontation. Internal political opposition was at first discredited and subsequently disallowed. At the same time, Cuba and the Soviet Union expanded political and economic ties (see **Soviet Union, Cuba's Relations with the**). By the early 1960s, Cuba and the Soviet Union had arrived at a number of important trade protocols. The Soviets agreed to purchase Cuban sugar and pledged financial support in the form of credits, technical assistance, and crude and refined petroleum.

All through the 1960s, the Cuban government mobilized vast sectors of the population on behalf of the revolutionary programs. Nearly 300,000 men and women were incorporated into the civilian militia. Women were organized into the **Federation of Cuban Women (FMC)**, and local communities formed the **Committees for the Defense of the Revolution (CDRs)**. Youth was organized into the Association of Young Rebels, and farmers joined the National Organization of Small Agriculturalists (ANAP). In 1965, the **Cuban Communist Party (PPC)** was organized.

At about the same time, many other Cubans were leaving the island, mostly emigrating to the United States (see **United States, Cuban Migrations to the**). In the decades that followed, the total number of émigrés would surpass 1 million. Even as their presence in the United States had a decisive impact on U.S. policy, their absence in Cuba had equally far-reaching consequences on the course of Cuban policies. The emigration represented the exportation of counterrevolution and all but foreclosed any possibility of a sustained and extensive internal challenge to the Revolution. Henceforth, organized opposition to the Revolution developed principally outside of Cuba, largely in the United States. Once the source of political opposition was transferred from within the island to outside it, the defense of the Revolution became synonymous with the defense of national sovereignty; once the question of sovereignty was evoked, a deep wellspring of national sentiment was tapped on behalf of the Revolution.

Economic development in the years following the consolidation of the new government followed an erratic course. Developmental strategies were initially driven by industrialization efforts and subsequently redirected to agricultural diversification driven by sugar exports. **Foreign trade** expanded increasingly with the So-

cialist bloc, with exports increasing during the early 1960s from 2.2 percent of the total to 74 percent. Imports increased from 0.3 percent to 70 percent. The Soviet Union accounted for more than half of Cuban exports and 40 percent of imports. In the decades that followed, the Soviets played a crucial role in financing Cuban trade deficits and otherwise providing the subsidies to sustained Cuban economic development between the 1960s and 1980s.

Many of the notable achievements of the Cuban Revolution were registered during these years. Illiteracy was virtually eliminated (see **Literacy Campaign**; **Educational System**). Educational opportunities expanded, and full-time school enrollments increased at all levels from elementary schools to graduate and professional education. Nutrition and health-care service improved; the number of trained health personnel increased steadily. Infant mortality rates declined; life expectancy rates increased (see **Nutrition and Food Rationing**; **Health-Care System**).

Increasingly, too, Cuba expanded its international presence, including moral and material support for guerrilla movements in Latin America and anticolonial struggles in Africa (see **Guerrillas, Cuba's support for**). Nor was the expanding Cuban international presence limited to military missions. Considerable resources were allocated to civilian socioeconomic projects, including construction workers, physicians, teachers, engineers, and agronomists.

In 1986, as the Soviet Union entered into a reformist phase under the tenets of Glasnost and Perestroika, the Cuban Government veered in the opposite direction, affirming socialist values and the virtues of moral incentives rather than material ones (see **Rectification of Errors Campaign**).

Everything changed during the late 1980s and early 1990s with the collapse of the Socialist bloc. These were decisive years, for Cubans found themselves caught up in momentous changes, not all of their making and far from their capacity to control but nonetheless of direct and vital national interest. The loss of trading partners and the suspension of economic relations with the former Socialist bloc produced disarray and distress and plunged Cuba into a crisis that threatened to undo thirty-five years of social gains and economic achievements. Cuba found itself increasingly unable to import the goods it consumed and without markets to export the goods it produced. Soviet trade and aid so vital to Cuban development strategies during the 1960s and 1970s began to dwindle in the late 1980s and virtually ceased altogether by the 1990s. The old Socialist bloc had accounted for almost 85 percent of Cuban trade, transactions conducted almost entirely in nonconvertible currency. Commercial relations with the former Soviet Union declined by more than 90 percent, from $8.7 billion in 1989 to $4.5 billion in 1991 and $750 million in 1993. Soviet oil imports decreased by almost 90 percent, from 13 million tons in 1989 to 1.8 million tons in 1992.

The economic crisis deepened through the early 1990s. For the second time in thirty years, Cuba experienced calamitous dislocations associated with disengagement from its principal trading partners. The effects were immediate and far-reaching and, in fact, of far more serious consequences the second time, for on this occasion Cuba was unable to obtain easily alternative sources of aid and assistance. Scarcities increased and shortages of almost every kind became commonplace. Fuel shortages resulted in the closing of industrial plants and factories, which in turn created another round of production shortfalls and consumer shortages. An estimated 50 percent of industrial plants, and perhaps more, suspended operations due to short-

ages of fuel, inputs, and replacement parts. Work animals replaced tractors, harvesters, and trucks. Domestic production of meat, milk, and eggs declined; the sugar crop decreased in successive years.

Cuba responded with a new regimen of rationing, and the nation at large was summoned once more to mobilization and prepared for new austerity measures. The government announced the implementation of the *período especial* (**Special Period**), a series of contingency plans conceived originally for use in a time of war, based on austerity measures and new rationing schedules.

The loss of aid from old allies made Cuba more vulnerable to pressure from old adversaries. The United States seized the occasion of the deepening crisis to enact new measures and expand economic sanctions against Cuba. First in 1992 with the Torricelli Law and later in 1996 with Helms-Burton, the United States expanded the scope and increased the severity of economic sanctions (see **U.S. Trade Embargo and Related Legislation**).

Government reactions to the deepening economic crisis were mixed, a combination of ideological rigidity with pragmatic adjustments, some economic reforms with political control. The official posture remained initially unchanged. Public pronouncements were often defiant and intransigent. But the Cuban response was not limited to the reaffirmation of the primacy of ideology. More pragmatic initiatives were introduced, measures that were themselves often in direct contradiction to official pronouncements and contrary to some of the central tenets of the Revolution. The harsh realities of the crisis gradually took their toll on the resolve of Cuban leaders. The defiant oratorical flourishes of earlier years softened as a much-subdued and sober Cuban leadership sought ways to relieve desperate and deteriorating conditions. The mood passed from the celebration of heroic struggle to the contemplation of grim sacrifice. Ideological rigidity yielded to pragmatic improvisations. The need to generate new sources of foreign exchange resulted in far-reaching changes of economic policies. New developmental strategies encouraged **foreign investment**, principally in the form of joint ventures and profit-sharing enterprises, changes that themselves were portents of a transition to a mixed economy. Joint venture projects expanded into **tourism**, pharmaceuticals (see **Pharmaceutical Industry**), construction, **transportation**, food processing, textiles, and **mining**.

Other reforms followed, mostly improvised adjustments in the form of ad hoc measures, a way to meet immediate needs while long-term strategies were developed. Cubans were authorized to receive and possess dollars. The state monopoly on employment, production, and distribution ended, and **self-employment** in more than 100 trades and services was authorized. This measure effectively established private enterprise. Under the provisions of the new self-employment law, automobile mechanics, taxi drivers, photographers, hairdressers, carpenters, cooks, and computer programmers, among others, were authorized to operate businesses and offer their services to the public at large at competitive prices. Artisans, artists, painters, and sculptors were authorized to sell their work directly to the public, both national and foreign, for *pesos* and dollars (see **Currency**). By the mid-1990s, more than 200,000 individuals had obtained self-employment licenses. Farmers were authorized to sell their surplus production on the open market after the quota for state markets was met. Heavy taxation and numerous restrictions and regulations, however, have kept the private sector from further expansion.

Economic experimentation and political reforms, if they were to succeed at all, would require time as authorities sought ways to adjust national modalities to changing international conditions. But it was clear, too, in the meantime, that Cuban leaders were determined that hard times would not be the occasion to challenge the authority of the government. The leadership may have been willing to introduce market mechanisms into a moribund economy and, further, to consider ways to make existing political institutions more representative and responsive to popular will, up to a point. The parameters of change were always to be contained within existing political structures. No opposition press was permitted. The primacy of the Communist Party in a one-party state was not open for debate. A multiparty system was rejected outright.

As Cuba entered the twenty-first century, it appeared to have survived both the worst effects of the collapse of socialism and increased economic sanctions from the United States. Conditions across the island began to improve, not always dramatically and not equally for everyone. The combination of modest economic recovery, tourist receipts, and especially **remittances** from family and friends abroad acted to underwrite modest improvements. But these gains have not been without some cost, and the long-range consequences of newly emerging social disparities and maldistribution of resources remain to be seen.

Further Readings

Domínguez, Jorge I. *Cuba: Order and Revolution.* Cambridge, MA: Belknap Press, 1978.

Halebbsky, Sandor, and John M. Kirk, eds. *Cuba: Twenty-five Years of Revolution, 1959 to 1984.* New York: Praeger, 1985.

Montaner, Carlos Alberto. *Viaje al corazón de Cuba.* Barcelona: Plaza & Janés Editores, 1999.

Pérez-Stable, Marifeli. *The Cuban Revolution: Origins, Course and Legacy.* 2nd ed. New York: Oxford University Press, 1999.

Thomas, Hugh. *The Cuban Revolution.* New York: Harper & Row, 1977.

Louis A. Pérez, Jr.

Revolutionary Armed Forces (Fuerzas Armadas Revolucionarias [FAR])

The Fuerzas Armadas Revolucionarias [FAR] (Revolutionary Armed Forces) constitutes one of Cuba's most powerful, prestigious, and important institutions. With **Fidel Castro** as its commander in chief and **Raúl Castro** as minister of the FAR, Cuba's military has played, and continues to play, important roles not only in the area of defense but also in the political and economic spheres.

Cuba's FAR has its immediate roots in the Rebel Army that toppled **Fulgencio Batista** in 1959. A few months into the **Revolution**, the Ministry of the FAR was established, and the paramilitary National Revolutionary Militias were organized. The FAR consolidated its reputation and power as a result of its victory during the **Bay of Pigs Invasion** in April 1961 and thereafter in the mid-1960s when it defeated the counterrevolutionary bands that opposed the regime from the **Escambray Mountains** and other foci (see **Segundo Frente del Escambray**). At the time, the FAR consisted of close to 300,000 troops. Beginning in the mid-1960s Cuba's military increasingly shifted its attention to economic development tasks. In 1965 it formed the infamous Unidades de Ayuda a la Producción (Military Units to Aid Production) units of unarmed conscripts who were deemed social deviants (e.g., homosexuals, religious individuals) who were forced to cut cane and perform other labor-intensive tasks; these units were disbanded in 1967 in the light of mounting international criticism. Regular army troops also provided labor support during the sugarcane harvests of the late 1960s and 1970s (see **Ten Million Ton Harvest**). In 1973 the FAR underwent a profound reorganization aimed at the professionalization of the armed forces. Changes included improved training for officers and regular soldiers as well as a new law of military service, which established that all males between the ages of sixteen and fifty had to serve three-year terms either on active duty or as reservists. During the Angolan War (1975-1976) and its aftermath the Cuban armed forces had their first major international war experience. At the time, Cuba's military consisted of 117,000 regular army troops, 90,000 ready reserves, and an additional 419,000 reserves; at its peak in 1976, the Cuban presence in Angola was 36,000 troops; some 30,000 remained there as late as 1985.

The size and budgets of the military have fallen sharply during the 1990s. In 1997 there were 60,000 regular forces and 39,000 reserves; over a million Cubans, however, were part of the paramilitary Territorial Troop Militias. During the 1990s the percentage of the gross domestic product designated for defense dropped to around 5 percent, half the level of the previous decade. A 1998 Pentagon report described Cuba's military as "weak" and not posing "a significant military threat to the U.S. or to other countries in the region." Over the past few years, the FAR has played an increasingly important role in government and the economy; several high-ranking retired or active officers head key government ministries and government corporations. The FAR is likely to play a key role in the post-Castro transition. *See also* Angola, Cuba's Involvement in; Ethiopia, Cuba's Involvement in; Gays and Lesbians; Guerrillas, Cuba's Support for; Sugar Industry

Further Readings

Domínguez, Jorge I. *Cuba: Order and Revolution*. Cambridge, MA: Belknap Press, 1978.

Fermoselle, Rafel. *The Evolution of the Cuban Military, 1492–1986*. Miami: Ediciones Universal, 1987.

Judson, C. Fred. *Cuba and the Revolutionary Myth: The Political Education of the Cuban Rebel Army*. Boulder, CO: Westview Press, 1984.

"Pentagon Calls Cuba 'No Significant Military Threat.'" *CubaNews*. May 1998, 9.

Pérez, Louis A. "Army Politics in Socialist Cuba." *Journal of Latin American Studies* 8, no. 2 (November 1976): 251–271.

Suchlicki, Jaime, ed. *The Cuban Military under Castro*. Miami: Research Institute for Cuban Studies, 1989.

Walker, Phyllis Greene. "Cuba's Revolutionary Armed Forces: Adapting in the New Environment." *Cuban Studies* 26 (1996): 61–74.

Luis Martínez-Fernández

Roa, Raúl (1907–1982)

Raúl Roa was one of Cuba's most distinguished intellectuals and activists whose career spanned the period from the mid-1920s to the first decades of the Cuban **Revolution**. While a law student at the **University of Havana** in the mid-1920s he helped establish the Directorio Estudiantil Universitario, or DEU (University Student Directorate) in 1927 and took an active role in anti-Machado politics (see **Machado, Gerardo**). He was the author of the DEU's October 1930 Manifesto Program that called for free speech, an honest university, and an end to Machadista corruption and violence. In 1931 he helped form the Ala Izquierda Estudiantil (Student Left Wing), a left-wing breakaway from the DEU, many of whose members were close to the communists (see **Partido Comunista**). During a period in jail between August 1931 and January 1933, he penned the first of his major writings, *Presidio Modelo*, one of a number of key sources (along with *Retorno a la alborada, La revolución del 30 se fue a bolina*, and *La bouffa subversiva*) for the history of the anti-Machado struggles of the early 1930s and the efforts to create a united anti-imperialist movement following the **Revolution of 1933**.

The repression following the crushing of the March 1935 general strike forced Roa into exile in the United States where he helped form the non-Stalinist Marxist group Organización Revolucionaria Cubana Anti-Imperialista, or ORCA. In the

1940s Roa became professor of the history of social doctrines at the University of Havana, and for a brief period during the presidency of **Carlos Prío Socarrás** he held the position of director of culture in the Ministry of Education. Forced into exile by **Fulgencio Batista**'s **coup of 1952**, Roa later returned to Cuba to collaborate with the young radicals of the Revolutionary Directorate and the **26th of July Movement**. He was appointed minister of foreign affairs in the revolutionary government in 1959, a position he held until the early 1970s. *See also* Foreign Relations; Students' Movement (Republican Era)

Further Reading

Domínguez, Jorge I. *Cuba: Order and Revolution* Cambridge, MA: The Belknap Press, 1978.

Barry Carr

Roca Calderío, Blas (1898–1987)

Born Francisco Calderío, the mulatto Blas Roca was a labor organizer and the best-known communist in pre- and post-**Revolution** Cuba. Trained as a shoemaker in the port city of Manzanillo, he joined the first Cuban Communist Party in 1929 (his nom de guerre being "Julio") and then moved to Havana in the early 1930s. At the end of 1933 he was elected general secretary of the Communist Party, which he led through the repression unleashed against the Left in 1934 and 1935. Following the Comintern's move toward the Popular Front strategy initiated in 1935, Roca welcomed the overtures made to the party by **Fulgencio Batista**, which culminated in the legalization of the communists in September 1938 and the creation of a pact with Batista for the 1939 elections to the Constituent Assembly (see **Constitution of 1940**). Following the dissolution of the U.S. Communist Party in January 1944 he altered the name of the Communist party to Partido Socialista

Popular (PSP) (see **Partido Comunista**), a change that was to last for the next twenty years.

The Cold War and the 1952 coup led by Batista dissolved the special relationship enjoyed by the communists in the first half of the 1940s. Roca led the PSP's clandestine organizing during the second Batista regime, although the communists denounced **Fidel Castro**'s attack on the **Moncada Army Barracks** and remained hostile to the early phase of the armed struggle launched in the **Sierra Maestra** by the **26th of July Movement**. After the 1959 Revolution, Roca, along with **Carlos Rafael Rodríguez**, advocated close relations between the PSP and the Castroites and remained a leading figure within the various intermediate organizations that preceded the inauguration of the present **Cuban Communist Party (PCC)** in 1965. He remained a senior figure within the PCC, as a member of the Politburo and the Central Committee, until his retirement due to old age in 1986. Also see Coup of 1952 (March 10)

Further Reading

Domínguez, Jorge I. *Cuba: Order and Revolution.* Cambridge, MA: The Belknap Press, 1978.

Barry Carr

Rodríguez, Carlos Rafael (1913–1997)

One of the most astute and durable Cuban politicians of the twentieth century, Carlos Rafael Rodríguez served in the cabinet of both **Fulgencio Batista** and **Fidel Castro**. He was one of the first old-line communists to recognize the revolutionary potential of the armed **struggle against Batista**. Rodríguez joined forces with Castro in the middle of 1958 and gradually convinced a reluctant Partido Socialista Popular (see **Partido Comunista**) to support the revolutionary struggle. After the triumph of the **Revolution**, he became one of its biggest

boosters as editor of the Communist Party newspaper *Hoy*. Castro appointed him head of the National Institute of Agrarian Reform (see **Agrarian Reform Acts**) in 1962, a post that he held until 1965. From there he was appointed minister without portfolio in Castro's cabinet. During the purge of old-line communists in the mid-1960s, Rodríguez was given a series of low-key positions, but he emerged again as a major policy maker in 1970 when he was given control of foreign policy, specifically relations with the Soviet Union. By the mid-1970s, he was a member of the Communist Party Politburo, a member of the Council of State, and vice president. On occasion, Rodríguez advocated greater tolerance by the Castro government, but he never formally broke with the regime. He remained in the Politburo until two months prior to his death in 1997.

Born to a middle-class family in **Cienfuegos**, he became that city's mayor at the age of twenty, during the **Revolution of 1933**. Rodríguez was originally a member of the Directorio Estudiantil Universitario (University Student Directory), which allied itself with the enlisted men and Sergeant Fulgencio Batista to topple the U.S.-backed government of Carlos Manuel de Céspedes y Quesada. He later broke with the Directorio, moved to Havana, and helped organize a national labor strike in March 1935 against the government of **Carlos Mendieta**, a government backed by the ever-growing power of Batista and the military. He joined the Communist Party in 1936 and quickly became one of its most influential members. In 1938, the communists and Batista formed an alliance that led to the party's legalization. As part of the deal, the communists supported Batista in his successful run for the presidency in 1940. In 1944, Rodríguez was named to Batista's cabinet.

In addition to his extraordinary political career, Rodríguez was a prolific author of essays, articles, and books. Among his works are *José Martí, guía y compañero* (1981), *Problemas de arte en la Revolución* (1979), *Cuba en el tránsito al socialismo, 1959–1963*, and *En defensa del pueblo* (1978) (which he coauthored with **Blas Roca** and Manuel Luzardo). *See also* Newspapers (Republican Era); Soviet Union, Cuba's Relations with the; Students' Movement (Republican Era)

Further Readings

Dillon, Sam. "Carlos Rodríguez, Castro Ally and Leftist Leader, Dies at 84." *New York Times*, December 13, 1997, C8.

Thomas, Hugh. *Cuba: The Pursuit of Freedom*. New York: Harper & Row, 1971.

Frank Argote-Freyre

Sánchez Manduley, Celia (1920–1980)

Celia Sánchez was a close confidante to **Fidel Castro** and an important revolutionary leader. Sánchez sent supplies and food to Castro and his colleagues during their imprisonment on Isla de Pinos (later renamed **Isla de la Juventud**) after the failed attack on the **Moncada Army Barracks** in 1953. Later she organized support in the days leading up to the disembarkation of the *Granma* in Oriente Province (see *Granma* **Expedition**).

Sánchez was one of the first women to take part in the armed struggle in the **Sierra Maestra**, and she was regularly assigned dangerous and sensitive missions by Fidel Castro. While in the Sierra Maestra, she took part in the battle at El Uvero, and she remained in the guerrilla camp permanently after October 1957. With the triumph of the **Revolution**, she promoted and oversaw various public works projects, including Lenin Park outside of Havana, the **Coppelia** ice cream factory, and the National Zoo. Sánchez's participation in government projects was varied and diverse. She promoted the development of rural areas and supervised the construction

Celia Sánchez Manduley with 26th of July Movement's uniform. Fidel Castro Photograph Collection, Manuscripts Division, Department of Rare Books and Special Collections, Princeton University Library.

of hotels in Santa María del Mar (see **Beaches**). She founded the Empresa de Producciones Varias (Factory for Various Products), including one specializing in the cultivation and distribution of flowers. In 1964, she founded the Oficina de Asuntos Históricos (Office of Historical Affairs), where she collected an impressive collection of documents on the Revolution. She was a member of the State Council and a Central Committee member of the **Cuban Communist Party**. *See also* Federation of Cuban Women (Federación de Mujeres Cubanas [FMC]); Batista, Struggle Against

Further Readings

Mujeres ejemplares. Havana: Ediciones Orbe, 1974.

Mujeres en Revolución. Havana: Dirección Política de las FAR, 1974.

Julio César González Pagés

Haydée Santamaría, long time head of the Casa de las Américas. Photograph courtesy of the Biblioteca Nacional José Martí, Havana.

Santamaría Cuadrado, Haydée (1922–1980)

Haydée Santamaría was active in the **struggle against Batista**, participating in some of its most dramatic moments, and later became one of the most strident supporters of the **Revolution** of 1959. She was a witness to the torture and execution of her brother, Abel Santamaría, one of the principal leaders of the 1953 assault on the **Moncada Army Barracks**. It was in this period that she gained national and international notoriety after she was photographed, along with colleague Melba Hernández, in their jail cell. On November 30, 1956, she took part in the uprising in **Santiago de Cuba**, timed to coincide with the disembarkation of **Fidel Castro** and a band of guerrilla fighters in Oriente Province (see *Granma* **Expedition**). She was married to **Armando Hart**. From its founding in 1959, she was the director of

Casa de las Américas, a cultural organization that supported numerous Cuban artists, including **Pablo Milanés** and **Silvio Rodríguez** and their Movimiento de la **Nueva Trova** (New Song Movement). She committed suicide in Havana on July 28, 1980.

Further Readings
Mujeres ejemplares. Havana: Edición Orbe, 1974.
Mujeres en Revolución. Havana: Dirección Política de las FAR, 1974.

Julio César González Pagés

Segundo Frente del Escambray

The Segundo Frente del Escambray (Second Front of the Escambray) had its roots among the revolutionary fighters who did not agree with the leadership of **Fidel Castro** and even more strongly opposed the sectarian policies and ideas of the pro-Moscow Partido Socialista Popular (**Partido Comunista**), whose prestige grew in direct proportion to U.S. hostilities (1959–1962). Using U.S. military supplies, the Second Front's counterrevolutionary campaign reached its height in 1963–1964 in the **Escambray Mountains** of south-central Cuba.

The Cuban government's response was to destroy the base of food support, by rounding up thousands of residents, mostly rural farm families, and resettling them in distant parts of the island. Women and children were relocated to Havana for medical attention and instruction in hygiene and the use of modern appliances and indoor plumbing, prior to reuniting with the men who for months had been constructing **housing** facilities. They have lived for decades "neither as prisoners, nor as free people," according to residents of Ciudad Sandino, a complex of apartment buildings, single homes, and community centers built by the Escambray refugees in the northwest province of **Pinar del Río**.

The consolidating revolutionary state mobilized thousands for the sweep of the Escambray, or the so-called "war against the bandits," the last vestige of armed political opposition on the island. Moving in concentric circular patterns of pursuit, the state forces and civilian volunteers moved inward until victory was assured. Second Front leader **Eloy Gutiérrez Menoyo** was captured and served a prison term of twenty-two years in Cuba and now lives in Miami. *See also* Dissent and Defections (1959–); Revolutionary Armed Forces (Fuerzas Armadas Revolucionarias [FAR])

Further Reading

Encinosa, Enrique G. *Escambray: la guerra olvidada*. Miami: Editorial SIBI, 1989.
Thomas, Hugh. *The Cuban Revolution*. New York: Harper & Row, 1977.

Eloise Linger

Soviet Union, Cuba's Relations with the

One of the principal factors that ensured the survival of the Cuban **Revolution** was the island's relationship with the now-defunct Soviet Union. Cuba received military, economic, political, and diplomatic support from the Soviet Union without interruption between 1960 and 1991. Whether the building of a communist system in Cuba and the alliance with the Soviet Union were among the original aims of the leaders of the Cuban Revolution, or this became the only option for resisting U.S. hostility, remains a contentious question.

Whatever the historical truth, whether in 1959 the Cuban leaders were prepared to deceive in order to gain time, the international context was favorable for a small state interested in changing sides during the Cold War. The international system was structured around a bipolar competition between the United States and the Soviet Union. The Soviets, led by Nikita

Khrushchev, considered the Third World an area where they could strike "imperialism" and offered aid to developing countries interested in the "noncapitalist path." The growing conflict between the Soviet Union and communist China for influence over the communist and progressive forces in the world also drove the Soviets to take a more active role in the Third World.

There were several stages in the evolution of Soviet-Cuba relations. In April 1959, **Fidel Castro** went to the United States, where he repeatedly claimed that the revolutionaries in Cuba were not communists but sought to build a democratic state. At the same time, **Raúl Castro** requested from the Soviet Union military advisers of Spanish origin (communists who fled to the Soviet Union at the end of the Spanish Civil War in 1939). Although the Soviet Union was still cautious of the new revolution due to its location in the heart of the U.S. sphere of influence and insufficient knowledge about the new leaders, they accepted Castro's request. In October 1959, Alexander Alexeev, a KGB officer, arrived in Havana as the main Soviet interlocutor of the Cuban leaders. Through him, Fidel Castro expressed interest in the visit to Cuba of Anastas Mikoyan (Soviet deputy prime minister) after his trip to Mexico (November 1959) and later asked Alexeev to postpone the visit because the internal situation was not favorable. By the end of the year, the Soviet Politburo had discussed the Cuban situation and was prepared to broaden trade relations and send arms if requested. In February 1960, Mikoyan visited the island, and a bilateral agreement was signed. The Soviet Union would provide credit for $100 million and would buy Cuban sugar, partly bartered for Soviet oil (see **Sugar Industry**). In April 1960, Cuba established diplomatic relations with Moscow and requested military aid. In July 1960, in a context of increased confrontation between the United States and Cuba, Khrushchev announced publicly that the Soviet Union was prepared to aid Cuba if the United States attacked it. Days later, Raúl Castro visited Moscow, cementing the new relations. Fidel Castro and Khrushchev met two months later in New York. In April 1961, just before the **Bay of Pigs Invasion**, Fidel Castro declared the socialist character of the Revolution. In December 1961, he stated his "Marxist-Leninist" beliefs. Cuba had become part of the Socialist bloc and dependent on Moscow for economic and military support.

By 1962, the Cuban leaders considered a U.S. invasion to be a high probability, a perception shared by the Soviet leaders, who decided to deploy Soviet nuclear missiles to the island in the spring of 1962. Cuban leaders accepted the missiles despite the risks, as a defensive strategy to avoid a U.S. attack and because they desired to participate in the strengthening of the Socialist bloc. The Soviet Union's motives for the deployment, whether the only feasible defensive strategy for Cuba or an opportunity to strengthen their own position against the United States, remain debatable. When the United States became aware of the presence of nuclear missiles in Cuba, in October 1962, the most dangerous crisis of the Cold War era escalated. The **Missile Crisis** was solved by bilateral negotiations between Khrushchev and John F. Kennedy without consulting the Cuban leaders, who were upset, as they had hoped that other issues of the U.S.-Cuba agenda might have been solved. The final agreement included the withdrawal of the Soviet missiles and a U.S. pledge not to invade Cuba. Although Cuban-Soviet relations cooled momentarily, Mikoyan visited the island in November 1962, and Khrushchev invited Fidel Castro on a visit to the Soviet Union in early 1963, when they signed a new economic agreement more favorable to Cuba.

By 1966 a new rift was developing between Havana and Moscow. At the Tricontinental Conference (1966) Castro advocated the strategy of armed struggle as the main way to transform underdeveloped countries, while the Soviet leadership disagreed, its main interests being peaceful coexistence and accommodation with the West. Moreover, Cuba denounced the relations between the Soviet Union and authoritarian regimes in Latin America. By 1968 the Soviet Union was reducing its supplies of oil to Cuba, but Castro's support for Soviet intervention in Czechoslovakia (August 1968) represented the beginning of a rapprochement. Furthermore, the Cuban economy was in trouble, especially after the 1970 failure of the **Ten Million Ton Harvest** (of sugar), which drove the Cuban government to seek further economic assistance from Moscow.

In July 1972 Cuba became a member of the CMEA (Council of Mutual Economic Aid) and began a process of remodeling Cuba's institutions and practices along Soviet lines. Although Castro expressed his support for détente during Leonid Brezhnev's visit to Havana (1974), in the second half of the 1970s Cuba sent troops to the conflicts in Angola and Ethiopia. One of the contentious issues of these interventions was the rationale of Soviet-Cuban relations. One approach explained the Soviet-Cuba relations with the "surrogate" thesis, Cuba acting as Soviet "proxy" that tried to advance Soviet interests in the Third World. Another approach acknowledged Soviet influence over Cuba but accepted a significant degree of initiative and autonomy on the Cuban part.

In 1979, Cuba supported the Soviet intervention in Afghanistan, though it injured its stand in the **Nonaligned Movement**. In the early 1980s Cuba succeeded in persuading the Soviet Union to aid the Nicaragua and Grenada revolutions, although the policies of the new U.S. administration of Ronald Reagan (1981–1989) increased the dangers of confrontation in the Caribbean Basin. The Soviet Union signalled to Cuba that they were in no po-

Fidel Castro in the Soviet Union flanked by Soviet dignitaries. Fidel Castro Photograph Collection, Manuscripts Division, Department of Rare Books and Special Collections, Princeton University Library.

sition to provide military aid if the United States decided to attack Cuba, but they increased the arms supply to the island. By 1986, Cuba and the Soviet Union, under Mikhail Gorbachev's leadership, began to develop divergent approaches to the construction of socialism and in their foreign policies (see **Rectification of Errors Campaign**). Although Gorbachev visited Havana in 1989 and signed a new treaty of friendship and economic cooperation, relations continued to deteriorate. In 1990 the Soviet Union failed to fulfil its economic commitments to Cuba, a situation that worsened considerably in 1991. In 1991, following a request from the United States, the Soviet Union decided to withdraw a Soviet army brigade stationed in Cuba since the Missile Crisis (1962), without consulting the Cuban leaders, who resented the unilateral decision. The disintegration of the Soviet Union in 1991 put an end to thirty years of close alliance. The relations between Cuba and the new Russia almost ceased between 1992 and 1994. In 1995 they reestablished ties. Russia maintained its intelligence-gathering base in Cuba; trade relations continued, mainly the barter of sugar for oil; and they agreed to reinitiate the construction of the Jaraguá Nuclear Plant of **Cienfuegos**. High-level visits had increased by 2002. *See also* Angola, Cuba's Involvement in; Ethiopia, Cuba's Involvement in; Foreign Relations; Grenada, Cuba's Involvement in; Guerrillas, Cuba's Support for; Nicaragua, Cuba's Relations with; United States, Cuba's Relations with the

Further Readings

Domínguez, Jorge I. *To Make a World Safe for Revolution: Cuba's Foreign Policy*. Cambridge, MA: Harvard University Press, 1989.

Fursenko, Aleksandr, and Timothy Naftali. *One Hell of a Gamble: Khrushchev, Castro, Kennedy and the Cuban Missile Crisis 1958–1964*. London: John Murray, 1997.

Pavlov, Yuri. *Soviet-Cuban Alliance: 1959–1991*. New Brunswick, NJ: Transaction Publishers, 1994.

Smith, Wayne S. *Castro's Cuba: Soviet Partner or Nonaligned?* Washington, DC: Woodrow Wilson Center for Scholars, 1984.

Zenén Santana Delgado

Spain, Cuba's Relations with

Cuba and Spain have a long-standing "special relationship" developed under the influence of strong historic, economic, and cultural ties, involving not only the two governments but also the Cuban and Spanish peoples. The Cuban revolutionary government maintained diplomatic relations with Francisco Franco's regime, in spite of political and ideological differences, the U.S. pressure on Franco's government, and some serious diplomatic incidents. Trade and transport relations actually expanded and helped the Cuban government break the U.S. policies of isolation and embargo. Spain's Christian Democratic governments continued relations after Franco's death (1975).

Difficulties appeared in the late 1980s, when the Spanish socialist government (1982–1996) reappraised the situation in Cuba. Although Prime Minister Felipe González visited the island in 1986, by 1990 the Spanish government reached consensus that Cuba's economic and political system needed to change. Spain designed a strategy to engage the Cuban government and aid a peaceful transition. In the second half of 1995 they worked unsuccessfully toward an agreement between the European Union and Cuba.

Relations with Spain became even more important for Cuba after the collapse of the Berlin Wall (1989). Cuba became interested in increasing Spanish investment, **tourism**, and credits and in maintaining good political and trade relations with Spain as a way to break the international isolation and the increased U.S. hostility. Spanish people and local authorities established several nongovernmental organizations to send aid to the Cuban people and particularly to Cubans of Spanish birth.

In 1996 the new conservative Spanish government of José María Aznar increased pressures for change in the Cuban government and strengthened communication with the opposition to the Cuban regime. Spain was one of the main promoters of the common policy toward Cuba adopted by the European Union in December 1996,

in which improvement of the relations would be conditioned by changes in the internal situation of Cuba. The reaction of the Cuban government was to freeze almost completely political relations with Spain. By 1998 the relations started to improve somewhat. In 1999 Cuba hosted the ninth Ibero American summit with the support of the Spanish authorities, though the latter renewed the criticism of the Cuban internal situation. While at first, the Spanish government did not accept the invitation for an official visit of the king of Spain to Cuba, the monarch visited the island in November 1999 heading the Spanish delegation to the Ibero American summit held in Havana. *See also* Foreign Investments; Foreign Trade; Immigration (Twentieth Century)

Further Readings

Domínguez, Jorge I. *To Make a World Safe for Revolution: Cuba's Foreign Policy*. Cambridge, MA: Harvard University Press, 1989.

Hennessy, C.A.M., and George Lambie, eds. *The Fractured Blockade: West European–Cuban Relations during the Revolution*. London: Macmillan Caribbean, 1993.

Paz Sánchez, Manuel de. *Zona de Guerra: España y la Revolución Cubana (1960–1962)*. Tenerife, Canary Islands. Taller de Historia, 2001.

Vásquez Montalbán, Manuel. *Y Dios entró en La Habana*. Madrid: El País Aguilar, 1998.

Zenén Santana Delgado

Ten Million Ton Harvest

The so-called Ten Million Ton Harvest was the name given to the sugarcane harvest of 1970. It marked the culmination of the reorientation of Cuba's revolutionary economic policy following the failure of earlier plans of industrialization and economic diversification, which had deemed the sugar-based economy a vestige of past capitalist exploitation.

Between 1959 and 1961 sugar production remained high (6 to 7 million tons) in spite of the government's antisugar policies. This was partly the result of previously planted cane and the continued use of infrastructure built before the **Revolution**. Production levels fell later, reaching 4 million tons in 1963. This drop endangered the government's goals of funding a more diversified economy, which by then was deemed impossible without capital from sugar exports. At about the same time, the Soviet Union offered Cuba much of its vast national market, granting the island a preferential price for its raw sugar: 6.1 U.S. cents per pound. This turned out to be a generous subsidy, given that the world market price for sugar averaged only 3.1 cents per pound during 1963–1970. Likewise, the Soviets subsidized the Cuban economy by providing it with crude oil at prices well below the world market (see **Energy**).

In spite of these subsidies, sugar production remained relatively low, fluctuating between 4.5 and 6.2 million tons between 1963 and 1969. Although the exact amount of sugar produced during the harvest of 1970 is the subject of debate, it appears that it may have reached 8.5 million tons. The accelerated pace at which the harvest was carried out and the unskilled, so-called voluntary labor it employed help explain the failure to reach the desired 10 million tons. The harvest of 1970 is also blamed for the low output of subsequent harvests.

The Ten Million Ton Harvest marked Cuba's return to sugar specialization for a single market, the difference now being that the Soviet Union replaced the United States. Although the return to sugar monoproduction diverted resources that could have been channeled to diversify the economy, the focus on subsidized sugar allowed economic growth rates not seen since 1959. Following a few poor harvests after 1970, production levels through the 1980s fluctuated between 6 and 8 million tons. The average during the 1990s was short of 5 million tons. The 8.5 million tons produced in 1970 still constitute

Cuba's largest harvest ever. *See also* Soviet Union, Cuba's Relations with the; Sugar Industry

Further Readings

Mesa-Lago, Carmelo. *Breve historia económica de Cuba socialista. Políticas, resultados y perspectivas*. Madrid: Alianza Editorial, 1995.

Pérez-López, Jorge E. *The Economics of Cuban Sugar*. Pittsburgh: University of Pittsburgh Press, 1991.

Santamaría García, Antonio. "Azúcar y Revolución. El sector azucarero de la economía cubana durante los primeros doce años de la revolución, 1959–1970." *Revista de Historia Económica* 12, no. 1 (1994): 111–141.

Antonio Santamaría García

United States, Cuba's Relations with the

Cuba is—without doubt—the second most important Latin American nation for the United States—after Mexico. Since the United States began expanding and dreaming of empire in the nineteenth century, Cuba has been an important territory for U.S. policy makers (see **U.S. Expansionism [Nineteenth Century]**). Conversely, the United States has always been a major foreign policy concern for all Cuban governments since independence. To this day, and after a sweeping social revolution changed the nature of U.S.-Cuban relations, the island remains at the forefront of U.S. foreign policy concerns in Latin America, and vice versa.

Cuba's relations with the United States have often been characterized as a "love-hate affair," meaning that Cubans have historically loved trading and interacting with their northern neighbor but have also hated its proclivity to intervene in—and influence—Cuba's national affairs. Cuba, after all, received its independence (in 1902) not from Spain but from the United States, who had invaded the island during the course of the Cuban **War of Independence**. Cuba's republican history from then on is of a dependent state (more like a protectorate), ruled by leaders pliant to U.S. interests, economically penetrated by U.S. companies, and shackled by the imposition of the **Platt Amendment** and **Reciprocity Treaty**. Many of these traits had begun to change by the 1950s, when Cuba was rocked by a social revolution sparked by the people's desire to rid themselves of corrupt dictator **Fulgencio Batista**.

The Cuban **Revolution**—with its unexpected turn toward socialism—brought about a quick reversal of the traditional trends in U.S.-Cuba relations. **Fidel Castro**, who had initially promised a democratic government for Cuba, quickly clashed with U.S. interests. Castro's courting of the Soviet Union and his rerouting of the Revolution into a Marxist-Leninist path brought the Cuban case to the forefront of the Cold War. Contrary to other Cold War "hot spots," Cuba was not a distant land (like Korea or Vietnam) but right on the front porch of the United States. Moreover, Cuba had historically been considered a client state within the U.S. sphere of influence, and that made the Cuban case more contentious. Castro's first revolutionary measures, such as the agrarian reform law (see **Agrarian Reform Acts**), were seen with apprehension by U.S. interests, but Castro was still considered nothing more than a nationalist, populist strongman. There would soon be, however, three main sources of conflict between the Castro revolutionary government and the United States. First, Castro's nationalist socializing agenda threatened U.S. economic interests in Cuba by seeking to nationalize foreign assets on the island. By late 1960, all U.S. investments in Cuba had been nationalized without compensation. Second, Castro's overtures toward the Soviet Union and his eventual alignment with the Soviet camp threatened to create a Soviet satellite state in the Americas—just ninety miles away from the United States.

Following the U.S. policy of "containment" applied in Korea and Vietnam, Castro's communist government had to be contained and—if possible—subdued. And third, the Cuban revolutionary government had attempted to export the revolution to Latin America by providing training and support to insurgents from various countries. Such a policy threatened several Latin American strongmen, some of them close allies of the United States (e.g., Rafael L. Trujillo, Anastasio Somoza).

The United States responded to Cuba's revolutionary policies with increasingly hostile measures. In February 1960, First Deputy Prime Minister Anastas Mikoyan of the Soviet Union visited Cuba and established the groundwork for what eventually became a "special relationship" between revolutionary Cuba and the Soviet Union. The Soviets would buy Cuba's sugar and provide the island with oil, machinery, military supplies, and technical assistance. On July 1960, the United States canceled Cuba's sugar quota. Cuba then began nationalizing U.S. properties on the island. On October 19, 1960, the Dwight D. Eisenhower administration imposed an economic embargo on Cuba, and on January 3, 1961, it broke diplomatic relations with the island's government. The John F. Kennedy administration then approved plans for an invasion to be carried out by Cuban exiles—but supported and coordinated by the Central Intelligence Agency (CIA) (see **Bay of Pigs Invasion**). Political concerns and gross miscalculations doomed the invasion from the start. The exile force of over 1,200 men was rapidly defeated, and hundreds were captured. Castro had achieved a huge political victory, while the Kennedy administration had been utterly embarrassed.

In January 1962, at the urging of the United States, Cuba's revolutionary government was excluded from the **Organization of American States**. Eventually, all member states—except Mexico—broke diplomatic relations with Cuba. Another major crisis erupted in October 1962, when the Kennedy administration announced that Cuba was installing Soviet missiles with nuclear capabilities (see **Missile Crisis**). A naval quarantine was declared by the United States on October 22, and for a few days the world came as close as it has ever been to the brink of nuclear war. On October 28, the United States and the Soviet Union (without consulting Castro) reached an agreement: The missiles would be removed, and in exchange, the United States promised not to support another military invasion of Cuba. Though the agreement guaranteed the survival of the Revolution, it was an embarrassment for Castro, who was considered a minor player in this dispute between superpowers. On the other hand, the 1962 Cuban missile crisis marks the zenith of the Cold War, and it gave the island and its revolution an importance way beyond its human and economic resources.

Relations between Cuba and the United States did not begin to improve until the Jimmy Carter administration (1977–1981), when the first flights of Cuban exiles returning to visit their relatives were allowed. Interests sections in both countries were opened, and several hundred political prisoners were released. In mid-1980, a massive wave of Cuban migrants reached the United States. Castro—in a surprising move—announced that those who wanted to leave the island could do so through the port of Mariel. Within weeks, over 125,000 Cubans had arrived in southern Florida in what was later called the **Mariel boatlift**. The U.S. government was forced to spend millions of dollars in helping these refugees relocate and in subsidizing state and local governments for their expenses during the crisis. Castro, on the other hand, used the crisis to his advantage by ridding the system of "un-

desirables," including some common criminals and the mentally ill.

The inauguration of Ronald Reagan in 1981 brought back a freeze in U.S.-Cuba relations. In 1983, U.S. combat troops fought against Cubans when the Reagan administration ordered the invasion of the tiny island of Grenada, where Cuban workers had been building an airport for the sympathetic government of Maurice Bishop (see **Grenada, Cuba's Involvement in**). Moreover, the U.S. government accused Cuba of supporting guerrilla struggles in Central America and of swaying Nicaragua's Sandinista government into the Soviet camp. Another source of friction was Cuba's involvement in African conflicts in Angola and Ethiopia. It was not until the end of the Cold War and the election of Democrat Bill Clinton that a thaw in U.S.-Cuban relations developed. The collapse of communism in the Soviet Union (now Russia once again) and Eastern Europe meant the end of their special relationship with Cuba. Without the billions of dollars that Cuba received every year in supplies and aid from the Soviet camp, its economy almost collapsed, and its international engagements were severely curtailed. Cuba no longer represents a political or military threat to U.S. security interests in the hemisphere. Instead, the main concern of the U.S. government vis-à-vis Cuba is the issue of uncontrolled migration (see **Cuban Adjustment Act; Migration Accords**).

Shortly after assuming office in 1993, the Clinton administration engaged in migration talks with Cuban officials. In 1994, after thousands of Cubans had ventured into the Florida Straits in what seemed like an uncontrollable flood, the Clinton administration changed the long-standing policy of almost automatically accepting all Cuban immigrants as political refugees. Instead, Cubans were now required—as all other immigrants—to prove political per-

Mural near the United States Interests Section compound in Havana: "Imperialist gentlemen, we have absolutely no fear of you!" Photograph by Celestino Martínez Lindín.

secution. Moreover, the U.S. Coast Guard was authorized to deport Cubans back to the island, and the Cuban government agreed to take them back. On its part, the United States agreed to issue several thousand immigrant visas per year for Cubans who wanted to leave the island legally. That agreement abated the "rafters' crisis," which has since then become the usual trickle of isolated cases (see **Balseros**). In May 2002, former president Jimmy Carter visited Cuba, where he criticized the U.S. embargo while calling for democratic reforms for the island. Carter also met with political dissidents and in an unprecedented televised speech from the **University of Havana** expressed his support for the Proyecto Varela. The George W. Bush administration has responded by publicly restating its continuing support for the embargo (see **Dissent and Defections**).

After over forty years of revolutionary government, the main concerns of U.S.-Cuban relations have changed. For the United States, revolutionary Cuba represented a major security threat in its own sphere of influence. Nowadays, it represents a potential migratory concern. For Cuba, the U.S. economic embargo continues to be its main economic predicament. For decades, the Castro administration has blamed Cuba's economic woes on the embargo. Recent developments seem to suggest a relaxation of the U.S. embargo and a willingness of U.S. companies to reinvest in Cuba. It remains to be seen, however, if that will bring about a political rapprochement between Castro and the United States. *See also* Angola, Cuba's Involvement in; Ethiopia, Cuba's Involvement in; Foreign Investments (Republican Era); Foreign Relations; Guerrillas, Cuba's Support for; Nicaragua, Cuba's Relations with; Soviet Union, Cuba's Relations with the; U.S. Trade Embargo and Related Legislation

Further Readings

Domínguez, Jorge I., and Rafael Hernández, eds. *U.S.-Cuban Relations in the 1990s*. Boulder, CO: Westview Press, 1999.

Kaplowitz, Donna Rich. *Anatomy of a Failed Embargo: U.S. Sanctions against Cuba*. Boulder, CO: Lynne Rienner Publishers, 1998.

Morley, Morris H. *Imperial State and Revolution: The United States and Cuba, 1952–1986*. Cambridge, United Kingdom: Cambridge University Press, 1987.

Paterson, Thomas G. *Contesting Castro: The United States and the Triumph of the Cuban Revolution*. New York: Oxford University Press, 1994.

Pérez, Louis A., Jr. *Cuba and the United States: Ties of Singular Intimacy*. Athens: University of Georgia Press, 1997.

Pérez, Louis A., Jr. *On Becoming Cuban: Identity, Nationality, & Culture*. Chapel Hill: University of North Carolina Press, 1999.

Welch, Richard E., Jr. *Response to Revolution: The United States and the Cuban Revolution, 1959–1961*. Chapel Hill: University of North Carolina Press, 1985.

Ernesto Sagás

Urrutia Lleó, Manuel (1901–1981)

Manuel Urrutia was a renowned jurist and short-time president of Cuba during the early days of the **Revolution** (1959). Urrutia was born in Yaguajay, old Province of Las Villas, in 1901. He studied law at the **University of Havana**, graduating in 1923. He served as judge in Jimaguaní and later as magistrate in the Audiencia of Oriente, where he had the courage to absolve a group of Fidelistas in 1957. Soon thereafter, Urrutia went into exile.

Fidel Castro selected Urrutia to serve as president upon the anticipated fall of the **Fulgencio Batista** regime; the Miami-based Junta Revolucionaria backed him as

well. He took possession of his office in **Santiago de Cuba** on January 2, 1959, and three days later arrived at Havana's **Presidential Palace**. Urrutia's most urgent steps included the removal of Batista supporters from government and the state bureaucracy. He also went after gambling interests. A moderate politician, Urrutia soon clashed with Fidel Castro, who maneuvered to secure extraordinary powers for himself as prime minister. He tried to resign repeatedly from the presidency but was kept from doing so for fear that it might reflect negatively on the revolutionary government. By mid-1959 tensions between Urrutia and Castro had reached a climax. On July 17 Castro resigned and proceeded to castigate the president over the media, including accusing him of treason. Mobilized by Castro's incendiary speech, crowds gathered around the Presidential Palace to demand Urrutia's resignation. He fled the executive mansion and sought asylum in the Venezuelan embassy. Urrutia went into exile and settled in New York, where he worked as a teacher. He died in 1981. *See also* Batista, Struggle Against; Presidents

Further Reading

Thomas, Hugh. *The Cuban Revolution*. New York: Harper & Row, 1977.

Luis Martínez-Fernández

U.S. Trade Embargo and Related Legislation

The U.S. trade embargo is perhaps the most visible sign of the conflictive relationship between the United States and revolutionary Cuba. What the public generically calls "the embargo" and Cuban officials call "the blockade" is really a collection of superimposed presidential orders and laws that restrict or forbid U.S. trade with **Fidel Castro**'s socialist government. Though the embargo began as a sort of retaliatory policy, with the short-term objective of bringing about Castro's downfall, it has acquired a sense of permanency and a life of its own after over four decades of implementation and modifications.

The origin of the U.S. trade embargo dates back to July 5, 1960, when the United States, concerned about the policies of Cuba's revolutionary government and its close friendship with the Soviet Union, canceled Cuba's sugar quota. Castro responded by nationalizing—without compensation—most U.S. companies on the island. Finally, on October 17, 1960, a few remaining U.S. banking institutions were also nationalized. The Dwight D. Eisenhower administration reacted by imposing an economic embargo on the island on October 19, 1960, so that only food and medicines could be exported to Cuba. The embargo was further tightened within the next few months to include a ban on U.S. ships from carrying cargo to Cuba, the declaration of a complete commercial embargo, and a ban on the importation of products that in whole or in part contained any material from Cuba (even if manufactured elsewhere). Later, in 1962, Cuba's revolutionary government was expelled from the **Organization of American States** (OAS), and in 1964, the OAS joined the United States by also declaring a commercial embargo on the island (which Mexico did not join). In short, Cuba ceased to exist as an economic entity for U.S.—and many Latin American—investors, and for many years thereafter, few U.S. citizens visited Cuba. Conversely, Cuba, now isolated from much of the Western world, developed close commercial partnerships with the Soviet bloc countries.

The embargo was somewhat relaxed in 1975, when the OAS lifted its ban on trading with Cuba. The Jimmy Carter administration followed suit in 1979 by allowing Cuban exiles to visit their relatives on the island. However, the Ronald Reagan and George Bush administrations retightened the embargo. The collapse of communism

in Europe and the end of the Cold War brought about renewed hopes regarding the downfall of Fidel Castro. It was widely believed in the United States that given the grave economic crisis that Cuba was facing then, a tightening of the embargo would cause Castro's government to teeter and fall (see **Special Period**). In 1992, President George Bush signed into law the Cuban Democracy Act (or Torricelli bill), which prohibited subsidiaries of U.S. companies located in third countries from trading with Cuba. It also banned ships that had departed a Cuban port from visiting the United States for six months, authorized the curtailment of aid to nations that provided assistance to Cuba, and allowed the Treasury Department to fine companies that violated the embargo up to $50,000 and to seize their property.

The Bill Clinton administration, inaugurated in 1993, followed a seesaw policy regarding the embargo; it tightened some aspects of the embargo legislation while relaxing others. For example, it allowed students to visit Cuba for study purposes and facilitated the establishment of long-distance telephone communication with the island, as well as the sending of **remittances**. On the other hand, the Clinton administration eliminated the longstanding policy of accepting all Cuban immigrants. Cubans were now to be deported unless they could show evidence to classify as political refugees. However, the zenith of the U.S. trade embargo is marked by the Helms-Burton bill (or Cuban Liberty and Democratic Solidarity Act), signed into law by the Clinton administration in 1996.

The Helms-Burton legislation (see **Appendix 13**) is the most overarching attempt to bring about a political change in Cuba and to prevent a detour in the "hardline" policy followed by U.S. presidents so far. The act takes away the president's power to modify U.S. policy toward Cuba by requiring the Cuban revolutionary government to fulfill a number of conditions before the trade embargo is to be lifted. For example, a Cuban transitional government must be in place, **political prisoners** must be released, all political activity has to be legalized (including the formation of opposition political parties), free elections (monitored by international observers) must take place within eighteen months, the state security apparatus must be dismantled, and both Fidel and **Raúl Castro** must be absent from this process. Moreover, in one of its most controversial points, Title III, the Helms-Burton Act seeks to punish foreign companies for "trafficking in confiscated property." That is, foreign companies who invest in areas of the Cuban economy or properties that were seized by the Cuban government are liable in U.S. courts. Presumably, U.S. citizens (including Cuban Americans) whose property was nationalized by the revolutionary government could now sue foreign companies profiting from those seized assets. The implied extraterritoriality of Helms-Burton has caused an uproar among U.S. allies, many of whom currently have investments in Cuba. Mexico, Canada, and the European Union states already have retaliatory legislation in their books allowing their citizens to countersue U.S. companies for any losses that they suffer as a result of Helms-Burton verdicts. Finally, the act also denies U.S. entry visas to the officers and stockholders of delinquent foreign companies.

The Helms-Burton Act, however, contains an important clause that allowed President Clinton to temporarily suspend its most conflictive portions. The president may suspend implementation of certain clauses of the law for up to six months, if necessary to the U.S. national interest. Clinton indefinitely postponed the implementation of Title III of Helms-Burton, given the intense criticisms that it received from U.S. allies—many of them important

trading partners. Following George W. Bush's election to the presidency, late in 2000 the U.S. Congress eased the embargo by allowing cash sales of food and medicine to Cuba. Castro rejected the overture because it banned credit sales. In the aftermath of Hurricane Michelle in November 2001, however, the Cuban government announced plans to purchase up to $30 million worth of food and medical supplies. By mid-December 2001, the first shipments of U.S. products left bound for Havana, the first such shipments in thirty-eight years. The George W. Bush administration has followed the traditional dictum of conditioning the lifting of the embargo to the implementation of deep democratic reforms in Cuba, most of them already outlined in the Helms-Burton Act.

The U.S. trade embargo against Cuba has failed to achieve its main goal: the removal of Castro and his socialist regime from power. Critics of the embargo label it a "fixation" of U.S. politicians and an anachronistic relic of the Cold War. Moreover, the embargo more often than not seems to follow the imperatives of U.S. domestic politics, as it is maintained and reinforced to court the favor of anti-Castro groups in the United States and not to really further the U.S. national interest. Defenders of the embargo argue that its removal would be a triumph for Castro and a capitulation by the U.S. government. Moreover, the embargo remains one of the few weapons that the United States still has at its disposal to apply pressure on the Castro regime. Particularly in the early 1990s, when the Cuban economy was in deep trouble, defenders of the embargo convincingly argued that tightening it was their best shot to bring Castro down. One way or the other, the formerly multinational commercial embargo of the 1960s is nowadays a unilateral measure maintained only by the United States. Its allies—including Canada and many European nations—have since long achieved a modus vivendi with revolutionary Cuba and are now major investors in the island's economy. *See also* Foreign Trade; Organization of American States (OAS), Cuba and the; Soviet Union, Cuba's Relations with the; Sugar Industry; United States, Cuba's Relations with the

Further Readings

Kaplowitz, Donna Rich. *Anatomy of a Failed Embargo: U.S. Sanctions against Cuba*. Boulder, CO: Lynne Rienner Publishers, 1998.

Roy, Joaquín. *Cuba, the United States, and the Helms-Burton Doctrine: International Reactions*. Gainesville: University of Florida Press, 2000.

Ernesto Sagás

6

Contemporary Economy and Society

Abortion

Cuba is the only nation in Latin America in which early term legal abortions are universally available upon demand and without charge. Despite the widespread availability of contraception and the promotion of sex education in Cuba, abortion rates are among the highest in the world. In the mid-1990s approximately one in three pregnancies ended in abortion.

Abortion was technically illegal from the colonial era through the first twenty years of the Cuban **Revolution**. Spanish colonial and subsequent penal codes provided lesser sentences to women who aborted in order to avoid the shame of an illegitimate birth. The 1936 penal code included two new decriminalized categories of abortion: "necessary" abortion to save the life of the mother, and "eugenic" abortion in order to prevent congenital disease or defect. Despite its general illegality, anecdotal evidence suggests that clandestine abortion was widely available in urban areas prior to the Revolution.

The revolutionary government began to more rigorously enforce abortion laws after taking power in 1959, but concern over rising maternal death rates led to a reversal in policy. Beginning in the mid-1960s the Ministry of Public Health used a broad interpretation of the "necessary abortion" provision of the criminal code to expand the availability of hospital abortions. The 1979 Cuban penal code decriminalized all abortions performed according to Ministry of Health guidelines. Special permissions are required, however, for second and third trimester abortions. In recent years officials of the Cuban government have expressed concern and frustration over Cuba's continuing high abortion rates, and policies to discourage "irresponsible" abortion, such as charging for the procedure, have been discussed but not implemented. *See also* Crime; Federation of Cuban Women (Federación de Mujeres Cubanas [FMC]); Health-Care System; Medical Sciences; Women's Rights

Further Readings

Álvarez Vázquez, Luisa. *La fecundidad en Cuba*. Havana: Editorial de Ciencias Sociales, 1985.

Lewis, Oscar, Ruth M. Lewis, and Susan M. Rigdon. *Living the Revolution: Four Women*. Urbana: University of Illinois Press, 1977.

Smith, Lois M., and Alfred Padula. *Sex and Revolution: Women in Socialist Cuba*. New York: Oxford University Press, 1996.

Lois Mamie Smith

Academy of Sciences (Academia de Ciencias)

The Academia de Ciencias (Academy of Sciences) was founded on May 19, 1861, by a royal decree of Queen Isabella II. Its original name was the Real Academia de Ciencias Médicas, Físicas y Naturales (Royal Academy of Medical, Physical and Natural Sciences). The Academy was originally housed at the Convent of Saint Augustine, remaining there until 1962 when it was relocated to the **Capitol Building**; it included a library and a museum of natural history. Several other professional organizations were affiliated with the Academy including the Anthropological Society (1877–1892) and the Society for Clinical Studies of Havana (1879–1960). A wide range of scientific issues were debated within the Academy, from medicine and natural science to **agriculture** and technology. The findings and debates of the Academy were regularly published in its journal *Anales* (1864–1962).

Among the prominent scholars and scientists affiliated with the Academy were Nicolás J. Gutiérrez, the Academy's first president from 1861 to 1890, **Carlos J. Finlay**, Felipe Poey, Juan C. Gundlach, Luis Montané, Carlos de la Torre, and Álvaro Reynoso. The Academy maintained strong professional ties with other scientific organizations in the United States, Spain, and France, among other countries, and took part in numerous international expositions such as Philadelphia (1877), Paris (1878), and Amsterdam (1883).

On February 20, 1962, the institution was renamed the Cuban Academy of Sciences. Among its members of the post-1959 period were **Fernando Ortiz**, Antonio Núñez Jiménez, **Emilio Roig de Leuchsenring, Salvador Massip**, Julio Le Riverend, and José López Sánchez. In addition to the name change, the Academy replaced several professional societies and was charged with a wide variety of scientific projects including the study of the island's natural resources. It administers research on ecology, geography, physics, oceanography, and meteorology. It also established a museum containing collections from the former Academy and other exhibits. In 1994, the Academy was elevated to a government ministry—the Ministry of Science, Technology and the Environment. *See also* Medical Sciences; Science and Scientists (Eighteenth and Nineteenth Centuries)

Further Readings

Anales de la Academia de Ciencias Médicas, Físicas y Naturales de La Habana. Havana: Academia de Ciencias de Cuba, 1864–1962.

García González, Armando. *Historia del Museo de la Real Academia de Ciencias Médicas, Físicas y Naturales de La Habana.* Havana: Editorial Academia, 1994.

Núñez Jiménez, Antonio. *Academia de Ciencias de Cuba: nacimiento y forja.* Havana: Academia de Ciencias de Cuba, 1972.

Armando García González

Afro-Cubans

Exact statistics are impossible to come by, but roughly 60 to 70 percent of Cuba's population is estimated to be composed of people of African descent. The term *Afro-Cuban* is rarely used among Cubans, whether in popular usage or among academics. It is more common for people to refer to *negros* (blacks) and *mulatos* (mulattoes). The reason the term *Afro-Cuban* is not widely used in Cuba is because nationalist ideology has emphasized both black resistance to oppression and black membership in the Cuban nation as a whole. The implication is that by adding the "Afro" to "Cuban" national identity is somehow diminished. This nationalist rejection of racial differences became official policy with the Cuban **Revolution** of 1959. Nonetheless, the term *Afro-Cuban* is frequently used by U.S.-based scholars, and younger generations of Cubans are becoming more comfortable with the designation.

The contested meanings of the term Afro-Cuban indicate the complex realities lived by Afro-Cubans since the Revolution. Few serious scholars would deny that Afro-Cubans have benefited greatly from the Revolution. Before 1959, blacks and mulattoes were disproportionately poor, and the socialist revolution's attempts to eliminate racist practices encouraged upward social and economic mobility among Afro-Cubans. Although they continue to be disproportionately poor, Afro-Cubans have experienced improvements in their literacy, employment, fertility, interracial marriage, and mortality rates. In addition, the internationalist policies of the Revolution highlighted antiracist and anticolonialist solidarity among Africans, Latin Americans, and Afro-Americans. As a result of these gains, many government officials and supporters argued that racism had been eradicated in Cuba. Meanwhile, black representation in the higher echelons of the government and the **Cuban Communist Party** has improved little since the 1960s. In the 1980s **Fidel Castro** and other leaders spoke about the need to increase black representation (as well as the percentages of white women and youth) in party and state bodies (see **Government Structure**).

The reason for Afro-Cuban underrepresentation in Cuban institutions is a topic of great controversy among Cuban specialists. While some researchers emphasize the undoubted historic gains made by Afro-Cubans since 1959, others highlight the reality that eliminating institutional racism does not eliminate racial prejudice. This debate has intensified since the onset of the social and economic crisis of the **Special Period** since 1990. On the one hand, optimistic observers of Cuba focus on how well Cubans society has weathered such an unprecedented and profound crisis; on the other hand, many crit-

ics argue that the crisis has disproportionately affected blacks, youth, and women. There is a widespread perception both within and outside Cuba that there are higher rates of unemployment and underemployment, crime and delinquency, and **black market** activity and **prostitution** among Afro-Cubans and mulattoes than there are for white Cubans. Afro-Cubans are also less likely to receive monetary **remittances** from relatives living abroad, given the predominantly white composition of Cubans in the United States. Scholars and policy makers are only beginning to carry out serious and systematic research on the social impact of the Special Period crisis, and the political implications of this research make doing such work extremely difficult.

Another development that has surfaced in recent years is the commercialization of Afro-Cuban culture. Cuba's dependence on **tourism** has increased dramatically since 1990, and the tourist industry has promoted Afro-Cuban music, religion, dance, and some would argue, sexuality as an "exotic" attraction for foreigners. The problem of the commodification of culture is by no means unique to Cuba, but given the cultural, nationalist, and political implications of Cuba's gradual reinsertion into the international economy, the subject of Afro-Cuban identity promises to be a topic of intense debate in the years to come. *See also* Population and Demographic Indicators; Racial Composition

Further Readings

Clytus, John. *Black Man in Red Cuba*. Coral Gables, FL: University of Miami Press, 1970.

De la Fuente, Alejandro. *A Nation for All: Race, Inequality, and Politics in Twentieth-Century Cuba*. Chapel Hill: University of North Carolina Press, 2001.

Fernández Robaina, Tomás. *Cultura afrocubana*. Havana: Biblioteca Nacional José Martí, 1994.

Fernández Robaina, Tomás. *El negro en Cuba, 1902–1958: apuntes para la historia de la lucha contra la discriminación racial*. Havana: Editorial de Ciencias Sociales, 1994.

Moore, Carlos. *Castro, the Blacks and Africa*. Los Angeles: UCLA Center for Afro-American Studies, 1988.

Moore, Robin. *Nationalizing Blackness: Afrocubanismo and Artistic Revolution in Havana, 1920–1940*. Pittsburgh: University of Pittsburgh Press, 1997.

Pérez Sarduy, Pedro, and Jean Stubbs. *Afro-Cuban Voices: On Race and Identity in Contemporary Cuba*. Gainesville: University Press of Florida, 2000.

Robert W. Whitney

Agriculture

With the advent of Spain's **conquest** and colonization, Cuba's agricultural resources became increasingly devoted to export crops, principally sugar, coffee, and tobacco. Cuba's present-day dependency on sugar, as its main export and second leading foreign exchange earner, was essentially established during four centuries of **Spanish colonialism**. Only in the 1990s did **tourism** displace sugar as Cuba's principal hard **currency** earner. The island's sugar monoculture, first on the basis of **slavery** and subsequently sustained through other coercive labor mechanisms, continues to shape Cuban economy and society today.

Over the last century and a half, vast areas were leveled, irrigated, and planted in sugarcane. In addition to sugar, tobacco, coffee, citrus fruits are also exported. Rice, the chief source of calories in the traditional diet, is another major crop (see **Cuisine**). Other significant agricultural crops include bananas, pineapples, sweet potatoes, potatoes, corn, cassava, and beans. Due to its large agro-export sector, Cuba has historically found it necessary to import annually large amounts of food (principally rice), cotton, and oilseeds.

Beginning in the late nineteenth century but even more so during the twentieth, the Cuban **sugar industry** attracted foreign investors, particularly from the United States (see **Foreign Investments** [Republican Era]). An upward spiral of world sugar prices in the period 1918–1920 brought unprecedented prosperity to the industry, a time known as the "Dance of the Millions." By 1919, approximately half of the island's sugar mills were owned by U.S. companies, accounting for more than half of total production. The precipitous rise in sugar prices enticed U.S. companies, such as the United Fruit Company, the Cuban American Sugar Company, and Hershey, to invest heavily in sugar mills and plantations. When sugar prices fell at the end of 1920, the First National City Bank of New York, a principal source of capital for U.S. sugar investments in Cuba, gained control over about sixty bankrupt mills. Then, after 1922, sugar prices entered a protracted period of stagnation or decline.

In the 1950s, Cuba's sugar mills and plantations continued to dominate the island's agriculture. There had been little diversification in agriculture. Tremendous land concentration and income inequality also marked Cuban agriculture. The largest 9 percent of farm owners owned 62 percent of the land, while the smallest 66 percent of farm owners had only 7 percent. Approximately 100,000 tenants, squatters, and sharecroppers had no land at all. The vast majority of those engaged in farming—70 percent—did not own land, enduring rents that equaled as much as 40 percent of their crop value. Fewer than 10 percent of farmworkers had full employment, and in general, farmworkers could find work only 123 days a year. Some 570,000 farmworkers and their families, constituting one third of the nation's 7 million inhabitants, subsisted on 5 to 10 percent of the national income.

Agricultural transformation was a priority of the Cuban **Revolution**. Nationalizations and **agrarian reform acts** placed limits on private ownership of land. U.S. investments ended. Within a few short years the Cuban government virtually socialized agriculture by requiring all farmers, private or collective, to sell their products to the state. While these measures gave land access and full employment to the rural population and achieved a more equitable distribution of food among Cuba's inhabitants, it did not lessen Cuba's dependence on sugar. Neither did it end large concentrations of land within the sugar industry and **cattle ranching**. A major reason for this was the long-term sugar purchase agreements Cuba negotiated with the USSR. Beginning in 1960, the Socialist trading bloc led by the Soviets purchased Cuban sugar at prices averaging four times the level of world market prices. Consequently, Cuba's sugar dependency deepened as annual production reached 8.5 million tons by 1970, double what it had been in the 1950s. Whereas sugarcane had covered 60 percent of cultivated land in Cuba in 1958, it covered 75 percent of cultivated land in 1982. Sugar export earnings also increased their share of total foreign exchange from 80 percent in 1957 to 83 percent in 1982.

At first the Cuban revolutionary government hoped to use its favored trading status with socialist nations and its sugar income to diversify its economy. As part of this effort, 12,000 middle and large farms that existed before 1959 were incorporated into 920 state farms and ranches. By the 1980s, state farms further consolidated into 427 units, averaging 50,000 acres per state farm, producing 82 percent of the island's sugar, 66 percent of noncane agricultural production, and 80 percent of livestock. Diversification, however, has continued to elude Cuban agricultural and economic planners.

After the failure in 1970 to reach the state's production goal of 10 million tons of sugar, the emphasis on large collectivized state-run farms was modified to allow the pooling of private farms into producer cooperatives (see **Ten Million Ton Har-**

vest). Furthermore, cooperatives were permitted to sell their surplus produce in **farmers' markets** established by the government. The number of cooperatives grew from 725 in 1977 to 1,480 by 1983. Because private production cost less and produced more than state-managed agricultural production, the state goal was to place 90 percent of agricultural land in the private or nonstate sector by 1990. Moreover, sugar exports to the USSR allowed Cuba to purchase fertilizers and pesticides, as well as further mechanize agriculture. By 1990, Cuba had the most capital-intensive agriculture in Latin America.

Cuba's agriculture entered yet another dramatic stage in 1990 as the USSR disintegrated and Cuba's favorable sugar contract ended (see **Special Period**). In the 1980s Cuba had been the world's leading producer of sugar as its harvests reached 8 million tons annually. While benefiting from its sugar trade with socialist nations, Cuba became dependent on imports of virtually everything needed to grow sugar—fertilizers, pesticides, fuel, machinery, and financing. After 1990, without sugar contracts to support its capital-intensive agriculture, Cuba's sugar production plummeted, and Cuban agriculture was thrown into crisis. One fifth of Cuba's 156 sugar refineries closed after 1990. Sugar harvests fell to 3.3 million tons in the 1995–1996 season. Availability of fertilizers and pesticides dropped by 80 percent; fuel and spare parts were cut in half. In general, the island's agricultural production fell 50 percent between 1990 and 1994, and consequently Cubans' caloric and protein intake declined one third (see **Nutrition and Food Rationing**).

Cubans were forced to shift to more organic means of agricultural production. As a result, Cuban agriculture has been markedly transformed. Since 1993, Cuba has been breaking up the large state-managed farms and distributing land to workers, a kind of innovative profit-driven cooperative movement. Supporters of the changes over the last decade argue that the shift in agriculture helped pull Cuba out of agricultural and economic collapse. They point to the increased availability of food in the **farmers' markets** and report that new cooperative production increased yields in ten of thirteen principal food items in 1997. More than 200 factories were established in the 1990s to produce beneficial insects and pest pathogens for agricultural application. The Cuban government has also trained extension agents in the new ecological methods. Since 1991, in the metropolitan area of Havana, 27,000 gardens and farms producing more than 1 million tons of food annually have been created.

Outside observers argue that production per acre actually declined during the 1990s. In a recent visit to Cuba by U.S. Farm Bureau leaders, they characterized the agricultural changes as an ecological and economic disaster. With 58 percent of its total land under cultivation, they charge that Cuba barely feeds its 11 million people.

At the dawn of the twenty-first century Cuba continues to be a net importer of food, approximately $650 million annually. At the same time, Cuba has increased food production acreage and is once again reconsidering its emphasis on sugar production. With world market sugar prices down in recent years, Cuba has emphasized the production and marketing of sugar derivatives, such as **rum**, and its specialty tobacco products. In general, while agricultural conditions have improved since hitting bottom in the early 1990s, Cuba is not soon expected to regain the economic growth and sugar production rates of the 1980s. *See also* Coffee Industry; Foreign Trade; Soviet Union, Cuba's Relations with the; Tobacco Industry

Further Readings
Borque, Martin. *Transforming the Cuban Countryside*. Oakland, CA: Food First Books, 2000.
Deere, Carmen Diana, et al. "The View from Below: Cuban Agriculture in the 'Special Period in Peacetime'." *Journal of Peasant Studies* 21, no. 2 (January 1994): 191–234.
Feer, Jason L., Teo A. Babun, Jr., et al. *CubaNews Business Guide to Cuba*. Washington, DC: CubaNews, 2000.
Funes, Fernando, et al. *Sustainable Agriculture and Resistance: Transforming Food Production in Cuba*. Oakland, CA: Food First Books, 2002.
MacEwan, Arthur. *Revolution and Economic Development in Cuba*. New York: St. Martin's Press, 1981.

John Ripton

AIDS (Acquired Immunodeficiency Syndrome)

In 1999 the Cuban government reported 977 AIDS cases, with an additional 2,621 testing HIV-positive (HIV = human immunodeficiency virus). Half of AIDS victims reside in Havana, according to these figures. Of infected men, 77 percent are homosexual (see **Gays and Lesbians**). Doctors without Borders and Cuba's Ministry of Public Health recently undertook a public educational campaign to promote the use of condoms and protected sex, since sexual contact with infected persons is reported in 95 percent of the cases.

Cuba's first cases of AIDS were discovered in 1985 among soldiers returning from African duty. Cuba immediately embarked on an aggressive effort to combat the disease. The government constructed fourteen sanitariums for HIV/AIDS patients. Critics charge, however, that efforts to identify, quarantine, and treat victims violated individuals' civil and **human rights**. By 1993, in response to escalating criticism, Cuba developed a flexible treatment program allowing patients the opportunity to remain in sanitariums or

HIV+ and AIDS in Cuba, 1986–1998

Year	HIV+ cases	AIDS cases	AIDS deaths
1986	99	14	2
1987	75	17	4
1988	94	20	6
1989	120	22	5
1990	137	21	24
1991	180	23	22
1992	146	21	17
1993	195	24	24
1994	238	39	31
1995	273	53	39
1996	308	65	31
1997	316	86	47
1998	344	104	49

Source: Theodore H. MacDonald, *A Developmental Analysis of Cuba's Health Care System since 1959* (Lewiston: Edwin Mellen Press, 1999), p. 171.

receive ambulatory care at home. Nearly all patients prefer sanitariums where **housing** and food, in addition to medical care, are provided without cost. Ambulatory patients also receive treatment at no cost. The recent growth in **tourism** has led to the expansion of **prostitution** and the spread of AIDS.

Cuba's strategy against AIDS has kept the spread of the disease under control. According to physician Michele Barry in the *Annals of Internal Medicine* (January 2000), Cuba's AIDS campaign suffered, however, from the ongoing U.S. embargo, limiting "the availability of antiretroviral therapy and reagents for HIV testing and CD4 cell counts." In 2000, however, the embargo was softened to allow U.S. food and medicine exports to the island. *See also* Angola, Cuba's Involvement in; Health-Care System; U.S. Trade Embargo and Related Legislation

Further Readings

Johnston, David W. "Cuba's Quarantine of AIDS Victims: A Violation of Human Rights?" *Bos-* *ton College International and Comparative Law Review* 15, no. 1 (Winter 1992): 189–212.

Leiner, Marvin. *Sexual Politics in Cuba: Machismo, Homosexuality, and AIDS*. Boulder, CO: Westview Press, 1994.

Lumsden, Ian. *Machismo, Maricones and Gays: Cuba and Homosexuality*. Philadelphia, Temple University Press, 1996.

John Ripton

Biblioteca Nacional José Martí (José Martí National Library)

Cuba's first national library, later named Biblioteca Nacional José Martí, was established in October 1901 during the U.S. occupation of Cuba. Originally housed at the Castillo de la Real Fuerza (see **Fortifications of Havana**), the following year it was relocated to the facilities of the Maestranza de Artillería (old artillery armory). The library's first director was Cuban intellectual Domingo Figarola Caneda, who donated his 3,000-volume collection to be-

Biblioteca Nacional José Martí in the Plaza de la Revolución. Photograph by Celestino Martínez Lindín.

come the library's founding core of books and other materials. Later directors during the Republican era included Luis Marino Pérez, Francisco de Paula Coronado, and Lilia Castro de Morales. In 1909 the library began publishing a journal, *Revista de la Biblioteca Nacional José Martí*, until 1912. Publication was resumed, albeit irregularly, since 1949 (see **Literary Journals**).

The imposing sixteen-story building that houses the Biblioteca Nacional was inaugurated in 1958, shortly before the triumph of the **Revolution**. It sits on the eastern side of the **Revolution's Square**. The library's holdings of approximately 2 million volumes are divided into several collections and reading rooms: General, Cuban Collection, Children, Braille, Art, and Music, among others. The library also houses important collections of newspapers, magazines, photographs, audio recordings, and maps (see **Newspapers and Magazines**).

In 1959 the library was placed under the Education Ministry (see **Educational System**), but transferred two years later under the jurisdiction of the National Cultural Council. María Teresa Freyre de Andrade, who had been trained in library science at the Sorbonne, became the first director of the library during the Revolutionary period. Since 1997, Eliades Acosta

Matos has served in that capacity. In 2001, the Biblioteca Nacional celebrated its hundredth anniversary and a postage stamp was issued to commemorate the occasion.

Further Readings

Centenario de la Biblioteca Nacional José Martí, 1901–2001 [Special volume of]: *Revista de la Biblioteca Nacional José Martí* 92, no. 3–4 (July–December, 2001).

Eberhart, George M. "Cuba's National Library." *American Libraries* 32, no. 2 (February 2001): 30–32.

Manuel de Paz Sánchez

Biotechnology

Despite its status as a Third World country, Cuba has made considerable strides in the area of biotechnology. In biotechnology as it relates to public health, Cuba is one of the world's leaders (see **Health-Care System**). The government invested more than $1 billion in biotechnology between the mid-1980s and 2000. Of its 1999 science budget (officially U.S. $125 million), Cuba earmarked 30 percent for biotechnology-related projects. Most of these projects' applied research related to human health issues.

In 1981, Cuba produced its first biotechnological product, interferon, useful in cancer treatment. It also developed the world's first recombinant vaccine against hepatitis B and is the largest producer of this vaccine. Cuba also developed and produces the world's only vaccine against the bacterium that causes meningitis B. Other important biotechnological products researched and developed in Cuba include an epidermal growth factor cream; a cholesterol-lowering drug (PPG-S), streptokinase, for heart attacks; and monoclonal antibodies for diagnosis of pregnancy, **AIDS**, and other infections. Through its biotechnological and medical investments, Cuba eradicated polio, malaria, and meningitis from its population, as well as effectively controlling hepatitis B. It is currently seeking to find vaccines for solid-tumor cancers, hepatitis C, and dengue fever.

Cuba's biotechnology also supports **agriculture** and industry. In sugarcane milling, a recombinant enzyme increases efficiency, reducing oil consumption up to 45 percent. Cuba also produces organic and biological fertilizers and pesticides, as well as pest-resistant sugarcane and potatoes. A promising recombinant vaccine that protects cattle against disease-bearing ticks was recently developed. A faster-growing variant of a freshwater fish was also developed.

Cuba's centrally networked scientific infrastructure includes thirty-eight institutes and thousands of scientists and engineers. Havana's Center for Genetic Engineering and Biotechnology, established in 1986, and its marketing arm, Heber Biotech, established in 1991, employ approximately 2,000 highly skilled technicians and scientists involved in manufacturing products that have generated several hundred million dollars in foreign sales in the last few years. Cuba's biotechnology establishment is linked with researchers, scientists, and companies in eighty countries and receives substantial international funding. Currently Cuban biotechnological products for anticancer therapeutics, a cancer vaccine, antifungal and antibacterial treatments, and a meningitis vaccine are in clinical testing in Canada and the United Kingdom. Dr. Agustín Lage, director of Cuba's Center for Molecular Immunology and a graduate of the Louis Pasteur Institute in Paris, leads a staff of 300, including 120 researchers and scientists, in cutting-edge research on the human immune system.

Currently, Cuba seeks to ally its biotechnological infrastructure with Western corporations who have the financial and technical expertise to market its products.

In the meantime, as Cuba markets its biotechnology products as widely as it can,

there is some concern that its products may, inadvertantly or otherwise, help rogue states develop bioweapons. In 2001, the former director of research and development of Cuba's Center for Genetic Engineering and Biotechnology, now in exile, claimed that Cuba had sold to Iran Technologies which could be used for bioweapons, a claim that the Cuban government denies. *See also* Medical Sciences; Pharmaceutical Industry; Sugar Industry

Further Readings

Biotechnology in Cuba: A Report on a Scientific Mission to Cuba (June 28–July 4, 1997). Washington, DC: American Association for the Advancement of Science, 1998.

Carr, Kimberly. "Cuban Biotechnology Treads a Lonely Path." *Nature* 398 (1999): A22–A23.

Feinsilver, Julie Margot. *Healing the Masses: Cuban Health Politics at Home and Abroad*. Berkeley: University of California Press, 1993.

John Ripton

Black Market

The black market serves as a principal vehicle for the public to resolve diverse needs. It is a direct result, albeit an unexpected one, of Cuba's failing political-economic model. The expansion and diversification of the black market were the result of a severe economic crisis caused by the state's inability to address the demands of the population for a wide variety of quality goods. The unsatisfied demand for quality goods is generally subjective and signals the nonacceptance by the public of the state's efforts to control consumption. This phenomenon manifests itself particularly when it comes to clothing and electronic goods.

The black market functioned differently before and after 1994, when reforms were introduced that permitted elements of a market economy. Before 1994, the black market operated in the context of a rigid system of rationing. This system guaranteed a restricted but egalitarian quota of food and some essential goods products to all inhabitants, regardless of their actual needs and their personal tastes. As a result, the black market met the unsatisfied demands of the population, but at considerably higher prices than permitted by the state economy.

After 1994, the black market continued to compete with the official economy, but in this case by offering lower prices than the state's, while at the same time commercializing scarce industrial products or those prohibited in the **farmers' markets**. *See also* Nutrition and Food Rationing; Self-Employment; Special Period

Further Readings

Moses, Catherine. *Real Life in Castro's Cuba*. Wilmington, DE: Scholarly Resources, 2000.

Pérez-López, Jorge F. *Cuba's Second Economy: From Behind the Scenes to Center Stage*. New Brunswick, NJ: Transaction Publishers, 1995.

Gerardo González Núñez

Cattle Ranching

Cattle ranching has historically been one of Cuba's primary industries. Beginning in the early 1990s, the cattle-raising industry in Cuba faced its most severe crisis in over a century due to prolonged neglect and other structural problems. The ranching sector was severely affected by the collapse of trade with the former Soviet bloc, but the roots of the current crisis date back to the 1970s, when the national cattle herd declined by a quarter in a short period of time.

When compared to the general human population, the herd's reduction is particularly striking. On a per capita basis, the number of cattle per person grew from 0.7 to 0.75 during the early 1950s, to 0.86 in 1957–1958, the highest pre-**Revolution** level. The rate remained stable until 1971, except for a period between 1960 and 1963 when the initial economic chaos (including the indiscriminate slaughter of even champion stud bulls) provoked a 15 percent drop. From a record stock of 7.2 mil-

lion head in the period 1968–1971, the size of the herd was reduced to an average of 5.4 million head for the rest of the 1970s, and in the next decade it barely reached 5 million. In 1978, there were only 0.56 head of cattle per capita (the lowest since 1902), and four years later the figure was reduced further to 0.51 head; by 1989, it was down to 0.47. In 1994 the herd reached its lowest relative size ever: 0.38 head per capita.

After 1959, a radical change was introduced into the composition of the herd, which previously consisted primarily of the *cebú* and *criollo* breeds, low milk producers but well adapted to the island's **climate**. By relying on genetics and artificial insemination, government experts developed other breeds that produce more milk but have greater difficulty in tolerating the tropical climate. Severe droughts during the 1990s and early 2000s produced a high rate of mortality in the national herd. In addition to the increase in mortality resulting from poor husbandry, illegal slaughtering has become a serious problem (see **Crime**).

Meat consumption reflects these trends. In the 1950s, meat production had reached 250,000 tons annually. With 4 more million inhabitants to feed, meat production reached only 271,400 tons in 1991. Currently the food-rationing system allows for less than ten pounds of meat and related products per person per year. *See also* Black Market; Foreign Trade; Nutrition and Food Rationing; Population and Demographic Indicators; Soviet Union, Cuba's Relations with the; Special Period

Further Reading

Álvarez Díaz, José R. *La destrucción de la ganadería cubana*. Miami: Agencia de Informaciones Periodísticas, 1965.

Feer, Jason L., Teo A. Babun, Jr., et al. *CubaNews Business Guide to Cuba*. Washington, DC: CubaNews, 2000.

Pérez, Rena. "La ganadería Cubana en transición." *Revista Bimestre Cubana* 73, no. 8 (January–June 1998): 112–136.

Armando H. Portela

Coffee Industry

Coffee is Cuba's third most important export, following sugar and tobacco. Approximately 120,000 hectares (296,532 acres)—2 percent of Cuba's arable land—is devoted to coffee. Over 250,000 coffee pickers harvest the crop yearly. Cultivators grow two basic species: *arabica* coffee (85 percent), for the export market, cultivated at the highest, coolest elevations, and the lower-quality *canephora* (or *robusta*) coffee (15 percent), for domestic consumption, cultivated in the lowlands. Regions of greatest production are the central **Escambray Mountains**; in the east, the **Sierra Maestra** and Nipe and Sagua-Baracoa mountains; and Guaniguanico in the west. Although Cuba hopes to earn more hard **currency** expanding the export of *arabica* and other quality varieties, coffee's world market price fell 19 percent near the end of 1999.

Cuba's original coffee producers were mostly French planters who fled Haiti and Louisiana in the 1790s. Coffee's subsequent expansion increased the use of slaves (see **Slavery**). A series of devastating **hurricanes** in the 1840s and a tariff war between Spain and the United States greatly reduced the production and exportation of coffee beginning in the middle decades of the nineteenth century; by century's end, Cuba had become a large importer of coffee, mostly from Puerto Rico.

During the first quarter of the twentieth century, Cuba continued to import coffee, averaging 25 million pounds per year. In response to protectionist tariffs put in place in 1928, Cuba once again became a coffee exporter. Production reached 53.5 million kilograms (118 million pounds) in the harvest of 1955–1956.

Before the **Special Period** coffee production levels were at 29,000 tons per year (1988). Since 1994 Cuba has attempted to reinvigorate coffee cultivation through giving over 50,000 hectares (123,555 acres) to peasants organized in cooperative associations. The 1998 coffee harvest was the largest in five years, suggesting coffee cultivation, which in recent decades suffered from neglect of plantations and rural-to-urban migration, may overcome its cyclical pattern of good harvests followed by poor ones. Despite the use of modern equipment and techniques, coffee production suffered again in 1999 from drought. *See also* Agriculture; Cuisine; Foreign Trade

Further Readings

Agete y Piñeiro, Fernando. *El café*. Havana: Cultural, S.A., 1937.

Pérez de la Riva, Francisco. *El café. Historia de su cultivo y explotación en Cuba* Havana: Jesús Montero, 1944.

John Ripton

Communications

Cuba's Ministry of Communications controls all communications, including mail and telecommunications. Since Cuba's telecommunications infrastructure is obsolete and fast deteriorating, the government in the 1990s privatized the telephone system and sought foreign financing for improvements. In the late 1990s a joint venture by an Italian company and Cuban Telecommunications Company (ETECSA) completed an overhaul of the telephone system. Reports of poor service persist, however. There are an estimated 300,000 telephones in Cuba, and the basic system was built by International Telephone and Telegraph (ITT) back in the 1930s. In the early 1990s, with the assistance of another Italian firm, Cuba introduced cellular phones. The calls were routed through Italy via satellite, but only 1,152 cellular subscribers enlisted. The international telecommunication circuit connections to Cuba are fully modernized. The 1,020 circuits connecting Cuba and the United States are owned and maintained by U.S. companies. Long distance telephone agreements with foreign telephone companies have come to represent one of Cuba's main sources of foreign exchange.

China and Cuba agreed in June 2000 to collaborate on modernizing Cuba's telecommunications and computer capabilities. China will help Cuba in expanding Internet service to the population without relinquishing government control of its access, as the Beijing government has done. At this point, all Internet servers in Cuba are controlled by the government. While there are schools and clubs throughout Cuba that offer instruction in computers, few have up-to-date models, and none are connected to the Internet. Very few individuals own or have access to a personal computer.

Cuba has fifty-eight television broadcast stations, 150 AM radio stations, five FM radio stations, and one shortwave broadcast station. In actuality there are only two state-run TV channels, which broadcast only during part of the day. Cubans have over 2 million radios and 2.5 million television sets. Cubans can sometimes receive television and radio broadcasts from U.S. channels in southern Florida. The U.S. government established in the 1990s two broadcast stations in Miami, Florida, to send programming and propaganda into Cuba, **Radio Martí** and TV Martí (see **Radio in South Florida, Cuban**). These signals, however, are successfully scrambled by the Cuban government.

The most important Cuban print publications are *Granma*, the official **Cuban Communist Party** newspaper, and *Juventud Rebelde*, the evening paper of the **Communist Youth Union**. Cubans can also read the daily newspaper *Tribuna de La Habana*, the trade union newspaper *Trabajadores*, the monthly women's magazine *Mujeres*, and *Contactos*, published bimonthly by the Chamber of Commerce. *Bohemia* is the most important Cuban

magazine; in its previous incarnation before the **Revolution** it was considered one of Latin America's best.

Several transnational companies have been interested in creating a fiber-optic system. At this point, however, Cuba has limited capabilities in data and fax transmission. *See also* Independent Journalists (Periodistas Independientes); Newspapers and Magazines; Newspapers (Republican Era); Foreign Investments

Further Readings

Feer, Jason L., Teo A. Babun, Jr., et al. *CubaNews Business Guide to Cuba*. Washington, DC: CubaNews, 2000.

Moses, Catherine. *Real Life in Castro's Cuba*. Wilmington, DE: Scholarly Resources, 2000.

Press, Larry. *Cuban Telecommunications, Computer Networking, and U.S. Policy Implications*. Santa Monica, CA: Rand, 1996.

Valdés, Nelson P. "Cuba, the Internet, and U.S. Policy." *Cuba Briefing Paper Series*, no. 13 (March 1997).

John Ripton

Crime

Although over the past few decades Cuba has had one of the lowest crime rates in the Western Hemisphere, crime has emerged as an important public concern in recent years. Sporadic robberies and murders have shocked Cubans. In **La Habana Province**, in 1994, there were fifteen murders for every 100,000 residents. A few tourists have been murdered; other foreigners have been arrested on drug charges. In the first eleven months of 1998, authorities rounded up 6,714 prostitutes and seized 3.52 tons of marijuana, cocaine, and hashish in 269 raids.

In February 1999, the **National Assembly of People's Power** approved stringent new laws to curb rising crime. The new laws delineated 112 capital offenses, 76 involving breaches of state security and 33 involving common crimes such as drug trafficking, corruption, and even cattle rustling (see **Cattle Ranching**). Critics charge that the new draconian measures are a legal mechanism for repressing political dissidence and masking socialism's failings. It is illegal to speak critically of the government to foreign journalists or to attempt to leave the country without official clearance. Recently authorities have banned television antennas capable of receiving U.S. broadcasts (see **Communications**). Cuban law concerning state security is so broad and harsh, opponents contend, that it intimidates **independent journalists** and frightens dissidents.

Cuban President **Fidel Castro** blames **tourism**, market forces, and the **U.S. trade embargo** for the surge in crime. Cuba is currently waging an aggressive anticrime campaign, enlisting thousands of special police and organizing 4,000 local vigilante groups to assist neighborhood defense committees in rooting out crime. *See also* Abortion; Black Market; Dissent and Defections (1959–); Political Prisoners; Prostitution

Further Reading

"Cuba's Repressive Machinery: Human Rights Forty Years after the Revolution." *Human Rights Watch Report* (June 1999): 117–123.

John Ripton

Currency

Cuba's official currency is the peso. Until 1990 no other currency was permitted to circulate on the island. While the official exchange rate was established at 1 peso = U.S. $1, in actuality the dollar's street value is several times higher.

With the expansion of **tourism** and other anticrisis, economic reform measures, other currencies began to circulate alongside the peso. One of the currencies was known as the *certificado de divisas* (certificate of hard currency), created for tourists and other foreign travelers in Cuba. Since the circulation of foreign cur-

Bills circulating in Cuba: one peso Cuban bill is roughly the equivalent of 5 U.S. cents. U.S. bills also circulate widely in Cuba since 1993. The convertible peso began circulating in 1994 and is the equivalent of one U.S. dollar.

rencies was illegal, foreigners were required to use the certificates in special shops and businesses established for them.

In 1993, the use of foreign currency was decriminalized, and the U.S. dollar and other currencies began to circulate with the same legal standing as the peso. This decision along with the excess of money in circulation unbalanced the exchange rate between the peso and the dollar, reaching a high of 150 pesos for each dollar in 1994. After a series of measures aimed at reforming the island's internal finances, an exchange rate of about 22 pesos for each dollar was established and remained fairly constant until 2002, when the rate changed to 26 pesos = 1 dollar.

In 1994, the government issued the convertible peso (*peso convertible*) for the use of tourists at stores and businesses permitted to deal in foreign currencies. The introduction of the convertible peso was aimed at replacing the older certificados. The exchange rate was established at U.S.$1 = 1 convertible peso. The convertible peso cannot be exchanged for the Cuban peso, and it does not eliminate the circulation of dollars and other currencies in the economy. *See also* Black Market; Crime; Farmers' Markets (Mercados Agropecuarios); Special Period

Further Reading

Ritter, Archibald R.M. "The Dual Currency Bifurcation of Cuba's Economy in the 1990s: Causes, Consequences, and Cures." *Revista del CEPAL* 57 (December 1995): 113–131.

Gerardo González Núñez

Divorce

The history of divorce in Cuba reflects the general progressiveness of Cuban social legislation in the twentieth century with its emphasis on the modern ideals of secularization and egalitarianism. Spanish colonial law in Cuba had allowed only legal separation or the ecclesiastical annulment of an existing marriage. Cuban independence forces adopted a provision legalizing no-fault divorce in 1896 during the **War of Independence**, which was rescinded by the U.S. occupying forces in 1900 (see **U.S. Interventions**). Cuba adopted its first peacetime divorce law in 1918, among the earliest in Latin America. The 1918 divorce law provided a no-fault, mutual consent option, expanded **women's rights** over their own dowries and other financial resources, made provisions for the assignment of alimony and child support, and established the general rule that custody of children under age five would be awarded to mothers while older children could choose with which parent to reside. Subsequent pre-Revolutionary divorce laws increased the list of faults for divorce, expanded state power particularly with regard to arrangements for custodial

children, and extended both the rights and the responsibilities of divorcing women.

The 1975 Cuban **Family Code** implemented under the government of **Fidel Castro**, in addition to allowing divorce by mutual consent, eliminated specific fault provisions and instead established that the court would determine when the marriage has "lost its meaning for the couple and for the children and, thus, for society as a whole" (Title I, Chapter III, Section Four, Article 51 of Cuban Family Code). As in the past, women retained preference in custody decisions.

Divorce remained relatively rare throughout the first half of the twentieth century. The divorce rate per 1,000 stood at 0.4 in 1958. In accordance with international divorce trends, divorce rates in Cuba began to climb dramatically during the social, economic, and political upheavals of the 1960s, averaging 1.1. They leveled off in the 1970s (at 2.66) and rose again in the 1980s and 1990s when approximately one in three marriages could be expected to end in divorce. The divorce rate hit its highest level during the first years of the **Special Period**, averaging 5.3 during 1991–1994. The Castro government expressed concern over the apparent instability of conjugal life and experimented with a range of policies to promote stable *legal* marriages and to combat Cuba's long-standing tendency to high rates of consensual unions. *See also* Federation of Cuban Women (Federación de Mujeres Cubanas [FMC]); Feminist Movement (Republican Era); Housing; Population and Demographic Indicators

Further Readings

Catasús Cervera, Sonia Isabel. *La nupcialidad cubana en el siglo XX*. Havana: Centro de Estudios Demográficos, 1991.

Martínez-Alier, Verena. *Marriage, Class and Colour in Nineteenth-Century Cuba*. Cambridge, United Kingdom: Cambridge University Press, 1974.

Smith, Lois M., and Alfred Padula. *Sex and Revolution: Women in Socialist Cuba*. New York: Oxford University Press, 1996.

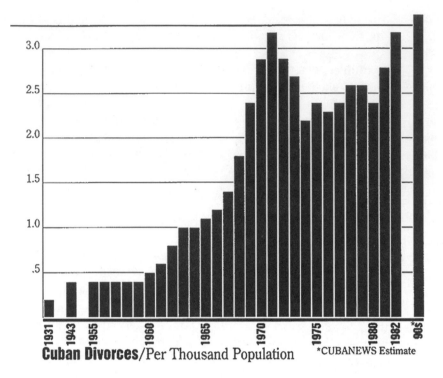

Divorce rates, 1931–1990s. Courtesy of *CubaNews*.

Stoner, Kathryn Lynn. *From the House to the Streets: The Cuban Women's Movement for Legal Reform, 1898–1940*. Durham, NC: Duke University Press, 1991.

Lois Mamie Smith

Educational System

There is general agreement that the level of Cuban education is very high, even by the standards of industrialized nations. With an average of one teacher for every 42 inhabitants and a half-million university-trained professionals in a nation of around 11 million, Cuba ranks among the world's most educated nations. Literacy in 1995 was estimated at 96 percent. In 1997, about 95 percent of all children ages six to sixteen were in school. At a time when most developing countries are struggling for universal education, 3 of every 5 Cuban adults have enrolled in some form of part-time education offered in workplaces and centers throughout the island.

During the Spanish colonial period, there was virtually no education available in the countryside where the peasants and slaves lived. In the cities and towns, however, the children of more affluent Cubans had access to some form of educational instruction. At first, the Catholic Church (see **Catholicism**) took the lead in education, establishing what eventually became the **University of Havana** in 1728. But, by 1842, the Spanish government, fearing the power of the Church, pushed it aside and issued the first comprehensive plan for education in Cuba. Under the new plan the colonial government assumed control of the University and closed many of the schools established by the Church and its charitable institutions. At the time of the **War of Independence**, less than 900 schools existed, and the university enrollment had dwindled to 229 from a high of 1,000. Literacy stood at 44 percent for whites over ten years of age and 24 percent for blacks.

As the United States imposed its influence in Cuba after the war, access to education dramatically increased. Within two years 3,500 new schools were opened in Cuba. The percentage of school-age population registered in school rose from 16 percent in 1899 to 40 percent in 1902. The **Constitution of 1901** guaranteed free, compulsory education for all children ages six to fourteen. These impressive gains were not sustained, however. While literacy reached 72 percent by 1931, education was generally not a priority of the Cuban government. Education levels stagnated as only 60 percent of school-age children enrolled in school, and the education system suffered from low attendance, shortages of schools and teachers, and few students moving beyond the primary grades.

With the rise of **Fulgencio Batista**, education became a clear concern of the state once again. Batista paid attention to public education because teachers and students became politicized in the turbulent politics of the 1930s and were organizing resistance to government repression. He assigned military personnel to head many rural schools and further "militarized" the educational system by allowing the military to construct schools, design curricula, and select textbooks. Problems persisted within the educational system into the 1940s and 1950s. A 1950 World Bank report blamed the overall poor quality of Cuban education on inadequate planning and administration, as well as corruption in the national government. Meanwhile, several Institutos (public high schools) in and around Havana offered education of the highest quality to their students, many of whom went on to the University of Havana.

Overall, the educational system was not responding to the real labor needs of the Cuban economy and society. While the national administration absorbed 20 percent of appropriated education funds in post–World War II Cuba, only 4 percent was allocated to vocational and technical education. Although 23 percent of the state budget was dedicated to education in 1956, less than 6 percent of the population had any secondary education, and only 2 percent had any university education. In 1953, 52 percent of Cubans had not progressed beyond third grade, and 44 percent had between four and eleven years of education. Only 1 percent of Cubans held a university degree. At the same time, the findings of the 1953 National Census demonstrated how little comparative emphasis was placed on scientific and technical preparation. The census recorded 309 engineers, 355 veterinarians, and 294 agronomists but more than 6,500 lawyers.

In the absence of effective public education, many Cubans turned to private and parochial schools. In 1958 there were 1,300 such schools and four private universities. Generally, private schools adopted U.S. curricula, emphasized English, and relied on U.S. textbooks. Segregation along race, economic, and gender considerations was even more apparent in private schools than in public schools. Moreover, after a strike by university students in 1956, the Cuban government closed the nation's universities (see **Students' Movement [Republican Era]**).

With the ascension of **Fidel Castro** and a revolutionary government in 1959, education received immediate and critical attention. The government closed down parochial and private schools while opening many new schools throughout the country. Education from primary school through university became free to everyone as the new Cuban government proclaimed "access for all" in education. Castro declared 1961 as the "Year of Education." In that year Cuba embarked on a national literacy campaign. All formal schools were suspended for the year, and 271,000 adolescent and adult students were sent into the countryside to teach more than 700,000 illiterate Cubans. According to the Cuban government, the literacy campaign reduced illiteracy in Cuba from 23.6 percent to 3.9 percent. Within the next ten years, every Cuban child had access to primary education, with 90 percent in preschool and more than 80 percent enrolled in secondary schools. More teachers were hired, and the government printed 500,000 preprimary books and 4.5 million primary books in its first two years. Also by 1961, 671 new rural schools and 339 urban schools, as well as 99 secondary schools, were built. Between 1962 and 1980, moreover, secondary school graduates increased from 17,583 to 510,957.

The Castro-led government had clear economic and cultural reasons for improving the access and quality of education. Literate Cubans, educated in a curriculum that has explicit ideological goals as part of the broader acquisition of useful skills and knowledge, would not only contribute to the reconstruction of the society and economy, but they would commit themselves politically to the new government. In this manner the government hoped to create a new Cuban culture in which collectivism would replace individualism, and socialism would eclipse capitalism. Accordingly, the government expanded educational access to groups and regions that had been previously underserved. The remote rural population, the economically disadvantaged, people of color, women, and the handicapped were among those to whom education became more readily available. The new Cuban government also extended preschool education (*círculos infantiles*) to children of working mothers and initiated adult education programs throughout the country. From adult education courses held in factories and in parks to the rural schools in former plantation mansions, education in Cuba since 1959 has elevated the level of public discourse.

Opponents of the Castro regime con-tend that education in Cuba is largely political indoctrination. They question the notion of "free education" when all secondary students must spend thirty days each year working in **agriculture**. They point out that medical students must take an "oath of unconditional support for the Revolution" and its principles and that all university-trained students must forfeit their degree if they do not accede to doing a three-year "social service" stint, usually in a distant province. Moreover, dissident critics contend that the Cuban state refuses to permit professionally trained individuals to leave the country. They say that the state imposes a political and moral rectitude in education, that it demands background checks of any students wishing to take the university entrance examination, and that youths are pushed to join communist youth groups such as the Young Pioneers or the **Communist Youth Union**.

Despite the economic stress of the early 1990s (see **Special Period**) and the continuing **U.S. trade embargo**, education in Cuba remains nominally free and universal. There are seven universities—University of Havana, Central University of Las Villas, University of **Camagüey**, University of Oriente; University of **Pinar del Río**, University of **Matanzas**, and University of **Cienfuegos**—and scores of professional and training institutes. But enrollment in higher education fell precipitously from a high of 3 million in the late 1980s to 176,228 by the mid-1990s. In 2002 the government began to provide university students with stipends in order to increase the student population. As education expenditures decline, school materials are in short supply. Many schools have no paper and only a few textbooks. While the Cuban national curriculum calls for education in computer technology, it does not have the foreign exchange needed to purchase computers for schools. Although Cuban schools have responded to

School girls during recess in Havana. Photograph © 1997 by Tony Mendoza.

the rising tourist industry by making English—in the place of Russian—the foreign language studied in schools, teachers of English often leave the classroom to work in **tourism**. While Cuba's educational system is the envy of developing countries throughout the world, new economic and political uncertainties jeopardize whatever gains it may have made. *See also* Federation of University Students (Federación de Estudiantes Universitarios [FEU])

Further Readings

Berube, Maurice R. *Education and Poverty: Effective Schooling in the United States and Cuba.* Westport, CT: Greenwood Press, 1984.

Kozol, Jonathan. *Children of the Revolution: A Yankee Teacher in the Cuban Schools.* New York: Delacorte Press, 1978.

Mikleson, Roslyn Arlin, ed. *Children of the Streets of the Americas: Education and Globalization in the United States, Brazil and Cuba.* New York: Routledge, 1999.

"Universities and Other Educational Centers." *CubaNews* (September 1995): 12.

John Ripton

Energy

One of the long-term weaknesses of the Cuban economy has been its dependence on imported sources of energy. Recently, the oil and gas and electricity sectors were among the hardest hit areas after the loss of economic support from the Soviet Union (see **Special Period**). Prior to 1989, Cuba imported as much as 230,000 barrels per day of Soviet crude and produced little of its own. As the Soviet Union's economic problems grew in the 1980s, Cuba came under pressure to increase its own oil production as a way of allowing the USSR to sell more of its oil elsewhere at market prices for hard currency. Cuba's own practice of reselling Soviet crude for a profit helped accelerate these demands.

In recent years, **foreign investments** and active exploration efforts by the state oil company, Cupet, have boosted oil production substantially. Cuban oil production in 2000 was about 48,000 barrels per day, up from 37,900 in 1999. Most Cuban oil is heavy and contains high levels of sulfur, which Cuban refineries cannot process. As a result, nearly all Cuban crude is burned in the island's power plants or cement factories. Natural gas production in 2000 was about 64 million cubic feet per day, up from about 44 million cubic feet per day in 1999. Nearly all natural gas production, which used to be burned as a waste product, is now used to generate electricity as part of a joint venture between the Cuban power company Unión Eléctrica and Canada's Sherritt Power Corp. Some gas also is piped to Havana to be sold via a small distribution system.

A boom in natural gas production is partially responsible for a dramatic improvement in the reliability of the electricity system. The island has just over 4,400 megawatts of installed generating capacity. The transmission system is generally in poor repair; however, since 1994, system performance has improved. In that year, there were more than 344 serious power outages, a total that had dropped to well under 100 by 2000. Efforts to provide Cuba with nuclear energy capabilities began in 1982 with the construction of the Jaraguá nuclear plant in **Cienfuegos**. Building of the plant, however, ended in 1992 before completion.

The government is finding that it is increasingly running short of power supplies as the economy grows and consumption rises. Efforts to reduce consumption through efficiency programs and the distribution of high-efficiency light bulbs have saved energy, but most experts agree that these efforts have reached the limits of effectiveness and that new generating capacity will have to be built soon. In ad-

dition, Cuban officials agree that major investments are needed in the country's distribution and transmission systems. *See also* Manufacturing; Mining Industry; Soviet Union, Cuba's Relations with the

Further Reading

Feer, Jason L., Teo A. Babun, Jr., et al. *CubaNews Business Guide to Cuba*. Washington, DC: CubaNews, 2000.

Jason Feer

Family Code (Código de Familia)

The Family Code (Código de Familia) was passed in 1975 with the goal of eliminating discrimination against women and creating economic equality within marriage. It was the first law of its kind in Cuba. The Código consists of 166 articles that address a broad range of family matters including marriage, **divorce**, parental issues, nutrition, adoption, and guardianship. The law specifies the legal responsibilities of couples when they enter into marriage, and parts of it are read during nuptials. Prior to its approval, the law was debated at workers' meetings and within the **Federation of Cuban Women** and other mass organizations. The legislation generated lively debate over the articles pertaining to **women's rights**. The law established the age of majority for men and women at eighteen. **Fidel Castro** presented the law to the nation on March 15, 1975, at a special ceremony held at the **Presidential Palace**. The Código has been revised on several occasions, particularly regarding the issues of adoption, children's homes, and substitute families. *See also* Machismo

Further Readings

Sé Jorné, Laurette. *La mujer cubana en el quehacer de la historia*. Mexico City: Siglo Veintiuno, 1980.

Smith, Lois M., and Alfred Padula. *Sex and Revolution. Women in Socialist Cuba*. New York: Oxford University Press, 1996.

Julio César González Pagés

Farmers' market in Marianao, Havana. Photograph by Celestino Martínez Lindín.

Farmers' Markets (Mercados Agropecuarios)

On October 1, 1994, the establishment of small farmers' markets (*mercados agropecuarios*) throughout Cuba was permitted. In allowing the markets, the government hoped to stimulate the production of crops and cattle, counter the spread of the **black market**, and provide another nutritional alternative for the population.

In the early 1980s, a similar experiment had been permitted, known as *Mercados Campesinos*, but these markets were eliminated in 1986 as part of the policies implemented during the **Rectification of Errors Campaign**. Unlike the earlier mercados, the new farmers' markets not only allow farmworkers to participate but also state farms, cooperatives, military farms, individual families farming small parcels,

and other small producers. The only exception to participation are the sugarcane growers, and the only limitation placed on farmers is that they sell only their excess crops after meeting their contractual requirement to the state. At the markets, prices are fixed based on negotiations between buyer and seller. The operation of the markets is quite simple. At each market, an administrator rents space, at an agreed-upon price, to a vendor. Taxes are based on sales declared by the vendor. *See also* Agriculture; Bodegas; Nutrition and Food Rationing; Self-Employment; Sugar Industry

Further Readings

Foster, Nancy. "Cuban Agricultural Productivity: A Comparison of State and Private Farm Sectors." *Cuban Studies* 11–12 (July 1981–January 1982): 106–125.

Rosenberg, Jonathan. "Cuba's Free-Market Experiment: Los Mercados Libres Campesinos,

1980–1986." *Latin American Research Review*
27, no. 3 (1992): 51–89.

Gerardo González Núñez

Fishing Industry

Fishing constitutes one of Cuba's principal
industries and sources of hard **currency**.
In 1997 it produced $180 million in reve-
nues, and it stands as the country's fourth
source of foreign exchange behind **tourism**, sugar, and nickel (see **Sugar Industry; Mining Industry**). While nearly 150
species of fish and seafood are commer-
cially exploited, lobster and shrimp account for over 90 percent of the exported
value. The Ministry of the Fishing Industry oversees Cuba's fishing and fish processing activities.

During the late 1950s, the fishing industry produced between 25,000 and
30,000 tons per year. Production increased
substantially during the 1960s and 1970s
as Cuba's fishing fleet grew and expanded
its activities to many of the world's fishing
areas. Changes in international fishing
laws during the late 1970s, however,
closed off many of the areas where Cuban
ships had been active, forcing the Cuban
industry to shift its focus to waters close
to the island. The fishing industry endured
an even harsher blow in the late 1980s and
early 1990s, when fish production and fish
consumption among Cubans fell by more
than half. Tonnage fell from 192,000 in
1989 to 87,700 in 1994. While the fishing
industry rebounded in the mid-1990s,
overfishing over the previous few decades
reduced the potential for marked growth.
In 1999, the industry produced 144,900
tons of fish. *See also* Fauna

Further Reading

Feer, Jason L., Teo A. Babun, Jr., et al., *CubaNews
    Business Guide to Cuba*. Washington, DC:
    CubaNews, 2000.
Sánchez Roig, Mario, and Federico Gómez de la
    Maza. *La pesca en Cuba*. Havana: Ministerio
    de Agricultura, 1952.

Luis Martínez-Fernández

Foreign Debt

The high level of foreign debt, and the difficulty in reducing it, remains one of the
greatest pressures on the Cuban economy.
There are two principal sources of debt:
the debt owed to capitalist nations and the
debt owed to the former socialist states of
Europe.

The amount of Cuba's foreign debt to
the capitalist nations grew at an accelerated pace throughout the 1970s. In 1969,
the debt amounted to $291 million, but by
1982 the amount exceeded $3 billion. The
impossibility of repaying the foreign debt
led Cuba to renegotiate the terms in 1982,
a process that ultimately led the government to suspend payments in 1986. That
decision has made it difficult for Cuba to
obtain further loans from international financial institutions, forcing the government to secure short-term loans at high
rates of interest. Estimates as of 2002
place Cuba's debt with the European Union at 11 billion; Cuba's debt to Japan—
its single largest lender—stands at 1.7 billion. Debt levels with Argentina follow
closely with 1.58 billion owed.

Cuba's debts to former Socialist countries are under dispute but are estimated to
be around 27 billion dollars, most of it
owed to the former Soviet Union. The
loans from the socialist countries were
used to cover deficits in the commercial
markets and to finance development programs. *See also* Currency; Soviet Union,
Cuba's Relations with the; Special Period

Further Readings

Comisión Económica para América Latina (CE-
    PAL). *La economía cubana: Reformas econ-
    ómicas y desempeño en los 90*. Mexico City:
    Fondo de Cultura Económica, 1997.
Pérez-López, Jorge. "The Cuban Economic Crisis
    of the 1990s and the External Sector." *Cuba in
    Transition*. Washington, DC: Association for
    the Study of the Cuban Economy, 1998.

Gerardo González Núñez

Foreign Investments

The collapse of the Soviet Union and the socialist camp, coupled with an internal economic crisis (see **Special Period**), created the impetus for widespread economic reforms in the early 1990s aimed at encouraging the investment of foreign capital. Foreign investment remains crucial to the Cuban government's plan to gain access to foreign markets, capital, and modern technologies.

The goal of attracting foreign investment dates back to the early 1980s, when the government concluded that the only way to diversify the Cuban economy was to work out agreements with capitalist corporations. In 1982, the Cuban government implemented Decree-Law 50 in an effort to regulate foreign investment, a measure that was superseded in 1995 by the Foreign Investment Law (Ley de Inversión Extranjera). The law permits foreign investment in most areas of the economy with the exception of the health and education sectors. It allows for varying degrees of participation by foreign investors.

The government went further in 1996 with the promulgation of Decree-Law 165, which created free trade zones and industrial parks on the island. As part of the plan, the trade zones and industrial parks were placed in special judicial districts to consider disputes within those zones. The reforms are permitted under constitutional changes approved in 1992 that recognize the property rights of foreign businesses. Restrictions remain in place, however, that make it illegal for a foreign company to hire Cuban workers directly. The Council of Ministers retains the right to approve or reject any foreign investment enterprise.

Since the establishment of the first foreign enterprise in 1988, 379 others have been formed. Of those, 63 have failed. In 1999, foreign investment in the island economy totaled approximately $2.2 bil-lion. **Manufacturing** and **tourism** have proven the most attractive avenues of foreign investment, with 121 business ventures in the industrial sector and 71 in tourism. The **mining industry** attracted another 33 business ventures. Spain leads in the area of foreign investment, with Spanish nationals accounting for 81 of the foreign enterprises, followed by 65 by Canadian companies and 54 by Italian firms. *See also* Foreign Investments (Republican Era); Foreign Trade; Spain, Cuba's Relations with

Further Readings

Comisión Económica para América Latina (CEPAL). *La economía cubana: reformas económicas y desempeño en los 90*. Mexico: Fondo de Cultura Económica, 1997.
Suchlicki, Jaime, and Jorge Antonio, eds. *Investing in Cuba: Problems and Prospects*. New Brunswick, NJ: Transaction, 1994.

Gerardo González Núñez

Foreign Trade

Cuba's economy has historically depended on foreign trade, mostly the export of tropical staples and the importation of fuels (see **Energy**) and manufactured goods. Before the **Revolution**, Cuba's foreign trade was dominated by the United States, where 74 percent of Cuba's exports (mostly sugar) were destined and where 65 percent of Cuba's imports originated. During the first six decades of the twentieth century Cuba enjoyed trade surpluses, averaging about 14 percent of its trade volume. The deterioration of Cuba-U.S. relations in the early 1960s and the imposition of the **U.S. trade embargo** forced Cuba to seek new markets for its sugar and new sources for its fuels and manufactured goods. By 1961, 74 percent of Cuba's exports and 70 percent of its imports resulted from trade with socialist countries, the bulk of it with the Soviet Union. Cuba's new trade relations were heavily subsi-

Cuba, Imports and Exports, 1998

	Millions of U.S. Dollars	Percent
Main Sources of Imports		
Spain	584	22.3
France	285	10.9
Canada	263	10.1
Italy	213	8.2
Venezuela	145	5.5
China	140	.4
Total	2,613	100
Main Destinations of Exports		
Russia	37	21.7
Netherlands	230	13.4
Canada	227	13.2
Spain	130	7.6
China	85	4.9
Egypt	79	4.6
Total	1,721	100
Principal Imports		
Fuels and lubricants	1,048	
Chemicals	564	
Food	414	
Machinery	263	
Raw materials	226	
Principal Exports*		
Sugar	601	
Nickel	263	
Tobacco	184	
Seafood	128	

*Data refers to 1997.

Source: The Economist Intelligence Unit, *Cuba: Country Report 1st Quarter 2000* (London: The Economist, 2000).

dized by the Soviet Union through credits, preferential prices, and other subsidies. In contrast with the pre-Revolutionary era, Cuba's trade balances during the 1960s, 1970s, and 1980s were increasingly negative.

The collapse of the Soviet Union and the Socialist bloc in 1989–1991 generated the most severe economic crisis in the island's history (see **Special Period**). Cuba's foreign trade, which had been dominated by the Soviet Union, fell precipitously from $11.7 billion in 1990 to $2.7 billion in 1993. As a result, Cuba was forced to diversify its exports and to integrate itself into the world market. Cuba's foreign trade has rebounded since its low points of the early and mid-1990s; in 1998 it reached $4.3 billion. In 1998 Cuba's main exports were sugar, nickel, tobacco, and seafood; its main markets were Russia, the Netherlands, Canada, Spain, and China. The island's main imports were fuels and lubricants, food, and machinery, mostly from Spain, France, Canada, Italy, and Venezuela. Cuba's trade imbalance has reached dramatic levels in the past few years. In 1998 the negative trade balance reached $892 million, or 21 percent of the volume of trade. *See also* Foreign Debt; Foreign Investments; Mining Industry; Soviet Union, Cuba's Relations with the; Spain, Cuba's Relations with; Sugar Industry; Tobacco Industry; United States, Cuba's Relations with the

Further Readings

The Economist Intelligence Unit. *Cuba: Country Report 1st Quarter 2000.* London: The Economist, 2000.

González Núñez, Gerardo. "Cuba y el mercado mundial." In *Cuba en crisis: perspectivas económicas y políticas,* ed. Jorge Rodríguez Beruff. Río Piedras: Universidad de Puerto Rico, 1995. 43–58.

Naciones Unidas, CEPAL. "Cuba: evolución económica durante 1998." Mexico City, 1998. Mimeographed.

Luis Martínez-Fernández

Gays and Lesbians

In Cuba gays and lesbians have long confronted restrictive gender roles and a *machista* culture that tolerates homophobia and associates masculinity with heterosexuality. In the 1960s, the government actively advocated these values as it tried to curtail the prerevolutionary visibility of gays and lesbians, who sometimes found acceptance in Havana's permissive tourist world. In its efforts to fashion a revolutionary "new man," the government classified homosexuals as social deviants and drafted them into special military units for "rehabilitation." Beginning in 1965, the army's high command sent homosexuals to work camps called Military Units to Aid Production (UMAP) to fulfill their compulsory military service. Pressure from the international community and from the

Unión de Escritores y Artistas de Cuba (UNEAC; Union of Cuban Writers and Artists) forced the military to phase out the brutal camps between 1967 and 1969. But laws against the public display of homosexuality remained intact and led to police raids, public sweeps, and the repression of literary and artistic groups such as the *El Puente* literary circle, prompting some gays and lesbians to emigrate: They figured prominently in the 1980 exodus from Mariel to south Florida (see **Mariel Boatlift**). Open questioning of the Public Ostentation Law that forbids "public displays of homosexuality" signaled a loosening of public strictures in the 1980s. So, too, did the positive national and international response to the 1993 film *Fresa y chocolate*, about the friendship between a gay artist and a communist youth, and the formation of the Gay and Lesbian Association of Cuba in 1994. But private and unofficial attitudes still remain ambivalent about the full equality of gays and lesbians in Cuban society. *See also* Arenas, Reinaldo; Crime; Machismo; Mariel Generation; Revolutionary Armed Forces (Fuenzas Armadas Revolucíonarias [FAR]); Tourism

Further Readings

Arenas, Reinaldo. *Before Night Falls.* New York: Viking Press, 1993.

Arguelles, Lourdes, and B. Ruby Rich. "Homosexuality, Homophobia, and Revolution: Notes toward an Understanding of the Cuban Lesbian and Gay Male Experience." *Signs* 9, no. 4 (Summer 1984): 683–699.

La Fountain-Stokes, Lawrence. "De un Pájaro las Dos Alas: Travel Notes of a Queer Puerto Rican in Havana." *Gay and Lesbian Quarterly* 8, no. 1 (2002): 7–33.

Leiner, Marvin. *Sexual Politics in Cuba: Machismo, Homosexuality, and AIDS.* Boulder, CO: Westview Press, 1994.

Lumsden, Ian. *Machos, Maricones, and Gays: Cuba and Homosexuality.* Philadelphia: Temple University Press, 1996.

David A. Sartorius

Health-Care System

Cuba enjoys a long tradition of excellence in the **medical sciences** and mutual aid health-care delivery systems (*clínicas* and *quintas*), dating back to the nineteenth century. Before 1959, however, most physicians, hospitals, and medical services were located in Havana and the major towns, leaving outside of their protection broad segments of the poor and rural population. The emigration of about half of Cuba's nearly 6,300 physicians between 1959 and 1964 posed a major challenge to the revolutionary government, which made free, universal medical care one of its priorities as it promised to turn Cuba into a medical world power.

Cuba's health-care system, as well as the island's medical schools, falls under the Ministry of Public Health. The system includes various levels of medical services beginning with the Médicos de la Familia (Family Doctors and Nurses). The Family Doctors program was established in 1984 with one doctor and nurse providing attention to each nucleus of 120 families. An estimated 30,000 doctors and about the same number of nurses operate within the Family Doctors network, emphasizing primary care, prevention, and regular checkups. The next level is composed of the Polyclinics. Outpatient units, the Polyclinics were first established in 1964; ten years later the model was adjusted, and the units were renamed Community Polyclinics. Presently some 440 such clinics operate throughout the island, each serving a few thousand patients residing in their vicinity. Besides the Family Doctors offices and Polyclinics, a broad network of urban and rural hospitals operate throughout Cuba. According to 1999 statistics, there were 276 hospitals and some 700 clinics of various sorts, totaling 76,500 beds. Statistics dating to 1996 reflect 62,624 doctors, 9,816 dentists, and over 75,000 nurses. The number of Cuban health-care workers serving abroad is in the thousands and is considered a major component of Cuba's **foreign relations**.

For decades the envy of other Third World nations, Cuba's health-care system has successfully provided free medical services to virtually every citizen. Cuba's high life expectancy and low infant death rate reflect the achievements of the system. In recent years, however, the system has shown serious signs of deterioration. Doctors and other health-care workers are chronically underpaid and do not make living wages; hospitals and other medical facilities are in disrepair; and medicines and medical supplies are in short supply. As a result, the quality of care provided to most patients has fallen markedly. The number of operations has fallen since the early 1990s, and the rising incidence of infectious diseases reflects the crisis of the island's health-care system. The citizenry is painfully aware, however, of the high-quality medical services offered to government officials and military officers and to foreign patients who pay for excellent services with hard **currency**. *See also* Biotechnology; Pharmaceutical Industry; Population and Demographic Indicators

Further Readings

Amador Torres, Fernando. *Cuba: la cultura de la salud*. Bogotá: T.M. Editores, 1995.

Díaz Briquets, Sergio. *The Health Revolution in Cuba*. Austin: University of Texas Press, 1983.

Feinsilver, Julie Margot. *Healing the Masses: Cuban Health Politics at Home and Abroad*. Berkeley: University of California Press, 1993.

MacDonald, Theodore H. *A Developmental Analysis of Cuba's Health Care System since 1959*. Lewiston NY: Edwin Mellen Press, 1999.

Luis Martínez-Fernández

Housing

The shortage of adequate and affordable housing has been one of Cuba's most enduring and pressing problems. Before the **Revolution**, large segments of the population lived in substandard housing. Two thirds of rural dwellers lived in the traditional *bohíos*, palm-thatched huts, while thousands of urban residents inhabited crowded tenements called *solares* and *cuarterías*. Many other families spent large proportions of their income renting houses or apartments. Within a few weeks of the triumph of the Revolution, **Fidel Castro**'s government issued decrees that cut rents between 30 and 50 percent. Meanwhile the growing flow of exiles made available thousands of housing units for redistribution; it has been estimated that emigrants vacated some 130,000 housing units between 1959 and 1995. The Urban Reform Law of October 14, 1960, socialized rented properties and set house payments at 10 percent of the dwellers' income.

New housing construction was negligible during the 1960s and demand far outpaced supply. Construction crews called microbrigades were organized in the 1970s to help combat the housing shortage. These construction crews eventually disbanded but have been reestablished since 1986. Housing problems have aggravated in the 1990s, particularly in Havana, which continues to attract internal migrants from other parts of the island. While Havana's population increased 70 percent between 1958 and 1995, the number of housing units grew only 28 percent during the same period. Some 10,000 Habaneros, whose homes have collapsed or are about to collapse, live in temporary shelters, while another 100,000 reside in unsafe housing. According to official Cuban statistics, less than half of Cuba's 2.73 million housing units are in good repair, and there are still a few hundred thousand bohíos on the island. One quarter of dwellings are over sixty-five years old. The chronic shortage of housing is doubtless partially responsible for the falling marriage and fecundity rates and the growing **divorce** rate. While the population contin-

ues to suffer from a shortage of adequate housing, government construction resources in the recent past have focused on the construction of tourist infrastructure and luxury condominiums for sale to foreign investors. *See also* Population and Demographic Indicators; Tourism; Architecture (Colonial Era); Architecture (Twentieth Century)

Further Readings

Hamberg, Jill. *Under Construction: Housing Policy in Revolutionary Cuba*. New York: Center for Cuban Studies, 1986.

"The Housing Problem." *CubaNews* (February 1996): 11.

Luzón, José L. "Housing in Socialist Cuba: An Analysis Using Cuban Census of Population and Housing." *Cuban Studies* 18 (1988): 65–83.

Pérez de la Riva, Francisco. *La habitación rural en Cuba: el bohío, la quinta, el barracón y la casa de vivienda*. Havana: Lex, 1952.

Tabío, Juan Carlos, director. *Se permuta*. Cuban film, 1983.

Luis Martínez-Fernández

Human Rights

The struggle for socioeconomic and political rights in Cuba has long roots in the nation's history. By world standards, the **Constitution of 1901** that established the Republic was a progressive document in that it recognized key civil and economic rights of the individual citizen. The "frustrated" **Revolution of 1933** also resulted in an expansion of economic guarantees for workers and a legal strengthening of the civil liberties of the people. The culmination of this trajectory of expansive socioeconomic and civil legislation reached a zenith in the **Constitution of 1940**, one of the most advanced legal documents of its time. In terms of human rights, the 1940 document was particularly favorable to labor and women. The dictatorship of General **Fulgencio Batista** (1952–1958) undermined the Constitution of 1940 and, as a result, the protection of individual and collective rights. Groups opposed to the dictatorship launched a civil, and eventually an armed, campaign to topple the military from power, pledging to restore the Constitution of 1940 and to redress many of the political and economic grievances of the people (see **Batista, Struggle Against**).

The human rights activities in revolutionary Cuba emerged from this current of social activism. Soon after the takeover of the Rebel Army, human rights dissidents raised concerns inside and outside the island. Summary executions, people's courts, persecution, and imprisonment of political opponents and nonconformists foreshadowed a bleak future in terms of civil liberties and indicated the authoritarian/totalitarian nature of the regime. Yet the Cuban revolutionary government satisfied basic economic rights. The first formal human rights association in post–1959 Cuba, the Comité Cubano pro Derechos Humanos (Cuban Committee for Human Rights or CCPDH), was established in 1976 by a handful of individuals who had supported the Marxist-Leninist course the **Revolution** took after the early 1960s. These individuals, such as Ricardo Bofill, one of the founders of the CCPDH, became convinced, over time and through personal experience, that individual human rights had to be defended in a civil manner. In 1988, **Gustavo Arcos Bergnes** became the organization's president. Since 1976 the dynamics of the formation of other human rights groups has resembled a chain reaction. By 1993 over 100 minuscule human rights and opposition groups were in existence.

Human rights groups in Cuba have been instrumental in sparking a small but steady and unprecedented chain reaction of independent group formation inside Cuba. In so doing, they have been a force of political development, planting the seeds of an embryonic civil society and calling into question, at least symbolically, the practices and legitimacy of the entire political system. The state has responded to the challenge of human rights in a variety of ways, from brutal repression to cooptation. Human rights activists and Cubans who dissent have suffered intimidation, cessation of employment (until the 1990s the state was the only sanctioned employer), incarceration, beatings, separation from family and friends, psychological abuse, and exile. Cooptation of the message of the human rights movement has been another official response to the human rights movement. Human rights groups continued to operate under considerable risks. In spite of severe constraints, the movement has been able to survive and erode, at least theoretically, the state's monopoly on political organizations and plant the seeds of civil society. International nongovernmental organizations such as Amnesty International and multilateral associations such as the United Nations have repeatedly condemned Cuba's human rights record. As of 2002 the Cuban government has paid no heed, as it refuses to reform widespread practices that violate human rights on the island. *See also* Crime; Dissent and Defections (1959–); Political Prisoners; Women's Rights

Further Readings

del Águila, Juan M. "The Politics of Dissidence: A Challenge to the Monolith." In *Conflict and Change in Cuba*, ed. Enrique A. Baloyra and James A. Morris. Albuquerque: University of New Mexico Press, 1993. 164–188.

Clark, Juan. *Human Rights in Cuba: An Experimental Perspective*. Miami: University of Miami Press, 1991.

Griffith, Ivelaw L., and Betty N. Sedoc-Dahlberg, eds. *Democracy and Human Rights in the Caribbean*. Boulder, CO: Westview Press, 1997.

Damián J. Fernández

Independent Journalists (Periodistas Independientes)

Despite the Cuban government's complete control over the press, a small group of journalists work independently of state authority. *Periodistas independientes* (independent journalists) report events that the official press does not cover, discuss **human rights** issues, and sometimes criticize the government and its policies. However, their writings are not published on the island. Some of their stories are broadcast back to the island via **Radio Martí** or other stations based in Miami. In addition, independent journalists submit their work to newspapers overseas or, with the help of colleagues outside Cuba, post their writings on the Internet. These journalists risk imprisonment or involuntary exile because the government may view their work as subversive. They come from a variety of backgrounds, ranging from those who have no journalistic training to those who have been prize-winning journalists for the official media. Those with official media experience generally became independent after having political problems with the regime. Independent journalists receive a small amount of international funding but must struggle to find paper and to keep their typewriters from being confiscated. *See also* Communications; Crime; Dissent and Defections (1959–); Newspapers and Magazines

Further Readings

DePalma, Anthony. "Cuba Moves to Silence a Growing Voice of Journalism." *New York Times*, April 7, 1996, sec. 1, 6.
Moses, Catherine. *Real Life in Castro's Cuba*. Wilmington, DE: Scholarly Resources, 2000.

Catherine Moses

Machismo

Machismo is a term used pejoratively to mean what has been described as a "cult of masculine virility" that places value on aggressiveness and physical and sexual prowess. It is often used in juxtaposition with *Marianismo*, equally stereotypical notions about female gender roles. At its core, the social, ideological, and cultural concepts of machismo seek to preserve the dominance and privileges of men over women.

Machismo is deeply rooted in Cuban culture and more generally Latin American culture, and despite being the target of sharp criticism for two decades, it persists at all levels of Cuban society both on the island and in exile. Since at least the nineteenth century, machista concepts of masculinity have been applied to young boys from the time they are born. The male, instilled with a sense of machismo, feels it necessary to constantly demonstrate his virility. The phrase "demuestra que eres un hombre" (prove that you are a man) exemplifies this way of thinking. Women that attempt to redefine gender boundaries and perform tasks traditionally considered in the male domain are sometimes attacked as *marimachos* (tomboys). Gender studies and research encourage reflection and analysis of these issues and promote change. *See also* Family Code (Código de Familia); Gays and Lesbians; Women's Rights

Further Readings

Con el lente oblicuo. Aproximaciones cubanas a los estudios de género. Havana: Editorial de la Mujer, 1999.
Fowler, Víctor. *Rupturas y homenajes*. Havana: Ediciones Unión, 1998.
Smith, Lois M., and Alfred Padula. *Sex and Revolution: Women in Socialist Cuba*. New York: Oxford University Press, 1996.
Vega, Pastor, director. *Retrato de Teresa*. Cuban film, 1979.

Julio César González Pagés

Manufacturing

The significance of manufacturing to the Cuban economy dates back to the nineteenth century and the all-important **sugar industry**, which combined the agrarian and industrial phases of sugar production (see **Sugar Plantations; Colonos**). Although remaining heavily dependent on sugar exports throughout most of the Republican era, by the 1950s, the Cuban economy had increasingly incorporated manufacturing activities to satisfy local demand for beverages, paint, chemicals, processed foods, perfumes, matches, and similar manufactured goods.

In the aftermath of the **Revolution** of 1959, the Cuban government sought to diversify the manufacturing sector of the economy by investing in industries vital to the everyday life of its citizens with the ultimate goal of spurring economic development. An analysis of Cuban investment strategies shows a high emphasis on expanding electrical capabilities, food production, mining, and nonferrous metallurgy. The investment strategy did not meet with the desired result. A large portion of the investment went to industries that required intensive labor and in which it was difficult to increase and maintain production capacities. As a result, the Cuban economy failed to diversify and keep pace with the demands of the international economy.

During the crisis of the 1990s (see **Special Period**), the manufacturing sector was virtually paralyzed, production declined, and investment was curtailed. The priority became attracting dollars for foreign exchange and encouraging **foreign investments**. *See also* Cigars and Cigar Making; Mining Industry; Rum

Further Readings

Comisión Económica para América Latina (CEPAL). *La Economía Cubana: reformas económicas y desempeño en los 90*. Mexico City: Fondo de Cultura Económica, 1997.

Rodríguez, José Luis. *Desarrollo económico de Cuba: 1959–1988*. Mexico City: Editorial Nuestro Tiempo, S.A., 1990.

Gerardo González Núñez

Medical Sciences

The medical profession in Cuba dates back to at least the eighteenth century when the island's physicians came under the supervision of the Real Protomedicato (Royal Board of Physicians) of Mexico. In 1755 a separate supervisory board was established in Cuba, which governed the profession until 1833. A royal decree in 1830 established a Superior Board of Medicine and a Superior Board of Pharmacy. There were two major centers of medical learning during the colonial period: the **University of Havana**, founded in 1728 by the Dominican order, and the Anatomical Museum of the Military Hospital of San Ambrosio, where medicine was taught from 1823 to 1842. Among the more prominent physicians at the latter institution were Nicolás José Gutiérrez and Tomás Romay. Romay introduced vaccines to Cuba in 1804. Gutiérrez introduced to the island important operating techniques he learned in France. He was also the founder of Cuba's first medical journal, *Repertorio Médico Habanero*, in 1840. Shortly thereafter, several other important medical journals were established, including *Anales de la Academia de Ciencias* (1864–1962) and *Crónica Médico-Quirúrgica de La Habana* (1877–1960) (see **Press and Journalism [Eighteenth and Nineteenth Centuries]**). One of the most notable areas of research during the second half of the nineteenth century was the work by **Carlos J. Finlay** on the mosquito as a contributor to yellow fever. Research on a wide variety of other topics was also conducted including cholera, vaccines against rabies, antiviral vaccines, and hygiene and medical/legal issues.

Over time, a number of other medical learning centers were established including the Colegio Farmacéutico de La Habana (Pharmaceutical College of Havana) in 1880, the Laboratorio y Centro Histobacteriológico (Laboratory and Center of Bacteriology Research) in 1879, the Sociedad de Estudios Clínicos (Society of Clinical Studies) in 1879, Asociación Médico Farmacéutica (Association of Medical Pharmacology) in 1900, Instituto de Medicina Tropical (Institute of Tropical Medicine) in 1937, and the Sociedad Cubana de Radiología y Fisioterapia (Cuban Society of Radiology and Physical Therapy) in 1929. Other professional organizations were established for specialists in hygiene in 1891, odontology in 1921, legal medicine in 1922, oncology in 1925, cardiology in 1938, tuberculosis in 1938, neurology and psychiatry in 1947, endocrinology in 1953, gastroenterology in 1952, and the history of medicine in 1954.

After the triumph of the **Revolution** in 1959, the medical profession has relied on a variety of research and teaching institutions, including the universities of Havana, Las Villas, and Oriente. Other important research centers include the Laboratorio Técnico de Medicamentos (Technical Laboratory of Medicines), founded in 1964, and the Centro Nacional de Investigaciones Científicas (National Center of Scientific Research), founded in 1965. The two facilities specialize in chemical analysis, electronic microscopy, neurophysiology, and genetic research. In 1966 eight national institutes were created for endocrinology, cardiology and cardiovascular surgery, neurology and neurosurgery, oncology and radio biology, gastroenterology, and hematology. These institutes in conjunction with the Centro de Biotecnología (Biotechnology Center), founded in 1981, have made a series of scientific breakthroughs in vaccine research and drug development. *See also* Biotechnology; Health-Care System; Pharmaceutical Industry; Science and Scientists (Eighteenth and Nineteenth Centuries)

Further Readings

Feinsilver, Julie Margot. *Healing the Masses: Cuban Health Politics at Home and Abroad.* Berkeley: University of California Press, 1993.

López Sánchez, José. *Cuba: Medicina y civilización, siglos XVII y XVIII.* Havana: Editorial Científico-Técnica, 1997.

López Sánchez, José. *Curso de historia de la medicina.* Havana: Escuela de Medicina, Universidad de La Habana, 1961.

Roig de Leuchsenring, Emilio. *Médicos y medicina en Cuba. Historia, biografía, costumbrismo.* Havana: Academia de Ciencias de Cuba, 1965.

Armando García González

Mining Industry

Although Cuba possesses a wide variety of mineral resources, nickel production has dominated the mining sector during the island's recent history. Other significant mining activities include the extraction of oil, gold, iron, chromium, copper, cobalt, and several nonmetal minerals.

Nickel production has historically ranked near the top of Cuba's export industries. Cuba has about 37 percent of the world's nickel reserves—about 19 million tons. The island currently has three major nickel production operations, all within **Holguín Province**, Cuba's most prolific nickel producing zone. The René Ramos Latour plant in Nicaro (24,000 tons per year capacity) dates from 1943 and produces nickel oxide and synther. The Pedro Soto Alba plant in Moa (24,000 tons per year capacity) began operation in 1960 and is one of the most efficient plants in Cuba. Its main products are nickel, sulfur, and cobalt. The **Ernesto "Che" Guevara** plant, also in Moa (30,000 tons per year capacity), built in 1986 with Soviet technology, uses the ammonia carbonate leaching technique. The incomplete Las Camariocas plant was supposed to have an annual capacity of 30,000 tons but has been stalled since the early 1990s after the Soviet Union pulled out of the project. Attempts to reactivate the project with Russian and other foreign assistance have been fruitless, and authorities in 2001 announced the plant might be abandoned entirely.

In the late 1990s, nickel production began to revive as **foreign investments** and the general recovery of the economy took hold. From a low point of just over 30,000 tons in 1993, production has recovered to more than 73,000 tons in 2000.

Some of the improvement is due to the entrance in 1994 of Canada's Sherritt International Corp. to the sector. The company operates nickel and cobalt mining near Moa in Holguín Province. Final refining takes place in Sherritt's Fort Saskatchewan facility in Canada. The joint venture has a concession to mine 60 million tons of ore in an area of 1,500 square kilometers (600 miles), with estimated reserves to sustain production for fifty years. Cuba's nickel customers include Canada, Italy, Germany, Sweden, and India. Currently 90 percent of Cuba's sales go to Western countries, while 10 percent are destined for China.

Prospectors, primarily from the former Soviet bloc as well as Australia and Canada, have searched for commercial reserves of gold, zinc, and other minerals. However, while there have been some discoveries, most are thought not to be of commercial scale. There also is some exploration work under way to identify copper deposits. At one point in Cuba's early colonial history, copper mining was a major industry, with production in the early 1950s reaching 18,000 tons per year. However, as reserves were exhausted, production sank to less than 2,400 tons per year by the early 1990s and came to an end when the last copper mine closed in 2001. *See also* Foreign Trade; Soviet Union, Cuba's Relations with the

Further Reading

Feer, Jason L, Teo A. Babun, Jr., et al. *CubaNews Business Guide to Cuba*. Washington, DC: CubaNews, 2000.

Jason Feer

Newspapers and Magazines

The government or **Cuban Communist Party** organizations control the press in Cuba. Newspapers and magazines are intended to further the state's revolutionary goals, and their main purpose is to inform the people of the government's activities and policies. In addition to presenting and interpreting speeches by **Fidel Castro** and other government officials, newspapers address topics of interest to particular segments of society or geographical areas. For example, the newspaper *Juventud Rebelde* is published by the **Communist Youth Union**: the newspaper *Trabajadores* focuses on the concerns of workers; and *Tribuna* is for the residents of Havana. The most important newspaper on the island is the daily *Granma*, the press organ of the Communist Party. It was created in 1965 after a merger of the newspapers *Hoy* and *Revolución. Granma* was patterned on the Soviet paper *Pravda*. Magazines also focus on particular audiences, like the **Federation of Cuban Women**'s *Mujeres* and *Verde Olivo* for the **Revolutionary Armed Forces**. *Bohemia*, a general interest cultural magazine that was one of the most prominent weekly publications in Latin America before the **Revolution**, continues to be published. The print media tend to have a greater variety of information than the broadcast media, but the reading is dull and lackluster. While the press has been encouraged by Castro to constructively criticize failures in government processes, it is not to criticize the Revolution or any decisions that have already been made.

Despite the importance of mass media to the Revolution, the **Special Period** of the 1990s took a toll on newspapers and magazines. Newsprint, paper, and ink became scarce commodities, as did replacement parts for aging Soviet-made printing presses. As a result, many magazines stopped publication. Most newspapers became weekly papers instead of dailies. Only *Granma* continued to be published on an almost daily basis. As the necessary products became available again in the late 1990s, printing of various publications gradually resumed.

Before 1959, there were between sixty and seventy newspapers in Cuba. Unfortunately, there were also extensive problems with censorship, patronage, and bribery by government and business sources to obtain favorable coverage. When Castro stopped this monetary support in 1959, many newspapers had to close their doors. As businesses and industries were nationalized, advertising revenue for the surviving papers dried up, ultimately leaving the state in control by 1961. *See also* Communications; Independent Journalists (Periodistas Independientes); Literary Journals; Newspapers (Republican Era); Press and Journalism (Eighteenth and Nineteenth Centuries)

Further Readings

Moses, Catherine. *Real Life in Castro's Cuba*. Wilmington, DE: Scholarly Resources, 2000.

Nichols, John Spicer. "The Press in Cuba." In *The Cuba Reader: The Making of a Revolutionary Society*, ed. Philip Brenner, William LeoGrande, Donna Rich, and Daniel Siegel. New York: Grove Press, 1989. 219–227.

Rius. "The Meaning of Cuba." *NACLA Report on the Americas* 29 (September–October 1995): 45–46.

Catherine Moses

Nutrition and Food Rationing

Severe food shortages dating to the early years of the **Revolution** and the revolutionary government's goals to more equally distribute food sources led to the establishment of a food-rationing system known a *la libreta*. The system provides each Cuban household with a rationing book each year that entitles citizens to purchase basic food items at government-owned food stores, the so-called *tiendas del pueblo*. Among the items that individuals can purchase with the libreta are bread (one small bun per day); eggs (seven units per month); sugar (four pounds per month); rice (six pounds per month); and beans (ten to twenty ounces per month). These and a few other libreta items are sold at low, subsidized prices and are usu-

ally of low quality. By all accounts, the amount of food allotted through the rationing system is not sufficient for the proper nutrition of individuals. Cubans are thus forced to complement the official food rations with items purchased at the much more expensive *mercados agropecuarios* (**farmers' markets**), the **black market**, and other outlets. While a pound of rice is sold through la libreta at 25 Cuban cents, it is sold at 5 pesos in the mercados agropecuarios. A pound of pork at the mercado agropecuario costs 25 pesos (the average monthly salary in Cuba is 217 pesos).

Nutrition levels among Cubans did not improve with the advent of the revolutionary regime in 1959. The already low levels of nutrition fell precipitously during the crisis of the early 1990s (see **Special Period**) when food imports and domestic production of food staples dropped by more than half. During those years the average per capita caloric intake fell from 2,940 to 2,100 (in some instances to near starvation levels of 1,450); while the average daily protein consumption fell from seventy-eight grams in the 1980s to forty-six grams. The falling levels of nutrition sparked an epidemic of optic myeloneuropathy and other deficiency diseases and have resulted in lower birth weights and an increase in mortality among the elderly. In recent years the government has sought to supplement the Cuban diet with a number of new processed food items: *cerelac* is a milk and cereal substitute; *masa cárnica, pasta de oca*, and *picadillo de soya* are meat substitutes made up mostly of unidentified ingredients. *See also* Cuisine; Foreign Trade; Health-Care System; Paladares

Further Readings

Gordon, Antonio M., Jr. "The Nutriture of Cubans: Historical Perspective and Nutritional Analysis." *Cuban Studies* 13, no. 2 (Summer 1983): 1–34.

Libreta (rationing book). Each family unit receives a libreta that entitles them to purchase food at the *bodegas*. Luis Martínez-Fernández Collection.

Medea, Benjamin. *No Free Lunch: Food and Revolution in Cuba Today*. San Francisco: Institute for Food and Development Policy, 1984.

Portela, Armando H. "Food Shortages Damage Nutrition, Health." *CubaNews* (March 1998): 10.

Luis Martínez-Fernández

Paladares

A *paladar* is a small private restaurant, usually located in a home. Operating a paladar became a legal occupation in June 1995 when the **Fidel Castro** government added it to the list of areas in which Cubans could work for themselves instead of for the state (see **Self-Employment**). Paladares quickly opened across the island. By law, these restaurants are to have no more than twelve seats and are to be run by families. In reality, many of them have back rooms with additional tables and employ individuals who are not relatives. The restaurants range from simple one-room setups to elaborate arrangements in large old houses. The food served also varies according to the expected clientele. Some paladares serve plain meals to peso-earning Cubans. Others, catering to tourists who pay with dollars, offer a varied menu including appetizers, seafood, and wine. To cover the cost of starting a paladar, the owner will often use money from relatives overseas (see **Remittances**). Even though taxes on these restaurants are high, successful paladares serving tourists can earn a tidy sum. *See also* Andiarenes, Nitza; Cuisine; Farmers' Markets; Nutrition and Food Rationing; Tourism; Villapol

Further Readings

Ritter, Archibald R. M., "Entrepreneurship, Microenterprise, and Public Policy in Cuba: Promotion, Containment, or Asphyxiation." *Journal of Inter American Studies and World Affairs* 40, no. 2 (Summer 1998): 63–94.

"Seafood Platter, Havana-Style." *The Economist*, March 1, 1997, 44.

Catherine Moses

Pharmaceutical Industry

The **biotechnology** and pharmaceutical sectors are among the leading areas for Cuban scientific research and product development. Heavily subsidized at a time when the government is requiring most sectors of the economy to become self-sufficient, the biotechnology and pharmaceutical industry receives funding equivalent to about 1.5 percent of gross domestic product on an annual basis. Between 1991 and 1997, the sector received a reported 1 billion pesos and close to $400 million dollars, a large investment by Cuban standards.

The industry is grouped together in a number of interdisciplinary teams (called *polos científicos*) that include research organizations, production facilities, and business and marketing units. The government's control of the main agricultural sectors, such as the **sugar industry**, as well as state control of the **health-care system** ensures that researchers have unrestricted access to raw materials needed for research, including tissues and organs and a wide range of agricultural products.

Cuban biotech and pharmaceutical companies have developed a number of important products that are sold internationally. The VA-Mengoc-BC vaccine against the meningococcus B bacteria is one of the most notable. The vaccine, developed by Cuba's Finlay Institute (see **Carlos J. Finlay**), is already used in twelve countries, including Brazil. In 1999 Cuba signed an agreement with the British drug company SmithKline Beecham to test it with an eye toward eventual joint sales.

Cuban scientists also have developed vaccines against strains of hepatitis, drugs to relieve the symptoms of a number of skin ailments, treatments for serious animal infections, and a number of diagnostic tests. The sector also produces a wide range of antibiotics, biopreparations, radioactive isotopes for medical use, various types of interferon, and genetically engineered seeds. Cuban research institutions continue to work on projects to develop effective vaccines against cholera and several types of cancer as well as products to stimulate neuron growth.

Biotech exports are reportedly about $100 million per year, still less than the annual government funding for the sector. Backers argue that the investment also has saved the government tens of millions of dollars per year in medical imports. *See also* Foreign Trade; Manufacturing; Medical Sciences

Further Readings
Biotechnology in Cuba: A Report on a Scientific Mission to Cuba (June 28–July 4, 1997). Washington, DC: American Association for the Advancement of Science, 1998.

Carr, Kimberly. "Cuban Biotechnology Treads a Lonely Path." *Nature* 398 (1999): A22–A23.

Feer, Jason L., Teo A. Babun, Jr., et al. *CubaNews Business Guide to Cuba*. Washington, DC: CubaNews, 2000.

Feinsilver, Julie Margot. *Healing the Masses: Cuban Health Politics at Home and Abroad*. Berkeley: University of California Press, 1993.

Jason Feer

Political Prisoners

The revolutionary regime's first political prisoners were individuals who were associated with the **Fulgencio Batista** dictatorship. Those who disagreed with the course of the **Revolution** soon joined their ranks, as individuals were charged with committing counterrevolutionary activities that threatened the security of the state. In November 1959, such charges became Fundamental Law and continue to the present day.

Criminal acts varied from overt political opposition to the more salient activities as described by the Penal Code article 108. Cases were seen in front of revolutionary courts, often with the denial of habeas corpus. Sentences were usually harsh, as much as sixty to ninety years of imprisonment, with the frequent use of execution by firing squad. It was not until the introduction of the Penal Code of 1979 that sentences were reduced to twenty years for crimes not punishable by death and thirty years as an alternative to the death penalty. Limitations on sentences were applied to crimes committed before this law's enactment.

Political prisoners are held in high-security prisons known as *Centro Penitenciario Combinado del Este*. Prisoners are said to be provided with indispensable living conditions, such as medical services, education, and social activities. These conditions are seen as privileges not extended to those political prisoners that refuse to take part in the country's rehabilitation program called the Progressive Plan. The Progressive Plan seeks to reeducate prisoners in skilled and unskilled labor at work camps.

The *plantados*, "those who stand firm," are political prisoners who refuse to take part in rehabilitation programs. They often engage in hunger strikes and refuse to wear uniforms as protest. They are denied the most basic human needs and are often placed in steel-plated cells that deny sunlight and fresh air for weeks at a time as punishment. Prison sentences of plantados have been extended for one to two years, and medical care has been withheld as a form of punishment.

While the number of plantados has decreased over the years, the exact number imprisoned or executed is not known. In a recent book, however, **Carlos Alberto Montaner** cites estimates of 150,000 political prisoners for the revolutionary period and between 5,000 and 18,000 executions. In 1965, **Fidel Castro** admitted to 20,000, though it was suspected by ex-

iles that the number was closer to 40,000. Through December 1978 and 1979, 4,000 political prisoners were released with the advent of the Penal Code of 1979. Further changes to the Penal Code in 1987 reduced these numbers by reducing sentences and providing contingent releases. While the Cuban government denies the existence of political prisoners as of July 2000, 314 remained imprisoned.

One of the most notorious cases of political imprisonment in recent years has been that of four Cuban dissidents (Vladimiro Roca, Félix Bonne, René Gómez, and Marta Beatriz Roque) who were arrested in July 1997, having authored and distributed a document outlining the shortfalls of the regime: "La Patria es de todos" (The Homeland Belongs to Us All), (see **Appendix 14**). Bonne, Gómez, and Roque served three-year terms in prison and Roca remained behind bars until the eve of the visit to Cuba by Jimmy Carter in May 2002. *See also* Crime; Dissent and Defections (1959–   ); Human Rights

Further Readings

Amnesty International. *Political Imprisonment in Cuba*. London: Amnesty International, 1987.

Clark, Juan. *Human Rights in Cuba: An Experimental Perspective*. Miami: University of Miami Press, 1991.

Gómez Treto, Raúl. "Thirty Years of Cuban Revolutionary Law." *Latin American Perspectives* 69, no. 2 (Spring 1991): 114–112.

Montaner, Carlos Alberto. *Viaje al corazón de Cuba*. Barcelona: Plaza y Janés, 1999.

Valladares, Armando. *Against All Hope*. New York: Alfred A. Knopf, 1986.

Kevin Rente

Population and Demographic Indicators

At the end of 1999 Cuba had a population of 11,180,099 and a population density of 100.8 per square kilometer (261 per square mile). More than 75 percent of the population is composed of urban dwellers, and

Cuba's Population

1774	171,620
1792	273,979
1817	553,033
1827	704,487
1841	1,007,642
1861	1,366,232
1877	1,509,291
1887	1,609,075
1901	1,572,797
1907	2,048,980
1919	2,889,004
1931	3,962,344
1943	4,778,583
1953	5,829,029
1970	8,569,121
1981	9,723,605
1990*	10,694,465
1999*	11,180,099

Source: Cuba, Oficina Nacional de Estadísticas, *Anuario Estadístico de Cuba 1996* (Havana, 1998); and Jason Feer et al., *CubaNews' Business Guide to Cuba, 2000* (Washington, DC: *CubaNews*, 2000).
*1990 and 1999 are official estimates.

nearly one in five Cubans lives in Havana. Life expectancy hovers around seventy-six years, close to the level of industrialized nations, and the island's population is graying, with 9.7 percent over sixty-five years of age. Population growth has virtually stagnated, exhibiting a yearly growth rate of .55 percent during the 1990s. In 2001 it was estimated at 0.37 percent. This has been the result of falling birthrates and growing death and emigration rates. In 1999 the birthrate was 13.5, the death rate was 7.1, and the infant mortality rate stood at 8.0. Fecundity rates have dropped significantly to 1.44 children per woman. About 39.9 percent of the population is married, and close to 24 percent have formed consensual unions. Greater emigration rates and mortality among men have recently produced a slight female majority within the island's population. In 2001 the migration rate was estimated to be 1.36 per thousand.

The population sizes of the island's fourteen provinces and special municipality of Isla de la Juventud ranked as follows at the end of 1998:

Ciudad de La Habana	2,197,706
Santiago de Cuba	1,022,105
Holguín	1,018,899
Villa Clara	830,085
Granma	823,481
Camagüey	778,772
Pinar del Río	726,929
La Habana	689,364
Matanzas	649,994
Las Tunas	521,793
Guantánamo	509,210
Sancti Spíritus	456,294
Ciego de Ávila	400,720
Isla de la Juventud	78,259

See also Divorce; Racial Composition

Further Readings
Cuba, Oficina Nacional de Estadísticas. *Anuario Estadístico de Cuba 1996*. Havana: 1998.

Feer, Jason, et al. *CubaNews Business Guide to Cuba*. Washington, DC: CubaNews, 2000.

Luzón, José Luis. *Economía, población y territorio en Cuba, 1899–1983*. Madrid: Ediciones Cultura Hispánica, 1987.

Luis Martínez-Fernández

Prostitution

Prostitution in Cuba and particularly in Havana, while not a new problem, had become increasingly widespread and visible during the 1940s and 1950s. It was intimately associated with a parallel boom in **tourism**. It has been estimated that in 1958 some 270 brothels and 11,500 prostitutes operated in Havana. After the fall of **Fulgencio Batista**, combating prostitution became one of the main social agendas of the **Revolution**. A 1961 law declared illegal all forms of prostitution, and special schools were established to reeducate former prostitutes. While not eradicating prostitution completely, the government closed down all brothels and significantly reduced the practice of prostitution.

Since the early 1990s, however, prostitution has resurfaced with a vengeance, spurred by the crisis of the so-called **Special Period**, the boom in tourism, and the dollarization of the economy (see **Currency**). Prostitution has taken the form of what in Cuba is referred to as *jineterismo. Jineteras* are young—some in their early teens—attractive women who earn a living by exchanging sexual favors for money and material goods. Jineteras sometimes establish long-term relations with foreign tourists that in some cases even lead to marriage. Unlike typical Third World prostitutes, Cuban jineteras are often educated women whose desperate economic situation forces them into prostitution. In a joke of very poor taste, **Fidel Castro** cynically acknowledged that prostitution had resurfaced but bragged that Cuba had the world's healthiest and best-educated prostitutes. Jineteras and their male counterparts, *jineteros*, tend to congregate in and around tourist areas such as Havana's hotels and nightclubs and beach resorts such as Varadero (see **Beaches**). A new variant of transvetite prostitution has become increasingly visible as well. Authorities have cracked down in a few instances when prostitution has become too visible. In 1996, for instance, nearly 7,000 prostitutes were detained in a single raid in Varadero. For the most part, however, the government appears to turn a blind eye on the problem, accepting it as a necessary by-product of the lucrative tourist industry. Unfortunately, Cuba has recently earned a reputation as a prime sex tourism destination. A sharp increase in sexually transmitted diseases is attributed in great measure to the rise in prostitution (see **AIDS**).

Further Readings

Fernández Robaina, Tomás. *Historias de mujeres públicas*. Havana: Editorial Letras Cubanas, 1998.

Fusco, Coco. "Hustling for Dollars." In *Imported: A Reading Seminar (Semiotexte Ser.)*, ed. Rainer Ganahl. Brooklyn, NY: Autonomedia, 1998. 139–156.

Smith, Lois M., and Alfred Padula. *Sex and Revolution: Women in Socialist Cuba*. New York: Oxford University Press, 1996.

Luis Martínez-Fernández

Racial Composition

Cuba's population is racially heterogeneous, the result of intense and prolonged processes of free and forced immigration and racial miscegenation over the past five centuries. The island's aboriginal population, estimated to have been about 112,000 at the time of the Columbian encounter, was virtually exterminated within a few decades of the arrival of the first Spanish conquistadors. Traces of aboriginal biological ancestry are still visible among some Cubans, particularly in the province of **Guantánamo**. The **conquest** and colonization of the island produced the immigration of Spanish settlers and importation of African slaves, processes that continued well into the nineteenth century, when other populations, notably the Chinese, contributed to Cuba's racial diversity. The census of 1861 reflected a racial makeup of 56.8 percent white and 43.2 percent of color (black and mulatto). Nearly four decades later, following the end of the **slave trade** and the massive arrival of Spanish settlers, the census taken during the U.S. occupation of the island reflected a population of 67 percent white; 15 percent black; 17 percent mixed; and .9 percent Chinese. White immigration, mainly from northern Spain, contributed to the further whitening of the Cuban population during the first half of the twentieth century to the point that the census of

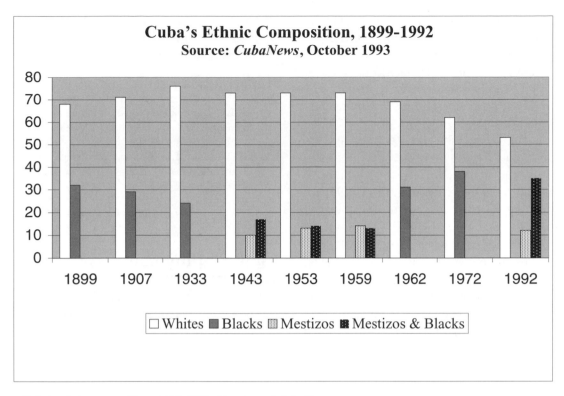

Cuba's Ethnic Composition, 1899-1992
Source: *CubaNews*, October 1993

Legend: □ Whites ■ Blacks ▦ Mestizos ▩ Mestizos & Blacks

Cuba's ethnic composition, 1899–1992. Courtesy of *CubaNews*.

1953 reflected a population consisting of 73 percent whites, 12 percent blacks, and 15 percent mulattos. The disproportionate participation of white Cubans in the exile process since 1959, particularly the earlier migratory waves, and the higher fecundity rate among **Afro-Cubans** have resulted in the gradual darkening of the population on the island. According to the census of 1981, 66 percent of the population described itself as white, 22 percent as mulatto, and 12 percent as black. More recent estimates place the proportion of Cubans of African descent on the island at over 60 percent. By contrast, racial patterns among Cubans in the United States point to a whiter population. According to the 1990 U.S. census, 86.3 percent of Cubans in the United States classified themselves as white; 0.2 percent as black; 0.3 percent as Asian; and 13.2 percent as other (most probably mulattos). *See also* Asian Con-

tract Laborers; Caribbean Immigration; Colonization and Population (Nineteenth Century); Immigration (Twentieth Century); Indigenous Inhabitants; Population and Demographic Indicators

Further Reading
Aguirre, Benigno E. "The Differential Migration of Cuban Social Races." *Latin American Research Review* 11 (1976): 103–124.
Masferrer, Marianne, and Carmelo Mesa-Lago. "The Gradual Integration of the Black in Cuba: Under the Colony, the Republic and the Revolution." In Robert Brent Toplin, ed. *Slavery and Race Relations in Latin America*. Westport, CT: Greenwood Press, 1974. 348–384.

Luis Martínez-Fernández

Remittances

The remittance of foreign **currency** by Cuban exiles to family members on the island has played an important role in energizing the economy and in satisfying the personal needs of the population. Remittances increased after the possession of foreign currency was decriminalized in 1993. Another factor in the increase is the growing number of stores accepting foreign currency.

Between 1989 and 1993 remittances reached $1 billion, but between 1994 and 1996 the figure climbed to $2 billion, of which $800,000 was received in 1996, according to official government statistics and those provide by CEPAL (Comisión Económica para América Latina). Remittances emerged as the second biggest source of foreign currency, ahead of sugar exports, and only surpassed by **tourism**. This statistic is even more significant when one considers that this figure was reached during a year in which the government of the United States adopted a series of sanctions against Cuba, in response to the shooting down of two planes flown by members of **Hermanos al Rescate** (**Brothers to the Rescue**). The sanctions restricted the free travel and communication between the Cuban immigrants in the United States and family members on the island.

The access of the Cuban population to foreign currency has increased substantially as a result of the increase in remittances. In 1993, about 20 percent of the population had access to foreign currency, a figure that grew to 62 percent by 1999, according to official estimates.

Many believe that remittances actually exceed $1 billion a year. This estimate is likely correct, considering the cumulative demand for dollars as a result of the economic crisis and the goods sent directly to family members. In many cases these goods are converted into currency as part of informal business arrangements. Remittances not only provide for personal needs; they are also a source of capital to establish small businesses such as **paladares** now that **self-employment** op-

portunities are expanding. *See also* Afro-Cubans; Foreign Investments; U.S. Trade Embargo and Related Legislation

Further Reading

Comisión Económica para América Latina (CE-PAL). *La economía cubana: reformas económicas y desempeño en los 90.* Mexico City: Fondo de Cultura Económica, 1997.

Monreal, Pedro. "Las Remesas familianes en la economía Cubana." *Encuentro de la Cultura Cubana* 14 (1999) 44–62.

Gerardo González Núñez

Self-Employment

Beginning in September 1993, self-employment became a viable option for Cuban workers as part of a series of economic reform measures adopted by the government in the wake of the economic crisis created by the collapse of the Socialist bloc (see **Special Period**). In theory, self-employment predated the 1993 reform measures, but the number of self-employed workers was so low—25,000, or less than 1 percent of the workforce—as to render it inconsequential. In essence the state was the nation's only employer.

While the decision to allow self-employment was motivated by the profound economic crisis, rising unemployment, and a decline in the standard of living, the Cuban government continues to maintain policies that discourage its full development. The imposition of high taxes on self-employment earnings and excessive controls and prohibitions discourage growth in this area. The limitations of the internal market also serve as a barrier to self-employment.

The number of self-employed workers reached a peak of 200,000 in 1995 but declined to 150,000 just two years later. Cuban authorities estimate that for every declared self-employed worker there is one working illegally. Taking that estimate into account, there are approximately 300,000

Stands of independent book sellers in Havana's Captains-General's square; Colombian novelist Gabriel García Márquez, a long-time supporter of the Castro regime, browses through books. Photograph by Luis Martínez-Fernández.

self-employed workers in Cuba, or approximately 7 percent of the national labor force. Among the several categories of self-employed workers are operators of beauty parlors, book stands, bicycle parkings, and watch and lighter repair stands. *See also* Paladares

Further Reading

Ritter, Archibald R. M. "Entrepreneurship, Microenterprise, and Public Policy in Cuba: Promotion, Containment or Asphyxiation." *Journal of Interamerican Studies and World Affairs* 40, no. 2 (Summer 1998): 63–94

Smith, Benjamin. *The Self-employed in Cuba: A Street Level View. Cuba in Transition.* Vol. 9. Washington, DC: Association for the Study of the Cuban Economy, 1999.

Gerardo González Núñez

Special Period

"Período especial en tiempos de paz" (Special Period in Time of Peace) is the euphemistic term applied to the period of economic crisis beginning in 1990. As of the mid-1980s, Cuba's rate of economic growth began to decline, a clear sign of the shortcomings of the island's economic model. The crisis deepened with the collapse of the socialist camp in 1989–1991. Within a matter of a few years, Cuba lost its principal export markets and sources of goods and the favorable financing terms upon which the economy relied. As a result, in just four years, Cuba's capacity to import foreign goods declined by 80 percent, leading to a dramatic decline in production and standard of living for Cuban workers. The importation of consumer goods including foodstuffs was greatly affected (see **Foreign Trade**).

Faced with an economic crisis of enormous proportions, the Cuban government implemented a series of emergency measures aimed at ensuring the survival of the population and regime. Economic growth and development goals were set aside in an effort to ensure subsistence. An emphasis was placed on providing a minimum diet for each family. As part of the overall shift in economic policy, the Cuban government encouraged **foreign investments**, particularly in the **tourism** sector, as part of an effort to stimulate the internal economy.

By 1993, it was clear that the new economic measures were insufficient to stem the decline of the economy. In a few short years, Cuba's gross national product fell by 36 percent. As a result, market reforms were introduced into the economy in 1993 and 1994. The reforms included allowing foreign **currency** to circulate in the economy, permitting Cuban workers more latitude in developing **self-employment** opportunities, the transformation of most

One of the measures enacted during the Special Period was the partial dollarization of the economy. This evocative photograph by Ángel Antonio la Rosa portrays a large Cuban bill while the sign behind reads: "Do not enter. Restricted access." Luis Martínez-Fernández Collection.

state-run farms into cooperatives, and the opening of small **farmers' markets**.

The reform measures stemmed the decline of the economy and improved living conditions, but they did not end the crisis. Severe financial problems persist as a result of a deformed economic structure, poor living conditions, strong foreign restrictions, and imbalances in the internal economy. *See also* Nutrition and Food Rationing; Soviet Union, Cuba's Relations with the

Further Readings

Comisión Económica para América Latina (CEPAL). *La economía cubana: reformas económicas y desempeño en los 90*. Mexico City: Fondo de Cultura Económica, 1997.

González Núñez, Gerardo. "Cuba y el mercado mundial." In *Cuba en crisis: perspectivas económicas y políticas*, ed. Jorge Rodríguez Beruff. Río Piedras: Universidad de Puerto Rico, 1995. 43–58.

Lage, Carlos. *El desafío económico de Cuba*. Havana: Ediciones Entorno, 1992.

Mesa-Lago, Carmelo. "Cuba's Economic Policies and Strategies for Confronting the Crisis." In *Cuba after the Cold War*, ed. Carmelo Mesa-Lago. Pittsburgh: University of Pittsburgh Press, 1997.

Valdés, Zoé. *Nada cotidiana*. New York: Arcade Publishers, 1997.

Gerardo González Núñez

Sugar Industry

The sugar industry has been Cuba's most important economic activity since the nineteenth century; it has just recently been displaced by **tourism** as the biggest revenue producer. Enjoying favorable trade conditions in the U.S. market, Cuban sugar production averaged 1 million tons per year from 1892 to 1895. Following the Cuban **War of Independence**, even more favorable circumstances pushed Cuba further into the path of sugar specialization, production reaching 2.5 million tons in

Cuba's Raw Sugar Output (millions of tons)

1985	7.8
1986	7.1
1987	7.0
1988	7.4
1989	8.1
1990	8.0
1991	7.6
1992	7.0
1993	4.2
1994	4.0
1995	3.3
1996	4.5
1997	4.2
1998	3.2
1999	3.8
2000	4.1

Source: Jason Feer et al., *CubaNews' Business Guide to Cuba, 2000* (Washington, DC: *CubaNews*, 2000).

1913 and soaring to 4.2 million tons in 1919. The largest pre-**Revolution** harvest was that of 1953: 7.2 million tons.

During the early years of the Revolution, the government nationalized sugar production and early on attempted to diversify the economy to reduce its dependence on one product, as had been the case for over 100 years. By the late 1960s, however, with generous Soviet subsidies in place, Cuba's leadership made a push for increased sugar production, targeting the **Ten Million Ton Harvest** for 1970. While failing to to reach that goal, the Cuban government invested in the industry's mechanization and purchased larger amounts of pesticides and fertilizers in response to favorable prices throughout the 1970s. All of this boosted production levels.

Favorable conditions persisted until 1989, when the Soviet Union's collapse signaled the end of Soviet subsidies for Cuban sugar. Falling production rates soon evidenced these changes. An average production level of 7.5 million tons during 1985–1992 dropped almost 50 percent to 3.9 million tons during 1993–2000. At the same time sugar dropped from 74.3 percent of all exports in 1985 to 42.5 percent in 1993.

Currently there are 156 mills in Cuba; only 107 of them functioned during the harvest of 2000; and only about 36 of them managed to produce a profit in 1999. Overall, sugar has become a losing sector of the economy, with production costs outpacing the worth of sugar in the world market. About half a million Cuban workers are tied to the sugar sector, and several thousand others work in related industries, such as **transportation** and by-products **manufacturing**. A total of 1.7 million hectares (4.2 million acres) are planted in sugarcane, equivalent to 36 percent of the cultivated surface. *See also* Agriculture; Foreign Investments (Republican Era); Foreign Trade; Hawley-Smoot Tariff Act; Jones-Costigan Act; Soviet Union, Cuba's Relations with the; Special Period; Sugar Plantations

Further Readings

Álvarez, José, and Lázaro Peña Castellanos. *Cuba's Sugar Industry*. Gainesville: University Press of Florida, 2001.

Brunner, Heinrich. *Cuban Sugar Policy from 1963 to 1970*. Pittsburgh: Pittsburgh University Press, 1977.

Feer, Jason L., Teo A. Babun, Jr., et al. *CubaNews Business Guide to Cuba*. Washington, DC: CubaNews, 2000.

Ortiz, Fernando. *Cuban Counterpoint: Tobacco and Sugar*. Durham, NC: Duke University Press, 1995.

Antonio Santamaría García

Tobacco Industry

The tobacco industry has historically been one of Cuba's main economic sectors, and Cuban cigars are universally recognized as the world's finest. The Europeans' first en-

Young woman sorting tobacco leaves in Viñales, Pinar del Río. Photograph by Ernesto Sagás.

counter with tobacco actually took place in eastern Cuba during **Columbus**'s 1492 voyage. During the sixteenth and seventeenth centuries tobacco production developed in small farms called *vegas* that catered to the demands of European smugglers (see **Contraband Trade**). The Spanish colonial state gradually gained increasing control over the production and marketing of tobacco, culminating in 1717 with the imposition of a monopoly through the Real Factoría de Tabacos de La Habana. Cuban tobacco farmers reacted with violence to the new controls in what came to be known as the **Vegueros' Revolts**. One of the results of the clash between producers and the state was the relocation of many farmers to the western part of the island, where particularly in La Vuelta Abajo, **Pinar del Río Province**, optimal conditions for tobacco farming were found. The abolition of the tobacco monopoly in 1817 led to a period of increased production, and Cuba's reputation as the producer of the world's finest tobacco was firmly established. The ravages of the **War of Independence** destroyed hundreds of tobacco vegas, and the subsequent influx of U.S. capital led to the acquisition of tobacco land by U.S. interests. By 1906 the U.S. Tobacco Trust had gained possession of 91,000 hectares (225,000 acres) in the Province of Pinar del Río. Production levels during the first half of the twentieth

century remained low; production averaged 37,900 metric tons during 1952–1958.

Production levels since 1959 have remained at about the same level as during the 1950s, and tobacco farming, unlike most other major agricultural activities, remains in private hands. A record harvest of 54,000 metric tons was accomplished in 1981; production fell sharply in the early to mid-1990s, reaching only 30,000 metric tons in 1996. By the beginning of the twenty-first century production had rebounded to about 45,000 tons, 70 percent of which is produced in the Province of Pinar del Río. Six cigar factories in Havana produced 47 million cigars for export in 1994; by the end of the twentieth century, exports reached 150 million cigars, nearly a third heading for Spain. While the importation of Cuban cigars to the United States remains illegal, U.S. aficionados manage to get hold of them. The most renowned cigar brands are Cohiba, Montecristo, Partagás, and Romeo y Julieta. There is also a major cigarette factory in Boyeros, outside of Havana, with mixed Cuban and Brazilian capital. *See also* Agriculture; Cigars and Cigar Making

Further Readings

Feer, Jason L., Teo A. Babun, Jr., et al. *CubaNews Business Guide to Cuba*. Washington, DC: CubaNews, 2000.

Ortiz, Fernando. *Cuban Counterpoint: Tobacco and Sugar*. Durham, NC: Duke University Press, 1995.

Stubbs, Jean. *Tobacco in the Periphery: A Case Study in Cuban Labour History, 1860–1958*. Cambridge, United Kingdom: Cambridge University Press, 1985.

Luis Martínez-Fernández

Tourism

Cuba's primary source of foreign **currency**, tourism has been a bulwark of the economy since the middle of the 1990s. The history of tourism to Cuba in the

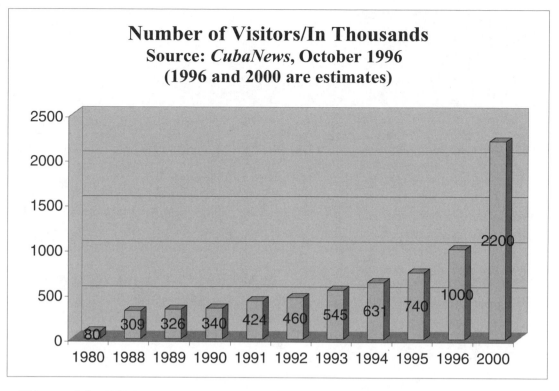

Number of Visitors/In Thousands
Source: *CubaNews*, October 1996
(1996 and 2000 are estimates)

Visitors to Cuba, 1980–2000. Tourism has recently outpaced sugar as Cuba's main source of revenue. Courtesy of *CubaNews*.

twentieth century consists of many unexpected twists and turns. Before 1959, Cuba was the principal vacation destination for travelers to the Caribbean, attracting about 25 percent of the visitors to the region. After the **Revolution**, the Cuban government sought to reduce the importance of tourism to the economy, a policy it maintained until 1990. The economic crisis, brought about by the collapse of the Soviet bloc (see **Special Period**), created a fundamental change in government policy. The Cuban government then saw tourism as central to its strategy of reentering the international economic system.

Since 1990, efforts to rebuild the tourism infrastructure, create new accommodations, and attract investment have intensified. As a result, the number of hotel rooms tripled, growing from about 13,000 in 1990 to nearly 36,000 by 2000. The areas of greatest development are Havana

and Varadero Beach, where 46 percent of the rooms are located (see **Beaches**). Roughly 32 percent of the rooms have been built in the north and central parts of the island, much of it resulting from **foreign investments** and mixed ventures.

With the improvement in accommodations has come a 20 percent annual increase in the number of visitors. In 1990, the number of tourists visiting Cuba was about 327,000. By 2000, the number of tourists climbed to just under 1.8 million. The vast majority of visitors, 55 percent, come from Europe. Visitors from North America and Latin America contribute another 20 and 15 percent, respectively. The largest percentage of national visitors are Canadian (16 percent), followed by Italians (13 percent), Germans (11 percent) and Spaniards (10 percent). While U.S. tourists are banned from visiting Cuba by their government, an estimated 30,000 un-

A Cuban *camello* (camel-shaped bus) traversing Havana's streets. Photograph by Celestino Martínez Lindín.

authorized visits by U.S. citizens took place in 1999. U.S. visitors remain legally barred from Cuban tourism by the restrictions imposed by the **U.S. trade embargo**.

The island is currently experiencing an annual growth rate of 26 percent in tourist receipts. At the present time, tourism accounts for 53 percent of Cuba's foreign exchange. In 1990, Cuba obtained $243 million as a result of the tourist trade, a figure that skyrocketed to $1.9 billion by the end of the decade. Cuba's share of the Caribbean tourism market grew to about 9 percent in 1999, eclipsed by only Puerto Rico, the Dominican Republic, and the Bahamas. *See also* Prostitution

Further Readings

Maribona, Armando R. *Turismo en Cuba*. Havana: Editorial Lex, 1959.

Pattullo, Polly. *Last Resorts: The Cost of Tourism in the Caribbean*. London: Cassell and Latin American Bureau, 1996.

Schwartz, Rosalie. *Pleasure Island: Tourism and Temptation in Cuba*. Lincoln: University of Nebraska Press, 1997.

Gerardo González Núñez

Transportation

The island of Cuba is crisscrossed by a network of roads that extends over 18,750 miles, half of which are paved. The system's principal artery is the Central Highway. A 1,144 kilometer-long (711 miles) highway built in the early 1930s, the Central Highway runs between **Pinar del Río** and **Santiago de Cuba**. Of more recent construction, the National Expressway connects Pinar del Río and Taguasco in the Province of **Villa Clara**. Also of major importance is Vía Blanca, a highway that runs between Havana and **Cárdenas**. By most accounts, Cuba's roads are poorly maintained, and gas stations are few and far between. Relatively few automobiles circulate through Cuba's streets, and roads—many, if not most—date back to the 1950s. Around 4,000 buses offer service to Cubans; several thousand more would be needed to meet actual transportation needs. Many of the circulating buses are the so-called *camellos* (camels): humped trailers pulled by diesel trucks. Recently, the government has allowed the circulation of *boteros*, private cars that pick up passengers along Havana's main thoroughfares for 10 pesos (less than 50 cents U.S.). Land transportation needs are supplemented by the railway system. It consists of 12,800 kilometers (7,955 miles) of track, 4,900 kilometers (3,045 miles) of which provide both cargo and passenger transportation.

The civilian air transportation system consists of eighteen airports, ten of which service international flights. The island's main airport is Havana's **José Martí** International Airport, with a daily average of 450 flights. In 1999 it had more than 4 million passengers entering or leaving. The **Juan Gualberto Gómez** International Airport near Varadero (see **Beaches**) is the island's second busiest. Cubana de Aviación, with a fleet of twenty-eight airplanes, is the island's largest carrier.

Cuba has a large number of harbors and bays that serve as ports; those that handle the largest volume of cargo are Havana, Santiago, Mariel, **Cienfuegos, Matanzas**, and Cárdenas.

During the **Special Period** access to transportation was curtailed. According to official statistics, between 1988 and 1997 the number of buses fell 57 percent and the number of passengers transported dropped 83 percent. *See also* Railroads (Nineteenth Century); Tourism; Self-Employment

Further Reading
Feer, Jason L., Teo A. Babun, Jr., et al. *CubaNews Business Guide to Cuba*. Washington, DC: CubaNews, 2000.

Luis Martínez-Fernández

University of Havana (Universidad de La Habana)

The oldest and best-known institution of higher learning in the country, the University of Havana was founded in 1728 by the members of the Dominican priestly order and soon became a symbol of cultural development and sophistication in the Spanish colony. It did, however, exclude women, non-Catholics, and people of color. Historically, it has been the birthplace of radical student organizations, as well as the site of rallies and protests. Today, more than 8,000 students attend the university, which includes fourteen different schools and fifteen independent centers.

The original site of the university, then known as the Real y Pontificia Universidad de San Gerónimo de La Habana, was the Convent of San Juan de Letrán in **Habana Vieja (Old Havana)**. It became a secular institution in 1842 and officially became known as the University of Havana in 1899. It relocated to its current location on a hill overlooking the Vedado section of Havana in 1927. Gardens and terraces surround the university grounds. The most dominant feature is the monumental staircase of eighty-eight steps, known as the "Escalinata," which forms the entrance to the grounds. Cuban architects Raúl Otero and César Guerra and French urban planner Nicolás Forestier drew up the plans for the university. At the top of the staircase is a large statue of a seated woman, known as *Alma Mater*, created by Czech sculptor Mario Korbel.

The tradition of student activism at the university dates back to the colonial period when many at the institution backed the independence movement. In November 1871, Spanish authorities executed eight University of Havana medical students charged with desecrating the grave of a Spanish officer. In 1922, students led by

Main entrance to the University of Havana. Photograph by Celestino Martínez Lindín.

Julio Antonio Mella supported a reform movement aimed at cleaning up the government and addressing socioeconomic inequities in Cuba. The students seized several buildings on campus and demanded reforms such as free higher education, university autonomy, and the dismissal of incompetent professors, some of whom were sinecure holders. The rector eventually resigned, corrupt professors were fired, and faculty and students thereafter elected the position of rector every two years. In that same year, the students organized the First Congress of Cuban Students and a formal governing body, known as the Federación Estudiantil Universitaria (FEU) (**Federation of University Students**). Activism reached new levels in the 1930s during the struggle to oust President **Gerardo Machado** from power. In an effort to clamp down on student opposition, Machado closed the uni-

versity in 1930, which, contrary to his plan, left the students more time to plot against the government. Two student organizations, the Directorio Estudiantil Universitario (University Student Directorate) and the Ala Izquierda Estudiantil (Student Left Wing), played key roles in the struggle against Machado and the subsequent ouster of his U.S.-backed replacement, Carlos Manuel de Céspedes y Quesada. The Directorio would ultimately form an alliance with the enlisted men of the army and select university professor **Ramón Grau San Martín** as president of the nation.

In 1934, the university was reopened and later that year granted autonomy, which meant it was free from the **Ministry of the Interior** and Ministry of Education. As a result of this autonomy, the campus provided a sanctuary in downtown Havana where police and soldiers were not permitted to enter. Once students reached the famous steps leading to the university, they could no longer be pursued. Thus, the campus became not only a safe place for political meetings, but also a center for violent antigovernment conspiracies. In the 1940s and 1950s, the university was dominated by so-called action groups, which in some cases were nothing more than gangsters allied to different political factions. Students pursued weapons and revolution rather than an education. These gangs moved into the business of monopolizing the sale of textbooks as well as examination papers and grades. One of the more famous student radicals from the university was **Fidel Castro**. His student years were spent mostly in political activity. The university was home to anti–**Fulgencio Batista** groups following his coup in 1952. Like Machado before him, Batista closed the university for several years to crack down on dissent. University students, including most notably FEU President **José Antonio Echeverría**, led a failed attack on the **Presidential Palace** and CMQ radio station in 1957. Echeverría and many other students were killed. After the triumph of the **Revolution**, a committee was established to purge Batista supporters from the faculty and administration. The revolutionary government has kept a tight grip on student organizations, and the days of violent student protest against the government are over. As part of its educational policy, the government has sought to expand the number of subjects at the university to provide a greater emphasis on the sciences, economics, and agriculture. *See also* Students' Movement (Republican Era).

Further Readings

Armas, Ramón de, Eduardo Torres-Cuevas and Ana Cairo Ballester. *Historia de la Universidad de La Habana*. Havana: Editorial de Ciencias Sociolog, 1984.

Cabrera, Olga, and Carmen Almodóvar, eds. *Las luchas estudiantiles universitarias*. Havana: Editorial de Ciencias Sociales, 1975.

Suchlicki, Jaime. *University Students and Revolution in Cuba, 1920–1968*. Coral Gables, FL: University of Miami Press, 1969.

Paula J. Pettavino

Women's Rights

Prior to the triumph of the **Revolution**, Cuban women had already won some very significant victories, including the right to vote. Many of these advances were codified in the **Constitution of 1940**. The structural changes created by the Revolution further broke down social and class barriers for poor Cuban women, so that rural women, domestics, orphans, and prostitutes were able to attend schools and enter professions. Legislation was subsequently passed allowing women greater equality and access to the workplace. The Código del Trabajo (Labor Code) established Comisiones de Empleo Femenino (Commissions of Feminine Employment) in all segments of the workforce to eliminate prohibitions on female employment. The 1975 **Family Code** further established women's rights, particularly addressing family matters including marriage, **divorce**, parental issues, nutrition, adoption, and guardianship.

The **Constitution of 1976**, amended in 1992, stipulates that women must be treated equally for all employment. It also established within the **National Assembly of People's Power** a Permanent Commission on Infancy, Youth, and Equal Rights for Women. The government also supported a National Action Plan on women's rights as proposed by the IV United Nations Conference on Women and established the necessary government commissions to monitor progress.

As of 2000, women made up 42.5 percent of the workforce in the state-sponsored civil sector. In the nonstate sectors of the economy, including private companies, cooperatives, and **agriculture**, women comprised 18 percent of the workforce as of 1997. Almost 65 percent of all Cuban professionals and technicians are women. Approximately 28 percent of Cuba's **National Assembly of People's Power** (Legislature) are women. As of 2000, there were fourteen women ambassadors and eleven female consul generals. Women occupied two ministerial positions: the Ministry of Science, Technology and the Environment and the Ministry of Internal Commerce. There are now seventeen vice ministers serving in the various departments, including two in the Ministry of Foreign Affairs. *See also* Federation of Cuban Women; (Federación de Mujeres Cubanas [FMC]); Feminist Movement (Republican Era); Prostitution; Women's Suffrage Movement; Abortion; Espín Guillois, Vilma; Santamaría Cuadrodo, Haydeé

Further Readings

Molyneux, Maxime. "State, Gender and Institutional Change. The Federación de Mujeres Cubanas." In *Hidden Histories of Gender and the State in Latin America*, ed. Elizabeth Dore and Maxine Molyneux. Durham, NC: Duke University Press, 2000. 291–321.

Smith, Lois M., and Alfred, Padula. *Sex and Revolution: Women in Socialist Cuba*. New York: Oxford University Press, 1996.

Julio César González Pagés

7

Literature and the Social Sciences

Abolitionist Literature

Abolitionist literature was the response of the nineteenth-century Cuban intelligentsia to the tension generated by the Haitian Revolution (1791–1803), a slave revolt in the French colony of Saint Domingue that led to the exile of planters to Oriente, transforming that Cuban region into an important sugar producer and a major slave importer (see **Slave Trade**). This resulted in a presence of blacks that outnumbered white Creoles as well as major slave rebellion plots that included the **Aponte** Conspiracy (1812) and the **Conspiracy of La Escalera** (1844). In addition, European abolitionist humanitarianism of the period (in Great Britain, France, Denmark, and the United States, for example) was also influential among a group of Cuban writers such as Emilio Blanchet, **Domingo del Monte, José Jacinto Milanés**, Pedro José Morillas, **Ramón de Palma y Romay, José Antonio Saco**, Anselmo Suárez y Romero, Félix Tanco y Bosmeniel, **Cirilo Villaverde**, and José Zacarías González del Valle, who wrote against the institution of **slavery**. In the 1830s there were a great number of abolitionist narratives caught in a politico-literary discourse that depicted the injustices to which blacks and slaves

were subjected and also the colonial situation of the country under Spanish rule. Antislavery literature encompassed multiple agendas, the most notable of which included ending the slave trade in order to reform Cuba's social, economic, and political institutions, gaining support from Europe, and exalting the vitality of black culture as an integral part of Cuba's search for cultural independence from Spain. Mentored by the intellectual Domingo del Monte, the young group of *delmontinos* started producing abolitionist texts that challenged slavery and developed a sentiment of regional consciousness by incorporating Cuban themes and characters. This perspective made their writings an integral part of Cuban cultural identity and literature. Among the most significant of these are **Juan Francisco Manzano**'s *Autobiografía*, written in 1839; **Gertrudis Gómez de Avellaneda**'s novel *Sab* (1841) (although she was not a direct member of this group, the antislavery topic of this novel affiliated her with them ideologically); Félix Tanco y Bosmeniel's articles *Escenas de la vida privada en la isla de Cuba* and the novel *Petrona y Rosalía*, both published in 1838; Anselmo Suárez y Romero's novel *Francisco: el ingenio o las delicias del campo* (1839); Pedro José

Morillas's *El rancheador* (1839 and 1858); Antonio Zambrana's novel *El negro Francisco* (1873); and Cirilo Villaverde's novel *Cecilia Valdés o la loma del Ángel: novela de costumbres cubanas* (1839, 1882).

Further Readings

Luis, William. *Literary Bondage: Slavery in Cuban Narrative*. Austin: University of Texas Press, 1990.

Williams, Lorna Valerie. *The Representation of Slavery in Cuban Fiction*. Columbia: University of Missouri Press, 1994.

Ilia Casanova-Marengo

Acosta, Agustín (1886–1979)

Agustín Acosta is a poet recognized as the precursor of a poetic movement that emerged during the 1920s reaffirming Cuban nationalism and criticizing foreign monopolistic influences on the island.

Acosta was born in **Matanzas** and became an attorney in 1918. Along with poet Regino Boti and José Manuel Poveda, Acosta inspired poetic activities and a cultural renaissance in the provinces rather than in the capital, the usual center of literary enterprise. His most important book of poetry was *La zafra*, published in 1926. Two poems in this collection, "Las carretas de la noche" and "Mediodía en el campo," transformed him into Cuba's national poet. His books included *Los camellos distantes* (1941), *Las islas desoladas* (1943), *Últimos instantes* (1941), and *Caminos de hierro* (1963).

In the 1930s, Acosta was arrested during the regime of **Gerardo Machado**; when Machado was overthrown, Acosta was appointed governor of **Matanzas Province**. From 1936 to 1944 he also served as senator. Leaving Cuba in 1973, he settled in Miami, where he passed away in 1979. In 1988, a posthumous book titled *Poemas escogidos* was published in Cuba.

Further Readings

Capote, María. *Agustín Acosta: el modernista y su isla*. Miami: Ediciones Universal, 1990.

Forés, Aldo R. *La poesía de Agustín Acosta, poeta nacional de Cuba*. Miami: Ediciones Universal, 1976–1977.

Wilfredo Cancio Isla

Alonso, Dora (1910–2001)

Dora Alonso was born and educated in **Matanzas**. She also went by the pseudonyms Nora Lin and D. Polimita. Best known for her novel *Tierra inerme* (1961), for which she won the **Casa de las Américas** prize, Alonso was one of the pioneers in the children's and juvenile genres, which experienced a strong resurgence following the **literacy campaign** of 1961. Though she was born into a **cattle ranching** family and her education was limited to the primary grades, a young Alonso made a name for herself early on when she was published in the newspaper *Prensa Libre*, **Cárdenas**, in 1930 and was active in politics at the local and national levels. Winner of literary prizes in all of the genres she cultivated, Alonso was awarded the short-story prize by the magazine *Bohemia* in 1936; the Ministry of Education's national award for her novel *Tierra adentro* in 1944; the "E.J. Varona" journalism award in 1946 (see **Enrique José Varona**). In 1947, one of Alonso's short stories won first prize in the prestigious Hernández Catá literary contest. The same year, her play *La hora de estar ciegos* won the Luis de Soto award, and in 1959 she was granted the Ministry of Education's award for her comedy *La casa de los sueños*.

Alonso's fiction concentrates on marginalized characters, the reality of the Cuban peasantry, and their struggles against the forces of nature and governmental indifference (see **Guajiros**). Her children's stories and novels are written in a conversational style with an easy-to-follow plot and narrative and often render tribute to Cuba's natural beauty.

The recipient of the 1988 National Literature Award, Alonso also wrote for radio and television. *See also* Newspapers (Republican Era)

Further Reading
Perdomo, Omar, ed. *Dora Alonso: letras y cubanía.* Matanzas, Cuba: Editorial Matanzas, 1999.

Pamela María Smorkaloff

Arenas, Reinaldo (1943–1990)

Reinaldo Arenas was born in **Holguín**, old Oriente Province. After completing a degree in accounting, Arenas moved to Havana in 1962. In 1964 he entered the **University of Havana**, first pursuing a degree in economics, later in arts and letters, but never completed his studies. Arenas worked at the **Biblioteca Nacional José Martí**, the Instituto del Libro, and **Casa de las Américas** and collaborated with the journals *Unión, Casa de las Américas, El Caimán Barbudo,* and *La Gaceta de Cuba,* where he worked as an editor (see **Newspapers and Magazines**). In Cuba, he published the novel *Celestino antes del alba* in 1967. His second novel, *El mundo alucinante: una novela de aventuras,* was published in Mexico in 1969. Based on the life, times, and published memoirs of Fray Servando Teresa de Mier, *Fray Servando* embodies Latin America's ongoing quest for liberation and the right to self-representation. Arena's re-creation of the life of the Mexican friar raised important questions of historical interpretation and cultural practice at a time when Cuban society was in the process of remaking itself. An outspoken dissident and openly gay man (see **Gays and Lesbians**), Arenas fled Cuba in 1980 as part of the **Mariel boatlift**. He established himself in New York, where his literary production continued and grew more prolific. Arenas remained steadfast in his attitudes, casting a critical eye on New York society as he had once done in Havana. Author of numerous

Reinaldo Arenas, leading literary figure of the Mariel Generation. Reinaldo Arenas Papers, Manuscripts Division, Department of Rare Books and Special Collections, Princeton University Library.

literary works and an autobiography, *Antes que anochezca* (1992), Arenas committed suicide in New York in 1990 rather than succumb to **AIDS**.

Of those Cuban writers who emigrated in 1980, Arenas distinguished himself by remaining productive. After his arrival, he founded the magazine and publishing house *Mariel* in 1983 (see **Mariel Generation**). Though he was marginalized on the island, outside of Cuba Arenas is considered a major figure in contemporary Latin American literature. Almost all of Arenas's oeuvre has been translated into English, including his autobiography, published in 1993 with the title *Before Night Falls.* This book was adapted for the screen in 2000. *See also* Dissent and Defections (1959–   ); Literary Journals; Literature of the Revolutionary Era

Further Readings

Arenas, Reinaldo. *Before Night Falls*. Trans. Delores M. Koch. New York: Viking Press, 1993.

Ette, Ottmar, ed. *La escritura de la memoria: Reinaldo Arenas: Textos, estudios y documentación*. Frankfurt am Maim: Vervuert Verlag, 1992.

Soto, Francisco. *Reinaldo Arenas: The Pentagonía*. Gainesville: University Press of Florida, 1994.

Pamela María Smorkaloff

Árrate y Acosta, José Martín Félix de (1701–1765)

Author of one of the first texts of the Cuban historiography of the eigteenth century, José Martín Félix de Árrate y Acosta was the son of lieutenant Santiago de Árrate y Vera, treasurer of the Royal Treasury, and Juana María de Acosta y Martínez, a native of Havana. He studied law in Mexico and, as a member of the Cuban oligarchy, was appointed alderman of the municipality of Havana in 1734 and was elevated to mayor in 1752. His texts *Llave del Nuevo Mundo* and *Antemural de las Indias Occidentales* earned him a place in Cuba's history. *La Habana descripta: noticias de su fundación, aumentos y estados* was written between 1750 and 1761—a short time before the **British occupation of Havana**. The original manuscript is unknown, but a version of it was published by the **Sociedad Económica de Amigos del País** in 1830. With a sober style and based on several reputed sources, Árrate expressed in its forty-nine chapters the pride of being a part of Havana's community and the native oligarchy confronting the centralist directives of the Spanish crown. Without challenging the institution of **slavery**, he recognized the advantages there might have been to conserving the **indigenous inhabitants**. In addition to their historical relevance, Árrate's works are also important for their political context.

Further Reading

Fornet, Ambrosio. *El libro en Cuba, siglos XVIII y XIX*. Havana: Editorial Letras Cubanas, 1994.

María Dolores González-Ripoll Navarro

Arrufat, Antón (1935–   )

Antón Arrufat is an independent-minded intellectual and writer associated with many of the principal Cuban cultural and **literary journals** of the 1950s–1990s. Widely recognized as a playwright, he is also a respected poet, novelist, and critic. A member of the post-***Orígenes*** fourth literary generation, Arrufat remains in Cuba writing works that reflect his interest in time and its effects on people.

Born in **Santiago de Cuba** and educated in the city's Jesuit elementary school, Arrufat also attended the Instituto de La Habana (1950–1955) from which he earned his high school degree, and in 1979 he received a degree in philology from the **University of Havana**. From 1957 to 1959 he resided in the United States. Early in his literary career he contributed to ***Ciclón*** along with **Virgilio Piñera**, who became his close friend and mentor-confidant. Interest in the theater of the absurd, the avant-garde, and surrealism shapes much of his work, but it was his first work as a mature writer—*Los siete contra Tebas* (1968), a play based on the Greek tragedy by Aeschylus—that was interpreted as counterrevolutionary by some of the **Cuban Communist Party** leadership. Nevertheless, *Los siete contra Tebas* received the **Unión de Escritores y Artistas de Cuba**'s (UNEAC's) José Antonio Ramos Prize upon publication. But as a result of the **Padilla Affair**, stricter state censorship of cultural production followed the release of the play, which was not performed, like his other works, for nearly twenty-five years.

Arrufat held important positions as a contributor to and editor of many Cuban journals. He served on the staff of ***Lunes*** *de Revolución*; from 1960 to 1965 he was editor of *Casa de las Américas* (see **Casa de las Américas**); and he worked as a collaborator for *La Gaceta de Cuba* and *Revolución y Cultura*, for which he was also editor. His contributions appear in *Unión* and *Cuba en la UNESCO*. Among his principal books are *De las pequeñas cosas* (1997), *Lirios sobre un fondo de espadas* (1995), *Las pequeñas cosas* (1988), and *La caja está cerrada* (1984).

In 2000, Arrufat was awarded Cuba's National Literary Prize. *See also* Newspapers and Magazines

Further Reading

Arrufat, Antón. *Antología personal*. Barcelona: Mondadori, 2001.

Peter T. Johnson

Balboa Troya y Quesada, Silvestre de (1563–1634?)

Silvestre de Balboa is best known for his epic poem *Espejo de paciencia* (1608) the first important text in the Cuban literary corpus. A native of the Canary Islands, it is not known precisely when he arrived in Cuba. It is clear, however, that he lived in Puerto Príncipe (**Camagüey**), where he served as notary of the Religious Council. The poem was written in royal octaves and divided in two sections: The first part narrates the kidnapping of the Bishop Juan de las Cabezas Altamirano by the French pirate Gilberto Girón and his subsequent rescue after the delivery of a booty that consisted of money and provisions (see **Corsairs Attacks**); the second part focuses on how the inhabitants of **Bayamo** took revenge on the abuses suffered by the bishop. The inclusion of Salvador, an African slave who killed the French corsair, made this poem a pioneer text in that it presented positively a black character in Cuban (and, therefore, in Latin American) literature. *Espejo de paciencia* draws its title from the virtuous personality by means

of which the bishop suffered his captivity that ultimately made him a "mirror" to reflect upon, a model worthy of imitation. Balboa's poem has been valued for its description of the **flora**, **fauna**, and seventeenth-century Cuban society, but it also has awakened a series of debates on whether or not it was used by the nineteenth-century Cuban intelligentsia to trace the origin of a national literary discourse in its nation-building stage.

Further Readings

Bueno, Salvador. *Historia de la literatura cubana*. Havana: Editorial Minerva, 1959.

Laurencio Aparicio, Ángel. Introduction. *Espejo de paciencia*. By Silvestre de Balboa Troya y Quesada. Miami: Ediciones Universal, 1970.

Ilia Casanova-Marengo

Baquero, Gastón (1918–1997)

Poet and essayist Gastón Baquero was one of the original members of a group who published the literary journal **Orígenes**. Though Baquero favored free verses and explored nationalistic themes, his poetry also reveals literary influences from the Spanish poets of the Golden Age as well as the British Romantic poets. Baquero's poetry examined reality and everyday events from the perspective of a detached philosophical observer interested in understanding the power of words and symbols; a poem representative of this approach is "Palabras escritas en la arena por un inocente." As a journalist, Baquero wrote editorials and columns on literature as well as on political events in and out of Cuba. His most popular and best-known nonfiction book is *Indios, blancos y negros en el caldero de América* (1991).

Of humble origins, Baquero published his first poems and articles when he was eighteen years old. At the beginning of the Cuban **Revolution**, Baquero supported the new regime, but as the government demanded more political participation from writers, Baquero felt the need to leave the island. In 1959, Baquero went into exile in Spain, where he died in 1997.

Though Baquero received numerous awards, including the Order of Alfonso X, the Wise, and the José Antonio Rivero national prize for poetry, he has not attracted as much critical attention as some of his contemporaries and colleagues, including **José Lezama Lima** and **Cintio Vitier**. His many books of poetry include *Memorial de un testigo* (1966), *Poemas invisibles* (1991), and *Poesía completa* (1998). *See also* Literary Journals

Further Reading

Ortega, Alfonso C., and Alfredo Pérez Alecant. *Celebración de la existencia: homenaje al poeta cubano Gastón Baquero*. Salamanca: Universidad Pontificia de Salamanca, 1994.

D.H. Figueredo

Barnet, Miguel (1940–   )

Internationally renowned novelist, poet, and ethnographer, Miguel Barnet was born in Havana and studied social sciences at the **University of Havana**. He continued his studies in 1960 at the Seminario de Etnología y Folkore. He has been a professor of folklore and a researcher at the Instituto de Etnología of the **Academy of Sciences** and is currently president of the Fundación **Fernando Ortiz** in Havana.

Author of numerous volumes of poetry, much of it collected in the book *Con pies de gato* (1994), Barnet is perhaps best known for his groundbreaking testimonial work *Biografía de un cimarrón* (1966), widely translated and disseminated (see **Cimarrones**). German composer Hans Werner Henze's opera *Cimarrón* is based on that work. Barnet's testimonial novel *Canción de Rachel* (1969) served as the basis for the film *La bella del Alhambra* (1989). *Gallego* (1981), the third testimonial novel of the trilogy initiated with *Cimarrón*, chronicles the life of one of many

Spanish immigrants on the island (see **Immigration [Twentieth Century]**). It too served as the basis for the film *Gallego* (1987). Barnet's most recent novel, *La vida real* (1986), researched in New York with a Guggenheim award, follows the life of Julián Mesa, one of the many Cuban labor migrants who arrived in New York in the 1940s and 1950s.

Considered by some Cuba's most celebrated contemporary author, Barnet's short story "Miosvatis" was the central fiction piece in the 1998 *New Yorker* magazine's special issue on Cuba. Some of his ethnographic writings include *La fuente viva* (1983) and *Cultos afrocubanos: la regla de Ocha, la regla de Palo Monte* (1995). *See also* Literature of the Revolutionary Era

Further Reading

Azougarh, Abdeslam. *Miguel Barnet: rescate e invención de la memoria*. Geneva: Slatkine, 1996.

Pamela María Smorkaloff

Benítez Rojo, Antonio (1931–   )

Essayist, narrator, and literary critic, Antonio Benítez Rojo is highly regarded as one of the most original literary figures of our times. He was trained in economics and finance, at institutions both in Havana and in Washington, D.C., and worked as a statistician. He has also held positions as vice director for theater and dance for the Cuban Council of Culture and as director of the Center for Caribbean Studies of **Casa de las Américas**. Benítez Rojo came to the immediate attention of readers with the publication of *Tute de Reyes* (1967), a collection of short stories that earned him the prestigious Casa de las Américas prize. His recognition continued with *El escudo de hojas secas* (1969), awarded the **Unión de Escritores y Artistas de**

Cuba (UNEAC) prize. He also published *Heróica, and Los inquilinos* (1976), *La tierra y el cielo* (1978), *Fruta verde* (1979), and the novel *El mar de las lentejas* (1979), in which the English merchant-privateer John Hawkins is one among four narrative voices in a historic novel with an absent center. He has also written three screenplays; *Los sobrevivientes* received the UNEAC Best Screenplay prize for 1979. Benítez Rojo's writings reflect his vast knowledge of history and culture.

In 1980 Benítez Rojo left Cuba and currently resides in the United States. He has held visiting appointments at various universities and since 1983 has taught at Amherst College, where he is the Thomas B. Walton, Jr. Memorial Professor. In the United States, Benítez Rojo has established himself as an exceptional literary critic, especially with his writings on the Caribbean and **Alejo Carpentier**. This is especially the case with his *La isla que se repite* (1989), as he applies concepts of the plantation and chaos theory to the Caribbean. He has also published *Estatuas sepultadas y otros relatos* (1984), *Magic Dog and Other Stories* (1990), *Antología personal* (1997), and *A View from the Mangrove* (1998). Most recently, Benítez Rojo completed *mujer en traje de batalla* (2001), a work about Henriette Faber who hid her sexual identity to study medicine and fight in the Napoleonic Wars. In this exceptional and ambitious novel, the author follows Faber from Europe to Cuba to New Orleans. *See also* Literature of the Revolutionary Era

Further Readings

González Echevarría, Roberto. Prólogo. *Estatuas sepultadas y otros relatos*. Hanover, NH: Ediciones del Norte, 1984.

Ortega, Julio. "Los cuentos de Antonio Benítez Rojo." In *El cuento hispanoamericano ante la crítica*, ed. Enrique Pupo Walker. Madrid: Editorial Castalia, 1973. 264–278.

Sklodowska, Elzbieta. "La cuentística de Antonio Benítez Rojo: La experiencia revolucionaria desde la marginalidad." *Cuban Studies*, no. 1 (Winter 1984): 17–24.

William Luis

Betancourt, Luis Victoriano (1843–1885)

Luis Victoriano Betancourt was the secretary and president of the House of Representatives of Cuba's provisional government during the **Ten Years' War**. A journalist and poet, Betancourt wrote for numerous publications that espoused Cuban independence from the Spanish crown. His most famous poem is titled "Simpatías del destino." The poem praises the courage and loyalty of the Cuban insurgents fighting against the Spanish government. In the poem, Betancourt promises his mother that he will not see her again until Cuba is freed from Spanish rule.

Betancourt was an attorney, a frequent contributor to numerous pro-independence newspapers, including *El Cubano Libre, La Estrella Solitaria*, and *Boletín de la Revolución*, and the founder of the satirical magazine *Rigoletto* (see **Press and Journalism [Eighteenth and Nineteenth Centuries]**). He was also a well-known orator. His articles, essays, and poetry, published in the volume *Artículos de costumbres y poesías* (1867), depicted Cuban life during the nineteenth century as well as patriotic themes. After the Ten Years' War, he worked as an attorney and a teacher.

Further Reading

Rodríguez Cuetara, Eva. *Luis Victoriano Betancourt, vida y obra*. Havana: Centro de Estudios Políticos y Sociales de Cuba, 1949.

D.H. Figueredo

Borrero, Juana (1877–1896)

Juana Borrero, together with her sister Dulce María and her father **Esteban Borrero Echeverría**, presided over one of the most influential literary *tertulias* (alternate spaces in which culture and the arts flourished) of the day. Their home in the Marianao district of Havana, where she was born, became known as the "House of Poets" in the difficult period characterized by the demise of Spanish colonial rule and growing uncertainty over what the Republic would bring. A painter and poet, her poems appeared in the anthology *Grupo de familia, poesías de los Borrero* as well as journals such as *La Habana Elegante, El Fígaro*, and *Gris y Azul*. In 1892, she traveled to New York with her father and met **José Martí**, who hosted a literary soirée in her honor. In 1895, as a result of Esteban's involvement in the insurrection, the entire family was forced to emigrate to Key West, Florida. That same year, she published a book of poetry titled *Rimas*. A vast selection of her correspondence was published posthumously in two volumes, *Epistolario*. *See also* Political Exile (Nineteenth Century); Press and Journalism (Eighteenth and Nineteenth Centuries); Uhrbach, Carlos Pío

Further Reading

Cuza Malé, Belkis. *El clavel y la rosa: biografía de Juana Borrero*. Madrid: Ediciones Cultura Hispánica, 1984.

Pamela María Smorkaloff

Borrero Echeverría, Esteban (1849–1906)

In 1863, Esteban Borrero Echeverría opened a night school for adults in **Camagüey**. So devoted was this young teacher to his students that in 1868 the students followed him into the Cuban countryside where they joined the insurgents fighting against the Spanish government during the **Ten Year's War**. In the battlefields, Borrero Echeverría founded two schools and continued teaching, while also proving himself a brave soldier, earning the rank of colonel. Captured by the

Spanish, he persuaded the authorities not to sentence him to death. He then relocated to Havana, where again he worked as a teacher. In the 1890s, he lived in the United States, returning home after Cuba achieved independence in 1902 (see **Political Exile [Nineteenth Century]**).

Highly educated, Borrero Echeverría was a trained physician and a teacher. He edited numerous pedagogical and scientific journals, including *Revista Cubana* and *Revista de Ciencias Médicas de La Habana* (see **Press and Journalism [Eighteenth and Nineteenth Centuries]**). He was a prolific author of articles and books on teaching, science, and medicine. As a poet, he wrote melancholic pieces on the pain of separation from loved ones and the loneliness of exile. In 1878, he published the book *Poesía*. He also wrote fiction and autobiographical essays, using both genres as avenues for social, philosophical, and political comments. *See also* Borrero, Juana; Science and Scientists (Eighteenth and Nineteenth Centuries)

Further Readings

Garrandés, Alberto. *Tres Cuentistas Cubanos*. Havana: Editoral Letras Cubanas, 1993.

Remoz y Ratio, Juan J. *El genio de Esteban Borrero Echeverría en la vida, en la Ciencia y en el arte*. Havana: Imprenta "Avisador Comercial," 1930.

D.H. Figueredo

Byrne, Bonifacio (1861–1936)

Born in **Matanzas**, Bonifacio Byrne showed literary talent as an adolescent and wrote poetry, fiction, and drama. His first book of poems *Excéntricas* (1893) was well received by the *modernistas*. Byrne's separatist beliefs sent him into exile to Tampa in 1896, where he wrote and agitated for the independence cause.

Byrne returned to Cuba in 1899 and there penned his most famous poem, "My Flag," expressing dismay at seeing the

U.S. flag flying alongside his own (see **National Flag**). Byrne published three books of poems between 1897 and 1903, then turned to theater, writing six plays from 1905 to 1920. But poetry was his true metier, and he is known as a civic poet in the best sense of the word. His patriotic verse *Efigies* (1897) may now seem like a historical relic, but Byrne was a solid writer of sonnets, knew his craft well, and produced a work that was an intriguing blend of romanticism, realism, *modernismo*, and classicism.

Byrne founded several newspapers, among them: *La Mañana, La Juventud Liberal* and *El Yucayo*. Byrne was voted Prominent Son of Matanzas in 1915 and was a corresponding member of the Cuban Academy of Arts and Letters. In 1920 he was awarded a pension for life by the Cuban Legislature. When he died in 1936, he left some forty unpublished books. *See also* Political Exile (Nineteenth Century); Press and Journalism (Eighteenth and Nineteenth Centuries)

Further Readings

Febles, Jorge. "Bonifacio Byrne." In *Dictionary of Twentieth-Century Cuban Literature*, ed. Julio A. Martínez. Westport, CT: Greenwood Press, 1990. 94–96.

Martínez, Carmenate Urbano. *Bonifacio Byrne*. Havana: Editora Política, 1999.

Moliner, Israel. *Índice bio-bibliográfico de Bonifacio Byrne*. Matanzas: Carreño, 1943.

Alan West-Durán

Cabrera, Lydia (1900–1991)

Lydia Cabrera was a scholar and short-story writer whose works are rooted in the traditions, beliefs, and customs of the Afro-Cuban culture (see **Afro-Cubans**). Born in Havana, Cabrera went to Paris in 1927 to study painting at the École du Louvre. In 1936 she published her first book, *Contes nègres de Cuba* (*Cuentos negros de Cuba*, 1940), a collection of twenty-two short stories that describe the

Anthropologist Lydia Cabrera was a pioneer in Afro-Cuban studies. Courtesy of the Cuban Heritage Collection of the Otto G. Richter Library of the University of Miami.

customs, language, and spirituality of the Afro-Cuban culture and blur the borders between magic and reality. The primary influence in this work is the awakening interest in African culture and values developed by French-speaking African authors in France during the 1930s and tales that she heard during her childhood from black servants at her father's house.

After her return to Cuba from Paris in 1939, Cabrera embraced the study of superstitions, traditions, legends, and religious beliefs of black Cubans. As a result, she published an extensive collection of texts dedicated to their music, dance, medicine, language, and tales. Of special importance is *El monte: Igbo, finda, ewe orisha, vititi nfinda: notas sobre las religiones, la magia, las supersticiones y el folklore de los negros criollos y del pueblo de Cuba* (1954), a study that describes the Afro-Cuban religious, curative, and ritual cosmos. In 1959 she abandoned Cuba and established herself in Miami, where she wrote *Ayapa, cuentos de jicotea* (1971) and *Yemayá y Ochún* (1974). An endowment that she left funds the Lydia Cabrera Prize, awarded yearly by the Conference on Latin American History. *See also* Palo Monte; Santería; Abakuá, Sociedad de

Further Readings

Castellanos, Isabel, and Josefina Inclán, eds. *En torno a Lydia Cabrera: (cincuentenario de cuentos negros de Cuba), 1936–1986.* Miami: Ediciones Universal, 1987.

Madrigal, José Antonio, and Reynaldo Sánchez, eds. *Homenaje a Lydia Cabrera.* Miami: Ediciones Universal, 1978.

Ilia Casanova-Marengo

Cabrera Infante, Guillermo (1929–)

Guillermo Cabrera Infante, major figure of contemporary Cuban literature. AP/Wide World Photos. Photograph by S. Barrenechea/EFE.

Also known as G. Caín, Guillermo Cabrera Infante is a provocactive writer in every sense of the word: aesthetically, politically, and personally. One need not agree with him to recognize he is a consummate word master, a man of refreshing (if not galling) candor, a writer entranced by the powers of fiction. Cabrera's ear is extraordinary; his ability to recreate Cuban popular speech is unparalleled. His work is hard to classify since his plots are often fragmented; the narratives are interrupted by wordplays, parodies, and a self-conscious narrator who often digresses. Within a single work, Cabrera Infante veers from fantasy to autobiographical reflection, from mock essay to stream-of-consciousness, from refined satire to vignettes laced with locker room humor.

Born into a family of communists, Cabrera Infante was never politically active, although he was opposed to the **Fulgencio Batista** dictatorship. A self-proclaimed addict of **cinema**, Cabrera was one of the cofounders of the Cuban Cinemateca (1951) and was film critic for *Carteles* magazine from 1954 to 1960 (see **Literary Journals**). While all of his work has cinematic influences, he has published three books specifically on the subject: *Un oficio del siglo XX* (1963), *Arcadia todas las noches* (1978), and *Cine y sardina* (1997).

Cabrera Infante was an early supporter of the **Revolution** and cofounder of *Lunes de Revolución*, the weekly cultural supplement of the newspaper *Revolución*, closed in November 1961 following the controversy over his brother Saba's film *P.M.* and the infamously tense meetings between the regime and intellectuals in June 1961.

Cabrera Infante was made cultural attaché in Brussels in 1962. In 1965, he returned to Cuba to attend his mother's funeral, and upon his return to Belgium, he resigned his post and moved to London (1966), where he still resides. In 1968 he openly broke with the regime and has been a trenchant critic ever since. *Mea Cuba* (1992) features political writings, speeches, and lectures from 1968 to 1992.

His first book of short stories *Así en*

la paz como en la guerra (1960) is a traditional work that imaginatively reveals the sordid dimensions of Cuban life under the Batista dictatorship. In 1964 Cabrera won the prestigious Biblioteca Breve Prize. Originally with a different title, when it was published in 1967 it was called *Tres tristes tigres* and had been radically revised. *Tres tristes tigres* was an immediate success and is one of the cornerstone novels of the 1960s Latin American Boom. It is an imaginative and hilarious re-creation of 1950s Havana as seen through five unruly protagonists. The author has described the theme as "betrayal in language, literature and love." The novel is also about writing and the adventures of the word.

In 1974 Cabrera Infante published *Vista del amanecer en el trópico*, using the material he had removed from *Tres tristes tigres*. It is a spare and unsparing work, offering a moving, poetic, and sometimes bleak view of Cuban history. *La Habana para un infante difunto* (1979) is a series of tales about sexual adventure and frustration, written with his customary verbal pyrotechnics and humor.

Cabrera Infante has written a book of essays *0* (1975), *Holy Smoke* (1985), a witty history of the cigar, and *Exorcismos de estilo* (1976), a series of verbal collages and word experiments. Most of Cabrera's work has been translated to English.

Cabrera Infante won the prestigious Cervantes Prize in 1997, the third Cuban author to do so in its quarter century of existence. Despite his fame and recognition, he has not published a major work of fiction in over twenty years. But his place is secure in Cuban letters. *See also* Literature of the Revolutionary Era

Further Readings

Nelson, Ardis. *Cabrera Infante in the Menippean Tradition*. Newark, DE: De la Cuesta, 1983.

Souza, Raymond. *Major Cuban Novelists*. Columbia: University of Missouri Press, 1976.

Alan West-Durán

Carpentier, Alejo (1904–1980)

Considered one of the world's greatest writers, Alejo Carpentier was a literary innovator who helped to develop the genre known as Magical Realism. His novels, usually based on historical and political incidents, are complex narratives where ideology is as important as character and plot development; often, fantastic events color the action.

Carpentier was born in Havana in 1904. His father was a French architect and his mother a Russian medical student. Expected to study architecture, Carpentier chose music instead. He studied in Paris and later attended the **University of Havana**. When he was in his early twenties, he organized concerts and wrote music criticism. He was one of the founders of the journal *Revista de Avance* (1927–1930), a highly influential literary vehicle, and became the editor of *Carteles*, an avant-garde periodical (see **Literary Journals**).

In 1927, Carpentier was imprisoned for opposing the **Gerardo Machado** regime. While in prison, he wrote his first novel *¡Écue Yamba-Ó!*, an exercise in Afro-Cuban culture (see **Afro-Cubans**). The novel was published in Madrid six years later. After his release from prison, he traveled to Paris in 1928 where he participated in the surrealist movement. His sojourn in France coincided with Europe's interest in Latin American mythology, which was fashionable at the time. This interest prodded Carpentier to explore Latin American and Cuban cultures.

Carpentier returned to Cuba in 1936, where he worked as director of a radio station, edited a newspaper, and taught music at the Conservatorio Nacional. In 1943, the French actor Louis Jouvet asked him to accompany him to Haiti. The trip proved fateful for Carpentier. While in Haiti, he researched the government of

Alejo Carpentier, one of the world's most re-nowned writers and precursor of the genre known as Magical Realism. Photograph courtesy of the Biblioteca Nacional José Martí, Havana.

Henri Christophe, a black tyrant who ruled from 1811 to 1820. The research culminated in Carpentier's first major novel, *El reino de este mundo* (1949).

From Haiti, Carpentier went on to Venezuela—after a brief stay in Cuba. He stayed in Venezuela from 1945 to 1959, where he organized a publicity agency while working on his next novel, *Los pasos perdidos*. Published in 1953, the novel was an international bestseller, establishing Carpentier as a major writer. He returned to Cuba in 1959. A supporter of the **Revolution**, Carpentier directed the Imprenta Nacional, the government printing office, and served as minister-consul to the Cuban embassy in Paris.

In 1962, he published the novel *El siglo de la luces* about the impact of the French Revolution in the Caribbean. Other works followed, including *Concierto barroco* (1988) and *El recurso del método* (1974) both issued in 1974. His last complete work was *El arpa y la sombra* (1979), a meditation on **Christopher Columbus**. In 1977, he was awarded Spain's prestigious Miguel de Cervantes literary prize.

Aside from writing fiction, Carpentier was also a musicologist, publishing the important study *La música en Cuba* in 1946.

In addition, he wrote literary criticism and essays. Carpentier died in Paris at seventy-six years of age. *See also* Literature of the Revolutionary Era

Further Readings

Campuzano, Luisa. *Carpentier entonces y ahora*. Havana: Editorial Letras Cubanas, 1997.

González Echevarría, Roberto. *Alejo Carpentier: The Pilgrim at Home*. Austin: University of Texas Press, 1990.

D.H. Figueredo

Casa de las Américas

Casa de las Américas is an important cultural center that holds literary contests and publishes the famed journal *Casa de las Américas* (1960–), along with award-winning books and other publications. The oldest and best known of Cuba's postrevolutionary literary contests is that of Casa de las Américas, held for the first time in October 1959. It was the desire to break out of isolation and establish channels of cultural, intellectual, and artistic communication throughout Latin America and the Caribbean that led to the decision to put out the call for original manuscripts and initiate what would become an important cultural tradition. At the time, all Latin American governments, with the exception of Mexico, had severed relations with the island (see **Organization of American States [OAS], Cuba and the**). Casa de las Américas thus served as a vehicle for keeping a range of channels and mechanisms for international exchange open. This was the principal focus of the gamut of activities carried out by Casa in literature and the arts, beginning in 1959. Since it was first established, the Casa de las Américas literary contest has received over 10,000 manuscripts, with prizes awarded to over 200 international writers and scholars. The categories for the first Casa contest covered five genres: novels, poetry, drama, short stories, and essays in Spanish. Throughout the 1960s Casa received a growing volume of testimonial narratives and in 1970 added a new award for works in that genre, corresponding to a shift in Casa's mission as a literary magazine, from 1960 to 1965, to a vehicle concerned in equal measure with historiography and international politics in their relation to culture, from 1965 to 1971. That period marked its transformation into "an aggressive intellectual review rather than a literary magazine," as Judith Weiss suggests in her study *Casa de las Américas: An Intellectual Review in the Cuban Revolution*. In the 1970s the categories were expanded to include works by Latin American and Caribbean writers in Portuguese, French and English, as well as works of children's literature. The essay category was open to all international writers whose works dealt with Latin American and Caribbean topics. The fact that Casa's publishing house began to function in 1960, in order to publish the award-winning works, is what sets the Casa prize apart from its predecessors.

Casa de las Américas' evolution is rife with tension and controversy, including the well-known **Padilla Affair**, yet because of its transformation from yet another literary magazine into a provocative, internationally oriented review, it became one of the most far-reaching channels for the dissemination of Latin American literature. *See also* Literary Journals

Further Readings

Lie, Nadia. *Transición y transacción: la revista cubana* Casa de las Américas, *1960–1976*. Gaithersburgh, MD: Hispamérica, 1996.

Weiss, Judith. Casa de las Américas: *An Intellectual Review in the Cuban Revolution*. Chapel Hill, NC: Estudios de Hispanófila, 1977.

Pamela María Smorkaloff

Casal, Julián del (1863–1893)

Julián del Casal entered the Real Colegio de Belén in Havana in 1870, where together with classmates he established the handwritten underground paper *El Estudio*. It was there that he published his first poems. After graduating in 1880, he pursued a degree in law at the **University of Havana** but never completed it. By 1885, he had begun to write for *La Habana Elegante, La Caricatura*, and *El Fígaro*. Casal traveled to Spain in 1888 and upon his return settled into a position as proofreader and journalist with *La Discusión*. Despite his modest circumstances, he achieved extraordinary fame as a man of letters in Cuba. Many of the writers of stature frequented his *tertulias*; he counted the young poet **Juana Borrero** and Nicaraguan modernist poet Rubén Darío among his friends. His first book of poems, *Hojas del viento*, came out in 1890. But it was his second work, *Nieve* (1892), that drew the acclaim of French poet Paul Verlaine. His third volume of poems, *Bustos y rimas* (1893), was published posthumously.

Casal's journalistic prose described social life in nineteenth-century Cuba. These pieces were published weekly and sought to encourage Cubans to develop intellectually and culturally. His poetry, on the other hand, was not concerned with Cuba nor nationalism but rather with cosmopolitanism and aesthetics. His poetry tended to be philosophical yet simple and direct in its diction.

Casal, who suffered from tuberculolis, had a short life but his contribution to Latin American modernism was far-reaching and profound. As a poet, his style is often compared with and contrasted to that of his contemporary **José Martí**. *See also* Press and Journalism (Eighteenth and Nineteenth Centuries)

Further Readings

Armas, Emilio de. *Casal*. Havana. Editorial Letras Cubanas, 1981.

Glickman, Robert Jay. "Julián del Casal." In *Latin American Writers*, ed. Carlos A. Sole, and María Isabel Abreu. New York: Scribner's Sons, 1989. 3: 365–370

Pamela María Smorkaloff

Casey, Calvert (1924–1969)

A son of a North American father and a Cuban mother, Calvert Casey embodied the encounter of the cultures of his parents. Born in Baltimore, he was raised in Havana, where he learned the language and culture of his mother, he went back to the U.S. at the age of 10, but returned to Cuba in 1958, participating in the construction of Cuba's revolutionary society. He worked for **Casa de las Américas** and became affiliated with *Lunes de Revolución*, edited by **Guillermo Cabrera Infante**. However, with the changing politics and the persecutions of homosexuals, Casey fell from grace (see **Gays and Lesbians**). He left the island in 1965 and committed suicide in Rome in 1969. His stories are characterized by existential concerns evident in a troubled society that produces human alienation.

A short-story writer and literary critic, Casey is best known for *El regreso* (1962, expanded in 1967) and *Notas de un simulador* (1969), which contains a novella and four stories. He published his first story, "El paseo," in English, but it is about the culture of his mother, allowing for a U.S. reader to view Cuban culture from the point of view of someone who understands both cultures. The introduction to manhood with a prostitute does not produce the expected euphoria but rather a feeling of complacency and alienation.

"El regreso" refers to a double return and alienation. The protagonist was born in Cuba but lived in the United States. He travels to Cuba, then returns to the United States, only to go back once more to the island. In Cuba, he is judged as a stranger, and dictator **Fulgencio Batista**'s henchmen detain and torture him. The story has a political interpretation but is also existential and philosophical and underscores the impossibility of any return to one's past and origin.

Relatively unknown outside of Cuba, the publication of his collected works by Duke University Press in 1998 introduced Casey to a new generation of North American readers and critics. Literary reviews praised the author's ability to render man's loneliness, alienation, and uprootedness in the modern world. *See also* Literary Journals

Further Readings

Cabrera Infante, Guillermo. "¿Quién mató a Calvert Casey?" *Quimera* 3, no. 26 (December 1982): 42–53.

Calvert Casey. The Collected Stories. Trans. John H.R. Polt. Ed. Ilán Stavans. Durham, NC: Duke University Press, 1998.

Luis, William. "El lugar de la escritura." *Encuentro de la Cultura Cubana* 15 (1999–2000): 50–60.

William Luis

Castillo de González, Aurelia (1842–1920)

Aurelia Castillo de González, a poet, biographer, translator, and travel writer, had to leave Cuba in 1875 when her husband, a colonel in the Spanish army, criticized the Spanish government for its abusive treatment of Cuban insurgents (see **Ten Years' War** and **Political Exile [Nineteenth Century]**). While living in exile in Spain, Castillo de González published articles and poems in well-known literary journals and magazines. Returning to Cuba after the war in 1878, she wrote extensively about her travels throughout Europe; a series of letters she penned in 1889, published as *Un paseo por Europa* (1891), describing the Paris World Fair, brought her national recognition. In 1887, she wrote a biography of her contemporary **Gertrudis Gómez de Avellaneda**. In 1912, she wrote a biography of the patriot **Ignacio Agramonte**. Castillo de González's translation into Spanish of the Italian classic *La figlia d'Iorio*—by Gabriel D'Annunzio—was well received by literary critics. She spent the last years of her life editing the works of Gómez de Avellaneda and **José Martí**. The Cuban revolutionary government has named a public library after Castillo de Gónzalez.

Further Reading
Martínez Fernández, Luis. *El lugareño y otros próceres*. Camagüey, Cuba: Ayuntamiento de Camagüey, 1954.

D.H. Figueredo

Ciclón (1955–1957, 1959)

Ciclón was an innovative literary journal emphasizing cultural values while attempting to internationalize Cuban exposure to literature that addresses such issues as the social responsibility of writers, homosexuality, and critical thinking. This journal was founded and edited by José Rodríguez Feo (Harvard, 1943; Princeton, 1949) after his break with **José Lezama Lima** over policies concerning *Orígenes*. *Ciclón* rejected the influence of **Catholicism** implicit in the writings and thinking of the major Cuban novelists and poets appearing in *Orígenes* and sought instead contributions from such authors as **Severo Sarduy, Calvert Casey, Antón Arrufat, Tomás Gutiérrez Alea, Virgilio Piñera**, José Triana, and Fayad Jamis. Among the foreign contributors were Lionel Trilling, W.H. Auden, Julio Cortázar, and Ernesto Sábato.

In the Cuba of the 1950s Rodríguez Feo editorialized about the journalism that passes as culture and criticized the state's attempt to promote culture. In the only issue for 1959, writers addressed the **Revolution** and what culture might become.

Although *Ciclón* did not circulate widely, it received attention from major writers in the Americas by maintaining a dialogue and providing them a venue for new fiction. Like Victoria Ocampo's *Sur*, *Ciclón* reflects the sophisticated literary taste of its founder and principal patron.

See also Literary Journals; Gays and Lesbians; Newspapers and Magazines

Peter T. Johnson

Cofiño López, Manuel (1936–1987)

Manuel Cofiño López was a short-story writer, novelist, and author of children's literature. Initially, Cofiño López worked as a college professor, academic administrator, and a researcher for the Ministerio de Industrias (Industries Ministry). After contributing to numerous newspapers and journals, the likes of *Bohemia* and *La Gaceta de Cuba*, he published his first book, *Tiempo de cambio* (1969), a collection of short stories, at the age of thirty-three. Two years later, his novel *La última mujer y el próximo combate* was awarded the prestigious **Casa de las Américas** prize; subsequently, the book became a bestseller in Cuba. In 1975, the **Unión de Escritores y Artistas de Cuba (UNEAC)** awarded his novel *Cuando la sangre se parece al fuego*, with its rich descriptions of **Santería** beliefs, honorable mention in a literary contest. His works sold well throughout Latin America and Europe and were translated into English and Russian.

Cofiño López wrote about life in Cuba. The characters in his stories and novels were based on actual people the author knew and befriended. His prose was realistic but also experimental, though the author believed that it was the writer's responsibility to write in a style accessible to all readers. *See also* Literary Journals; Newspapers and Magazines

Further Reading
Vidal, Hernán. *Para llegar a Manuel Cofiño: estudio de una narrativa revolucionaria cubana*. Minneapolis, MN: Society for the Study of Contemporary Hispanic and Lusophone African Revolutionary Literature, 1984.

D.H. Figueredo

Cruz Varela, María Elena (1953–)

A poet and **human rights** activist, María Elena Cruz Varela was born in **Matanzas**. At the age of twenty she moved to Havana, where she attended the **University of Havana**. Her aspirations were to study art, but she was attracted to the writing of poetry. Her first book, *Afuera esta lloviendo* (1987), brought her instant recognition and fame on the island and in Latin America. Her poetry celebrated the human spirit and protested political oppression.

In 1991, Cruz Varela chaired an organization that offered a political alternative to **Fidel Castro**'s regime; she also signed a document criticizing the Cuban government. For these actions Cruz Varela was arrested and sentenced to two years of imprisonment. She was actually forced to eat her own writings. In 1992, she was nominated for the Nobel Peace Prize. In 1993, PEN awarded her the Poetry International Prize. A year later, Cruz Varela went into exile in Spain.

Her best-known book is *El ángel agotado* (1992). It is because of this volume of poetry that many admirers describe Cruz Varela as the "angel" of freedom. *See also* Dissent and Defections (1959–); Political Prisoners

Further Reading

Cámara, Madeline. *Vocación de Casandra: poesía femenina cubana subversiva en María Elena Cruz Varela*. New York: Peter Lang, 2001.

D.H. Figueredo

Cuban American Literature

There has been long-lasting Cuban diaspora, one that predates the **Revolution** of 1959 and extends across Europe, Latin America, and the United States. Many of Cuba's most prized writers—from **Esteban Borrero Echeverría** and his daughter **Juana Borrero** to **Cirilo Villaverde** and

José Martí, toward the close of the nineteenth century—have lived, written, and published in the United States, long before the tensions of the 1950s erupted. Cuban anthropologist **Fernando Ortiz** arrived in the United States in 1931 and stayed for four years, teaching and militating against then-president **Gerardo Machado** before he returned to Cuba for good. That none of these earlier displaced writers ever became "hyphenated" Cuban Americans is an important distinction. By contrast Cuban American hyphenated writers live and create on a permanent axis that connects their ties to their country of origin with their daily American lives. Fueled by the Cold War, which deeply affected the lives of Cubans on and off the island, the historical debate over what it meant to be Cuban acquired a new urgency when it came to revolve around the Revolution of 1959. That year unleashed a massive new exile, concentrated in Miami.

Among Cuban American literature's most notable scholars is **Gustavo Pérez Firmat**, whose 1994 study *Life on the Hyphen: The Cuban-American Way* offers a comprehensive vision of contemporary Cuban American culture. Interspersed between essays on pop culture icons such as **Desi Arnaz** and **Gloria Estefan** are thoughtful meditations on the cultural, geographic, and historical trajectory of contemporary Cuban American writers such as novelists **Cristina García, Oscar Hijuelos**, Roberto G. Fernández, and **Virgil Suárez** and poets José Kozer and Pablo Medina. According to Pérez Firmat's analysis of language, text, and context in Cuban American literature, the writing itself can move in either of two directions, toward or away from Cuba, indicating the two extremes and everything in between. Pérez Firmat's "directional" sense of the spirit and letter of contemporary Cuban American writing is theoretically valid and useful for understanding the vast, differentiated world of Cuban American literature, as well as the relationship between the Cuban canon and the writers of the diaspora. Accordingly, those who write "from" Spanish into English and "from" the United States "toward" Cuba have a stronger grounding in and relationship to the Cuban literary tradition. On the other hand, the writers who belong on the axis that moves from Cuba toward the United States are claiming their place "among American 'ethnic' writers." Pérez Firmat goes on to distinguish between Cuban Americans who, even if they wrote in English, wrote for other Cuban Americans and newer generations of writers whose audience may include Cuban Americans but also transcends the community, observing that "only in the last couple of years, with the appearance of novels by Oscar Hijuelos, Virgil Suárez, and Cristina García, have Cuban-American authors sought to reach a broader audience. The language of these most recent novels is strikingly different from that of earlier texts."

In distinction to their predecessors, the Cuban American characters of contemporary authors like García, Suárez, and Achy Obejas question identity and rigorously explore what it means to be Cuban American in the United States today. The conscious examination of Cuban American identity propels the characters, quite literally in the case of the protagonist of Suárez's *Going Under* (1996), to Cuba, back to the source, the origins, to sort things out. The same journey back to Cuba, into historical consciousness, together with the theme of intergenerational conflict, structures the fiction of García, most notably in *Dreaming in Cuban* (1992), and Achey Obejas, in *Memory Mambo* (1996).

Cuban American narratives have, in recent years, transcended the boundaries of the enclave, undertaking a journey of return, sharing many of the characteristics of the larger Latino literary "boom" whose writers, such as Dominican American Julia Alvarez or Mexican American Rolando Hinojosa, cross and recross borders in their works, mapping the route back. Contemporary Latino and Cuban American narratives tend to stand poised between origins and diaspora, scrutinizing both land of origin and adopted homeland with equal passion and rigor. A new wave of Cuban American writers is now engaging actively and critically with the reality that surrounds them, giving expression to the contradictions inherent in a hyphenated life and vision within the United States, as their counterparts in Cuba begin to take stock of the moment, the present juncture. With greater numbers of Cuban émigrés traveling to the island in recent years and with Cuban American and Cuban writers attempting to create literary bridges—as demonstrated by Ruth Behar's edited book *Bridges to Cuba* (1995)—an increasing level of exchange may make nostalgia in its purest form a relic of the literary past. In studying Cuban American and other dual-heritage literatures, Ramón Gutiérrez and Genaro Padilla suggest, in *Recovering the U.S. Hispanic Literary Heritage* (1993), that categories overlap "when the author lives a transnational reality" and there are no easy answers to the question "where does one end and the other begin." That is certainly true of the works of consecrated diaspora writers **Reinaldo Arenas** and **Antonio Benítez Rojo**, among others. *See also* Cuban Playwrights in the United States; Cuban Migrations to the United States

Further Readings
Behar, Ruth, ed. *Bridges to Cuba: Puentes a Cuba.* Ann Arbor: University of Michigan Press, 1995.
Pérez Firmat, Gustavo. *Life on the Hyphen: The Cuban-American Way.* Austin: University of Texas Press, 1994.
Smorkaloff, Pamela María. *Cuban Writers on and off the Island.* New York: Twayne Publishers, 1999.

Pamela María Smorkaloff

Cuban Playwrights in the United States

Cuban theater in the United States originated in nineteenth-century Cuban exile enclaves in Florida, where large numbers of independence patriots and tobacco workers settled. In Tampa–Ybor City, touring Cuban and Spanish companies performed for Cuban exiles. By the 1920s, the popularity of Afro-Cuban music and dance and **teatro bufo** had spread to Latino theaters in New York City. The exodus produced by the 1959 Cuban **Revolution**, however, marks the beginning of significant Cuban theatrical activity in U.S. regions with large Cuban communities, principally South Florida and New Jersey–New York.

The first generation of post-Revolution U.S.-Cuban playwrights was intellectually formed in Cuba and had begun writing before leaving the island. Plays written in exile in Spanish by Matías Montes Huidobro, Julio Matas, Jorge Corrales, and Fermín Borges have reached limited, mostly academic audiences. Montes Huidobro, also a literary critic and professor, is the most anthologized and produced playwright of this generation. He uses symbolic language and metatheatrical techniques to examine Cuban themes such as **machismo**, authoritarianism, Afro-Cuban myths, and exile (see **Afro-Cubans**). Two of his more recent pieces include *La navaja de Olofé* (1986) and *Exilio* (1988).

While criticism of the Revolution and a nostalgic longing for the land and culture left behind characterize Cuban American theater of the 1960s, a second generation educated in the United States began to produce plays in the late 1970s and early 1980s. Iván Acosta's *El súper* (1977) and Manuel Martín, Jr.'s *Union City Thanksgiving* (1982) are emblematic of many realist family dramas that treat such issues as acculturation, bilingualism, and generational conflict. Dolores Prida's *Coser y cantar* (1981) breaks realist molds and uses two characters, Ella and She, to present the conflicts of bicultural U.S.-Cuban identity. With over a dozen plays staged, Prida is one of the most successful Cuban playwrights in the United States. A *Little Something to Ease the Pain* (1980) by René R. Aloma and *Nadie se va del todo* (1991) by Pedro Monge Rafuls transcend typical nostalgia plays by dramatizing the difficult encounters between those who stayed on the island and those who emigrated. Eduardo Machado's cycle *The Floating Island Plays* (1991) spans the history of twentieth-century Cuba and thus covers many of the themes found in Cuban American drama. As evidenced by the titles, the playwrights of this generation are as likely to write their works in English as in Spanish.

The work of these authors, and others too numerous to name here, as playwrights, actors, directors, and founders of theaters and theater publications created a space for Cubans in a national U.S.-Latino theater movement. Exciting voices of the 1990s such as Nilo Cruz and performance artist Carmelita Tropicana are reaching ever-wider audiences. U.S.-Cuban theater today dismantles national and ethnic stereotypes and addresses such formally taboo themes as sexual orientation and **AIDS**. Finally, any survey of U.S.-Cuban theater must highlight María Irene Fornés, one of the most innovative playwrights in the United States. Fornés differs from the authors noted above because she emigrated from Cuba before the Revolution, and her plays, written in English, do not address explicitly Cuban themes. Since 1980, she has mentored emerging U.S.-Cuban playwrights through her writing lab at International Arts Relations (INTAR). *See also* Cuban American Literature; Mariel Generation; Theater

Further Readings

Cortina, Rodolfo J., ed. *Cuban American Theater*. Houston: Arte Público Press, 1991.

Sandoval-Sánchez, Alberto. *José, Can You See? Latinos on and off Broadway*. Madison: University of Wisconsin Press, 1999.

Camilla Stevens

Díaz, Jesús (1941–2002)

Author and film director Jesús Díaz taught philosophy at the **University of Havana**, where he also served as editor of the journal *Pensamiento Crítico* (1967–1971) until it was shut down by the government. Díaz also founded the monthly *El Caimán Barbudo*, which he edited from 1966 to 1967.

He began writing in 1966 and received the prestigious **Casa de las Américas** literary award for his collection of short stories *Los años duros*, categorized in Cuba as a work representative of the revolutionary struggle. In 1979, he published *De la patria y el exilio*, a collection of interviews conducted with young Cubans who had left the island in the 1960s and were returning to visit (see **Brigada Antonio Maceo**). The book complemented his documentary *55 Hermanos*, filmed in 1978. After a lengthy absence from publishing, due to political pressures, in 1987 he published the novel *Las iniciales de la tierra*, which portrayed a Cuban caught between political dogma and social inertia. In 1991, he wrote *Las palabras perdidas*, a novel about the conflict between personal ambition and the revolutionary process. That same year, Díaz went into exile, first in Germany and later in Spain, where he resided until his death in 2002.

In 1996, Díaz founded in Madrid, Spain, the journal *Encuentro de la Cultura Cubana*, meant as an avenue for exchange between Cubans on the island and those in exile. Later on, he edited an electronic version of the journal—www.cubaencuentro.com. His other books include *La piel y la máscara* (1996), *Dime algo sobre Cuba* (1998), and *Siberiana* (2000). He directed dozens of documentaries and feature films, including *Polvo rojo* (1981) and *Lejanía* (1985). *See also* Cinema; Literary Journals

Further Reading

Collman, Lilliam O. *Jesús Díaz: el ejercicio de los límites de la expresión revolucionaria en Cuba*. New York: Peter Lang, 1999.

Wilfredo Cancio Isla

Diego, Eliseo (1920–1994)

Along with **Nicolás Guillén** and **José Lezama Lima**, Eliseo Diego is considered one of Cuba's greatest twentieth-century poets. As an author, Diego wanted his words, and his poetry, to capture the very essence of objects: He longed for his words to give life to inanimate objects. He was also intensely preoccupied with the passing of time and the temporality of space.

Diego attended law school at the **University of Havana** but dropped out after two years to pursue a literary career. From 1942 to 1943, he was member of the editorial board of the journal *Clavileño*. Later on, he was one of the cofounders of the influential literary publication, *Orígenes*; he published many of his poems in both journals (see **Literary Journals**).

In 1949, he published the book of poetry, *En la Calzada de Jesús del Monte*. Initially, the volume did not sell well—but gradually the book gained national recognition. Today, this book of poetry is regarded as a classic of Latin American letters.

During the 1940s and 1950s, Diego taught English in night school and worked as a school inspector for the Ministry of Education. After the triumph of the Cuban **Revolution**, he was appointed head of the Children's Department of the National Library (**Biblioteca Nacional José Martí**).

During the 1960s and 1970s, he traveled throughout Europe, attending numerous literary conferences. In the meantime, he continued to write poetry, publishing dozens of books of poems and submitting short stories and essays to literary journals. Among his most important books are *Por los extraños pueblos* (1958), *El oscuro esplendor* (1966), *Noticias de la quimera* (1975), *Los días de tu vida* (1977), and *Libro de quizás y de quién sabe* (1989). In 1986, he received Cuba's Premio Nacional de Literatura. In 1993, he was awarded in Mexico the Juan Rulfo international award for literature.

Diego translated into Spanish children's stories by Hans Christian Andersen and the Grimm Brothers as well as Russian and Hungarian poets. He passed away in Mexico in 1994.

Further Readings

Abreu, Mauricio. *Asomado al mundo de Eliseo Diego*. Havana: Urbe, 1993.

Bella Abellan, Salvador. *L'univers poétique d'Eliseo Diego*. Paris: L'Harmattan, 1999.

D.H. Figueredo

Estévez, Abilio (1954–)

Poet, dramatist, and fiction writer, Abilio Estévez was born in Havana where he attended the **University of Havana**, graduating in 1977 with a degree in literature and language. Influenced by **Virgilio Piñera**, Estévez belongs to that generation of writers who emerged during the 1980s and questioned the accomplishments and ethics of the **Revolution**. His work *La verdadera culpa de Juan Clemente Zenea* (1987) received the national theater award. His many plays, including *Perla marina* (1993), *Santa Cecilia* (1994), and *El enano en la botella* (1994), have been performed in Cuba and the United States. The drama *La Noche* was awarded the 1996 Tirso de Molina prize in Spain.

His book of poems *Manual de las tentaciones* (1989) was well received in Eu-

rope, obtaining the Luis Cernada Award in Spain. His novel *Tuyo es el reino* (1997) brought him further recognition. It is an allegorical story about an eccentric family living in a decaying mansion filled with phantasmagorical images. The novel was translated into English, French, German, Greek, and Finnish. He has written two collections of short stories, *Juego con Gloria* (1987) and *El horizonte y otros regresos* (1998) as well as several film scripts (see **Cinema**).

Estévez has also worked as editor and literary critic for the journals *El Caimán Barbudo* and *La Gaceta de Cuba*. See also Newspapers and Magazines; Theater; Literary Journals

Further Reading

Carreo Mendía, Raquel. "La verdadera respuesta: apuntes para una lectura del tercer personaje." *Conjuntos*, 71 (Jan–Mar 1987), 65–80.

Wilfredo Cancio Isla

Fernández Retamar, Roberto (1930–)

Poet, essayist, critic, lecturer, and cultural representative of the revolutionary government, Fernández Retamar has taught as a visiting professor at Yale University and the **University of Havana**, has served as diplomat for the Cuban government, and has worked as the editor of the literary journal of **Casa de las Américas**.

Fernández Retamar studied architecture at the University of Havana but switched to the study of linguistics and literature. An accomplished student, he received numerous awards and scholarships. He continued his graduate studies in France and in England. In 1950, Fernández Retamar published his first book of poetry, *Elegía como un himno*. In this volume, the poet expressed the loneliness and isolation that an artist often experiences. After the triumph of the Cuban **Revolution**, his poetry manifested an interest in social and political issues. Notable among his many volumes are *Revolución nuestra, amor nuestro* (1976) and *Juana y otros poemas personales* (1981).

Outside of Cuba, Fernández Retamar is better known for his work as an essayist, particularly the book *Calibán* (1971), which explored postcolonialism in Latin America and the region's right to assert its own political destiny without the influence of powerful countries such as the United States, and his collection of essays, *Para el perfil definitivo del hombre* (1981).

Fernández Retamar's poems and essays have been translated into ten languages, including English and Russian. *See also* Literary Journals; Literature of the Revolutionary Era

Further Reading

Sklodowska, Elzbieta, and Ben A. Heller. *Roberto Fernández Retamar y los estudios latinoamericanos*. Pittsburgh, PA: Instituto Internacional de Literatura Iberoamericana, Universidad de Pittsburgh, 2000.

D.H. Figueredo

García, Cristina (1958–)

Born in July 1958 in Cuba and raised since age four in the United States, Cristina García embodies both U.S. and Cuban cultures. In 1984 she visited her place of birth, an experience that permitted her to better understand her Cuban past. She has written two successful novels in a poetic language that brings her native and adopted countries together.

Her first novel, *Dreaming in Cuban* (1992), based on aspects of the author's life, narrates the life of Pilar, a child of the 1960s, who attempts to reconcile her mother's pro-U.S. and anti-Castro sentiments and her grandmother's support of the **Revolution**. Pilar's trip to Cuba allows her to uncover her family past, represented by letters her grandmother, Celia, wrote to her Spanish lover, Gustavo. The family problems are evident before the Revolution, in the early part of the century, and

Cristina García. Cuban American author whose first novel *Dreaming in Cuban* became an overnight success. David Lavin Agency, Inc.

unfold in the present. The novel ends during the takeover of the Peruvian embassy in 1980 and alludes to the **Mariel boatlift**, when 125,000 Cubans abandoned the island. Pilar's actions to help her cousin Ivanito escape, and her denial of having seen him at the embassy, represents a coming to terms with the Cuban Revolution and her family trauma.

The theme of Cuban and U.S. cultures is further examined in García's second novel, *The Agüero Sisters* (1997), as Reina, who lives in Cuba, and Constancia, who resides in the United States, represent the separation of the Cuban family caused by the Revolution. Their parents, Ignacio and Blanca, were ornithologists and collected rare and extinct Cuban birds. The family history serves as backdrop for understanding events in the Revolution. History, culture, ornithology, cosmetics, and Afro-Cuban religions make up some of the layers of the novel. Similar to the almost extinct specimens collected by Ignacio and Blanca, when Reina joins her sister in Miami, she only brings her memories. Cuban culture, whether on the island or abroad, can only be represented metonymically. *See also* Cuban American Literature; Santería

Further Readings

Álvarez Borland, Isabel. *Cuban-American Literature of Exile*. Charlottesville: University of Virginia Press, 1998.

Luis, William. *Dance between Two Cultures: Latino Caribbean Literature Written in the United States*. Nashville, TN: Vanderbilt University Press, 1997.

Pérez Firmat, Gustavo. "Cuba sí, Cuba no. Querencias de la literatura cubano/americana." *Encuentro de la cultura cubana* 14 (Fall 1999): 131–137.

William Luis

García Marruz, Fina (1923–   )

A poet and literary critic, Fina García Marruz was also a member of the *Orígenes* group. On several occasions she has won the National Award for Literature and the National Award for Criticism. A Catholic and committed revolutionary, García Marruz, like her husband **Cintio Vitier**, has been a mainstay of Cuban cultural life for six decades. Although her work has an almost mystical transcendentalist streak, on the one hand, and a commitment to social justice, on the other, her best poetry is neither "pure" nor "militant." She cautions about poetry with definite ends (or aims), saying that a poet inhabits poetry, a realm that exceeds the poet's limitations and intentions, not the other way around. The bulk of her wide-ranging poetry has been published in *Visitaciones* (1970) and *Habana del centro* (1997).

As a critic, she coauthored with Vitier *Temas martianos* (1969), where she examines themes of Cuban identity in the work of **José Martí**. A major collection of her criticism *Hablar de la poesía* (1986) contains essays on Gustavo Adolfo Béc-

quer, Juana Inés de la Cruz, Juan Ramón Jiménez (the Spanish poet who was a major influence on her work), nineteenth-century Cuban literature, and **José Lezama Lima**, among other subjects. García Marruz, despite praise for her fine poetry and insightful criticism, has not achieved the international recognition that the male authors, such as Lezama Lima and Vitier, of her generation have. *See also* Literary Journals; Literature of the Revolutionary Era

Further Readings

Arcos, Jorge Luis. *En torno a la obra poética de Fina García Marruz*. Havana: UNEAC, 1990.

"Homenaje a Fina García Marruz." in *Encuentro de la Cultura Cubana*, 11 (Winter 1998–1999): 4–7.

Roc, Ana. "Fina García Marruz." In *Dictionary of Twentieth Century Cuban Literature*, ed. Julio A. Martínez, Westport, CT: Greenwood Press, 1990. 187–189.

Alan West-Durán

Gómez de Avellaneda, Gertrudis (1814–1873)

Gertrudis Gómez de Avellaneda is considered, along with the poet **José María Heredia**, one of the most important literary figures Cuban Romanticism produced. Whereas Romanticism in literature emerged on the Latin American continent in the years immediately following Independence (1820s), in Cuba and Puerto Rico it arose under Spanish colonial domination (see **Spanish Colonialism [Nineteenth-Century]**). The Romantic sensibility in Cuban letters was characterized by hostility toward Spain and the struggle for political freedom on the island, affirmation of a Cuban national identity, and the will to forge an independent national literature.

Gómez de Avellaneda was born in **Camagüey**, to a Spanish father and a Cuban mother, and went to live in Spain at the age of twenty-two, after rejecting the offer

Gertrudis Gómez de Avellaneda, pioneer feminist whose poetry and prose criticized slavery and the culture of *machismo*. Courtesy of the Cuban Heritage Collection of the Otto G. Richter Library of the University of Miami.

woman. She later married Colonel Domingo Verdugo, who accepted an official posting in Cuba, and returned to Havana with him in 1859. In Havana she presided over the journal *Album Cubano de lo Bueno y lo Bello* (1860). Upon Verdugo's death in 1863, she traveled with her brother Manuel to the United States, London, and Paris before returning to Madrid, where she died in 1873. Gómez de Avellaneda wrote for numerous literary journals, translated poetry from the French, and utilized the pseudonym "La peregrina." *See also* Abolitionist Literature; Press and Journalism (Eighteenth and Nineteenth Centuries); Theater

Further Readings

Gómez de Avellaneda y Arteaga, Gertrudis. *Autobiografía y epistolarios de amor*. Newark, DE: Juan de la Cuesta, 1999.

Jiménez Faro, Luzmaría. *Gertrudis Gómez de Avellaneda: la dolorida su pasión*. Madrid: Ediciones Torremozas, 1999.

Pamela María Smorkaloff

Govantes, José Joaquín (?–1881)

José Joaquín Govantes was born in Havana, the son of a judge. As a young man, he expressed interest in literature and writing and contributed poems to the journals *Aurora* and *Aguinaldo Habanero*. During the **Ten Years' War**, he joined the insurgents and moved to the United States to advocate the Cuban cause. In New York City, he founded the newspaper *La Voz de la Patria*, which featured pro-independence writings, vivid descriptions of battles, and updates on the war. Financial restraints forced him to cease publication a year later.

Govantes published two books of poetry, *Horas de amargura* and *Poesías de José Joaquín Govantes*, and wrote a comedy for the stage, *Una vieja como hay muchas*, but he is better known for his patriotic activities while living in exile (see **Political Exile [Nineteenth Century]**).

of a "good marriage" in Cuba. Though her oeuvre consists of theater, poetry, and epistolary prose, she is best known for her six novels and nine *leyendas*, or short stories, the most well known being the abolitionist novel *Sab* (1841). An abolitionist, and equally fervent early feminist, Gómez de Avellaneda bore a daughter out of wedlock in 1845 with Spanish poet Gabriel García Tassara, but the child died a few months later. She married Pedro Sabater the following year, but he died in Burdeos three months later. After a conventional period of mourning, Gómez de Avellaneda returned to Madrid and entered a period of intense intellectual activity. Between 1846 and 1858 no less than thirteen of her plays had their debuts in Madrid theaters, often to great acclaim. In 1853 she tried to become a member of the Academia Española but was denied entry because she was a

Further Reading

Diccionario de literatura cubana. Vol. 1. Havana: Editorial Letras Cubanas, 1980.

D.H. Figueredo

Guerra y Sánchez, Ramiro (1880–1970)

Ramiro Guerra was a teacher, an economist, historian, and journalist who was also the director of the influential newspaper *El Diario la Prensa*. A Harvard University graduate—through a program specifically designed to train Cuban teachers at the turn of the twentieth century—Guerra later earned a doctorate in education from the **University of Havana**. He was the national superintendent of public schools during the 1920s and founded numerous private and public schools as well as educational organizations (see **Educational System**).

Guerra wrote dozens of pedagogical textbooks, including the *Libro primero de lectura* (1917), biographies of prominent Cuban patriots and educators, histories of Cuba's wars of independence, and books on economics. His volume *Azúcar y población en las Antillas* (1927) was regarded for many years as the definitive study of sugar production in the Caribbean. Along with José M. Pérez Cabrera, Juan J. Remos, and Emeterio S. Santovenia, he edited the monumental and valuable ten-volume *Historia de la nación cubana* in commemoration of the fiftieth anniversary of Cuba's independence, published in 1952.

Further Readings

Cuba en la mano. Havana: Imprenta Úcar, García y Cía. 1940. 903–904.

Pérez, Jr., Louis A. *Essays on Cuban History: Historiography and Research*. Gainsville: University Press of Florida, 1995.

Villarreal, Juan Jérez. *La historia de Cuba y Ramiro Guerra Sánchez*. Havana: Ediciones Atenas, 1930.

D.H. Figueredo

Guillén, Nicolás (1902–1989)

A native of **Camagüey**, Nicolás Guillén was considered Cuba's "national poet." In his hometown he learned typography skills at the printing press where his father published the newspaper *La Libertad*. After graduating from high school in Camagüey in 1920, he moved to Havana to study Law at the **University of Havana** but had to abandon his studies shortly thereafter because of lack of funds and unemployment. Back in Camagüey, he published his first verses in the journal *Camagüey Gráfico*. Guillén spent the better part of the 1920s moving back and forth between Camagüey and Havana, alternating between law school, which he never finished, and various jobs as editor of newspapers and literary journals, until he made the definitive move back to Havana in 1926.

Guillén's poetry is rooted in the cross-cultural imagination of Caribbean *mestizaje*, as he himself defined it, and resistance to any kind of dogmatism. There is a strong sense of Cuban history and its relationship to the wider Caribbean, Latin America, and the United States in his poetry. His verses are inhabited by Cubans from all walks of life and incorporate Cuban vernacular speech. In *Motivos del son* (1930), Guillén sought to speak "en negro de verdad," that is, to write an Afro-Cuban poetry of the everyday, devoid of the exotic so sought after in the Europe of the day, and achieved his goal to acclaim.

Guillén's connections to his contemporaries were vast. In January 1930, African American poet Langston Hughes visited Havana. The two met, became friends, and later translated one another. In 1942, Guillén traveled to Haiti on a cultural mission, invited by Haitian writer Jacques Roumain.

During the 1940s, Guillén joined the Communist Party and wrote for the Party's organ *Hoy* (see **Partido Comunista [Partido Socialista Popular, Republican**

Nicolás Guillén was Cuba's national poet; his poetry celebrated the island's African heritage. Photograph by William Luis.

Era]). After dictator **Fulgencio Batista** took over the Cuban government in 1952, Guillén went into exile for six years until the triumph of the Cuban **Revolution**. In 1961, Guillén assumed the presidency of the Writers and Artists Union, **Unión de Escritores y Artistas de Cuba (UNEAC)**, which had been established that same year, and traveled widely in that capacity.

His poetry appears in numerous anthologies and has been translated into more than a dozen languages. Among his many books are *Songoro cosongo* (1931), *West Indies, Ltd.* (1934), *El gran zoo* (1967), and *El diario que a diario* (1972). *See also* Afro-Cubans; Literary Journals.

Further Readings

Santana, Joaquín G. *Nicolás Guillén, juglar Americano: un poeta por la revolución*. Havana: Editora Política, 1989.

Smart, Ian. *Nicolás Guillén, Popular Poet of the Caribbean*. Columbia: University of Missouri Press, 1990.

Pamela María Smorkaloff

Hemingway, Ernest, in Cuba

Although scores of writers of international fame—from Graham Greene to Gabriel García Márquez—have visited and lived in Cuba, Ernest Hemingway (1899–1961) is the foreign author most closely associated with the island. He lived in Cuba on and off for nearly forty years, spending more time on the island than anywhere else in the world. Cuba stimulated his creative impulses and provided him with adventures. More important, as Hemingway often told his visitors, Cuba afforded him tranquility and peace.

The author first visited the island sometime in the 1920s. During that decade he was living in Key West and often sailed to Havana. From his constant sailing in Cuban waters and his trips to Havana and the port came the inspiration for his book, *To Have and Have Not* (1937).

During the late 1930s Hemingway spent many days and nights at Havana's Hotel Ambos Mundos, where he finished his 1940 novel *For Whom the Bell Tolls*. In 1940 Martha Gellhorn, his third wife, persuaded him to move to the island, where the author bought a farm on the outskirts of Havana. In many ways, the farm was luxurious: it included a mansion, a pool, and forty acres of lush tropical vegetation. Atop the farm stood a tower from which the author contemplated the surrounding Cuban landscape and the sea.

During the early days of World War II, Hemingway scouted the Cuban coastline, on a secret mission for the American government: to detect German U-boats—an activity that he later recounted in his book *Island in the Stream*, published posthumously in 1970.

Hemingway hired Cuban fishermen to go sailing with him. One of these fishermen, Gregorio Fuentes, provided the author with the material for one of his most famous novels, *The Old Man and the Sea* (1952). The protagonist of the story, Santiago, is an old Cuban who is at the end of his fishing career. Everyone in the fishing village—probably the town of Jaimanita—thought that Santiago was no longer able to fish, but one evening the old man caught a marlin, which was then hunted down by sharks. The novel tells of the mythic struggle first between Santiago and the marlin and then between Santiago and the sharks that surround his tiny boat. The novel brought about Hemingway's nomination for the Nobel Prize for literature in 1954. The author did not attend the ceremonies in Oslo; instead, he delivered his acceptance speech live over Cuban radio.

When Hemingway was neither writing nor fishing or hunting, he was found at one of the Havana bars, which he made famous: El Floridita and La Bodeguita del Medio. He also liked to roam about the streets of **Old Havana**, where he was a sight. He was often spotted wearing shorts and sandals, attire that contemporary Cubans did not deem acceptable but that they attributed to the author's eccentricities. Well liked by Cubans—the sentiment was reciprocal—Hemingway was referred to as Ernesto during the 1950s and as Papá after his death. Hemingway befriended Cuban artists and writers, among them **Antonio Gattorno** and **Lino Novás Calvo**, and publishers and journalists.

Feeling infirm, the author left Cuba shortly after the triumph of the **Revolution** in 1960, never to return. Today his farm, Finca Vigía, is a national museum, where things still stand the way Hemingway left them. The Cuban government also sponsors a fishing tournament named after the author, and a marina frequented by foreign yachts bears his name.

Further Readings

Fuentes, Norberto. *Hemingway in Cuba*. Secaucus, NJ: L. Stuart, 1984.
Hemingway, Gregory H. *Papa: A Personal Memoir*. Boston: Houghton Mifflin, 1976.

D.H. Figueredo

Heredia y Heredia, José María (1803–1839)

José María Heredia is known as the most prominent Romantic poet of nineteenth-century Cuban literature. Born in **Santiago de Cuba**, Heredia was a self-taught writer, introduced to the classics from an early age by his father. In 1818 he began studying law in Havana, and a year later, his play *Eduardo IV o el usurpador* was performed. In 1820, due to his father's job, he went to Mexico where he wrote "En el Teocalli de Cholula," an ode in which Heredia transforms the ruins of an Aztec temple into a poetic memory of the civilizations that inhabited Anáhuac, Mexico's ancient capital. The poem is also a philosophical reflection on the inevitable fugacity of time. That same year he was obliged to return to Cuba after his father's death. On the island, he finished his law degree and became involved with a group of young revolutionaries brought together under the Soles y Rayos de Bolívar conspiracy. This activity led to his exile to the United States in 1823, where he stayed for two years teaching language classes. His visit to the Niagara Falls in 1824 inspired his celebrated work "Oda al Niágara" in which the poet treats the Romantic description of an imposing nature reflected on the astonishing waterfall and is reminded about his exiled condition as well as his nostalgia for Cuba by means of the distinctive image of some palms that appear behind the cascading water (see **National Tree**). His first poetry collection *Poesías* was published in 1825, the year in which President Guadalupe Victoria invited him to move to Mexico, where he played an active part in public life and also directed and worked as literary critic for the magazines *El Iris* (1826) and *La Miscelánea* (1829–1832). In 1832, Heredia published in Toluca, Mexico (with the help of his wife, Jacoba Yañéz), the second edition of *Poesías*. The constant social and political upheavals in that country took him back to Cuba in 1836 after he obtained permission from Captain-General Miguel Tacón. Heredia wrote him a letter in which he renounced his former separatist endeavors. As a result, his visit lasted two months, during which he was exposed to

José María Heredia. Nineteenth-century romantic poet. Sketch by Esteban Valderrama.

his friends' reproaches. He returned to Mexico, where he died in 1839. *See also* Political Exile (Nineteenth Century)

Further Readings

Bueno, Salvador. "José María Heredia, el poeta romántico". In *Figuras cubanas del siglo XIX*. Havana: Unión de Escritores y Artistas de Cuba, 1980. 77–84.

Lazo, Raimundo. *Historia de la literatura cubana*. Mexico City: Dirección General de Publicaciones, 1974.

Ilia Casanova-Marengo

Hernández Espinosa, Eugenio (1936–)

Dramatist and theater director Eugenio Hernández Espinosa started his professional affiliation with **theater** in 1960 in the Seminario de Dramaturgia del Teatro Nacional, where he met the most important playwrights of his generation. Seven years later, he staged his work *María Antonia*, a classic of Cuban contemporary theater. The piece—a sort of Caribbean *Carmen*—fleshes out racial stereotypes to offer a new theatrical vision of the Afro-Cuban universe (see **Afro-Cubans**). The play is enriched by the use of popular **Santería** rites.

A prolific writer, Hernández Espinosa has explored Cuba's African roots and popular idiosyncracies. His most famous works are *Mi socio Manolo*; (1971), *La Simona* (1977), which won the **Casa de las Américas** prize; *Calixta Comité* (1980); *Odebi, el cazador* (1982); *Oba y Shangó* (1983); and *Alto riesgo* (1996). In 1991, he founded the Teatro Caribeño where he has staged his most recent works. *María Antonia* and *Mi socio Manolo* were recently adapted to the screen. *See also* Theaters

Further Reading

Hernández Espinosa, Eugenio. *Teatro*. Havana: Editorial Letras Cubanas, 1989.

Wilfredo Cancio Isla

Hijuelos, Oscar (1951–)

Oscar Hijuelos was the first Latino novelist to receive the Pulitzer Prize (1990) with his second novel *The Mambo Kings Play Songs of Love* (1989), which was also transformed in 1992 into the film *The Mambo Kings*, directed by Arne Glimcher. Born in New York of Cuban parents, he attended the City University of New York, finishing a B.A. in 1975, followed by an M.A. in 1976, both in English (creative writing). In 1983, he published his first novel *Our House in the Last World*, which narrates the complex living experiences of a Cuban immigrant family in New York's Spanish Harlem. His award-wining *The Mambo Kings Play Songs of Love*, is the story of César and Eugenio Castillo, two Cuban musicians who immigrated to the United States in the late 1940s in search of the American Dream; it is also a re-creation of the influence of Latin music through the 1950s in mainstream North America. Though exploring Cuban themes in these two novels, and subsequent works,

Hijuelos attempted to create a narrative and situations that were not entirely Cuba-centric.

Oscar Hijuelos has been the recipient of highly competitive scholastic awards: the American Academy in Rome Fellowship (1985), the National Endowment for the Arts Fellowship (1985) and the Guggenheim Fellowship (1990). He also has published the novels *The Fourteen Sisters of Emilio Montez O'Brien* (1993), *Mr. Ives' Christmas* (1995), and the *Empress of the Splendid Season* (1999).

Further Reading

Pérez Firmat, Gustavo. "Oscar Hijuelos." In *Modern Latin-American Fiction Writers*, ed. William Luis and Ann González. Detroit: Gale Research, 1994. 148–154.

Ilia Casanova-Marengo

Jorge Cardoso, Onelio (1914–1986)

Born in the Cuban countryside, in Calabazar de Sagua, old Las Villas Province, Onelio Jorge Cardoso wrote his first short stories while still in his teens. He won the first prize for short stories in the journal *Social* in 1936, and over the course of a long and prolific literary life, he came to be known as Cuba's national short-story writer. Author of more than a dozen volumes of short stories depicting the lives of farmers and laborers, Jorge Cardoso worked as a rural schoolteacher, a traveling salesman of medical equipment, and writer for radio and television and later for documentary films produced by the Cuban Institute of Art and Motion Picture Industry (ICAIC) and the Ejército Rebelde. His stories have been dramatized and presented by the **theater** companies El Teatro Escambray and the Conjunto Dramático de Oriente and translated into Chinese, German, English, French, Russian, and Bulgarian. In addition to numerous pres-

tigious literary prizes, Jorge Cardoso was awarded the 26 de Julio Journalistic Prize in 1964. He has also authored several collections of short stories for children. His most famous short story, "El caballo de coral," was choreographed for ballet by Cuba's **Ballet Nacional**. *See also* Literary Journals.

Further Readings

Chaple, Sergio. *Estudios de narrativa cubana*. Havana: Ediciones UNIÓN, 1996.
Hernández Azaret, Josefa de la C. *Algunos aspectos de la cuentística de Onelio Jorge Cardoso*. Santiago de Cuba: Editorial Oriente, 1982.

Pamela María Smorkaloff

Labrador Ruiz, Enrique (1902–1991)

Novelist and short-story writer Enrique Labrador Ruiz was the creator of the *novelas gaseiformes*, a type of novel that had no clear beginning and ending and where the lack of a narrative allowed the reader to open up the book anywhere. It was an experimental literary style that heralded the innovative works of later writers, especially the Latin American Boom authors who emerged during the 1960s.

Self-educated, Labrador Ruiz began his writing career as a journalist. During the 1920s, he worked for several newspapers, including *El País, Prensa Libre*, and *El Mundo*, as well as numerous magazines of wide circulation, such as *Bohemia, Chic*, and *Social* (see **Newspapers [Republican Era]**). In 1951, he received the **Juan Gualberto Gómez** award for journalism.

What brought him fame, however, was the novel *El laberinto de sí mismo*. Labrador Ruiz wrote the novel in 1933, a period when many Cuban authors were experimenting with different literary techniques. The novel was a psychological game between the "I" of the creator and the world of words. Not an easy work to read, the novel, nevertheless, received critical and scholarly attention. Two other novels followed, *Cresival* (1936) and *Anteo* (1940). Scholar Max Henríquez Ureña compared reading these three works to piecing together a broken mirror. In 1947, the author published another experimental work, *Carne de quimera*. In 1950, he returned to a more traditional style with *La sangre hambrienta*; this novel earned him the national prize for fiction issued by the Ministry of Education. He also continued writing short stories and articles, which he submitted to international literary journals.

During the 1960s, Labrador Ruiz worked for a publishing house, Editorial Nacional, and traveled throughout Russia and China. In the 1970s, he went into exile, settling in Miami. He toured many universities in the United States, lecturing on literature and reading from his works. Though his novels are taught and used in some U.S. universities, he has not received as much scholarly attention as his friends and colleagues **José Lezama Lima** and **Reinaldo Arenas**. *See also* Literary Journals

Further Readings

Henríquez Ureña, Max. *Panorama histórico de la literatura cubana, Tomo II*. Havana: Editorial Arte y Literatura, 1979.

Sánchez, Reinaldo. ed. *Homenaje a Enrique Labrador Ruiz: textos críticos, sobre su obra*. Montevideo, Uruguay: Editorial Ciencias, 1981.

D.H. Figueredo

Leante, César (1928–)

As a novelist, short-story writer, and essayist, César Leante emerged with the Cuban **Revolution**. Prior to 1959, Leante was a minor writer who made a living writing for television and radio. Afterward, he worked as a journalist for *Revolución* and

César Leante, journalist, editor of several important Cuban journals, and winner of Cuba's national award for fiction. Photograph by William Luis.

collaborated in ***Lunes de Revolución***. He also worked for Prensa Latina, the Ministry of Foreign Affairs in Paris, the **Unión de Escritores y Artistas de Cuba (UNEAC)**, and the Ministry of Culture, before seeking exile in Spain in 1981.

Leante is a prolific writer. He published *Con las milicias* (1962), a journalistic-testimonial account of Castro's militia; *El perseguido* (1964), based on the March 13, 1957, attack on the **Presidential Palace**; *Padres e hijos* (1967), a fictionalized autobiography narrated in the second person; and *Muelle de caballería* (1973), an experimental novel that moves back and forth between the nineteenth and twentieth centuries. He has also published three collections of short stories, *La rueda y la serpiente* (1969), *Tres historias* (1977), and *Propiedad horizontal* (1978), and a collection of essays, *El espacio real* (1975). His *Los guer-rilleros negros* (1977) received UNEAC's **Cirilo Villaverde** prize in 1975.

Outside of Cuba, Leante has written opinions and essays critical of the Cuban government but has not abandoned totally the art that gave him his reputation. He has published *Calembour* (1988), about the first years of the Revolution; *Fidel Castro: el fin de un mito* (1991); *Hemingway y la revolución cubana* (1993); and *Desnudo femenino y otros cuentos* (1995), which gathers new and previously published sto-ries. Currently Leante resides in Madrid and is the editor of the publisher's series Pliegos de narrativa. *See also* Literary Journals; Literature of the Revolutionary Era; Newspapers and Magazines

Further Readings

Álvarez García, Imeldo. *La novela cubana en el siglo XX*. Havana: Editorial Letras Cubanas, 1980.
Luis, William. "La novelística de César Leante." *Cuadernos Americanos* 244, no. 5 (1982): 226–236.

William Luis

Lezama Lima, José (1910–1976)

José Lezama Lima, next to his sister, Eloisa. He was a poet and novelist with Baroque style who influenced much of Cuban culture during the 20th century. Courtesy of the Cuban Heritage Collec-tion of the Otto G. Richter Library of the Univer-sity of Miami.

A central figure in twentieth-century Cu-ban culture, poet, novelist, and essayist José Lezama Lima fostered a resurgence of Cuban poetry with the founding of the journal *Orígenes* (1944–1956) and the Grupo Orígenes, a grouping of Cuban writers of which he was a leading member.

Lezama Lima received a doctorate in law from the **University of Havana** in 1938 and worked as a lawyer until 1945, when he took an administrative post with the Ministry of Education's Cultural Di-vision. Pillar and lifeblood of Cuban cul-ture in his day, Lezama Lima founded four successive **literary journals**, the first of which was *Verbum* (1937), created with René Villanova out of the University of Havana Law School; followed by *Espuela de Plata* (1939–1941), created with Guy Pérez Cisneros and Mariano Rodríguez; *Nadie Parecía* (1942–1944), with Angel Gaztelu; and finally, *Orígenes*, in 1944. Following the politically charged decade from 1920 to 1930, the revolt against then-president **Gerardo Machado**, and general repression in all areas of national life, the 1940s witnessed a mass-media onslaught. Against this backdrop, the Orígenes Group, with their journal and book pub-lishing initiative, created its own channels for literary and artistic efforts of a minor-ity, but a minority with a far-reaching aes-thetic and cultural program. The journal *Orígenes* soon earned international ac-claim and provided an invaluable stimulus for literary and artistic production with few outlets to society at large.

Lezama Lima's own volumes of poetry with their journal and book publishing initiative include *Muerte de Narciso* (1937), *Enemigo rumor* (1941), *La fijeza* (1949), and *Dador* (1960). His books of essays include *Analecta del reloj* (1953), *La expresión americana* (1957), *Tratados en La Habana* (1958), *La cantidad hechizada* (1970), *Las eras imaginarias* (1971), and *Fragmentos de un imán* (1977). Many consider the poetic novel *Paradiso* (1966) to be his master work. Lezama Lima redefined the baroque literary style, which he perceived as sensuous, colorful, full of life, and playfully intellectual, rather than academic and abstruse.

Though he held a succession of important positions within Cuban cultural institutions over the course of a lifetime—he was one of six vice presidents of the **Unión de Escritores y Artistas de Cuba** (**UNEAC**) in 1962, was a researcher and adviser to the **Academy of Sciences**' Institute of Literature and Linguistics, and was later affiliated with the **Casa de las Américas**—he was marginalized by the Cuban government. From 1969 to 1976, he lived in virtual isolation. Government officials later reevaluated his work, considered it appropriate, and reprinted limited editions during the 1970s and 1980s. Lezama Lima left an unfinished manuscript, *Oppiano Licario*, which was published in 1971. His works have been widely translated, and his fame has grown since his death. *See also* Literary Journals; Literature of the Revolutionary Era

Futher Readings

Martínez, Pedro Simón, ed. *Recopilación de textos sobre José Lezama Lima*. Havana: Casa de las Américas, 1970.

Vizcaíno, Cristina, ed. *Coloquio internacional sobre la obra de José Lezama Lima*. 2 vols. Madrid: Editorial Fundamentos, 1984.

Pamela María Smorkaloff

Literary Journals

Cuba has a long and rich history of cultural institutions that have lent indirect support to writers. The oldest of these is the **Sociedad Económica de Amigos del País**, established in 1792 by royal decree. The journal founded by the Sociedad, the *Revista Bimestre Cubana* (published in three phases, 1831–1834, 1910–1959, and 1994–   ), played an important role among the first generation of writers in the Cuban Republic. The first phase of the journal underlined the cultural lag suffered in the colony and announced its intent to serve as an organ for literature. In the second phase, under the direction of **Fernando Ortiz**, the journal continued to promote literary creation and incorporated a new section, "Cuban Poetry," open to the nation's unpublished poets. The Sociedad contributed to the establishment of two new institutions specializing in Cuban literature and culture: the Hispano-Cuban Cultural Institute (1926–1948) and the Society for Cuban Folklore (1936–1947). The former put out *Ultra* (1936–1947), a journal that published articles by international authors, and the latter, *Archivos de folklore cubano* (1924–1931), which was devoted to fables, *décimas*, **boleros**, and other expressions of national popular culture.

Other major literary journals born in the first two decades of the Republic were *Chic* (1917–1927, 1933–1959?), *Cuba Contemporánea* (1913–1927), and *Social* (1916–1933, 1935–1938), the most influential of them. Like *Social, Orto* (1912–1957), of the town of Manzanillo, had a sturdier base of support than most equivalent journals. In the decade from 1920 to 1930, a group of activist intellectuals calling themselves the **Grupo Minorista** founded the *Revista de Avance* (1927–1930), typical of the journals that voiced the social and artistic concerns of the progressive intelligentsia of the 1920s and

1930s. The 1930s brought forth other journals that, like *Avance*, wedded literary concerns to social commitment; among these were *Gráfos* (1933–1946), *Baraguá* (1937–1938?), *Isla* (1936), and *Mediodía* (1936–1939). The most important literary journal of the 1940s, lasting over a decade, was *Orígenes* (1944–1956), founded by the intellectuals of the Orígenes Group. Toward the end of this period, two Orígenes members, **Virgilio Piñera** and José Rodríguez Feo, split from the group and edited the journal *Ciclón* (1957–1959). From 1954 to 1960 a new journal, *Revista de Nuestro Tiempo*, flourished. It featured literary, film, and music criticism by such figures as **Tomás Gutiérrez Alea**, Mirta Aguirre, and Juan Blanco, among others.

After 1959, Cuba's major periodicals were those published by the **Casa de las Américas**, among them *La Revista Casa de las Américas*, published since 1960; *Boletín de Música* (1970–   ), devoted to Latin American music; *Conjunto* (1964–   ), a specialized journal devoted to Latin American drama; *Criterio: Revista de Teoría Literaria, Estética y Culturología* (1982–   ), copublished with the **Unión de Escritores y Artistas de Cuba (UNEAC)** and devoted to theory and criticism; and *Anales del Caribe* (1981), for Caribbean specialists. Other important journals are *Unión* and *La Gaceta de Cuba*, published by UNEAC, and *Lunes de Revolución*, shut down by the government in 1961.

Throughout the economic crisis known as the **Special Period**, many of these journals ceased publication, and others, such as *Temas* (1994–   ), have emerged. *See also* Press and Journalism (Eighteenth and Nineteenth Centuries); Newspapers and Magazines

Further Readings

Pérez León, Roberto, ed. *Tiempo de Ciclón*. Havana: Unión de Escritores y Artistas de Cuba, 1991.
Weiss, Judith A. Casa de las Américas: *An Intellectual Review in the Cuban Revolution*. Chapel Hill, NC. Estudios de Hispanófila; Madrid: Editorial Castalia, 1977.

Pamela María Smorkaloff

Literature of the Revolutionary Era

The year 1959, the year of the "triumph of the Cuban **Revolution**," was witness to a cultural explosion and at the same time a kind of catharsis. In terms of literature, there was no initial "avalanche" of production following the Revolution. In the early 1960s, Cuban society was forced to examine existing resources and determine how they might be combined to forge the foundations for a graphics and book publishing industry, following on the heels of the massive **literacy campaign**. New definitions of the role of the Cuban writer, reader, and literature itself, from 1959 to 1962, had grown out of the literacy campaign, the efforts of the newly formed National Printing House, **Casa de las Américas**, and the **Unión de Escritores y Artistas de Cuba (UNEAC)**. New institutions such as the municipal libraries, writers' workshops, and local bookstores began to spring up all over the island to reinforce the literacy and postliteracy campaigns. Cuban critic and literary historian Ambrosio Fornet has spoken of an initial silence, a catharsis, on the part of writers in the first months and years in response to revolutionary change and the new reading public for Cuban literature.

If we take stock of Cuban literary production from 1959 through the 1960s, poetry stands out as the most widely cultivated genre, followed by the novel and prose narrative in general, which includes the essay and testimonial literature in addition to the short story, all of which caught up with poetry in the 1970s. Cuban poetry reflected the revolutionary period as it was unfolding, drawing its raw material from the everyday life of Cubans.

The major poets to emerge during the 1960s were **Nancy Morejón, Roberto Fernández Retamar**, and Heberto Padilla (see **Padilla [Affair], Heberto**), capturing the world's attention over the next four decades with a poetry that both celebrated and criticized the Revolution. Novelists such as **Guillermo Cabrera Infante, César Leante**, and **Reinaldo Arenas** achieved international recognition. Short-story writers, like **Antonio Benítez Rojo** and **Jesús Díaz**, among others, were also acclaimed. And children's literature experienced a renaissance, as a result of the Revolution, through the editions of Gente Nueva, a publishing house devoted to the genre. Established writers also enjoyed an increased appreciation of their work. Among these writers were **Nicolás Guillén, Alejo Carpentier**, and **José Lezama Lima**.

In the 1970s, the Letras Cubanas publishing house was founded to disseminate classic and contemporary works of Cuban literature. It arose in response to a "boom" in national literary output from the mid-1970s to the mid-1980s. Though the revolutionary era was witness to the emergence of Cuban writers too numerous to mention individually, two works in particular stand out as approximations of a novel of the Cuban Revolution. The first is *Consagración de la primavera* (1978), by one of Cuba's major novelists, Alejo Carpentier, who died two years later, in 1980. The second is *Las iniciales de la tierra* (1987) by Jesús Díaz, considered to have ushered in a new era in Cuban literature with his collection of short stories *Los años duros* (1966).

Cuban critic and women's studies scholar Luisa Campuzano, in "La mujer en la narrativa de la Revolución: ponencia sobre una carencia," one of the few existing studies of gender in contemporary Cuban literature, addresses gender issues in Cuban literary production on three levels: women's access to education and the labor force, women as protagonists in Cuban literature, and women as authors of literary works. While noting women's major advances in higher education and as active members of a labor force beyond traditional roles, Campuzano admits that by 1983, when research for her study was conducted, these gains had not been translated into a greater presence of women authors on the contemporary literary scene (see **Women's Rights**). Taking stock of the novels of the revolutionary era, Campuzano notes, in the same study, only 12 novels written by women as compared to more than 160 written by men.

To date, numerous works of national literature have been translated into film: *El siglo de las luces, Cecilia Valdés*, and *El otro Francisco*, on or from the historical past; *Canción de Rachel* and *Memorias del subdesarrollo*, from the early years of the Revolution; and more recently, *Fresa y chocolate*, adapted from the short story "El lobo, el bosque y el hombre nuevo" (1994), by Senel Paz (see **Cinema**).

Recent works of Cuban literature, such as Pedro Juan Gutiérrez's *Trilogía sucia de La Habana* (1998), begin to chronicle the little or unexplored themes of gay life and the contradictions of the **Special Period. Miguel Barnet**, one of Cuba's most celebrated contemporary writers, was featured author of the central fiction piece in *The New Yorker* magazine's 1998 "Cuba Issue." In that short story, "Miosvatis," Cuba is a site of estrangement, and the narrator's condition is one of seemingly permanent in-betweenness, signaling a new perspective on "home" and "nation," viewed from a critical distance and with the intent to take stock of Cuba's present.

Further Readings

Campuzano, Luisa, ed. *Mujeres latino-americanas: historia y cultura*. Iztapalapa, Mexico: Universidad Autónoma Metropolitana; Havana: Casa de las Américas, 1998.

Fornet, Ambrosio. *Cine, literatura y sociedad*. Havana: Editorial Letras Cubanas, 1982.

Pamela María Smorkaloff

López, César (1933–   )

The winner of the 1999 Cuban National Literature Award, César López is a poet, short-story writer, and translator. His writings include the book of poetry *Libro de la ciudad* (1983), a collection of short stories titled *Circulando el cuadrado* (1967), as well as hundreds of articles and poems published in international journals. He has translated works by Lawrence Durrel and Yannis Ritzo.

López was born in **Santiago de Cuba**. A physician by training, López attended the **University of Havana** and the University of Salamanca, in Spain. From 1960 to 1962, he served as consul in Scotland and then returned to Cuba to work in the Ministry of Foreign Relations. He worked as secretary of the **Unión de Escritores y Artistas de Cuba (UNEAC)** and conducted research for the Instituto de Documentación e Información Científica. From 1968 to 1983, he was one of the many authors who experienced censorship, as a result of the **Padilla Affair** when the government censored writers who were critical of the revolutionary process, and was not allowed to publish his works. In 1991, he re-emerged with a book of poetry, *Doble espejo para muerte denigrante*. Five years later new editions of his works were published in Cuba.

Further Reading
Diccionario de la literatura cubana. Vol. 1. Havana: Editorial Letras Cubanas, 1980.

D.H. Figueredo

Loynaz, Dulce María (1903–1998)

Dulce María Loynaz's life and literary career is one of quiet but enduring revelations, written in a finely chiseled, transparent poetry or prose. Loynaz comes from the Independence struggle aristocracy: Her great uncle and father fought in the **War of Independence**, alongside **Antonio Maceo, José Martí**, and **Máximo Gómez**.

Despite her admirable prose, Loynaz is better known as a poet. Her literary career began early: At ten she published a poem in the newspaper *La Nación*. She later wrote journalism for the same publication. Her first book of poems was *Versos, 1920–1938* (1938). It was followed by *Juegos de agua* (1947), *Poemas sin nombre* (1953), *Carta de amor al Rey Tut-Ank-Amen* (1953), and *Últimos días de una casa* (1958), a detailed and poetic portrait of a world about to vanish. In 1993, *Poesías completas* was published in Cuba.

Loynaz's prose works consist of three books: *Jardín* (1951), deemed by the author a lyrical novel; *Un verano en Tenerife* (1958), about her long visits to the Canary Islands; and *Ensayos literarios* (1993), which contains an important 1950 essay called "Mi poesía: autocrítica," an excellent overview of her artistic views and a definition of her poetics. Loynaz's poetic universe speaks of love, solitude, and nature with a disarming simplicity, beneath which lies a richly layered world that is complex, unsentimental, and philosophical.

Loynaz was a loner and avoided literary schools or movements. She said that for a writer there is "nothing more dangerous than to establish a school." Her influences were far-ranging: Rabindranath Tagore, St. John, St. Augustine, Francisco de Quevedo, Azorín, the French Symbolists and Parnassians, and Gabriela Mistral, as well as Cuban writers like **Juan Clemente Zenea, Gertrudis Gómez de Avellaneda, José Martí**, and **Julián del Casal**.

In 1959 she withdrew from all public literary life and stopped writing poetry. The Cuban **Revolution** signified an end to the world she grew up in and wrote about. She remained at the margin of political debates in Cuba and was largely ignored for two decades. In the 1980s, as the Cuban literary climate opened up, her work was reappraised.

Loynaz won many awards, from the Orden **Carlos Manuel de Céspedes** (1947, Cuba) and the Order of Alfonso X, the Wise (1947, Spain) to the more recent National Prize in Literature (1987), the Orden **Félix Varela** (1987), and the **Alejo Carpentier** Medal (1983). The Cervantes Prize, in 1992, brought her international renown and has led to reeditions of her poetry and prose and more critical attention.

Further Readings

Rodríguez, Ileana. *House, Garden, Nation*. Durham, NC: Duke University Press, 1994.
Simón, Pedro, comp. *Dulce María Loynaz: valoración múltiple*. Havana: Casa de las Américas, 1991.
West-Durán, Alan. *Tropics of History: Cuba Imagined*. Westport, CT: Greenwood Press, 1997.

Alan West-Durán

Luaces, Joaquín Lorenzo (1826–1867)

Joaquín Lorenzo Luaces was a nineteenth-century poet and pioneer dramatist who, along with **Gertrudis Gómez de Avellaneda**, attempted to create a Cuban consciousness and identity. His works echoed the contemporary interest in a national expression, emphasizing Creole traits and seeking a cultural and sentimental connection with the Siboney Indians, aborigines wiped out by Spaniards during colonization (see **Indigenous Inhabitants** and **Conquest**).

Many of Luaces's poems were written during a stay in Isla del Pinos (now **Isla de la Juventud**) in the late 1840s. His first published piece was "La hija del artesano," which came out in the journal *El Artista* in 1849. From 1855 onward, he wrote for several **literary journals**, including the *Revista Habanera*. In 1857, he published *Poesías*, and in 1859 he was awarded the Liceo de La Habana prize for

his poem "A Ciro Field, or la inmersión del cable submarino."

Luaces's best-known plays, which belonged to a dramatist tradition called **Teatro Bufo**, or comic theater, were *El mendigo rojo* (1859), *El becerro de oro* (1859), and *Aristodemo* (1867), a classically inspired drama. These plays were never performed during his lifetime, however.

Some of his plays were published in 1964 in a volume titled *Teatro*. A selection of his poetry appeared in 1981 under the title *Poesías escogidas*. *See also* Theater; Press and Journalism (Eighteenth and Nineteenth Centuries)

Further Readings

Salazar, Salvador. *Milanés, Luáces y La Avellaneda, como poetas dramáticos*. Havana: A. Miranda, 1916.

D.H. Figueredo

Lunes de Revolución (1959–1961)

Lunes de Revolución, published from March 23, 1959, to November 6, 1961, was the weekly literary supplement of the newspaper *Revolución*, of the **26th of July Movement**, edited by **Carlos Franqui**. Under the direction of **Guillermo Cabrera Infante** and assistant editor Pablo Armando Fernández, *Lunes* became the most important Cuban and arguably Latin American literary supplement of its time. In a short period of time, its circulation surpassed 250,000 copies.

Lunes attempted to provide a direction for the unfolding of literature and culture in the **Revolution**. The supplement was anti-imperialistic but supported a broad definition of culture, as expressed by its varied themes and diverse collaborators. Contributors included Pablo Neruda, Jorge Luis Borges, Federico García Lorca, and Jean Paul Sartre but also **Fidel Castro** himself. Special issues were dedicated to individuals like Emilio Ballagas (issue

26), **José Martí** (93), and Pablo Picasso (129) and countries like Guatemala (22), Vietnam (116), and the People's Republic of China (108).

Lunes became a threat as Castro shifted his allegiance from the 26th of July Movement to that of Cuba's Communist Party (see **Partido Comunista**). *Lunes*'s demise was precipitated by its support of *P.M.*, an innocuous short documentary by Sabá Cabrera Infante and Orlando Jiménez Leal, about the nightlife of Havana's Afro-Cuban population (see **Afro-Cubans**). The government's decision to censor the film and close *Lunes* culminated on June 30, 1961, with Castro's famous "Words to the Intellectuals," where he stated, "Within the Revolution, everything. Outside the Revolution, nothing." Castro's speech set the stage for judging literature and culture within a binary framework: Whether a work of art was revolutionary or counter-revolutionary. The closing of *Lunes* signaled an end to a period of plurality and openness in Cuban society and culture. *See also* Literature of the Revolutionary Era; Padilla (Affair), Heberto; Cinema; Literary Journals

Further Readings

Franqui, Carlos. *Retrato de familia con Fidel*. Barcelona: Editorial Seix Barral, 1981.
Luis, William. "Autopsia a de *Lunes de Revolución*: entrevista a Pablo Armando Fernández." *Plural* 17, no. 126 (1982): 52–62.
Luis, William. "*Lunes de Revolución*: Literature and Culture in the First Years of the Cuban Revolution." In *Guillermo Cabrera Infante: Assays, Essays, and Other Arts*, ed. Ardis L. Nelson. New York: Twayne Publishers, 1999. 16–38.

William Luis

Luz y Caballero, José de la (1800–1862)

José de la Luz y Caballero was a teacher and philosopher who promoted the formation and spread of nineteenth-century Cuban national discourse. Born in Havana, he received a philosophy degree in 1817 at the Convento de San Francisco, where he began ecclesiastic studies that he left unfinished to go into teaching. His travels took him to the United States in 1828 and Europe in 1821, where he met intellectuals such as Henry W. Longfellow, Walter Scott, and Goethe.

On his return to Cuba in 1831, he contributed articles to many Cuban periodicals including *Revista Bimestre Cubana* and *Diario de La Habana*. In 1833, he published his *Libro de lectura por el método explicativo* and also became director of Colegio de San Cristóbal, where he created a chemistry professorship and taught a philosophy class from 1834 to 1835. He became a lawyer in 1836. In 1843, he went to New York and then to Paris, having to return to Cuba in 1844 to be tried for his alleged involvement in the **Conspiracy of La Escalera**. He was freed on a lack of evidence. In 1848, he established the boarding school Colegio El Salvador, where he disseminated his political, philosophical, and educational ideas, all based on his vision of a reformed **educational system** and the end of Cuba's colonial status. *See also* Press and Journalism (Eighteenth and Nineteenth Centuries)

Further Readings

Esténger, Rafael. *Don Pepe, retrato de un maestro de escuela*. Havana: Editorial "Alfa" 1940.
Henríquez Ureña, Max. *Panorama histórico de la literatura cubana*. Vol. 1. Havana: Editorial Arte y Literatura, 1978.

Ilia Casanova-Marengo

Mañach Robato, Jorge (1898–1961)

Author, journalist, university professor, and political thinker, Jorge Mañach was born in Sagua la Grande in what was then Las Villas Province. As a child he lived in Spain and received part of his primary education there. He later went to the

Jorge Mañach Robato, one of Cuba's leading essayists. Photograph courtesy of the Biblioteca Nacional José Martí, Havana.

United States to pursue college studies and graduated from Harvard University in 1920. After graduation, he spent a year at Harvard teaching Romance languages. In 1922 Mañach returned to Cuba and became a leading figure in intellectual circles, while at the same time working as a journalist for various publications including the magazine *Social* and the newspapers *Diario de la Marina* and *El País*. During this period, Mañach obtained doctoral degrees in civil law and philosophy and letters from the **University of Havana**. In the 1920s, Mañach became associated with the **Grupo Minorista**, a group of intellectuals that advocated ethical government and political and social reforms. As part of the movement, he founded the magazine *Revista de Avance*, which promoted the group's agenda. An innovative educator, Mañach helped create *Universidad del Aire*, a radio program dedicated to teaching Cuban culture and history to a mass audience.

Mañach was forced into exile in 1935 because of his opposition to the **Fulgencio Batista**–backed government of **Carlos Mendieta**. While in the United States, from 1935 through 1939, he undertook an ambitious scholarly agenda that included editing parts of the *Revista Hispánica Moderna* and directing the Instituto de las Españas at Columbia University in New York. He was elected as a delegate to the Constitutional Convention and returned to Cuba in 1940 to help draft a new constitution (see **Constitution of 1940**). For a short period he served in the cabinet of President Batista. He returned to teaching at the University of Havana and revived his old radio program, which ran from 1948 to 1952. He founded the popular television program *Ante la prensa* (Before the Press) and served as the show's moderator. Mañach left Cuba in 1960 because of dissatisfaction with the revolutionary government. He settled in Puerto Rico, where he taught briefly at the University of Puerto Rico at Río Piedras. He authored numerous works including *Glosario* (1924), *Estampas de San Cristóbal* (1926), *Indigación del choteo* (1928), *Martí, el apostol* (1933), *Pasado vigente* (1939), and *Historia y estilo* (1944). A book of his lectures and conferences, *Teoría de la frontera*, was published posthumously in 1970. *See also* Newspapers (Republican Era); Puerto Rico, Cubans in

Further Reading

Valdespino, Andrés Alberto. *Jorge Mañach y su generación en las letras cubanas*. Miami: Ediciones Universal, 1971.

Wilfredo Cancio Isla

Manzano, Juan Francisco (1797?–1854)

Juan Francisco Manzano was the author of *Autobiografía de un esclavo* (parts of which were published in English in 1840;

the actual work was published in Cuba in 1937), a portrayal of Cuban **slavery** and the only life account by a former Cuban slave known in nineteenth-century Latin American literature. Manzano's destiny changed after the death of his first owner the Marchioness Jústiz de Santa Ana in 1809, when he became the property of the Marchioness de Prado Ameno who constantly punished him. He escaped and remained in Havana roughly between 1814 and 1817. In 1818 Juan Francisco served under his former mistress's son, Don Nicolás de Cárdenas y Manzano. He was able to become literate by imitating his new master's handwriting. After three years, he returned to the Marchioness's service from whom he ultimately ran away. In 1821 he published *Poesías líricas*, followed in 1830 by *Flores pasageras* [*sic*]. In 1835, he started writing his life story at the request of **Domingo del Monte** who, in 1836, obtained Manzano's freedom through a collection organized in conjunction with other Cuban intellectuals. After his liberation, he earned a living as a confectioner, tailor, and cook, and from 1837–1838 on he continued publishing in journals such as *Aguinaldo Habanero* and *El Album*. His *Autobiografía* and some poems were published in England by British abolitionist Richard R. Madden as *Poems by a Slave in the Island of Cuba* in 1840. He published a play, *Zafira*, in 1842 and in 1844 was falsely accused and imprisoned for participating in the **Conspiracy of La Escalera**. Released in 1845, he never wrote again. *See also* Abolitionist Literature; Cimarrones (Runaway Slaves)

Further Readings

Friol, Roberto. *Suite para Juan Francisco Manzano*. Havana: Editorial Arte y Literatura, 1977.

Molloy, Sylvia. "From Serf to Self: The Autobiography of Juan Francisco Manzano." In *At Face Value: Autobiographical Writing in Spanish America*. Cambridge, United Kingdom: Cambridge University Press, 1991. 36–54.

Ilia Casanova-Marengo

Mariel Generation

The *Mariel Generation* is a term applied to a group of writers, intellectuals, and artists who left Cuba through the port of El Mariel during the mass exodus of 1980 and settled in the United States (see **Mariel Boatlift**). Consisting mostly of men, this group had achieved maturity under **Fidel Castro**'s regime. Censored by the government, they were often marginalized and even imprisoned. Because of this oppression, they fled the island.

The members of this generation published several **literary journals**: *Término*, published in Spanish in Cincinnati, Ohio; *Unveiling Cuba*, published in English in New York; and *Mariel*, which was the most prominent and popular publication, lasting from 1983 to 1985. The journals were the first steps many of these writers and artists took to develop their careers in exile.

The journal *Mariel* was directed and edited by **Reinaldo Arenas**, the most famous member of the generation. Other writers who contributed to the periodical were the novelist Carlos Victoria, the poets Roberto Valero, Esteban Luis Cárdenas, and Andrés Reynaldo, and the short-story writers Miguel Correa, Rolando Morelli, René Cifuentes, and Carlos A. Díaz. Novelist Guillermo Rosales and playwright René Ariza were considered part of the group even though they did not leave Cuba during the 1980 exodus. One of the few women connected to the Mariel Generation was Marci Morgado, who had in fact left Cuba in 1961. Artists **Carlos Alfonzo**, Gilberto Ruiz, Juan Abreau, Ernesto Briel, Jesús Selgas, Héctor Niebas, and Juan Bozo illustrated the publication.

The Mariel Generation did not create a unique artistic and literary movement and did not share a common artistic style. What united its members as a group was their formation and intellectual foundation in Cuba's socialist regime and their opposition to Fidel Castro, as well as their commitment to establishing a literary and artistic presence in the United States. *See also* Literature of the Revolutionary Era

Further Readings
Arenas, Reinaldo. *Before Night Falls*. New York: Viking Press, 1993.
Bertol, Lillian. *The Literary Imagination of the Mariel Generation*. Miami: Endowment for Cuban American Studies, Cuban American National Foundation, 1995.

Wilfredo Cancio Isla

Marrero Artiles, Leví (1911–1995)

Leví Marrero was a recognized and prolific author of an extensive and unparalleled body of research on Cuba's history and geography and also a journalist and outstanding professor in his homeland and abroad. Born in **Santa Clara**, in the former province of Las Villas (currently **Villa Clara**), on July 16, 1911, Marrero graduated in 1940 from the **University of Havana**, where he was a disciple of the prominent historian **Ramiro Guerra y Sánchez**, receiving the degree of Doctor of Philosophy.

In 1952 Marrero completed a postgraduate course at McGill University, with the support of a Guggenheim Fellowship he earned after the publication of his *Geografía de Cuba*. In 1953 he conducted comprehensive studies on methods of scientific research while working at the University of Florida, under the guidance of geographer Raymond Christ and demographer Lynn Smith.

Marrero served as professor of geography at the Instituto de La Víbora in Havana from 1940 through 1955. After the founding in 1955 of the Higher Institute of Economic Research at the University of Havana, Marrero held the chair of Economic History of Cuba. In 1959, he was appointed to a diplomatic position with the Organization of American States (OAS) in Washington.

Marrero sought exile in Venezuela in 1961 where he was appointed professor of geography at the Pedagogical Institute of the University of Barquisimeto (1961–1964). He moved to Puerto Rico in 1965 where he served as chair of the Department of Social Sciences at the College of Humacao of the University of Puerto Rico. He lived in Puerto Rico until his death in Guaynabo on March 10, 1995.

Marrero wrote over a hundred articles, essays, and journalistic pieces, ranging the subjects of historical and human geography, economy, demographics, education, natural resources, and history. He also authored dozens of books on geography and history, among them the *Geografía de Cuba* (1950), which was used as a textbook in Cuban high schools and universities until it was banned by the government and the remaining copies were destroyed in 1961. Other books and writings by Marrero were also proscribed after his exile.

His inexhaustible creativity and commitment to scholarship produced extraordinarily documented, superbly illustrated, and gracefully edited works of geography and history. The most important and ambitious of his works is the fifteen-volume *Cuba: economía y sociedad*, published between 1972 and 1988; also important were his *Historia económica de Cuba* (1956), *La tierra y sus recursos* (1957), and *Venezuela y sus recursos* (1964).

Further Reading
Pérez, Jr., Louis A. *Essays on Cuban History: Historiography and Research*. Gainesville: University Press of Florida, 1995.

Armando H. Portela

Martí, José (as Writer) (1853–1895)

Journalist, poet, novelist, critic, and orator, José Martí was a leading literary figure of the late nineteenth century. His writings, chiefly his journalism and his poetry, were a major influence on Spanish and Latin American writers. Martí achieved this standing despite the fact that he dedicated most of his time, energy, and ultimately his life to the cause of Cuban independence. Though a prolific writer, Martí published few books during his lifetime. With the exception of his books of poems *Ismaelillo* (1882) and *Versos sencillos* (1891) and a short novel *Lucía Jerez* (1885), all published in small editions at the author's expense, Martí was known throughout Latin America for his journalistic pieces. Martí wrote columns for major Latin American newspapers—*La Nación* (Argentina), *Revista Universal* (Mexico), *La República* (Honduras), *La Opinión Pública* (Uruguay), *El Partido Liberal* (México)—as well as literary and art criticism for New York's *The Sun* and *The Hour*. Most of these articles, entitled *Escenas norteamericanas*, were written in the form of letters addressed to the editors of the newspapers. They contain Martí's observations of life, culture, and politics in the United States from 1881 to 1895. Martí thereby became Latin America's window to the United States. After his death and Cuba's independence from Spain, two books of poems, *Versos libres* (1913) and *Flores del destierro* (1933), were published. His collected works have been published in multivolume editions.

The extent of Martí's influence on the Latin American and Spanish literary movement known as *Modernismo* continues to be a matter for critical debate. Nevertheless, it is generally acknowledged that the prose of his newspaper articles, full of vigor and unexpected poetical images, had a major impact on *modernista* writers. Although he did not fully share the enthusiasm of many modernistas for escapism, the exotic, and the decadent, Martí was a pioneer in the blending of traditions taken from the classics of Spanish literature with newer forms of expression, which would become one of the hallmarks of the modernista movement. It is also clear that Martí found North American writers like Ralph Waldo Emerson and Walt Whitman more congenial than Paul Verlaine and Charles Leconte de Lisle, two French poets greatly admired by the modernistas. Ultimately for Martí, art in all its forms offered a temporary refuge where the soul was purified and strengthened in order to return to the work of life.

Of all of Martí's essays, *Nuestra América* (1891; *The America of José Martí*, 1954) continues to be part of the dialogue regarding Latin American identity more than a century after it was published. In it he identifies the mistakes of the leaders of the former Spanish colonies and proposes solutions for the future. Martí also articulates his formula for a harmonious relationship between the young American republics and the "Colossus of the North." All the citizens of the Americas must learn about each other, and the fruit of this knowledge will be mutual respect. The essay culminates in one of Martí's characteristic lapidary phrases: "There can be no racial hatred because there are no races." In his essays, as in his speeches, Martí captures the attention of his public with memorable phrases and dazzling metaphors that help to encapsulate his ideas. It is significant that the illiterate as well as the more educated members of his public responded powerfully to his words. Interviewed years after the **War of Independence**, a Cuban veteran who had heard Martí's speeches declared: "We didn't always understand everything he said, but we knew we had to die for him."

Ismaelillo, Martí's first book of poems, was dedicated to his infant son born in 1878. Unable to adjust to a life of poverty and exile in New York, Martí's wife, Carmen Zayas Bazán, returned suddenly to Cuba with their son, whom Martí would never see again. The title alludes to the biblical Ishmael, the infant son of Abraham who, banished to the desert with his mother, becomes the father of the nomadic Arab peoples. In these poems Martí conjures up the image of his absent son and speaks to him with great tenderness. Martí describes his son's birth as the catalyst for his own ethical and poetic rebirth: "I am my son's son!/He has made me again!" His son is a shield that protects his tired father from all that is evil and sordid in the world, leaving him purified and invigorated to resume the struggle for the good in life.

In the preface to *Versos libres*, poems written about the same time as *Ismaelillo*, Martí expresses forcefully the birth of his poems: "Not one has come out reheated, artificial, recomposed, from my mind; but as tears come out of the eyes and blood spurts from a wound. . . . They are written, not with academical ink, but with my own blood." These free verses where Martí dispenses with rhyme but adheres to the eleven-syllable meter of classical Spanish poetry are so daring in their images as to pose challenges to their readers. The poem "Copa con alas" is phantasmagorical and elusive until one realizes that the whole poem is an otherworldly description of a kiss, culminating in the declaration: "Oh love, . . . You, only you, know how to/ reduce the Universe to one kiss." Love, here as elsewhere in Martí's poems, is equated with art and its power to condense the experience of the universe.

Flores del destierro is a compilation of poems written between 1882 and 1891, many of which follow the pattern of *Versos libres*, and Martí's preface describes them as "notes taken on the run." In the poem "Dos patrias," Martí states that his two countries are Cuba and the night but immediately wonders if they are actually one. In this poem of unrelieved melancholy and alienation (unusual for Martí), Cuba/Night is depicted as a widow dressed in mourning and plucking at a red carnation that is identified as the poet's heart.

Martí's poetic fame, however, rests on the enduring popular success of his *Versos*

sencillos. Written in the Catskill Mountains of New York during a doctor-enforced rest from his feverish political activities in 1891, they summarize Martí's thoughts about human existence. Love in its carnal and spiritual forms, nature, art, beauty, exile, Cuba, Spain, friendship, and the role poetry itself plays in his life are evoked not in the free verses of his two previous collections but in the rhymed, eight-syllable quatrains of traditional Spanish ballads. In the preface to these simple verses, Martí states: "I love simplicity, and I believe in the need to express feelings in forms that are straightforward and sincere." These poems, identified only by Roman numerals, are indeed direct and simple but also remarkable for the originality of the images they contain. A good example of Martí's ability to transform even a geological fact into a metaphor is the following quatrain taken from poem I : "Everything is beautiful and constant,/Everything is music and reason,/And everything, like a diamond,/Before pure light is just coal." The book's best known poem is "La rosa blanca," which explores the subjects of friendship and reconciliation (see **Appendix 8**).

Martí is often and incorrectly described as a nationalist. Poem VII, the impressionistic description of a flamenco dancer, and poem X, a loving evocation of the region of Aragón in Spain, its land, history, and its freedom-loving people, demonstrate that this enemy of the Spanish empire was an admirer of its culture and its people: "I esteem whoever turns and/ brings down a tyrant:/I esteem him, if he is Cuban;/I esteem him, if Aragonese."

José Martí's two *Campaign Diaries* (1895), written during the invasion of Cuba with their telegraphic, urgent style and the former exile's euphoric descriptions of the island's landscape, are the last words he wrote. *See also* Martí, José (as Political Leader); Press and Journalism (Eighteenth and Nineteenth Centuries); Political Exile (Nineteenth Century)

Further Readings

Rodríguez-Luis, Julio, ed. *Re-reading José Martí (1853–1895): One Hundred Years Later*. Albany: State University of New York Press, 1999.

Rotker, Susana. *Fundación de una escritura: las crónicas de José Martí*. Havana: Casa de las Américas, 1997.

Gustavo Pellón

Massip y Valdés, Salvador (1891–1978)

Salvador Massip was a renowned geographer and pioneer of the scientific research and teaching of geography in Cuba. He was born in Artemisa, **Pinar del Río Province**, on April 19, 1891, and died in Havana on October 17, 1978. He earned the degree of Doctor of Philosophy from the **University of Havana** in 1915 and a Master of Arts from Columbia University under the guidance of the well-known geomorphologist Douglas Johnson, disciple of the founder of modern geomorphology William Morris Davis.

Appointed by concourse, professor of geography at the Philosophy and Arts Faculty of the University of Havana in 1924, he created the Department of Geography at the University of Havana in 1925. He also founded and became the first director of the Institute of Geography of the **Academy of Sciences** of Cuba (1962–1965). Massip was also professor of geography at the Universidad Nacional Autónoma de México (1935–1936). Later on he taught at the University of Miami (1941–1942), Smith College in Massachusetts (1943–1944), the University of Puerto Rico (1946–1947), Northwestern University (1948), and the University of Texas at Austin (1949).

In his work *Introducción a la geografía de Cuba* (1927), which became a masterpiece and foundation of Cuba's modern geographical studies, Massip was the first to describe the structure, composition, and evolution of the natural regions of the island. He wrote hundreds of scientific articles, essays, books, and journalistic pieces on regional, historical, and physical geography and the teaching of geography. Some of his writings, such as the *Elementos de la geografía regional* (1942), were long used as official texts in Cuban high schools and universities and also in some Latin American colleges.

As a constant traveler and participant in international congresses of geography, Massip for decades enlightened the Cuban academic world with modern concepts in geography through his writings and conferences.

He was a member of the **Ortodoxos (Partido del Pueblo Cubano)** until 1959 and was appointed ambassador to Mexico and Poland between 1959 and 1961.

Further Readings

Campoamor, Fernando G. *Vendimia en Capricornio*. Artemisa, Cuba: Editorial Proa, 1947.

Nuñez Jiménez, Antonio. "Salvador Massip." *Revista Canoa, Órgano de la Sociedad Cubana de Geografía* 2, no. 1 (1995): 15–28.

Armando H. Portela

Matamoros, Mercedes (1851–1906)

When Mercedes Matamoros was eighteen years old, she attracted the attention of Cuba's greatest poet, **José Martí**. It happened at a political rally in Havana (1869). The young woman was wearing the red-white-and-blue colors of the Cuban flag, a daring act that could have easily provoked the Spanish soldiers' anger. Years later, Martí befriended her and visited her regularly in Havana. Upon the death of the patriot in 1895, Matamoros wrote the poem titled "Elegía a Martí." This poem was one of the more than 500 works that Matamoros penned. During her lifetime, however, she was a neglected and little known poet. Most of her poems were published in such literary journals as *La Ha-*

bana Elegante, as well as newspapers, including *El Diario de la Marina*. Her poetry was lyrical and gently erotic, often describing doomed love affairs.

Often using the pen name Ofelia, Matamoros also wrote articles describing Cuban customs and traditions. Well versed in English, French, and German, she translated into Spanish works by Lord Byron, Geoffrey Chaucer, Alfred De Vigney, and Goethe. Having to work as a teacher and a private tutor, while nursing her elderly father, she absented herself from writing for a number of years. But toward the end of the nineteenth century she purchased a winning lottery ticket and the purse afforded her some financial freedom. In 1892, she published *Poesías completas*, a modest bestseller that brought her some national attention.

In 1997, many of her poems were published in a single volume titled *La poesía de Mercedes Matamoros*. In Cuba, a poetry contest has been named after her. *See also* Press and Journalism (Eighteenth and Nineteenth Centuries)

Further Reading

Varona, Alberto J. ed. *La poesía de Mercedes Matamoros*. Miami: San Lázaro Graphics, 1997.

D.H. Figueredo

Mendive, Rafael María (1821–1886)

For some, Rafael María Mendive deserves recognition only because he taught and greatly influenced **José Martí**. Mendive, aside from being an important educator, was a journalist, poet, and political activist. While not a great poet, Mendive's work was elegant, well crafted, and melodious; their musicality prompted composers such as Gottschalk and Bottesini to use his verses. Mendive also wrote an opera libretto for Luigi Arditi.

As a promoter of culture, Mendive was tireless in his efforts as a journalist,

educator, translator (Hugo, Lamartine, Byron, Moore); he also sponsored literary contests and magazines. His pro-independence views had him jailed, then deported to Spain. He spent most of the **Ten Years' War** in New York; he returned to Cuba in 1878, where in his last years he was director of a **Matanzas** newspaper.

He published a first book of poems *Pasionarios* (1847), and another titled *Poesías* (1860), with several editions. Along with **Joaquín Lorenzo Luaces**, Mendive is credited with restoring a certain refinement to mid-nineteenth-century Cuban poetry, which, according to some critics, had fallen prey to prosaicness and vulgarity.

Further Readings

Diccionario de la Literatura Cubana. Vol. 2. Havana: Editorial Letras Cubanas, 1984.
Ureña, Max Henríquez. *Panorama de la literatura cubana*. Vol. 1. Havana: Editorial Arte y Literatura, 1978.

Alan West-Durán

Milanés, José Jacinto (1814–1863)

José Jacinto Milanés belongs to the first group of Cuban Romantic poets that also includes **José María Heredia** and **Gabriel de la Concepción Valdés**, known as Plácido. His poetry is characterized by its fine poetic expression, vivid pictorial fancy, and explicit quintessential Cubanness. Some of Milanés's poems demonstrate the typical amorous passion of Romanticism ("La madrugada"), while others hint at his social scorn ("La ramera") or reflect his patriotism ("Los dormidos"). Born in **Matanzas**, his family's financial misfortunes forced him to abandon school. He then moved to Havana in 1832 to work at a hardware store but came back home in 1833 due to a cholera epidemic ravaging the capital. By 1837 he began publishing poems in *El Aguinaldo Habanero*, and his play *El conde Alarcos*, which recreates a

Spanish folk romance legend, was performed in 1838. His friendship with the Cuban intellectual **Domingo del Monte** in 1841 enabled him to obtain a position with the Matanzas's Railroad Company (see **railroads**). Though the subject of some speculation, it is believed that Milanés's hypersensitive personality or strongly emotional reaction to the representation of *El conde Alarcos* resulted in a mental illness that overcame him in 1843 and from which he never recovered. In 1846 he published his *Obras completas*. He also wrote *El mirón cubano*, which is a collection of articles that criticizes nineteenth-century Cuban customs, and the plays *El poeta en la corte* and *A buen hambre no hay pan duro*, which is based on an incident in Miguel de Cervantes Saavedra's life. *See also* Abolitionist Literature

Further Reading

Arias, Salvador. *Tres poetas en la mirilla: Plácido, Milanés, la Avellaneda*. Havana: Editorial Letras Cubanas, 1981.

Ilia Casanova-Marengo

Morejón, Nancy (1944–)

After receiving a high school degree in 1961 from the Instituto de La Habana, the city of her birth, Nancy Morejón worked as a French teacher and translator for the **Ministry of the Interior**. In 1966 she graduated from the **University of Havana** with a degree in French language and literature. That same year her collection of poems *Richard trajo su flauta y otros argumentos* was awarded honorary mention in the **Unión de Escritores y Artistas de Cuba (UNEAC)** literary contest. Her writing has since appeared in the journals *Unión, El Caimán Barbudo, La Gaceta de Cuba*, and *Casa de las Américas*. Morejón is the author of numerous volumes of poems, among them *Mutismos* (1962), *Amor, ciudad atribuída* (1964), *Parajes de una*

época (1979), *Poemas* (1980), *Piedra pulida* (1986), *Paisaje célebre* (1993), and *El río de Martín Pérez* (1993). As a literary scholar, Morejón authored a study on the work of poet **Nicolás Guillén**, titled *Nación y mestizaje en Nicolás Guillén* (1982), edited the volume *Recopilación de textos sobre Nicolás Guillén* (1974), and coauthored *Lengua de pájaro: comentarios reales: monografía histórica* (1967) with Carmen Gonce. In poems that are fast paced and imaginative, Morejón celebrates Cuba's racial and cultural heritage, advocating the concept that in Cuba many and diverse races came together to forge one culture. *See also* Literature of the Revolutionary Era; Literary Journals

Further Readings

DeCosta-Willis, Miriam. *Singular Like a Bird: The Art of Nancy Morejón*. Washington, DC: Howard University, 1999.
Flores, Ángel. *Spanish-American Authors: The Twentieth Century*. New York: Wilson Company, 1992.

Pamela María Smorkaloff

Moreno Fraginals, Manuel (1920–2001)

An accomplished and prominent historian, Manuel Moreno Fraginals redefined the study of nineteenth-century Cuban history with his groundbreaking study on the **sugar industry**. The three-volume *El ingenio*, first published in 1964, focused on the business aspects of the sugar industry and the technological innovations introduced by the planters to maximize profits. It was one of the first historical works to employ quantitative measures as an analytical tool (see **Sugar Plantations**). There was resistance within the revolutionary government to publishing the work, but that was overcome by the strong support of **Ernesto "Che" Guevara**.

The son of a sugar mill administrator, Moreno Fraginals studied at the **Univer-**

Nancy Morejón. Leading figure of Cuban literature whose poetry and essays often praise the achievements of the Revolution. Photograph by William Luis.

sity of Havana in the early 1940s and thereafter in Mexico and Spain. In the course of his studies, he compiled academic degrees in law, the humanities, and business administration. For much of the 1950s, he lived in Venezuela where he worked as an executive at a brewery. There he gained a knowledge of business that would serve him well in his historical research on the sugar industry. After the triumph of the Cuban **Revolution** he returned to Cuba where he became one of its most respected historians. In the 1990s, Moreno Fraginals became disillusioned with the Revolution and came to live in the United States, where he taught Cuban history at Florida International University. The author of numerous essays and books, among his important works are *Cuba/España, España/Cuba: historia común* (1995) and *La historia como arma: y otros estudios sobre esclavos, ingenios y plantaciones* (1983).

Further Readings

De la Fuente, Alejandro. "In Memoriam, Manuel Moreno Fraginals." *Perspectives* (Newsmagazine of the American Historical Association) 39, no. 7 (October 2001): 46–47.

"Homenaje a Manuel Moreno Fraginals." *Encuentro de la Cultura Cubana* 10 (1998): 3–10.

Frank Argote-Freyre

Novás Calvo, Lino (1905–1983)

Best known for his short stories, Lino Novás Calvo was an influential precursor of modern Cuban fiction with his incisive exploration of how individuals confront adversity and the portrayal of marginalized characters. Born in Galicia, Spain, his family sent him to Cuba in the care of a maternal uncle. He was unable to get a formal education and worked instead at a variety of jobs. In 1927 his literary career began with the publication of the poem "El camarada" in *Revista de Avance*. A job at a major bookstore in Havana introduced him to the intellectual life of his time. Novás Calvo published his first short story "Un hombre arruinado" in 1929. Two years later, he departed for Spain as a journalist for *Orbe*, a Cuban magazine. The same year he published three short stories in the renowned *Revista de Occidente*. His novel about the slave trader Pedro Blanco Fernández de Trava, *El negrero*, came out in 1933. In 1940 he returned to Cuba and began to achieve recognition as a writer after winning the 1942 Hernández Catá prize for the tale "Un dedo encima" and the publication of *La luna nona y otros cuentos*. Afterward, he published the stories "Cayo Canas" in 1946 and "El otro cayo" in 1959.

Novás Calvo left Cuba in 1960 to live in the United States, where he took a teaching position at Syracuse University in 1967. His second collection of short stories *Maneras de contar* was published in 1970. He died in New York in 1983. *See also* Literary Journals; Literature of the Revolutionary Era; Slave Trade

Further Readings

Gutiérrez de la Solana, Alberto. *Maneras de narrar: contraste entre Lino Novás Calvo y Alfonso Hernández Catá*. New York: Eliseo Torres & Sons, 1972.

Roses, Lorraine Elena. *Voices of the Storyteller: Cuba's Lino Novás Calvo*. Westport, CT: Greenwood Press, 1986.

Ilia Casanova-Marengo

Oliver Labra, Carilda (1924–   )

Poet and winner of Cuba's 1997 National Literary Prize, Carilda Oliver Labra was born in **Matanzas** and attended the **University of Havana**, from where she graduated with a law degree. In 1946, she published her first poem, "Me desordeno, amor, me desordeno," a frankly sexual poem describing the act of lovemaking. The style and contents of this poem laid the foundation for her book of poetry *Al sur de mi garganta*, published in 1949. Other books followed: *Canto a Martí* (1953), *Canto a Matanzas* (1956), *Memoria de la fiebre* (1958), *Desaparece el polvo* (1984), and *Sonetos* (1993), among others.

A feminist and erotic poet, Oliver Labra has found a large readership in Europe and in the United States. In Spain, a cultural foundation bears her name. *See also* Feminist Movement (Republican Era)

Further Reading

González Castro, Vicente. *Cinco noches con Carilda*. Havana: Editorial Letras Cubanas, 1997.

D. H. Figueredo

Orígenes (1944–1956)

Orígenes was the most important Cuban literary journal of its era, directed by **José Lezama Lima**, with emphasis on abstract poetics, lyricism, and modern art. Influenced by the Catholic religious convictions of many of its contributors, *Orígenes* promoted an esoteric aesthetic ranging from baroque to surrealism, yet remained cosmopolitan in coverage of Cuban and leading foreign contributors (see **Catholicism**).

Dedicated to freedom of expression, *Orígenes* featured works by **Cintio Vitier, Fina García Marruz, Eliseo Diego, Virgilio Piñera**, Octavio Smith, **Gastón Baquero**, Ángel Gaztelu, and **Lydia Cabrera** and reproduced the art of **Wifredo Lam, René Portocarrero, Julián Orbón, Amelia Peláez**, and **Mariano Rodríguez**. Foreign writers ranged from Juan Ramón Jiménez to Octavio Paz, Albert Camus, and Witold Gombrowicz. Many of the English and French pieces were translated by cofounder and principal financial supporter José Rodríguez Feo.

Although the magazine leaned heavily toward poetry, it also published fiction, philosophical essays, reviews, and criticism on art and music. Rodríguez Feo sought to create a journal as intellectually significant as Victoria Ocampo's *Sur*, but conflicts with Lezama Lima led to Rodríguez Feo's departure (after issuing double numbers 35 and 36 in 1954 under individual editorship!). *Ciclón* emerged as a result.

Orígenes did not enter directly into political debate, yet Lezama referred to the state's poor relationship with culture. Many of the contributing writers and artists remained in Cuba after 1959, assuming, to varying degrees, roles in state-supported journals and publishing. *See also* Literary Journals

Further Readings

Barquet, Jesús J. *Consagración de La Habana: las peculiaridades del grupo Orígenes en el proceso cultural cubano.* Miami: Iberian Studies Institute, University of Miami, 1992.

Barradas, Efraín. *La revista Orígenes.* Ann Arbor, MI: University Microfilms International, 1978.

Rodríguez Feo, José. *Mi correspondencia con Lezama Lima.* Havana: Unión de Escritores y Artistas de Cuba, 1989.

Peter T. Johnson

Ortiz Fernández, Fernando (1881–1969)

Anthropologist, ethnologist, lawyer, and linguist, Fernando Ortiz Fernández was one of the most influential Cuban scholars of his generation. Ortiz attended the universities of Havana, Barcelona, and Madrid and received a law degree from the latter in 1901. While in Madrid he was influenced by evolutionists, positivists, and followers of the philosopher Karl Christian Krause, such as Rafael Salillas, Manuel Sales y Ferré, and Francisco Giner de los Ríos. These different sources influenced his scholarly methods and conception of history and society, particularly when it came to the issues of **crime** and atavism. In Ortiz's thought and writings, one observes the rapid transition from the concepts of criminal anthropology to the perception of a more open society, one in which the past, traditions, folklore, and material culture form the nucleus of individuals and communities. For Ortiz, history was the fundamental tool to understand the present and prepare for the future.

As his career developed, Ortiz began to move away from racial conceptions, emphasizing the importance of culture over race, concluding by the 1940s that race was not a biological category and must be understood within a cultural framework. As an intellectual he came to define *cubanidad* as an *ajiaco* (Cuban stew) in which all the ingredients were slowly dissolved and mixed to make a new cultural concoction. The dissolution and reintegration of all these different cultural and ethnic elements was possible through the process of transculturation, a concept he coined.

Ortiz dedicated his life to research, writing, and teaching. He was a professor at the **University of Havana** in the Department of Public Law from 1908 through 1917. During the same period, he practiced law and participated in politics. His intellectual pursuits were deeply interwoven with profound feelings of nationalism. He was a member of the Partido Liberal and a member of the **Grupo Minorista**, a group of intellectuals dedicated to ridding corruption from public life, strengthening national unity, and combating the decline in moral values. A cultural activist, Ortiz reorganized the *Revista Bimestre Cubana* in 1910, managing it for forty-nine years, and promoted, organized, and directed the Colección Cubana de Libros y Documentos Inéditos o Raros (Collection of Rare and Unpublished Cuban Books and Documents) in 1927. He founded *Mensajes de la IHCC* (1926), *Surco* (1930), and *Ultra* (1936). In addition to membership in several scientific academies, Ortiz founded a number of cultural organizations, includ-

Anthropologist Fernando Ortiz Fernandez, author of the classic *Contrapunteo cubano del tabaco y el azúcar* (1940).

ing the Institución Hispano-Cubana de Cultura (1926) and the Sociedad de Estudios Afrocubanos (1937).

Ortiz was the author of many influential scholarly works, including the groundbreaking *Hampa afrocubana. Los negros brujos* (1906), which was edited in Madrid and which initiated a series of works, beginning in 1916, titled *Hampa Afro-Cubana: los negros esclavos*. Other important works included *La reconquista de América* (1910); *Entre cubanos. Psicología tropical* (1913) and *La identificación dactiloscópica* (1913); *La crisis política de Cuba* (1919); *Proyecto de Código Criminal Cubano* (1926); *Contrapunteo cubano del tabaco y el azúcar* (1940) and *El engaño de las razas* (1946). In the 1950s, he wrote several noted works on Afro-Cuban dances and music, among them *La africanía de la música folklórica de Cuba* (1950) and *Los instru-*

mentos de la música afro-cubana, published in five volumes between 1952 and 1955.

In 1961, Ortiz was named honorary president of the Cuban **Academy of Sciences**. *See also* Afro-Cubans

Further Readings

García Carranza, Araceli. *Bio-bibliografía de don Fernando Ortiz*. Havana: Biblioteca Nacional José Martí, 1970.

García Carranza, Araceli, Norma Suárez, and Alberto Quesada. *Miscelanea II de estudios dedicados a Fernando Ortiz (1881–1969)*. New York: InterAmericas, 1998.

Le Riverend, Julio. Selección y prólogo. *Órbita de Fernando Ortiz*. Havana: Unión de Escritores y Artistas de Cuba, 1973.

Consuelo Naranjo Orovio

Padilla (Affair), Heberto

Heberto Padilla (1932–2000) was one of Cuba's most popular poets of the twentieth century as well as one of its most controversial, the result of the so-called Padilla Affair.

The Padilla Affair refers to the events surrounding his arrest in April 1971, his alleged actions against the government, his release from detention several weeks later, and his staged confession before a meeting of the **Unión de Escritores y Artistas de Cuba (UNEAC)**, in which he accused his wife and his friends of being critical of the government. The event produced an international scandal among European and Latin American intellectuals who supported the **Revolution**.

Padilla's problems were not new and began when writing for the weekly literary supplement *Lunes de Revolución* (1959–1961). *Lunes* became controversial, and the government closed it down. Its editor **Guillermo Cabrera Infante** later abandoned the island. Padilla's problems increased in 1967 when he wrote a critical review of Lisandro Otero's *La pasión de*

Urbino and praised Cabrera Infante's *Tres tristes tigres*. Both novels were finalists for Spain's Biblioteca Breve prize, which Cabrera Infante won. By then Cabrera Infante was considered an enemy of the Revolution, and Otero served as the vice minister of the National Council of Culture. In a subsequent article, Padilla recanted his position.

In 1968 Padilla won the UNEAC poetry prize for his *Fuera del juego*, a collection of poems, which members of the government denounced as counterrevolutionary. The government was obligated to publish the prize-winning book, but it also included a "Declaration from the UNEAC," a government letter critical of Padilla. After the failed **Ten Million Ton Harvest** of sugar in 1970, the government became increasingly defensive and restricted liberties further. The Padilla arrest and subsequent staged confession produced two letters published in *Le Monde* and signed by intellectuals who supported the Revolution but were outraged by the events surrounding Padilla's arrest. In **Fidel Castro**'s speech before the First National Congress of Education and Culture (1971), he rejected criticism of his government and broke with friends of the Revolution who were critical of him. This signified a true hardening in cultural policy that did not open up until the 1980s. In the meantime, many writers lost jobs, were demoted to menial labor, and were not published for several years.

Padilla's works include the book of poems *El justo tiempo humano* (1962) and *El hombre junto al mar* (1981), the novel *En mi jardín pasean los héroes* (1984), and the memoir *La mala memoria* (1989). *See also* Literature of the Revolutionary Era

Further Readings
Casal, Lourdes, ed. *El caso Padilla: literatura y revolución en Cuba; documentos*. Miami: Ediciones Universal, 1971.
Padilla, Heberto. *La mala memoria*. Barcelona: Plaza y Janes, 1989.

Quesada, Luis Manuel. "*Fuera del juego*: Poet's Appraisal of the Cuban Revolution." *Latin American Literary Review* 6 (1975): 89–98.

William Luis

Padura, Leonardo (1955–)

Novelist, essayist, and journalist Leonardo Padura is a leading figure in the new generation of writers who emerged in the 1980s and who are critical of Cuban society.

Padura was born in Havana and graduated from the **University of Havana** in 1980. He began his writing career as a literary critic and journalist but soon became a novelist and a screenwriter. His first book was *Con la espada y la pluma* (1984), a collection of essays, followed by the novel *Fiebre de caballos* (1988) and the collection of short stories *Según pasan los años* (1989). In the 1990s, he achieved international recognition and fame with his tetralogy "Las cuatro estaciones," consisting of the four novels: *Pasado perfecto* (1991), *Vientos de Cuaresma* (1994), *Máscaras* (1995), and *Paisaje de otoño* (1998). These novels—three of which received international literary awards—feature a disillusioned detective who questions the accomplishments of the **Revolution** over the past forty years.

Padura's nonfiction works include *El alma en el terreno* (1989), *El viaje más largo* (1994), *Los rostros de la salsa* (1997), and *Un camino de medio siglo: Carpentier y la narrativa de lo maravilloso* (1994). In 2001, Padura finished the work of fiction *La novela de mi vida*, an account of the life of the poet **José María Heredia**. Padura's works have been translated into English, French, German, and Portuguese.

Further Reading
Epple, Juan Armando. "Leonardo Padura Fuertes." *Hispanoamericano* 24, no. 71 (Aug. 1955), 49–66.

Wilfredo Cancio Isla

Palma y Romay, Ramón de (1812–1860)

Ramón de Palma y Romay was a lawyer, journalist, and writer associated early on with the **Domingo del Monte** literary circle through which he became one of Cuba's foremost nineteenth-century narrators along with Anselmo Suárez y Romero, José Antonio Echeverría, **Cirilo Villaverde, Gertrudis Gómez de Avellaneda**, and José Ramón de Betancourt. Born in Havana, Palma was also the founder, with José Antonio Echeverría, of two journals: *El Aguinaldo Habanero* (1837) and *El Plantel* (1838). In 1842 he received a law degree from the **University of Havana**. His prose writings include short stories and short novels, notably *El cólera en La Habana* (1838) and *Una Pascua en San Marcos* (1838), a book that describes the amorous triangle between Don Claudio de Meneses, a playboy, Aurora, the daughter of a rich planter of San Marcos, and Rosa, the wife of a Spanish army captain. This novel received a great deal of critical attention because it is inserted in Romanticism by means of its idealization of Cuban landscape and types as well as through the passionate relationships of its characters. The novel also incorporates another literary current of its time, Realism, which enables it to reflect the customs and social dilemmas of nineteenth-century Cuba. *Una Pascua en San Marcos* was criticized for its portrayal of the immoral conduct of upper-class life in terms of extramarital relationships, gambling, and idleness. Also a poet, Palma published these verse collections: *Aves de paso* (1842), *Hojas caídas* (1848), and *Melodías poéticas* (1848). *See also* Press and Journalism (Eighteenth and Nineteenth Centuries)

Further Readings

Bueno, Salvador. *Historia de la literatura cubana.* Havana: Editorial Minerva, 1959.

Lazo, Raimundo. *Historia de la literatura cubana.* Mexico: Dirección General de Publicaciones, 1974.

Ilia Casanova-Marengo

Pérez Firmat, Gustavo (1949–   )

Gustavo Pérez Firmat's most well-known books, *Life on the Hyphen: The Cuban American Way* (1994) and the bestseller *Next Year in Cuba* (1995), are thoughtful meditations and explorations on what it means to be Cuban and to remain one while spending a lifetime away from the island. *Life on the Hyphen* is a scholarly yet playful study of such Cuban American icons as **Desi Arnaz** and **Gloria Estefan** and their successful careers. In *Next Year in Cuba*, Pérez Firmat comes to terms with the knowledge that most Cubans in exile will not be able to return to the island and that for most Cuban Americans Miami has become the country of origin rather than Cuba. In this book, he also essays on what makes Cubans different from other migrant groups and the social and cultural characterisitics that affirm "Cubanness" among Cuban Americans.

Pérez Firmat left Cuba at the age of eleven and settled in Miami with his parents. Earning a doctorate in literature from the University of Michigan, he went on to teach at Duke University, where he achieved recognition as a scholar. Then he started to write poetry, first in Spanish, later on in English, and eventually combining both languages. As a poet, he captures the nuances, ambivalences, and pathos of living in two countries and thinking in two languages: "The fact that I/ am writing to you/ in English/ already falsifies what I/wanted to tell you./My subject:/ how to explain to you that I/don't belong to English/ though I belong nowhere else."

While his books on being Cuban make him popular with Cuban American readers, his poetry appeals to Latinos in general. His essays and poetry are often anthologized. His novel titled *Anything But Love* (2000) was well received by critics. He currently teaches at Columbia University.

His books of essays include *Literature and Liminality* (1986), *The Cuban Condition* (1988), *Cuban Literature* (1989), *Idle Fictions* (1993), and *Cincuenta lecciones de exilio y desexilio* (2000). His books of poetry are *Carolina Cuban* (1987), *Equivocaciones* (1989), and *Bilingual Blues* (1995). He is credited with coining two terms: ABC, meaning American-born Cubans, and "one and a halfer," referring to those Cubans who left the island as young children and reached adulthood in the United States. In 1995, he was nominated for the Pulitzer Prize for *Next Year in Cuba*. *See also* Cuban American Literature; United States, Cuban Migrations to the

Further Readings
Dick, Bruce Allen. *"A Conversation with Gustavo Pérez Firmat." Michigan Quarterly Review* 41 (2001): 682–694.
Pérez Firmat, Gustavo. *Next Year in Cuba.* New York: Anchor Books, 1995.

D.H. Figueredo

Pérez y Montes de Oca, Julia (1841–1875)

Julia Pérez y Montes de Oca celebrated Cuba's natural beauty in her poetry. She published numerous poems in such popular nineteenth-century journals as *El Siglo* and *El Kaleidoscopio*. She was also an actress and artist.

Born on a farm in the old Oriente Province she spent some time in **Santiago de Cuba**, where she contributed poems to the literary journal *El Redactor*. In 1858, she moved to Havana, where she studied astronomy as well as painting. In 1875, she published in Spain a book of poetry, *Poesías*, which was well received by the critics.

Her modest oeuvre was neglected during her short lifetime, but in the 1960s writers and critics of the caliber of **José Lezama Lima** reevaluated her contributions to the national literature, promoting her work and including her poems in the important anthology *Antología de la poesía cubana* (1965).

Further Reading
Lezama Lima, José. *Antología de la poesía cubana.* Havana: Consejo Nacional de Cultura, 1965.

D.H. Figueredo

Piñera, Virgilio (1912–1979)

A prolific writer of poems, short stories, plays, novels, and articles as well as a major figure in twentieth-century Cuban literature, Virgilio Piñera's writings are marked by the concept of the absurd, through which life in modern society is portrayed as chaotic and meaningless; yet underneath this bleak assessment, there is a profound ethical concern and a search for justice.

Born in **Matanzas**, he moved to Havana with his family in 1940 where he studied philosophy and literature, although he never finished his studies, refusing to present his doctoral dissertation on **Gertrudis Gómez de Avellaneda** to the university's academic committee. His literary career began as a poet with the publication in 1943 of the collection of poems *Las furias* and *La isla en peso*. His play *Electra Garrigo*, written in 1941 and published in 1945, proved popular and was staged in 1948. Other plays published and staged were *Jesús* (1943) and *Falsa alarma* (1957).

In 1946, he moved to Argentina, where he worked as translator, proofreader, and functionary at the Cuban embassy and contributed articles and short stories to the Argentine magazine *Sur*. His first novel *La carne de René* was published in 1952, followed by a first collection of short fiction, *Cuentos fríos* (1956). When he returned to Cuba in 1958, he became actively involved in the island's cultural life after the Cuban **Revolution** in 1959. Two years later he was arrested for homosexual activities but was released within a day. Piñera's later novels are *Pequeñas maniobras* (1963) and *Presiones y diamantes* (1967).

In 1968 he was awarded the **Casa de las Américas** prize for his play *Dos viejos pánicos*. But as a result of the **Padilla Affair**, his latter works were not published in Cuba until nearly twenty years later.

Further Readings

Quiroga, José. "Fleshing out Virgilio Piñera from the Cuban Closet." In *Entiendes?: Queer Readings, Hispanic Writings*, ed. Emilie L. Bergmann and Paul Julian Smith. Durham, NC: Duke University Press, 1995, 169–180.

Valerio-Holguín, Fernando. *Poética de la frialdad: la narrativa de Virgilio Piñera*. Lanham, NY: University Press of America, 1997.

Ilia Casanova-Marengo

Piñeyro, Enrique (1839–1911)

Piñeyro was Cuba's foremost literary critic of the nineteenth and early twentieth centuries. A true renaissance man, Piñeyro was a scholar, an academic administrator, an attorney, and a judge. He was involved in the **War of Independence** for which the Spanish authorities sentenced him to death. During the 1870s, he toured South America seeking financial support for the struggle against Spain. In 1902, after Cuba gained independence and elected its first president, Piñeyro devoted his energy and intellect to literary criticism.

Piñeyro was a prolific essayist, publishing hundreds of articles in dozens of journals and writing studies on such literary figures as **Juan Clemente Zenea, Gabriel de la Concepción Valdés (Plácido)**, and **José María Heredia**. In 1880, he published *Estudios de conferencias de historia y literatura*, and in 1904 he wrote his popular volume *El romanticismo en España*.

Translated into English as *The Romantics of Spain* (1934), this book was part of the critical and literary canon well into the mid-twentieth century.

Further Reading

Cancela, Gilberto. *Enrique Piñeyro, su vida y su obra*. Miami: Ediciones Universal, 1977.

D.H. Figueredo

Portell-Vilá, Herminio (1901–1993)

Herminio Portell-Vilá was one of Cuba's most distinguished and influential historians of his time. Throughout his career he combined his scholarly activities with political activism on behalf of Cuba's freedom.

Portell-Vilá was born in Cárdenas in 1901. He received degrees in law and philosophy from the **University of Havana**, whose faculty he later joined as professor of Latin American history. He also taught at various institutions of higher learning in Latin America and the United States. In 1933 he represented Cuba as delegate to the Seventh International Conference of American States, where he denounced the evils of the U.S.-imposed **Platt Amendment**, which limited Cuba's autonomy and development.

Among Portell-Vilá's numerous works of history stand out his four-volume *Historia de Cuba en sus relaciones con los Estados Unidos y España* (1938–1941), his three volume *Narciso López y su época* (1930–1958), and *Nueva historia de la República de Cuba* (1986).

Exiled from Cuba, Portell-Vilá became a vocal opponent of the **Fidel Castro** regime and served as adviser to the American Security Council in Washington, D.C.

Further Readings

Pérez, Louis, A., Jr. *Essays on Cuban History: Historiography and Research*. Gainesville: University Press of Florida, 1995.

Portell-Vilá, Herminio. *Nueva historia de la Républica de Cuba*. Miami: La Moderna Poesía, 1986.

Luis Martínez-Fernández

Quintero, José Agustín (1829–1885)

José Agustín Quintero led a life of adventure that took him to Mexico and the United States. Born into a wealthy family, Quintero studied at Harvard University, where he befriended Ralph Waldo Emerson and Henry Longfellow. Upon his return to Cuba in the 1850s, he espoused annexation to the United States; because of this stance, he was arrested and sentenced to death (see **Annexationism**). Quintero escaped to the United States, where, as a result of his friendship with Jefferson Davis, he joined the Confederate army. Afterward, he traveled to Mexico where he supported Benito Juárez and fought against the French army. Returning to Cuba in 1869, he quickly joined the **Ten Years' War** and was forced once again to flee to the United States, where he died.

Quintero edited several journals including *El Picayune* and published his writings in numerous literary publications. His poems were anthologized in *Laúd del desterrado*, published in New York City in 1858. *See also* Press and Journalism (Eighteenth and Nineteenth Centuries)

Further Reading

Tucker, Phillip Thomas. *Cubans in the Confederacy: José Agustín Quintero, Ambrosio José González, and Loreta Janeta Velázquez*. Jefferson, NC: McFarland, 2001.

D.H. Figueredo

Rodríguez, Manuel del Socorro (1754–1819)

Manuel del Socorro Rodríguez was a poet, journalist, and librarian who wrote more than 600 poems. A descendant of Siboney Indians, Rodríguez was born into a poor family of **Bayamo**. Intelligent and creative, he designed and crafted by hand the altar for the local church. During the **Ten Years' War**, when the city of Bayamo was burned, the altar survived the flames.

At the age of thirty, he was awarded a teaching post at Havana's prestigious San Carlos Seminary. From there, he journeyed to Colombia, where he lived the rest of his life, working as a librarian and founding and managing several newspapers, including *El Semanario* and *Últimas Noticias*. This activity earned him the title of "The Father of Journalism" in Colombia. *See also* Press and Journalism (Eighteenth and Nineteenth Centuries)

Further Reading

Torre Revello, José. *Ensayo de una biografía del bibliotecario y periodista Don Manuel del Socorro Rodríguez*. Bogotá: Instituto Caro y Cuervo, 1947.

D.H. Figueredo

Roig de Leuchsenring, Emilio (1889–1964)

The official historian of the city of Havana, Emilio Roig de Leuchsenring was a journalist, an editor, and energetic promoter of Cuban culture who dedicated his life to the production of Cuban history and the preservation of Cuban monuments and historic buildings.

In 1912, Roig de Leuchsenring achieved national recognition with his humorous essay "¿Se puede vivir en La Habana sin un centavo?" and established himself as a practitioner of the literary genre known as *costumbrismo*—essays on local customs and traditions. In 1917, he became an attorney and began to write articles on judicial matters and political issues while editing such popular journals as *Carteles* and *Social*. Six years later, he joined the **Grupo Minorista**, an informal group of intellectuals critical of political conditions on the island and promoters of a national culture; the members of this group often held their meetings in Roig de Leuchsenring's office.

In 1935, he was appointed official historian of the city of Havana and immediately created the office of the Historiador de la Ciudad. Through this office, he supervised the publication of dozens of monographs on history and culture, sponsored cultural activities, and lobbied for the creation of museums and the preservation of colonial buildings and monuments in the city. He also continued to work as an editor and a writer while remaining active in archeological, legal, and literary societies. In 1943, he was placed in charge of the city's historic archives. He managed the office of Historiador until his death in 1964 at which time **Eusebio Leal Spengler** replaced him.

Roig de Leuchsenring wrote hundreds of articles and books. Among his works are *Martí en España* (1938), *Banderas oficiales y revolucionarias de Cuba* (1950), *Cuba no debe su independencia a los Estados Unidos* (1950), *Los monumentos nacionales de la República de Cuba*, a three-volume set (1957–1960), and *Los Estados Unidos contra Cuba republicana* (1964). Throughout his writings, Roig de Leuchsenring insisted on the development of Cuba's national identity and was critical of the U.S. government's interference in the island's political and economic affairs.

Further Reading

Hart Dávalos, Armando. *Roig de Leuchsenring, promotor de la cultura del antimperialismo*. Havana: Dirección de Información, Ministerio de Cultura, 1989.

D.H. Figueredo

Santa Cruz y Montalvo (Condesa de Merlín), María de las Mercedes (1789–1852)

The Countess of Merlín is best known for her memoirs, letters, and diaries, which constitute a travel corpus that recalls her early years in Cuba and her life in Europe. For some critics, her writings are controversial in terms of their upper-class ideology, promotion of **slavery**, and their support of Cuba's colonial status. Others argue not only that she has been marginalized from the nineteenth-century Latin American literary canon but that her personal situation as a Cuban living in the metropolitan centers of empires in Spain and France has been misunderstood. Born in Havana to a wealthy family, she emigrated from Cuba to Spain in 1802 with her parents. In 1809 she married the French count Antoine Merlín, a general of José Bonaparte's Regal Guard, and in 1812 both headed for Paris, where the countess partook in an intense cultural life surrounded by significant intellectuals of her time, including Victor Hugo, Alfred de Musset, George Sand, and Honoré de Balzac. In 1831 she published her first book of chronicles, *Mes douze premires années*, which recounts her former years in Cuba, followed in 1832 by *Histoire de la Soeur Ines*, which narrates the story of a nun who helped her to escape from the Franciscan convent where she was taken by her father in order to facilitate her education. Her subsequent volume of diaries was *Souvenir et memoires* (1836). In 1839 her husband died, and the following year she returned to Cuba to claim her father's inheritance. While there, she published *La Havane*, (1844), a depiction of nineteenth-century Cuban society. A more succinct version in Spanish, *Viaje a La Habana*, also appeared. Then she returned to Paris, where she was associated with French philosopher Philarete Charles, a man who influenced her emotional life during her last years.

Further Readings

Bueno, Salvador. "Una escritora habanera en francés: la condesa de Merlín." In *Figuras cubanas del siglo XIX*. Havana: Unión de Escritores y Artistas de Cuba, 1980. 297–304.

Méndez Rodenas, Adriana. *Gender and National-ism in Colonial Cuba. The Travels of Santa Cruz y Montalvo, Condesa de Merlín*. Nash-ville, TN: Vanderbilt University Press, 1998.

Ilia Casanova-Marengo

Santacilia, Pedro (1826–1910)

Pedro Santacilia was a patriot, a journalist, and a poet. Born in **Santiago de Cuba**, his mother came from the Dominican Repub-lic and his father was a Spaniard. When Santacilia was ten years old, his father, who was critical of the treatment the Span-ish government afforded Cubans, was or-dered to return to Spain. There, Santicilia studied pedagogy. In 1846, Santicilia was able to go back to Cuba. He became a teacher as well as a journalist. The poems and essays he published in the journal *En-sayos* brought him recognition.

After joining a revolutionary group seeking Cuba's independence, Santacilia was arrested, sentenced to prison, and ban-ished to Spain in 1852. Later on, in 1853, he made his way to the United States, where he wrote for the annexationist jour-nal *La Verdad* and befriended Benito Juárez. Relocating to Mexico, he was ap-pointed personal secretary of President Juárez and married his daughter. Though he never went back to Cuba, Santicilia served as the representative of Cuba's Republic-in-Arms before Mexico in 1895 (see **War of Independence**).

Santalicia wrote essays and anecdotes depicting Cuban traditions. His works were published in dozens of newspapers and literary magazines; his poetry is an-thologized in *El laúd del desterrado*, pub-lished in New York in 1848. It is believed that his poem "Al ruiseñor" was the basis for Costa Rica's national anthem. "Adios," about his departure from Cuba, is his most popular poem. *See also* Annexationism; Press and Journalism (Eighteenth and Nineteenth Centuries)

Further Reading
Puig Casauranc, J.M. comp. *Archivos privados de D. Benito Juárez y D. Pedro Santacilia*. Mexico City: Secretaría de Educación Pública, Bibli-oteca Nacional, 1928.

D.H. Figueredo

Sarduy, Severo (1937–1993)

Although not Cuba's first gay writer, nor the first to deal with the subject of ho-mosexuality, Severo Sarduy made his gayness a celebratory, erotic affirmation: a hilarious mix of baroque **theater**, **rumba** wiggle, postmetaphysical philos-ophy, and religious mysticism, all per-formed as a kind of writerly "voguing." As a young artist he was linked to the iconoclastic writers around *Ciclón* mag-azine such as **Virgilio Piñera**, José Rod-ríguez Feo, **Antón Arrufat**, and Fayad Jamís. Soon after the **Revolution**, Sarduy went to Paris in 1960 on an art scholarship and never returned.

Sarduy was equally brilliant as novel-ist, poet, and essayist. His critical success began with *De dónde son los cantantes* (1967), an unorthodox and irreverent ex-ploration of Cuban identity. Sarduy's work grew more experimental with *Cobra* (1973) and *Maitreya* (1978), both about transformations of identity with strong Tantric influences. He published three more novels in his lifetime: *Colibrí* (1984), a parody of jungle novels and Latin Amer-ican boom writers; *Cocuyo* (1990), which describes the rite of passage of a pica-resque, grotesque child; and *Pájaros de playa* (1993), set on an island where a group of young people are ravaged by a terrible affliction. It is Sarduy's rueful, po-etic, and searing meditation on **AIDS**, which terminated his life in 1993. His books of essays include *Escritos sobre un cuerpo* (1969), *Barroco* (1974), and *La si-mulación* (1982). Sarduy was a gifted poet, publishing *Un testigo fugaz y disfra-zado* (1985) and *Epitafios* (1994). His

Severo Sarduy, Cuban novelist, essayist, and poet, in France, where he lived from 1960 until his death in 1993. Couresty of Roberto González Echevarría.

neobaroque aesthetics was informed by cosmological and scientific models and metaphors. Sarduy practiced and preached an erotics of reading/writing, and his rich and sensuous prose prompted Colombian novelist, Gabriel García Márquez to say that "he wrote in the most beautiful Spanish of our time." The richness of his prose is even evident in the numerous English translations of his works.

A rarity in Cuban intellectual circles, Sarduy did not cave in to the inevitable polarization that has been (and still is) the Cuban intellectual's staple for decades: Either you are a revolutionary and progressive or a counterrevolutionary and, thus, a reactionary. In Sarduy's fiction, issues of identity, ideology, and even gender are fluid notions, not opposing camps. While keenly aware of the ideological nature of art and culture, Sarduy was inimical to reductively defining a work of art. He let his art do the talking: a work of witty complexity, poetic flash, spiritual warmth, and plain outrageousness. *See also* Gays and Lesbians

Further Readings
González Echevarría, Roberto. *La ruta de Severo Sarduy*. Hanover, NH: Ediciones del Norte, 1987.

West-Durán, Alan. *Tropics of History: Cuba Imagined*. Westport, CT: Greenwood Press, 1997.

Alan West-Durán

Secades, Eladio (1904–1976)

A journalist, Eladio Secades is regarded as an innovator of "crónica costumbrista," that is, stories about local customs, social types, and events. Born in Havana, Secades worked as a sports journalist for the dailies *La Noche, Heraldo de Cuba*, and *El País*. From 1935 to 1943, his pieces on sports and local customs were published in the newspaper *Alerta*; his articles were very popular and brought him national fame. Subsequently, he became a writer for the newspaper *Diario de la Marina* and the influential weekly *Bohemia*. He worked for these two publications for nearly twenty years. In 1962, Secades went into exile in Mexico. Five years later, he relocated to Miami where he wrote for the humorous weekly *Zig Zag Libre*.

Secades's stories reproduced Cuba's popular parlance as well as a portrayal of Cuban idiosyncracies. His numerous writings are collected in the books *Estampas de la época* (1941, 1943), *Estampas* (1958), and *Las mejores estampas de Eladio Secades* (1969). *See also* Newspapers (Republican Era)

Further Reading
Secades, Eladio. *Las mejores estampas de Eladio Secades*. Miami: Ediciones Universal, 1998.

Wilfredo Cancio Isla

Serpa, Enrique (1900–1968)

A Havana-born novelist, short-story writer, and poet, Enrique Serpa befriended **Rubén Martínez Villena** and became politically active with the **Grupo Minorista** in the 1920s. Also a journalist, he was press attaché for the Cuban embassy in Paris (1952–1959). Poverty, crime, and degradation are his important themes. Though considered a naturalist writer, Serpa's literary techniques and supple handling of personal and social psychology go much further than mere description or denunciation.

Contrabando (1938), his most accomplished novel, won him the Premio Nacional. Narrated in first person, it involves a clandestine shipment of liqueur to the United States during Prohibition. Serpa deftly combines the realism of dockside lowlife culture with a poetic intuition about the inner life of the characters. *La trampa* (1956), his second novel, is the story of two gangsters and their diverging and converging lives.

Felisa y yo (1937) was his first book of short stories and focuses on personal, social, and political fears; his second, *Noche de fiesta* (1951), deals with characters trapped by certain social restrictions. Serpa's contribution was in his ability to evoke the psychological and sexual dimensions of social conditions such as poverty and injustice, thereby giving a nuanced and poetic portrait of life's darker side.

Further Readings

Benítez Rojo, Antonio. "Enrique Serpa." In *Dictionary of Twentieth Century Cuban Literature*, ed. Julio A. Martínez. Westport, CT: Greenwood Press, 1990. 65–71.

García Ronda, Denia. Prólogo. *Contrabando*. Havana: Editorial Arte y Literatura, 1975.

Alan West-Durán

Suárez, Virgil (1962–)

Virgil Suárez is a novelist, poet, and essayist whose works portray the life of Cuban Americans in the United States and who belongs to the generation of writers who were born in Cuba but chose to write in English rather than in Spanish. After spending a short time in Spain, Suárez came to the United States in 1974, settling with his parents in California. He graduated from California State University at

Virgil Suárez. Cuban American writer representative of the generation that chose to write in English rather than in Spanish. Photograph courtesy of Virgil Suárez.

Long Beach and received a master's degree in creative writing from Louisiana State University in 1987.

He published his first novel, *Latin Jazz*, in 1990. It tells the story of a Cuban family rushing to Cuba during the **Mariel boatlift** to pick up relatives. A year later, he published *The Cutter*, about a man working in a Cuban labor camp. For his subsequent novels, Suárez shifted from writing about the island to chronicling the life of middle-class Cubans trying to assimilate into North American culture. His novels are quick-paced and provide insight into the human condition at large. Most of his characters are either Cubans or Latinos.

Suárez has been active in promoting Latino culture in the United States. With that purpose, he edited—with his wife Delia Poey—the anthology *Iguana Dreams* (1992). As a poet, he captures the complexities of family life and mourns the passing away of the older generations of Cubans living in exile.

Suárez contributes regularly to literary journals and teaches creative writing at Florida State University. Some of his other books are *Welcome to the Oasis and Other Stories* (1992), *Havana Thursdays* (1995), *Little Havana Blues* (1996), *Going Under* (1996), *Spared Angola* (1997), and *Banyan* (2001). *See also* Cuban American Literature

Further Reading
Smorkaloff, Pamela M. *Cuban Writers on and off the Island.* New York: Twayne Publishers, 1999.

D.H. Figueredo

Teurbe Tolón y de la Guardia, Miguel (1820–1857)

During the summer of 1848, the Venezuelan **Narciso López**, who was in the United States planning an invasion of Cuba, asked his friend Miguel Teurbe Tolón to design a flag he could take into battle. Teurbe Tolón drew a sketch that his wife then sewed into a fabric that would become Cuba's **national flag**. Teurbe Tolón also designed the island's **national coat of arms**, which he printed in the annexationist newspaper he was editing in New York City, *La Verdad* (see **Annexationism**).

Though better known for his patriotic participation in the struggles for independence, Teurbe Tolón was an accomplished poet. His poems, patriotic in nature, were fast paced and lyrical and meant to excite the reader. Some of the poems were included in the anthology *El laúd del desterrado*, published in New York City in 1848. A gifted translator, Teurbe Tolón wrote poetry in English for the journal *Waverly Magazine*, was a correspondent for the *New York Herald*, and translated into Spanish Thomas Payne's *Common Sense*. His most famous book was *Flores y espinas*, issued in Cuba in 1857. *See also* Press and Journalism (Eighteenth and Nineteenth Centuries)

Further Reading
Montes-Huidobro, Matías, ed. *El laúd del desterrado.* Houston: Arte Público Press, 1995.

D.H. Figueredo

Trelles y Govín, Carlos (1866–1951)

Carlos Trelles y Govín was a librarian, historian, and bibliographer. In 1892, he established a branch of the **Partido Revolucionario Cubano** in the city of **Matanzas**. Persecuted by the Spanish authorities for his independence views, Trelles relocated to Tampa where he collected funds for the Cuban insurgents. At the end of the **War of Independence** in 1898, he returned to Cuba. He worked as librarian at the Matanzas Public Library before serving as librarian of the Chamber of Deputies—a role similar to the United States Librarian of Congress—in 1923. He represented Cuba before numerous international cultural and literary associations, including the Hispanic Society of the Americas, based in New York City, the Sociedad Chilena de Historia y Geografía, and the Sociedad Mexicana de Geografía y Estadística. He was vice president of the Asociación Interamericana de Bibliógrafos y Bibliotecarios.

Though he wrote many books on the history of Cuba, he is best remembered for his bibliographic research, culminating in the monumental multivolume *Ensayo de bibliografía cubana* (1907–1915), which listed thousands of Cuban works published from the 1600s to the 1910s. *See also* Political Exile (Nineteenth Century)

Further Reading
Asociación de la Prensa de Cuba. *Homenaje al Señor Carlos M. Trelles y Govín, socio de honor.* Matanzas: Imprenta de J. F. Oliver, 1919.

D.H. Figueredo

Turla y Denis, Leopoldo (1818–1877)

Leopoldo Turla y Denis was a poet and playwright whose patriotic poems appeared in the famous anthology *El laúd del desterrado*, published in New York City in 1848. He contributed regularly to literary journals; many of his poems, written in a romantic vein, were translated into English.

In 1851, Turla y Denis, who was conspiring against the Spanish government, learned of his imminent arrest by the Spanish authorities and escaped from Cuba, seeking asylum in New Orleans. In the United States, he worked as a teacher, corresponded with Cuban patriots who were plotting war against Spain, and was one of the organizers of the **Narciso López** expedition in 1852. Favoring annexation to the United States, he wrote numerous essays on the topic (see **Annexationism**).

Turla y Denis used the pen name Un quidam. He is the author of the poetry book *Ráfagas del trópico*, published in 1842.

Further Readings
Carbonell, José M. *Leopoldo Turla, su poesía y su actuación revolucionaria*. Havana: Imprenta "El Siglo XX", 1926.
Montes-Huidobro, Matías, ed. *El laúd del desterrado*. Houston: Arte Público Press, 1995.

D.H. Figueredo

Uhrbach, Carlos Pío (1872–1897)

Born in **Matanzas**, Carlos Pío Uhrbach was a romantic figure and poet of the **War of Independence**.

Uhrbach published numerous poems in such important **literary journals** as *La Habana elegante* and *El Fígaro*. In 1896, he left Cuba on a secret mission to the United States. There he met with **Tomás Estrada Palma**, a revolutionary leader and the man destined to be Cuba's first

president. Later he returned to Cuba to fight against the Spanish army. He died in battle at the age of twenty-five. When his body was retrieved from the battlefield, a friend found on his chest a poem written to him by his fiancée, the writer and poet **Juana Borrero**. On the other side of the sheet, Uhrbach had penned a stanza where he sensed an early death.

His most famous poems are "A Colón," an ode to **Christopher Columbus**, and "Camafeos." His brother Federico (1873–1932) was also an accomplished writer.

Further Reading
Borrero, Juana. *Poesías y cartas*. Havana: Editorial Arte y Literatura, 1978.

D.H. Figueredo

Unión de Escritores y Artistas de Cuba (UNEAC; Union of Cuban Writers and Artists)

The Unión de Escritores y Artistas de Cuba (UNEAC) is one of several important revolutionary institutions established to facilitate the work and direct the artistic production of Cuba's intellectual vanguard. Poet **Nicolás Guillén** headed the organization from its founding in 1961 until 1988, when Abel Prieto Jiménez succeeded Guillén as president for the next ten years. In 1998, union members, numbering over 5,000, elected Carlos Martí Brenes as the UNEAC's third president. Since 1962, UNEAC has published *La Gaceta de Cuba*, a bimonthly journal that discusses performance, the plastic arts, literature, music, film, and radio, as well as studies of sociocultural interest. In addition, UNEAC prints the quarterly magazine *Unión* and operates a publishing house, Ediciones Unión, which specializes in publishing authors associated with the union and major figures in the history of Cuban literature (see **Newspapers and**

Magazines and **Literary Journals**). Ediciones Unión also publishes the winners of UNEAC's annual literary contests. As a large cultural institution, UNEAC has been at the center of controversies involving artistic freedom in the **Revolution**. In 1968, it awarded prizes to two writers, Heberto Padilla and **Antón Arrufat**, whose works *Fuera de juego* and *Los siete contra Tebas* contained what was officially deemed questionable ideological sentiments (see **Padilla [Affair] Heberto**). Although some officials condemned the writings as counterrevolutionary, UNEAC published them with a disclaimer and an explanation of their artistic merit. Throughout the years, the changing composition of the union's leadership and its changing relationship to the **Cuban Communist Party** has shed light on shifts in cultural policy and the status of the artist in Cuban revolutionary society. In the 1990s, both *Unión* and *La Gaceta* began publishing pieces by Cuban authors in exile. *See also* Literature of the Revolutionary Era; Casa de las Américas

Further Readings

Casal, Lourdes. "Literature and Society." In *Revolutionary Change in Cuba*, ed. Carmelo Mesa-Lago. Pittsburgh: University of Pittsburgh Press, 1971. 447–469.

Johnson, Peter T. "The Nuanced Lives of the Intelligentsia." In *Conflict and Change in Cuba*, ed. Enrique A. Balroya and James A. Morris. Albuquerque: University of New Mexico Press, 1993. 137–163.

Camilla Stevens

Valdés, Gabriel de la Concepción (Plácido) (1809–1844)

Considered one of Cuba's most popular Romantic poets of his time, Plácido's tragic death has strongly contributed to the evolution of his fame as a legendary figure. Born in Havana from the illicit relationship between a white Spanish dancer,

Nineteenth-century sketch of Plácido. He was executed during the repression of La Escalera in 1844.

Concepción Vázquez, and a mulatto hairdresser, Diego Ferrer Matoso, he was abandoned by his mother at the Casa de Beneficiencia y Maternidad and later was cared for by his paternal relatives. Although his last name Valdés was from the name of the Orphanage Founder, he decided to call himself Plácido, the title of a French novel by Madame de Genlis. He ended his formal schooling early on and survived by making ornamental combs for women's hair and by working as a typesetter between 1826 and 1832. His first poem, "A una bella," was written in 1821 when he was twelve. "La siempreviva" was the lyric composition that brought him fame when, in 1834, he wrote it as part of an homage paid to the Spanish poet Francisco Martínez de la Rosa. In 1837 he worked for the newspaper *La Aurora de*

Matanzas, which paid him for writing a weekly poem. He published his first book, *Poesías de Plácido*, in 1838 and *Poesías escojidas* [*sic*] *de Plácido* in 1842. He also published a chivalric tale, *El hijo de maldición*, in 1843, the same year that he was accused and taken prisoner for his alleged involvement in the **Conspiracy of La Escalera** (1844), an abolitionist revolt. He was executed by firing squad in 1844. *See also* Abolitionist Literature; Press and Journalism (Eighteenth and Nineteenth Centuries)

Further Readings

Arias, Salvador. *Tres poetas en la mirilla: Plácido, Milanés, la Avellaneda.* Havana: Editorial Letras Cubanas, 1981.

Stimson, Frederick S., and Humberto E. Robles, eds. *Los poemas más representativos de Plácido (Edición crítica).* Chapel Hill, NC: Estudios de Hispanófila, 1976.

Ilia Casanova-Marengo

Valdés, José Policarpo (1807–1858?)

José Policarpo Valdés was born in Havana into an aristocratic family. Shy and withdrawn, he favored literature and the arts, writing poetry at an early age. Under the name of the Polidoro, as well as El Silencioso, he submitted his poetry to such literary journals as *El Album, El Lucero, La Moda*, and *Revista de La Habana*. In 1833, a friend collected some of the poems Valdés had published in *La Moda* and included them in the book *Rimas americanas*. His poems were lyrical and sentimental, addressing such universal topics as love and beauty.

Though he did not publish a book, and left upon his death a collection of unpublished poems, Valdés enjoyed a certain reputation as a poet during his lifetime. Late in the nineteenth century, scholar Antonio López Prieto included Valdés in the volume *Parnaso cubano* (1881), which was a study of the evolution of Cuban po-

etry. In 1928, another anthology, *La poesía lírica en Cuba*, featured some of his works. But overall Cuban critics tend to dismiss his importance as a poet and read his works only within the frame of Cuban literary production during the nineteenth century.

Further Reading

Diccionario de la literatura cubana. Vol. 2. Havana: Editorial Letras Cubanas, 1984.

D.H. Figueredo

Valdés, Zoé (1959–)

Zoé Valdés is an erotic and feminist writer whose novel *La vida cotidiana* brought her international recognition when it was first published in 1995. The novel portrayed the lives of ordinary citizens in contemporary Cuba and the frustrations they experienced as they tried to make a living during the **Special Period**, a time of enormous difficulties and shortages on the island. Tired of political slogans and material deprivation, the protagonist of the novel, a young Cuban woman, sought escape through love affairs and sexual encounters (see **Prostitution**).

Valdés was born and raised in Havana. Before becoming a novelist, Valdés, a college dropout, worked for the United Nations Educational, Scientific, and Cultural Organization (UNESCO) and the Cuban embassy in Paris. She was also assistant director of the journal *Revista Cine Cubano*. Raised in a household dominated by women—her father had deserted the family—Valdés became conscious of women's struggles for self-assertion in a male-driven society (see **Machismo**). An ardent reader, a friend once gave her a set of novels by Marcel Proust. Valdés was fascinated by Proust and considers him the writer that influenced her the most.

La vida cotidiana has been translated into several languages. Other works that followed include *Te di la vida entera* (1996), *Café Nostalgia* (1997), *Traficante de belleza* (1998), *Milagro en Miami* (2001), the book of poems *Vagón para fumadores* (1996), and *Cuerdas para el lince* (1999), all written in exile. In Cuba, Valdés wrote *Respuestas para vivir* (1986), *Toda una sombra* (1986), *Sangre azul* (1993) and *La hija del embajador* (1995).

Valdés's language reproduces Cuba's slang and vernacular but with a poetic and philosophical touch. Her major characters are women who tend to be liberated, free-spirited, and filled with love and passion.

Further Reading

Strausfeld, Michi. *Nuevos narradores cubanos*. Madrid: Ediciones Siruela, 2000.

D.H. Figueredo

Villaverde, Cirilo (1812–1894)

Cirilo Villaverde is the author of *Cecilia Valdés o La Loma del Ángel; novela de costumbres cubanas*, the most important novel written in nineteenth-century Cuba. It is the story of the incestuous love between the mulatto woman Cecilia Valdés and her white half brother Leonardo Gamboa. Villaverde's novel is a political accusation against the Spanish colonial regime and a document that depicts the racial tensions undermining the nineteenth-century Cuban nation (see **Spanish Colonialism [Nineteenth Century]**).

Born in the sugar mill Santiago, in the province of **Pinar del Río** in 1812, Villaverde received a law degree, but his disillusionment with corrupt lawyers made him leave the profession soon thereafter. After becoming an active member of the **Domingo del Monte** literary circle, he published his first tales and short novels in 1837. Two years later, he published the first version of *Cecilia Valdés* in the Havana magazine *La Siempreviva*. Villaverde was taken prisoner in 1848 for his involvement in the **Narciso López** conspiracy

(1848–1851) (see **Annexationism**). After a few months he managed to escape to the United States in 1849, where he served as General Narciso López's secretary, worked as a teacher and translator, and continued aiding the Cubans in their struggle for independence from Spain. In 1858 Villaverde returned to Cuba, where he remained until 1860. While on the island, he founded the literary magazine *La Habana* with Francisco Calcagno and also worked on the publication of his complete oeuvre. After returning to New York, he and his wife, Emilia Casanova, founded a school in Weehawken, New Jersey, in 1864. Although he finished *Cecilia Valdés* in 1879, the novel as it is now was not published until 1882. Villaverde revisited Cuba for two weeks in 1888. He died in New York in 1894, but his body was sent back to Cuban soil.

Though he wrote and published other volumes, including *Excursión a Vueltabajo* (1891), *La joven de la flecha de oro* (1841), *Dos amores* (1858), *El guajiro* (1890), and *El penitente* (1925), *Cecilia Valdés* remains his most important work. The novel was made into a famously popular **zarzuela** in 1932 by the composer **Gonzalo Roig**, was serialized on Cuban television during the 1960s, and was adapted for the screen by **Humberto Solás** in 1982 (see **Cinema**). *See also* Press and Journalism (Eighteenth and Nineteenth Centuries)

Further Readings

Álvarez Imeldo, ed. *Acerca de Cirilo Villaverde*. Havana: Editorial Letras Cubanas, 1982.

Lamore, Jean. Introduction. *Cecilia Valdés o La Loma del Ángel*. By Cirilo Villaverde. Madrid: Cátedra, 1992. 11–48.

Ilia Casanova-Marengo

Vitier, Cintio (1921–   )

Cintio Vitier is one of the key poets of the ***Orígenes*** group, author of a classic study on Cuban poetry, and a leading literary scholar, especially on the work of **José Martí**. Born in Key West, Vitier spent his childhood in **Matanzas**, then studied at the **University of Havana**, where he graduated in, but never practiced, law.

Vitier is a deeply religious poet, imbued with a sense of the absolute in his early work (1938–1959) and, afterward, seeking a synthesis of Catholic belief and revolutionary commitment (see **Catholicism**). One of the editors of *Orígenes* magazine (1944–1956), Vitier published several books of poetry in the 1940s, most notably *Capricho y homenaje* (1946). His *Canto llano* (1956), written in a direct, but never simple language, reveals a poetry of pain and suffering viewed from a Catholic philosophy of justice and redemption.

His poetry has been grouped in four major collections: *Vísperas* (1953; work from 1938 to 1953), *Testimonios* (1968; from 1953 to 1968), *La fecha al pie* (1981; 1969–1975), and *Nupcias* (1992; 1979–1992). Vitier has also published three novels.

Vitier's *Lo cubano en la poesía* (1958) is a seminal work on Cuban poetry that is more than literary criticism; it delineates the poetic imagination as central to Cuban history and identity. His *Ese sol del mundo moral* (1975) is a book-length essay on a history of Cuban ethnicity. *Temas martianos* (1969), coauthored with his wife **Fina García Marruz**, is a key critical work on the writing and thought of José Martí. Despite criticism by younger writers who say he is an "official writer," Vitier's compassion, lucidity, and imagination have been, and continue to be, influential in Cuban letters. *See also* Literature of the Revolutionary Era

Further Readings

Díaz Quiñones, Arcadio. *Cintio Vitier: la memoria integradora*. San Juan, Puerto Rico: Editorial Sin Nombre, 1987.
García, Enildo. "Cintio Vitier." In *Dictionary of Twentieth Century Cuban Literature*, ed. Julio A. Martínez. Westport, CT: Greenwood Press, 1990. 487–492.

Alan West-Durán

Xenes, Nieves (1859–1915)

Nieves Xenes devoted her life to an impossible love. When she was twenty years old, she met the popular orator José Antonio Cortina, an autonomist politician, and fell in love with him (see **Autonomism**). It is not clear whether they had any relationship, but his early death saddened her deeply and inspired her to write poems about heartache and the loss of love. In this vein, she wrote "El primer beso" and "Una confesión," for which she received great acclaim.

Xenes submitted her poetry to many **literary journals**, including the prestigious *La Habana Elegante*. She also read her works at gatherings of writers and intellectuals. A founding member of the Academia Nacional de Artes y Letras, Xenes did not publish a book during her lifetime. But soon after her death in 1915, the Academia issued *Poesías*, an anthology of her works.

Further Reading

Xenes, Nieves. *Poesías*. Havana: Imprenta "El Siglo XX de A. Miranda", 1915.

D.H. Figueredo

Zenea, Juan Clemente (1832–1871)

Unlike most Cuban poets of his time, Juan Clemente Zenea was deeply influenced by the French (Alfred de Musset in particular) and U.S. poets, as opposed to Spanish writers. He published his first poems at the age of fourteen and became editor of *La Prensa* in 1849. Not only an accomplished poet, Zenea led a fascinating and adventurous life. At seventeen he began a torrid liaison with poet and actress Adah Menken. Forced to leave Cuba in 1852 for publishing anti-Spanish poetry, he renewed his affair with Menken in New Orleans, then moved to New York. He was condemned to death for subversive activities by Spanish authorities in 1853, but an amnesty allowed him to return to Cuba in 1854. He taught, wrote for many magazines and newspapers, and founded *La Revista Habanera* (1861–1863), subsequently closed by the Spanish authorities. In 1870, while again living in New York, he clandestinely returned to Cuba with a double mission: to pass on information to the Cuban revolutionaries and to offer a deal from the Spanish government for greater Cuban autonomy, but not independence, if they surrendered (see **Ten Years' War** and **Autonomism**). Trying to return to the United States, Zenea was captured by Spanish troops, despite having a safe conduct from the Spanish embassy. Held incommunicado for eight months, he was shot by firing squad on August 25, 1871. In 1926 documents from his trial were released that suggest he agreed to work for the Spanish government, but his last poems written in prison, and his execution, cast doubt on this thesis.

His books of poems are *Poesías* (1855), *Cantos de la tarde* (1860), and a posthumous edition, *Poesías completas de Juan Clemente Zenea* in 1872. A sensual and lyrical poet, Zenea's poetry has a dreamy quality, what **Cintio Vitier** has called "an unending softness, that we can infinitely pierce." *See also* Press and Journalism (Eighteenth and Nineteenth Centuries)

Further Readings

Ureña, Max Henríquez. *Panorama histórico de la literatura cubana*. Vol. 1. Havana: Editorial Arte y Literatura, 1978.

Vitier, Cintio. *Lo cubano en la poesía*. Havana: Editorial Letras Cubanas, 1970.

Alan West-Durán

Zequeira y Arango, Manuel de (1764–1846)

Manuel de Zequeira was the author of one of the most popular poems ever written in Cuba, "Oda a la piña," a lyrical ode describing the pineapple and celebrating the beauty of nature and the Caribbean. Born in 1764, he attended the Seminario de San Carlos, where he befriended philosopher and educator **Félix Varela**. After excelling at literary studies, he joined the Spanish Army in 1780. He traveled to the Dominican Republic and participated in the campaign against the French who were trying to takeover the island. In 1813, he sailed to Gran Colombia, where he served as governor of the province of Río Hacha. Returning to Cuba in 1817, he was transferred to **Matanzas** in 1821, where he commanded the Spanish armed forces. Around this time, Zequeira became mentally ill and never recovered.

Zequeira was editor of the journal *Papel Periódico de La Habana* from 1800 to 1805. He wrote a book of poetry, *Poesiás* (1829), and published numerous historic epics on figures such as Hernán Cortés while also attempting to define a Cuban identity in his writings. He is regarded as one of the first poets to emerge in Cuba. *See also* Press and Journalism (Eighteenth and Nineteenth Centuries)

Further Reading

Cuevas Zequeira, Sergio. *Manuel de Zequeira y Arango y los albores de la literatura cubana*. Havana: "Tipografía Moderna" de A. Dorrbecker, 1923.

D.H. Figueredo